State and Local Politics

The Individual and the Governments

SECOND EDITION

W. B. Stouffer
Cynthia Opheim
Susan Bland Day
Southwest Texas State University

HarperCollins*CollegePublishers*

Dedicated with love and respect to our strongest supporters:
Sandy, Cinnamon, and Brewer Stouffer
Jeff Opheim
Jo and Wallie Bland

Acquisitions Editor: Leo A.W. Wiegman
Developmental Editor: Margaret Loftus
Project Coordination and Text Design: Ruttle, Shaw & Wetherill, Inc.
Cover Design and Photo Montage: Wendy Fredericks
Cover Photographs: Wyoming capitol building by Norris Taylor/Photo Researchers, Inc.
                    N. Wisconsin Town Hall by Chromosohm/Sohm/Photo Researchers, Inc.
Photo Research: Julie Tesser
Electronic Production Manager: Christine Pearson
Manufacturing Manager: Helene G. Landers
Electronic Page Makeup: Ruttle, Shaw & Wetherill, Inc.
Printer and Binder: R. R. Donnelley & Sons Company
Cover Printer: Phoenix Color Corp.

State and Local Politics: The Individual and the Governments, Second Edition

Library of Congress Cataloging-in-Publication Data

Stouffer, Willard B.
    State and local politics : the individual and the governments /
  W.B. Stouffer, Cynthia Opheim, Susan Bland Day. – 2nd ed.
        p.   cm.
    Includes bibliographical references and index.
    ISBN 0-673-99661-1
      1. State governments–United States.   2. Local government–United States.   3. Federal government–United States.   4. Pressure groups–United States.   5. Political participation–United States.
  I. Opheim, Cynthia.   II. Day, Susan Bland.   III. Title.
  JK2408.S857   1996   95-31706
  353.9–dc20   CIP

96 97 98 99   9 8 7 6 5 4 3 2 1

BRIEF CONTENTS

DETAILED CONTENTS

PREFACE

We are very grateful that our book has survived the process that separates a first edition from oblivion. The second edition has made room for some new things without making the book much longer or sacrificing what we hope was useful in the first. We also hope that a theme implicit in the first edition is explicit in this one. This is the notion that most individuals realize their highest potential as human beings by participating in their communities.

This edition includes a new chapter on the media in state and local politics. Each chapter begins with a vignette that—in most cases—emphasizes that individuals can make a difference.

Another new feature is the option of obtaining a disk containing a copy of the State of Vermont's Constitution which is a good example of a brief document for comparison with states with long meandering constitutions. The disk also contains a great deal of comparative data on the states which some instructors or students may wish to use for research and instructional purposes. The Instructor's Manual will address this more completely.

Naturally we have attempted to bring the book up-to-date where appropriate. In keeping with our belief in ongoing reform we have added more material on reinventing government. Although it is possible that the term itself may become dated as the decade wears on, the basic concepts associated with it will not.

As we said in the first edition, our point of view is that the individual matters, that individual action makes a difference in what government does. From this premise comes our concern with reform, with providing a lucid book that will encourage individuals to study the institutions and processes on which they are most likely to have an impact—state and local governments. From our concern with the inividual also comes our emphasis on the intergovernmental context. To be effective, individuals have to become informed about the interacting, overlapping, and sometimes competing units of government of which they are citizens, voters, and taxpayers.

As teachers, we are concerned about the fact that students come to our text with different skills and levels of preparation. That is why Chaper 1 spends some time addressing this issue and why every chapter ends with a glossary and study objectives on which both learning and testing can be based.

As teachers, we are also aware that some colleagues with whom we hope to be sharing students may find our organization of material a little different. In developing our intergovernmental theme we have tried to avoid causing difficulties for colleagues who may wish to treat local government separately from state government. We have placed the local government portions at the end of chapters that include material on local institutions. We hope that reading assignments can be more easily organized simply by referring to the table of contents instead of skipping all over a chapter to mold our work to your needs.

As idealists, we believe that politically skilled and motivated individuals can increase the rationality and effectiveness of our intergovernmental system. Thus, our book has an unabashed participatory outlook. We believe also that virtually anything humans make can be improved; more important, we believe that it is essential to improve our state and local systems of governing so that we can better deal with the myriad problems that confront us. As we point out more than once, our students—the future leaders of our states and communities—will be asked to make decisions about changing their state and local political systems. Exploring some of these proposals in the classroom as early as possible makes a lot of sense to us.

We are serious about teaching. We feel that we are coteachers with the instructors who adopt this book for their courses. Producing a textbook that challenges students and encourages them to read beyond the assigned text was one of our motivations for taking on this project. We have tried very hard to make this book readable, and we would like to think that at times it's even interesting. Our major intent is to be as lucid and straightforward as possible without sacrificing substance. We've seen too many cute, shallow texts that grab your attention and then don't do much with it. However, we also know how difficult it is to get students to stay with encyclopedia-like texts. We've tried to walk a fine line between being merely interesting and being merely informative. We hope you approve of the result.

We would like to thank all the people who have assisted us during the revison. First and foremost we express our appreciation to Leo Wiegman, Poltical Science Editor, not only for selecting our text from the many available for revision but for providing advice and counsel, support and e-mail information which has been most valuable.

Associate Editor, Margaret Loftus, has done a great deal to make our text more presentable through photo research and copy coordination. Chris Korintus, Political Science Assistant, deserves a word of thanks for making sure that the reviewing process proceeded in an orderly fashion. Gloria Klaiman has rendered our prose more readable, for which we are eternally grateful.

We'd also like to thank colleagues on other campuses who, until listed below, were anonymous reviewers for the advice and helpful suggestions they provided.

David Bowers Jr.
University of Southern Mississippi

Edgar C. Leduc
University of Rhode Island

Larry Elowitz
Georgia College

Timothy Martinez
Black Hills State University

David G. Houghton
Western Michigan University

Antonia C. Moran
Central Connecticut State University

William Lammers
University of Southern California

Many of our colleagues at Southwest Texas State have been most helpful. In particular, we appreciate the efforts of Dan Farlow, Patricia Shields, and Landon Curry, who read parts of the manuscript and provided insightful criticisms. The staff members of the Southwest Texas State University library, especially Ryana Wright, Robert Harris, Ann Blakely, Al Quinn, and Margaret Vaverek, were extremely patient in helping us locate necessary documents and useful data. Karim Aziz provided useful maps and figures, for which we thank him and his mentor Dennis Fitsimons.

W. B. Stouffer

Cynthia Opheim

Susan Bland Day

CHAPTER

1

The Community and the Individual

Of Those who have much to offer, much is asked.

   No Man is an island.—John Donne

Outside the community man is either a beast or a god.—Aristotle

It takes a whole village to raise a child.—African Proverb

Kimi Gray is a mother of five children. A few years ago she was receiving welfare and lived in Kenilworth-Parkside, a Washington D.C. public housing project. Very little in the project worked including the people. Crime as well as unemployment was rampant. An open-air drug market dominated the streets, and the Public Housing Authority had virtually given up on trying to maintain the place.

   Some teenagers in the project asked Ms. Gray if she knew anything about college. They had questions like: Would any college take seriously applications from kids in the projects? If one gets in, how does one pay for college?

   With kids of her own to think about, Ms. Gray decided to check out the possibilities. She learned about the procedures and recruited volunteers to offer tutoring and application help. Together with interested students and a few parents she created an organization called "College Here We Come."

   She found part-time jobs for some of the teenagers and started a scholarship fund financed in part by bake sales and community service projects. In August of that same year, 17 kids from the project went to school. Within a decade, 700 had attended with a 75 percent graduation rate (the national rate is about 50 percent).

   Each set of college students from the projects provides a growing cadre of role models for children living in poverty whose previous models for success were drug dealers and pimps. This growing center of success provides living proof that opportunities exist even in "the projects" because an individual acted constructively and got other individuals involved.

Beyond ourselves and our families is a loosely defined set of relationships called community. Most of us belong to more than one community (neighborhood, city or town, profession, workplace, school, church, synagogue or temple). Within these communities we have rights which we deserve as long as we agree to meet our obligations.[2]

Violent crime, babies having babies, teenage gangs, environmental degradation, and homelessness are among the many problems confronting our communities. Most of our problems can be related to two themes that pervade discussions of American society's current ills. The first is the decline of community. At least in part this demonstrates the failure of the whole village to take responsibility for raising the child. The children who drop out, have babies, commit crimes, and waste their potential to be productive citizens will cost society a lot more money in the long run than could have been spent now on day care, job training for their mothers and fathers, and other programs involving intervention. You can pay now for preventive social programs or you can pay 10 times as much later in annual prison tuition at $30,000 a bed, not to mention the cost of the crimes committed. In communities with active voluntary agencies and enlightened leadership many of these problems either don't happen or are severely curtailed.

It is the active participation by individuals that makes a collection of dwellings into a community. The term "community" is often used in a wishful thinking, whistling past the graveyard, kind of way. To refer to any neighborhood, town, city, or state as a community is to make a statement of hope, that it is indeed or soon will become one. In this text we will do it too, as a demonstration of our optimism about the future of our society. After all, with you as future leaders of it, how can one not be optimistic?

An organizational response to the growing concern for the community is the Communitarian Movement. According to a founding member, Emitai Etzioni,

> The eighties was a decade when 'I' was writ large in which the celebration of the self was a virtue. . . . Now the time has come to push back the pendulum. The times call for an age of reconstruction, in which we put a new emphasis on 'we,' on values we share, on the spirit of the community.[3]

The "living democracy" notion described in The Quickening of America by Lappé and DuBois has the same basic goal as Etzioni's movement but it moves the emphasis from fulfilling obligations to enjoying meaningful activity.[4] Lappé and DuBois are also teachers and community activists. They know personally about the self-fulfillment associated with participating in the life of one's community and have collected case studies from around the country, some of which we will mention in the pages that follow.

Most authors who write about community agree that the ideal community is one in which people have personal feelings about the well-being of other individuals in the community, even if we do not know them personally. The idea of community is not too far different from that of extended family. Communities make demands on us, just as our families do. Sometimes it seems as if the communities to which we belong ask too much. Balancing our sanity and our need for time and energy for ourselves against family and community demands is part of the human condition. That we cannot please everyone does not mean we shouldn't try to meet at least some of our responsibilities.

The second theme that relates to the problems facing our society is the failure of individuals to take responsibility for what happens in their lives. Books with titles like A Nation of Victims provide copious evidence that too many Americans blame others for their misfortunes or for accidents that happen to them. While some would blame all of this on plaintiffs' lawyers (also known as ambulance chasers), more insightful thinkers attribute this failure to take responsibility to the fact that for the past two decades there has been an overemphasis on rights while responsibilities have too often been ignored. The recent reaction against the various efforts to protect the environment in the form of "Landowners' Rights" is a recent manifestation of this theme. We hasten to admit that some regulators are overzealous, that some regulations and some procedures for enforcing regulations need to be reexamined. The notion, however, that landowners do not have responsibilities as well as rights is the concern here.

The assertion that there are rights available to everyone (whether they own land or not) is part of our cultural heritage. In *The Declaration of Independence* we find them stated as part of self-evident truth—life, liberty, and the pursuit of happiness. That document also contains a central idea so obvious at the time *The Declaration of Independence* was written that the idea didn't even need to be stated. That self-evident truth is presented in different ways in the quotations that begin this chapter. They all suggest directly or indirectly that freedom is really freedom to realize one's highest potential for good as a human being, usually as a contributing member of a community. Social contract and natural law theory both assert that we do not have freedom to do as we damn well please. What we do have is the right, and the obligation, to figure out for ourselves what our highest potential is and how to realize it, and then—whether church, state, or family agree with us—we attempt to realize that potential.[5]

You are certainly on the right track toward realizing some of your potential by having read this far. Patience is, after all, an important virtue. The purpose of this book is to help you meet your obligations as a future leader of one or more of your communities. If you are reading this book as a course assignment, then you assumed some obligations simply by enrolling. You implicitly took on this obligation for leadership in accepting the highly subsidized education you are receiving. Even if you are paying tuition at a private institution, it is very likely that generous individuals with gifts large and small have defrayed part of the cost of your education. Even national, state, and local governments are subsidizing your education—by granting tax deductions to those who give gifts to your institution and by not taxing the property of your school at full value or in some cases at all.

Your obligations as future leaders may not necessarily lead you to run for public office. These obligations arise almost naturally. In the years to come as a consequence of your enhanced thinking and communication skills, in addition to your larger fund of factual knowledge, others will ask your opinion. You are more likely than the 75 percent of your generation that did not graduate from college to have an informed opinion. You, and your peers, will be asked to vote on changing your state constitution and local government charters. You will be asked to vote for candidates and propositions. You may even confront the possibility that your community would be better off with its own government or that the existing government should be merged with another.

There are many people like Kimi Gray with far less formal education than you have now who have taken on a task in the interests of their community and been the better for it.

WHY STUDY STATE AND LOCAL POLITICS?

Preparing for informed participation and community leadership is certainly a good answer to the foregoing question. Although Kimi Gray worked within a housing project she soon learned that in order to help students get scholarships she had to learn about sources of private and of government aid, and about admission procedures at public as well as private schools. In a rudimentary way she was learning (and teaching) about the way that state and local communities attempt to find ways to offer higher education and train leaders. There are many other reasons for studying state and local politics but, for the sake of brevity, we have listed only eight.

It Was Good Enough for Plato and Aristotle

State and local politics is a legitimate and traditional subject of study. Plato and Aristotle lived in and studied a type of community called the *polis*, the city-state of ancient Greece. In attempting to develop a science of the well-ordered, harmonious *polis*, the founders of political science dealt with the units of government closest to the individual. They were concerned with issues that are still relevant at local and state as well as national levels of governance.

These issues include corruption (why it occurs and how to avoid it), justice (what it is and how to try to obtain it), the appropriate role of money in politics (should those who have the gold make the rules?), who really governs (the one, the few, or the many?), who ought to govern, and a modern variation of these questions most relevant for metropolitan America, "Is anybody governing?"

That's Where the Action Is

Exciting things are happening at the state and local levels, and have been happening there for some time. Osborne and Gaebler's *Reinventing Government* contains dozens of examples of innovative ways to solve problems confronting our communities. Most of the innovations were developed in or involve cooperation with state and local government. It is no mistake that when the Clinton administration looked for people to help reduce costs and increase the quality of government at the federal level it turned to a state official—John Sharp, Comptroller of Texas—to help Vice President Al Gore organize the National Performance Review. This review is patterned after a cost-cutting process that saved the State of Texas $6.2 billion in the $67 billion 1993–94 budget.[6]

The Ford Foundation gives annual awards to ten exemplary programs developed by innovative state and local governments. Since 1986 when the first set of winners received their grants nearly 10,000 programs have been considered for awards. The purpose of the awards is to recognize and publicize these innovations, thus encouraging others in and outside of government to think creatively about making their communities work better.

In the 1993 round, the Seattle Worker Center received an award for helping the homeless find jobs via a voice-mail system. Once prospective employers had a place to leave a message, job hunting became a realistic activity. Many of the homeless found jobs and eventually places to live. Of the first 148 homeless to use the voice-mail system, 126 found jobs, and 78 found housing in just a few weeks.[7]

In Columbia, South Carolina, police officers and their families are provided the opportunity to become homeowners in neighborhoods throughout the city. Police officers are welcome neighbors in family-oriented areas of any city, whether they can afford to live there or not. In Columbia, the Police Homeowner Loan Program offers low-interest, no-down-payment mortgages. The result is a more secure neighborhood, and a police force based in the community it serves.[8]

In 1994 the John F. Kennedy School of Government at Harvard University, which reviews innovative programs, examined 1,300 applications. The 10 winning entries came from six state agencies, three city or county agencies, and a junior-senior high school in Winchester, New Hampshire. The diversity of levels of government and members of the communities involved in making innovation work is understated somewhat in the numbers given. Many programs brought together the talents and energy of volunteers as well as private businesses, nonprofit organizations, and other state or local agencies.

The Tulsa Police Department's SANE program is a good example of the many resources in a community to be integrated in problem solving. This program attempted to solve the problem confronting the long wait endured by rape victims waiting in crowded emergency rooms for doctors pressed to deal first with heart attacks, gunshot wounds, and other life-threatening situations. The solution involved numerous individuals and organizations including: nurses trained to become Sexual Assault Nurse Examiners (skilled in preserving vital evidence that might help to identify and convict the rapist); the Hillcrest Medical Center, which provides a suite (where victims are now taken instead of to emergency rooms); volunteers from Call Rape, a local victims' advocacy organization (at least one who stays with the victim and one who provides emotional support and comfort to the family); a research grant from United Way; the University of Oklahoma College of Medicine (which provides medical supervision); the Tulsa City-County Health Department (which provides malpractice insurance for the nurses); and the district attorney's office (which helps to compensate the Hillcrest Medical Center and SANE nurses).[9] The study of state and local politics naturally involves conflict but, as we shall point out more than once,

The LiteRail system that will connect Long Beach to Los Angeles is, like many public works projects, a partnership between private business and public agencies.

it requires a great deal of cooperation and creativity in dealing with the needs of a diverse population in an increasingly complex society.

The states have long been considered laboratories for experimentation. Many of the major problems facing this country today will be ameliorated and even solved by the nationwide application of experiments being planned or taking place as you read this paragraph. There is a lot more to state and local government than most people are aware. Whether you help these governments as an active citizen promoting the spread of cost-cutting innovations or as a public servant making them work, state and local governments can put your time and talent to good use.

State and Local Governments Are Major Employers

There are over 15 million jobs in state and local government. It is unlikely that the state and local government payroll will ever again be less than $19 billion a year. That payroll includes six times as many civilians as the national government employs.[10]

When you graduate from college there will be thousands of new positions in state and local government created since this book went to print. Some of them will be training people, whose jobs have become obsolete, to perform new jobs that haven't even been invented yet. The variety of jobs in state and local government is about the same as that in the private sector, from using computers to detect cellular phone number thieves to helping the state legislature deal with problems arising from genetic engineering and the creation of new chemicals and life forms. Therefore, it makes sense for those considering employment after college to take a look at some of the major employers in our economic system. State and local governments do more than collect taxes and build highways, much more.

Since state and local governments are major employers, many of them are also concerned with one of the major sources of conflict in our political system as well as one of the major opportunities for cooperation. Resolving the differences in the interests of employers and employees in a complex society such as ours is a major activity that goes on within government as well as outside of it. Some agencies of state and local government are involved in resolving disputes between private sector employers and employees.

The issue of collective bargaining—the right of employees to pool their resources and pay for an individual or agency to represent them—is an important one within and outside of government. The political battles that have been fought over this issue have consequences that affect not only the workplace but the political system in many states and communities. In recent years private employers have been more successful than public employers in limiting the efforts of their employees to seek collective bargaining rights. Thus, the percentage of public sector employees represented by collective bargaining organizations or labor unions is more than three times higher than in the private sector.[11]

State and Local Governments Are Major Customers

Many state and local governments are big operations. Each of the top 50 general purpose governments (states, cities, counties, and townships) spend more than $3 billion a year. Collectively, the big ones and the many small ones spend $1.3 trillion a year, just a little less than the $1.6 trillion that the federal government spends. If every state were a private company they would all be listed in the *Fortune* 500. Sixteen states have revenues that would place them in the top 50 organizations in the country, right up there with IBM and Exxon.[12]

For the rest of this decade state governments alone will spend more than $7 billion a year on equipment and over $35 billion on construction. In addition to these sums, a goodly portion of the more than $320 billion they will spend on current operations will go for purchases of supplies from local businesses and directly from the manufacturer.[13]

State and local governments often make decisions about their purchases that have effects beyond their borders. The state of California purchases thousands of automobiles and trucks each year. The specifications for pollution control or safety that it requires for fleet purchases have a great deal of influence on auto manufacturers. Some manufacturers find it makes economic sense to use these specifications for all their models; others may decide to modify standard vehicles for the California market.

State and Local Governments Are Major Actors in the National Political Economy

Not only do state and local governments employ a lot of people and buy a lot of goods and services, they also influence the political economy in other very important ways. The political economy is the collection of reward (and penalty) systems that affect choices available in a given society.[14] The political economy is that part of society where politics and economics overlap. The study of political economy focuses on the variety of taxes, tax breaks, fees, permits, licenses, and regulations that governments use to promote and pay for various social goals such as safe highways, fair competition, safe workplaces, environmental protection, and to promote the offering of goods and services to rural as well as urban areas.

The political economy involves many dimensions and many actors who do not share the same interests. It includes the interaction of buyers and sellers, employees and employers, firms that produce in one's state or community and those outside producers who wish to compete with them. It also involves small local businesses and giant outside corporations.

With the headline "Up Against the Wal-Mart" *Time Magazine* recounted a struggle as yet unresolved between the state and local governments in Vermont (annual state budget $1.9 billion) and Wal-Mart ($67.3 billion). Wal-Mart was told as a condition of receiving permits and permission to build stores in the state that it must build them small and build them downtown. The practice of turning small town business districts into wastelands by constructing large stores on farmland on the outskirts of cities has earned the company the nickname "Sprawl-Mart."[15] As this book goes to press there are active anti-Wal-Mart campaigns in seven cities in New York, two in Vermont, four in Massachusetts, and one each in Connecticut and Rhode Island. In recent years plans for Wal-Marts have been rejected in Lebanon, New Hampshire; Bath, Maine; and Westford and Greenfield, Massachusetts.[16]

The state governments of California, Florida, Massachusetts, Minnesota, New York, Texas, Washington, and Wisconsin have been involved in one or more of the following legal actions against large corporations: major insurance firms for damaging competitors; a major cereal company for false advertising; and a chemical company for falsely labeling their products biodegradable.[17]

Many government requirements act as incentives affecting economic decisions by individuals and organizations. The state of Maine initiated a program of identifying firms that produced all or most of a product in the state and then encouraged state and local agencies to purchase from them. The directory produced has been made available to the public. Now Maine firms and Maine residents are using it. Employment in the listed firms went up 22 percent in the three-year period after the program began. Naturally, more than a few states have asked Maine how they did it. States and local governments learn from one another. [18]

State and local governments also affect the economy in terms of decisions about whether or not to own and operate economic enterprises such as cable television, railroads, liquor stores, and utility companies.

Each social science studies political economy from a slightly different perspective. This book was written by two political scientists and a sociologist. We tend to emphasize a basic conflict between the haves and the have-nots over the decisions that governments make that affect the political economy—decisions about fairness in taxation, about whether to have government offer services and tax breaks to businesses or whether they should provide social services that may develop human potential or whether they should try to offer both. Thus in the chapters to come we will be suggesting reforms to strengthen the opportunities for the have-nots to have a realistic influence on the making of public decisions. As V. O. Key pointed out many years ago, political structures are not neutral. Some make it easier for one side to influence policy than another. Political institutions and procedures influence what kinds of policies, not simply how many policies, we get.[19]

Thus, we may not see things in exactly the same way as your economics or history instructors. This diversity of viewpoints is a healthy thing. It leaves the final decisions on what programs and solutions to invest your time and energy in up to you.

What *won't* be up to you is making decisions with political and economic consequences. Like it or not, you will face numerous decisions from signing petitions, to voting for or against a local bond issue or school board candidate. Unless you choose an active role in the political system, you simply leave to others decisions about changing or maintaining the economic regulations, taxes, tax expenditures, and legal rights that exist in your state and community. Whether you act politically or not, the political economy will be there to influence you by means of rewards, penalties, choices, and opportunities.

In sum, individuals who anticipate playing a role in the free enterprise system may consider it useful to know something about one of the biggest sets of economic decision makers in our economy. Even business majors can learn something useful from a course in state and local government.

The Federal Government Depends upon State and Local Governments

John Naisbitt, the author of *Megatrends*, has asserted that "In politics, it does not really matter any more who is president, and Congress has become obsolete . . . State and local governments are the most important political entities in America."[20]

While our belief in the importance of the individual causes us to protest that it *does* matter who is president of the United States, or in a leadership position of any other organization, we share Naisbitt's optimism about the subject matter of this book: the 50 states and the 86,693 local governments. The study of the state and local governments as they currently exist is an excellent way to develop the background necessary to make informed choices about whether to change them at all and, if necessary, what to change in the years to come.

Furthermore, while we are inclined to feel that Naisbitt understates the importance of the national government, we agree that state and local governments are a very important part of the American political system. Most national policies, such as care for the aged, assistance for the unemployed, and education for all those able to benefit from it, are carried out by state and local employees.

The federal government seldom sets up its own service delivery system. Instead, it usually creates a grant program to encourage state and local governments to perform certain important services. This year the federal government will channel more than $180 billion into the economy via grants.[21] It is important to note that most grant money does not arrive automatically. It must be applied for by state or local officials.

Some State and Local Governments Try Harder than Others

The fact that not all state or local leaders are equally willing to go after federal grant opportunities is part of the reason why Kansas, Virginia, Texas, Indiana, and Nevada received federal aid amounting to less than $600 per capita in 1992 while the states of Wyoming, Louisiana, and New York received over $1,000 per capita.[22]

Not only do governments differ in how hard they try to obtain federal funds, they also differ in how hard they work to serve their citizens. The variety of service delivery systems in our intergovernmental system is amazing. As a citizen with many years of paying taxes ahead of you, it may be a good investment of time and energy to learn something about the services that your governments provide as well as how much they cost and the way they pay for them (see Box 1.1).

One example of the differences that exist from state to state is the tuition at state colleges and universities. These differences are the results of political decisions made by state governments. The average tuition and fees for full-time students range from $8,330 in Vermont to $1,020 in Nebraska. Two of the largest states have considerable differences in tuition and fees. In California the average is $2,301; in New York it's $5,296.[23]

Naturally, state and local governments vary widely in their ability to pay for services and benefits. Even more important to students of politics is the fact that the governments also vary widely in the efforts they make to use the resources at hand. Too often we hear more about failure and corruption than we do about success. However, there are successful governments to which you can compare your own. Part of our mission is to suggest to you some reliable places to look for success.

We will explore this concept more thoroughly in Chapter 16. For the present we'll simply note that a state or local government's wealth *is not the only factor* in determining whether that government makes an effort to solve problems involving human needs. There is a school of thought that we'll call the "politics is an artifact of economics" school which uses statistical techniques to point out what happens more often than not.

> *Economic development shapes both political systems and policy outcomes, and most of the association that occurs between system characteristics and policy outcomes can be attributed to the influence of economic development . . . rather than a direct product of political variables.*[24]

Although a state, community, or individual's wealth is important, wealth doesn't explain why one rich state makes a concerted effort to deal with the problems of the have-nots and why another doesn't seem to try; or why some poor states achieve far beyond reasonable expectations given their economic base. For that we need to look to the individuals who make decisions, to the individuals and organizations who influence them, and to the institutions for state and local governance.

> ### BOX 1.1
>
> ## PLACES TO LOOK FOR COMMUNITY SUCCESS IN MAKING STATE AND LOCAL GOVERNMENT WORK
>
> *Governing: The Magazine of States and Localities.* Available in the current periodical shelves of most college libraries, or call 800–829–9103.
>
> *The Spirit of Community: Rights, Responsibilities, and the Communitarian Agenda.* Emitai Etzioni. (New York: Crown Publishers, 1993).
>
> *Innovations in State and Local Government.* Published annually by the John F. Kennedy School of Government, Harvard University, Cambridge, MA 02138.
>
> *The Quickening of America: Rebuilding Our Nation, Remaking Our Lives.* Frances Moore Lappé and Paul Martin DuBois. (San Francisco: Jossey-Bass, Inc., 1994). Pages 303–315 contain an extensive list of organizations involved in solving community problems.
>
> *Reinventing Government: How The Entrepreneurial Spirit Is Changing America.* David Osborne and Ted Gaebler. (Reading, MA: Addison-Wesley, 1992). Available now at bookstores in paperback or in your local library.
>
> *Activist's Almanac: The Concerned Citizen's Guide to the Leading Advocacy Organizations in America.* David Walls. (New York: Fireside, 1993).

Learning more about whether the governments that serve you can "afford" to offer the services you think they should is an important reason for studying state and local government. In the course of this endeavor you may also gain some insight into how to go about influencing the decisions that state and local governments make.

State and Local Governments Are Launching Pads for Careers

If you are considering a political career, state and local governments are good places to get experience. The opportunities are there. More than 500,000 state and local officials are elected in each election cycle.

If you are thinking in terms of the "number one office" in the land, there are precedents for obtaining state and local experience first. George Washington, for example, served from 1759 to 1774 as a delegate to the Virginia House of Burgesses before taking on the job of commander in chief of the revolutionary army. During the war Thomas Jefferson served as governor of Virginia.

Among the presidents in this century who have held state and/or local office one finds:

Bill Clinton	Governor of Arkansas
Ronald Reagan	Governor of California
Jimmy Carter	Governor of Georgia
Harry S. Truman	Judge, and county executive in Missouri
Franklin Delano Roosevelt	State senator and governor of New York
Woodrow Wilson	Governor of New Jersey

Calvin Coolidge

City council member, mayor, state senator, and governor of Massachusetts

THE INDIVIDUAL, THE COMMUNITY, AND THE GOVERNMENTS

There are essentially five reasons why we used the word "individual" in the subtitle of this book: (1) the importance of individual action, (2) the inherent value of each individual, (3) the collective bias of the social sciences, (4) the validity of humanizing the world in order to increase our ability to cope with it, and (5) the Aristotelian proposition about participation.

Individual Action Matters

A few months after graduating from Vanderbilt University, Marie Ragghianti was hired to work for the Tennessee state board of pardons and paroles. She was a single mother with two children who had spent many years in the threadbare existence of part-time jobs at starvation wages to feed her kids and get herself through school. At long last she achieved a fairly comfortable life-style.

After several months of hard work, she was promoted to the position of the chairperson of the board. Now she had an office and a secretary in addition to decent pay, reasonable hours, and meaningful work. Once she became chairperson of the board of pardons and paroles of the state of Tennessee, it looked as if Ragghianti could breathe easily for a while. For her, the middle-class dream had arrived: no more tight-pants cocktail waitressing; no more typing dull theses for graduate students who couldn't spell. She could save some money, contribute to her church, buy new clothes for her kids, and take them out to eat in a decent restaurant occasionally.

It soon became clear, however, that her superiors expected Ragghianti to cooperate in a bribery scheme to sell pardons and paroles. All she had to do was sign off on recommendations to Governor Ray Blanton to free or reduce the sentences of undeserving but well-connected criminals. Money, not rehabilitation, became the criterion for releasing rapists, drug dealers, and murderers from state prison.

To her superiors, Ms. Ragghianti must have seemed perfect for the job. She was a devout Catholic—"Hey, they're used to accepting authority, aren't they?" She had an Italian name—"Those people 'understand' about bending rules, don't they?" She had three kids to support, having left a wife-beating husband to work her way through college—"She needs her paycheck, doesn't she? Besides, she knows the way things are." She had worked in the Tennessee Young Democrats while she was in college. "Marie ? She'll cooperate." Unfortunately for them, her superiors forgot that stereotypes, though sometimes useful, are *always* imperfect pictures of reality.

When Ragghianti heard about the payoff, she thought at first that Governor Blanton was being used. She soon learned better—either he knew what was going on, or he didn't want to know. After some fairly explicit warnings from the governor's office to keep quiet about what she had learned, Ragghianti felt certain that if she spoke out she would soon lose her job, maybe more. Friends told her to keep quiet and to cooperate. " 'The system' is too big," they said.

To Ragghianti, it just didn't seem right, no matter how big the system, to let the corruption she could see every day continue. As the pressure mounted, she wrote the following entry in her diary:

I thought back to all the hard times that the kids & I had known, & all the meals of macaroni & cheese, & the cups of milk I'd borrowed, & the post-dated checks that we lived on, & the juggling of bills & the tears, & the marriage proposals, & the other proposals, & how easy it would have been, at any time, how easy it would have been to 'sell out'. . . .[25]

And so she resolved not to sell out. Against the advice of others, including her priest, Ragghianti told the FBI about the governor, his legal counselor, and the rest of the crew. Pretty soon her diary contained the entry, "I am afraid now, really afraid. In fact, I am terrified."[26] In the course of the next three years, Ragghianti was fired, a smear campaign was initiated in an attempt to discredit her, and she received death threats. Four people were murdered.

Ultimately the FBI investigation resulted in arrests and convictions of Governor Blanton's legal counsel and other conspirators as well as the termination of Blanton's governorship and the end of his political career. This all took place in the 1970s. Now, Marie Ragghianti and her grown children are safe. She was reinstated in her job but left it shortly afterwards to seek a law degree. A best selling book and the sale of film rights have brought her some income and removed any doubts generated by the smear campaign. The governor and his coconspirators have served or are serving time in prison.

The business of pardon and parole selling in Tennessee is bankrupt, as is the liquor license business, for which Blanton ultimately was convicted. It's safe to assume that officials in other states will now think twice about pardons and paroles as sources of income. They will do so not because of recent constitutional amendments, or new laws, or new anticorruption strike forces, but rather because an individual stood up to say, "No, this is wrong!"

Individual actions, individual courage, individual talents, and individual tenacity *matter*. Even in a society of over 250 million people, they still make a difference. Perhaps that is one reason why social scientists tend to employ words such as "frequently, often, most, many, seldom, and infrequently" instead of words like "always, invariably, everyone, all, and never." Although there are patterns, the patterns do not apply to *each* individual in a given objective category.

Individuals overcome gender, class, ethnic, and religious prejudice to do noble things for their fellow sufferers and sometimes for their ignorant tormentors. Individuals overcome poverty, racism, and physical handicaps to do great things for themselves and for the society of which they are members. Thus we generalize about human beings very carefully.

While some individuals are clearly superstars, or have faced unusual sets of circumstances, most of us are not superstars. We never get the opportunity to put a governor in jail. Thus the study of the institutions, processes, and patterns by which our society offers rewards and makes progress possible is important. Whether you are a potential superstar or one of the rest of us you need to learn about these things in order to discover how an individual can contribute to progress and help prevent the continuation of bad practices or the initiation of new ones that move us backward. The study of both our political system and the individuals who have helped it improve is an obligation to ourselves and to the generations that will follow. We can improve and preserve our state and local communities and our nation by identifying what is worth saving as well as what needs changing. If we don't, there are individuals who will make the changes for us in ways we may not appreciate.

To a very great extent the survival of our system depends on individuals standing up for what is right. Without hundreds of individual statements affirming that prejudice is wrong, the damage it does today would be far greater. Racial and ethnic prejudice is still here. Unlike the bad old days, there are more individuals around who no longer accept prejudice as something they can't do anything about. Box 1.2 is not the only example of individuals standing up for what is right, on this and many other issues.

Individuals Themselves Are Important

We used the word "individual" in our subtitle as a statement of value. Each individual human being is important. We make no claim to being unique in recognizing this fact. The inherent worth of each individual is a theme that runs through the art, music, and literature of the Western world. Perhaps no current conflict illustrates this more dramatically than the debate over whether a woman has the right to terminate a pregnancy.

Both sides consistently affirm the value of individual human life. The central question is, When does human life begin? This critical question is so well recognized that comedy routines—"Four weeks, four months, foreplay?"—have been built around it. The issue itself is far from comic, and unfortunately the debate is often far from genteel. Whichever side one takes, however, it is a side that firmly believes in the value of individual human life. Thus, not only does the discussion of this important public issue, and this incredibly

The violence in Oklahoma did not prove that "people are no damn good!" On the contrary it demonstrated conclusively how good most people are! Hundreds of volunteers from all over the state and nation rallied to help the survivors with material aid and comfort.

BOX 1.2

AN INCIDENT IN A SMALL TEXAS TOWN: INDIVIDUAL ACTIONS REINFORCE IMPORTANT VALUES

In Texas law, a rear-end collision at a stop sign automatically makes the driver of the second car the guilty party. Thus, in late January 1983, a fender bender just off the square in Chaw, Texas, appeared to be a simple matter of discovering whether or not there were any injuries, of getting the cars moved, and writing a ticket.

As Officer Jones, a former sergeant on the Houston police force and a decorated Vietnam veteran, approached the two vehicles he had no idea that he would be providing a lesson in human relations which would be the talk of the town for days, perhaps years to come. He had taken over as police chief in this small town to earn enough money to finish college in a nearby city and put some away for law school. Teaching human relations was nowhere on his agenda.*

"Anyone hurt?" he asked. The driver of the first vehicle, an elderly Mexican American just shook his head, sadly. His wife stared straight ahead and said nothing.

"Naw, I'm okay," said the driver of the second vehicle, a man of about the same age as the Mexican American couple but an Anglo like the police officer. "Guess I was going a little too fast and hit this greaser here."

Officer Jones raised an eyebrow at the "greaser," and then said, "I'm afraid I'll have to issue you a ticket, sir."

"Me, a ticket?" said the driver somewhat astonished. "But, son, he's a Mesakin. They alluz git the tickets, else at leas' a stern talkin' to." Then he smiled knowingly, "Yer new in town, ain't you, son?"

Officer Jones placed his hand on the man's shoulder and leaned toward him slightly.

"Could you just step over here a moment, sir?" He motioned to a spot a little further away out of the hearing of the other driver and the driver's wife, who was fighting back tears.

"Sure, son, anythin' you say."

poignant individual decision, become cheapened when each side screams epithets at the other it also denies the validity of individual human decision making.

To point out that other human beings merit courtesy and respect, even when we don't agree with them, is to risk dwelling on the obvious. Civilized behavior toward individuals with whom we intensely disagree has practical consequences, not the least of which is a reduction in the amount of bloodshed and violence.

Clearly individuals in a political system will have to make decisions of cosmic importance to themselves and to others. To recognize the right of individuals to make these decisions with the full understanding that they may be wrong is to recognize not only the value of the individual but also the value and uniqueness of our political system. It is, after all, less than three centuries old. Our nation, however we define it, is based in part upon the principle that individuals are bound to disagree on important issues but that the preservation of the system in which disagreements are worked out peacefully is a value which itself is an extension of the value of individual human beings.

BOX 1.2 (CONTINUED)

When they reached the spot, Officer Jones took a deep breath before he said, "I sure wish you were 30 years younger, sir."

The man smiled, "So do I son, but why?"

"Because then I could pound some manners into your ignorant, bigoted skull, sir. Now, pay very close attention," he said, carefully articulating every syllable. "When we go back to the vehicles, your language will have improved some. If I hear you utter one more racial slur in the hearing of that couple, you will be amazed at the things I can find to ticket you for. Besides following too closely, there are dozens of things wrong with your driving, as well as with your vehicle. Furthermore, I had better not hear about any problems with your insurance company paying for the damage to their vehicle. He paused, and smiled, "Now, go sit down and behave yourself while I do some paperwork here."

The driver swallowed, and nodded. Then he turned and walked slowly back to await his ticket.

The next day the mayor of this small town happened by the police chief's office.

"Understand you gave one of our citizens a little talking to."

"Yes, sir, I did."

"You know it's the main topic of conversation in the coffee shop, the post office, and the general store, don't you?"

"Yes, sir."

"Keep up the good work, son. But lighten up just a little, okay?"

"I'll try, sir. I truly will, sir.†

_____

*The names of the town and officer are changed. The officer is a former student whose language has been tidied up a bit but who affirms that this version of the incident is essentially accurate.

†Food for thought: When you stand up for your beliefs, there are other people involved. You not only affect the situation at hand; you help others, who share your beliefs, to know that they are not alone.

The survival of our political system depends to a great extent on a nonviolent approach to disagreements on some very big issues. Without a consensus on this point, scarce resources would have to be allocated simply to keep the peace—resources that could instead be used for hospitals, schools, and protection from activities that everyone agrees are criminal. Because the value of nonviolent conflict resolution is so important to the integrity of our nation and the communities therein, state and local governments exercise the responsibility to arrest and confine individuals—no matter how justified they may feel—who break the peace and inflict violence on others.

Collective Bias of Social Sciences

The third reason for using the word "individual" in our subtitle has to do with the social science perspective, the way we must view human behavior in order to understand it. All the social sciences, including political science, tend to emphasize the collective rather than the individual. We use collective words such as "the people," "the electorate," "the public," "social class," and "ethnic group." It is useful to remind ourselves every now and then that a central goal of our scholarly effort is to help individual human beings understand and thus better operate in the social part of their world. We will occasionally provide examples of individuals such as Ms. Ragghianti and Officer Jones in an attempt to counter the collective bias built into the subject matter of this book.

Humanizing Promotes Understanding

A fourth reason for including "individual" in the subtitle is to help make the world we are trying to explain not only more understandable, but also worth understanding. In a large, complex society such as ours it is often tempting to believe that large, complex entities— the media, big business, government, special interests—rule our lives. If, occasionally, we realize that these entities are made up of individual human beings, we may find the world to be a friendlier place in which to live and work.

Not only is such a world a less threatening place, it is also one we may be able to deal with more rationally and effectively. If we deal with other individuals as fellow humans instead of "things" that play roles, such as "bureaucrat" or "clerk," we may find these individuals responding to us as human beings. This may lead to cooperation in getting things done. Ms. Ragghianti, you may recall, was a bureaucrat, that is, an employee of the state of Tennessee. Officer Jones is a police officer, also a member of a bureaucracy. In discussing the future of our federal system, David Beam has observed:

> Although policy analysts have traditionally devoted most of their attention to the investigation of large impersonal forces in determining governmental events, the record shows that a decisive role is also played by personality, interests, values, and commitments of the decision makers themselves. Moreover, it is not just this very few "great" men and women of history, but a great many lesser individuals too, who sometimes have their stamp on governmental trends. Individuals tucked away at strategic locations in the legislature, the bureaucracy, interest groups, in the media, or elsewhere can influence outcomes by pointing out problems or proposing solutions.[27]

The Obligation to Contribute Our Talents to the Community

Our fifth, and final, reason for focusing on the individual has to do with the obligation to participate. Aristotle put it something like this: "If good people don't participate in the affairs of the community then others will." Because we believe that the vast majority of our readers are good people, we think it is important for them to participate. It is in their own interests to participate. Call this living democracy, enlightened self-interest, noblesse oblige, or whatever you choose. The fact remains that participating in our political system is worth the time and trouble it takes. More often than not, the individuals who participate not only have made ours a better system by participating in it, they have become better people because they participated.

Because individual actions are so important in maintaining what is good about our political system, an organization called the Giraffe Project (Box 1.3) was created a few years ago to give recognition to the actions of ordinary individuals across the country who have stuck their necks out to help others and to reaffirm the values that too many of us have come to take for granted.

Although this is not a how-to-do-it book, one of its major purposes is to equip the individual with a better understanding of how our political system works so that he or she can be more effective in dealing with it. Our basic assumptions about the American political system are that, for all its faults, it is a system worth attempting to understand and that informed participation is one of the best ways of understanding it. The more we know about the world of politics, the more comfortable we will be in acting constructively within it.

In sum, we believe that the individual matters because it is important who leads and the direction in which we are led. It also makes a difference when individuals speak up for what is right. Individual actions often have a ripple effect on the way other individuals see the world and thus on the way that world works.

WHY WE USE THE TERM *GOVERNMENTS*

In the title of this book, and from time to time in the pages which follow, we use *governments* in the plural because this word provides an occasional reminder that you, the citizen, are responsible for electing and keeping track of the leaders in charge of several interacting units of government.

Our use of the plural term "governments" also represents an attempt to emphasize the dynamics of the political system in which individuals and governments interact. Quite often, textbook authors use the term in the singular, to refer to any one of or all of the governments with which an individual must deal. When "government" is used in that way, it

---

BOX 1.3

THE GIRAFFE PROJECT

In 1983, John Graham, a retired foreign service officer, and Ann Medlock, a journalist, founded an organization to recognize people who "stick their necks out for the common good." Sticking one's neck out may involve discomfort, danger, or ostracism, or cause one to lose one's job; sometimes it involves devoting time and energy to a long-term project for the good of others when the time could have been spent on more profitable activities. It usually involves some kind of risk.

Almost daily, more than 500 radio stations report short accounts of people who are given a Giraffe award. Four times a year, *The Giraffe Gazette* reports on the deeds of individuals who have been commended for their actions by a screening committee consisting of Graham, Medlock, and friends and neighbors. "Each of these individuals' acts," says Medlock, "teaches the rest of us about learning to cope in an unsafe world."

Through the courtesy of the Giraffe Project, we will report in these pages on a few of the more than 300 Giraffes who have helped keep alive the notion that individuals matter. Should you wish to nominate someone for a Giraffe award or help the organization in other ways, here is the address:

The Giraffe Project, Box 759, Langely, Washington 98260.

Source: The Giraffe Gazette.

tends to give the impression of a seamless web of government reaching from city hall to the state capitol ("Got to go deal with the government") that the individual must confront in order to get anything done. This is often not the case.

Depending upon the business to be conducted, the individual actually confronts, one at a time, other human beings who work for a number of units of government which do not necessarily coordinate their activities, keep one another informed of what they are doing, or cooperate as much as they should. The individual deals with many governments. Unless we make it clear which one, "the government" could be any one of 86,000 units found within the borders of the United States of America.

State and local governments interact in a number of ways: they make contracts with one another, perform services for one another, sue one another, give money to one another, and compete with one another for new industries and tourist dollars. Not only do many of these governments deal directly with one another, but they may also deal with the same citizens. Many governments have authority over and responsibilities to the same land and people.

From our perspective, the fact that the individual may have more than one government to keep track of is an important feature of the political system. For an example of the number of governments that an individual may interact with in a not atypical urban area, see the case of Fridley, Minnesota, in Box 1.4. Each government's tax rate, service offerings,

---

BOX 1.4

LAYERS OF GOVERNMENT IN FRIDLEY, MINNESOTA

11. United States of America
10. State of Minnesota
9. Metropolitan Mosquito Control District
8. Minneapolis–St. Paul Metropolitan Airports Commission
7. Anoka County
6. Soil Conservation District
5. North Suburban Hospital District
4. Minneapolis–St. Paul Sanitary District
3. North Suburban Sanitary Sewer District
2. Independent School District
1. City of Fridley

The Individual Citizen of: 1, 2, 3, 4, 5 . . .

Believe it or not: A citizen of Fridley, Minnesota, is expected to exercise informed control over 11 superimposed governments. Most of them levy taxes through a board or council the citizen elects.

Source: Committee for Economic Development, Modernizing Local Government (New York: 1966), 12.

or both, will have an effect on other governments and on the individual. Many city residents finance two separate road or street departments (city and county) without ever inquiring as to whether combined operations or cooperative arrangements might save money. A local newspaper which fails to assign a reporter to look into the intergovernmental dimension of local politics is clearly shortchanging its subscribers. This is something you might think about if you are looking for part-time journalistic employment.

In the years to come it will be up to you to determine how well organized, well integrated, and efficient the system of government is in your state and community. One of the purposes of this book is to give you a few tools to make informed judgments about your governments.

Another term that you will see frequently in this text is intergovernmental relations (IGR); it officially entered the vocabulary of political science with creation of the Advisory Commission on Intergovernmental Relations (ACIR) in Washington, D.C. The term intergovernmental is another way of suggesting that state and local governments, as well as the national government, are part of a dynamic system of interaction. As a matter of fact that's what the ACIR studies and makes recommendations for improving — this dynamic system.

Whether we call it the study of state and local government, the study of state and local governments, the study of the interaction between the individual and the governments, or the study of intergovernmental relations, the study of this system is both important and quite compatible with our concern for the individual. According to Deil S. Wright, an authority on intergovernmental relations,

> Strictly speaking, then, there are no intergovernmental relations; there are only relations among officials who govern different units. The individual actions and attitudes of public officials are at the core of IGR.[28]

Thinking of governments in terms of the people who run them helps us to remember that mistakes are human and sometimes can be corrected. Furthermore, decisions by human beings can be overruled. After all, when the state of Vermont or the city of Los Angeles or Anoka County "speaks," it is actually a *person* who is saying something, and persons can be fired, voted out of office, or persuaded to change their minds. Thus the individual does not usually confront governments as such. Instead, the individual deals with other human beings who are government officials or employees.

WHY YET ANOTHER BOOK ON STATE AND LOCAL GOVERNMENT?

The authors of this book have been teaching long enough to know that at least two things that ought to be in textbooks cannot be found in many of them.

The first thing is a straightforward admission that textbooks form the basis for test questions. We have taught from textbooks which were well organized, but boring, and from books which were interesting but didn't seem to have much "meat." The problem with the first kind of book is that students don't want to read them. The problem with the second kind is that instructors find it rather difficult to determine whether their students have actually learned anything. While holding your interest is important to us, providing you with information useful for participating in your governments has a much higher priority. Thus, we will tend to favor "meat," or content, over style, or "cute."

How to Pass Tests on This Book

We will try to compensate for our lack of pizzazz by attempting to make it as painless as possible for you to meet one of your highest priorities: getting a decent grade on the tests based on this book. To this end we offer four pieces of advice: break your reading into digestible bits, outline, identify and learn study objectives, and use flash cards.

Break Your Reading into Digestible Bits

Don't attempt to read any chapter of this book all at once. Since it is a textbook, it lacks a sustained plot and character development. To attempt to read it all at once is to invite sleep. For your convenience, this book has already been broken into digestible bits through the use of chapters, headings within chapters, and subheadings between headings. Therefore, skim each chapter to identify the main courses and major dishes before you start your intellectual meal.

Outline

First, find the outline we provide by marking the headings in the book with appropriate outline identifiers (I, A, 1, a, and so on), and then write the outline of the chapter in your notebook before attempting to read the chapter. This will provide a road map of where you are going. It will also provide an opportunity to identify many, if not most, study objectives.

Identify and Learn the Study Objectives

By study objectives we mean any idea, or set of ideas, that can be the subject of a test question. You might also call them study questions, learning goals, or behavioral objectives. What you call them matters less than that you identify the meat of a chapter (or a lecture).

While it is possible for an instructor to test you on tiny details, it is more likely that he or she will focus on ideas associated with reasons why, characteristics of, differences between, or definitions of new terms and concepts. In this book we attempt to lead you to most of the study objectives with headings and subheadings. Not all authors do this, however, and sometimes study objectives are buried in the text of a chapter. We've probably done this ourselves a few times in this textbook.

A single study objective can be the subject of a vast array of exam questions. Once you have learned the study objective, you are ready regardless of the type of question about it. In most chapters there are usually from 10 to 15 study objectives, sometimes more if the chapter is particularly long. After checking your outline for study objectives, survey the chapter again to find objectives hidden away in "headless" paragraphs or buried in strings of "reasons why" that haven't been introduced with a topic sentence.

As you will soon observe, if you haven't already, we provide about ten study objectives at the end of each chapter. We hope that this will help. We cannot guarantee, however, that your instructor won't find objectives that we overlooked to add to his or her test question pool. Therefore, don't depend entirely on our list. Make a few more of your own. Remember, we are feeding you a few study objectives in order to teach you how to fish for them by yourself—in this and other texts.

Use Flash Cards

Once you have a list of study objectives, read the chapter, or at least the parts of the chapter in which you've identified study objectives, to see if you understand them. Then isolate each one on an index card.

On one side put the study objective (for example, to identify four steps in studying for a test on this book). If one or more of the items briefly listed on the flip side of your card requires some elaboration, make a separate card for that idea, concept, or point. For example, after you list our four pieces of advice, you may wish to make a card that defines study objective or a card that lists three advantages for using flash cards. Thus some study objectives will generate more than one index card.

Flash cards have at least three advantages. The first is to reinforce learning by writing the information out on the card in the first place. Second, making an individual copy of each study objective and its response forces you to concentrate on one item at a time, biting off the information in digestible bits. Ever notice how you lose track of ideas when you "review" a whole page of notes? A third advantage from making flash cards is that it becomes easier to quiz yourself before your instructor tests you. Either you know what is on the flip side of that card or you don't.

If you can pass your own tests, you will probably pass the instructor's. Making cards from lecture notes isn't a bad idea either. It helps separate main points from examples and helps identify places in your notes that need cleaning up, or need that fourth "reason why," for which you ought to check someone else's notes, or ask the instructor.

Stretching

The second thing we've yet to find in many textbooks is a willingness to confront the fact that there are many bright people who are poorly prepared for college. This lack of preparation may be a product of the wide differences in the resources available to local school districts, or it may have something to do with upbringing or with a late blooming of an individual's motivation to do something with his or her intellectual equipment. Regardless of the cause, the fact remains that the individual applied to and is enrolled in an institution of higher education. Almost by definition this education should challenge and stretch minds. Colleges and universities are about what *can be*, as well as what is. If some students have to work a little harder to realize their considerable potential, so be it.

It seems to us that too many texts are dummied down when they ought to challenge, push, and stretch. Some, for example, use a ninth-grade vocabulary to explain college level material. In order to avoid this inconsistency we've used our own vocabularies. We identify **in boldface type** some of the terms we think will be new to you. Whether or not we define them in the text, we have placed a glossary of most of the terms in boldface at the end of each chapter. Naturally, glossary entries are fair game for test questions. Thus, we recommend you make flash cards on the glossary terms that are new to you as well as the study objectives at the end of each chapter.

If we miss a term or two in the glossary, we assume you have a good dictionary and, if not, that you will buy one. There are also several good political science dictionaries available, so we won't recommend by name. We used our own vocabularies because we assume that no matter how poorly prepared for college an individual may be, he or she has the potential to rise to the occasion and look up a few words in a dictionary, or even ask questions in class based on the reading. We didn't start college with the vocabularies we are using.

Whether or not we really stretch you, make you mad enough to read further in other sources, or simply teach you some facts, we'll never know unless you tell us. Please do. Just write us care of the publishers. They'll forward our mail.

CONCLUSION

This chapter has attempted to explain a little bit about this book, its goals, and its approach to the subject matter. The major goal of this book is to encourage you to help make the more than 86,000 governments in this country more effective and more responsive to the communities they serve. We hope to show that you can do so through informed participation in state and local politics.

In the pages that follow we will use the term "community" more often than the term "society." In this way we emphasize the fact that individuals are bound to some set of relationships beyond the family. By community we mean more than simply the people in a territory that has a local or state government, although for some that's all it means.

STUDY OBJECTIVES

1. Identify seven reasons why studying state and local government may be important.
2. identify five reasons why attention to the individual is important in studying state and local government.
3. Identify Marie Ragghianti and her relationship to the study of state and local governments.
4. Identify the Giraffe Project and the Innovations in State and Local Government Program.
5. Why is the plural word "governments" rather than the singular word "government" used in the subtitle of the book?
6. Identify the four steps in effectively preparing for tests based on the material in this book.
7. Identify flash cards.

GLOSSARY

Anglo Among the many peculiarities of the political culture of the southwestern states is the fact that all people of predominantly European heritage are called Anglos (short for Anglo-Saxon) to differentiate them from Mexican-Americans and African Americans. The term "Anglo" is somewhat disconcerting to newcomers from other states, particularly those who are proud of their non-Anglo-Saxon heritage. Officer Jones, for example, is an Irish-American from Chicago.

Collective These nouns are used in the singular to describe or refer to a collection of many individuals. Collective nouns take singular pronouns and use the singular form of verbs, e.g., The army, . . . it.

Economics   The study of the relationships in society involving the use, management, or exchange of limited resources.

Grant   A sum of money given, not loaned, from one to another is called a grant, or a grant-in-aid. Private foundations, wealthy individuals, and units of government are the sources of most grants.

Political economy   Relationships in society involving politics and economics. These relationships usually involve regulations that affect economic choices.

Politics   Any human relationship that involves—to a significant degree—influence or power. Politics usually involves conflict or cooperation in attempting to solve problems that confront the community. Politics becomes heated because people don't always agree on what the problems really are, much less the proper solutions.

Rehabilitation   Repairing damage to the mind or body. To rehabilitate a criminal is to convert that person into a productive citizen. Rehabilitation usually involves training.

Society   Any collection of individuals among whom there exists regular patterns of behavior.

Stereotypes   Mental constructs used to simplify part of reality in order to cope with it. The more we go beyond merely coping and attempt to understand reality, the less likely we are to operate in terms of stereotypical thought. The problem with stereotypes is not only that they are partially true but that they provide no guidance as to how often they are not true.

Tax expenditures   Exceptions to tax laws that result in reductions, for those who benefit from them, in the amount of taxes paid. They also result in reductions in tax revenue collected. Tax expenditures result when legislatures give a tax break, or exception, to one category of individuals, business, or type of income or property and not to others.

ENDNOTES

1. David Osborne and Ted Gaebler, *Reinventing Government* (Reading, MA: Addison-Wesley, 1992), 60–65.

2. Emitai Etzioni, *The Spirit of Community: Rights, Responsibilities, and the Communitarian Agenda* (New York: Crown Publishers, 1993), 9–10.

3. Ibid., 25. See also Etzioni, *Rights and the Common Good: The Communitarian Perspective* (New York: St. Martin's Press, 1994).

4. Frances Moore Lappé, and Paul Martin DuBois, *The Quickening of America: Rebuilding Our Nation, Remaking Our Lives* (San Francisco: Jossey-Bass Inc., 1994).

5. Robert N. Bellah et al. *The Good Society* (New York: Vintage Books, 1991), 295.

6. Texas Comptroller of Public Accounts, "Reinventing Texas Government," *Fiscal Notes* (October, 1993), 1–2.

7. Charles Mahtesian, "Connecting the Phoneless to the Rest of the World," *Governing* (November, 1993), 42.

8. Penelope Lemov, "3BR, 2BA, and a Cop Next Door," *Governing* (November, 1993), 42–43.

9. John F. Kennedy School of Government, *Innovations in State and Local Government, 1994*

(New York: The Ford Foundation, 1994), 22.

10. U.S. Department of Commerce, Bureau of the Census, *Statistical Abstract of the United States 1993* (Washington, D.C., 1993), 318.

11. Michael A. Curme, Barry T. Hirsch, and David A. Macpherson, *Industrial and Labor Relations Review* 44 (October, 1990), 25–26.

12. Peter A. Harkness, "Publishers Note," *Governing: 1995 Resource Directory* (January, 1995), 3.

13. The Council of State Governments, *The Book of the States: 1994–95* (Lexington, KY: The Council of State Governments, 1994), 341.

14. Edmund S. Phelps, *Political Economy* (New York: W. W. Norton & Co., 1985), 5.

15. John Greenwald et al., "Up Against the Wal-Mart," *Time Magazine* (August 22, 1994), 58.

16. Jonathan Walters, "Store Wars," *Governing* (January, 1995), 29.

17. "Four Big Insurers Settle Texas Antitrust Case," *New York Times*, March 29, 1991. C2; "Kellogg Pays 6 States." *New York Times*, October 4, 1991, C5; and "Company Settles Lawsuits on Biodegradability Claims," *Wall Street Journal*, July 3, 1991, C18.

18. Karen Ann Coburn, "Maine Puts Its Stamp on Home-Grown Products," *Governing* (October 1991), 21.

19. V. O. Key, *Southern Politics* (New York: Knopf, 1949), 299–307.

20. John Naisbitt, *Megatrends* (New York: Warner Books, 1982), 97.

21. In 1992, *The Statistical Abstract of the United States 1993* (Washington, D.C., 1993), indicated that the grant total was $174 billion, p. 296. The sum of $180 billion is a conservative projection. From 1991 to 1992 the increase was from $154 billion to $174 billion.

22. Ibid.

23. Ibid., 345.

24. Thomas R. Dye, *Politics, Economics, and the Public* (Chicago: Rand McNally, 1966), 293. Cited in Thomas R. Dye, *Politics in States and Communities*, 8th ed. (Englewood Cliffs: Prentice-Hall, 1994), 131.

25. Peter Maas, *Marie: A True Story* (New York: Random House, 1983).

26. Ibid.

27. David R. Beam, "Forecasting the Future of Federalism," *Intergovernmental Perspective* (Summer, 1980), 7.

28. Deil S. Wright, *Understanding Intergovernmental Relations* (North Scituate, MA: Duxbury Press, 1978), 9.

CHAPTER

2

The State and Local Environment

Encouraged by the success of project "College Here We Come," Kimi Gray and her friends stepped up a long-standing effort to persuade the Housing Authority to let them take over management of the project. In 1982 the mayor, figuring it couldn't get much worse before it would probably have to be bulldozed, reluctantly agreed. In a series of well-attended meetings, much to the surprise of Housing Authority bureaucrats, the tenants:

1. *Drew up a constitution, bylaws, policy and personnel procedures, and job descriptions.*
2. *Created a system of elected building captains empowered to levy fines for littering and excessive noise and charged with the responsibility of helping explain the relationship between paying rent and getting things fixed.*

Over the course of the next few months the loosely structured tenants association became the Resident Management Corporation and began to transform the project into a community. They developed a survey of the needs of project residents. They created programs to respond to the needs surveyed by forming day-care, tutoring, and adult education centers, all of which were run by project residents either as volunteers or employees.

They also began to serve eviction notices to those who would neither pay nor contribute work to pay their rent. With funds coming in from increased rent collections they created businesses to do repairs and maintenance. This provided wages and income for tenants and kept money circulating in the project. The Corporation established initiatives to promote family stability such as the "Bring the Fathers Out of the Closets Campaign." Returning fathers were promised jobs within the project.

Residents also developed a new relationship with police. They were invited to attend meetings and locate a temporary station in the project. As a community they took a firm stand on drug dealers. Those dealers who were residents were evicted. Others were turned in and harassed by marches and demonstrations, and tenants actually went to court to testify against them.

In addition to a wide range of activities which suggested that the quality of life in Kenilworth-Parkside was getting better, there were some measurable results as well. First, by 1989 the crime rate had fallen from 15 crimes a month to two; this was the lowest in the city. Second, auditors reported in 1986 that during the first four years alone, resident management had saved the city over $785,000. Not only was rent collection increased to seven times that of public housing citywide, but the Resident Management Corporation had helped more than 130 persons get off welfare—hiring some, setting others up in business, and finding training and jobs for others.

In a little less than a decade of hard work and risk-taking, a housing project of 3,000 people, mostly impoverished, had become a community. In 1990, the Department of Housing and Urban Development sold the project to its residents. Kenilworth-Parkside is now not only a community but a community of homeowners. The people of Kenilworth-Parkside are no longer clients or subjects, they are citizens.[1]

Kimi Gray and her organization dealt with the city government in obtaining tenant ownership of Kenilworth Parkside. At minimum her efforts indicate (1) the importance of the individual; (2) the fact that government is not the only organization for solving problems in our communities; (3) the fact that sooner or later efforts to solve problems involving large numbers of people will bring most organizations or individuals into contact with one or more agencies of state or local government (either as a friend, an enemy, a resource, or an obstacle). Because the 86,000 units of state and local government are so central to solving problems in the communities of America they are the organizations to which this book will pay the most attention.

Kimi Gray's story also helps us make another important point. The context or the environment in which Kimi Gray operated may not be one familiar to you. Rural or suburban residents do not often have to deal with areas taken over by drug dealers, or with the complex of problems generally labeled urban poverty. Nevertheless, state and local politics take place in an environment. Some dimensions of this environment are common to all communities, some are not.

In this chapter we explore a few dimensions of the differences and the similarities found in the environment in which individuals attempt to solve problems that affect their communities. We have selected only those that seem essential to establish a common frame of reference for understanding the chapters that follow.

THE CHANGING TECHNOLOGICAL ENVIRONMENT

All political systems change. New leaders come to power, new problems arise, better solutions to old problems are discovered. The good news is that political systems can change for the better. The bad news is that they can also change for the worse.

The American system of governments was born in an agricultural era. It is still adapting to the consequences of industrialization and metropolitan living even as it enters the age of computers, robots, and the twenty-first century. In attempting to put rapid change in perspective, we present Box 2.1, which collapses the approximately 60,000 years of the history of *Homo sapiens* into one calendar year. Most of the technological advances we have come to take for granted have occurred rather late in that history, and more are occurring so fast that our social and political institutions have trouble adjusting to them. The theft of cellular phone numbers, for example, is a billion-dollar-a-year criminal activity with which we have yet to come to grips.

Today the individual and the governments interact in a world that is changing more rapidly than ever before. A critical feature of the rapid changes to which we must continue to adjust is the fact that human beings nearly always create technology faster than they create methods for dealing with its consequences. Whereas we had thousands of years to adjust to the technology of fire, metal, and agriculture, we are now dealing with several new generations of computers.

Technology and the Community

Technology can be defined as the knowledge available to make, store, use, or transmit energy, matter, or information. The root word of technology is *tekhnē* meaning "skill." The discovery that people could make and use fire resulted in technology for dealing with the materials for producing and using it—spits for cooking over it, pots for cooking on it, hearths and chimneys to manage and disperse heat and smoke, and developments in metallurgy, fuel discovery, and the preparation and refinement of fuels.

The social and political consequences of the next major technological discovery—agriculture—were enormous. The agricultural revolution made it possible for many people to live in one place all year round. It no longer mattered whether game and wild plants were available. Because one farm family could feed many other families, not everybody had to be a farmer.

Thus, while it involved the development of techniques for planting, harvesting, and storing crops, the agricultural revolution also made economic and other social specializations possible. The agricultural revolution also created a type of city to which the human race has had over 10,000 years to adapt. Plato, Christ, Charlemagne, Shakespeare and Thomas Jefferson all lived in essentially the same type of urban place. It was a walking city; that is, one could walk completely around it in less than a day. Its area was about two square miles. The metropolitan areas of the automotive revolution, by contrast, have been here for only about 50 years. Thus, in the context of human history, it will take some time to adapt to them.

Technological change may once have permitted a long leisurely process of getting used to new ways of doing things, but it no longer does. Because new problems and new opportunities arise long before we've fully solved the problems or explored the possibilities of the previous ones, rapid technological change is an important part of the environment in which individuals and their governments find themselves.

The Industrial Revolution, which really got rolling in the United States after the Civil War (about 1865), changed cities all over the world, as well as the world itself. Manufacturing activities required unskilled labor, thus increasing the size of the city's population. Technology made it possible for cities to grow both up (steel frameworks to build skyscrapers and elevators so that people could use them) and out (steel made light-rail streetcar systems possible, first horse drawn and then electric). The city of the Industrial Revolution was bigger, and more complex, with more opportunities and more problems than the city the human race had been adapting to for over 10,000 years.

BOX 2.1

THE YEAR OF *HOMO SAPIENS*

Homo sapiens appears at the last stroke of midnight as the new year begins. Fire is domesticated in early February. The agricultural revolution occurs in March, but most of the earth is still sparsely populated by hunters and gatherers clear through the summer. Recorded history begins about November. By this time the agricultural revolution has spread more widely. People begin a long adjustment to urban living which was not possible before the discovery of the science of seed collection.

Sometime after Thanksgiving, the pyramids are built. The navigational equipment to carry Columbus and later the Pilgrims across the Atlantic becomes available about the second week of December. On December 29 James Watt gets his steam engine to run in the morning. In the afternoon America wins its independence. The Industrial Revolution gets rolling just before dawn the next day.

December 30 is a pretty full day. By the time it is over, slavery will end and telephone lines will connect Europe and America. Ships made of steel (which actually float!)—each carrying a hundred times as many people from Europe to America as the wooden *Mayflower* did—will cross the Atlantic in one-third the time it took the *Mayflower*.

About midnight Edison finally gets a light bulb that works after trying about 200 different filaments. As dawn lights the skies of American cities they have ceased to be dependent at night upon gas lamps for reading and street lighting. Mass production of the automobile starts about noon on December 31. By dinner-time, electricity is beginning to reach rural America through the cooperatives financed by Roosevelt's New Deal.

World War II begins and ends about coffee break time in the afternoon of the thirty-first. About the time the New Year's Eve parties are under way, television (black and white) becomes available—but only to the well-off. In a few seconds these new devices become so widely available that millions of homes are ready to receive scenes of the civil rights revolution and later the war in Viet Nam. Politics is changed forever by the new technology of presenting the news.

The countdown to midnight just begins when the first commercial nuclear reactor begins to generate electricity, and two Americans not only land on the moon but return safely.

The first stroke of midnight has already sounded as Apple builds its first desk top computer. The echoes of the last stroke are dying out as most of you graduate from high school. It isn't even one o'clock in the morning, dawn is a long way off, and you are now enrolled in state and local government as another 60,000 years of human history begin.

The opportunity to adjust to this city did not last very long, because in the second decade of the twentieth century the mass production of the automobile began. We are still adjusting to the automotive revolution. Three of the many adjustments are as follows:

- First, for certain activities there is no difference between an automobile, a hotel room, a movie theater, or a restaurant. The implications in terms of morals and manners are considerable.

- Second, our perception of time has changed dramatically from the days when journeys were calendar events, not stopwatch events. People who walk or use horses and buggies (or even mass transit) are accustomed to waiting a few minutes here and there. People in cars become very quick tempered if the car ahead of them doesn't move within ten seconds after the light changes. To sit through an entire 90-second light cycle without moving causes some people to come unhinged.
- Third, our relationship to the land has changed in at least two major ways as a result of the automobile. (1) More people view land as an economic quantity, to be divided up and sold for a profit. Fewer people view land as a sacred trust from generations of the past to generations of the future. Recently several thousand people demonstrated at state capitols and in Washington, D.C., over their "rights" as landowners. (2) Second, urban land is put to more different uses than ever before. The walking city and the city of the streetcar devoted a relatively small amount of space to transportation. Today, our tendency toward two- and three-car families requires vast amounts of land for parking and for service locations as well as for roads, bridges, and interchanges.

When a unit of government considers requiring developers to set land aside for parks, in many communities this is viewed as confiscation of private wealth, a "taking" rather than enforcement of a responsible use of the land.

Given the short time we have had to adjust to rapid change, it is no wonder that the new metropolitan areas containing hundreds of homes, businesses, malls, and shopping centers sprawling for miles in every direction under the jurisdictions of dozens of different units of government present us with organizational challenges we have yet to meet adequately.[2]

The Metropolitan Paradox

Metropolitan Statistical Areas (MSAs) contain over 30 percent of the governments in this country, yet most metropolitan areas have no government. This is the metropolitan paradox. To appreciate the importance of this paradox, we must examine a definition and a process.

Metropolitan Statistical Area

An MSA is an area consisting of a county in which there is a city (or twin cities) with a total population of 50,000 people and any contiguous counties which are socioeconomically integrated with the core county.[3] Socioeconomically integrated means that unless a contiguous county meets certain standards regarding population density, urban population, and close economic and social ties with the core county, it is not included in the MSA.

Not only do MSAs include numerous communities and governments, many of them also form larger agglomerations called Consolidated Metropolitan Areas (CMAs). There are now nearly 20 CMAs. Some observers refer to this phenomenon as a megalopolis. Whether we call it a megalopolis, a CMA, or an MSA, it is a large complex of people and governmental units struggling to cope with traffic jams; air pollution; stray animals; water shortage in the summer and floods in the spring; fire; sewage, and solid waste management; juvenile delinquency; and a host of other problems that ignore the boundaries between one government and the next.

County boundaries are used to define MSA boundaries and CMA boundaries in all but six states (Connecticut, Rhode Island, Massachusetts, Vermont, New Hampshire, and

Maine). In those states, statistical data are collected by towns and cities. Most states designate their county governments to be the agency for collecting birth, death, land ownership, and other statistics.

While the more than 300 MSAs in the United States account for only 16 percent of the land area, they contain about 75 percent of the population, and most of the wealth, job, cultural centers, and problems in our political economy.

Because county boundaries are used to define MSA boundaries in most states, many parts of metropolitan America are not completely urbanized. Thus, while it is probably useful to know that not every square foot of metropolitan America is densely populated, paved, and polluted, it is probably more important to remember that metropolitan areas are gobbling up some of the best farmland on the continent.[4] Furthermore, while metropolitan areas occupy a relatively small land area, what happens on that land area affects the rest of the country in terms of air pollution, acid rain, and finding places to dump household, industrial, hazardous, and nuclear waste.

The Process of Metropolitan Sprawl

Metropolitan sprawl is the uncoordinated spread of economic, recreational, residential, and governmental development beyond the legal limits of the core cities of the metropolitan areas of America. Metropolitan sprawl is also known as suburban sprawl or urban sprawl. It means traffic jams, water shortages, pollution, vast shopping centers with asphalt parking lots smothering good farmland, downstream flooding because upstream the land can't absorb as much water, and large populations crowding inadequate parks and recreational facilities.

According to urban historian Lewis Mumford, "The city has burst open and scattered its complex organs and organizations over the entire landscape."[5] Not only have affluent urban workers migrated to live outside the central city, but many jobs have left as well. Furthermore, new cities and special districts are created outside the central cities every year. These new governments add to another problem found in the intergovernmental environment: the fragmentation of authority.

The Fragmentation of Authority

Authority is legitimate power. When power is divided into many small parts, at least two things can happen, one good and one bad. If individuals or units of government which have a small part of power have a common vision of what they want to do with it, they can cooperate in accomplishing great achievements. It is, of course, a major premise of democracy that the bits of power we each possess will be used for a common good. If power is used in such a way that each power holder is in a position to cancel out the effort of others, like a collection of clowns all fighting to get through a narrow doorway, then the fragmentation of authority can be very wasteful. Not only are resources lost, but so ultimately, is legitimacy.

One cause of fragmentation of authority in metropolitan America is the creation of approximately 500 new special districts a year for the past 20 years. Between the 1962 and 1992 Census of Governments 10,000 new special districts and 1,077 new municipalities were created. That is a great many new offices, new officials, and new jurisdictions.

To the frustrated citizen who doesn't want to take a short course in local jurisdictions and responsibilities, there seems to be little good that outweighs the proliferation of numerous local governments (see Box 2.2). A question that needs asking in many of the more than 300 MSAs is whether we can produce good results through a democracy of governments in metropolitan America, or whether the people need to create a single metropolitan

It was not until 1921 that three-fourths of the states ratified the Nineteenth Amendment granting women the right to vote in the states that had not yet followed the example of Wyoming, which had done so in 1869 while it was still a territory. In 1925 Wyoming became the first state to elect a woman governor, Nellie Taylor Ross. The state motto is "Equal Rights."

government in each area and hold it responsible by holding the individuals in charge of it responsible.

Different solutions will be appropriate to different conditions. For the present, it is sufficient to note that the metropolitan paradox, together with metropolitan sprawl and the fragmentation of authority, has yet to be eliminated in any MSA to the point where a model solution has emerged. Thus individuals and their governments will be experimenting with solutions for a long time to come.

PERVASIVE DIVERSITY

Our society is incredibly diverse. We've chosen in this chapter to touch two dimensions of that diversity—demographic and economic. However, there are many other dimensions of diversity which we will bring to your attention throughout this book. Some dimensions of diversity may seem to be mere diversions in the form of verbal cartoons, while others emphasize points being made in the chapter. That, of course, is what diversity is all about—things to be taken seriously and things not, and a sincere effort to differentiate between them.

BOX 2.2

THE STOPLIGHT AND THE LONG ISLAND SCHOOL CHILDREN

When more than one local government has jurisdiction over different matters in the same geographic area, it can be very confusing for ordinary citizens. It raises questions such as How many political systems does one have to contact to get something done? Who's in charge? Is *anyone* in charge?

In an article titled, "The Balkanization of Suburbia," written more than twenty years ago, Samuel Kaplan told of the troubles he and his neighbors encountered attempting to sort through the various local governments which shared jurisdiction over all or part of an area containing some 35,000 people located in the Port Washington peninsula of Long Island, New York.

Their objective was to get a traffic light installed on Main Street to make it safer for children to go from the elementary school on one side of the street to the library on the other side. Briefly, this is what they learned in 1971 about the boundaries of their various political systems.

The school on the south side of the street was located in an unincorporated area of Port Washington and therefore was controlled by the township. The library on the north side was located in the village of Baxter Estates. The street itself was a county road, but was located in and patrolled by the Port Washington Police District, which is independent of the village, town, and county. Traffic lights on county roads are the responsibility of the county. However, parking on the street that is also a county road falls under the jurisdiction of the town.

Although Mr. Kaplan wrote as much in sorrow as in anger (and with enviable style and charm), his cause was not lost. While it did take time ("A lot of time," Mr. Kaplan might say), the governments did respond.

First, the township of North Hempstead passed a parking ordinance. This, at least, gave the children and motorists a better view of one another. Second, the Nassau County Board of Supervisors ordered a traffic study.

Whether the traffic flow was great enough, according to existing standards, for it to order its public works department to install a traffic light—or whether the Nassau County Board simply caved in to public pressure, we don't know. We do know that an official of the Nassau County Board told us on the phone that there is now a traffic light on Main Street between the school and public library. We didn't ask when it was installed.

Source: Samuel Kaplan, "The Balkanization of Suburbia," Harper's Magazine, October, 1971, 72–74.

Diversity of People

The notion that America is a nation of immigrants is well established. *Homo sapiens* migrated to the new world more than 30,000 years ago. There is no evidence that man evolved in the continental United States or in Hawaii. Native Americans are the descendents of peoples who migrated from northwestern Asia. The first Hawaiians arrived there between 300 and 600 A.D. after a long voyage from the Polynesian islands across open sea.

Today Americans trace their ancestry to more than 100 places on the globe. In the past two decades 19 million immigrants (legal and illegal) have come here from more than 100 countries. There are some 42 languages spoken in the homes of American citizens.

We are probably the only nation on earth to contain such a variety of peoples, cultures, or races and to provide a system of governance than enables these diverse individuals to live together in relative peace, harmony, and prosperity. The story of this book is in part the story of how we do it. Ours is a system that works for nearly 250 million individuals, and one of the reasons why this book was written is to help make sure that it continues to work.

Extremes of Wealth and Poverty

In virtually all political systems political resources are distributed unequally. In some, however, the differences are greater than in others. It is generally understood that there is diversity in the distribution of wealth among individuals and among units of government. It is not generally understood that in recent years the differences among family incomes have been increasing rather dramatically. Should the trends of the 1980s continue into the next century the stability of our political system could be affected.

Take, for example, the rewards obtained by the Chief Executive Officers of large corporations in America. In Japan the top executives receive salaries 25 times that of the average factory worker; in Germany the ratio is 36 to 1. In the United States the ratio is 125 to 1. Now, if these American top executives paid larger portions of their income in taxes than do executives in other industrial nations, these differences might be understandable. However, they don't.

Donald L. Bartlett and James B. Steele, two Pulitzer Prize winning journalists, provide another way of looking at the size of the differences in income in America. They note that in 1959 the top 4 percent of income earners received the same amount of income as the bottom 35 percent. In 1989 it took more incomes to equal that of the top 4 percent; in that year they received the same amount of income as the bottom 51 percent.

Those deciding how to make companies leaner and more efficient seldom did so by taking a cut in pay, as several thousand American workers who became unemployed and sometimes homeless during that decade are well aware. The total salaries of people in and outside of corporate boardrooms earning more than $1 million in the 1980s increased by 2,184 percent while the incomes of people earning $20,000 to $40,000 a year went up by 44 percent. According to Bartlett and Steele this was "a phenomenon unlike any America had seen in this century."[6]

One of the original purposes of grants in aid whether from the federal government to the states or the states to local governments was to make it possible for all citizens to have equivalent if not equal schools, roads, water supplies and other essential services and facilities. It will be interesting to see if the tremendous increase in discretionary income available to the very wealthy is used politically to further reduce their share of the state-local tax bill and to change a long-standing commitment to provide opportunity and minimal services at the state and local level to rich and poor alike (see Box 2.3).

BOX 2.3

DIMENSIONS OF DIVERSITY: BANKRUPTCY

In 1992 almost a million Americans filed for bankruptcy, a 179 percent increase since 1984. Some of those declaring were hiding large resources, some were virtually destitute. In order to promote fairness and as a consequence of learning about rather large loopholes many states began to comb through state codes in which exemptions were stashed away "like a crazy uncle in the attic." Here are a few items located as the cobwebs were peeled back.

In Mississippi you can keep 40 gallons of molasses, 500 pounds of bacon, and 1,000 stalks of sugar cane.

In Michigan among the things you can shield from creditors are 100 hens, 10 sheep, five swine, and grain and hay to feed them. Unfortunately you can only protect $3,500 in home equity. If you owe more than that the home may have to be sold.

In Florida most homes would be protected because bankruptcy law there protects $250,000 in home equity. Texas, where leniency is on par with that in Florida, exempts the wages of a family's chief wage earner along with $60,000 in personal property and the homestead.

Five states—all in New England—don't allow any homestead exemption. If you run up debts you can't pay in Pennsylvania, you can lose everything including your home—well, almost everything. You can keep a Bible and a sewing machine.

Source: Charles Mahtesian, "Fifty Ways to Go Bankrupt," Governing, December 1993, 22–23.

THE ENVIRONMENT OF BELIEF: REGIONAL CULTURES AND NATIONAL IDENTITY

Political culture consists of attitudes, beliefs, values, and patterns of behavior that influence both the way we see the world and the way we deal with it. We are taught our political culture, it doesn't come with our genes. In this section, we will examine political culture in terms of three concepts: political socialization, regional subcultures, and four models of our national identity.

The notion of political culture is important not only because it helps us to understand ourselves, it also helps us to understand people we may wish to influence. If you understand the models and values that other individuals use to operate within the real world and you attempt to communicate in their terms instead of your own, not only will those individuals seem less irrational, so will you.[7]

Political Socialization

Political socialization is a process through which we learn our political culture—the beliefs, ideas, and attitudes about politics that are accepted as appropriate for our society. We are taught our political culture throughout our lives, but for many Americans the early years are most important because after we reach adulthood the :

political orientations of most individuals are simply not challenged very frequently. It is well known that politics in the conventional sense is not salient for most people on a day-to-day basis. . . Therefore, since politics is most often a peripheral concern, change typically comes about rather slowly; because the questions raised are seldom about the foundation of the political system, basic political beliefs are most likely not to shift.[8]

This is not to say that children are carbon copies of their parents; in fact a considerable body of research suggests that parental views explain very little about the positions take by children on social issues.[9] It simply suggests that by the time most Americans have made up their minds what they're going to accept from parents, neighbors, peers, and other sources of political learning they seldom reexamine their basic political orientations.

The reason that basic political orientations are seldom reexamined is that people pay so little attention to politics. If, however, one can get them to pay attention, then attitudes and orientations can be changed. As we shall see in Chapter 7, which deals with the media, there is a great deal of research available on political persuasion and evidence to support that attitudes can and do change.

This potential malleability of individual beliefs increases the importance of the individual in two ways. First, it suggests more rather than less potential for affecting change in others. Second, it suggests that we ourselves need to be more aware of our own vulnerability to manipulation. Openness to change also increases the importance of leadership. As Jennings and Niemi have noted:

perhaps the most important implication of all this is the emphasis it places on political leadership. Citizens are willing to change with the times, and occasionally demand change. But the possible directions of change are many. The task of political leadership is to channel development in a way that proves to be satisfactory.[10]

This information provides a pair of reasons why it is important for us to attempt to understand these patterns that have been laid down over time. First, we need to know what is worth saving if others attempt to change them. Second, confident in the knowledge that change for the better is possible, we need to know what it is that needs improving.

Moralistic, Individualistic, and Traditionalistic Subcultures

The beliefs and values that most Americans share as part of their political culture can be traced to the writing of John Locke, a seventeenth-century English philosopher. Locke's ideas were adapted by the political leaders who led the revolution which created the American political system. This ideology has become the core of American political culture.

Perhaps the most concise statement of this cultural core is found in the *Declaration of Independence* (see Box 2.4). The notion that all people are created equal was the basis for our second revolution, the civil rights revolution, which helped to redefine the American nation and to bring us closer to realizing the ideals found in the *Declaration of Independence*. Political leaders in the government may argue over the application of these principles in the real world, but they base their argument on the same system of ideas and beliefs. Thus, even liberals and conservatives have more in common than would appear to be the case, especially in the heat of the debate.[11]

Although the terms "liberal" and "conservative" are frequently used in the American political context, another set of differences also helps us to understand some of the diversity in the environment of the governments. Daniel Elazar has identified three American subcultures which he and his students have demonstrated to be important in shaping the way we

BOX 2.4

AMERICAN POLITICAL CULTURE: THE DECLARATION OF INDEPENDENCE

We hold these truths to be self-evident, that all men are created equal, that they are endowed by their Creator with certain unalienable rights, that among these are Life, Liberty, and the pursuit of Happiness. That to secure these rights, Governments are instituted, among Men, deriving their just powers from the consent of the governed, That whenever any Form of Government becomes destructive of these ends, it is the Right of the People to alter or to abolish it, and to institute new Government, laying its foundation on such principles and organizing its powers in such form, as to them shall seem most likely to effect their Safety and Happiness. . . .

think about politics. These subcultures are three versions of the same overarching American political culture. Elazar identifies them as moralistic, individualistic, and traditionalistic.[12]

Each subculture emerged in a particular region and type of community in eighteenth-century America, before the Revolutionary War and well before the Industrial Revolution. The moralistic subculture emerged in small farming communities of New England. The political unit of reference was a small rural town. New Hampshire and Connecticut farming communities tended to be homogeneous and thus people who came together to make decisions about what was good for the community tended to share a common vision of that good.

The individualistic culture was associated with the Middle Atlantic states and with the dynamic growing trading communities located there—New York, Philadelphia, Trenton, Baltimore. It was in these port cities and the rural areas surrounding them that new immigrants were settling. The political unit of reference was an urban center, a city. Thus the communities associated with the individualistic culture were more diverse, and there was more likely to be disagreements over what was good for the community. Furthermore, in the city there were more extremes of wealth and poverty than in the farming communities of New England.

The traditionalistic culture is associated with the plantation economy of the South. Here the typical political unit was the county in which several wealthy families dominated a society consisting of landed gentry; poor whites on scattered farms some of whom did menial work and crafts, and African Americans, most but not all of whom were slaves. There was more diversity in these rural areas than in New England and there was a much more hierarchical social order to keep it stable. Diversity was not associated with dynamic growth and competition as it was in the areas where the individualistic culture emerged.

As populations in each of these three areas multiplied and descendants moved westward, the cultures traveled along in their heads. Today these three cultures (or subcultures) are found in various combinations in each of the 50 states. As Figure 2.1 indicates, few states have only one of these cultures and the pattern of distribution reflects migration out of the states in which the cultures originated. Each culture embraces values that are part of the Lockean-American political culture but some emphasize some aspects more than others. In light of our concern about change for the better, Elazar's caveat is worth noting:

Each of the three political subcultures contributes something important to the configuration of the American political system and each contains certain characteristics that are inherently dangerous to the survival of that system.[13]

A growing body of research testifies to the importance of political culture as an influence on the actions of state governments and individuals. Ira Sharkansky, for example, using data on the contiguous 48 states, indicates that high levels of traditionalism were associated with low voter turnout, lower government expenditures on social programs, a low tax effort, and lower levels of expenditure on education.[14] Russell L. Hanson reviewed some of Sharkansky's findings and looked at what happens when individuals raised in one culture move to states where another culture predominates.[15] Others have shown relationships to party competition and innovative government policies. Even the way candidates campaign in elections appears to be influenced by the political culture in which the campaign takes place.[16]

The Equal Rights Amendment for Women, which ultimately failed to pass the requisite number of state legislatures, was adopted by at least some state legislatures in each type of culture. However, states with a predominantly traditionalistic political culture lagged behind other states in terms of the percentage of states ratifying. As Table 2.1 indicates, only 25 percent of traditionalistic states ratified the proposed Equal Rights Amendment for Women, while 88 percent of moralistic and 76 percent of individualistic states have done so. Each subculture provides a different orientation toward politics, government, and participation, and thus toward the way we go about solving problems in our states and communities.

Politics

The moralistic subculture promotes the view that politics is the process of seeking the common good.

Traditionalistic communities tend to see politics as a process for maintaining social order. To put it another way, the common good tends to be defined in terms of maintaining the status quo.

In communities influenced by the individualistic culture politics is likely to be seen as a contest for control of government. There is a basic assumption that not everyone has the same goals or view of the common good.

Government

The moralistic subculture promotes the view that government is a tool (one of several including the church, private enterprise, and third sector voluntary organizations) that can be used to solve problems or promote the common good.

The traditionalistic culture also views government as a tool. It is to be used to maintain the status quo. Control of it should be kept in the hands of those who know the community best—who understand "our way of life."

The individualistic culture sees government as a prize. Politics is a game played to win that prize. Once one controls government one can help one's friends and sometimes even punish one's enemies.

Participation

Participation in community affairs is an obligation in the moralistic culture. The concept of public service is more common in this culture than in the others where participation is seen

Figure 2.1

The Distribution of the Three American Subcultures

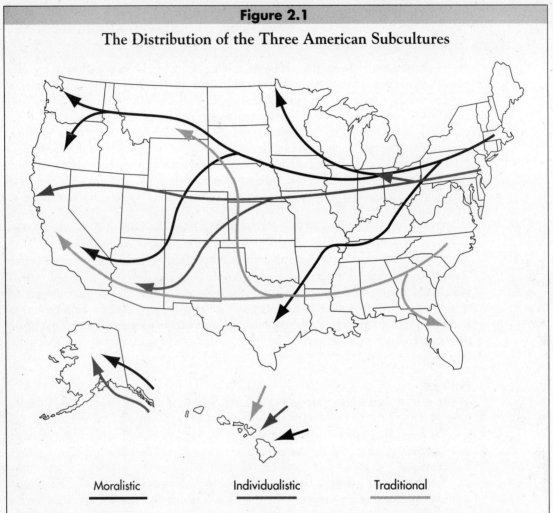

Moralistic   Individualistic   Traditional

Distribution of three American political cultures. Emerging in preindustrial colonial America, these cultures have been modified by time and transportation to new places. However, they still influence our views about politics.

Source: Daniel J. Elazar, American Federalism: A View from the States (New York: Harper & Row, Publishers, 1972).

as "getting involved in politics." The moralistic culture promotes the view that the public is best served when everyone offers their talents for accomplishing the common good. Today, the communitarian movement, river and beach cleanups, neighborhood watch groups, and urban parent patrols which try to make sure kids get to school safely are examples consistent with the moralistic idea of public service.

Table 2.1

POLITICAL CULTURE AND THE EQUAL RIGHTS AMENDMENT

Predominant State Political Culture*

	M	MI	IM	I	IT	TI	T	TM
Not Ratified	Utah		Illinois	Nevada	Missouri	Alabama Arkansas Florida Georgia Louisiana Oklahoma Tennessee	Mississippi South Carolina Virginia	Arizona North Carolina
Ratified and Rescinded	Idaho	Nebraska						
Ratified	Colorado Maine Michigan Minnesota North Dakota Oregon Vermont Wisconsin	California Iowa Kansas Montana New Hampshire South Dakota Washington	Connecticut Massachusetts New York Ohio Rhode Island Wyoming	Alaska Indiana New Jersey Pennsylvania	Delaware Hawaii Maryland	Kentucky New Mexico Texas West Virginia		

*Predominant culture is listed first.

M = Moralistic

I = Individualistic

T = Traditionalistic

Source: John Kincaid, ed., Political Culture, Public Policy and the American States (Philadelphia, PA: Institute for the Study of Human Issues, 1982), 21. Reprinted by permission.

Participation in the affairs of the community is also an obligation in American communities influenced by the traditionalistic culture. However, there is a hierarchy involved. For the better classes, the founding families, participation is an obligation. For the rest it is a privilege, earned by proving that one is qualified to use the privilege properly. On the whole, the upper classes would prefer to select candidates and identify solutions at private social occasions, then let the common folk ratify their decisions through the electoral process.

Participation in the affairs of the community in individualistic communities is a right rather than an obligation or a privilege. Hierarchy is often involved here also but in the sense of a hierarchy of merit rather than social class. If one wishes to enjoy the rewards of political participation and one is willing to learn the rules of the game, willing to pay one's dues, and wait one's turn, then one can participate in making decisions about who will run and how the issues will be decided. Amateurs and those concerned with issues and causes simply mess things up and create problems. Elections are contests in which team captains bring forth their players to engage in a contest of who can get the most supporters to "exercise their right to vote." Once the election is decided, the supporters go home and await the next election.

The Use of Office for Personal Gain

In the moralistic culture this is a betrayal of the public trust. Rooting out corruption is a major concern of people in the moralistic political culture. The tendency of some professional politicians to become wealthy in office is one reason why, in areas where the moralistic culture is strong, there have been so many efforts to promote reforms such as nonpartisan elections, term limits, and a willingness to equip government with tools to limit the use of money to influence the political process.

In the individualistic culture the use of office for personal gain is not a problem, unless it becomes an embarrassment that could affect the next election. That is why people put up with the grief and aggravation of politics, to obtain material rewards. One can overdo it, but a little graft lubricates social and political intercourse. Because they are more inclined to view politics as a game, participants have trouble understanding why moralists get so hot under the collar and behave in such an uncompromising fashion sometimes when a little trade-off here and a little payoff there would send everybody home with something.

In the traditionalistic culture the use of office for personal gain is a minor sin when one considers that those who serve the public have made sacrifices to do so, and that in the long run those who benefit from public office will probably reinvest their gains in the community anyway. However, if someone who is out of favor with the elite should engage in corruption, well then that is a horse of another color!

Three Political Cultures—Summary

For many participants in the political system, regardless of their political culture, politics can be a lot of fun. Even if it gets messy on occasion, it has its exhilarating moments. Sometimes one feels pretty good about accomplishing something in politics, whether it's for the ordinary working stiff or for posterity.

The three political cultures we have summarized are combined in several ways in different states and communities. The resulting combinations help shape what people expect of their governments and what they will tolerate from them. Elazar cautions us against "hasty judgments" of any or all of the political cultures. Each has contributed something worthwhile to the American political system:

> The moralistic political culture, for example, is the primary source of the continuing American quest for the good society. At the same time, there is a tendency toward fanaticism and narrow-mindedness noticeable among some of its representatives. The individualistic political culture is the most tolerant of out-and-out political corruption, yet it has also provided the framework for the integration of diverse groups into the mainstream of American life. The traditionalistic political culture contributes to the search for continuity in a society whose major characteristic is change, yet in the name of continuity, its representatives [have tried] to deny blacks (or Indians, or Hispanic-Americans) their civil rights.[17]

Elazar also observes that sometimes one serves to limit the excesses of another, as in the individualistic culture's protection, "though not for any noble reasons," of personal freedom in the face of moralistic efforts to use the power of government to produce a better social order. Adherents of the moralistic and traditionalistic cultures have been known to limit the individualistic tendency to stretch liberty into license.

National Identity

All three subcultures identified by Elazar were created during the early years of American history, before the Industrial Revolution and before massive immigration changed the nature of American society. Thus, they do not address the problem of defining the American nation. The three subcultures do not attempt to answer the question of who we are because they all were created when the only view of the American nation was that of a society most of whose members shared a common British heritage.[18]

The question of who we, the American people, are is an important one for the study of state and local government. Our common bond of membership in a nation is an essential link in holding together a political system in which there is a great deal of real and potential divisiveness. The breakup of the Soviet Union is but one example in modern times of the difficulty of keeping large political units from falling apart.

Today there are four competing myths or models of who we are: the Anglo core culture, the melting pot, cultural pluralism, and the multiracial society. Like all attempts to simplify reality in order to deal with it or understand it better, each myth or model leaves out part of the picture. Each is partially true and partially false. The trick is to determine which part is which.

A discussion of different models of who we are would not be very important if not for the fact that these models serve both as explanations for how things *are* and as patterns for how things *ought to be*. It is the "ought to be" dimension of each model that has important political consequences. To jump ahead a bit, people who operate in terms of the melting pot see bilingual education as a useful tool to promote assimilation. They are uncomfortable when it is used as part of a state-financed program to preserve and promote ethnic heritage. Those who think in terms of cultural pluralism are more likely to see this as a perfectly legitimate way to use state and local funds because for them America is (and thus ought to be) a collection of ethnic groups.

The Anglo Core Model

The Anglo core cultural model is based on the fact that our language is a dialect of English and our basic political institutions and our basic political values can be traced to the English philosopher John Locke. Thus, certain core symbols, institutions, and practices are so central to our self-concept that to alter them would be to risk severe damage to our national identity.

Although the Anglo core culture model was based on fact, it ignored other rather important facts. Even as John Jay wrote Paper Number Two of *The Federalist* (see Box 2.5), Americans of non–British or non–Anglo-Saxon ancestry and cultural heritage were making contributions to the American nation. In addition to numerous people from different parts of Europe, African Americans were also adding to the national wealth, through their labor, their music, and their contributions to our language. The Anglo core myth overlooks those facts.

A second error made by the Anglo core culture, in addition to stressing the importance of the Anglo contribution to the exclusion of other contributions, resulted from a confusion of ancestry and heritage. The first is biological or genetic; the second is cultural. Heritage is taught. It may be taught to us by people who are related to us, but it can also be taught by people who aren't. By confusing ancestry and heritage (genes and jeans as it were), the Anglo core culture became associated with the idea that people who weren't of Anglo-Saxon ancestry couldn't learn to be good Americans. The Anglo core culture became identified with the emergence of political movements such as the Know-Nothings, and the Ku Klux Klan.[19] It is a major reason why we had a racist immigration policy from 1924 until the 1950s. The National Origins Quota Act of 1924 gave a high quota to people of "correct" ancestry (Northern Europeans), a low quota to people from other parts of Europe, and no quota at all to people from China and Africa.[20]

It is no insult to anyone to assert that the American nation has a set of core values. To assert that they are only comprehensible to people with the right genes is both insulting and scientifically inaccurate.

The Melting Pot Model

The melting pot is the model that we celebrate most often in a culinary way. The selection of ethnic foods available and the entry of ethnic words into the language testify to the ability of the American society to accept new ways of doing things. The concept of assimilation—adopting a new culture and contributing to it—is central to the melting pot model. In this model, the American national identity is the result of contributions by individuals as well as by other cultures.

This interpretation also has some problems. The major one is that it does not contain a place for ethnic groups. In fact, it is rather impatient with them.

We define an ethnic group as a collection of people with a common sense of identity who seek to obtain the rights and benefits of citizenship in the state. Thus, an ethnic group is similar to a nation in that it can be created out of myths, language, shared version of history, common experiences, and heroes. However, it differs from a nation in that an ethnic group does not seek its own state. Thus, our definition is based on the notion that when a collection of people seeks their own state they are not an ethnic group but a nationalist movement.

BOX 2.5

THE ANGLO CORE CULTURE IN *THE FEDERALIST*

Providence has been pleased to give this one connected country, to one united people; a people descended from the same ancestors, speaking the same language, professing the same religion, attached to the same principles of government, very similar in their manners and customs.

The Federalist Papers, which we will learn more about in Chapter 3, were written by three of our founding fathers—John Jay, Alexander Hamilton, and James Madison—all writing under the pseudonym, Publius. *The Federalist Papers* first appeared as a series of newspaper articles written to convince the people of New York that they ought to elect Federalists to the constitutional ratifying convention in New York. They are generally regarded not only as one of the finest statements of American constitutional principles, but also as a classic in the field of political theory.

_____

Source: " Paper Number Two" in Roy P. Fairfield, ed., The Federalist Papers (Baltimore: Johns Hopkins Press, 1981), 6.

In America, unlike many other countries, it is possible for one to be a member of the nation and a member of an ethnic group. In part, this is because we have such a variety of definitions of who we the American people are. Thus, in the United States it appears that we have been able to keep the distinction between ethnic group and nation clear. The idea has gained fairly widespread acceptance that African Americans, Jewish Americans, Chinese Americans, and Hispanic Americans are among the many ethnic Americans who have an additional cultural identity of which they are proud yet who want and should receive the rights and the responsibilities of full citizenship in the American nation-state.

Ethnic identity, according to the melting pot model, is viewed as something that should disappear a generation or so after immigration to this country. Although many American families and individuals have shed their ethnic identity, and thus provide ample evidence that the model is partly true, others have not. Many other Americans do not wish to give up their ethnic identity and they resent the notion that being ethnic somehow means not being ready for prime-time Americanness.

The Cultural Pluralism Model

Cultural pluralism is perhaps the most popular image of America today. It is also known as multiculturalism. Because it is the most recent, there is a tendency to think of this model as being better than the others instead of simply the most recent imperfect explanation of who we are. "New" may be the favorite color of mall rats, but new isn't always best.

Cultural pluralism, like the other myths, has much to offer. It gives respectability to ethnic identity. It accurately reflects the notion that many Americans wish to keep and sometimes rediscover their pre-American ethnic heritage. Ethnic identity is here to stay. There are jobs, organizations, market niches, media audiences, and public policies that are based on ethnic identity. Ethnic identity isn't going away and thus a model of America that recognizes the validity of ethnic identity is one worth taking seriously whether it works for us or not.

According to this model, everyone is a part of an ethnic salad in which every ingredient maintains its identity. In *Megatrends* John Naisbitt asserts, "We have moved from the myth of the melting pot to a celebration of cultural diversity."[21]

The pluralist model, for all its many advantages, has some disadvantages as well. The most important one for the purposes of this discussion is that the model has no place for the fact that many Americans do not have and do not want an ethnic identity.

To the cultural pluralist this is not the way things ought to be. America is a collection of ethnic groups, says the cultural pluralist. If you say that you aren't ethnic, then you are either hiding something or you don't understand America. In the following passage Ricardo Garcia, a cultural pluralist, indicates the difficulty that this model of America has in dealing with a nonethnic American national identity:

The dominant ethnic group in American society is made up of much-maligned white, Anglo-Saxon, Protestants (WASPS). The power of our WASP heritage is still potent, manifested in major institutions, in people's attitudes and behaviors. The WASP group is so deeply

The "melting pot," which served as a symbol that all Americans of European ancestry ought to assimilate and become nonethnic Americans, was a symbol of America's industrial might. It was not a culinary device. The more recent multiracial model asserts that regardless of ancestry anyone can become a nonethnic American.

embedded in American society that its attitudes and values are perceived by some to be the American core ethos.[22]

The implications of the above statement are both interesting and potentially troublesome. First, it strongly suggests that there is something wrong with the notion that America has a set of core values (at all). Second, it implies that to learn the core values is to compromise one's ethnic integrity. Third, it fails to acknowledge the existence of a broad mainstream that is constantly changing, a mainstream to which individuals from nearly all ethnic groups make contributions in one way or another. In short, the notion that America has a "core ethos" troubles some cultural pluralists because they fail to appreciate the fact that one can have an American identity based on that ethos without having an ethnic identity.

This difficulty for cultural pluralists is understandable if we recall one of the flaws in the application of the Anglo core culture idea. Its early adherents wrongly assumed that people of color and people from other European nations could neither learn that core ethos nor make worthwhile contributions to the America which is still under construction. Once we admit that many individuals and peoples other than the English have contributed to what makes America worth protecting and preserving, then we can accept the reality that some of our basic institutions are our own (American) version of English institutions.

The second problem with cultural pluralism or multiculturalism is that it forces on a category of persons a group identity they may not want. Many people classified as WASPs are neither of British heritage nor of Protestant faith. WASP is a sort of catchall category for nonethnic whites.

If everyone *must have* an ethnic identity, then what do we do with people who say they don't have one? Do we honor that claim or not? Many Americans identify with the American nation and have no additional ethnic identity. They may have identities based on schools, professions, sports, hobbies, astrological signs, food preferences, and so on ("I'm a lacto-vegetarian." "You are? Well that's interesting, I'm a Sagittarius.")

For many Americans, ethnic identity is rather incomplete. After the 1970 Census, the Bureau of the Census found in a series of reinterviews in 1973 that only 64.7 percent of the surveyed individuals reported the same ethnic responses that they had less than five years earlier.[23]

A third problem with cultural pluralism is the difficulty in dealing with the notion of a national identity. If everyone is ethnic, what do we do with George Washington and Abraham Lincoln? Are they *merely* WASP heroes? Clearly they are more than that, just as Martin Luther King is both an ethnic and a national hero . It is worth noting that in the magnificent "I Have a Dream," speech he looked to the day when his children would be judged on "the content of their character, not the color of their skin." To this it seems reasonable to add, "or the cultural identity they do or do not choose to define themselves."

Multiracial Society

The fourth myth is perhaps less developed than the other three. It has fewer adherents, although that may change in the years to come. The idea of a multiracial society is implicit in Martin Luther King's "I Have a Dream" speech.[24]

A multiracial society is one in which the notion of "both" replaces the either/or orientation in dealing with race. In a multiracial society children of mixed ancestry are not forced to identify themselves as belonging to one or the other race. A law passed by the Georgia legislature in 1993 removes the "other" category from application forms used by the state and makes it possible for one to classify oneself as multiracial. An organization called project RACE (Reclassify All Children Equally) is working to have other states and the federal government abandon the use of "other" and use instead multiracial as a way of classifying people of more than one race. It is worth noting that the Georgia State legislator who sponsored the multiracial bill was the son of Ralph Abernathy, a stalwart in the civil rights movement.

Also worth noting is the fact that people are asked to place themselves in racial categories so that records can be kept for the purpose of monitoring social progress toward the goal of communities in which race is no longer a factor in hiring, promoting, admitting to schools or to professional organizations, granting loans, or selling insurance or homes.

The multiracial society is one in which people no longer assume that just because someone has a black ancestor one is supposed to be an expert on black issues or have an African American ethnic identity. If one chooses an ethnic identity one is not an outcast, but neither are people of color who do not choose an ethnic identity. Being ethnic and being nonethnic are both valid in a multiracial society.

The notion of situational ethnicity is also consistent with a multiracial society. At work a stockbroker may operate as an American who happens to be black. At home he or she may be an African American. "Ethnic or not," says the multiracialist, "we are all Americans regardless of our ancestries."

The empirical validity of the multiracial myth is supported by the fact that in America today there are large numbers of people of color who are of mixed ancestry, and there are thousands of people of ostensibly European ancestry who have unacknowledged African or Native American ancestors. Thus, a certain amount of hybridization has already taken place. As more interracial marriages and/or adoptions take place there will be several million young Americans who find the either/or thinking of racial or ethnic chauvinists —white, black, brown, red, or yellow—to be confusing, upsetting, and inappropriate for them.[25]

The major flaw in the multiracial myth is the fact that it is so threatening and offensive to some adherents of the other myths. On the one hand there are white racists who will make life difficult for those operating under the assumption that ours is a multiracial society. Race mixing is anathema to the Aryan Nation and the Ku Klux Klan. On the other hand there are ethnic group members who see the loss of members and support for ethnic organizations if too many people of their ancestry de-emphasize their ethnic identity. To cultural pluralists this is selling out. Consequently, they will recruit individuals into keeping their ethnic identity rather vigorously and sometimes in ways that—to some—might not seem fair.

Four Models—Summary

Each of these models is flawed. Each model is useful for many individuals but not for others. Each deserves respect, and in some societies, such as ours, each receives respect. One of the tragedies of other societies is that they lack political institutions that make it possible for people with different views on important matters to work out solutions peacefully.

As future leaders at the state, local, and national levels, you will have to deal with people who have models different from one another's and from yours. Our major reason for bringing this to your attention is to prepare you to respect these models and to communicate in terms of shared goals and beliefs rather than to insist upon ideological uniformity.

CONCLUSION

In this chapter we have introduced some terms and concepts we think are useful in the study of the individual and the governments. We will attempt to avoid jargon as much as possible. However, we find it extremely difficult to have readers "know what we mean" if they do not share a working vocabulary and a common frame of reference.

It is important to emphasize that the frame of reference in this book is simply one of many. We do not claim our definitions or our sets of concepts are the best for everyone. We offer them because you need to know that they exist and need to come to terms with them if you want to operate effectively in your state and community. Later in this book we will explain some institutions, such as political parties—and some policies, such as welfare or taxation, from a particular point of view. We do this to encourage you to think, to challenge yourself, and to prepare yourself for dealing with decisions you will be asked to make in the political system of your state and community. We do not do it to persuade you that a particular point of view is the right one.

A few paragraphs ago we asked, somewhat rhetorically, whether George Washington and Abraham Lincoln were American heroes, or merely WASP heroes. Equally significant is the question of whether or not Harriet Tubman, Sojourner Truth, Cesar Chavez, and Martin Luther King can be American heroes as well as ethnic heroes. The answer, we hope, is that they not only can be but *already are* American heroes

Respecting the right of other individuals to differ from us ideologically and then working with them through our state and local political institutions to resolve peacefully the consequences of our differences has been necessary for our political system and our nation for over two centuries. Understanding how they work, and endeavoring to make them work better will improve the chances that they'll be around for another 200 years.

In the American political system the possibility is worth considering that the good old days were not really all that good. When our nation was founded, slavery was tolerated, and women couldn't vote. During the Industrial Revolution leaders who proposed laws prohibiting child labor in mines and factories were regarded as being enemies of the free enterprise system. From 1877 until the 1960s segregation and daily humiliation for African Americans were upheld by the force of law in the states now covered by the 1974 Voting Rights Act and subsequent amendments. In short, our nation has changed, and for the better in many ways.

Where it goes from here depends upon you. Whether you become a leader willing to make tough decisions, or an individual willing to do your homework and let your leaders know you are watching, you will affect some part of the political system. In doing so, you will affect the whole because political systems neither exist in isolation nor remain forever the same.

STUDY OBJECTIVES

1. Define "technology" and identify three technological changes that have profoundly affected the social environment of the human race.
2. Explain what the metropolitan paradox is.
3. Explain the relationship between metropolitan sprawl and the fragmentation of authority.

4. Identify two dimensions of diversity that affect politics.
5. Define "political culture and political socialization."
6. Identify the significance of our potential malleability.
7. Identify the three American political subcultures.
8. Identify four dimensions of politics to which the subculture provides different orientations.
9. Compare and contrast ethnic group and nation.
10. Describe the four models that are used to define who "we the people" are.

GLOSSARY

Abstraction   A mental construction, a set of ideas that we use to simplify reality and organize our thinking about it.

Agglomeration   A collection of mixed items. In the metropolitan context it refers to the large areas of hundreds of square miles that include a hodgepodge of cities, towns, villages, trailer parks, slums, and industrialized and commercial areas.

Altruistic   The quality of being unselfish and concerned with the well-being of others.

Authority   Political power which is accepted as right and proper, as legitimate.

Category   A part of a classification scheme. We use category to refer to items or individuals included in a classification scheme. They share a characteristic. We contrast category with the term "group." A group is a collection of individuals who share a common identity. Members of a group have more links to one another other than simply sharing a characteristic. "Category" is objective; "group" is subjective.

Charisma   The gift of grace; special personality characteristics that enable one to lead other people. Charismatic individuals are usually believed to have superior moral qualities.

Community   A collection of people among whom there is some sense of fellow feeling, or the people who live in a neighborhood or larger territory.

Ethnic group   A collection of people with a common sense of identity who seek to obtain the rights and benefits of citizenship in a larger society or state. Members of ethnic groups can also be members of nations.

Government   A set of offices which make and enforce decisions that affect the membership of a political system.

Ideology   A set of beliefs about politics. It comes in two forms, manifest and latent. The latent form of an ideology is similar to political culture.

Jurisdiction   The subject matter or territory over which an individual or government has authority.

Legitimacy   The quality of being accepted as right, fair, proper, or in accordance with agreed upon standards.

Megalopolis   A large complex of people and governmental units struggling to cope with problems that ignore the boundaries between one government and the next.

Metropolitan Statistical Area (MSA)   An area consisting of a county in which there is a city (or twin cities) with a total population of 50,000 people and any contiguous counties which are socioeconomically integrated with the core county.

Metropolitan sprawl   The uncoordinated spread of economic, recreational, residential, and governmental development beyond the city limits.

Nation   A collection of people with a common sense of identity who seek to establish or maintain a state of their own. Members of nations may also be members of different ethnic groups.

Nation-state   The predominant form of political unit in the international community today. It consists of a self governing political unit—a state—in which a nation constitutes the majority of the politically relevant population.

Paradox   Something that appears to be false or absurd, but which is true—once one better understands it.

Political culture   Consists of attitudes, beliefs, values, and patterns of behavior that influence both the way we see the world and the way we deal with it. We are taught our political culture, it doesn't come with our genes.

Political power   The ability to get people to do something they might not otherwise do, also known as influence.

Political resource   Anything that can be used to obtain power or influence.

Political socialization   A process through which we learn our political culture—the beliefs ideas, and attitudes about politics that are accepted as appropriate for our society. We are taught our political culture throughout our lives, but for many Americans the early years are most important.

Political system   Any persistent pattern of human behavior involving to a significant extent control, influence, power, or authority.

Politics   Any human relationship involving, to a significant extent, influence or power.

State   A political system whose government is able to enforce its claim to unique authority to regulate the use of force among the people living in a defined territory.

Technology   The knowledge and skill available to make, store, use, or transmit energy, matter, or information.

ENDNOTES

1. David Osborne and Ted Gaebler, *Reinventing Government* (Reading, MA: Addison-Wesley, 1992), 60–65.

2. For an excellent overview of the history of the city and the emergence of the metropolis see Mark Schneider, *Suburban Growth: Policy and Process* (Brunswick, OH: King's Court Communications, 1980). The American classic is, of course, Louis Mumford, *The City in History* (New York: Harcourt Brace and World, 1961).

3. Census Bureau, U. S. Commerce Department, *County and City Data Book, 1992.*

4. Edward H. Glade, Jr., and Keith Collens, "State Agriculture," *The Book of the States: 1982–83*, (Lexington, KY: The Council of State Governments, 1982), 620–631.

5. Mumford, *The City In History*, 34.

6. Donald L. Bartlett and James B. Steele, *America: What Went Wrong?* (Kansas City: Andrews and McMeel, 1992), 1.

7. The two essential sources on political culture are: Daniel J. Elazar, *American Federalism: A View From the States*, 2d. ed. (New York: Harper and Row, 1972), 86–126; and Gabriel A. Almond and Sidney Verba, *The Civic Culture: Political Attitudes and Democracy in Five Nations* (Boston: Little, Brown & Co., 1965).

8. M. Kent Jennings and Robert Neimi, *Generations and Politics* (Princeton, NJ: Princeton University Press, 1981), 390.

9. Michael A. Milburn, *Persuasion and Politics: The Social Psychology of Public Opinion* (Pacific Grove, CA: Brooks/Cole Publishing Company, 1991), 37.

10. Ibid., 391.

11. Donald J. Devine, *The Political Culture of the United States: The Influence of Member Values on Regime Maintenance*, (Boston: Little, Brown & Co., 1972), 46–65.

12. Elazar, 93.

13. Ibid., 125.

14. Ira Sharkansky, "The Utility of Elazar's Political Culture: A Research Note," *Polity* 5 (Fall, 1972), 139–141.

15. Russell L. Hanson, "The Political Acculturation of Migrants," *The Western Political Quarterly*, 1992, 355–383.

16. An excellent collection of essays and research reports on political culture is John Kincaid, ed., *Political Culture, Public Policy and the American States* (Philadelphia: Institute for the Study of Human Issues, 1982).

17. Elazar, 125.

18. Edgar Litt, *Ethnic Politics in America: Beyond Pluralism* (Glenview, IL: Scott, Foresman and Co., 1970), 8–13. See also, Milton M. Gordon, "Assimilation in America: Theory and Reality," *Daedalus*, XC (Spring, 1961), 263–283. This article also appears as a chapter in a useful volume edited by Brett W. Hawkins and Robert A. Lorinskas, *The Ethnic Factor in American Politics* (Columbus, OH: Charles E. Merrill Publishing Co., 1970). Additional sources on this topic which may be of interest include: Stanley Feldstein and Lawrence Costello, eds. *The Ordeal of Assimilation: A Documentary History of the White Working Class*, (Garden City, New York: Anchor Press/Doubleday, 1974); Joseph Rothschild, *Ethnopolitics* (New York: Columbia University Press, 1981); Stephen Steinberg, *The Ethnic Myth: Race, Ethnicity, and Class in America* (New York: Antheneum Publishers, 1981); and Anthony D. Smith, *The Ethnic Revival* (Cambridge and New York: Cambridge University Press, 1981).

19. For an example of the literature that probes the wrongs caused by Anglo-Saxons in particular, and whites in general see: Lewis H. Carlson and George A. Colburn, *In Their Place: White America Defines Her Minorities, 1850–1950* (New York: John Wiley and Sons, 1972).

20. See Rogers M. Smith, "Beyond Tocqueville, Myrdal, and Hartz: The Multiple Traditions in America," *American Political Science Review* (November, 1993), 87:549–566, for a discussion of the unenlightened side of American intellectual traditions.

21. John Naisbitt, *Megatrends* (New York: Warner Books, 1982), 244.

22. Ricardo L. Garcia, *Fostering a Pluralistic Society Through Multi-Ethnic Education* (Bloomington, in: The Phi Delta Kappa Educational Foundation, 1978), 12.

23. Lieberson, Stanley, "Unhyphenated Whites in the United States," *Ethnic and Social Studies* 8 (January, 1985), 174.

24. For an exploration of some of the implications of what a multiracial society could be and the difficulties of getting there, see Shelby Steele, *Content of Our Character*, 1990. Steele's book is a challenging exploration of the difficulties facing black Americans in the post-Civil Rights era. It is not expressly a book about multiracial society.

25. Of the 52 million married couples in 1988, 956,000 were interracial couples. *The Universal Almanac* 1991 (Kansas City: Universal Press Syndicate), 196.

3

Federalism and Intergovernmental Relations

Several years ago, Mr. Moke, a chimpanzee was taken from his cage at the St. Louis Zoo by an individual who fled to Florida with him. The state of Missouri asked the Governor of Florida to return Mr. Moke and the person who had kidnapped him. The Governor of Florida learned that the chimpnapper was Mr. Moke's former owner. After selling Mr. Moke to the St. Louis Zoo, the former owner had tried unsuccessfully to buy him back once he realized how much he missed his hairy little friend. Furthermore, Mr. Moke's former owner had left $1,000 in the cage as partial payment.

   If you were the Governor of Florida what would you do? The U.S. Constitution obliges officials in one state to render up individuals fleeing from another. The enthusiasm of the Governor of Florida for meeting his "moral" obligation to render up Mr. Moke and his owner was well under control. Florida did not grant the request of Missouri.

   Most extradition cases are not this exceptional. Usually, officials are happy to see the last of the persons sought in another state and cheerfully turn them over; sometimes they even deliver. It isn't always necessary to send Dirty Harry.

   What is always involved in interactions between governments are real people with real names. We didn't provide any names of people to emphasize that point. The pages which follow examine the development of a system of relationships between people and governments that works for more than 250 million Americans. It is a system that is complex, but which can be understood reasonably well if one is willing to make the effort.

This chapter is about the development of American Federalism from an eighteenth century American contribution to the science of politics to an intergovernmental system involving interaction of 86,000 units of government with each other and with the national government.

E pluribus unum, it says on the Great Seal of the United States. That seal appears in many places, including the backside of one dollar bills. *E pluribus unum* means "from many, one." Creating an *unum* out of a plurality of peoples and governments was no small accomplishment; the process still continues.[2]

Our federal system began rather late in human history (about December 29, according to our Year of the Human Race); yet it has worldwide influence. One of the major features of federalism is that it has been adaptable to changing conditions. Although it was invented before the industrial revolution began, its growth and adaptations have paralleled the economic and geographic growth of the United States from 13 fledgling former colonies on the edge of a continent to a powerful nation-state that spans that continent and half an ocean.

Suggestions for reforming, restructuring, and altering the unity which is our federal system have included abolishing the states, granting statehood to major metropolitan areas, and proposing a constitutional amendment favoring a states' rights doctrine.[3] For your generation to make wise decisions about altering the American federal system it makes sense to start with a fairly clear picture of the essential nature of the system. This chapter will sketch some of its most salient features and some of the major changes that have occurred since it first appeared in 1787.[4]

FEDERALISM: A NOVEL AMERICAN COMPROMISE

Federalism is generally understood to be a system of government in which power is divided between a central government and regional or provincial governments.[5] This definition, however, doesn't do much to differentiate federal systems from confederal systems or from unitary systems in which the realities of politics require that central government officials pay attention on some issues to powerful mayors and provincial leaders. Distinctions which set federalism apart are to be found in a more detailed examination of how power is divided. Before we examine a more detailed definition, let's look at three things that federalism is and three things that it is not.

Three Things that Federalism Is

Federalism is a relatively recent American contribution to the vocabulary of politics. It was created and is maintained by compromising some very important principles upon which men and women of conscience were in disagreement then and are now.

A Relatively New Concept

The language of political science can be traced at least as far back as the fourth century before the Christian era began in ancient Greece. Thus, any political concept invented in the past 200 years is relatively new. In discussions of federalism found in medieval European documents as well as classical Greek political theory, the term "federalism" was used interchangeably with the term "confederation" to refer to any association of independent political units.[6] Today we take for granted that there is a distinction between these two terms. Until the system of government established by the American constitution had been in operation for several decades, the two terms were synonyms. The debate over the ratification of the U. S. Constitution was not between federalists and confederalists. It was between federalists and anti-federalists.

Alexis de Tocqueville, writing in the 1830s, attempted to explain the American system to Europeans. His task was a difficult one because he was really describing two different things: First he was explaining democracy to people who were used to aristocracy and monarchy, and second he was describing a new arrangement between the whole and its parts. In attempting to describe our federal system he wrote, "a form of government has been found out which is neither exactly national [unitary] nor federal . . . the new word which will one day designate this novel invention does not yet exist."[7]

Tocqueville was wrong, of course. There is a word to identify "this novel invention." The word is *federal*. Tocqueville was one of the first to bring to the attention of the wider world the existence of this new contribution to the science of politics. Because of this invention we now make clear distinctions between the ancient terms **federal** and **confederal**.

The terms **unitary, federal,** and **confederal** all refer to the relationship between the central government and local governments included within its boundaries. A unitary system of government is one in which one level of government can alter or abolish other levels without consulting them. For example, each of the 50 states can alter local government. In some states the people might have to approve the action, for example, in a constitutional amendment. However, only the people of the state, not their governments, would have to approve. Our 50 states have unitary systems of government.

In a confederal system the parts that make up the whole (the governments that are members of the confederation) have the final say. They can alter or abolish the confederation. A federal system has characteristics of both unitary and confederal systems as Box 3.1 indicates.

An American Contribution to the Science of Politics

Other countries which have created their own versions of federalism used the American model. Not only was it the oldest one available in written form, but its philosophical underpinnings were described in a classic work which is now printed in many languages. The *Federalist Papers* consists of 85 newspaper articles written between 1787 and 1789 to persuade the people of the state of New York to elect Federalist delegates to the state ratifying convention.

This classic was written by three delegates to the Constitutional Convention in Philadelphia—James Madison, John Jay, and Alexander Hamilton. They all used a single pen name, *Publius*. Their work is as well known among college students in Canada, Germany, India, and Australia as it is in the United States, perhaps even more so.[8]

BOX 3.1

UNITARY, FEDERAL, AND CONFEDERAL STRUCTURES

In examining the relationship between the central government and the major subunits which make up the whole, the terms unitary, federal, and confederal are used today. This set of distrinctions was not always apparent until well after the U. S. Constitution appeared in 1789.

Examples of Each Type

UNITARY	France, Japan, Turkey, Chile
FEDERAL	United States, Canada, Germany, Mexico
CONFEDERAL	The United Nations, The European Economic Community (Common Market) and various common defense organizations and treaty organizations such as NATO (The North Atlantic Treaty Organization).

The Sovereign, the Source of Authority for the Government

UNITARY	The people (or more accurately, the political system consisting of the the people living in a defined territory and a government they accept as legitimate).
FEDERAL	The people
CONFEDERAL	The political units (states) that created the central government.

Autonomy of the Governments of the Parts That Make Up the Whole

UNITARY	None. The governments of the subunits or parts can be overruled and the parts themselves can be abolished by the central political system.
FEDERAL	Modified. Subunits and the central government are partners in the union, not equal partners, but partners. Power is shared in such a way that the major subunits (provinces, states, *länder*) cannot be abolished.
CONFEDERAL	Total. States or subunits can abolish or restructure central government, or abolish the union. The American Civil War was a test of whether or not the states could withdraw from or destroy the union, once they joined it.

Relationship of the Individual to the Political System over Which the Central Government Has Authority

UNITARY	Direct. Individuals are citizens of the State whose government is the central or national government.
FEDERAL	Direct. Individuals are citizens of the State whose government is central or national government.
CONFEDERAL	Indirect. Individuals are citizens of states which belong to the Confederation. Confederations are unions of governments, but not unions of people.

A System of Government Based on Compromise

Federalism itself is a compromise. The government of the United States of America exists because advocates of a strong central government and advocates of state sovereignty were able to compromise. American Federalism was the only way to get the states to enter a union with a strong central government. [9]

Most students of American government are aware of at least one or two of the three great compromises briefly sketched in Box 3.2: the Connecticut, the three-fifths, and the slave trade compromises. What is sometimes understated is the fact that these compromises involved real issues to which strong emotions were tied.

Take the three-fifths compromise. Delegates from northern states weren't sure that it was right to let slaveholders in South Carolina and Virginia have a stronger voice in Congress than the numbers of free men in those states warranted. Since slaves, even though they were property, were also to be counted for purposes of representation, Elbridge Gerry of Massachusetts asked, "Why then should not horses and cattle have the right of representation in the North?"[10] The three-fifths compromise meant that the votes of free men in states such as Pennsylvania and New York were diluted. Southern slave owners ended up with a proportionately larger influence in the lower house of Congress than citizens in the northern states had, as Box 3.2 illustrates.

Black Power rhetoric often asserts that the U. S. Constitution treated a slave as three-fifths of a person. A careful reading of the document will reveal two things about the slave controversy: First, the terms "slave" or "slave trade" are never used. Many constitution writers regarded slavery as something they did not want in their document and hoped to do away with it in a generation or so.

Second, every time a reference is made to slaves they are referred to as "persons," not fractions of persons. For example, "Such persons as the states shall choose to admit" refers to slaves and the slave trade.

The three-fifths compromise was a formula dealing with allocating seats to states. In the political system of the time slaves were property but they were also *persons* who couldn't vote, though they could own property. Free men in the north were persons who were underrepresented in the House of representatives by the three-fifths compromise, and could be denied the vote if they didn't own enough property. Women were persons who were sometimes treated as property and also couldn't vote. It was a political system with a lot of shortcomings, but it was also one that contained mechanisms for fixing them.

For American federalism to come into existence, people of strong convictions had to suspend judgment and consider the possibility that they might not know everything. In the closing hours of the Constitutional Convention when a complete document had been prepared for signing, Benjamin Franklin advised reluctant delegates to set aside their reservations and sign. He said:

> I confess that there are several parts of this constitution that I do not at present approve, but I am not sure I shall never approve of them. . . . The older I grow, the more apt I am to doubt my own judgment, and to pay more respect to the judgment of others. . . . On the whole, I

BOX 3.2

FEDERALISM AND THREE COMPROMISES

The Connecticut Compromise

Also known as The Great Compromise, this involved the distribution of seats in the national legislature. There would be a two-house legislature. Representation in the upper house was to be based on equal representation for every state; in the lower house, it was to be based on population. Each state was given two seats in the Senate, and was guaranteed, regardless of population, at least one seat in the House of Representatives.

This compromise between large and small states made it possible for the Constitutional Convention to break out of an almost hopeless deadlock. Without some protection, the guarantee of representation in both houses, and significant representation in the senate, small states would not have entered the union. Representatives from large states, on the other hand, felt that they were being underrepresented in the national legislature.

The Three-Fifths Compromise

This was also about representation. It was decided that the formula for distributing seats in the House of Representatives among the states would use the census figures for three-fifths of the slave population of each state. The Northern representatives did not want to reward slaveholding states by giving them representation based upon the slave population. The southern representatives at the convention naturally wanted the entire slave population counted for the purposes of allocating seats.

Thus, slave owners, who could vote while their slaves could not, were overrepresented in the national legislature while other working people in non-slave states were underrepresented. Without this compromise the Southern states would not have entered the union.

The Slave Trade Compromise

This allowed the slave trade to go untaxed and unregulated until 1808. After that it could be regulated and taxed and probably abolished. Representatives of slaveholding interests believed that by that time the imported population of slaves would be large enough to maintain itself by natural increase.

This compromise involved several principles: abolishing the slave trade altogether; taxing the importation of slaves; taxing the export of slave-grown products such as sugar, cotton, and tobacco; and using the word "slave" in the Constitution.

Source: Catherine Drinker Bowen, Miracle at Philadelphia (Boston: Little, Brown & Co., 1966; reprint, Atlantic Monthly Press Book, Little, Brown & Co., 1986).

cannot help expressing a wish that every member of the Convention who may still have objections to it would with me on this occasion doubt a little of his own infallibility and to make manifest our unanimity, put his name to this instrument."[11]

Compromise is essential for the American federal system to work. The possibility of doubting the **infallibility** of our political wisdom is an important thing to remember in an age of nonnegotiable demands and political principles that seem carved in stone. We do not suggest that one's personal moral and ethical principles bend with every passing breeze. We simply emphasize the fact that if the founding fathers had not agreed to leave some issues very important to them for future generations to resolve, there would probably be no United States of America.[12]

Three Things Federalism Is Not

After a decade or so of discussing federalism with students, it seems apparent to us that there are three concepts with which federalism is frequently confused.[13] They are democracy, separation of powers, and decentralization.

Democracy

Many a blue book over the years has testified to the confusion that exists in many undergraduate (and graduate) minds about the relationship between federalism and democracy. Although many apples are red when ripe, it does not follow that *all* ripe apples are red. Thus, while it can be argued that federalism works best when combined with democracy, it does not follow that federalism and democracy are the same thing.[14]

Not all of the federal systems listed in Box 3.3, for example, are democracies. Federal systems may become dictatorships temporarily or permanently. The Weimar Republic of Germany, for example, was a federation and a democracy until Hitler took power in 1932 and dispensed with both principles.

The Principle of Separation of Powers

This principle divides power at one level of government. Federalism divides power *between* governments. In the U.S. Constitution, the **separation of powers** means that the power of the national government is divided into three branches: executive, legislative, and judicial.

Virtually all state constitutions separate the powers of state government into three branches as well. The laws and the charters that establish local governments may employ this principle, but to a lesser extent. In the commission form of local government, for example, the officials who approve the budget (legislative) are also assigned some administrative duties (executive).[15]

The confusion between federalism and separation of powers seems to arise from the failure to appreciate the fact that power can be divided or shared out in a number of dimensions. Federalism looks at power sharing in terms of the whole and its parts. The separation of powers is concerned with power within a single government, whether the government of the whole or the government of a part.

Decentralization

Federalism is not the only system of government in which there is a national government as well as regional and local governments. The superficial definition of federalism—a system of government in which power is divided between a central government and regional or provincial governments—certainly allows one to **infer** that in other types of systems such

BOX 3.3

COUNTRIES WITH A FEDERAL FORM OF GOVERNMENT

State	Number and Name of Divisions
Argentina	23 provinces
Australia	6 states
Austria	7 provinces
Brazil	27 federated states
Canada	10 provinces
Federal Republic of Germany	16 länder
India	22 states, 9 territories
Malaysia	13 states
Mexico	31 states
Federal Republic of Nigeria	21 states
Switzerland	22 cantons (19 full, 6 half)
United States	50 states
Venezuela	20 states

Source: 1995 Information Please Almanac (*New York: Houghton Mifflin Co, 1995*).

lesser or more local governments may not exist. However, this inference is wrong. In all large political systems there are local as well as central governments. Not only do local communities have governments in unitary systems of government, they also elect officials who exercise power and spend a fair amount of money.

An essential difference between federal and unitary political systems is in the way in that power is formally distributed. In a unitary system the political system that chooses the central government has the right to claim all power but delegates some of it to the political system which chooses subordinate units of government in the interests of efficiency. This is called **decentralization**. Decentralization can be reversed unilaterally by the central government or, to be more accurate, the political system that chooses the central government. In a political system with a unitary system of government the government could propose a constitutional amendment to abolish units of local government and the amendment could be approved in a national election without ever involving the units of government themselves. That cannot happen in American Federalism.[16]

Having provided a little context, we now turn to our four-part definition of American federalism. It exists as we define it only in the United States of America, though some variations are closer to it than others.

AMERICAN FEDERALISM: A FOUR-DIMENSIONAL DEFINITION

We define American Federalism as a political system in which a union of governments and a union of people establish and maintain a constitution that creates a central government which exercises sovereignty for the union while guaranteeing the continued existence of the member governments.

This is not the only and certainly not the best definition of federalism available, but it serves our needs because it enables us to point out four essential features of the American political system. Some but not all of these characteristics are shared by other federal systems.[17]

A Union of Governments

Each of the 50 American states could exist as an independent country. California's gross domestic product ranks fifth among the industrial nations larger than that of England, Canada, or Mexico. Twenty-three states have economies ranked in the top 50 worldwide. In area, many states are larger than half the countries in the United Nations. Even Rhode Island is larger than sixteen independent countries in both square miles and in population.[19]

Some federations are unions of governments which were once independent, such as the princely states of Germany.[20] That is also the case with three of our states. Before becoming a part of the United States, Vermont had declared itself a republic independent from England, and from New York. It was the first new state created after the federal constitution was ratified by the original 13 states.[21] Texas was an independent republic for nearly a decade and Hawaii had been an independent monarchy.

The concept of a union of separate polities is an essential aspect of federalism. If the unique identity of each part is not recognized then the parts are in danger of becoming mere administrative subunits of the central government.[22] Daniel J. Elazar expresses the notion of a union of governments very nicely in his definition of federalism:

> The mode of political organization that unites separate polities within an overarching political system by distributing power among general and constituent governments in a manner designed to protect the existence and authority of both.[23]

A Union of People

Implicit in the meaning of American federalism is the notion of a single nation. Its citizens may have additional ethnic, class, religious, or geographic defined identities, but they share or are encouraged to share a single national identity. As we noted in Chapter 2 there may be a number of different models of this nation in operation, but they are still models of a single nation. Thus, American federalism includes the notion of the nation-state. As John Jay observed in *Federalist Paper #2*, Providence has given "one connected country to one united people." See Box 3.4.

The **nationalism** built into American federalism is one reason for the tension, discussed in the previous chapter, between the notion of America as a union of people one people and the notion that America is a union of peoples—ethnic groups. This tension is neither unique to America nor necessarily unhealthy. The essential political meaning of ethnic identity (at least in the American context) is that ethnic groups organize in order to obtain full citizenship in the nation-state, they do not organize to create their own nation-state.

BOX 3.4

TO THE MEMBERS OF THE AMERICAN NATION: COME INTO THE UNION AND BRING YOUR STATE GOVERNMENTS WITH YOU

I have often taken notice that Providence has been pleased to give this one connected country to one united people . . . who, by their joint counsels, arms, and efforts, fighting side by side throughout a long and bloody war, have nobly established their general liberty and independence.

This country and this people seem to have been made for each other, and it appears as if it was the design of Providence that an inheritance so proper and convenient for a band of brethren, united to each other by the strongest ties, should never be split into a number of unsocial, jealous, and alien sovereignties.

Source: John Jay, "Federalist Number Two" in James Madison, Alexander Hamilton, and John Jay, The Federalist Papers (New Rochelle, NY: Arlington House, Circa 1975), 38.

The fact that a federation is a union of people as well as a union of governments is an essential difference between a federation and a confederation. As Box 3.1 indicates, in a federation there may be state, provincial, or territorial citizenship, but the people are also citizens of the nation-state. In a confederation there is no Confederal identity, no confederal citizenship. The people who live in a confederation have no obligations to it, their obligations to pay taxes and obey the law are obligations to their country, which is a member of the confederation.

The notion that the citizens of a federation have rights as well as responsibilities was the basis for the civil rights movement in America. Some American citizens demanded that the federal government meet its obligations to its own citizens by enforcing the requirement that those citizens be treated equally in every state regardless of state law and custom. Thus, in the 1960s the federal government became deeply involved in what had traditionally been state and local matters such as education and voting registration. Later in this chapter we will examine some of the current controversy over whether the federal government has carried its obligation too far in requiring state and local governments to meet certain standards in their treatment of American citizens.

The idea of a united people sharing a single national identity helps us appreciate the practical value of federalism in 1787. It is as if the authors of the Constitution had declared, "If the only way to bring the people of a single nation together under one government is to bring their separate governments into a union of governments, then that's the way we'll have to do it." Hamilton observes in the _Federalist_ that, "A nation without a national government is, in my view, an awful spectacle."[24]

In some federations, the customs, language, religion, geography, and other sources of identity may interfere with the recognition of a common identity. When these separate sources of identity reinforce one another, as they did in Yugoslavia and the Soviet Union, or in the slaveholding states in the American South over 100 years ago, then the federation may confront problems severe enough to threaten its continued existence.[25] Clearly nation-building is a difficult process. The governments of Yugoslavia and the Soviet Union were unable to carry it out. They failed to build a national identity among their citizens.

National identity can be created in at least two ways. First, individuals in a state are taught to think of themselves as members of the nation by education (and, if you will, propaganda). They are taught stories about national heroes and heroines, myths, symbols, a common language, and a common set of laws and customs. They may also be taught additional languages, or to respect additional cultures, but a common culture and language among a significant portion of each generation of leadership of the nation is essential.

The second way in which a national government can bring new people into the nation is by expanding the idea of what the nation or union of people really is. This expansion of the definition of the American nation occured during the 1960's and 1970's and to some extent it's still going on. It involved educating both those who were included in the old definition of nation and those who had accepted their exclusion as part of the nature of things.

The union of people—the American nation—was redefined during the civil rights era by the blood, sweat, and tears of many individuals and the martyrdom of a few. The new union included, as full citizens, millions of people (African American, Hispanic American, Native American, and Asian Americans) who previously were treated as second-class citizens in terms of the ability to buy property, ride where they chose in public transportation, attend the public schools and collages of their choice, and participate in electoral politics.

The process of national integration, bringing all Americans into the same large community, continues. Ultimately it does not matter whether they come into the nation singly or in groups. The ultimate objective, whatever our model of it, is a union of individuals who each possesses a national identity that links each of us to individuals in communities large and small which are served by 86,000 state and local governments within our federal system.

The Government of the Union Exercises Sovereignty

Sovereignty is a concept that includes two notions: supremacy in one's own sphere of influence and independence from the rule of others. In democratic political theory, sovereignty resides with "the people."[26] In small communities the people may actually exercise sovereignty themselves. In larger communities they delegate power to government to exercise on their behalf. Thus we use the phrase "exercise sovereignty" in our definition of federalism.

One Sovereign, One Government

Sovereignty tends to be indivisible. Only one government can exercise the sovereignty of the people of the United States of America—the national government. Within each of our 50 states, there is only one government empowered to exercise the sovereignty of the people of that state—the state government.

In confederal systems, the central government does not exercise sovereignty. It cannot act independently of the member governments. Under our first constitution, the Articles of Confederation, for example, there was no executive branch at the national level. The U. S. Congress could pass laws, but only unanimously, and it had no means to enforce them.

A modern confederacy, the United Nations, has an executive branch, but it has no power to carry out resolutions passed in the General Assembly unless the member governments give it permission and money. When the executive branch of the UN acts, it offers services in accordance with the laws of the state in which it happens to be acting, whether it is distributing food in Rwanda or distributing birth control information in India.

Three Dimensions of Sovereignty

In the American federal system the national government exercises sovereignty in three ways. First, it is independent of the control of the governments within its boundaries. When an agency of the U. S. government carries out the functions assigned it by the Constitution or by law, it does not need the permission of a state government to act. The F.B.I., for example, does not have to get the permission of the government of Michigan to arrest someone in that state who is suspected of breaking a federal law. Usually courtesy and custom result in cooperative action, but it is not legally necessary.

A second way in which the national government exercises sovereignty is as an actor in the international state system, independent of the rule of any foreign government. In the American federal system, the national government is the only government empowered to make binding agreements, with foreign states. Article I, Section 10, of the Constitution says, "No state shall, without consent of Congress . . . enter into any agreement . . . with a foreign power." State and local governments deal with foreign governments in terms of ceremonial matters, exchanging representatives with sister cities, attending international conferences of legislators, and promoting economic linkages including giving aid or receiving it. However, they do so with the tacit approval of Congress.

Third, in conflicts between the national government and member governments of the union, the federal government also exercises sovereignty. Even when a state government challenges the constitutionality of a federal law, it is the U. S. Supreme Court that decides the case.

The Constitution and Supremacy

The supremacy of the American national government is stated in Article VI:

> This Constitution, and the laws of the United States which shall be made in pursuance thereof; and all treaties made, or which shall be made, under the authority of the United States, shall be the supreme law of the land; and the judges in every State shall be bound thereby, any thing in the constitution or laws of the State to the contrary notwithstanding.

The intent here is both clear and impressive. The fact that representatives of 13 sovereign states agreed to this clause reminds us that some heavy compromising went into the construction of the constitution.

Closer examination of this clause indicates that the laws of the United States that are capable of becoming the "supreme law of the land" must be in accord with the Constitution. Since the Constitution can be amended and the Supreme Court can change its interpretation of the Constitution, it is clear that the process of exercising sovereignty is a dynamic, ongoing process.

If a federal law is enacted to which enough people (state officials included) are strongly opposed, then the constitutionality of that law may be tested (it remains supreme until it fails the test of constitutionality) or the law can be repealed or modified by a responsive Congress. Furthermore, the President can modify the executive branch's interpretation of the law by executive order.

Once the objections to the law have been clarified, it is not unusual for Congress to pass new laws refining the old, particularly in cases where unforeseen hardship may be placed on state or local governments.

The final decision on what really is the supreme law of the land can take generations to determine. For example, the final say on whether or not small children could be employed in factories and mines was not determined until 1941, when the Supreme Court upheld the Fair Labor Standards Act of 1938. Decades earlier the Court had found similar laws, both state and federal, unconstitutional. Attempts to abolish child labor in factories and mines by means of a constitutional amendment also failed. By 1937 only 28 states had ratified the child labor amendment proposed in 1924.[27]

Throughout the history of the development of the federal system there has been an effort to determine the boundary between the exercise of by the national government and the powers of the states. The most recent opinion of the Court on this matter is that there is no subject matter is reserved to the states and denied to the national government. According to the court, the states are protected by the dynamics of the federal system, not by drawing a line that the national government cannot cross.

In *Garcia vs. San Antonio Metropolitan Transit Authority*,[28] Justice Blackmun speaking for a (5–4) majority stated that:

> the founders of the Constitution chose to rely on a federal system in which special restraints on federal power over the States inhered principally in the workings of the National Government itself, rather than in discrete limitations on the objects of federal authority. State sovereign interests, then, are more properly protected by procedural safeguards inherent in the structure of the federal system than by judicially created limitations on federal power.[29]

The receptiveness of Congress to demands by state and local officials for legislative relief after the *Garcia* case was decided provides a good example of the safeguards to which Justice Blackman alluded.

The Supreme Court decided in 1985 that the overtime provisions of the Fair Labor Standards Act applied to virtually all state and local government employees, including those working for publicly owned mass transit systems. State and local officials protested that paying cash bonuses for overtime would create an undue financial hardship. They were, however, willing to reward employees who worked overtime with compensatory paid time off. In response to this cry for help, Congress came to the aid of the governments. It enacted the Fair Labor Standards Amendments of 1985 to buffer the effect of the Court's ruling, setting forth conditions under which compensatory time could be used in lieu of a cash payment by a state or local government. In effect, Mr. Garcia was told that he would get time and a half in compensatory time for each hour of overtime he worked, not time and half in his paycheck.[30]

The Union Is Made of Indestructible Parts: Six Guarantees

The fourth feature of our definition of American Federalism is that the viability of the parts must be maintained. The U. S. Supreme Court observed in 1869:

> The preservation of the states, and the maintenance of their governments are as much within the design and care of the Constitution as the preservation of the Union and the maintenance of the National government. The Constitution in all of its provisions, looks to an indestructible Union, composed of indestructible States.[31]

As Box 3.5 indicates, there are numerous guarantees in the Constitution that promote the continued existence and vitality of the states. The six safeguards we discuss by no means constitute the complete list. They provide enough evidence, however, to demonstrate that even though the central government possesses powers that sometimes appear awesome, there is some basis for the belief that states are unlikely to become mere administrative subdivisions in a unitary system.

Territorial Integrity

The territorial boundaries of a state cannot be altered without the consent of its legislature. Minor boundary disputes between states—and such disputes have been numerous—are decided by the U. S. Supreme Court acting as umpire of the federal system. Although the creation of the state of West Virginia during the Civil War may appear to be an exception to the notion of territorial integrity guaranteed to the state of Virginia, it is worth recalling that at the time the Commonwealth of Virginia was in a state of rebellion against the United States of America. Upon the conclusion of hostilities, in the course of officially recognizing that it had never left the Union, the Virginia House of Burgesses formally approved of the creation of West Virginia.[32]

Representation in Congress

Every state is guaranteed three seats in Congress—two in the Senate and one in the House of Representatives—regardless of population. Thus, it is difficult for any legislative action to occur in the absence of participation by representatives elected in each of the states. In other words, the states and portions of states are the electoral units for the national legislature.

While the actual number of seats in the House of Representatives allocated to a state may change as national population patterns change or as the Constitution is amended, representation in the Senate can only be changed with the consent of the state involved. Article V not only says that "no state without its consent, shall be deprived of its equal suffrage in the Senate," it also exempts that clause from constitutional amendment.

Members of Congress Must Be State Residents

The likelihood that Congress will pay at least some attention to the problems of the states is increased by the fact that the Constitution requires that members of Congress be inhabitants of the state they represent.

In some political systems the residence of a member of the national legislature is irrelevant. The national party finds safe constituencies for party leaders somewhere regardless of their places of residence. Imagine, for example, the kinds of decisions the national government might make if the legislature were elected not from state-based constituencies but instead on a party ticket that could obtain a majority of the popular vote nationwide.

The National Legislature Is Truly Bicameral

The requirement that all laws and proposals to amend the Constitution must pass both houses means that the House cannot overrule the Senate and vice versa. In the U. S. Congress each house must approve of a bill or proposed constitutional amendment in exactly the same language or the bill fails. Thus, all of the built-in protections for the states in constructing the national legislature must be dealt with in the creation of the supreme laws of the land.

BOX 3.5

GUARANTEES OF STATE VIABILITY IN THE CONSTITUTION

Article I

Section 2   No Person shall be a Representative. . . . who shall not, when elected, *be an Inhabitant of that State in which he shall be chosen.* *
Section 2   [E]*ach State shall have at least one Representative.*
Section 3   The Senate of the United States shall be composed of *two Senators from each State.*
Section 3   No Person shall be a *Senator* who shall not, when elected, *be an Inhabitant of that State for which he shall be chosen.*
Section 5   *Each House shall be the judge of* the elections, returns and qualifications of *its own* members.
Section 7   *Every bill* which shall have passed the House of Representatives *and the Senate,* shall, before it become a law, be presented to the President of the United States.

Article II

Section 1   *Each State, shall appoint,* in such manner as the legislature thereof may direct, a number of electors, equal to the whole number of Senators and Representatives to which the State may be entitled in the Congress.
Section 1   The electors shall meet *in their respective States* . . . The person having the greatest number of votes shall be the President, if such number be a majority of the whole number of electors appointed; and if there be more than one who have such majority, and have an equal number of votes, then *the House of Representatives shall immediately choose by ballot* one of them for President; and if no person have a majority, then from the five highest on the list the said House shall in like manner choose the President. *But in choosing the President, the votes shall be taken by States, the representation from each State having one vote.*

Article IV

Section 1   Full faith and credit shall be given in each State to the public acts, records, and judicial proceedings of every other State.
Section 2   The citizens of each State shall be entitled to all privileges and immunities of citizens in the several States.
Section 3   No new State shall be formed or erected within the jurisdiction of any other States; nor any State be formed by the Junction of two or more States, or parts of States, *without the consent of the legislatures of the States concerned* as well as of the Congress.
Section 4   *The United States shall.* . . . *protect each* of them [the states] against invasion; *and on application of the legislature,* or of the Executive (when the legislature cannot be convened) *against domestic violence.*

(Continued)

BOX 3.5 (CONTINUED)

GUARANTEES OF STATE VIABILITY IN THE CONSTITUTION

Article V

The Congress whenever *two thirds of both Houses* shall deem it necessary, *shall propose amendments to this Constitution*, or, on the application of the legislatures of two thirds of the several States, shall call a convention for proposing Amendments which. . . . shall be valid. . . . *when ratified by the legislatures of three fourths of the several States, or by conventions in three fourths thereof*. . . .

———————
Emphasis added throughout.

The relationship between the U. S. Senate and the House of Representatives stands in contrast to that found in many other national legislatures, including the British Parliament, where the upper house can only delay legislation. The House of Commons can in effect pass a law whether the House of Lords likes it or not.

The Electoral College Chooses the President

The electoral college never meets all in one place. The electors in each state constitute the college, but they cast their votes in the state capitals. Congress then counts those votes and confirms the election of the president. No president in this century has ever been elected who did not receive more popular votes than his opponent. The three times this happened were in the previous century, long before radio, television, and truly national campaigns. See Dimensions of Diversity, Box 3.6

Each state is guaranteed three electoral college votes regardless of its population. To be elected president or vice president, a candidate must win a majority of the electoral college votes cast in the state capital, not just more votes than anyone else receives. This forces some attention to be paid to the wishes of a fairly large number of states in constructing a majority coalition. If there is no majority in the electoral college the decision goes to the House of Representatives where each state delegation, regardless of its size, gets one vote for president.

The Constitution Cannot Be Amended Without State Participation

To say that the U. S. Constitution cannot be amended unless the states are consulted is to understate the point. The Constitution requires that any amendment proposed must be ratified by three fourths of the states. Moreover, the source of all proposed amendments since the Constitution went into affect has been Congress, a body in which states have some influence, as we have already indicated (Figure 3.1).

American Federalism: The Litmus Test

We summarize our four part definition of American Federalism with a simple test which can be used to determine whether another federal system approximates American Federalism.

BOX 3.6

DIMENSIONS OF DIVERSITY: FIFTY ELECTORAL COLLEGES

After every Presidential election there is an eruption of articles and radio talk show pontificators complaining about the electoral college. In nearly every case the author or talker points out that the popular election does not elect the president, it "only" determines the person whom each state will send to the state capitol to vote in the electoral college, a month after the popular election.

Most of those who denounce the electoral college identify the three elections when the electoral college chose a candidate without either a plurality in the popular election (more votes than any other candidate) or a majority (more than half of the votes cast). These elections were in 1824, 1876, and 1888. This suggestion is then made that we ought to have a constitutional amendment abolishing the darn thing. "Let the people decide who the President will be!" they declaim.

Oddly enough, rather than thwarting the popular will, the electoral college results tend to overstate the margin of victory. For example, in 1992 with only 43 percent of the popular vote, but still more than all his opponents, Bill Clinton won 69 percent of the electoral college votes.

Oddly enough, the problem isn't the remote possibility that in a two-candidate race the electoral college could elect a president whose opponent obtained a majority of the popular vote. The problem is that in a three-way race, a candidate with fewer popular votes than another candidate could win in the electoral college. This might occur if the candidate obtained narrow victories in enough states to win the electoral college vote despite the fact that the opposition won its states with large popular margins.

This potential for mischief exists because the states use the "winner take all" system to choose the Presidential Electors. To win *all* the votes in a big state a candidate needs to win a plurality by only a few votes. Then the party of that candidate gets to send all of the electors to the state capital to cast all that state's electoral college votes for its candidate. The second best and third best candidates send no one, even though they each may have garnered 30 percent or more of the vote in that state. This "all or nothing" procedure is not built into the U. S. Constitution.

A little appreciated, and perhaps little known fact about the electoral college is that its fate is largely in the hands of the states. They can change the way it works by state law. Each state election code determines the way that state's presidential electors are chosen. If a state wants to prevent the state's electoral college vote from being allocated on a "winner take all" basis, then all that state has to do is change its election code. It can decide that each state congressional district will send an elector to the state capital, according to the vote in that district. The electors allocated to the state because it has two senators could be determined by the statewide vote and thus give the statewide winner a slight, rather than a huge, advantage in the electoral college.

Why don't the states take advantage of this opportunity for diversity? Could it be that in each state the legislature sees the advantage of forcing presidential candidates to "go for broke" in their states? What other explanations might there be?

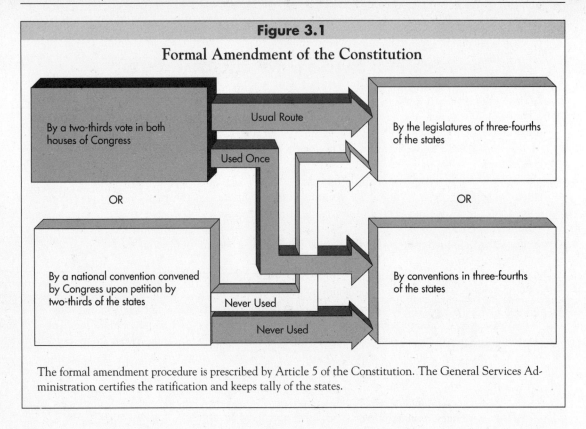

Figure 3.1

Formal Amendment of the Constitution

The formal amendment procedure is prescribed by Article 5 of the Constitution. The General Services Administration certifies the ratification and keeps tally of the states.

This litmus test is whether or not formal amendments to the Constitution must be approved by the member governments. If at least a majority must approve, then the system in question may resemble American Federalism: a political system in which a union of governments and a union of people establish and maintain a constitution that creates a central government which exercises sovereignty for the union while guaranteeing the continued existence of the member governments.

If the central government can go directly to the people to amend the constitution then it is probably not a federal system. If it claims to be one, it is certainly very different from the American version of Federalism.

FEDERALISM: A WORKING VOCABULARY

Thus far we have introduced several terms which are necessary for a better understanding of American Federalism in particular and state and local politics in general. We add to that list six concepts that are found in the Constitution or that emerged very early in the development of our federal system and continue to be relevant today.

Expressed Powers

Expressed powers are also called enumerated powers or delegated powers. They are listed, in Article I, Section 8, of the Constitution as subjects on which Congress has the power to make laws. Elsewhere in the Constitution, Congress is given the power to approve or reject certain actions that state governments may wish to take, such as entering into compacts or agreements with one another or with foreign nations. Congress is also given the power to admit new states to the Union under conditions that protect state territorial integrity.

A point worth emphasizing about powers given to the national government, whether expressed or otherwise, is that these powers come from a Constitution created by a sovereign people—not from the states.

> We the People of the United States of America in order to form a more perfect Union . . . do ordain and establish this Constitution for the United States of America.

The delegated powers of the national government can be altered or taken away by constitutional amendment but not by the states. What the states did not give, they cannot take away. A leading states' rights advocate, James Kilpatrick, has observed, somewhat wistfully, "The States have very few rights as the Ninth and Tenth Amendments make clear in their perfect choice of nouns, people have rights; States have powers."[33]

Implied Powers

This concept is such an important aspect of the history of intergovernmental relations in the United States that it merits a chapter by itself. In the interest of brevity, this discussion is limited to a few paragraphs here. The "foregoing powers" mentioned below are the enumerated powers we have already discussed. The constitutional source of implied power is Article I, Section 8, which contains the statement that Congress shall have the power:

> to make all laws which shall be necessary and proper for carrying into execution the foregoing powers, and all other powers vested by this Constitution in the Government of the United States, or in any Department or Officer thereof.

The phrase "to make all laws which shall be necessary and proper" is also known as the elastic clause because it allows the expressed (enumerated) powers of the national government to apply to new topics and situations unforeseen by the authors of the Constitution.

The implied powers doctrine was set forth in the landmark case McCulloch vs. Maryland (1819), in which Chief Justice John Marshall, observed that the authors of the Constitution did not limit the power of Congress only to enumerated subjects. He wrote:

> Let the end be legitimate, let it be within the scope of the Constitution, and all means which are appropriate, which are plainly adapted to the end, which are not prohibited, but consistent with the letter and spirit of the Constitution, are constitutional.[34]

The doctrine of implied powers makes it possible for federal power to stretch to subjects unforeseen by the founding fathers. More than that, however, it provides a basis for arguing that almost anything is traceable to an enumerated power.

Imagine, for example, that Congress only had the power to regulate interstate commerce, that it had no other enumerated or specific power. With the doctrine of implied powers the regulation of interstate commerce can be stretched to cover almost anything on which Congress now legislates.

The regulation of interstate commerce is meaningless, it could be argued, if foreign countries can invade our shores and disrupt this commerce. Thus, Congress must regulate immigration and create a defense force to protect interstate commerce. Congress cannot do this without the power to tax and spend. Furthermore, healthy commerce requires a trans-

When this building was planned there were no mandates requiring that it be accessible to people in wheel-chairs. When this building was constructed states were not required to allow women and people of color to vote. Mandates may be a mixed blessing for some, but they are an essential part of intergovernmental relations.

portation network to carry goods and information. It also requires educated employees and informed consumers. Healthy commerce also requires protection from foreign competition and/or the opportunity to compete in foreign markets. Thus, as long as one interprets the phrase "necessary and proper" in a flexible manner, the elasticity of the implied powers of the national government seem almost limitless.

The regulation of interstate commerce actually has been the basis for extending federal involvement into many areas, from labor relations and industrial safety to inspections of food processing plants and nondiscriminatory provision of motel accommodations and transportation.

Although it appears that Chief Justice John Marshall issued a book of blank checks in 1819, each of these checks still has to be cashed in a political system in which Congress is not the only check writer. Thus, what Congress does with implied powers depends to a great extent on what the public and the president think it ought to do, what the courts decide is a "legitimate" end, a legitimate means to that end, and the willingness of state and local officials to (enthusiastically or reluctantly) enforce a law that Congress claims is "necessary and proper."[35]

Concurrent Powers

Concurrent powers are powers that both the states and the federal government may exercise. For example, the Constitution gives to the federal government the power to tax and to regulate commerce. Since it does not deny that the states also have taxing authority and the power to regulate commerce, the two levels of government may both engage in these activities. If the concurrent exercise of power in a certain area becomes unworkable, the regulations of the federal government are supreme. Without a specific statement by Congress that it intends to preempt a field of law, it is up the Supreme Court to decide whether or not federal laws overrule state laws.[36]

Powers Denied the National Government

Both Article I, Section 9, and the Bill of Rights specifically list certain things that the national government cannot do. Furthermore, Article IV, Section 3, prohibits the creation of new states from the territory of existing states without the permission of the state legislatures. The prohibitions found in Article I, Section 9, such as to suspend the writ of habeas corpus, pass ex post facto laws, and give preference to the ports of one state over those of another, seem to be fairly straightforward.

However, the limitations on the national government in the Bill of Rights are the source of a vast body of constitutional law dealing with the interpretation of the meaning of terms such as "unreasonable searches" and "cruel and unusual punishments" and stating whether there really are limits to what one may call a religion, how freely one may exercise it, and at what point state and federal governments may or may not assist religious institutions in promoting education or care for the elderly.[37]

Obligations of the States to One Another

In discussing the relationships among the 50 states, the term "horizontal federalism" sometimes is used to differentiate this dimension of our Constitution from the state-national dimension ("vertical federalism"). The Constitution places three major interstate obligations on the states. The first is that each state must give full faith and credit to the public acts, records, and judicial proceedings of every other state. The importance of this is apparent if one imagines taking an automobile trip from Bangor, Maine, to San Diego, California, without interstate obligations of full faith and credit. In each state one would have to stop at the border to take a test for a driver's license and have one's vehicle inspected to make sure that one and one's vehicle pose no threats to the safety and health of the residents of that state. Naturally, one would do a fair amount of hanging around service stations and government offices, filling out forms and paying fees.

For the most part, states recognize one another's public acts, records, and judicial proceedings. The exceptions are what help to keep lawyers employed, and occasionally sell newspapers. Technical matters, such as whether a resident of State A has lived long enough in State B to establish residency there so that a divorce, recognized in the courts of State A, can be obtained in State B are the reason why this part of the Constitution is sometimes referred to as "the lawyer's clause."

The second interstate obligation is for each state to grant to the citizens of other states the same privileges and immunities enjoyed by its own citizens. The Supreme Court has recognized some exceptions. For example, states are allowed to charge out-of-state students a higher tuition for attending state colleges and universities than students who are residents of the state. The same exception is applied to hunting or fishing license fees, which can be higher for those from out-of-state. The justification for this is that state taxpayers subsidize higher education and game management activities and thus have earned the right to a lower cost.

The third interstate obligation is to release to officials of another state any person accused of a crime who has fled from that state. This action is sometimes referred to as rendition. More commonly, the complete process of rendering up, or handing over, a person to be taken from one state to another state is also called extradition. It also happens between countries.

Extradition, a process which is usually routine, sometimes involves headline-making exceptions. Those exceptions give the impression that extradition is a rare and delicate matter. From time to time governors have refused to "render up" persons who have fled from another state because over a period of several years those persons have become model citizens, because it appears that they have more than paid for their crime through the time already served in the other state's prison system, or because there is strong evidence that the individual was not dealt with fairly in the first place.

When asked to umpire these situations, the Supreme Court has found no machinery to force a state to render up a person to another state. It is a moral duty, the Court has declared, not a legal one. Thus, it seems that the federal government has no power to require state officials to behave morally.[38] The federal government wisely stayed out of the case of Mr. Moke, who was taken from his cage at the St. Louis Zoo by a person who fled to Florida with him.[39]

Powers Prohibited to the States

Article I, Section 10, lists several things states cannot do, such as coin money, and a few things they can do only if permitted by Congress, such as enter into agreements or compacts with other states.

One of the most important sources of constitutionally imposed limitations on state government is the clause in the Fourteenth Amendment which says: "nor shall any State deprive any person of life, liberty, or property, without due process of law; nor deny to any persons within its jurisdiction the equal protection of the laws."

Brown vs. *The Board of Education* is perhaps the best known example of the application of the Fourteenth Amendment clause "equal protection of the laws." In 1954, the Supreme Court declared that state laws enforcing segregated education were unconstitutional. This case marked the end of legally enforced segregation in public schools and the beginning of the end of segregation, period.[40]

The Fourteenth Amendment also limits state and local government via the doctrine of incorporation. The Supreme Court gradually, case by case, determined that the "due process" and "equal protection of the laws" provisions of the U. S. Constitution mean that almost the whole of the Bill of Rights protects individuals from state and local government laws and officials as well as from the laws or actions of officials of the national government.

Concern over the excessive broadening of individual rights via the doctrine of inclusion has been supplanted by the rediscovery of the bills of rights in the several states. State constitutions, rather than the U. S. Constitution, are now being cited as the source of new protections for individuals from injustices within each state (Box 3.7). According to Professor Stanley H. Friedelbaum, director of the Burns Center for State Constitutional Studies at

---

BOX 3.7

DIMENSIONS OF DIVERSITY: FREEDOM OF SPEECH

Can one exercise one's right to freedom of speech to override another's private property rights by entering a private mall, retirement village, or the waiting room of an abortion clinic to express an opinion, distribute literature, or circulate petitions? Not according to the U. S. Constitution.

The standing opinions in the U. S. Constitution have been interpreted in favor of private property on this issue. However, rights to freedom of speech have been located in state bills of rights which override the rights of private property in some cases. Furthermore, distinctions have been made between different types of private property. The waiting rooms of abortion clinics have generally been ruled off limits for political activity. However, some state bills of rights do give the right to exercise freedom of speech in shopping malls, others don't.

The state supreme courts in California, Massachusetts, New Jersey, and Washington have held that rights found in the state constitution give individuals the right to set up tables in a privately owned shopping mall to solicit signatures on petitions while the courts in Connecticut, Michigan, and Pennsylvania have not found this right in their state constitutions. In New Jersey one can even enter a retirement village to distribute literature. Just another example of the diversity within our federal system.

Source: Western Pennsylvania Social Workers 1982 Campaign v. Connecticut General Life Insurance Company 512 Pa. 23, 515 A.2d 1331 (1986), reprinted in Advisory Commission on Intergovernmental Relations, State Constitutional Law: Cases and Materials (Washington, D.C.: 1988), 136–137.

Rutgers University, "there are close to 500 cases nationwide in which state courts have construed their state constitutional provisions to provide guarantees more substantial than their federal counterparts. . . ."[41]

MODERN AMERICAN FEDERALISM: INTERGOVERNMENTAL RELATIONS (IGR)

Intergovernmental relations (IGR) is a term that focuses our attention on the dynamic nature of our federal system. It emphasizes the fact that more than two levels of government interact. American Federalism began in preindustrial America as a compromise between representatives who wanted to create a national government and those in each of 13 independent states who feared the loss of state sovereignty. Today, American Federalism has been so altered by national and international events that it would be almost unrecognizable to those who designed it. The accomplishment of the framers can be appreciated if we note that the foundation they laid was for a 13-state federation that now includes 50 states. Not only do the 13 original states cover less than 10 percent of the area of United States, the state of Alaska would include them all with room to spare.

Our intergovernmental system is a system of relations between more than 86,000 interdependent units of government of which only a small fraction existed in 1789.[42] Our system is no longer simply a matter of one-dimensional national-state relationships. It now involves cooperation and conflict among more than 86,000 governments, the numerous agencies and offices in each one, the interest groups that represent them, and interest groups that represent individuals and corporations who do or do not want the states to regulate certain activities.

As we noted in Chapter 2, the pace and the volume of technological and demographic change have become so great that we tend to lose sight not only of what we have accomplished but also of the fact that we *can* accomplish constructive change.

A brief overview of some of the ways in which our federal system has responded to changing conditions seems appropriate. Some changes have taken place as the capacity of the national government increased, and some changes have been solutions introduced to reduce confusion and render the intergovernmental system more manageable. Thus, by examining what seems to be working, we will be in a better position to evaluate future suggestions for making the federal system more accountable to the needs of individuals and more effective in attempting to meet them.

SOME OF THE SOLUTIONS IN OPERATION

Among the many significant features of modern federalism, we have identified five that seem most appropriate for our discussion of efforts to make this system more understandable by the average citizen, a bit more efficient, and a little more sensitive to the needs of individuals.

The ACIR: Advice and Attention

The Advisory Commission on Intergovernmental Relations (ACIR) was created in 1959. It is composed of 26 members. Nine of them represent the federal government: three from the Senate, three from the House, and three from the executive branch. Fourteen represent state and local governments: four mayors, three governors, three state legislators, and three county officials. Three are private citizens.

Most of the members are chosen by the president with the advice of appropriate organizations: the National Governors Association, the National Conference of State Legislatures, the National League of Cities, and the National Association of Counties. The Senate and House members are chosen by the presiding officers.

The commission members who serve part-time are assisted by a full-time staff of approximately 20 persons headed by a full-time executive director. The director is usually someone with excellent academic credentials who has studied or served in government (or both) for a long time.

The purpose of the ACIR is to study the workings of the federal system and to make recommendations for improving it. The considerable body of research that the commission has published is available, at least in part, in most university libraries and upon request by writing to the ACIR, Washington, D.C., 20575. Although the ACIR is a relatively small federal agency, it is a very influential one whose studies and recommendations are taken seriously at all levels. Many recommendations have been enacted into law at the national and state levels.

The success of the national ACIR in identifying and suggesting solutions to problems has led to the creation of state-level ACIRs in about 30 states. Over the years some states have abolished their ACIRs while others have created new ones. Currently the number hovers around 25.[43] In 1993 the U.S. ACIR itself had a narrow escape. The House of Representatives eliminated the $1.8 million appropriation for this small but effective agency. The Senate approved the appropriation and the Clinton administration was happy to work with a variety of state and local officials and organizations to convince House members that the agency was worth saving. As a former governor, President Clinton appreciated the advocacy role that the ACIR plays for state and local government. The funding was partially restored in the compromise budget emerging from the House-Senate conference committee.

Fiscal Federalism

Fiscal federalism represents an attempt to take advantage of the superior financial resources of the national government to deal with the tremendous diversity of the American intergovernmental system. Among the national government's superior resources are its power to (1) tax individuals and business firms, (2) borrow, (3) print money to pay off what it borrowed, and (4) regulate interest rates. State and local governments can tax and borrow, but they have no control over the money supply and very little influence over interest rates.

The two features of fiscal federalism we will briefly examine are grants in aid, and mandates. Grants in aid are mechanisms through which the national government attempts to promote national goals while recognizing that some communities have fewer resources and more problems than others. Mandates are requirements placed on states and local governments. Often, but not always, these mandates are linked to grant funds.

Grants in Aid

At the beginning of this century the national government had five grant programs which distributed $3 million. Today the national government sends many times that amount of money to state and local government—nearly $200 billion by 1994. Currently the national government provides 17 percent of the funds that finance the activities of state and local governments.[44] These funds are a major reason why there are so many intergovernmental relationships.

A grant-in-aid is a transfer of funds from one unit of government to another. It is not a loan. There are a variety of ways in which governments distribute money. Table 3.1 indicates four of the ways in which grants can be classified. The type of grant used has consequences that may have an impact that goes beyond the grantor and grantee. For example, from 1972 to 1986, the national government's General Revenue Sharing Program distributed over $60 billion to states and certain kinds of local governments including municipalities.

The fact that virtually no conditions were attached to this money encouraged many unorganized communities to create their own municipal governments instead of continuing to depend on county and township governments for services. In 1985 there were 1,098 more municipal governments than there had been in 1972, an increase of about 6 percent. It is probably not a coincidence that the rate of municipality creation has declined since the General Revenue Sharing Program was canceled.[45]

There are now hundreds of organizations of public officials (elected and appointed) that lobby state and national legislatures for laws and for grant programs to advance the goals of those governments and agencies, whether they are township supervisors, waste management technicians, fire marshals, or nursing home supervisors.

Table 3.1

A BRIEF GRANTS-IN-AID VOCABULARY

This table indicates that our grant in aid programs have several dimensions including: scope of activity, federal commitment, methods for acquiring grants, and the local commitment. These four dimensions cover most—but not all—grant programs.

Category	Scope of Activity
Project	Specific activity such as a sewage treatment plant or a summer program for children
Categorical	Narrow range of activities within a functional area
Block	Broad range of activities within a functional area
General revenue sharing	Virtually anything except to match funds for other federal grants or meet requirements that archaeologic and historic preservation studies and environmental impact studies be conducted before construction can take place.

Category	Federal Commitment
Fixed-amount	Limited to specific amount of money
Open-ended	Unlimited as long as the recipient meets criteria such as matching money for unemployment compensation or aid to dependent children

Category	Method of Allocation
Formula	Units of government are allocated funds according to formulas that take into account factors such as unemployment or school-age population
Competitive	Usually applies to project grants for which a limited amount of money is available and only a few applicants receive grants

Category	Recipient Participation
Matching	Recipient government supplies some funds or equivalent of funds in the form of hours of work by personnel, or supplies, or the use of facilities such as buildings or equipment
Nonmatching	Recipient government simply meets guidelines for spending money

Source: George F. Break, "The Economics of Intergovernmental Grants," in Laurence J. O'Toole, Jr., ed., American Intergovernmental Relations (Washington, D.C.: Congressional Quarterly Press, 1985), 144–145.

Few state or local chief executives are aware of what all these intergovernmental spokespersons are asking of Congress. Since many grants involve matching money from the grant-recipient, keeping track of the obligations incurred is a challenging and more or less permanent feature of intergovernmental relations.[46] As Box 3.8 suggest sometimes chief executives have been unpleasantly surprised at how "well" their subordinates are doing in obtaining grants.

Fortunately, the situation in San Jose is less likely to occur because of changes, recommended by the ACIR, in the grant application process which now require that a unit of

BOX 3.8

THE PROLIFERATION OF GRANT PROGRAMS IN SAN JOSE

In 1970, to find out where he stood in terms of matching requirements that committed local funds, office space, and employee time, Mayor Norman Mineta of San Jose, California got a $200,000 grant to discover the number of grants in which his city was involved.

From this study came two revelations which were unsettling, to put it mildly. First, it was virtually impossible to see the total picture in detail. No local, state, or federal agency had the data on how many federal grants entered the city of San Jose. Not only were there school districts, the county, and other special districts involved, there was no way to find out the total dollar amount even for city government agencies. It took every penny of that grant to put together a booklet summarizing the known commitments involving the city of San Jose, a city of 450,000 people.

Second, to Mayor Mineta's surprise, it was learned that San Jose was committed to come up with matching money of about $20 million in order to get $56.4 million from various federal agencies for a range of services and programs that the mayor and the city council had never sat down to review and approve.

Source: *Deil S. Wright*, Understanding Intergovernmental Relations (*North Scituate, MA: Duxbury, 1978*), 57–58.

government's chief executive review and comment on all grant applications from that unit. Furthermore, grants to states and regions must be coordinated at the state level through clearinghouses designated by the state.

Mandates

The conditions or requirements that one level of government imposes on another are called, **mandates**. The federal government imposes them on state and local governments, and state governments impose them on local governments. Mandates first appeared in intergovernmental relations as conditions attached to grants. They were designed to ensure fiscal and programmatic accountability in the use of funds. By using mandates, the national government has altered the way state and local governments do business. It has introduced requirements intended to increase accountability and efficiency. For example, most grants now require that public hearings be held before decisions are made about spending federal grant money. This has increased participation in government by local citizens. Affirmative action efforts must be made by state and local officials who spend grant money to hire new employees. In some cases state and local budgeting has been improved by the installation of effective accounting methods to keep track of federal funds (Table 3.2).

In recent years, however, it has been observed that the pendulum may have swung too far. There is real concern that may compromise the realization of the goals they are intended to achieve.[47] Examples include the conditions attached to grants from the Highway Trust Fund which forced several states to enact seat belt, and drinking age laws, and the 55 mph speed limit, in order to avoid reductions in their formula share of the money.[48]

The figures for the 1970–1990 period are the only ones available. During that period about half of the 500 preemptions that have occurred in the history of the federal system took

Table 3.2

MANDATES: RECENT CONGRESSIONAL ACTS REGULATING STATE AND LOCAL GOVERNMENTS

AMERICANS WITH DISABILITIES ACT 1990   CC, DO
Comprehensive national standards prohibiting discrimination in public services and accommodations and promoting handicapped access to public buildings.

CLEAN AIR ACT AMENDMENTS OF 1990   PP
Imposed strict new deadlines and requirements dealing with urban smog, municipal incinerators, and toxic emissions; enacted new programs for controlling acid rain.

COMMERCIAL MOTOR VEHICLE SAFETY ACT OF 1986   CO
Minimum national standards for licensing and testing commercial and school bus drivers; directed states to issue and administer licenses by 1992 or risk losing 5 to 10 percent of major highway grants.

CONSOLIDATED OMNIBUS BUDGET
RECONCILIATION ACT OF 1985   DO
Extended Medicare hospital insurance taxes and coverage to all new state and local government employees.

EMERGENCY PLANNING AND COMMUNITY
RIGHT TO KNOW ACT OF 1986   PP
National hazardous waste clean-up standards and timetables; required community right to know program, state and local notification of potential hazards and dissemination of information to public.

SAFE DRINKING WATER ACT AMENDMENTS 1986   PP, DO
New procedures and timetables for setting national drinking water standards, established new monitoring requirements for public drinking water systems, tightened penalties for noncompliance.

CC—Crosscutting Requirement—applies to all grants
CO—Crossover Sanction—denies funds from different program
DO—Direct Order—requires actions not in context of grant program
PP—Partial Preemption—sets standards which state may exceed

Source: ACIR, Federal Regulation of State and Local Governments: The Mixed Record of the 1980s (A-126) (Washington, D.C.: U. S. Advisory Commission on Intergovernmental Relations. 44–45

place.[49] The ACIR has consistently advocated a reduction in mandates, especially those requiring the expenditure of funds. In 1993 it published a study titled, *Federal Regulation of State and Local Governments: The Mixed Record of the 1980s*, indicating that new regulations enacted between 1983 and 1990 imposed costs estimated to be more than $9 billion on state and local governments.[50]

It appears that some relief may be in sight. In 1993 President Clinton issued executive order 12875 directing federal agencies "to reduce unfunded mandates and increase flexibility for state and local compliance." Leaders of the GOP-dominated Congress of 1995 promised mandate relief bills as part of the Contract with America.[51] In terms of practicing what one preaches, some state governments have begun to limit themselves in terms of the imposition of costs to local governments through unfunded mandates (Box 3.9). In 1994 half the states had imposed restrictions that require the state to fund new expenditures or reimburse local governments for expenditures that result from the imposition of mandates.[52]

BOX 3.9

DIMENSIONS OF DIVERSITY: THE MANDATE ISSUE

The mandate issue is often too easily simplified into a state-national conflict. Mandates are also symptoms of problems we will deal with in Chapter 8 when we discuss interest groups. Take, for example, the current controversy over preemption, a form of mandate. Congress has the power to preempt a field of legislative activity either partially—by setting minimum standards the states can exceed—or totally by excluding the states altogether from making regulations in this area. States don't regulate the use of nuclear fuel in power plants; the federal government has totally pre-empted that field, placing the Atomic Energy Commision in charge of seeing that nuclear plants are safely operated.

Sometimes a preemption occurs because a powerful interest feels that a state is regulating too rigorously. Interest groups may seek congressional help from state regulation by asking Congress to totally preempt the field and make the federal minimum regulations the only regulations. A recent example is the credit industry that tried in 1994 to get Congress to preempt the area of regulating credit reporting and thus render null and void a strict Vermont law protecting consumers from sloppy work by credit reporting firms.

As this book goes to press Congress has not responded favorably to the lobbying efforts of the credit industry against Vermont, nor has it responded favorably to demands by the oil companies to set a liability cap preempting state oil spill laws. In the 1980s auto manufacturers asked the Federal Trade Commission (FTC) to preempt state "lemon laws" imposing strict quality standards on new cars. The FTC was not amused. It told the states to do as they pleased.[53] Before making a judgment on any one mandate as to whether or not this was a federal invasion of state and local spheres of activity, it is well to ask the question, who wanted the preemption to take place? Who benefited? To see issues as national government versus state government is to miss an important dimension of American politics. Our system is one in which competition takes place among individuals, communities, and various interest groups—business and otherwise—and each one may prefer the competition to take place at a different level—national, state, or local.

Councils of Governments

Councils of Governments (COGs) are an excellent example of a local innovation at the local level in one state which the national government encouraged other state and local governments to put to use. A **Council of Government** is a voluntary association of local governments. The first council of government began in 1954 in the multicounty metropolitan area of Detroit, Michigan. It was called the Supervisor's Inter-County Committee. By 1968 it evolved into the Southeast Michigan Council of Governments, including cities and townships as well as the original three county governments.[54] Today there are nearly 600 COGs nationwide, serving their regions and regional governments in a variety of ways, from managing a zoo in the Portland, Oregon, area to developing programs for at-risk children in the 12-county San Antonio, Texas, area.[55]

James Madison, the Father of the American Constitution, was a major contributor to the *Federalist Papers*. He and his co-authors, Alexander Hamilton and John Jay, wrote under the pen name "Publius." Madison was also a founder of the American party system and the Democratic Party (Jeffersonian Republican) in Virginia. While Jefferson was governor, Madison carried most of his reform legislation in the Virginia House of Burgesses.

The basic idea of COGs is coordination. The proliferation of governments, particularly in metropolitan areas, has made it difficult for decision makers in each government to keep track in the normal course of a nine hour day of how their actions may affect or be affected by actions of neighboring governments. The council of government idea formalizes interaction between these decision makers.

Representatives of each government meet once or twice a month with one another to discuss mutual problems, review reports and proposals from a staff devoted to helping them plan and coordinate everything from highway and drainage construction to human service activities.

The national government helped promote the spread of the COG idea by building rewards and requirements for planning and metropolitan area coordination into various grant programs, beginning with Section 701 of the Housing Act of 1954. The ACIR studied COG activities and accomplishments and recommended in 1962 that state and local governments use COGS to reduce confusion and fragmentation of resources in metropolitan areas.[56]

The federal government has attempted to promote coordination within each state by requiring that the states create or designate existing agencies as clearinghouses for reviewing grant applications. These agencies could prevent the advancement of applications that interfere with long-range planning. The mechanism that states almost universally adopted to act as clearinghouses for federal grant applications was the council of governments. Busy chief executives serving on these councils found them to be a useful source of information in conducting their own oversight functions. Many states have now designated state planning regions, using county lines as boundaries, and have assigned major coordinating functions to the COG for that region.[57]

Federal funding for COGs was virtually eliminated by the Reagan administration and federal pressure to use COGs as designated coordinating bodies was reduced. Nevertheless, in 37 states COGs have proven to be so useful that they are still used by the statewide clearing agencies.[58] The member governments in some states have found COGs to be valuable not only for coordinating grant applications but for actually performing services on an area wide basis. In some states COGs have been given authority usually assigned to local governments such as taxing (16 COGs), zoning (15 COGs), and the power of eminent domain. More often, however, the activities of COGs consist of planning (highways, mass transit, water, and solid waste management), disseminating information, and coordinating services.[59]

Table 3.3 reports on the uses that are made of several small COGS within Allegheny County in Pennsylvania. This county was the subject of a study by the ACIR because of the large number of governments within it. In addition to the city of Pittsburgh, Allegheny County includes 330 local governments including 8 COGS and 128 municipalities. Al-

Table 3.3

ALLEGHENY COUNTY COUNCILS OF GOVERNMENTS

This table indicates ways in which a cluster of relatively small COGs are used by communities within one Pennsylvania county to deliver services. In many states COGS are countywide or even multi-county organizations.

Name	Members	Major Services
Turtle Creek Valley	17	Payroll and billing, street maintenance
Steel Valley	9	Planning, shared finance manager
Twin Rivers	11	Joint dispatch, firing range
Quaker Valley	15	Joint purchasing
Char-West	20	Planning
North Hills	12	Credit union, planning emergency management and street maintenance
Allegheny Valley North	15	Credit union
South Hill Area	15	Credit union, joint purchasing council

Source: ACIR, Metropolitan Organization: The Allegheny County Case (Washington, D.C.: U. S. Advisory Commission on Intergovernmental Relations, 1992), 18.

legheny County thus represents an extreme case of the complexity of intergovernmental relations in America.

The Council of State Governments

For more than 50 years the Council of State Governments (CSG), a voluntary organization, has operated as an information broker for the states. From its national headquarters in Lexington, Kentucky, and from regional offices in Atlanta, Chicago, New York City, and San Francisco, the CSG has worked to "improve decision-making and promote effective and innovative problem-solving and partnerships across the states."[60]

The variety of services performed by the council is indicated in part by Box 3.10 which lists publications by the Council of State Governments; these are available to public officials and interested citizens.[61] Within the Council of State Governments there are more than 35 types of national associations of state officials classified as cooperating with the Council. They include organizations representing probation and parole officers, dam safety officials, foresters, telecommunications directors, fleet administrators, printing associations, and utility regulators.[62]

Ten Federal Administrative Regions

For the purposes of administering federal programs, including grants-in-aid, each of the 50 states has been placed in one of ten Standard Federal Regions. Most major federal agencies

---

BOX 3.10

PUBLICATIONS OF THE COUNCIL OF STATE GOVERNMENTS

This is a selected list. Some of these publications such as *The Book of the States* are available in public libraries. Many of the others are available in university libraries.

The Book of the States: A biennial reference book. It contains essays by experts on state operations and hundreds of tables with comparative data on the 50 states.

State Elective Officials and the Legislatures: A directory of names, addresses, and telephone numbers.

State Administrative Officials Classified by Function: A directory of names addresses, and telephone numbers.

State Government News: A monthly magazine about state innovations and issues.

Suggested State Legislation: An annual volume of draft legislation selected by a committee of state officials.

Spectrum: The Journal of State Government: A quarterly publication that provides a forum for discussing state issues from the viewpoints of academics, political leaders, and practitioners.

Innovations: A series of reports focuses on award winning state programs that contribute to innovation in state government.

Source: Deborah A. Gona, "The Council of State Governments," The Book of the States: 1994–95 (Lexington, KY: Council of State Governments, 1994), 626.

Figure 3.2

Ten Federal Administrative Regions

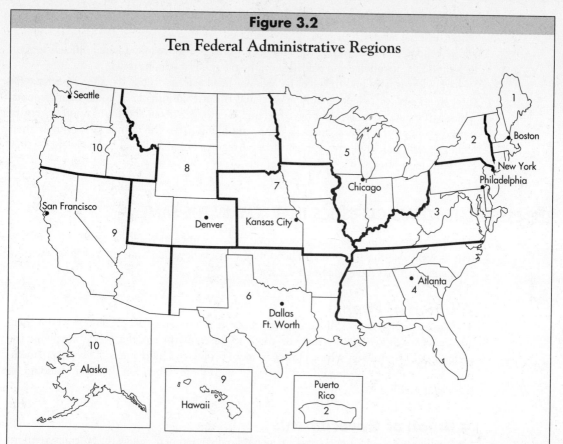

Ten Federal Administrative Regions. Not all federal Agencies use them, but enough do so that life has been made less complicated for state and local officials.

Source: *Strengthening Public Management in the Intergovernmental System. A report prepared for the Office of Management and Budget by the Study Committee on Policy Management Assistance, Executive Office of the President, (Washington, D.C., Executive Office of the President, 1975), 15.*

which deal with the state and local governments have been required to adopt the same regional map and put their own regional headquarters in the cities that have been designated for the ten regions.[63]

The top executives of these agencies constituted the membership of each of the ten Federal Regional Councils. Until 1983, when the Reagan administration abolished them, their mission was to improve the coordination of federal activities, including grant programs, in each region. Whether the regional councils are ever reconstituted, the continued existence of the standard regional headquarters has greatly reduced travel and confusion for state and local officials. Prior to the establishment of the regions, each federal agency divided the country into its own regions without consulting the others.[64]

For example, Idaho, as Figure 3.2 indicates, was located in a region for one agency whose regional headquarters was in San Francisco, another agency located Idaho in a region whose headquarters was in Denver, and yet another agency required Idaho officials to look to Kansas City for advice and guidance on the programs it administered.

Individuals who had to travel to regional headquarters to put together a package for their state, city, or county greatly appreciated the streamlining of regional arrangements. Thus, while state officials might have had mixed emotions about abolishing another coordinating agency—the federal councils—they are likely to let the White House know their feelings pretty quickly if the standard federal regions are abandoned by the agencies they deal with most often.[65]

THE ESSENTIALS: CHARACTERISTICS THAT REMAIN THE SAME

Although our nation-state has become an intergovernmental system, it is still a federal system as well. Among the many indicators of consistency, one finds at least four essential characteristics that have remained the same.

A Union of People

The American nation is still a union of people. It is a union of people among whom there are occasional disagreements, some of which are based on the fact that we do not all use the same model to define ourselves. However, more people and more kinds of people are members of our nation, enjoying citizenship rights with more dimension than our founding fathers ever imagined.

A Union of Governments

Originally a union of 13 states and a new national government, today the federal system includes 50 states. When some people use the term "federal," they refer only to the state-national relationship outlined in the constitution. Others include all 86,000 governmental entities of the intergovernmental system. However many governments we refer to with the term federalism, we are talking about a system that is still a union of governments after 200 years.

Constitutional Guarantees Still Work

The parts of the union remain indestructible. The states are still the key units within the federal system. Veteran journalist Neal R. Pierce puts it this way:

> Virtually all 50 states today are strong enough entities to take on almost any program the national government might hand over to them. Twenty or 30 years ago this wasn't the case. [However,] a quiet revolution of state-level reform, centered on new constitutions, broadscaled executive branch reorganizations, "one-man, one vote" reapportionment, and professionally staffed legislatures has changed all that.[66]

Today the states are better equipped then ever before and, as observed earlier, all of them could stand alone in the world community of nations. Thus, our system is still a union of state and national governments.

A Government of the Union Still Exercises Sovereignty

The government of the Union exercises sovereignty. The notion that the government of the Union may or may not exercise too much sovereignty will continue to be debated as long as the system exists. The task that we, the sovereign people, face today is to make sure that the reforms we support are dedicated to strengthening the whole system, not simply weakening a particular part of it. Quite often in our discussions of the relative strength of the states and the federal government we forget how strong and economically healthy the states really are.

CONCLUSION

The American federal system involves not only tension between the center and its parts but also competition and conflict among the parts themselves. The Frostbelt and Sunbelt disagree over which federal military installations ought to be closed, and communities within states as well as states themselves compete with one another and with foreign countries to attract new industries. We argue among ourselves over federal purchasing contracts which benefit local industries, the formulas of major grant programs, and the ability of states to tax the exploitation of natural resources such as oil, gas, and coal. These are all serious matters with intergovernmental consequences. Conflict in various forms is a continuing feature of a large, complex society. Fortunately, in our federal system compromise and negotiation are also built in. The federal system itself is part of the conflict-resolving equipment.

STUDY OBJECTIVES

1. Identify three things which federalism is and three which it is not.
2. Identify the three compromises that were necessary for the creation of the U. S. Constitution.
3. Identify the four parts of our definition of federalism.
4. Identify three dimensions of sovereignty.
5. Identify the significance of *Garcia* v. *San Antonio Metropolitan Transit Authority*
6. Identify the six protections guaranteed the states.
7. Identify the litmus test of federalism
8. Identify and define the terms in a working vocabulary of federalism.
9. Identify five changes in the American federal system which have helped it deal with the fact that it has become a system of intergovernmental relations.
10. Identify the role of interest groups in mandates and preemption.
11. Identify the two major features of fiscal federalism.

GLOSSARY

Confederation, confederal   In classifying the relationship between the central government and the governments at the next level (the whole and its parts) the terms confederal, federal, and unitary are used. A confederation is a system of government in which the central government is subordinate to the governments at the next level. They are usually legally free to leave the confederation at any time. Citizens of member governments do not usually feel a sense of confederation citizenship.

Council of government   A voluntary association of local governments.

Decentralization   The process of delegating functions (education, fire protection) to a local unit of government in the interests of efficiency.

Federal   Describes a system of government in which power is divided between a central government and specific subunits of government.

Fiscal federalism   The dimension of our federal system that involves the use of superior financial resources at the national level to assist units of government with fewer financial resources.

Fiscal note   A statement attached to a proposed law to indicate what it would cost to carry it out that law.

Infallibility   The characteristic of being not subject to error.

Infer   To deduce or reason from. We point this out because many people use imply and infer interchangeably. What you infer from someone's words is not necessarily what that person meant to imply.

Mandates   The conditions or requirements that grant recipients must meet to receive funds. A mandate is a command; thus mandates are not always grant-related. Laws that assign new responsibilities or limitations on other governments are also called mandates.

National integration   The process of bringing all Americans into the same society.

Nationalism   A belief system whose central value is the nation-state.

Pre-emption   The act of taking over a field of legislative activity. Pre-emption may be total or partial.

Salient   The quality of being noticeable. A salient issue is one of which many people have become aware.

Separation of powers   A principle of government that divides power within a single level of government. The usual division is three branches; executive, legislative, and judicial.

Sovereignty   A concept which includes two notions: supremacy in one's own sphere of influence and independence from the rule of others. In democratic political theory, sovereignty resides with "the people".

Unitary   In classifying the relationship between the central government and local governments the terms confederal, federal, and unitary are used. A unitary system of government in which one level of government can alter or abolish other levels without consulting them. Each of the 50 states can alter local government. In some states the people might have to approve the action, for example, in a constitutional amendment. However, only the people of the state, not their governments would have to approve. Our 50 states have unitary systems of government.

ENDNOTES

1. Thomas H. Eliot, *Governing America*, 2d ed. (New York: Dodd, Mead & Company, 1964), 759.

2. While all eleven volumes of the comprehensive overview of the federal system, *The Federal*

Role in the Federal System: The Dynamics of Growth, would be heavy going, the serious student is encouraged to examine the summary volume: *An Agenda for American Federalism: Restoring Confidence and Competence*, vol. 10 (Washington, D.C.: U. S. Government Printing Office, 1981, A–86), as well as Richard Leach, *American Federalism*, (New York: W. W. Norton, 1970).

3. "Amendments Are the Talk of the Season," *Governing* (October, 1988), 13. See also, Robert T. Golembiewski and Aaron Wildavsky, *The Costs of Federalism* (New Brunswick: Transaction Books, 1984), Roy V. Peel, *State Government Today* (Albuquerque: University of New Mexico Press, 1948); and Stanley D. Brunn, "Geography and Politics of the United States in the Year 2000," *The Journal of Geography* (April 1973) 42–49, and G. Etzel Pearcy, *A 38 State U.S.A.*, (Fullerton, CA: Plycon Press, 1973).

4. The student interested in keeping abreast of significant changes in the federal/intergovernmental system is advised to monitor the following two quarterly publications: *Intergovernmental Perspective*, published by the Advisory Commission on Intergovernmental Relations and *Publius*, Published by the Center for the Study of Federalism.

5. K. C. Wheare, *Federal Government* (Westport: Greenwood Press, 1980).

6. Martin Diamond, *A Nation of States*. See also David F. Epstein, *Political Theory of the Federalist* (Chicago: University of Chicago Press, 1984).

7. Alexis de Tocqueville, *Democracy in America*, vol. 1, trans. Henry Reeve (New Rochelle, NY: Arlington House), 144.

8. Ivo D. Duchacek, *Comparative Federalism* (New York: Harper and Row Publishers, 1970). See also David F. Epstein, *Political Theory of the Federalist* (Chicago: University of Chicago Press, 1984).

9. For a very readable account of the negotiations and compromises in Philadelphia in 1776, see Catherine Drinker Bowen, *Miracle at Philadelphia* (Boston, Little, Brown, & Co. 1986).

10. Bowen, *Miracle*, 92.

11. Ibid, 255–256.

12. Ibid., quoting Hamilton on the three-fifths compromise, without which, ". . . no union could possibly have been formed," 200.

13. For a more elegant example of ex adverso definition, see "What Democracy is Not," in Giovanni Sartori, *Democratic Theory* (Detroit: Wayne State University Press, 1962), 135–157.

14. Franz Neumann, "Federalism and Freedom: A Critique," in Arthur W. MacMahon, ed. *Federalism: Mature and Emergent* (Garden City, NY: Doubleday and Co., 1955), 44–57. See also William H. Riker, *Federalism, Origin, Operation, Significance* (Boston: Little Brown & Co., 1964).

15. Herbert S. Duncombe, *Modern County Government* (Washington: D.C. National Association of Counties, 1977), 51.

16. See Murray Greensmith Forsyth, *Unions and States: The Theory and Practice of Confederation* (New York: Leicester University Press, 1981).

17. For additional definitions of federalism see, K. C. Wheare, *Federal Government* (Westport: Greenwood Press, 1980) and Arthur Maas ed., *Area and Power* (Glencoe: Free Press, 1959).

18. Daniel J. Elazar, "A View from the Commission," *Intergovernmental Perspective* (Fall, 1988), 2.

19 *The World Almanac, 1987*. With an area of 1,049 square miles Rhode Island is more than twice the size of all but four of those fifteen.

20. Ivo D. Duchacek, *Comparative Federalism* (New York: Harper and Row Publishers, 1970).

21. Ralph Nading Hill, *Yankee Kingdom: Vermont and New Hampshire* (New York: Harper and Brothers, 1960), 170. T. R. Fehrenbach, Clifton McCleskey et al., *The Government and Politics of Texas*, 7th ed. (Boston: Little, Brown & Co, 1982), 3. See also *Lone Star: A History of Texas and Texans* (New York: Macmillan, 1968).

22. For a discussion of attempts to create and maintain federalism in new nations see Thomas Franck, ed. *Why Federations Fail* (New York: New York University Press, 1968).

23. Daniel J. Elazar, *American Federalism: A View from the States* (New York: Harper and Row Publishers, 1972), 2.

24. Alexander Hamilton, "Federalist Number 85" in James Madison, Alexander Hamilton, and John Jay, *The Federalist Papers* (New Rochelle, NY: Arlington House, Circa 1975), 527.

25. Karl Deutsch, *Nationalism and Social Communication: An Inquiry Into the Foundations of Nationality* (Cambridge, MA: M.I.T. Press, 1966), 162–166, and 181–186.

26. James Bryce, *Modern Democracies* (New York: Macmillan Co., 1924), 20.

27. John A. Garraty, *The American Nation*, vol. 2 (New York: Harper and Row Publishers, 1983), 573. See also Walter I. Trattner, *Crusade for the Children* (Chicago: Quadrangel Books, 1970); Viviana A. Rotman Selizer, *Pricing the Priceless Child* (New York: Basic Books, 1985); and Ronald B. Taylor, *Sweatshops in the Sun* (Boston: Beacon Press, 1973).

28. *Garcia v. San Antonio Metropolitan Transit Authority.* Supreme Court of the United States, 1985. 469 U.S. 528 S.Ct. 1005, 83 L. Ed. 2nd 1016.

29. William D. Valente, *Local Government Law: Cases and Materials*, 3d ed., (St. Paul, MN: West Publishing Co., 1987), 325.

30. Ibid., 330–331.90

31. *Texas v. White*, (1869). Quoted in C. Herman Pritchett, *The American Constitutional System* (New York: McGraw Hill Book Co., 1981), 21.

32. Oscar D. Lambert, *West Virginia and Its Government*, (Boston: Heath, 1951).

33. James Jackson Kilpatrick, "The Case for States' Rights," in Robert A. Goldwin, ed., *A Nation of States: Essays on the American Federal System*, (Chicago: Rand McNally, 1974) 24.

34. Quoted in Joseph T. Keenan, *The Constitution of the United States: An Unfolding Story* (Homewood: The Dorsey Press, 1988), 98.

35. In *South Carolina v. Baker*, 1988 48 CCH S./ Ct Bull. Justice Brennan's majority opinion: "States must find their protection from congressional regulation through the national political process, not through judicially defined spheres of unregulable state activity." 1646–1647.

36. Pritchett, *The American Constitutional System*, (1981), 18.

37. Ibid. 91–101.

38. Ibid., 23.

39. Thomas H. Eliot, *Governing America*, 2d ed. (New York: Dodd, Mead & Co., 1964), 759.

40. The Court, as is its practice, combined similar cases from several states in deciding this one. The School District of Topeka, Kansas, was not the only intergovernmental litigant.

41. Stanley H. Friedelbaum, "Supreme Courts in Conflict: The Drama of Disagreement," *Intergovernmental Perspective* (Fall 1991), 27. For an extensive list of rights found in state constitutions see: Mark Glasser and John Kincaid, "Selected Rights Enumerated in State Constitutions," *Intergovernmental Perspective* (Fall, 1991), 35.

42. Among the excellent overviews of the shift from Federalism to intergovernmental relations upon which this chapter has relied are: David B. Walker, *Toward a Functioning Federalism* (Cambridge, MA: Winthrop Publishers, Inc., 1981); Daniel J. Elazar, *American Federalism: A View from the States* (New York: Harper and Row Publishers, 1972); David C. Nice, *Federalism: The Politics of Intergovernmental Relations* (New York: St. Martin's Press, 1987); and Deil S.Wright, *Understanding Intergovernmental Relations* (North Scituate, MA: Duxbury Press, 1978).

43. ACIR, *Directory of Intergovernmental Contacts* (Washington, D.C.: Advisory Commission on Intergovernmental Relations, 1994) 17–18. See also, ACIR, *State-Local Relations Organizations* (Washington D.C.: Advisory Commissions on Intergovernmental Relations, 1991).

44. ACIR, *Significant Features of Fiscal Federalism*, vol. 1 (Washington: Advisory Commission on Intergovernmental Relations, 1989), 26.

45. Joel C. Miller, "Muncipal Annexation and Boundary Change," in *The Municipal Year Book 1988* (Washington, D.C.: International City Management Association, 1988), 62.

46. For a similar example in Muncie, Indiana, see David B. Walker, *Toward a Functioning Federalism* (Cambridge, MA: Winthrop Publishers, 1981) 3.

47. Ibid., 193.

48. ACIR. *Federal Regulation of State and Local Governments: The Mixed Record of the 1980s* (A–126) (Washington, D.C.: U.S. Advisory Commission on Intergovernmental Relations) 1993, 7.

49. Ibid., 53.

50. Ibid., 57.

51. *Intergovernmental Perspective* (Fall 1993/Winter 1994), 8.

52. The Business of Government." *Governing* (August, 1994), 53.

53. Ellen Perlman, "The Gorilla That Swallows State Laws," *Governing*. (August, 1994), 47–51.

54. National Association of Regional Councils *New and Notes* (November 18, 1988), 2, and telephone interviews with Carole Anne Boileau, Communications Associate, National Association of Regional Councils, Washington, D.C. November 18, 1988.

55. National Association of Regional Councils *New and Notes* (November 18, 1988), 2, and telephone interviews with Al Notzen, Executive Director of the Alamo Area Council of Governments, San Antonio, Texas, November 18, 1988.

56. National Association of Regional Councils *New and Notes* (November 18, 1988), 39.

57. *Intergovernmental Perspective* (Fall, 1984) 5.

58. Office of Management and Budget, *Implementation of Executive Order 12372: The First Year: Background Document for the Report to the President*, (Washington, D. C: Executive Office of the President, March, 1985), Appendix 4.

59. Sherman M. Wyman, "Profiles and Prospects: Regional Councils and Their Directors," *The Municipal Yearbook 1994* (Washington, D.C.: The International City/County Management Association, 1994), 48.

60. Deborah A. Gona, "The Council of State Governments," *The Book of the States: 1994–95*, (Lexington, KY: Council of State Governments, 1994), 622.

61. Ibid., 626–628.

62. Ibid., 628.

63. *U.S. Government Organization Manual*, (Washington, D.C. : 1988–1989), 784. See also Office of Management and Budget circular A-105 for restrictions on agencies seeking to use other regional arrangements.

64. For a brief history of Federal Regional Councils see "Federal Regional Councils," in Martha Derthick, *Between State and Nation: Regional Organizations of the United States* (Washington, D.C. Brookings Institute, 1974), 157–181.

65. Among them are the Environmental Protection Agency, Housing and Urban Development, Department of Transportation, Health and Human Services, Department of Labor, and the General Services Administration, see individual agency listings in the *U. S. Government Manual: 1988–89*, (Washington, D.C.: Office of the Federal Register, National Archives and Records Administration, revised June 1, 1988). See also Office of Management and Budget, "Circular A-105, Standard Federal Regions."

66. *Public Administration Times* (December 1, 1981), 2.

4 Foundations of the Governments: State Constitutions

Cody McGannon, a 10 year old grounded for a week because he told a lie, gained his 3 minutes of fame when Missouri Governor Mel Carnahan granted him a pardon. The public response was mixed. For some TV news directors it was an interesting human interest story which merited a 15-second slot; some newspaper editors put it on the front page while others put it inside. Few ignored it. Phil Donahue, Jay Leno and others have invited Cody to appear on their shows.

Somewhat less amused was Robin Scott of the National Institute of Ethics who said that the Governor's pardon sends the wrong message. Cody told his parents he had not opened his bedroom window. It turns out that he had. "How is that child going to learn from his mistakes if he doesn't take the punishment that his parents set for him?" Scott asks.

Since everyone else seems taken with this case, we might as well weigh in by suggesting that not only is a little lightening up in order, but also that the most important part of the story is often left out. Cody's parents gave the Governor the authority to grant the pardon. Had they not done so, the Governor would not have become involved. What Governor wants to get into the middle of a family feud?

Cody's stepfather, Alex Jones, had responded to Cody's complaints about the harshness of a whole week of grounding by suggesting that if he didn't like it, maybe he should take it up with the Governor. After serving four days of his punishment, Cody wrote to Carnahan. Cody's mother, Elizabeth Jones, faxed the letter to the Governor along with one of her own putting in a good word for Cody and letting the Governor know that the family would accept his decision.

Much to her amazement, the Governor faxed back a pardon the same day: "I hope the authorities (your parents) are not too upset with me, and that they decide to accept my act of clemency in the same spirit of good will in which it was given," the Governor wrote.

Cody was happy to accept the pardon, his parents were happy for the opportunity to appear reasonable, and especially happy that Cody learned his lesson. He won't ever try to get another pardon. "One shot. That's all," Cody said.[1]

Just as Cody's parents granted the governor of Missouri the authority to issue a pardon, some state constitutions grant a governor authority to do the same for convicted criminals, others do not. As we observed in Chapter 1, Marie Ragghianti helped put a governor who abused this power behind bars. In some states governors no longer have the authority to grant pardons because of the sins of previous governors; in other states the constitution has not been amended to deny the power of clemency to all governors, the public has simply decided to monitor their activity in this area a little more closely.

Constitutions grant and limit the power of public agencies and officials. This chapter explores the nature of state constitutions and examines the difficulty of finding an appropriate position on granting too much or too little authority to government in general, and to state government in particular.

STATE AND LOCAL SOURCES OF AUTHORITY

The 50 state constitutions are the basis for each state government's claim to exercise the sovereignty of the people of that state. Like the U. S. Constitution, the state constitutions establish the structure of government by identifying the major offices, the qualifications of those eligible to hold them, the method of selecting public officials, and the procedures for amendment. For these reasons alone, an examination of state constitutions is worthwhile. However, there are at least six additional reasons for studying the constitution of your state in particular, and state constitutions in general.

Six Reasons to Study State Constitutions

1. To Better Understand the U. S. Constitution

There are significant differences between state constitutions and the U. S. Constitution which are useful in understanding both. According to Janice C. May, these differences are so numerous that "we may be justified in speaking of 'two constitutional traditions.'"[2] May pays particular attention to three differences between state constitutions and the U. S. Constitution.

The first is that only governments or conventions selected by governments are involved in amending the U. S. Constitution. As we noted in Chapter 3, this is the litmus test of American Federalism. State constitutional amendment, however, involves the people in all but one state, Delaware.

The second difference is the frequency of amendment. Most state constitutions have more than three times as many amendments as the 27 additions to the U. S. Constitution.

Thirdly, the U. S. Constitution tends to serve as a set of guidelines for conducting politics; too many state constitutions are part of the prize for political victory. The recent efforts to amend the U. S. Constitution suggest that it too is in danger of becoming a prize rather than a set of guidelines for conducting politics.

2. To Better Understand One's Rights

Our concern with obligations and responsibilities, you may have noted, has more to do with our concern with unrealized human potential than it does with simply being a good citizen, although we value that as well. It is no contradiction for people with potential to realize that they need to invest some time in understanding the rights they can exercise while attempting to realize that potential. Thus, we are also concerned with the rights of individuals.

State constitutions contain many rights that the U. S. Constitution does not.[3] For example, in *Robinson* v. *Cahill* (1973), the New Jersey Supreme Court—not the U.S. Supreme Court—found the state's method of financing education was unconstitutional technically because it failed to meet the state constitution's requirement that the education system be "thorough and efficient." In this decision and in decisions in other states a state's highest court has found that the right of school children to a *state defined* standard of educational opportunity was denied by the existing system. In New Jersey the state court then ordered all of the state's school systems shut down until the legislature found a way to finance them equitably.[4]

Glasser and Kincaid inventoried the rights listed in state constitutions. They discovered more than 370 that they classified in ten categories, which we have placed in Table 4.1. We suggest that you take a look at this table since, as elsewhere in this book, we often place important things in boxes and tables without repeating them in the text. For example, where does one find most states bill of rights?

One of their 10 categories is "Limits on Rights," many of which are attempts to protect the rights of the many while restricting the rights of a few. For example, North Carolina has a prohibition against "secret political societies," which was clearly an anti-Klan amendment. Glasser and Kincaid note that some of these limitations are ignored by practice. Plural marriages, they observe, "exist openly in the four states that constitutionally prohibit them: Arizona, Idaho, Oklahoma, and Utah."[5]

Approximately 110 of the rights (or limitations) identified in their survey are listed in only one state constitution, which is not to say that those particular listed rights are unique to one state. An unlisted right is not necessarily denied nor unprotected. Some rights are so taken for granted that constitution-makers or amenders may not have felt it necessary to include them.[6]

3. To Better Understand One's Own State Political System

Not all state constitutions are the same. This has at least two important implications. First, since there is no "one size fits all" state constitution, in each state people who wish to influence the political system need to know about the constitution that influences that state's political system. Second, because some states share economic and social similarities, there may be something that works in one state that could be applied in another. In some cases these innovations may require constitutional amendments. You can't amend something if you don't know much about it.

Table 4.1

TEN CATEGORIES OF RIGHTS FOUND IN STATE CONSTITUTIONS

If one is familiar with the Bill of Rights in the U. S. Constitution, one may experience a little déja vu in reading some of the items on this list. It is well to recall that the U. S. Constitution was the product of several generations of state constitution writing. Protecting individuals from excessive government was what early state constitutions were all about.

1. Fundamental Principles
   The U.S. Constitution is the only one in the federal system that puts a bill of rights at the end. State constitutions begin with one. Most declare the following five principles to be basic:
   (1) there are natural or inalienable rights, (2) all persons are equal,
   (3) the people are sovereign, (4) government derives its just powers from the consent of the people, and (5) government exists only to promote the common good.
2. Basic Rights of Human Freedom
   The four most common are: religion, speech, the press, bearing arms.
3. Rights to Participate in Governance
   The three most common are: suffrage, the right of the people to ratify or reject amendments to the constitution, and peaceable assembly.
4. Rights Against Tyranny
   The nine listed by 40 states or more are:
   (1) Private property cannot be taken without just compensation
   (2) No unreasonable search and seizures
   (3) Procedures for warrants
   (4) No government-established religion
   (5) No ex post facto laws
   (6) No special government created privileges or monopolies
   (7) Life, liberty ,or property cannot be deprived without due process of law
   (8) No quartering of soldiers in private homes without consent
   (9) The military must be kept in strict subordination to civil power
5. Rights in Civil and Criminal Proceedings
   Most of these rights protect persons accused of a crime or convicted of a crime. Five are found in 45 or more state constitutions.
   (1) Habeas corpus cannot be suspended
   (2) No excessive bail
   (3) No self-incrimination
   (4) No excessive fines
   (5) Executive authority to grant reprieves or pardons
   (6) No cruel or unusual punishment
   (7) The right to be informed of charges
6. Natural Resources and Environment
   Most of the 33 rights listed are mentioned in only one or two states. They range from very broad—
   "All public natural resources are held in trust by the state for the benefit of the people." (Hawaii)
   To fairly specific—"Free Navigation of the Mississippi." (Tennessee)
7. Occupational Rights
   21 rights, none mentioned for more than nine states.
8. Other Rights
   A small residual category.
9. Limits on Rights
   24 in all, only one listed by more than ten states. Thirteen state constitutions deny state citizenship to persons stationed there because of military service, a provision clearly in conflict with the U.S. Voting Rights Act of 1974 and amendments, and therefore null and void.
10. Reserved Rights
    Much like the 10th amendment. Rights not listed are still rights.

Source: Mark Glasser and John Kincaid, "Selected Rights Enumerated in State Constitutions," Intergovernmental Perspective (Fall, 1991), 38–44.

4. To Learn About Five Hundred Pound Gorillas

Where does a 500-pound gorilla sleep? —— Anywhere he wants to.

In many states officials other than judges are involved in the interpretation of the state constitution. This means that in your state, there may be a 500-pound gorilla or two in the constitutional jungle. You may want to know who these officials are.

In at least twenty states state attorneys general issue opinions interpreting the state constitution. Thomas R. Morris reports that even though they are not legally binding, these opinions are "regularly sought and almost always followed by state officials."[7] In other words these opinions are, more often than not, politically effective. Few individuals, organizations, or units of local government in those states wish to invest the political resources necessary to test these opinions in court.[8]

5. To Better Understand Local Government

State constitutions are critical to the study of city, county, and other local governments. In addition to setting forth the structure of state government, they also are the ultimate source of authority for many local governments. Perhaps nothing symbolizes the linkage between state constitutions and the fate of local government better than the fact that since 1921, when it published its first model state constitution, the National Municipal League has sponsored research on state constitutional issues.[9]

Some state constitutions devote few pages to local government, but give the authority to create local governments to the legislature. Other state constitutions describe some dimensions of the local government system in copious detail. Usually, county government is described in some detail, including the officers that must be elected. Thus in many states, for the citizens of a given county to restructure their county government, it is necessary to push a constitutional amendment through the legislature and get it approved by all the voters in their state.

6. To Better Evaluate Suggestions for Change

Within the next 10 years, most of you will be asked to decide whether or not to change your state constitution. Frequent amendment is certainly one of the major differences between the U. S. and state constitutional traditions. Among the 50 state constitutions there have been 5,503 amendments as of 1994.[10] Janice C. May reports that in the 1990–1993 period alone, an additional 465 amendments were proposed, of which 305 were adopted (Table 4.2).[11]

Thus, a little knowledge about your state's constitution as it is now, how it compares to models such as the U. S. Constitution, and how it compares with other state constitutions is in order. With this information you will be better equipped to make informed decisions and perhaps influence the decisions made by others. In the pages that follow we will compare and contrast major features of state constitutions, leaving a closer examination of your own state constitution up to you and your instructor.

CONSTITUTIONAL GOVERNMENT: TWO IDEAS IN CONFLICT

The idea of government implies that there is a need for something to be done. This usually results in the selection of a set of officials to exercise power in the name of the community. The idea of *constitutional* government implies limits on the use of that power so that individ-

Table 4.2

STATE CONSTITUTIONS CURRENT IN 1994

State	Date Effective	Approximate Word Count	Number of Amendments
Alabama	1901	174,000	556
Alaska	1959	13,000	23
Arizona	1912	28,876	119
Arkansas[a]	1874	40,720	76
California	1879	33,350	485
Colorado	1876	45,679	124
Connecticut	1965	9,564	28
Delaware	1897	19,000	123
Florida	1969	25,100	65
Georgia	1983	25,000	39
Hawaii	1959	17,543	86
Idaho	1890	21,500	109
Illinois	1971	13,200	8
Indiana	1851	9,377	38
Iowa[a]	1857	12,500	46
Kansas[a]	1861	11,865	89
Kentucky	1891	23,500	32
Louisiana	1975	36,146	54
Maine	1820	13,500	162
Maryland	1867	41,134	205
Massachusetts	1780	36,690	117
Michigan	1964	20,000	17
Minnesota	1858	9,500	113
Mississippi	1890	23,500	116
Missouri	1945	42,000	81
Montana	1973	11,866	18
Nebraska	1875	20,048	197
Nevada[a]	1864	20,770	107
New Hampshire	1784	9,200	143
New Jersey	1948	17,086	44
New Mexico	1912	27,200	123
New York	1895	80,000	213
North Carolina	1971	11,000	27
North Dakota	1889	31,000	129
Ohio	1851	36,900	151
Oklahoma	1907	68,800	141
Oregon	1859	25,965	192
Pennsylvania[b]	1968	21,675	56
Rhode Island	1843	19,026	36
South Carolina	1896	22,500	463
South Dakota	1889	23,300	99
Tennessee	1870	15,300	32
Texas	1876	62,000	353
Utah	1896	17,500	82

(Continued)

Table 4.2 (Continued))

STATE CONSTITUTIONS CURRENT IN 1994

State	Date Effective	Approximate Word Count	Number of Amendments
Vermont	1793	6,600	50
Virginia	1971	18,650	23
Washington	1889	29,400	88
West Virginia	1872	25,600	64
Wisconsin[a]	1848	13,500	127
Wyoming	1890	31,800	61
United States	1789	10,000	27

(a)Does not include amendments nullified by State Supreme Court, or U.S. Supreme Court decisions
(b) The Pennsylvania Constitution of 1973 was significantly revised in 1968

Source: The Book of the States 1994–95 (Lexington, KY: Council of State Governments, 1994), 19–20.

Representative government involves formal deliberation, negotiation, and compromise. Its product is usu-ally—but not always—something different than the first drafted proposal.

uals or the community as a whole will be protected from arbitrary behavior on the part of those who govern.

The conflict between the idea of government (using power to do something) and the idea of limits (preventing the abuse of power) cannot be easily resolved. Almost anything that weakens the ability of government to do mischief also weakens its ability to act in the public interest.

For some people government is best kept on the sidelines assuming that the free market, or natural law, or fate will decide things. If this appeals to you, then Box 4.1 needs to be carefully studied. Actually, it needs to be carefully studied whether you want government handcuffed or not. The points mentioned in Box 4.1 are not only key points in chapters that follow but they are the basis for much of the discussion of state constitutional revision that will occur in the years to come.

As we noted in Chapter 2, the status quo is seldom preserved permanently. Change always takes place. Thus, if weak government does nothing, then other parts of the political system may be able to make sure that change occurs the way they want it to. In addition to the folks whose suspicion of changes that strengthen government are based on a legitimate concern for abuse of power, there are others who benefit from weak government: organized crime, street gangs, people who do not want anyone inquiring too closely into how they prepare food, treat their employees, make loans or chemicals, dispose of waste products, build buildings, or contribute to political campaigns.

BOX 4.1

HOW TO KEEP GOVERNMENT ON THE SIDELINES

1. Fragment power within the executive branch of government. Distribute it among numerous officials; it becomes so difficult for any of them to get much done that they either stop trying or conserve their energy for a very few projects. (Chapter 11)*
2. Create numerous veto points. Before any significant action takes place, require formal approval from numerous actors in the political system: the legislature, the governor, the courts, and/or the public via a referendum. (Chapters 4 and 5)
3. Make it easy to remove officials by providing a recall system that is easy for a small number of people to put into motion. (Chapter 4)
4. Keep officials busy at nonproductive activities by giving them short terms of office, thus requiring them to spend a lot of time and energy running for reelection. (Chapters 4, 10, 11).
5. Provide no resources for taking action (money, personnel, equipment). Keep the budget low. (Chapter 16).
6. Limit the grant of power in the constitution to a short list of enumerated powers. Without a "necessary and proper" clause, public officials must get the constitution amended in order to do anything new. (Chapter 5).

---

* Indicates chapter in which this item is discussed

John P. Wheeler, Jr., a noted constitutional scholar, is one of several observers who believe that keeping government weak is not an effective protection from arbitrary rule. A constitution that excessively limits government, according to Wheeler, has:

> consistently proved self-defeating for it has prevented states from meeting the needs of a dynamic society. It is better to give power to the organs of government and then seek means to keep public officials honest and responsible than seek to deny them power. The constitution is a poor place to seek complete insurance against irresponsible government.[12]

Weak government does little to assure that change occurs in the public interest. In the game of politics, weak government simply stays on the bench and keeps its uniform clean.

If one is concerned about protecting the environment, or promoting social justice, it really doesn't matter very much whether one has a government too weak to provide these things or whether one has a government strong enough to provide these things but controlled by the "wrong" people.

The authors of the 145 or more constitutions, which have been in force in the 50 states since 1776, have used a variety of methods to reduce the risks of excessive strength and excessive weakness. Throughout this book we will compare the results of these experiments. In this chapter we focus on the fact that all 50 state constitutions employ at least four basic principles to resolve the too weak/too strong dilemma of constitutional government.

FOUR PRINCIPLES OF LIMITED GOVERNMENT

State constitutions all embrace, with some variation, four principles that serve to limit government: liberalism, republicanism, separation of powers, and democracy.

Liberalism

Liberalism (Box 4.2) is a term used to identify both an ideology whose central value is the freedom of the individual and a basic principle of constitution making that is consistent with that ideology. The principle is the protection of the individual from abuse of power by public officials. The notion that governments are created to protect individual freedom is firmly established in all state constitutions by a bill of rights (see "fundamental principles" Table 4.1).

For many years state constitutional bills of rights were regarded as virtually useless because the national government seemed to be more able and more willing to protect individual freedom than were many state governments. During the 1970s, however, the U. S. Supreme Court began to identify limits to the rights the U. S. Constitution guarantees under the equal protection clause of the Fourteenth Amendment.

Attorneys and schools re-examined state constitutions to see if they might guarantee equal rights such as educational opportunity. During the past two decades the state supreme courts of California, Connecticut, New Jersey, and Texas have declared that the methods for financing public schools conflicted with the constitutions of those states. According to their state constitutions, not the U.S. Constitution, individuals were guaranteed the right to equal educational opportunity. As Table 4.1 indicates other rights have been discovered as well.

The protection of the individual is based on two concepts central to liberalism. First, that solutions to problems facing the communities come from individuals. Absent protec-

BOX 4.2

THE "L" WORD

1. Liberalism originated in the era of John Locke and Adam Smith when government was viewed as the personal property of kings, dukes, earls, and czars, many of whom used their power to take property, and sometimes life, away from individuals without due process of law.

2. Conservatism is a first cousin to, not an opposite of, liberalism. After the French Revolution (1789), when the Parisian mobs began to use the guillotine with reckless abandon, Edmund Burke wrote a critique of liberalism, which he believed the French philosopher Jean Jacques Rousseau had carried to extremes, thus leading to the carnage of the French Revolution. On the whole, Burke agreed with Locke more than he disagreed with him. Burke rejected French, not English, liberalism.

3. After the Industrial Revolution a new social institution emerged upon which liberals and conservatives disagreed. That social institution was capital. What to do about capital, defined as the ownership of large-scale economic enterprises, lies at the heart of the liberal-conservative debate over the economy. For conservatives, capital was simply another form of private property. It was to be afforded all the protections Adam Smith had intended for a small family business. For liberals (and a lot of others: progressives, utopian socialists, Marxists, nihilists, and Luddites), capital (or large economic enterprises such as DuPont Chemical, General Motors, or IBM) was a new kind of power that could be used to dominate and oppress workers and whole communities.

4. Since conservatives and liberals disagreed about what capital was, they disagreed about what to do about it. Conservatives wanted it left alone. Liberals wanted it regulated in the interests of free enterprise, (the Sherman Anti-trust Act), employees (child labor acts, collective bargaining agreements, minimum wage laws), and the next generation (environmental protection laws).

5. The disagreement about how to respond to the industrial revolution has affected the responses of liberals and conservatives to modern government. Liberals see government as the only available tool to control the damage that can be done by the abuse of power by capital. Conservatives continue to mistrust government and are more inclined to trust capital (the market, the free enterprise system) than to trust government to deal with major social problems. Thus, conservatives are prepared to give large tax breaks to corporations and wealthy individuals, assuming that this will promote economic development, which in turn will provide jobs, which in turn will enable everyone to rise from poverty. Liberals, by contrast, are more prepared to tax the wealth of corporations and wealthy individuals to provide services directly to citizens for whom the economy does not seem to be working, while at the same time attempting to keep the free market competitive.

6. Over time many conservatives have come to accept liberal proposals once they are convinced that these proposals will not destroy society, the free enterprise system, or individual freedom. Although liberals value individual freedom and society far more than they value the free enterprise system, they are prepared to go along with conservative proposals to preserve the free enterprise system as long as the other two values are not endangered.

Modern management techniques in business and government attempt to involve workers in decision making. The workers on this assembly line in a Macintosh computer factory in California contribute more than their labor to the final product. Workers on assembly lines during the early age of the factory system were treated as little more than part of the raw materials of production.

A major disagreement between modern liberals and conservatives is whether or not *private property* such as a neighborhood shoe repair shop is essentially the same thing as a large factory employing hundreds of people.

tion of the ability of individuals to exchange ideas, create organizations, and seek creative solutions to problems, the political system will not be able to adapt to change.

The second concept is that the protection of the individual has a price. Individuals are not free, at least morally, to squander their talents and deny their use to the community. They are protected by the community so that they will benefit the community. The beauty of this relationship is found in Plato's observation that individuals reach their highest potential by participating in the affairs of the community, the *polis*.

A more recent statement of this important concept comes from a 1994 work by Lappé and DuBois, *The Quickening of America*. In debunking the notions that public life is only for "big shots," and that public life is unrewarding and conflict ridden, Lappé and DuBois state what they believe is the core insight about public life:

Whether [democracy] works or not depends on how each of us lives our public life, our lives outside our families. Without meaningful public lives we can't protect and further the well-being of those we care about most in our private lives.

Democracy requires a lot more of us than being intelligent voters. It requires that we learn to solve problems with others—that we learn to listen, to negotiate, and to evaluate, to think and speak effectively. To go beyond simple protest in order to wield power, becoming partners in problem solving. This isn't about so-called good work; it's about our vital interests. And it is not about simply running our government; it's about running our lives.[13]

We will discuss the many permutations of democracy later in this chapter, at present we simply note that liberalism means that the majority cannot prevent the individual or numerical minorities from publicly disagreeing, or from organizing to change what the majority thinks. Liberalism means that majority rule is tempered with the rights of individuals and those in the minority . When Lappé and DuBois use the term *democracy* they consistently imply that they mean liberal democracy.

Given the controversy over the "L" word in several recent statewide elections, it seems appropriate to note, as we have done in Box 4.2, that in America, liberals and conservatives have as much or more in common than they have differentiating them. They are first cousins, and sometimes family feuds become rather emotional.

Republicanism

The term **republicanism** is associated with two related but separable concepts: representative government and community.

Representative Government

Representative government is a principle that attempts to limit the abuse of power by making power harder to get. It does this by reducing the likelihood that government will be overly responsive to short-run enthusiasms or to the whims of temporary majorities. The republican principle requires that government decisions be made by representatives of the people, not by the people themselves. This slows the decision-making process and allows representatives to deliberate about whether or not government should translate the current demands of the general public into public policy. The republican principle builds in delay. It prevents a majority—whether moral, amoral, or immoral—from turning all its goals instantly into law.

Of course, if a majority stays around long enough to elect representatives to control the government, it may enact the policies for which there seems to be public enthusiasm. In short, the first meaning of republicanism attempts to limit the abuse of power by removing control of government at least one step from the hands of a temporarily aroused public.

A Community Of Enlightened Citizens

The second meaning of republicanism involves the notion of a community of enlightened citizens who share many of the same values. This meaning of republicanism views participation in the affairs of the community as an obligation, not merely a right. Government is not the enemy or something to be taken "off our backs" but a tool for accomplishing agreed upon goals. As we have observed in Box 4.2, conservatives and liberals are members of the same ideological family. Both those who support the notion of republicanism and those who support liberal democracy value the notion of community, and the obligation to participate in it.

The republican idea of a community in which politics consists in the search for the common good, is found most frequently in states with a moralistic political culture. Daniel Elazar notes that the constitutions of the New England states "are basically philosophic documents designed first and foremost to set a direction for civil society and express and institutionalize a theory of republican government.[14] According to this theory, the abuse of power can best be checked by an active and informed citizenry deciding who governs and advising them how to govern. The phrase "the price of liberty is eternal vigilance" is consistent with the notion of republicanism. People stay free by carefully watching those who govern them. It is a labor intensive, participatory method of checking abuse.

Stripped to its essentials, our discussions of the obligation to participate in the affairs of the community may sound somewhat idealistic. However, it is no more so than the idea of politics as dirty and the idea that only the worst people participate and win. We simply view the glass of water as half full instead of half empty. Ideals by their very nature are difficult to attain; that we do not always attain them does not mean we should not try. Ideals provide goals to achieve and a yardstick by which to measure our behavior in achieving them. Without some idea of what the community *should* be, we leave government unchecked, because then whatever is, is right.

This little essay on ideals is not limited to republicanism alone. Democracy (trust the people) and liberalism (free the individual) both imply that "the people" and "the individual" can be trusted to use power or freedom wisely. We know, of course, that both freedom and power have been used unwisely from time to time. That is probably why state constitution makers often build more than one principle into their documents. The possession of ideals does not prevent realistic behavior. Trust your fellow citizens, but count your change.

Separation of Powers

Separation of powers as noted in Chapter 3, is a principle that divides power at a single level of government. At the state level, separate branches of state government are created, and each is assigned certain specific functions. All 50 states have three branches: legislative, executive, and judicial. By dividing control over the different functions—rule making, rule administration, and adjudication—and by assigning them to the different branches of a government, we can check the abuse of power by those who hold it because these people don't have all of it.

The principle of separation of powers is usually coupled with the principle of checks and balances; that is, each branch is supposed to serve as a check on the abuse of power by the others. At the state level, for example, the governor, who is chief of the executive branch, is given the power to veto laws passed by the legislature. The legislature is given the power to make or approve the budget and can deny operating funds to executive agencies and to the judicial branch. The judicial branch can be appealed to by citizens or by public officials who believe that laws are not being enforced properly or that a particular law is not consistent with the state constitution.

Democracy

All state constitutions embrace this principle, some more thoroughly then others. **Democracy** is a term that we shall use first to indicate the source of authority on which both state and local governments base their claim to rule and second to describe the techniques for linking this principle to decision making.

A Source of Authority

Many ancient and medieval governments were theocracies. In a **theocracy** those in power base their claim to rule on the will of God. They assert that God put them in power and that only God could hold them responsible for their actions. Although in the very long run this may work out, the very long run may take decades. In the meantime, a lot of human potential and even lives may be lost.

Although we invoke divine blessings on our currency and in the Pledge of Allegiance —"one nation, under God, with liberty and justice for all," state governments in America depend on a source of authority that is quite limited and imperfect. The source of authority for state constitutions is "we the people." The entire system of governments based on our national and state constitutions has the power to make laws and collect taxes because it has our permission to do so.

Democracy As a Method of Governing

As a principle of government, democracy is essentially the principle of majority rule. When combined with republicanism and liberalism, democratic systems of government are those in which members of a community attempt to make decisions by means of a majority vote after a free and open discussion of the issues.[15]

Without the concern of liberalism for the rights of individuals who may or may not be in the minority and without the concern of republicanism for the long-run survival of the community, democracy can be reduced to mob rule. Indeed, the Greek word *demos*, which is the source of the word *democracy*, is also the source of the word **demagogue**. Untutored by liberal and republican guidance, democracy can result in whatever a majority of ill-informed, self-centered nitwits want at any particular point in time.

Nevertheless, considerable social science research has confirmed that the vast majority of the American public supports the general principles of liberalism and republicanism.[16] Since 1970, when given the opportunity to change state constitutions in the direction of individual freedom and tolerance, more often than not the voters make such a change. In examining the impact of state constitutional amendments on civil rights, Janice C. May has observed that:

> In a democracy, support for civil rights must ultimately find an anchor in public opinion. For better of worse, the state constitutional tradition tips the scales toward voter participation in preserving or reducing civil rights. The record of civil rights protection during the past 15 years, while mixed, holds out hope for the state amendment process.[17]

During two periods of our history, a large portion of the general public felt that the principles of republicanism had been overemphasized in a way that prevented ordinary people from influencing decision making. The first period is associated with Jacksonian Democracy, the second with Plebiscitary Democracy. These two attempts to apply the principle of democracy to the practical world of politics continue to influence state constitutions. Since they will affect the way constitutions change in the future, it is worth spending some time examining them.

Jacksonian Democracy

Early state constitutions embraced the republican idea of government in the name of, but not by, the people. They limited the ability of all adult citizens to participate in decision making. Age, property ownership, gender, and race were criteria that kept many adults from even voting, not to mention governing. During the early nineteenth century several states introduced changes in their constitutions and laws that are traditionally represented by the term **Jacksonian democracy**. Historian Edward Pessen has marshaled considerable evidence that Andrew Jackson and his supporters were beneficiaries of democratic changes rather than the initiators of them.[18] Nevertheless, we will use this traditional term to describe a cluster of changes that emerged during the last three-quarters of the nineteenth century that made state government more accessible to some members of the political system— white males. Women, African Americans, and other traditionally underserved categories of people were not enfranchised by Jacksonian Democracy.

Jacksonian Democracy removed property qualifications so that men of modest means could vote and run for office. It also increased the number of offices that were elective. It wasn't expressly intended that way, but one could argue that Jacksonian Democracy was a kind of political job benefits program for lower class white males.

Andrew Jackson, elected in 1828 and again in 1832, was the first president whose power base was west of the Appalachian Mountains. More important, although he became a wealthy man, he wasn't born that way. Associated with neither the Virginia planter aristocracy nor the New England merchant-banker elite, Old Hickory had little patience with the idea that leaders should be chosen from the families that could provide formal education for their sons and subsidize them while they served an apprenticeship in governance. "No man has any more intrinsic right to official station than another," said Jackson. "The duties of all public officers are so plain and simple that men of intelligence may readily qualify themselves for their performance."[19]

However, the legacy of Jacksonian democracy went beyond providing an opportunity to serve in the jobs that existed. It also changed the structure of government to provide for more elective offices. This change had several consequences. First, it provided more opportunities to obtain a government job through the ballot box. Second, and perhaps more important, it placed upon each individual more responsibility for keeping track of those in government. Instead of electing one chief executive official at the county or state level who hired and fired the rest, the electorate was expected to be responsible for the hiring and firing of a multitude of public officials through the ballot box.

Jacksonian democracy lives on in the constitutions of many states that were influenced by it. Eighteen states still place supreme court judgeships on the ballot, and even more elect lower court judges. A majority of states elect more than six executive officials, including the governor and lieutenant governor. In California, for example, voters choose the governor, secretary of state, attorney general, treasurer, the comptroller, and members of the board of property tax equalization. In Colorado, voters who want to be responsible must become informed about the qualifications of the three elected members of the University of Colorado Board of Regents. The superintendent of public instruction is elected in Montana, and in 15 other states. In Oklahoma and seven other states the voters elect a Commissioner of Insurance.[20]

Many opponents of constitutional reform assert the Jacksonian belief that the best way to keep a public official honest is to make his or her job elective rather than appointive. For voters overwhelmed by the long list of offices to keep track of, this aspect of Jacksonian democracy sounds rather like the dubious proposition, "More is better."

Sometimes the public responds to all these elective offices and all this responsibility by making a joke of it. From 1940 until his death in 1977, a man named Jesse James was regularly reelected to the office of state treasurer in Texas. While this Jesse James was not guilty of robbing banks, he did cost the taxpayers of Texas a lot of money by leaving large amounts of state funds in non-interest bearing checking accounts in various banks around the state. This practice continued under his successor, Warren G. Harding. Naturally, the bankers who received interest-free loans via the state treasurer were quite happy to contribute to that person's reelection campaign. Eventually this practice was halted by the first female State Treasurer of Texas, Ann Richards.[21]

Plebiscitary Democracy (PD)

Plebiscitary democracy (PD) is an attempt to provide the general public with an opportunity to make public decisions directly without waiting for state legislators, city councilors, or county commissioners to reach agreement. Plebiscitary democracy consists of three activities: initiative, referendum, and recall. The New England town meeting in which the whole community makes major budgetary and personnel decisions once a year, is the ideal for PD.[22] Whether PD is an appropriate mechanism for reaching that ideal remains to be seen.

There may be a limit as to how effective direct democracy can be when large numbers of people are involved, even in New England.[23] A large football stadium packed with several thousand citizens aroused and divided over an issue does not leap immediately to mind as the best way to make decisions on important public matters. David B. Magleby observed, "One of the most persuasive criticisms of direct legislation is that it allows us to vote our passions and our prejudices."[24]

The most significant difference between plebiscitary democracy and representative government is that PD has no built-in process of deliberation. As we will see in Chapter 10, the legislative process of representative government does. Plebiscitary democracy is a method of making decisions in which there is no formal provision for exploring alternatives, talking things over, or seeking compromises. Plebiscitary democracy involves voting on yes or no questions.

Before discussing PD further, it is important to emphasize four reasons why we are devoting this much space to it. First, for all its apparent shortcomings, PD is here to stay (Figure 4.1). Forty-nine states use at least one dimension of PD referendum in the constitutional amendment process, when they refer proposed amendments to the voters. Only Delaware uses the legislature alone to propose and ratify amendments to its constitution.[25] Twenty-four state constitutions contain a provision for PD to be used to propose legislation, and 25 state constitutions provide for the referral of some proposed state laws to the voters before they go into effect.[26]

Second, PD is widely used at the local government level, particularly in municipalities. Local PD is found in many states which do not use PD at the state level.

Third, in states that do not have PD at the state level there will be efforts to amend the state constitution to include it.

Fourth, PD has much to offer and should not be rejected simply because of its more obvious shortcomings. A number of reforms may refine PD so that it becomes a method for reflecting the legitimate concerns of an informed public. In sum, we recall the familiar refrain,

"This subject is important for you to know something about because you will be tested on it, in life as well as in the classroom."

Initiative is the process of getting propositions on the ballot. These proposals or propositions are initiated by individuals and groups using petitions signed by an appropriate number of citizens. The proposition may involve constitutional ammendments, laws, or proposals to remove (recall) public officials.

Initiative involves at least three steps: (1) writing a petition for government action, (2) circulating copies of that petition for registered voters to sign, and (3) making sure all the legal formalities have been followed before submitting the petitions to the appropriate government official.

The initiative process usually requires a certain percentage of the electorate to sign the petitions. The signatures are then verified by a designated public official such as the secretary of state or the county clerk. When enough people sign the initiative petition and the number of valid signatures is declared sufficient, the proposal or proposition is put on the ballot and referred to the voters.

Referendums are sometimes referred to as elections because the public uses balloting to make a decision. The distinction between a referendum and an election is further blurred because they often occur on the same day. Referendum is the process of referring decisions to the public. In a referendum the public votes yes or no on propositions that can be placed on the ballot by at least three different procedures. The one traditionally associated with referendum is the initiative process. A second procedure exists because some state or local constitutions require that certain measures automatically be referred to the people. In addition to the ratification of proposed constitutional amendments and laws, referendums may be required to approve of bond issues (the pledging of the public credit for a loan to government). A third procedure occurs when a legislative body wants a formal but nonbinding statement by the public to guide it. Instead of taking public opinion polls, the legislators hold a nonbinding referendum. Thus, referendums come in two styles: binding and nonbinding. When the government must abide by the results of the vote in a referendum such as the ratification of a constitutional amendment, the referendum is binding.

Recall is a process that involves both initiative and a referendum. A petition is circulated (initiative) proposing to remove an elected public official in a specially called referendum. Usually recall referendums occur in local governments, particularly municipalities. However, in 1984 for the first time in 30 years in the United States, a recall election at the state level resulted in the removal of a public official. Two state legislators who had voted to raise the income tax to help pay for increased educational spending and welfare payments were recalled in Michigan. In 1988 the governor of Arizona, was hit with a double whammy. A recall petition drive obtained more than enough signatures to force a referendum, but before it took place he was impeached.

Assessing PD

Proponents of PD argue that it provides an opportunity to force legislatures dominated by powerful interest groups to pay attention to the public interest.[27] Opponents argue that PD simply gives wealthy interest groups even more influence because voters already overwhelmed with other electoral decisions respond to referendums by voting for the side with

Figure 4.1

STATES USING ONE OR MORE PD ITEMS

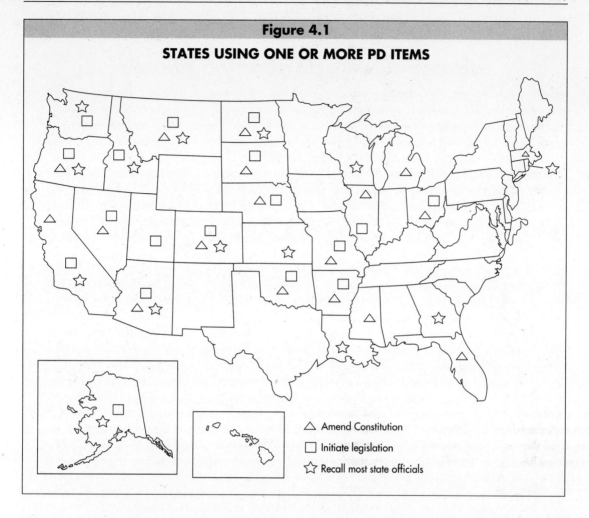

△ Amend Constitution

☐ Initiate legislation

☆ Recall most state officials

the biggest advertising budget and the cleverest slogans.

Betty Zisk reports that in 78 percent of the campaigns she studied in four states between 1976 and 1982, the biggest spenders won. In twenty of 32 cases on which polling data were available an "initial majority approval of voters was changed in the direction of the high-spending side to create electoral victory for the spenders."[28]

Magleby summarizes his effort to empirically test some of the assertions in favor of PD with the following observation:

> *The practice of direct legislation has by and large fallen short of the reformer's expectations and is prone to abuse. The people who rule in direct legislation are those who have mastered the process at the petition-qualification and voting stages. Large numbers of citizens are effectively excluded from participation, and what issue concerns they might have do not reach the direct legislative agenda. Because of the participation biases fostered by the direct legis-*

BOX 4.3

SELECTED SAFEGUARDS FOR PLEBISCITARY DEMOCRACY

1. *Sponsorship* A petition for an initiative should have a number of sponsors before it is registered to begin the signature collection process. Requiring a significant number of sponsors discourages frivolous uses of the process. This requirement will ultimately save taxpayers a good deal of money, and help to preserve the integrity of the process.

2. *Filing Fee* A fee of between $200 and $1,000 to file the petition before initiating the process will further discourage frivolous and publicity-seeking efforts.

3. *Official Statements* Too many initiatives use inflammatory and emotional language in order to get public attention. To prevent this from interfering with an objective view of the issue, a public agency should be charged with the task of preparing the language of the petition before it is circulated.

4. *Geographic Distribution* Some states limit the percentage of signatures that come from one area to make sure that the petition reflects the wishes of the general public. In Massachusetts no more than 25 percent of the signatures can come from one county. At the local level this could apply to voting precincts.

5. *Hearings* One of the most serious shortcomings of PD is that no required deliberative process is involved. Screening out frivolous petitions prepares the way for requiring appropriate governing bodies (state legislative committees, county commissioners courts, city councils) to hold public hearings on petitions that have completed the initiative stage. These hearings should take place early in the referendum campaign. Thus the media will have an opportunity to report the facts and issues raised by the hearings.

6. *Voter Information Pamphlets* These are officially prepared digests of the issues, the pros and the cons. Some newspapers take a position on an issue and local residents hear only one side. Thus, although this costs money in the short run, it may save money in the long run by promoting a fully informed vote.

7. *Financial Disclosure* The source and amount of funds that organizations spend in initiative and referendum campaigns should be reported. Any contribution or expenditure over a minimum amount, say $200 should be reported.

8. *Fairness in the Media* Disclosure is of little use if the information is not made readily available to the public in an easily understood format. Thus, it may be necessary to require the press to publish this information in accordance with a prescribed format. In addition to reporting expenditures, the mass media should be required to make an effort to give both sides a fair hearing.

Source: Thomas E. Cronin, Direct Democracy: Initiative, Referendum, and Recall Cambridge (*Harvard University Press, 1989*), 234–238.

lation process and the inability of many voters to translate their opinions into policy, the process has fallen short of the mark in the areas of participation and representation as well.[29]

In short, PD is not universally admired. As Thomas Cronin, the author of the most thorough study of PD, suggests, there are many points worth considering before deciding whether PD is appropriate for a given state or community. We think his suggestions are important enough to devote Box 4.3 to a few of them. As we note elsewhere, the box is not intended as optional reading. It is a way of emphasizing important material.

If you live in a state that already has PD, or one in which the proposition of applying it statewide is under consideration, you may want to consult Cronin's book. In the final chapter Cronin concludes his analysis of PD by observing that while he favors it for some state and local governments, he does not recommend it at the national level:

> *Not until these processes can be proved to work with greater integrity at the subnational level should anyone seriously consider amending the [U. S.] Constitution to permit them for the national government.*[30]

Four Limiting Principles: Summary

The four principles found in all 50 state constitutions are combined in different ways to limit the abuse of power. Each state's bill of rights limits the use of the power by the governments in their dealings with the individual, thus tempering the impact of majority rule. Separation of powers limits the ability of any individual or group to control all three branches of government at the same time. It also makes it difficult for any branch to dominate state government.

Representative government requires deliberation and discussion before action. By removing the levers of power from temporary majorities and requiring that the people act indirectly through representatives, representative government reduces the abuse of power through miscalculation or appeals to emotion.

Democracy requires the popular election of those who do the deliberating. Thus, those in power are limited by the possibility that they will be held to account by the public at the next election. In many states not only the chief executive but many other officials who carry out the laws are elected. Furthermore, the people are consulted in amending the constitution in every state but Delaware. In 24 states, if elected representatives fail to enact laws supported by the public, then the public can do so without involving the legislature.

None of these limitations alone or in combination make it impossible for the abuse of power to occur, or for circumstances to arise in which a majority or a large determined minority can impose its will on the rest of a state's inhabitants. Indeed, it can be argued that it is impossible to design such a constitution, unless human nature is redesigned.

GUIDELINES FOR CONSTITUTIONAL DESIGN

In its decision on a particularly knotty constitutional case, the Supreme Court of Pennsylvania observed with apparent weariness, that the state constitution is:

*[A]n instrument prepared by human beings, and contains within itself the proof of their frail-
ties, as we are frequently advised by the arguments presented on the many questions arising
under it. Although being a Constitution, it should contain only that which is fundamental, we
are constantly made aware of the fact that many details are embodied in it which more properly
belong in legislation.*[31]

Although an absolutely foolproof constitution may be impossible to design, many state
constitution writers attempted to combine the four principles outlined above into a long,
detailed legal code that would prevent future generations from suffering from the abuses of
power by government officials. Before we examine the shortcomings of state constitutions,
and some of the ways to fix them, we briefly examine guidelines for designing an effective
constitution.

In *McCulloch* v. *Maryland*, Justice John Marshall provided us with good reasons why a
constitution should not be as detailed as a legal code, "It would probably never be understood by the public." He also suggested that in writing a constitution, "only its great outlines
should be marked, its important objects designated."

Thus, the generation that writes a constitution should create a document with four basic features. The constitution should describe in general terms: (1) its goals, (2) the most
important offices and institutions of government, (3) the method of their selection, and (4)
the method of adopting and amending the constitution itself. Then it should allow each
succeeding generation to interpret the meaning of the constitution and make its own
mistakes.

STATE CONSTITUTIONAL FLAWS

The major problem with too many state constitutions is that they are too restrictive. They
keep state and local government from dealing with the problems that confront us. Numerous scholars have added to the list of shortcomings that build on the main problem. On
most lists one finds the following observations about state constitutions.

They Are Too Long

The average state constitution is 26,150 words long. This is three times as long as the U. S.
Constitution. As Table 4.2 indicates, there is a considerable range in the length of state
constitutions. Note that the Alabama Constitution is approximately 174,000 words long
while that of Alaska contains only 13,000 words.

They Are Too Detailed

The details come from restrictions on the state legislature, on the executive agencies, and
on local government as well as from topics best left to laws (or even interoffice memos
within agencies). The Oklahoma Constitution, for example, requires that "Stock feeding"
be taught in public schools.

Excessive detail makes many constitutions more of a legal code than a concise statement of principles. The excessive detail involved is one reason why the constitutions have
to be amended so frequently. It isn't age that makes a constitution obsolete or difficult to
adapt to modern conditions, it is detail. The shortest state constitution, Vermont's, has

"only" been amended 50 times since its adoption in 1793.

They Contain Numerous Obsolete References

Once they've become too long and too detailed *and* too frequently amended it becomes expensive and time consuming to identify the parts everyone will agree on as outmoded and therefore removable. Few political leaders want to invest resources in getting rid of useless verbiage to which no one pays much attention.

Nevertheless, we are happy to report that the citizens of Mississippi were recently given the opportunity to remove obsolete requirements that segregation be enforced in the state prisons and that its U. S. Senators be elected by the state legislature. Furthermore, although the treasurers and the governors of Mississippi have long since ceased to count state revenues by hand twice a year, they are no longer required to do so by the Mississippi Constitution.[32]

They Contain Excessive Verbiage

We used excessive verbiage instead of "wordy" to make a point. Too many state constitutions contain empty phrases such as the following from Pennsylvania's Constitution: "the sessions of each House and of committees of the whole shall be open, unless when the business is such as ought to be kept secret."[33]

They Are Poorly Organized and Repetitive

State constitutions are often repetitive, poorly written, and poorly organized which, of course, adds to their length. As we've noted earlier, this isn't necessarily a problem of the distant past. The Texas Constitution contains two section 16s in Article 7, the Education Article. The first was added in 1928, the second in 1930. In the same document, county sheriffs are dealt with in Sections five, eight, and sixteen.

FOR THE TWENTY-FIRST CENTURY: CONSTITUTIONAL CHANGE, OR NOT?

The notion that the "average" state constitution needs improvement tends to imply that all states have seriously flawed foundations. This just isn't so. Some have needed relatively little change since their adoption. Among them one finds constitutions from three different centuries: Connecticut (1965), Indiana (1851), and Vermont (1793). All of the foregoing contain less that 10,000 words. The Vermont Constitution is shorter, by about 1,000 words, than the U. S. Constitution, itself a model of brevity.

Nevertheless, there seems to be a consensus among many students of state government that more than one or two state constitutions are badly in need of revision. Terry Sanford, a former governor of North Carolina has referred to them as, "drag anchors of state progress, and permanent cloaks for the protections of special interests."[34]

As Table 4.3 indicates there has been some progress in recent years toward longer and multiple terms for governors and giving legislatures annual sessions. However, since 1972 there has also been little reduction in the Jacksonian ballot. According to Beyle, there were 306 separately elected executive officials in 1972 and only two fewer in 1992.[35]

In the 40-year period prior to 1960 there were only five new constitutions created, two of which were those of Hawaii and Alaska. In the twenty year period since 1960 there have been eleven new state constitution, and no new states.

Constitutional change can be discussed in three general categories: first, they can be altered gradually as the individuals in charge of the institutions of government respond to new problems and circumstances. Second, if a constitution must be formally changed in order to make adjustment possible they are usually added to (amended). Third, if significant formal change is required they are revised (significantly rewritten or replaced).

Constitutional Change Via Institutional Development

Constitutions that follow Justice Marshall's advice are flexible. They can be adapted to changing conditions gradually from within the government itself in one of three ways.

1. Legislative Elaboration

Flexible constitutions allow state governments to deal with nuclear power, toxic waste, theft by computer, and other problems (which the constitution framers never dreamed of) simply by passing laws or statutes. Each law is based on a legitimate grant of general authority in the constitution (to promote the general welfare, or to regulate commerce, and so on). In turn, this law grants authority and/or resources to a new or to an existing state or local agency. No constitutional amendment is required.

2. Judicial Interpretation

As conditions change, and as new judges are chosen, so does the interpretation of the constitution as well as the laws which elaborate on it. State Bills of Rights which didn't mean much in the 1950s, have been interpreted by the state courts in the 1980s and 1990s to guarantee equal educational opportunity. By interpreting the constitution in a new way the courts help to adapt the constitution to changes in the environment of the governments.

These state judicial interpretations do not all point in the same direction. For citizens who wish to collect petitions or demonstrate in a privately owned shopping mall this is a

Table 4.3

SELECTED INDICATORS OF CONSTITUTIONAL CHANGE: 1960–1990

Feature	Number of State Constitutions Years		
	1960	1980	1990
Two-year terms for governors	15	4	2
Governors prevented from running for a second term	16	5	1
Legislature meets every other year (biennial sessions)	31	14	7

Sources: David B. Walker, "The States and the System: Changes and Choices," Intergovernmental Perspective, 6:4 (Fall, 1980), 7 and Book of the States 1994, 50–51, 109–1109.

right protected by the state constitutions of California, Massachusetts, New Jersey, and Washington. State supreme courts in Connecticut, Michigan, and Pennsylvania have not found that right in their state constitutions.

3. Executive Action

Governors and other executive officials use the powers of their offices in new ways to change the meaning of that office as well as the constitution which created it. Naturally, some of the laws passed by the legislature, and some actions by executive officials will be challenged by individuals and groups opposed to them. These individuals and groups can attempt to remove the offending officials by recall (if that is available) or challenge the constitutionality of the law in the courts.

Constitutional Change Via Formal Amendments

Constitutional amendment usually, but not always changes the document in a piecemeal fashion by making it possible to do things that the Constitution writers did not foresee as necessary, like allowing counties to have home rule or creating new organizations such as housing authorities or ethics or sunset commissions. There is no strict boundary differentiating amendment from complete revision. It is rather like the difference between a little and a lot.

Constitutions are divided into articles just as books are divided into chapters. When proposals dealing with more than one or two articles are offered, revision rather than amendment is probably occurring. As a rule of thumb, amendment usually involves adding a new article to the constitution, or rewording portions of one article. Revision usually involves rewriting all or a significant number of articles.

Amendment: Two Steps

The amending process involves two steps: proposal and ratification. All state constitutions provide for the legislature to propose constitutional amendments. While 19 states require only a simple majority (one half plus one), the rest require a **special majority** to propose an amendment. Special majorities are usually two-thirds, three-fourths, or three-fifths of each house. The larger the majority required, the more difficult it is to propose amendments. Some states require that two successive legislatures must each approve a proposed amendment before it goes to the people.

In 18 states, amendments also can be proposed by initiative under a variety of arrangements as Box 4.4 indicates. As noted in the discussion of plebiscitary democracy, initiative involves obtaining a required number of eligible voters to sign a copy of a petition before it can go onto the ballot. Once the petition has been certified, in most states by the secretary of state, the proposal is placed on the ballot for consideration by the public.

The second step in the amendment process is ratification, whether the amendment was proposed by the legislature or by initiative. This is usually done by referendum, a procedure also discussed in the section on plebiscitary democracy (Table 4.4). Delaware, the only state that does not routinely ratify amendments via referendum, requires special majorities in two different sessions of the legislature.

The 50 state legislatures represent the only governments involved in amending the state constitution. There is no required vote of county governments, or municipalities, or

---

BOX 4.4

DIMENSIONS OF DIVERSITY: AMENDMENT OF STATE CONSTITUTIONS

There is considerable variety in the procedures for amending state constitutions by initiative and referendum in the 18 states where this is possible

The signature requirements on initiative petitions some states vary from 4 percent of the state population in North Dakota to 15 percent of the total votes cast for all candidates for governor at the last election in Arizona. Several states have requirements intended to keep amendments from being added because no one is paying attention. In Nebraska the majority which approves of an amendment must be at least 35 percent of the total votes cast in the election. In Mississippi it's 40 percent. Nevada's restriction makes sure that adequate time and opportunities for putting the spotlight of public attention on proposed amendments are provided. It requires that majorities must be generated in two consecutive general elections.

Thirteen states make it possible for a small percentage of the electorate in a low turnout election to approve of an amendment by a simple majority vote.

Source: The Council of State Governments, The Book of the States 1994–95 (Lexington, KY: The Council of State Governments, 1994), 23.

---

school districts. Only the federal constitution requires that amendments involve two levels of government.

Constitutional Change or Replacement

Constitutional revision involves writing a new constitution, or so significantly rewriting parts of the old one that the process produces virtually a new constitution. For example, in Table 4.2 the current Pennsylvania Constitution is assigned the date 1968 because on that date significant changes of the Constitution of 1873 took effect.

Revision by Convention

Fourteen state constitutions require that the electorate be asked periodically to vote on whether or not it wants a constitutional convention to meet for the purpose of revising the constitution or proposing a new one. The periods vary, from nine years (in Hawaii) to 20 years (in eight states). All but nine states, however, have some provision in their constitutions for calling a constitutional convention. Since the first state constitutional convention took place in Pennsylvania in 1776, there have been 232 state constitutional conventions, 62 in this century.[36]

Like everything with a beginning, a middle, and an end, important decisions are made at each stage of the convention process. We use the term process to suggest that the actual convention itself is the middle stage, even though it too has a beginning, middle, and end.

Chief among the decisions to be made prior to calling a convention is that of determining the scope of the mandate. Are certain subjects like the education fund to be off-limits for the convention? If it is to be a limited convention, will it have a broad or a narrow focus?

Other important preconvention decisions involve the methods for selecting delegates

Table 4.4

STATE AMENDMENT PROCEDURE: LEGISLATIVE ROLES

State	Vote Required to Propose	Number of Legislative Sessions
Alabama	3/5	1
Alaska	2/3	1
Arizona	Majority	1
Arkansas	Majority	1
California	2/3	1
Colorado	2/3	1
Connecticut	(a)	(a)
Delaware	2/3	2
Florida	3/5	1
Georgia	2/3	1
Hawaii	(b)	(b)
Idaho	2/3	1
Illinois	3/5	1
Indiana	Majority	2
Iowa	Majority	2
Kansas	2/3	1
Kentucky	3/5	1
Louisiana	2/3	1
Maine	2/3	1
Maryland	3/5	1
Massachusetts	Majority	2
Michigan	2/3	1
Minnesota	Majority	1
Mississippi	2/3	1
Missouri	Majority	1
Montana	2/3	1
Nebraska	3/5	1
Nevada	Majority	1
New Hampshire	Majority	2
New Jersey	(c)	(c)
New Mexico	Majority	1
New York	Majority	2
North Carolina	3/5	1
North Dakota	Majority	1
Ohio	3/5	1
Oklahoma	Majority	1
Oregon	Majority	1
Pennsylvania	Majority	2
Rhode Island	Majority	1
South Carolina	(d)	2
South Dakota	Majority	1
Tennessee	(e)	(e)
Texas	2/3	1
Utah	2/3	1
Vermont	(f)	(f)
Virginia	Majority	1

(Continued)

Table 4.4 (Continued)

STATE AMENDMENT PROCEDURE: LEGISLATIVE ROLES

State	Vote Required to Propose	Number of Legislative Sessions
Washington	2/3	1
West Virginia	2/3	1
Wisconsin	Majority	2
Wyoming	2/3	1

(a) Connecticut: 3/4 vote in each house at one session, or majority vote in each two sessions, between which an election has intervened
(b) Hawaii: 2/3 in each house in one session or majority vote in two.
(c) New Jersey: 3/5 in one session or majority in two
(d) South Carolina: 2/3 in each house first passage, majority after approval in referendum
(e) Majority first passage, 2/3 second
(f) Vermont: 2/3 senate, first passage, majority house; majority both on second passage.

Source: The Book of the States: 1994–95 (Lexington KY.: Council of State Governments, 1992), 21.

to the convention and for compensating them. Will delegates be elected from small single member districts, which give minorities and the poor a better chance at serving as delegates, or will they be elected from large districts or appointed; if appointed, by whom?

Constitutional conventions are highly political activities. Not only do advocates of various causes clash but realists who see politics as the "art of the possible" who support the same causes as "true believers" may disagree on tactics and what can realistically be accomplished. The failure to compromise at all can have the same results as compromising too soon.

During the convention itself technical decisions are made that influence the final outcome on controversial matters. Should the voters be presented with an all or nothing package or with a series of choices? While in recent years all-or-nothing choices on a wholly new constitution have done less well than a series of choices on separate resolutions, the 53-item package that faced Louisiana voters in 1970 is an extreme that was voted down.

The third stage in the process is the ratification campaign. Whether one is revising a city charter, restructuring county government, or promoting state constitutional reform, there is an important lesson to be learned from the experiences of several state constitutional reform efforts. That lesson is that an all-out campaign effort involving as many people as possible will significantly improve the chances of adoption.

Commissions and Constitutional Revision

Commissions are created in various ways: by executive order, by law, by legislative resolution, and (in Florida) by Constitutional Provision. Members of Constitutional Commissions are usually appointed. Convention delegates on the other hand are usually elected. Commissions often include ex officio members, that is, members such as the Speaker of the House of Representatives, the Chief Justice of the Supreme Court, the governor, and other occupants of important state-wide offices.

The two major types of commissions associated with constitutional revision are study commissions and preparatory commissions. Study commissions hold public hearings around the state, research suggestions from the public, and prepare a report which usually includes a list of recommendations and/or a draft of suggested revisions. The report is then submitted to the state government—usually the legislature and/or the governor. The reports are usually published and available to the general public. Then the work of the commission is usually finished. It is up to the legislature to make formal revision proposals.

The fact that study commissions usually report to the legislature (which can then decide whether or not to act upon their recommendations) makes this approach a much more attractive one to most legislators than a state convention over which they usually have less influence.

If there really is going to be a constitutional convention then a commission is usually appointed to make preparations for it. Preparatory commissions take care of a number of necessary details such as arranging for printing, acquiring space for the convention and its several committees to meet, arranging for press credentials, media participation, scheduling, staffing, and perhaps even the interim rules and regulations for conducting the first day or so of the convention.

Or Not, Problems with Straitjacketed Government

A government based on a general and brief constitution is one with considerable potential for adapting to change effectively. Constitutions written like law codes place government in a straitjacket. They can only be adjusted to cope with change by amendment and or revision. However, among the available responses are three that have unfortunate consequences.

First, public officials can solve problems by bending (or ignoring) the rules. Fortunately this rarely happens. If it were to happen more often it could result in a loss of respect for the rules of the game among office holders and eventually the general public. Breaking the rules in a situation where it is "necessary" could lead to breaking the rules because it is merely convenient; then, breaking them because one can get away with it, and finally because everyone else is doing it.

In some states, for example, the constitution not only includes numerous details for passing legislation but also sets relatively short sessions for the state legislature to conduct its business. These sessions may have been adequate in a slower paced agricultural era but not for states with complex urban industrial societies. In the rush to deal with several hundred pieces of legislation including a multibillion dollar budget, technicalities in the procedures for passing laws required by the constitution have from time to time been ignored. The best known example does not occur every year in all legislatures but sometimes sessions destined to end at midnight on a certain date are prolonged by virtue of stopping the clock at about 11:58 P.M. When the session finally ends and the clock is allowed to reach midnight, legislators emerge from the chambers to see the sun rising in the east.

A second reason why an over-restrictive constitution is not healthy for a political system is that critical problems may not get solved. Public officials may justify their inability to solve problems by blaming the constitution for things like polluted aquifers, crime in the streets, or child abuse. Under these conditions, respect for the rules of the game declines and the foundation upon which government bases its claim to rule begins to crumble.

A third, and far more likely situation, is too frequent amendment. Frequently amending an inflexible constitution may sometimes help adjust government to changing conditions. While this sounds like a good idea, it does have one disadvantage. The difference between the fundamental rules of the game—the constitution—and the rules and regulations made in the course of governing can easily become confused. Some state constitutions have been amended hundreds of times. Not all of these amendments were to streamline or modernize. Some were to protect special interests which used their political resources to build advantages into the basic foundation of state government.

For example, few state constitutions amended under the influence of the National Rifle Association contain language asserting the need for regulation as does the second Amendment of the U. S. Constitution.

In a state where frequent amendment occurs, the constitution itself is in danger of becoming a political prize. It may cease to be a check on the misuse of political authority.

CONDITIONS PROMOTING CONSTITUTIONAL GOVERNMENT

Constitutions are mere pieces of paper unless certain conditions are met. Among the checks on the abuse of power that help make constitutions meaningful, four seem particularly important: adequate socialization of leaders, existence of more than one power center, open government, and an informed and active public. These conditions do not guarantee a liberal democracy. They simply increase the likelihood that one will survive and adapt successfully to changes in its environment.

1. Socialization of Leaders

As we noted in Chapter 2, political socialization is a process through which we learn the values and norms of our community and state. Because it is critical that public officials themselves accept the rules of the game as set forth in the constitution as legitimate, many states require that some civic or political education is provided in the schools and colleges of the state. This helps ensure that the participants in the political system accept the ideals that the constitution attempts to promote because they understand and believe in them.

2. Multiple Power Centers

Separation of power distributes resources within a single level of government. Constitutions are best protected when there is also power available to individuals outside of government—in the free enterprise system or in consumer and employee organizations such as labor unions. It is important for public officials to know that other political actors both in and out of government have political resources which can be used to punish them for breaking the rules. A few people may get away with breaking the rules. No system is perfect. However, if the abuse of power frequently results in punishment, then those who want to behave themselves will feel better about doing so and those who are tempted to abuse their power will be more circumspect. This principle also occurs, of course, in the political economy. Businessmen who want to pay fair wages are more likely to do so if everyone is required to do so. Chemical firms that want to install expensive refining equipment to prevent the escape of toxic gases or chemicals are more likely to do so if all chemical firms are required to do so.[37]

3. Open Government

When public officials know that both the rules of the game and their own activities are a matter of record, they are much more likely to act in accord with their beliefs about the constitution. If the rules of the game are a big secret, then who's to know if they are being followed? Even when the rules of the game are easily available, if the actions of public officials are not a matter of public record, then who's to know whether or not these actions were taken according to the rules? Thus, in a society with open meetings, open records, a free press, and an informed and active public, government officials are more easily held accountable should they attempt to misuse their power.

4. An Informed Public

Without an informed public, the constitution is unlikely to serve as an adequate check on the abuse of power. The public, "we the people," must learn the rules and insist that they be followed. Not every single individual can become an expert, but if a significant portion of the public pays attention to and remembers the promises of the candidates and reminds them occasionally what they promised to do or not to do then constitutional government is protected. Clearly, the "significant portion" cannot always be the same people. All of us must know at least something and all of us must be prepared to vote the rascals out when it seems appropriate. In short, if no one attends the open meetings, reads the open records, consults the free press, or makes themselves heard, government officials, and for that matter, people with a lot of power in the political economy, can operate pretty much as they please.

CONSTITUTIONAL REVISIONS AND YOU

The opportunity to participate in revising a state constitution does not come along every year or even every decade. However, when it does arrive it is worth considering some of the ways in which you might participate. In addition to the role of voter there are other possibilities. We suggest only three.

First, the early stages of most constitutional revision attempts involve a series of public hearings, held at various locations around the state. They may be conducted by a legislative committee or a revision commission. This is an excellent opportunity for the average citizen (you) to see how political leaders in your state operate and also for you to influence the course of events.

In most states, elaborate efforts are made to promote attendance. Participation in commission hearings provides a real opportunity to influence events. It is for this reason that organized interest groups make sure they have their local representatives at each public hearing in each city.

Hearings are sometimes carefully organized in order to make the optimum use of time. A common arrangement is for staff members to circulate a sign-up sheet, or distribute forms on which individuals who wish to address the commission identify themselves and the topic they wish to address. Staff members then use this information to make a schedule for calling on people.

Second, all conventions require staff. Once it is announced that a commission will be formed, the creation of the staff for the commission begins. While many staff members are borrowed from existing agencies and from legislative staffs, it is still possible to serve on the commission staff or to work on a more temporary basis by helping to make arrangements for the hearings which will take place in your home community.

Third, today's indispensable volunteer is tomorrow's employee. Volunteering to work in the ratification campaign or in some other phase of the constitutional revision process is not the worst way to spend some of your time. The pay isn't all that great but the opportunity to meet interesting people and learn about the political process from the inside is not only something that looks good on job application forms later in life but also provides some interesting stories to tell your grandchildren. A volunteer effort may lead to useful contacts, you might simply obtain material for a term paper or two, or even meet Mr. or Ms. Right.

CONCLUSION

In concluding our introduction to state constitutions, it is worth noting that while our discussion has been biased in the direction of change, we are aware that change can be for the worse as well as for the better. In fact, the 50 states among them have operated under 145 different constitutions not all of which were improvements over the previous ones.

Nevertheless, knowing something about constitutional revision is important since you may wish to help the revision process have a happy ending in your state.

STUDY OBJECTIVES

1. Identify five reasons for studying the state constitution.
2. Identify the ratification date, the number of words, and the number of amendments added to your state constitution.
3. Identify the two ideas in conflict in most state constitutions.
4. Identify six ways to keep government on the sidelines.
5. Identify four principles of limited government.
6. Identify the similarities and differences between conservatives and liberals in America.
7. Identify Republicanism and the two terms associated with it.
8. Identify the major features of Jacksonian Democracy.
9. Identify the consequences of making more offices elective rather than appointive.
10. Identify plebiscitary democracy and the three procedures that go along with it.
11. Identify the advantages and disadvantages of plebiscitary democracy.
12. Identify six ways to promote the integrity of plebiscitary democracy.
13. Identify the conditions that promote constitutional government.
14. Identify the major shortcomings of most state constitutions.
15. Identify the guidelines for writing a constitution, which are found in *McCulloch v. Maryland*.
16. Identify the three ways in which constitutional change usually occurs.
17. Identify the formal methods for changing the state constitution.
18. Identify three ways in which you might participate in amending a state constitution.

GLOSSARY

Demagogue   One who appeals to the emotions and lesser instincts of others (selfishness, greed, fear of strangers).

Democracy   A system of government in which the majority rules. In America we usually think of liberal democracy (majority rule and minority rights) when we use the term democracy. To the ancient Greeks and to some of the authors of the U. S. Constitution, however, democracy meant little more than mob rule (rule by the demos).

Initiative   The process of getting propositions on the ballot.

Jacksonian Democracy   A term used to describe a number of changes in our political system which took place during the early nineteenth century. Among them are the long ballot, universal suffrage, and short terms of office, all of which were intended to make government more democratic.

Liberalism   A term used both to identify an ideology whose central value is the freedom of the individual and to identify a basic principle of constitution-making consistent with that ideology.

Plebiscitary democracy (PD)   An attempt to approximate the direct democracy associated with rural communities in which the adult population is small enough in number so that its members can meet to talk things over and make collective decisions.

Recall   A process that involves both initiative and referendum. A petition is circulated (initiative) proposing a referendum to remove an elected public official in a specially called referendum.

Referendum   The process of referring policy decisions to the public, and is sometimes referred to as elections because the public uses balloting to make a decision.

Republicanism   A principle that is most often associated with representative government. It also implies a community of enlightened citizens who share many of the same values.

Special majority   Larger than a simple majority, which is one half plus one. Special majorities are usually two-thirds, or three-fourths of the relevant body (house, senate, the electorate). They are required for procedures that do more than routine business—propose a constitutional amendment, suspend the rules, impeach a governor, and so forth.

Theocracy   A system of government in which those in office claim that their authority is based on the will of God, not on election or heredity.

ENDNOTES

1. Associated Press, "Boy Decides to Call in Governor When Parents are 'Unreasonable.' " *Austin American Statesman*, January 28, 1995, 1.

2 Janice C. May, "Constitutional Amendment and Revision Revisited," *Publius* (Winter, 1987), 153.

3. Thomas C. Marks Jr. and John F. Cooper, *State Constitutional Law* (St. Paul, MN: West Publishing Company, 1988), 48–49.

4. *Robinson v Cahill*, cited in John J. Harrigan, *Politics and Policy in States and Communities*, (Glenview, IL: Scott, Foresman and Company, 1987), 300–301. See also "State Constitutions and Public Education" in *State Constitutional Law: Cases and Materials* (Washington, D.C.: U. S. Advisory Commission on Intergovernmental Relations, 1988). Major portions of the court's decision in *Robinson* v. *Cahill* are presented on pp. 400–403.

5. Mark Glasser and John Kincaid, "Selected Rights Enumerated in State Constitutions," *Intergovernmental Perspective* (Fall, 1991), 38.

6. Ibid., 36.

7. Thomas R. Morris, "State Attorneys General As Interpreters of State Constitutions," *Publius* (Winter, 1987), 133.

8. For an extended discussion of the agencies and nuances of interpreting state constitutions see: "Interpretation of State Constitutions" in *State Constitutional Law: Cases and Materials*. (Washington, D.C.: U. S. Advisory Commission on Intergovernmental Relations, 1988), 179–234.

9. National Municipal League, *Model State Constitution, 6th ed., rev.* (New York: NML, 1968). Since 1921 the NML Model has been significantly revised six times. The sixth edition was first published in 1963 and then further revised for a 1968 publication. The Alaska constitution is cited by the NML as being the State Constitution that comes closest to its model, and Elazar identifies Alaska as an example of a Managerial Pattern constitution.

10. Author's calculations based on Table 1.1 in the *Book of States: 1994–95*. (Lexington, KY: Council of State Governments), 19.

11. Janice C. May, "State Constitutions and Constitutional Revision: 1992–1993," *The Book of the States 1994–95*, (Lexington, KY: Council of State Governments, 1994), 2.

12. John. P. Wheeler Jr., ed. *Salient Issues of Constitutional Revision* (New York: National Municipal League, 1961), xiii.

13. Frances Moore Lappé and Paul Martin DuBois, *The Quickening of America: Rebuilding Our Nation, Remaking Our Lives* (San Francisco: Jossey-Bass Inc., 1994), 13–15.

14. Daniel J. Elazar, *American Federalism: A View from the States*, 2nd ed. (New York: Harper & Row, 1972), 96.

15. For more sophisticated attempts to define democracy or liberal democracy see: Robert A. Dahl, *A Preface to Democratic Theory* (Englewood Cliffs, NJ: Prentice-Hall, 1956). See especially p. 84 for a concise presentation of the definitional characteristics of what Dahl calls, "polyarchy, an inadequate, incomplete, primitive ordering of the common store of knowledge about democracy."

16. Donald J. Devine, *The Political Culture of the United States* (Boston: Little Brown & Co., 1972), 286. For an opposing view see James A. Stever, *Diversity and Order in State and Local Politics* (Columbia: University of South Carolina Press, 1980), 24–26.

17. Janice C. May "Constitutional Amendment and Revision Revisited," *Publius* (Winter, 1987), 178. A 1970 study conducted for CBS News found that things had not changed very much, Robert Chandler, *Public Opinion: Changing Attitudes on Contemporary Political and Social Issues* (New York: R. R. Bowker Co., 1972), 6–13.

18. Edward Pessen, *Jacksonian America Revised Edition* (Champagne-Urbana: University of Illinois Press, 1985), 150. For a brief capsule account of the impact of Jacksonian Democracy on state constitutions see Albert L. Sturm, "The Development of American State Constitutions," *Publius* (Winter, 1982), 63–65.

19. John A. Garraty, *The American Nation*, vol I, 5th ed. (New York: Harper and Row, 1983), 238–239.

20. *The Book of the States 1994–95*, 209–212.

21. Ronnie Dugger, *Texas Observer* (October, 1983).

22. Joseph F. Zimmerman, *The Massachusetts Town Meeting: A Tenacious Institution* (Albany, NY: Graduate School of Public Affairs, 1967),15–24.

23. Ibid., 57

24. David B. Magleby, *Direct Legislation: Voting on Ballot Propositions in the United States* (Baltimore: Johns Hopkins University Press, 1984), 191. See also Thomas E. Cronin, *Direct Democracy* (Cambridge, MA; Harvard University Press, 1989).

25. *The Book of the States 1994–95*, 279. As do 10 other states, Delaware requires approval of a proposed amendment in two different legislative sessions.

26. *The Book of the States 1994–95*, 294.

27. For a summary and discussion of reform assertions in favor of PD see Magleby, pp. 27–28, and for the opposing assertions see pp. 29–30.

28. Betty Zisk, *Money, Media, and the Grassroots: State Ballot Issues and the Electoral Process*, (Newbury Park, CA: Sage Publications, 1987), 245.

29. Magleby, 199.

30. Thomas E. Cronin, *Direct Democracy*, p. 251.

31. *Armstrong v. King* 281 Pa. 207, 126 A. 263 (Penn.1924). Cited in Robert F. Williams, ed., *State Constitutional Law: Cases and Materials* (Washington, D.C.: The Advisory Commssion on Intergovernmental Relations, 1988), 223.

32. Janice C. May, "State Constitutions and Constitutional Revision, 1990–91." *The Book of the States 1992–93*. (Frankfort, KY: 1992), 8–10.

33. ACIR, *The Question of State Government Capability* (Washington D.C.: The Advisory Commission on Intergovernmental Relations, 1985), 39.

34. Terry Sanford, *Storm Over the States* (New York: McGraw Hill, 1967), 189.

35. Thad L. Beyle, "The Executive Branch: Organization and Issues, 1992–93, *The Book of the States 1994–95* (Lexington, KY: Council of State Governments, 1994), 65.

36. Janice C. May, "State Constitutions and Constitutional Revision, 1992–93," *The Book of the States 1994–95*, (Lexington, KY: Council of State Governments), 4.

37. See Edmund S. Phelps, *Political Economy* (New York: W. W. Norton and Co., 1985), 183, for a cogent discussion of the logic of collective action and problems of public choice.

CHAPTER

5

Foundations of the Local Governments

A MARINA BY ANY OTHER NAME MIGHT SMELL THE SAME, BUT . . . .

Local government makes local decisions, locally, and often pretty quickly.

A marina, at minimum, consists of a dock and the surrounding area. If it's on the ocean marinas are usually located in a harbor or inlet. Marinas come in all sizes. At a marina a person can fish from the dock or put a boat out for fishing or other pleasures. The marina in south Dade County that fisherman Frank Brown had enjoyed for 44 years was known locally as Black Point Marina.

In January, 1994, the Miami-Dade Metropolitan government announced a name change. Without consulting anyone the commissioners had decided to honor retired county parks chief Bill Bird by naming the marina after him. This seemed a minor matter to the Miami-Dade Commissioners. It would also have seemed a minor matter to the Florida Department of Parks and Recreation. Fortunately, for the latter, state government was not responsible for naming county parks, the Miami-Dade Commissioners were.

Frank Brown, and a few friends including an insurance agent and a nurse, discussed the name change over a few beers at a local restaurant. "It's a place we've known all our lives," said Brown. "For the county to suddenly change its name upset us, because it was a decision made without local knowledge or participation. . . .To take away a name that's been around longer than I've been alive is just wrong."

They decided to fight the decision. Before long other Black Point people joined in, petitions were circulated and meetings were held. A phone bank was improvised and each commissioner's office received calls. According to Jan Jordan, "No one actually got a commissioner on the phone but we still created a noise factor. There's a close-knit community of secretaries, clerks, and aides. They have to walk past one another to get to the soda machine, and when they do, dialogue occurs."

In addition to helping organize the phone operation, which did not involve any long distance charges, Jordan did some serious library research and interviewed longtime residents of the area. He dug up references to Black Caesar, a legendary pirate, and even found a 1775 reference to a "Black Caesar's Creek" flowing into the sea near the point.

Although he was never able to prove conclusively that Black Caesar really existed, residents have organized a festival which they hope will become an annual event honoring the legendary pirate and extending a sense of community into the future. The commissioners reversed their decision and it's Black Point Marina again.[1]

Miami-Dade (the cities of Miami, Miami Beach, and several others, and the County of Dade), in which Black Point Marina is located is generally referred to as a county. Actually it's a consolidated city of which there are less than 30 in the United States.[2] The Census Bureau recognizes five basic types of local government: county, city, township, school district, and special district. At last count there were 86,743 of them.

The purpose of this chapter is to briefly examine the local governments and their sources of authority. These are the tools nearest at hand for you to learn about how the system works in a practical way. We hope that you will use them to help make the place where you live into more of a community. While we acknowledge the intriusic value of local government, we think it is reasonable to ask why there are so many of them.

ARE LOCAL GOVERNMENTS REALLY NECESSARY?

Strange as it may seem, we could get along without local governments. We could eliminate nearly 86,000 units of government and 450,000 elective offices. Each of the 50 state governments could offer all the essential services through local offices of state agencies. With more personnel the state police, highway department, health department, education department, and other state agencies could provide local services.

This is not to say that we would be happier without an average of 1,734 units of local government per state, or that we would be better served. It is simply to suggest that conditions that we take for granted as what is, do not exhaust the possibilities of what could be. There are at least six reasons why local government is preferred over the local delivery of services by a state agency headquartered elsewhere.

We can divide these reasons into two groups: the first being why state officials think local government is a good idea and the second being why local folks think local government is a good idea. Sometimes the same reason suits both as the Black Point Marina story suggests.

WHY STATE OFFICIALS LIKE LOCAL GOVERNMENT

Delegation of "Minor" Details

From the point of view of state leaders, local government takes care of decisions that while important locally—determining what services people are willing to pay for, or what to name a park or marina—would constitute several hundred or several thousand details for the next level of government. Delegating local decisions to local people leaves state officials free to take care of policy concerns that affect a larger portion of the state's population. In virtually all large systems responsibility for decisions that affect one location differently than another are delegated to local decision makers whether the system governs, makes cars, or sells hamburgers.

Personnel Management

When the local officials take care of hiring and firing at the local level this takes the pressure off of the leaders of the wider political system who have enough hiring and firing problems of their own. When the local community takes responsibility for hiring and firing the local decision makers though the electoral process that also keeps problems from reaching the state level.

Maintaining System Legitimacy

Local government places some of the responsibility for making tough decisions about services and taxes in the hands of locally elected officials. These decisions are more likely to be accepted if they are made locally. Most of these decisions can be changed by local political action, without involving the wider system.

Some decisions, however, affect the wider system more than others. Thus, when the County commissioners' court (the county legislature) in Williamson County, Texas voted down a package of tax benefits intended to attract an Apple Computer manufacturing facility, a whirlwind of activity occurred.[3] The proposed agreement with Apple had been the result of a rather lengthy period of negotiations and many were surprised at the action of the commisioners' court. It seems that rather late in the game one or two of the commissioners who voted against the proposal decided that if the county provided a tax break, it would be subsidizing sin. Apple's employee health insurance program covers unmarried domestic partners.

As a result of the vote, Williamson county received more attention than it wanted. There were headlines in the metropolitan newspaper, an invasion of television cameras and reporters, stories on the five o'clock news, and even meetings with the governor. In a few days a vote or two changed and Apple signed on to locate a plant in Williamson County.[4]

Resource Management

Taxes locally raised may be managed a little more carefully than funds raised and redistributed by the state or by the national government. Just as important is the fact that tax dollars go further when voluntary contributions of labor, supplies, and even cash are donated to make local projects work. Most people are more likely to volunteer for local projects than for national or state projects. A few hours on something near one's home is more easily donated than to a distant project involving another level of government. Instances of statewide and nationwide responses to a tragedy or a dramatic case of need are newsworthy because they are unusual. Less often reported on are the millions of dollars worth of labor and resources donated by members of local churches, synagogues, temples, Lions, Elks, League of Women Voters, B'nai Brith, Shriners, and other local organizations that plug away all year long without even making the evening news. Every service or project they offer is one less that a public official has to raise taxes to pay for.

Why Local People Like Local Government

Access for the citizens to their government and control over various life-style decisions like zoning, educational quality, and police protection are the two major reasons why we have many local governments in each state. [5]

Access

Local government provides individuals with convenient access to decision makers for opportunities to express needs and seek explanations. While a relatively small percentage of the population takes advantage of these opportunities, it is important that the opportunity is there. It is easier to get to city hall or the county courthouse than it is to the state capitol or Washington, D.C.

Local Autonomy

In many communities some groups of citizens wish to be independent of other communities. Before the rapid urbanization of America, this desire was expressed in terms of the creation of new county governments. Now it is usually expressed in terms of municipal authority.

If you look at a map of county lines in states settled during the eighteenth and early nineteenth centuries, when population growth was fairly rapid in rural areas, you will find numerous counties with boundaries that were designed to fit local geography and settlement patterns. In contrast to this, observe the straight lines of surveyors that define the much larger counties farther west (see Figure 5.1). Many of the eastern counties were created for local autonomy and convenience—the convenience of two locales, usually. When an existing county found itself with two population concentrations, an older settlement, the population of which had run things for years and a new settlement which threatened to take over the county politics from sheer force of numbers, the sporting thing seemed to be to divide the county up. "Let the newcomers have their own county. Besides, if we don't they'll take over ours."

The machinery for creating new counties still exists in most states. But few of the states that were settled after the Industrial Revolution (and especially after the automobile went into mass production) have very many counties small in area, defining a community. The creation of a new county in the United States is an unusual event; five were created in the 1980s, the highest number in several decades. During the same period 336 municipalities were incorporated.[6] In the pages that follow we'll attempt to explain why.

SOURCES OF LOCAL GOVERNMENT AUTHORITY

Among the sources of authority for local governments in various states one finds state constitutions, state laws, local charters, local ordinances.

State Constitutions
Specific Governments

Articles in or amendments to many state constitutions create specific governments by name. For the first century of our existence that was the usual method for creating cities. In some states special districts have been created by constitutional amendment. This, of course, contributes to the length and clutter of state constitutions.

Figure 5.1

Eastern and Western Counties: Local Government Before and After the Automobile*

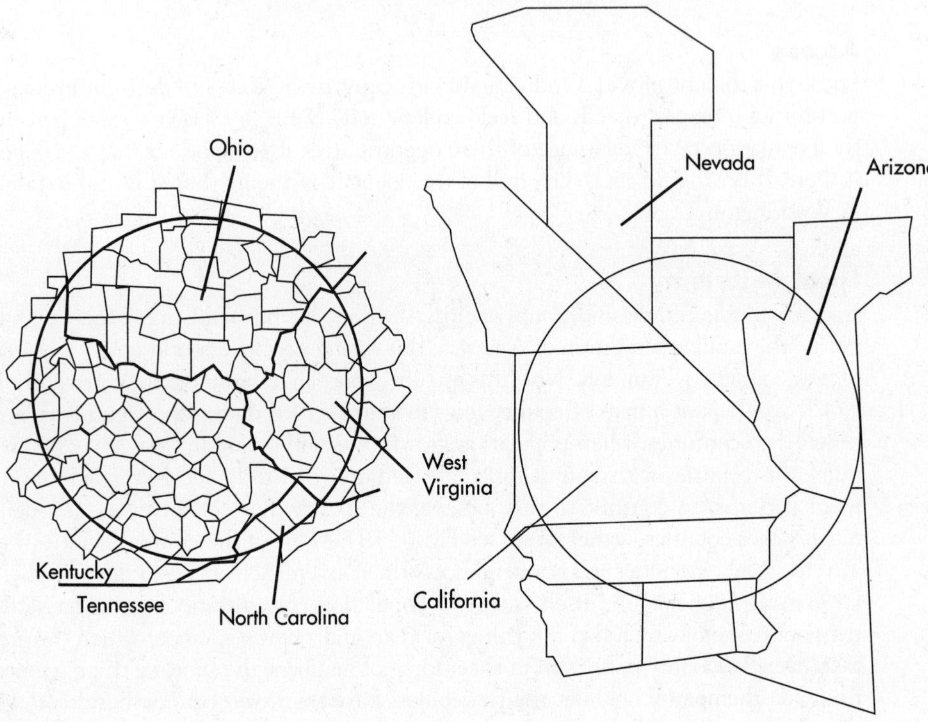

*Counties before and after the automotive revolution. Each area represents the same number of square miles—about 20,000. In the horse and buggy days, every good-sized community wanted its own county, with a centrally located county seat where most legal, financial, and political business would be conducted. After the automobile made travel to the county seat much easier, it seemed more practical for a community to have its own municipal government empowered to offer urban services. The county became at least temporarily less relevant. Thus, new small counties were no longer created as communities grew in the postautomotive area.

Source: Rand McNally, County Map of the United States.

Required Procedures

Most state constitutions today contain procedures for creating various types of local government. Some states set up a classification system according to population size. The larger the government, in most of these systems, the more authority it can be given. Usually these governments are cities. However, in some states counties are classified also. The State of Washington, for example, has a scheme that places counties in 11 categories from ninth (fewer than 3,300 inhabitants) to "AA" (500,000 inhabitants or more).[7]

State Laws

As with constitutions, there are also state laws which create specific local governments and state laws which set up procedures to be followed for creating types of local government.

Charters

Charters are local constitutions, and are usually given to cities. Although some states give this opportunity to counties, or to city-county consolidations, the more common reference is to cities. These charters are granted in accord with any one of the procedures mentioned above. Charters create two basic types of governments: general law and home rule.

General Law

General law governments follow a pattern set forth in the state law or the state constitution. Thus, to change anything in a general law city's charter would require—at minimum—an act of the legislature, if not a constitutional amendment.

Home-Rule

A home-rule charter is one that enables the community to revise its local government constitution without returning to the legislature for a law or a constitutional amendment.

Thus, if a city ordinance is declared null and void by a court because it is not consistent with the city's charter, the remedy is local instead of at the state level. The city charter can be amended and then the ordinance passed again, if that is what the community wants. No state law or state constitutional amendment need be guided through the state legislature.

Local Acts or Ordinances

New Jersey empowers its counties to create Beach Erosion Control Districts, County Bridge Commissions, County Improvement Authorities, County Industrial Pollution Control, Financing Authorities, and County Recreation Authorities.[8] Thus, the source of authority for these governments is an act or ordinance passed by another local government.

In each of the fifty states it is ultimately the state constitution upon which these various laws, enabling acts, and procedures for creating local governments are based. Thus, each state constitution provides a context for the study of local government. Each state constitution determines how easy or how difficult it is for local communities to manage, alter, or combine the local governments which serve them.

STRUCTURE (AND POLITICS)

At risk of some oversimplification to their almost infinite variety, local government structures can be classified along two basic dimensions: the relationship of the executive branch to the legislative branch, and the relationship of the executive departments to the chief executive.

1. In the legislative-executive dimension there are three basic arrangements: commission, council-manager, and independent executive and council.

2. In the executive branch-chief executive dimension there are two basic structural types: fragmented and unified.

Executive-Legislative Relations

In most of the governments we have been discussing the government is empowered, and sometimes required, by the state or federal government to offer services. These are paid for in large part by taxing and borrowing. The legislative branch sets the tax rate and approves the budget. The executive is responsible for carrying out the services. Although they may have different names from state to state, there are three basic patterns to the executive-legislative relationship: the commission form, the council-administrator form, and the elected chief executive form.

The Commission Form

In commission government the elected legislators are also executives. In addition to serving collectively as the legislative branch, each commissioner takes charge of one or more of the executive departments. This form of government clearly does not tightly embrace the principle of the separation of powers. Without checks and balances built in, the citizens have a greater responsibility for monitoring government.

The Council-Administrator Form

In this form the legislature appoints and can remove the chief of the executive branch. Some examples of this form include the elected school board which appoints the school superintendent, the elected city council which chooses the city manager, and an elected county commission which appoints the county executive.

The International City/County Management Association defines the council-manager form as one in which an elected council appoints a manager "to serve as chief administrative officer, to oversee personnel, development of the budget, proposing policy alternatives, and general implementation of policies and programs adopted by the council."[9]

School district superintendents also have much the same authority over principals, teachers, and other district employees as city managers do over department heads and the rest of city government.

Elected Chief Executive

This form of government follows most closely the separation of powers principle (Chapter 4). In theory, it places control of the executive branch in the hands of one elected official who is responsible to the voters rather than to the legislature. In cities this form is referred to as the strong mayor form. In counties it is usually referred to as the elected executive form. Whether or not the mayor of a city is elected by the electorate or by the city council is less important than the control that mayor has over the heads of the major departments in the executive branch.

Chief Executive—Executive Branch Relations

In those governments in which the elected mayor or county executive is in charge of the executive branch there are significant differences in the amount of influence the chief executive will be able to exert over that branch depending upon the way that branch is organized.

In a *unified executive branch*, the chief executive can hire, fire, and give direction to the heads of the various departments. In the *fragmented executive branch* the chief executive may not have much formal influence at all because some other person or authority chooses the heads of the major departments. They may even be elected independently of the chief executive.

As noted earlier not all elected mayors are chief executives. It depends upon that city's form of government. Many cities with elected mayors are really commission or council-manager cities. The mayor presides over council meetings but has no control over the executive branch. In many cities elected mayors have no executive authority. They preside over the city council but not the executive branch.

Political Limits and Opportunities

Many factors may modify the ability of a chief executive to get things done. Although they can hire, fire, and direct department heads, many city managers must deal with powerful city council persons who attempt to "meddle" in administrative matters. From another point of view, these individuals may see the line between policy-making and inquiring into administrative performance differently than the chief executive does.[10] That's why it is important for them and the manager to understand what the city charter or the city's source of authority means.

School superintendents may find it politically necessary to remove a coach who is an excellent teacher but can't win football games or to keep a poor teacher in the classroom because of his or her connections to a school board member. Furthermore, executives at all levels must make personnel decisions in the context of affirmative action, civil service regulations, state and federal grant mandates, and the realities of the political situation in which they find themselves.

Political skill can also make it possible for an official without much formal authority to persuade, motivate, and lead a government and a community to accomplish important goals. It matters which individual occupies a role or office.

Chief Administrative Officers and Political Leaders

The job of chief executive requires both technical and political skills. Some executive branches separate the political and the administrative roles. Many cities that have a strong mayor also have a chief administrative officer (CAO), who operates almost like a city manager in the council-manager system, except that he or she is hired and fired by the mayor (not the council). The mayor, in a strong mayoral system, then takes charge of the coalition building, the negotiation, the promotion of projects and plans, as well as the ceremonial functions associated with serving as the head of a unit of government.

The need to devote time and talent to both the technical-administrative and the political roles is one reason why Charles R. Adrian, an authority on city government, has observed that the council-manager system and the mayor-council system are becoming more alike.[11] Now that we have examined sources of authority and some of the possible relationships between the executive and legislative branches in local governments, let us examine the types of local governments themselves.

FIVE TYPES OF LOCAL GOVERNMENTS

Nothing testifies to the diversity of the American intergovernmental system more than the variety of local governments found within it. The Bureau of Census identifies five types of local governments: counties, townships, municipalities, school districts, and special districts. Yet within these five types there is more variety than we can fully explore in these

BOX 5.1

DIMENSIONS OF DIVERSITY: LOCAL GOVERNMENT NAMES AND FUNCTIONS

Although town governments exist in each county in NEW HAMPSHIRE, they do not cover the entire area of each county. Cities, gores, grants, purchases, unorganized locations, and unorganized townships exist outside the area of any town.

IOWA townships may provide fire protection, cemeteries, community centers, and township halls. Township trustees also serve as fence viewers, and resolve animal trespass problems upon request. Although Iowa township trustees may levy taxes, and may issue anticipatory bonds, the compensation of township trustees is paid by the county government. For this reason, townships in Iowa are classified as administrative subdivisions of the counties and are not counted as separate governments, in census statistics on governments.

The entire state of INDIANA is encompassed by 91 county governments, except for the former county of Marion. Marion County and the city of Indianapolis were consolidated to operate as one government, designated the City of Indianapolis.

CALIFORNIA law provides for the following types of school districts: elementary, high school, unified, and community college. Among the types of elementary districts are: city districts, regular districts, union districts, joint districts, and joint union districts.

In LOUISIANA, the county governments are legally designated "parish" governments. The entire area of the state is encompassed by parish government except for the parishes of East Baton Rouge, Orleans, and Terrebonne. These three parishes are substantially consolidated for government purposes with the cities of Baton Rouge, New Orleans, and Houma, respectively. The governing body of a parish is called the police jury, except in Jefferson Parish, which has a parish council, and in Plaquemines Parish, which has a commission council.

The entire area of the State of VIRGINIA is encompassed by county government, except for areas located within the boundaries of the 41 cities. Cities in Virginia exist outside the area of any county, and are counted as municipal rather than county governments. . . . [although] cities perform county-type as well as municipal functions. . . . In localities where a city and a county share the same Clerk of Circuit Court, Commissioner of Revenue, Commonwealth's Attorney, Sheriff, or Treasurer, the officials involved are classified for census purposes as county officials. . . .

Source: Bureau of the Census, 1992 Census of Governments, vol. 1: Government Organization (Washington, D.C., U. S. Government Printing Office 1988), A–1 to A–235.

pages, as our Dimensions of Diversity (Box 5.1) indicates. From state to state different names, forms, and functions are assigned to the five basic types of local government.

While all people may be created equal, all local governments are not. Counties and municipalities (or cities), are usually considered to be a **general purpose government**. They offer a wide range of services and usually contain all three branches of government: legislative, executive, and judicial.

Townships (which exist in 21 states) lie somewhere in between general purpose and special purpose government, depending upon the way in which they are structured in each state. In Iowa, for example, townships are subunits of county government and are not considered to be a separate governmental unit. In other states, townships offer a wide range of services.

Special purpose governments include independent school districts and special districts such as municipal utility districts (MUDs), soil conservation, rural fire control, and mosquito abatement districts, as well as metropolitan transit and port authorities. Most of these governments specialize in a limited number of services and lack a judicial branch. However, some—such as the New York Port Authority created by an interstate compact between New York and New Jersey—have become incredibly complex.[12] As Table 5.1 indicates, special purpose governments outnumber general purpose governments. Furthermore, they are increasing at a much faster rate. In the past 25 years 10,000 special districts have been created. In this chapter we hope to shed some light on why so many of these governments have been created.

The County

County governments are found in all but two states, Connecticut and Rhode Island. In two other states they exist under different names: Boroughs in Alaska, and parishes in Louisiana. Because they are the largest unit of government in land area, there are fewer counties than any other form of local government. Of the 85,000 local governments, there are only 3,043 of the county-type in the United States. After the state and the national governments, county governments include more people than any other type of government, yet for many Americans county government remains a "Dark Continent of American Government."[13]

Dual Identity

The county serves two basic purposes. It is both an agency of state government and a unit of local government. Most counties were created in the eighteenth and nineteenth centuries

Table 5.1	
GENERAL AND SPECIAL PURPOSE GOVERNMENTS 1992	
Type	**Number**
General Purpose	39,005
National	1
State	50
County	3,043
Municipal	19,296
Township	16,666
Special Purpose	45,977
School Dist.	14,556
Special Dist.	33,131
Total	86,743

Source: Bureau of the Census, 1992 Census of Governments vol. 1: Government Organization (Washington, D.C.: U. S. Government Printing Office.)3.

as arms of state government to provide limited services to an essentially rural population. As an agent of the state, county government provides: courts, jails, roads, bridges, schools, welfare services, record keeping (such as land sales and vital statistics), and county government conducts the general election every other year in November. County government enables the state to provide a more or less uniform system of law and order and a basic minimum standard of some services throughout the state.[14]

County as Local Government

Counties are units of government which are local, first, because the officials who run them are locally elected, second, most counties were created because local people wanted them, and third, each county determines its own budget using its power to tax local property or economic activities. These powers, of course, may be limited by the state constitution or state laws. An important county government role is determining the range of services that residents receive. In addition to the services that counties are required to perform for the state, a county may offer a wide range of additional services if its citizens demand them.

Local government is a term that embraces communities large and small with a wide range of problems and resources. Nevertheless, they have more in common than often meets the eye. Is air pollution, illegal dumping, or family violence likely to be a problem for the citizens who elect the government centered in this building? Think about it.

As Table 5.2 indicates, some services are offered as a result of counties contracting with other units of government or with private enterprise to offer them. While counties in metropolitan areas are likely to offer more services, some rural or non-metropolitan counties go considerably beyond the traditional law and order and roads functions.

Whether or not a county offers a service depends upon political action by the citizens within it, even those who live in cities. As county citizens, they can demand services paid for by county government rather than by the city government alone. If the county is prohibited from performing a service by state law or the state constitution, then citizens of the county can get those changed. County citizens, after all, are also state citizens.

Towns and Townships

In some states "town" is part of a classification scheme for urban locations. In those states towns are cities, some of considerable size, but with fewer powers and responsibilities than large cities.

In 21 states, and for over 52 million people the terms *town* or *township* refer to a unit of local government that is not simply a small city. Two terms are used in discussing towns and townships: the New England town and the congressional township. The latter was created with the former as a model.

The New England Town

The New England town (or sometimes township) is from 20 to 40 square miles in area, about half the size of the average county in New England. Towns include both rural and urban populations. New England town government existed even before the American Revolution.[15] It was designed for the technologically simple needs of a fairly homogeneous rural population, most of which lived on small farms.

Table 5.2

A FEW SERVICES OFFERED BY AMERICAN COUNTIES

Service	County Operated	Contracted Out
Airports	585	264
Electric power	18	50
Fire protection	607	191
Gas supply	14	49
Hospitals	476	259
Landfills	1,261	359
Libraries	1,128	202
Nursing homes	489	167
Public transit	148	98
Sewerage system	310	75
Stadiums, convention centers	140	40
Water supply	312	86

Source: Bureau of the Census, 1987 Census of Governments, vol. 1: Government Organization (Washington, D.C., U. S. Government printing office, 1988), 11.

Today in many parts of New England, annual town meetings still set the tax rate and the budget and make major decisions that affect the community, including the election of officials such as the town clerk, treasurer, selectmen, auditors, a road commissioner, a sewer commissioner, a tree warden, constables, members of the board of health, and a school committee. The major town official is the moderator of the meeting who may be elected for a term of as many as three years or who may be elected on a meeting-by-meeting basis.[16]

The Congressional Township

In 1787 when the Continental Congress set up procedures for surveying and selling public lands in the (Northwest) territory (which ultimately became the states of Michigan, Ohio, Indiana, and Wisconsin), it created a geographic unit known as the congressional township. The **Northwest Ordinance** attempted to set up New England town-sized blocks of land which might become future units of local government. Thus, much of Ohio, Michigan, Indiana, and some of the land further west which had yet to be purchased from France or taken by force or guile from Native Americans was destined to be divided up into townships, each the same size, 36 square miles. The one square mile sections were then divided into quarters of 160 acres each. These in turn into four fields or farms of 40 acres.[17]

Since lines on a map often ignore rivers, ridges, hills, valleys, and other geographic features that help shape communities, it is a wonder that any of these uniformly shaped townships actually became units of local government. Many did, however. The process was helped along by two political phenomena which we have already introduced. Political culture and "the rules of the game." The political culture of New England was carried into the congressional townships in the heads and hearts of the early settlers, many of whom were born and raised in New England. Along with the moralistic version of American political culture, they brought familiarity with the township as their "natural" form of local government.

The process of making the township part of the state pattern of local government, rather than geographically convenient boundaries, was helped along by the requirement established quite early in the laws of most states that when the citizens of an area wished to set up a new county they had to include whole townships.

Today, there are over 16,000 township governments located in the 21 states that stretch along the northern third of the United States from Cape Cod in Massachusetts to Puget Sound in Washington.

Municipalities

A **municipality** (or city) is a unit of general purpose local government created to meet the needs of an urban population. In the era of the walking city when the urban population was located in a fairly small area, it made sense for urban residents to have their own government, separate from the county or township. Such a government could offer services that the rural population didn't need, and deal with problems (fires in tall buildings) that the rural population didn't have.

Until the Industrial Revolution American cities were few and far between, islands in an agricultural sea. Terms such as *village*, *town*, and *city* provided a useful way of differentiating urban places in terms of population size, complexity of problems to be dealt with, the range of services offered, and the appropriate local government structure. The Industrial

Revolution and the automobile revolution promoted the dispersion of urban businesses and residential concentrations into the countryside.

Today distinctions among local governments which were appropriate for an agricultural America are difficult to apply consistently. There are some very densely populated villages and some very small cities. This confusion is also reflected in the fact that some counties, as well as townships, offer urban-type services to their "rural" as well as suburban and urban residents.

If this is so, you may ask, why should we even have separate municipal governments? Why can't county or township government do it all?

We have two answers. First, under some circumstances county or township government probably can do it all. It depends upon the constitution and laws of your state. Second, to understand the special role of the municipality we have to briefly summarize some intergovernmental history. This summary will involve three terms: *incorporation*, *Dillon's Rule*, and *home rule*.

Incorporation of Municipalities

A corporation is an artificial entity created by a group of people. It has legal standing. The corporation can sue and be sued. It can own property. It can buy and sell goods and services. It can borrow money. It exists independently of the individuals that create it. For people in the business world, incorporation —the act of creating a corporation—puts a buffer between the individual business owner and liability for anything done in the name of the corporation. Thus, a corporation can go bankrupt and that's that. The individuals who control the corporation aren't liable for its debts, or for other obligations that the corporation cannot meet.

For most of the nineteenth century, a distinction existed between municipalities and other local governments based on the belief that only municipalities were corporations. For better or for worse, the act of municipal incorporation was viewed as a local act, whereas the creation of a county (or township) government was regarded as a state act. When counties and townships tried to do the things that cities did—pass local ordinances to deal with health problems, regulate traffic, or offer certain services—they were stopped by many state courts because they were not corporations. The Ohio Supreme Court explained it this way in 1857:

> A municipal corporation proper is created mainly for the interest, advantage, and convenience of the locality and its people; a county organization is created almost exclusively with a view to the policy of the state at large with scarcely an exception; all the powers and functions of the county organization have a direct and exclusive reference to the general administration of that policy.[18]

Similar court decisions during this era can be found in many other states. At the national level, Chief Justice Roger B. Taney, whose place in history is linked forever to the Dred Scott Decision, declared that, "The several counties are nothing more than certain portions of the territory into which the State is divided for the more convenient exercise of the powers of government."[19]

Thus, for individuals to use government to deal with the problems industrial America created in their communities it became necessary to create municipal governments. There was no other form of local government with the authority to offer urban-type services and to deal with the problems of densely populated areas. This is one of the major reasons for the proliferation of cities historically.

Today, the distinction between governments based on local or state creation seems somewhat specious. New governments are created at all levels usually because local citizens ask the state to allow them to be created (or to create them). Nevertheless, for a goodly period of our history it appeared that city (or municipal) governments could make regulations (also called ordinances or local laws) just because they were a special entity called a corporation.

Lest we give the wrong impression about courts, we hasten to point out that courts did not decide on their own to interfere with local government. Courts become involved in questions of the ability of governments to do something because individuals go to court to stop a local unit of government from regulating economic activities or offering services. There are, after all, individuals, and businesses, who find it profitable to dump chemicals in lakes and streams, to employ children in the fields and factories, or who feel that city parking garages, utilities, or day care centers, will compete unfairly with theirs. Thus, they take government to court to overthrow laws or regulations they don't like. Sometimes they win.

Dillon's Rule

In the late nineteenth century the authority provided to cities by corporate status alone was weakened, if not destroyed, by an Iowa Supreme Court Judge named John F. Dillon. His specialty was a relatively new area of public law called municipal law. In the 1880s when the judge was writing his influential *Commentaries on the Law of Municipal Corporations* (which by 1911 had gone through five editions), America was engaged in rapid industrialization and in experimentation with the best way to bring order to its expanding urban areas.

Judge Dillon interpreted the city's legal powers in a rather narrow fashion. **Dillon's Rule**, as a famous passage from his commentaries is now known, states that:

> It is a general and undisputed proposition of law . . . that a municipal corporation possess and can exercise the following power, and no others: First, those granted in express words; second, those necessarily or fairly implied in or incident to the power expressly granted; third, those essential to the accomplishment of the declared objects and purposes of the corporation—not simply convenient, but indispensable. Any fair, reasonable substantial doubt concerning the existence of power is resolved by the courts against the corporation, and the power is denied.[20]

In short, Judge Dillon interpreted Iowa state law to mean that municipal governments had virtually no implied powers. "If it isn't in your charter, you can't do it," he told cities. Any individual or business that could raise a reasonable doubt that a city was doing something for convenience rather than necessity would be upheld in court. To those suspicious of the way some urban politicians were using their power, Judge Dillon's Rule was very appealing. Therefore, Dillon's Rule was widely accepted as the way things ought to be in most states during the late nineteenth and early twentieth centuries.

Dillon's Rule is worth remembering for at least four reasons. First, it provides an excellent example of the fact that expertise is important. With no legal authority beyond the borders of Iowa other than widespread respect for his expertise, Judge Dillon shaped the future of cities in other states. Knowledge can be a political resource. We hope that point is of some comfort, however cold, during the sometimes tedious process of acquiring it.

Second, Dillon's Rule indicates the importance of the rules of the game. Constitutions, charters, and other basic political documents are the rules of the game by which the political process of rule making and enforcement is played. State constitutions and city charters determine whether or not a city council or county commissioners court has the authority to regulate a new activity (massage parlors, junk yards, fireworks, video games) or to perform a new function (building sports stadiums, parking lots, or providing day care facilities). If someone doesn't want to be regulated or thinks tax money shouldn't be spent on activities that offend his or her sensibilities then he or she can take a local government to court. Following Dillon's Rule, the courts for many decades ruled against new activities unless that government had authority from state law or a clause in its charter that expressly grants or "clearly implies" that the local government is empowered to engage in the activity in question.

Third, Dillon's Rule made the careful drafting of local government charters very important. If a power wasn't in the original charter then getting it could be a time-consuming process. In most cases it would mean that citizens from each city who wanted their city to be able to give them regulatory protection would have to get the state legislature to amend the charter (if it were a charter granted to a specific city by name) or change the laws affecting all general law. In some cases the state constitution might have to be amended. All of these courses of action were potentially expensive and time-consuming procedures.

The fourth and perhaps most important feature of Dillon's rule is that it made the distinction between home rule and general law government an extremely important one.

Home Rule

Home rule became virtually essential for communities experiencing the problems associated with urban development. With home rule the charters drafted by local charter commissions could be more easily amended or revised locally—right in the old home town. General law cities might have to wait years to get the authority they needed from either state law or state constitutional amendments.

Home rule means that the citizens of a community can choose the charter of their government. Home rule has two basic dimensions: First, it allows the local community to determine the structure of the unit of local government. This structure can follow the Jacksonian long ballot model, or it can use any of the structural models that were discussed earlier. The community may choose to incorporate plebiscitary democracy (initiative, referendum, and recall). It can create a variety of departments—planning and zoning, nuisance abatement, parks and recreation—without seeking permission elsewhere.

Second, the community can decide whether or not its local government should have the power to pass ordinances, also known as local laws. The community can decide, within the limits of the state laws and constitution, how much authority to give their government and on what subject matters. Home rule invariably means that a local government can make and enforce ordinances. While there are limits, ordinance authority gives local governments considerable flexibility in dealing with local problems.

Local ordinance-making authority can be granted by the state to units of government that don't have home rule. However, having home rule makes ordinance authority a sure thing. General law governments are usually limited to enforcing the laws passed by the state. Home rule governments can react to new situations much more quickly by passing and enforcing local laws. If its home rule government lacks the authority to deal with a specific situation, the local community can still amend its charter to grant that authority a lot more quickly than it can get from the state.

In many states home rule is only available to cities of a certain size. Townships usually don't have it and only recently have counties been granted home rule. Only 18 states granted or made it possible for counties to obtain home rule in 1967. By 1992 this was the case in 38 of the 48 states that have county government.[21] Thus, in 10 states a county with a population of several hundred thousand may be stuck with a structure more suited for an earlier period of American history, and with few powers to deal with modern conditions such as the sprawl of populations and problems beyond the boundaries of the home rule cities within it.[22]

Since in many states county and township governments lack the power to deal with modern problems, other units of government (cities and special districts) are created to deal with them. Although municipalities with home rule are equipped to deal with modern problems within their borders, they are still vulnerable to problems originating outside those borders. The vulnerability of cities and the incapacity of some counties are one of the major pairs of misfortunes in the intergovernmental scene. This pair of misfortunes will not go away until the intergovernmental system is modified by state and local action. The suggested solutions range from city-county consolidation to simply granting counties home rule.

Independent School Districts

In five states and the District of Columbia, primary and secondary education are provided by general purpose governments: counties, townships, or municipalities. The school system run by these governments may have a board and be divided into geographic areas called districts for administrative purposes. These school districts are not considered separate units of government. They are merely agencies of whatever local government controls them.

In 30 states elementary and secondary education are given special recognition in the state constitution by requiring that they be administered by special units of government which are independent of county, city, or township supervision. Generally referred to as school districts, these units of government are more correctly called Independent School Districts (ISDs). A "mixed" situation exists in 15 states where general purpose governments provide education in some places and ISDs provide it in others.[23]

Special Districts

Sometimes called "non-school special districts," these units of local government each perform a range of services that is usually narrower than those performed by cities, counties, and townships. Many special districts only perform one service. As Table 5.3 indicates, special districts are created to perform many different types of functions. Most special districts are located within a single county, and one fourth of them share the same boundaries as an existing general purpose government. However, more than 2,400 special districts have territory in two or more counties and some cross state lines. The latter are usually involved in parks, bridges, ports, mass transit, or airports.

The significance of special districts is that the public knows so little about them and takes little interest in seeing to it that they use wisely their considerable powers to tax, spend, borrow, and duplicate efforts. Of the 19,675 special districts on which the Census

Table 5.3

SPECIAL DISTRICT GOVERNMENTS BY FUNCTION: 1992

Function	Number	Percent
Multiple-function districts	2,674	8.1
Single-function districts:	30,457	91.9
Natural resources	6,564	19.8
Fire protection	5,354	16.2
Housing and community development	3,663	11.1
Water supply	3,442	10.4
Cemeteries	1,646	5.0
Sewerage	1,850	5.6
Parks and recreation	1,212	3.7
Libraries	1,063	3.2
Hospitals	774	2.3
Education	870	2.6
Highways	666	2.0
Health	619	1.9
Utilities other than water supply	479	1.4
Airports	447	1.3
Other	1,808	5.5
Grand Total	33,131	100

Source: U. S. Bureau of the Census, 1992 Census of Governments, vol. I. Government Organization (Washington, D.C.: U. S. Government Printing Office), 7–9.

Bureau has financial data, nearly 40 percent have debts outstanding of more than one million dollars. Over a thousand have debts of five million or more.[24]

While we are inclined to share the view that special districts make the intergovernmental landscape more complex than need be, we think it is important for future leaders of the system to keep in mind the possibility that the proliferation of special districts is a symptom that something needs attending to rather than a problem in and of itself.

Just as there are a variety of causes for a puddle of liquid on the floor during a soap opera—a leaky roof, an untrained puppy, a spilled beverage, an overflowing bathtub, a freshly used umbrella, a defective dishwasher, or copious weeping—so there are a variety of causes for the creation of so many units of local government; special district, and otherwise.

REASONS FOR CREATING NEW LOCAL GOVERNMENTS

In the past 25 years the population of the United States has grown by 25 percent. The number of municipalities has grown by 5 percent. However, the number of special districts has grown by 60 percent. Special districts have increased at more than twice the rate that the population has.

Early in this chapter, we mentioned several reasons for having local government at all (delegation, local autonomy, access, personnel management, system legitimacy, and resource management). While an increase in population might require some new governments, it seems reasonable to look beyond population increase and the basic advantages of local government in general for an explanation for the proliferation of new ones.

The next time a proposal for a new unit of government surfaces in your community it might be interesting to see which of the five common reasons are causes for its creation. They are: constitutional restrictions, the power of interest groups, private profit, intergovernmental convenience, and defensive incorporation. In many, if not most cases, more than one reason is involved.

Constitutional and Statutory Restrictions

As Table 5.4 indicates, some states give more authority to one type of local government than to another. Furthermore, while cities nearly always have more flexibility than counties, the degree of flexibility varies considerably from state to state. At minimum this means that in some states, communities facing new problems may not be able to use existing governments such as the county or the township to solve their problems. Thus, they may create new units of government such as a municipality or a special district.

For citizens in a local community it is easier to create a new unit of local government than it is to go through the state political system to change the state law, or the constitutional provision that restricts one's county or township government. Table 5.5 shows the 10 states that lead the country in special district government. While there are parallels between population rank and interest group rank, the top 10 states in interest group numbers are not the 10 most populous states.

Interest Group Power

As Table 5.4 indicates, Texas ranks first among the several states in terms of the discretionary authority given to cities. However, it ranks forty-third among states in terms of authority given counties. With their county governments among the most restricted in the nation, it is no surprise that communities in Texas organize other units of government to obtain services, and to acquire the power to regulate various legal and illegal entrepreneurial activities. Texas led the nation in new municipal incorporations in the 1980s, and ranks third in total number of special districts.

While the reasons for creating new units of government are numerous, in the Texas case it seems resonable to assume that two powerful interest groups that do not want counties empowered to regulate land use and the sale of fireworks may have had an impact.

There have been numerous attempts to better equip counties in Texas to deal with urban problems. However, the Texas Association of Realtors and the fireworks lobby have worked very hard to maintain the status quo for county authority. Thus, late in December and around the Fourth of July, roadside stands selling fireworks open up just outside the boundaries of most cities. Texas cities can regulate fireworks, and usually ban their sale in the interest of health and fire prevention. However, Texas counties do not have that authority, even though they try to get it in almost every session of the legislature. Thus, the power of interest groups not only dooms Texas county governments to budget for and to fight grass fires every January and July, it also leaves communities with little choice but to create additional governments in order to solve problems associated with growth.[25]

As Table 5.5 indicates, population alone is not the only factor involved in the creation of special districts. The reasons we have discussed are but a partial explanation. Clearly, however, it is more than simply population or economic growth that leads communities to

Table 5.4

DEGREE OF AUTHORITY GRANTED TO LOCAL GOVERNMENT

State and Composite Rank*	State Rank By Cities	Rank by Counties
28. Alabama	23	37
5. Alaska	13	2
25. Arizona	14	38
21. Arkansas	34	6
18. California	17	17
42. Colorado	37	45
4. Connecticut	4	***
9. Delaware	26	5
26. Florida	30	14
30. Georgia	18	32
40. Hawaii	**	22
50. Idaho	47	44
12. Illinois	10	19
37. Indiana	40	24
44. Iowa	39	30
14. Kansas	15	11
29. Kentucky	36	16
10. Louisiana	16	8
2. Maine	2	20
6. Maryland	7	9
43. Massachusetts	41	48
16. Michigan	3	2
17. Minnesota	19	12
45. Mississippi	31	35
19. Missouri	8	47
31. Montana	38	18
41. Nebraska	24	41
46. Nevada	45	33
22. New Hampshire	27	36
36. New Jersey	35	31
48. New Mexico	49	23
35. New York	44	25
3. North Carolina	5	3
24. North Dakota	25	21
27. Ohio	11	42
13. Oklahoma	12	27
1. Oregon	6	1
7. Pennsylvania	20	4
38. Rhode Island	42	***
15. South Carolina	21	7
47. South Dakota	43	39
34. Tennessee	32	34
11. Texas	1	43
20. Utah	28	10
39. Vermont	48	46
8. Virginia	9	13
32. Washington	33	29

(Continued)

Table 5.4 (Continued)		
DEGREE OF AUTHORITY GRANTED TO LOCAL GOVERNMENT		
State and Composite Rank*	**State Rank By Cities**	**Rank by Counties**
49. West Virginia	46	40
23. Wisconsin	22	15
33. Wyoming	29	26

* A rank of 1 means that this state gives a particular type of local government a high degree of discretionary authority.

** Only 49 states. In Hawaii local governments are counties or city-county consolidations.

*** Only 48 states. Neither Connecticut nor Rhode Island have organized county governments

Source: ACIR, Measuring Discretionary Authority (Washington, D.C.: Advisory Commission on Intergovernmental Relations, November, 1981), 59.

choose the creation of additional governments to solve problems instead of making do with those they have.

Private Profit

In some states the creation of a special district is a very profitable activity. It usually involves gaining control over several acres of land within commuting distance of a good sized city and then developing that land using money borrowed by a government one has created for one's own purposes. As Virginia Marion Perrenod observes in her detailed study of Houston area developer districts,

> The old axiom of "never use your own money to make money" is certainly true for the developer who has discovered a bonanza for financing his development. Enabling laws that allow districts to be formed either by a percentage of property holders or by a percentage of holders in value are the key to this public development for private purposes.[26]

These governments are special districts and are registered under a variety of titles such as municipal utility district, water development district, and so on. The process usually involves the steps listed in Box 5.2. If all goes well, the developer sells all of the improved land at a handsome profit and moves on, leaving behind a unit of government which owes a lot of money and a community of property owners to run that government and tax themselves to pay off the debt.

Of course, all may not go well. First, all of the property may not be purchased. Then, those who did purchase the land including the developer, may have to shoulder the tax burden to pay off the bonds issued by the special district. Since the district (not the developer) owes the debt, the developer may decide he doesn't want to own the land any more and simply fail to pay off the mortgage owed to the bank. The bank then becomes the owner of the land. Other landowners may not be in so flexible a position. They may have invested their life savings in the land and the new house that is on it.

A second unfortunate possibility is that the development work in the district may be poorly planned or improperly performed. In unincorporated areas the land is cheaper than in cities but there is no city government to make inspections to ensure that utility construction or home building is performed properly. If the "improvements" don't last very long, then, in addition to paying off the bonds, the taxpayers of the special district might have to pay for expensive repairs and maintenance.

The foregoing unhappy scenarios are not the usual case, though they have happened often enough in the past to lead to the passage of laws in some states regulating land development and the creation of special districts. Nevertheless, many observers of the intergovernmental scene are less than enthusiastic about more special districts in the intergovernmental system, especially developer "owned" districts.

Intergovernmental Convenience

Special districts are sometimes created by other units of government, for two major reasons: in order to coordinate a large expensive service or to avoid the responsibility for offering new functions.

Coordinating a Large Expensive Service

A major reason why local governments may find it convenient to create a new special district is to offer a service such as mass transit to an area larger than that of any one of the local governments involved. The New York Port Authority, which operates in three states coordinating a vast array of transportation and construction activities, and the Bay Area Rapid Transit Authority linking many San Francisco Bay communities are two ex-

Table 5.5

LEADING SPECIAL DISTRICT STATES 1992

State	Rank in Population	Special District Ranking	Number of Special Districts
California	1	2	2,897
Texas	2	3	2,392
Pennsylvania	5	4	2,244
Illinois	6	1	2,995
Indiana	14	10	1,000
Missouri	15	6	1,443
Washington	16	8	1,192
Colorado	26	7	1,317
Kansas	32	5	1,506
Nebraska	36	9	1,075

Sources: U. S. Bureau of the Census, 1992 Census of Governments: Preliminary Report (Washington, D.C.: United States Government Printing Office, 1992), 6.
U. S. Bureau of the Census, Statistical Abstract of the United States 1992 (Washington, D.C.: U. S. Government Printing Office, 1992), 22–23.

BOX 5.2

CREATING PROFITABLE GOVERNMENTS

Major Steps Followed by Developers in Creating a Special District in Unincorporated Areas.

1. The developer acquires control over a large parcel of several hundred acres, usually by buying a little, and purchasing the option to buy the rest.
2. The developer moves employees onto the land and begins the survey and development work. While this is going on, the employees are establishing residency in order to be able to vote. As soon as residency is established, the developer makes sure they register.
3. The developer initiates whatever legal procedures are set forth in state law to create a special district. This usually involves a public hearing that few attend, and a referendum to determine whether the residents of the area approve. Since most of the voters are employees of the developer, little money is invested in public opinion polls to predict the outcome.
4. When the special district is finally created the developer has control of a virtually private government. This government can borrow money by issuing bonds. These bonds are attractive to people in certain income tax brackets because the interest earned on these bonds is not subject to income tax.
5. Having obtained the money to pay for engineering work, street construction, water lines, and whatnot by borrowing, the developer's special district then hires the developer to put in these improvements.
6. When all or most of the improvements are installed the developer advertises and sells the land to prospective home builders.

Source: Woodworth G. Thrombley, Special Districts and Authorities in Texas (Austin: Institute of Public Affairs, University of Texas, 1959), 1–25.

amples of special districts created to deal with problems larger than a single government's territorial jurisdiction. Large special districts offer four noteworthy political advantages.

The first advantage is that a multigovernment special district would move the day-to-day aggravations of offering the service a step further away from the existing elected officials.

Second, large special districts have a broader tax base. Furthermore, as taxing authorities, the bills they send do not reflect on the "no-new-taxes" promises of the elected officials of the general law governments.

Third, special districts can borrow money to build improvements. Therefore, the debt burden of existing governments won't be increased and their ability to borrow for their own projects is less likely to be directly affected.

Fourth, in cases where a metropolitan area crosses state lines, or when a complex of numerous local governments already exists, a large multigovernment special district may be a valuable coordinating device.[27]

Avoiding Responsibility for New Functions

The traditions, the rules of the game, or the personal preferences of some public officials may encourage them to avoid taking responsibility for offering a new service. Thus, they may encourage the creation of a special district to offer the service within their territorial jurisdiction. This is one reason for the proliferation of fire districts and road districts in some counties. The county is empowered to offer the service or improvement, but the county board must raise the tax rate to pay for it. Raising taxes takes more fortitude than many officials appear to possess.

Defensive Incorporation

To incorporate, as we recall from our Dillon's Rule discussion, is to create a new municipality and thus a government. Defensive incorporation is the process of creating a new municipality to avoid annexation by a nearby larger city.

Annexation is the act of adding land to the territory of an existing unit of government. In the American context we usually think in terms of unincorporated areas when we discuss annexation. An **unincorporated area** is land that lies outside the boundaries of an existing municipality. There may be a community in place, but if that community has not incorporated (and created a government), the land on which the community lives, farms, or does business is unincorporated land.

In some states it is very easy for a city to grow by annexing unincorporated land. It simply follows a procedure established by the state. Residents and businesses may be annexed whether they like it or not. In other states incorporation cannot occur unless the residents vote for it. Yet in others there is a review board that must approve.

Whether annexation is easy or hard, one condition always exists. The land to be annexed must be outside the boundaries of an existing city. Even though it lies within a special districts township, or a county, unincorporated land is eligible for annexation. For this reason, residents of areas outside the boundaries of large cities may find it useful to protect themselves from annexation by incorporating a city of their own. Incorporated land, on the other hand, is virtually impossible, for any city, large or small, to annex.

From the point of view of those who think that residents are incorporating to avoid responsibility for helping the larger city deal with its problems, their act of incorporation is sometimes called **defensive incorporation**.

Defensive incorporation is associated with pejorative terms such as **exclusionary zoning**, and **parasitism**. **Exclusionary zoning** is the practice of passing land use regulations which make it very difficult to build high density, low-cost housing of the sort that would enable some of the less affluent central city population to move to the suburban city to be closer to work. One of the major economic changes occurring in your lifetime has been the export of jobs to the suburbs. Over half the jobs in metropolitan America are now in the suburbs, not the central cities.[28]

One of the ongoing struggles of not only central cities but also other communities is the effort to require those who earn profits and salaries in them to put something back to pay for roads, streets, police protection, and other services. Since most central cities have a lot of expensive problems to solve, people who benefit from the city without contributing to its tax base are not highly regarded by central city political leaders.

Most of the terms we have just introduced are judgmental. They attribute selfish motivations to the actions of others. Whether or not these are the true motivations is not a matter for us to decide. We simply introduce these terms because they are part of the intergovernmental scene, especially in metropolitan areas. A less judgmental view of defensive incorporation is to consider three facts about community decision making. First, not everyone in a community is involved in making every decision. Second, decisions are usually made for more than one reason. Third, wrong decisions are sometimes made for altruistic reasons just as right ones are made for selfish reasons.

When a local population decides something, then, it is neither a unidimensional nor a totally homogeneous act. Defensive incorporation stripped of its emotional weight simply means that a suburban community goes through the procedures required by the state to become a municipality. In doing so it does not become part of a large city. Recalling the metropolitan paradox from Chapter 2, defensive incorporation, at minimum, contributes to the fragmentation of authority in the metropolitan area.

The central cities of many metropolitan areas today are completely surrounded by small and medium sized cities. Some of them are the products of defensive incorporation. Others were there all along, the big city just grew out to meet them.

ALTERNATIVES TO THE CREATION OF NEW GOVERNMENTS

For most of this century it has been convenient for communities to create new units of local government which had the authority to deliver one or more urban-type services. The alternatives were usually less convenient but are worth reviewing briefly. Yesterday's inconvenience may be tomorrow's opportunity.

Demand Accountability

Insist that one of your the existing governments use the authority it has to offer the service (even if it means an increase in taxes). To add a city police department when one already has a sheriff's department costs money and could ultimately increase taxes even more. It may be cheaper to increase the sheriff's budget so that more deputies can be hired and trained for patrolling urban areas.

If the existing county legislative body won't vote more funds, or if the existing sheriff won't attempt to even ask for them, then get some new county officials through the electoral process. This means entering the political arena. There's a first time for everything.

The tremendous potential for the 3,000 county governments to serve as area-wide units of government and thus reduce the proliferation of special districts; is best represented by the Lakewood plan; in California. There, Los Angeles county, which first contracted with the city of lakewood to offer urban-type services eventually was offering services such as trash collection, fire fighting and police protection to numerous small towns and cities within the county.

Structural Reform

If the existing government doesn't have the authority to do something, then help it get that authority through the passage of state laws or through constitutional amendment.

This is how the home rule movement began. Many cities created in the eighteenth century were given restrictive charters by the state legislature or were created by general laws which provided only expressed powers. Dillon's Rule didn't help things very much either. The individuals and groups who organized the movement to get home rule for cities were successful in a few states in getting it for counties. However, home rule is still not available to all counties and townships.

Consider the Virginia System

As some states do, Virginia empowers counties to perform many urban functions including land use regulation. Because counties can do some of the things that in other states only cities can do, Virginians who live in an urbanized area have a choice. State law allows them to vote for two different levels of independence and accountability.

In Virginia a community of at least 5,000 inhabitants can decide whether it wishes to be a town or a city.[29] When a town becomes a city, or when an unincorporated area with 5,000 or more inhabitants decides to become a city, it takes on all the legal powers and responsibilities of a county including welfare and education services. Even though it may be surrounded geographically by the county of which it was formerly a part, the city ceases to be part of that county. Each Virginia city is, in effect, a county.

Virginia towns, on the other hand, remain in the county. Residents of Virginia towns still pay county taxes, vote for and can serve as county officials but they also have a town government that performs other functions and may offer services that the county doesn't.

The decision on whether to become a town or a city in Virginia is essentially a decision about taking on more responsibility. Since Virginia counties are equipped with the authority to perform many city-type functions there is less motivation to incorporate or to create special districts. As James Campbell of the Virginia Municipal League has observed, "Our city-county separation is probably the reason why there are fewer taxing authorities in Virginia than any other state."[30] As a result, Virginians appear to have an easier job of keeping track of their governments. Although Virginia ranks fourteenth in the United States in terms of population, it ranks *last* in terms of units of government per county, and near the bottom in terms of total governments.

Privatization

Privatization is a growing trend wherein an existing local government contracts with a private business to provide a service that the local government itself formerly performed. Table 5.2, for example, indicates not only the variety of services offered by counties, but also the fact that every single one of the 12 services listed are sometimes offered via contracts with private firms.

ARE THERE TOO MANY LOCAL GOVERNMENTS?

As Table 5.6 indicates the total number of governments is less then it was since the early 1960s. Virtually all of this reduction has been the result of a state by state consolidation of rural school districts, a process that was complete by the early 1970s. Since that time, the number of units of local government has begun a steady increase. Municipalities and special districts are the major source of this growth.

Table 5.6

GOVERNMENT UNITS: 1967–1992

Type	1992	1987	1982	1977	1972	1967
National	1	1	1	1	1	1
State	50	50	50	50	50	50
County	3,043	3,042	3,041	3,042	3,044	3,049
Municipal	19,296	19,200	19,076	18,862	18,517	18,048
Township	16,666	16,691	16,734	16,822	16,991	17,105
School District	14,556	14,721	14,851	15,174	15,781	21,782
Special District	33,131	29,523	28,078	25,962	23,885	21,264
Total	86,743	83,237	81,831	79,913	78,269	81,299

Source: U. S. Bureau of the Census, 1992 Census of Governments (Washington, D.C.: U. S. Government Printing Office), 3.

The trend toward more local governments has slowed somewhat, yet the likelihood that it will continue is of concern to business, political, and scholarly observers. These are divided into two somewhat unequally sized camps. The largest is the traditional reformers. They believe the answer to the question is "yes." A more recently emerged school of thought is the public choice theorists who believe that the current situation is simply the result of market efficiencies.

Yes, There Are Too Many

The reformers believe that the multiplication of local governments can lead to citizen confusion, the fragmentation of authority, wasted resources, and ultimately a decline in legitimacy.[31]

Over 20 years ago The Committee on Economic Development, a prestigious organization consisting of top executives from major corporations and other leading American institutions, issued a two-part report on their analysis of the governmental system. The local government portion included the nine recommendations found in Box 5.3. Similar recommendations could be found in the literature of the ACIR or the National Municipal League.

We point out the work of the Committee on Economic Development to indicate the concern of the business community with the governments. Naturally, these executives all value economy and efficiency, especially in the governments to which their firms pay taxes, but the thrust of their argument is twofold: first, that American communities need to deal with problems facing us and second, that it is the obligation of those advantaged by the system to take on this task:

> . . . [T]he need for action is urgent; the responsibility of each citizen to share, to participate, and to exert initiative in constructive endeavors cannot be evaded. And that responsibility bears most heavily upon those favored in education, wealth, and positions of trust . . . To shirk this challenge is to deny our birthright of freedom and self-government.[32]

BOX 5.3

RECOMMENDATIONS COMMITTEE ON ECONOMIC DEVELOPMENT

1. The number of local governments in the United States, now about 80,000, should be reduced by at least 80 percent.
2. The number of overlapping layers of local government found in most states should be severely curtailed.
3. Popular election should be confined to members of the policymaking body, and to the chief executive in those governments where the "strong mayor" form is preferred to the "council-manager" plan.
4. Each local unit should have a single chief executive, either elected by the people or appointed by the local legislative body, with all administrative agencies and personnel fully responsible to him; election of department heads should be halted.
5. Personnel practices based on merit and professional competence should replace the personal or partisan "spoils" systems found in most counties and many other local units.
6. County modernization should be pressed with special vigor, since counties—everywhere except in New England—have a high but undeveloped potential for solving the problems of rural, urban, and most metropolitan communities.
7. Once modernized, local governments should be entrusted with broad legal powers permitting them to plan, finance, and execute programs suited to the special needs, interests, and desires of their citizens.
8. The fifty state constitutions should be revamped—either by legislative amendment or through constitutional conventions concentrating on local government modernization—to provide for boundary revisions, extensions of legal authority, and elimination of needless overlapping layers.
9. The terms and conditions of federal and state grants-in-aid should be revised to encourage the changes recommended in this statement.

Source: Committee on Economic Development, Modernizing Local Government : to Secure a Balanced Federalism (New York: Committee on Economic Development, 1966), 17–19.

The first suggestion the committee made was to reduce the number of local governments by more than 75 percent.[33] This point is worth considering for three reasons.

First, it indicates a fairly distant goal that may take a generation or more of state local leadership to achieve. These executives are well aware that the dismantling or consolidation of 50,000 to 60,000 thousand units of local government in the near future is highly unlikely.

Second, some reduction may well be a realizable goal. From 1962 to 1987 the number of school districts did decrease by more than 50 percent. Furthermore, 104 places surrendered their separate municipal identity, between 1980 and 1990, 34 by merger with another government. The creation of a city is clearly not an irreversible act.[34]

Third, it is important to consider the suggestions of the committee not only on their merits, but because they indicate that local government reform is not a merely parochial concern, nor one limited only to starry-eyed idealists. Hardheaded business people who lead national corporations are concerned with the shape of the intergovernmental system, just as we are.[35]

Kellogg and Battle Creek

Since actions sometimes speak louder than lists of recommendations, the Kellogg Company's use of its political resources in Battle Creek, Michigan is worth some attention. In 1978 Kellogg decided that it needed to expand its corporate headquarters. It had been in Battle Creek for over 70 years and wanted to stay. However, its executives were discouraged by the urban-suburban bickering that took place between the city of Battle Creek (1980 population, 35,700) and Battle Creek Township (population, 20,600). Furthermore, Kellogg was having trouble recruiting executive talent because of a reluctance to bring families into a no-growth, economically depressed area.

The company decided not to try to get the state to change its annexation laws which make it difficult for a city in Michigan to extend its boundaries and thus acquire the tax base to finance needed service improvements. Instead, the company applied its influence at the local level in Battle Creek at the city and township levels.

It looked around at other areas with similar problems where consolidations led to **economies of scale** and economic growth. The mergers of Toronto, Nashville, Minneapolis, Indianapolis, and a few others, all indicated that consolidating governments was difficult but not impossible.[36] If political resources (including carrots, sticks, leadership skills, and lots of time and energy selling the idea to the public) were carefully invested consolidations could and did occur. Next, Kellogg commissioned a Michigan law firm in another city to study the procedures for merging the city and the township, and to prepare a precise timetable for announcement and publicity prior to the referendum which would have to take place before the merger.

Finally, it prepared a plan for merger that would bring maximum benefits to as many political actors as possible. The plan included the creation of a fund to provide seed money for small business creation, and equal city and township representation on an expanded city council that would include all incumbent council persons. No one's seat would be at risk until the 1984–1985 elections. The showpiece of the plan was that Kellogg and its more than 700 headquarters staff would not leave Battle Creek for a better offer elsewhere. Not only would Kellogg stay, but it would build a new 20 to 30 million dollar worldwide headquarters and put the tax savings resulting from the merger into the seed money fund. The tax savings and thus the seed money fund would amount to more than $1.6 million over a five year period.[37]

In May of 1982, with no advance notice, Kellogg revealed its plan. The message was simple. Merge or we leave. The longer version was carefully explained in the media over the summer and early fall:

> Allow your governments to keep on bickering over who gets new economic development opportunities, or merge them and start thinking about the whole area of Battle Creek as one interconnected community. We have been, and we will be a responsible citizen of this community, that is why we are going to all this trouble.

On November 2, 1982, the citizens of Battle Creek voted "yes," to the merger of city and township, and to economic development. Since that referendum, the area has attracted new jobs, domestic and foreign plants, has become a regional retailing center, and is now another success story of corporate-government partnership.[38] Shortly after the election, noted intergovernmental reporter Neal R. Pierce observed, "For years, good government groups, lacking clout, have fought a lonely battle for metropolitan consolidations—rarely succeeding. But if forward looking corporations enter the ring, the odds could start to change dramatically."[39]

The Battle Creek merger was one of two mergers in the 1980s involving populations greater than 5,000.[40] Too many have used the competition for new jobs and industry to play off one community against another. As responsible corporate citizens, Kellogg went to a lot of trouble to give Battle Creek a chance to keep a major resource in its political economy. It is worth noting that Tony the Tiger acted a little differently than the tiger Exxon is trying to put in your tank. Exxon quietly left New York for Dallas in 1989, apparently having made no effort to use its resources to promote reforms in exchange for staying. That Battle Creek is much smaller than New York, and that Exxon's influence might thus be proportionately smaller are factors in the corporate-government relationship worth noting.

Nevertheless, the Kellogg example is worth some attention. It indicates that corporate America is not united in either altruism or greed. It depends in part upon the individuals in

Not only is Battle Creek, Michigan the place where Kellogg showed that business leadership can promote constructive political change, it is also one of the many U. S. cities involved in international relations.

charge of the corporation. Gary Costley, the Kellogg vice president in charge of the merger project, asked a question worth asking in many corporate boardrooms:

"We said to ourselves, we've been here 70 years. Is it fair just to pull up stakes and leave without giving the citizens of this community a chance to do something about what we regard as a fixable problem?"[41]

The answer, of course, depends upon who is doing the answering.

No, There Aren't Too Many Governments

Not all students of the intergovernmental system are equally committed to reforming local government by consolidation or dissolution. The public choice school takes the position that the proliferation of overlapping units of local government are the rational responses of local communities to problem solving. Each community offers a different array of services—some many, some just a few. Individuals can either move to an area that matches their needs, or organize politically to choose a new array of services for the community in which they live.

In 1988 two studies were released of the choices available, the kinds of people most able to take advantage of them, and the degree to which the governments in the St. Louis, Missouri, metropolitan area cooperated in serving their residents. In this area numerous governments engaged in an unequal competition for economic resources and development. These two studies came to radically different conclusions.

One study was sponsored by the ACIR. Its principle investigators were Ronald J. Oakerson, and Roger B. Parks. The title of their study is *Metropolitan Organization; The St. Louis Case.* Its purpose was to learn how a system with extensive jurisdictional fragmentation actually worked. After a careful examination of the 91 cities and many special districts in the St. Louis county area, Parks and Oakerson found a great deal of cooperation through formal and informal agreements among political leaders and public officials in the St. Louis area. Box 5.4 provides some examples of cooperative arrangements they found.

What they did not find, however, was that everyone had an equal opportunity to choose his or her community in which to live. Nor was there a system in place to deal adequately with communities inhabited largely by people unable to make the sorts of choices that families with incomes in the top 10 or 15 percent can make. The authors noted somewhat laconically, "A complex metropolitan area that has performed well in terms of service responsiveness and in finding efficient ways to deliver services may not perform equally well in assisting distressed communities."

The residents of most of the distressed communities were taxing themselves at relatively high rates, but were unable to raise revenues—in spite of locally imposed higher tax burdens—to make it possible to deliver to themselves and their children the kinds of services enjoyed by their more advantaged neighbors. This disparity in fiscal resources is not specific to St. Louis, nor to Missouri. It is one of the major problems confronting state and local government today.

In contrast to the ACIR study was one submitted by a group of local citizens, the Board of Freeholders, who had been appointed by city, county, and state officials to make reform recommendations. The freeholders' plan suggested a radical reorganization of the St. Louis County area. It pointed out that approximately 400,000 residents in unincorporated St. Louis County were not being well served. This was largely because the county did not have

BOX 5.4

EXAMPLES OF FUNCTIONAL COOPERATION IN THE ST. LOUIS CITY-COUNTY AREA

Police and Fire Services:

1. An area-wide major case squad pools investigative resources from a large number of separate police departments to respond to serious crimes.
2. The St. Louis County Police and Fire Training Academy supplies recruit training for all police and fire departments in the county.
3. Mutual aid agreements link all fire departments in the county and St. Louis City.
4. Joint dispatching arrangements are common among both police and fire departments.
5. The Regional Justice Information System (REJIS) links all police dispatchers in the city and county to a common data base for information related to crime and criminals. An area-wide 911 system operates through the county.
6. The Greater St. Louis Fire Chiefs' Association facilitates the sharing of specialized equipment among fire departments.
7. In public education:
   a) The Cooperating School Districts of the St. Louis Suburban Areas supply members with a large audiovisual collection and with joint purchasing of supplies and equipment.
   b) The Regional Consortium for Education and Technology supplies members with computer technology, software, training, and maintenance.

Source: Roger B. Parks & Ronald J. Oakerson, "St. Louis: The ACIR Study," Intergovernmental Perspective (Winter, 1989), 9–10.

an adequate tax base to provide municipal type services at anywhere near the quality offered in many of the municipalities.[42]

In his comparison of the freeholders' plan and the ACIR study, Donald Phares noted that the resource disparity between rich and poor municipalities, and between municipalities as a whole and the county has been worsened by "land grab annexation" and incorporation activity. "The most fiscally productive areas in unincorporated St. Louis County are literally being grabbed up," he observed, "while the less resource rich areas remained for the county to take care of as its diminishing resources allow."[43]

The freeholders recommended the creation of 37 new municipalities to cover the entire county. Some of these municipalities would consist of both formerly unincorporated areas and one or more existing cities. They would be consolidated into a larger new city. Although the freeholders' plan was supposed to come before a vote of all the residents of St. Louis County in the spring of 1989, legal action by individuals and organizations threatened by the plan successfully prevented the election.

There is no reason to believe, however, that had the election taken place it would have led to an overwhelming victory for the reorganization advocates. In 1926 a proposal to merge the city and county under a city government failed and since that time efforts to deal with the limited resources of the county have been defeated at the polls.[44]

The scholarly debate over consolidation or proliferation will not be decided in the near future in St. Louis, or in very many other metropolitan areas of the United States. Unless political actors with considerable resources and skill can be persuaded to act, as Kellogg did in Battle Creek, the real world debate will continue to be resolved in favor of proliferation.

We leave it up to you to decide whether the saturation point has been reached in your state and community and where to take it from there. We recommend that you take a close look at both of the studies conducted on St. Louis County as you prepare to make a positive contribution to the debate in your communities. Whether you come down on the side of proliferation or consolidation, or somewhere in between, it will be useful for you to know something about the dynamics that lead to the creation of additional units of government because those dynamics will continue to operate for a long, long time.

CONCLUSION

In addition to the seven reasons for the study of local government indicated in Chapter 1, it is worth noting that some top executives of corporate America have long expressed a concern with the effectiveness and efficiency of local government. This concern goes beyond decisions about where to locate new facilities. It involves an interest in the shape of the national pattern of local governance.

Restructuring efforts are underway in several states. As a result, it is very likely that sooner or later you will be asked to vote on or perhaps help promote state and local reforms that affect the number, the structure, and the powers of local governments. Therefore, it makes sense to prepare for informed discussion on remodeling, dismantling, or leaving as is.

We began this chapter by observing that 86,000 governments may be more than we need. While social, economic, and even political changes beyond the boundaries of any one state or community have created pressures for the establishment of more and more governments we have attempted to indicate that there are ways of slowing down the growth in numbers and even reducing the number of units of local government.

The thrust of our argument has been that the foundation document of a unit of government describes the government's source of authority and the limits established on what that government can and cannot do. In some states, general purpose governments such as the county are not allowed to deal with certain types of problems. If the problems are to be dealt with, then either these existing units will have to be given the authority or new ones created. We are suggesting that the former alternative—giving adequate power to existing units—may be a way to slow down the growth in the number of units of government and make local government a better servant of local communities. A logical place to begin the process of intergovernmental reduction is to examine the foundations of local governments, the power available to them, and the methods or procedures for altering, consolidating, or abolishing them.

In sum, it matters who runs our local governments. In the remaining chapters we will deal with ways to participate in state and local politics and either influence those who govern, or become one of those who govern. Local governments have great potential for problem solving. It remains to be seen whether our needs for local governance require us to create more governments or perhaps consolidate some of the units of government smaller in area than a county.

STUDY OBJECTIVES

1. Identify the reasons why we have local government.
2. Identify the major sources of authority for the local governments.
3. Identify the basic types of local government structure in terms of the legislative-executive dimension, and the chief executive-executive branch dimension.
4. Identify the major types of local government. Which type has decreased in numbers in the past 25 years? Which type has increased the most?
5. Identify reasons for creating new local governments.
6. Identify the steps in creating a special district.
7. Identify Dillon's Rule, and its relationship to home rule.
8. Identify the Virginia system of towns and cities.
9. Identify alternatives to the creation of new local governments.
10. Identify some of the reasons for merging existing governments or slowing the rate of creating new ones.

GLOSSARY

Annexation   The act of adding land to an existing unit of government, usually a municipality (or city). Since cities can not take land from one another, the only kind of land that can be annexed is unincorporated land. In some states it is very easy for cities to annex land, in others it is almost impossible.

Charters   Local constitutions, and are usually given to municipalities (or cities).

Defensive incorporation   The act of creating a new municipality to avoid annexation by a large one nearby.

Dillon's Rule   A principle of law that cities do not have implied powers, they can only do what is specifically granted by their charters.

Economies of Scale   Savings from consolidation and reduction in duplication that arise in any large enterprise whether it is a government or a business. At minimum, these savings occur first, from buying at wholesale rather than retail prices, and second, because one set of decision makers and procedures rather than several are involved in doing the buying or offering the service. Economies of scale have limits. They decline after a certain size is reached. This size varies from one type of service or function to another.

Exclusionary Zoning   The practice of passing land use regulations which make it very difficult to build high density, low cost housing of the sort that would enable people of modest means to live there.

General purpose government   A unit of government that offers a wide range of services and usually contains all three branches of government, although some may not perform judicial functions.

General rule cities Municipalities which do not have home rule. A contemporary term might be "generic cities." These are cities whose charters (or constitutions) all follow a pattern established by the state law or constitution.

Home rule Means that the citizens of a local government choose the charter of that government, and can amend or revise it without consulting the state legislature, or the state-wide electorate.

Municipality A unit of general purpose local government created to meet the needs of an urban population, a.k.a. a city.

Northwest Ordinance One of the last official acts of the Continental Congress. Passed in 1787, this law organized the lands ceded by several of the states to the confederation. These lands include the territory that now includes Ohio, Indiana, Illinois, Michigan, Wisconsin, and Minnesota.

Special purpose governments Governments that specialize in a limited number of services.

Unincorporated Area Land outside the boundaries of a municipality. In virtually all states the general purpose government responsible for unincorporated areas is the county, and in some states the township or both.

ENDNOTES

1. Patrick May, "Marina's Fans Make County Get Their Point," *Miami Herald,* May 15, 1994, 18A.

2. ACIR, *State and Local Roles in the Federal System,* (Advisory Committee on Intergovernmental Relations, 1982), 396, Updated in Joel Miller, "Annexation and Boundary Changes in the 1980s and 1990–91" in *The Municipal Year Book 1993* (Washington D.C.: International City/County Management Association), 107.

3. County legislatures in Texas are called Commissioners Courts, the term *Commission* is used for stylistic purposes. The events described occurred in May, 1994.

4. *Austin American Statesman,* May, 1994.

5. O. P. Williams, "Lifestyle Value and Political Decentralization in Metropolitan Areas," *Southwest Social Science Quarterly,* 1967, 48: 299–310.

6. Joel Miller, "Annexation and Boundary Changes in the 1980s and 1990–91," 106–107.

7. *1987 Census of Governments,* vol. 1, 221.

8. Ibid., 145–146.

9. *The Municipal Year Book 1993,* xiii.

10. For recent reexaminations of the virtues and shortcomings of appointed and elected chief executives see: *Public Management,* July, 1994, and *Publius,* April, 1994. Citations later.

11. Charles R. Adrian, "Forms of City Government in American History," in *The Municipal Year Book 1988* , (Washington, D.C.: International City Management Association, 1988), 9–10.

12. John C. Bollens, *Special District Governments in the United States* (Berkeley: University of California Press, 1957), 71.

13. Gilbertson, *The County: The "Dark Continent" of American Politics,* (New York: National Short Ballot Organization, 1917).

14. For the most recent thorough examination of county government in America, see David R. Berman, ed. *County Governments in an Era of Change* (Westport, CT: Greenwood Press, 1993).

15. David Thomas Konig, "English Legal Change and the Origins of Local Government in Northern Massachusetts," and Bruce C. Daniels, "The Political Structure of Local Government in Colonial Connecticut," in Bruce C. Daniels, ed. *Town and County* (Middletown, CT: Wesleyan University Press, 1978), 12–43, 44–71; and Edward Cooke, Jr., "Local Leadership and the Typology of New England Towns, 1700–1785," *Political Science Quarterly* (December, 1971), 586–608.

16. Joseph F. Zimmerman, *The Massachusetts Town Meeting, A Tenacious Institution* (Albany, NY: Graduate School of Public Affairs SUNY, 1967) 20, 30–35.

17. Ferris E. Lewis, *State and Local Government in Michigan, 8th ed.* (Hillsdale, MI: Hillsdale Educational Publishers, 1979), 127–140.

18. Cited in Robert Norwood, *Texas County Government: Let the People Choose* (Austin: Texas Research League, 1984), 46–47.

19. Ibid., 46.

20. John F. Dillon, *Commentaries on the Law of Municipal Corporations*, 5th ed. (Boston: Little, Brown & Co., 1911, vol. 1, see 237. Cited in Clyde F. Snider, Local Government in Rural America, (Westport, CT: Greenwood Press, 1957), 78.

21. Berman, *County Governments* 1993, 60.

22. Texas, with 254 counties, is one of these states. For a useful overview of the efforts to obtain home rule in Texas see Robert Norwood, *Texas County Government: Let the People Choose* (Austin: Texas Research League, 1984).

23. U. S. Bureau of the Census, *1992 Census of Governments. vol. 1: Government Organization* (Washington, D.C.: U. S. Government Printing Office,.1994).

24. *1987 Census of Governments, vol. 1, 22.*

25. Dave McNeely, "Bills Bottled Up On Construction Rules in Unincorporated Areas," *Austin American-Statesman*, May 5, 1985.

26. Virginia Marion Perrenod, *Special Districts, Special Purposes: Fringe Governments and Urban Problems in the Houston Area* (College Station: Texas A&M University Press, 1984), 44.

27. Bollens, *Special District Governments in the United States*, 66–71.

28. Terry Christiansen, *Local Politics: Governing at the Grassroots* (Belmont, CA: Wadsworth Publishing, 1995), 49.

29. Chester W. Bain, *A Body Incorporate: The Evolution of City-County Separation in Virginia* (Charlottesville: The University Press of Virginia, 1967), 37. Bain differentiates cities in terms of first class and second class, according to size. However, the *Municipal Yearbook* and common practice use the town-city distinction adopted in our brief overview. *1988 Municipal Yearbook*, 211, and James Campbell, Director of Intergovernmental Affairs, Virginia Municipal League, personal communication, December, 1988.

30. James Campbell, December, 1988.

31. Berkeley and Fox, or any reductionist text.

32. Committee on Economic Development, *Modernizing Local Government: to Secure a Balanced Federalism* (New York: Committee of Economic Development, 1966), 19.

33. Ibid., 67.

34. Joel C. Miller, "Municipal Annexation and Boundary Change," in *The Municipal Year Book 1994* (Washington, D.C.: International City/County Management Association), 105.

35. Bureau of the Census, *1987 Census of Governments, vol 1: Government Organization* (Washington, D.C.: U. S. Government Printing Office, 1988), vi.

36. For a brief and well-written case study of an ongoing battle for consolidation that keeps on failing, see Timothy D. Mead, "The Daily Newspaper as Political Agenda Setter: The Charlotte Observer and Metropolitan Reform," *State and Local Government Review.* 1994, 26:27–38.

37. Neal R. Pierce, "Kellogg to Battle Creek: Merge Governments or We Leave Town," *Today*, November 26, 1982, 5.

38. Interviews with Battle Creek City Manager, Rance L. Leader, and the City Manager at the time of the merger, Gorton Eager, November 10, 1989.

39. Pierce, "Kellogg to Battle Creek," 5.

40. Joel C. Miller, "Municipal Annexation and Boundary Change," 107.

41. Pierce, "Kellogg to Battle Creek," 5.

42. Donald Phares, "Reorganizing the St. Louis Area: The Freeholders Plan," *Intergovernmental Perspective* (Winter, 1989), 12–15.

43. Ibid., 1. See also: Donald Elliott, "Reconciling Perspectives on the St. Louis Metropolitan Area." *Intergovernmental Perspective* (Winter, 1989), 17–19.

44. Phares, "Reorganizing the St. Louis Area," 13.

CHAPTER

6

Political Participation Making the System Work: The Options

On a cool September morning several years ago, a stocky middle-aged man filled a 50-pound milk can with sewage that had floated downstream on the Fox River. He collected it near the outfall pipes of the U. S. Reduction Company's aluminum recycling plant in Aurora, Illinois.

That same afternoon, in East Chicago, Indiana, the man with the milk can entered the headquarters of the U. S. Reduction Company. After crossing the clean, tiled floor, he tipped the milk can and slowly emptied it near the reception desk. The contents, which had warmed and ripened somewhat since being collected that morning, oozed across the floor in an ever-spreading surface of stinking slime.

The man handed a note to a receptionist, one of the few who had yet to flee choking and gagging from the nauseating smell. Then the man with the milk can exited. The note he left behind demanded that the pollution of the river cease immediately.

The note was signed, "The Fox."[1]

THE FOX AND SIX FACTS ABOUT PARTICIPATION

The Fox is an appropriate character to begin our chapter on political participation. Too many people think politics is dirty and don't participate, so why not begin a chapter on participation right there in the muck? If, however, we get beyond what too many people think, and take a closer look at the Fox we find that he illustrates several facts about political participation that are worth serious consideration. We've identified at least six things for you to ponder as you decide on whether or not to participate, and if so, how.

AN INDIVIDUAL CAN ACT ALONE

Politics, by definition, involves more than one individual. Nevertheless, an ordinary individual acting alone can influence decision making in and outside of government.

The Fox did not bring about an immediate change in water quality in the Fox River. However, the Fox gained national publicity for the environmental movement and was featured in *Newsweek Magazine* for this and other acts such as dumping dead skunks on the front porches of the homes of executives whose companies pollute, and climbing smokestacks which annually dump tons of particles into the sky and sealing them off with home-made metal smokestack lids.

Individuals are the essential political actors. Each decision to participate or not is made by an individual. As you may recall from Chapter 1, the purpose of the Giraffe Project which provided the examples in Box 6.1 is to give recognition and publicity to individual acts of courage and integrity on behalf of others.[2] The motto of the organization is "Nobis es," which means "It's up to us."

Political Participation Involves a Wide Range of Activities

Pouring raw sewage on a corporate headquarters floor is not what most people have in mind when they think about political participation. We mention it, not to register approval, but to indicate that your imagination is about the only limit in terms of the methods used to participate in politics—your imagination *and* your sense of fair play. After all, the top-level decision makers at U. S. Reduction company weren't the individuals who had to mop up the mess in the reception room (and perhaps in the restrooms nearby). While it would have

---

BOX 6.1

A FEW INDIVIDUALS WHO'VE STUCK THEIR NECKS OUT

- Vickie Ceja, a mother of four, got tired of living on a muddy street so she organized her community and got the city to pave it. Getting results felt pretty good, so she kept on going. Now, as president of Metropolitan Organizations for People, she's leading her neighbors in working against polluted water and hazardous wastes—a serious problem in the Denver, Colorado, area.

- If you got mugged by a bunch of street kids, would you go to bat for them? Steve Mariotti did. He figured they were street-smart, tough, and independent—maybe they would do well in the business world, as he was. Eventually, after working part-time with the young entrepreneurs and going to work full-time, Mariotti quit his business altogether and now teaches teens in New York City public schools to be entrepreneurs; his students have started 45 new legitimate, profit-making companies.

- Ray Profitt of Delaware is known as "the river vigilante." A former test pilot and stockbroker, he has appointed himself protector of the Delaware River and its tributaries. He cruises the waterways to spot violations of state and local ordinances such as untreated sewage outfall, a new unregistered drainpipe pouring out industrial waste, dumping in the marshlands than run along a nearby highway. He traces the pollution to the source, lets the offender know that he has photographed and documented the violation and that he is prepared to take the violator to court if the mess isn't cleaned up. His success in court has led to lots of scrambling into compliance with the laws. So far he has a perfect record.

Sources: *Giraffe Broadcasting Service,* "Giraffe Spot #128," "Giraffe Spot #145," *and* The Giraffe Gazette (Spring, 1988) 1–3.

been more appropriate, had the Fox picked on a major polluter, the facts about U. S. Reduction were not the major feature of the *Newsweek* story, the activities of the Fox were. Box 6.2 just touches a few of the possibilities.

BOX 6.2

A PLETHORA OF PARTICIPATION OPTIONS

Writing a letter

Sending an e-mail message on the internet

Making a phone call

Organizing the production of dozens, hundreds, thousands of the above

Handing out literature

Typing envelopes

Stuffing envelopes

Helping someone figure out how to use a computer to do print merge or mail merge, or doing it for them

Joining a political party or an interest group

Founding a political party or an interest group

Attending a meeting of (an interest group, a political party, a candidate selection committee)

Walking a neighborhood door-to-door to hand out literature, to register voters, to get signatures on a petition

Tending a cardtable or booth in a public place where literature is distributed, contributions are collected, or petitions are signed

Baby-sitting for someone so they can participate

Organizing a group of baby-sitters for one or more fellow workers

Providing transportation for voters, for people walking neighborhoods door-to-door, or for fellow workers

Putting up yard signs

Assembling yard signs for someone else to put up

Delivering speeches

Writing speeches

Photocopying and mailing speeches

Running for office

Recruiting people to run for office

Organizing meetings

Reporting violations of rules to policemen, pollution control agencies, better business bureaus, election commissions, newspapers

Giving a party to let a candidate meet potential campaign workers or contributors

Negotiating a compromise between two individuals; or groups

Organizing contributions to pay for a newspaper ad, a radio spot, or a television spot; writing a newspaper ad, or a radio spot; or a television spot

Writing an article about or taking a picture of: tragedies, victories, violations, community problems, things to be rewarded, things to be stopped

Testifying before a committee, a commission or council

Attending a council meeting

Doing library research on a public issue

Expressing an opinion or providing information to: a decision-maker who is a government official; a voter, friend, or staff member of a government decision maker, a decision-maker outside of government (such as a party leader), a newspaper editor, or reporter, an interest group leader or member

You Can Lose Your Battles and Win the War

The Fox was unsuccessful in getting an immediate end to the pollution of the Fox River and had little direct impact on the U. S. Reduction Company. Thus, he lost his battle. However, he probably helped in the winning of a larger war. He helped to draw state and national attention to the Fox River and to environmental problems elsewhere. Eventually, state and federal officials took notice of the problem and efforts were made to clean up the river. Today, there are waterskiing contests on the Fox River.[3]

Although we can grant The Fox a long-run victory, a more important thing to keep in perspective about losing in the short run is that each political battle is often part of a larger war. Even when your side loses a battle, you have influenced your opposition in at least three important ways that will help win the war.

First, you have forced them to use political resources—they have had to make promises, expend funds, use time and energy dealing with you that might have been invested elsewhere.

Second, by fighting and losing you've also made the opposition think about the price of making you unhappy next time. Next time, they may negotiate.

Third, you have required the opposition to go on record for or against something. By making them go public, the opposition's behavior may come to the attention of others who agree with you, perhaps even a group of individuals who are already organized. Those individuals or that group may be allies in the next battle. In short, you have made the issue more salient.

Unless you bring a matter up, place it on the public agenda, power-holders don't have to establish a public record on an issue (see Box 6.3). They can quietly do it their way. Simply by making the opposition take a position, as Robert Dahl points out, you have acquired valuable information about what they really want.

BOX 6.3

MYTHS WITH SPECIAL MEANINGS. THE CONSEQUENCES OF BELIEVING THAT YOU CAN'T FIGHT CITY HALL

If power holders can convince you that participation is hopeless because you cannot win, then they are winning three battles, not just one.

1. They get their way.
2. They get to economize on the use of their political resources.
3. They don't have to take public action against a reasonable request.

In short, they win, cheaply, and quietly. Remember:
YOU CAN FIGHT CITY HALL, BUT IT HELPS IF YOU KNOW WHERE IT IS.

Political Participation Eventually Touches Government, Directly or Indirectly

If, as we noted in Chapter 1, public life involves participation in our communities however narrowly or broadly we define them, then political participation is a type of public life. Political participation can be defined as any activity which, like the Fox's, attempts to influence decisions on public issues. Eventually, political participation deals with decisions by people who are employees of, appointees to, or elected officials of government—national, state, or local. Implicit in most definitions of political participation is the notion that "attempts to influence" eventually affect government.[4]

An interesting thing about individual acts of participation is that they not only touch government but they often lead to the mobilization of many other people who were there, sort of waiting for an individual spark to ignite them as Candy Lightner's experience indicates (Box 6.4).

BOX 6.4

INDIVIDUALS WHO TAKE ACTION MAY START OUT ALONE—BUT THEY SELDOM END UP THAT WAY

Candy Lightner mobilized thousands of parents, many of whom had lost loved ones in accidents involving drunk drivers. Ms. Lightner's 13-year-old daughter, Cari, was killed in an accident caused by a frequently arrested but seldom punished drunk driver. Ms. Lightner dealt with her grief, in part, by creating Mothers Against Drunk Drivers (MADD) and soon heard from hundreds of parents who had had a child killed or permanently handicapped by a drunk driver.

There are now over 300 chapters in over 40 states. Recent victories include the enactment of laws in several states against possessing open alcoholic beverage containers in vehicles and for mandatory jail time for drunk drivers. Nineteen states have enacted statutes that take away the cars, license plates, or registrations of drunk drivers. In 1993 an Ohio law empowered state officials to confiscate a drunk driver's car and have it crushed.

Just as important as changes in the law are changes in attitude. "We're seeing *Fortune 500* companies providing taxi service for employees who had too much to drink at office parties," Ms. Lightner reports. Citizens with car phones are now provided with special 800 numbers to report suspected drunk drivers, and they are being put to use.

Attitude changes, laws, and stricter enforcement have led to a 32 percent reduction in deaths from drunk driving in a decade. However, the carnage is still too high. In 1992 there were 11,358 deaths resulting from drunk-driving accidents.

Sources: Ellen Perlman, "Moving Toward None for the Road," Governing (September, 1994), 25–26; Time, January 7, 1985, 41; and People, July 9, 1989, 102.

Political Participation Can Be a Meaningful Experience

It sounds kind of silly to say something like, "dumping raw sewage can be a lot of fun." But for the Fox it must have been so. The adrenaline flow of adventure, the glee of sticking it to the smug, the satisfaction of at least "doing something" about an important problem—these are rich sources of enjoyment.

Sewage redistribution is not high on our own personal lists of political activities. It is mentioned as evidence that some pretty far out activities can be considered political participation. Thus, there are many possibilities for finding enjoyment in politics, including meeting Mr. or Ms. Right.

Enjoyment is not always the first thing that comes to mind in identifying emotions associated with political participation. Candy Lightener found a way to deal with grief as have mothers in several states whose children have been killed or permanently disabled by other children in homes where gun owners left loaded weapons available.

Because of the activities of Candy Lightener, alcohol is now used more responsibly in most states and fewer people will die because of drunk drivers than would otherwise. Because of the publicity associated with efforts to pass gun ownership responsibility legislation, it is likely that fewer children will kill children in at least three states.

Participation Can Change the Political System for Better or for Worse

Because your battles are part of larger wars and because all political contests take place within a framework of rules and customs, it is a good idea to keep in mind that what you do in your current battles can affect not only your credibility and your chances of making alliances and achieving success in the battles to come. Your behavior also affects the political system itself.

We point this out at the risk of some redundancy because we've seen leaders who failed to impress their own values of fair play and common sense upon less informed followers. (Our premise, you may recall, is that you are a future leader, thus we assume you will have this opportunity.)

If you keep in mind the notion that the less people know about politics the less respect they have for it, you will appreciate the fact that it is the beginners who break the rules more often than the experienced political actives. Naturally, when leaders break the rules they get lots of unwelcome publicity. However, local political arenas are littered with the mistakes of amateur zealots who believe political activity to be something dirty and behave that way.

The Fox, depending upon your point of view, may be a zealot or a folkhero. The point here is not to judge him, but to point out that political systems can be seen as fragile environments that can be poisoned for a long time by what we do now. Hence the concern today about the apparent decline in civility at national if not state level politics.

The Fox broke some rules and made life unpleasant for the innocent as well as the guilty. On the state and national scene The Fox may be remembered as a hero among environmentalists for bringing discomfort to the polluters, and publicity to their cause.

On the local scene, however, he may have done as much harm as good to the prospects for communication, compromise, and constructive action. As an outdoorsman and nature lover The Fox, doubtless, understands the importance of preserving fragile systems and would not approve of fishing with dynamite sticks any more than most members of the Right-to-Life movement approve of murdering physicians and receptionists in abortion clinics.

As an environmental activist, The Fox, would be chagrined to learn, if he did not know already, that the U. S. Reduction Company was involved in an environmentally constructive business, the recycling of aluminum scrap.[5] The company claims that the only thing that the outfall pipe dumped into the Fox River was warm water from the non-contact pipes of the cooling system. Thus, it is very likely that the pollution The Fox collected came downstream to the outfall pipes, not from them. Whether the pipes were polluted or not, the fact remains that the Fox's mess on the floor was cleaned up by custodians who had nothing to do with corporate decision making.

To briefly summarize, The Fox has helped us to point out six things about political participation:

- Individuals can do it alone.
- It can involve innovation and creativity.
- It eventually involves one or more governments.
- Even when battles are lost, the effort put forth can contribute to the winning of a larger war.
- Political participation can be fulfilling, sometimes even fun.
- It has consequences for the environment in which it takes place.

PARTICIPATION: CONVENTIONAL AND UNCONVENTIONAL

Many observers divide participation activities into two types: conventional and unconventional. The Fox's was clearly unconventional while the activities of many people mentioned above such as Candy Lightener who founded MADD, or Vicki Ceja who founded Metropolitan Organizations for People, were more conventional—such as creating an organization to lobby state and city officals.

The problem with the conventional—unconventional distinction is that marches and demonstrations might be examples of inappropriate behavior in one community while in another they are almost passé.[6] Whether we call them traditional, or conventional, or essential, there are some strategies with which we must become familiar in order to begin to understand how the political system works. Despite minor differences from one set of categories to the next, political scientists mainly agree upon most of the conventional strategies for political participation. Besides being a subject matter upon which political scientists have produced a great deal of literature, conventional participation has immense practical virtue. Without it, unconventional participation is seldom effective.

Saul Alinsky, author of *Rules for Radicals* and *Reveille for Radicals*, is both an inventor of ways to influence decision makers and a great respecter of the need to organize, to do one's homework, and to understand the rules of the game. He regards this as necessary so that one can gain ground via conventional participation after the explosions of unconventional participation have cratered the mental landscape of the establishment. During the violence outside the 1968 Democratic Convention in Chicago where police and the National Guard personnel bashed antiwar demonstrators, his response to students who asked him if he still believed in working within the system was classic Alinsky:

Do one of three things. One, go find a wailing wall and feel sorry for yourselves. Two, go psycho and start bombing—but this will only swing people to the right. Three, learn a lesson. Go home, organize, build power and at the next convention, you be the delegates."[7]

The political system probably needs a few Foxes every now and then, but it needs more Saul Alinskys and many more people willing to do their homework to make the system responsive and responsible.

After a dramatic event has focused attention on the issue, somebody has to draft a bill and get a legislator to introduce it, then guide it through the legislative committees and through both houses, and then get it enforced. Before all that can happen, it may even be necessary to nominate and elect some somebodies to do that.[8] Although participation is good, informed participation is even more effective.

CONVENTIONAL PARTICIPATION STRATEGIES

Political strategies combine and point an almost infinite number of political activities toward a political goal. The strategy an individual or an organization chooses will depend upon the type of decision to be influenced. For example, influencing an appointment to the State Supreme Court involves different tactics and techniques than those involved in getting a bill passed in—or a candidate elected to—the state legislature.

Seven of the most well known strategies are: **lobbying, grassroots lobbying, attendance at public hearings, demonstrating, appointmenteering, litigation,** and **electioneering**. Organizations such as political parties and interest groups use these strategies. Individuals acting independently can use them as well. Even when organizations act, they do so through individuals—their leaders, spokespersons, chairpersons, lobbyists, and sometimes ordinary members.

Lobbying

Lobbying is a term, that can be defined to embrace a number of activities. As Box 6.5 suggests, the word *lobby* is a much misunderstood and misused term.

We define lobbying as any activity involving personal communication with a decision maker that is intended to influence a decision on a public issue.

Thus, writing a letter, sending a telegram, making a personal visit to the office of the decision maker, and talking to a decision maker about your issue at a social gathering are all lobbying activities.

Rationale

Since lobbying involves a higher investment of political resources than does responding to a public opinion poll taker or voting, decision makers pay more attention to it. Those willing to lobby are likely to be willing to work for another candidate if lobbying doesn't work. Thus, the number and types of individuals involved in lobbying are sometimes used as a measure of the intensity as well as the direction of public opinion.

Lobbying serves the decision maker as a source of information about the political environment. It also brings other kinds of information: technical, legal, economic, and even ethical, that may not otherwise be readily available to decision makers. In recent years the

BOX 6.5

THE MANY MEANINGS OF LOBBY

1. Verb. To attempt to influence a decision on a public issue by personally contacting a decision maker.

   "Mr. Councilman, don't vote for the ordinance on leashing dogs," barked A. Jones over the phone.

   "I won't fence with you, Mr. Jones," replied the Councilman, bitingly. "I'm tired of stepping into things without any warning. I'll make my decision after I read the staff report."

2. Verb. Any method of attempting to influence a decision of government.

   "Now rub this magic lantern," said the Elf, "and the city council will grant your wish."

   "Are you sure this is lobbying?" asked Charles Credulously.

   "Would a person with ears like mine lie to you?" the Elf asked, pointedly.

3. Verb. To attempt to influence any decision.

   Item: Fenwick lobbied his father for a new sports car.

   "Please, Daddy, all my friends have one."

   "Not until you floss more regularly," said his father.

   "Aw, gee, Dad," said Fenwick, "you are really mean."

   "That's tough-love, Son," said his father. "By the way, what color would you like?"

4. Noun. A collection of well-financed organizations or well-dressed individuals representing them.

   News Item: The Lobby won a major victory today when the legislature voted not to limit the amount of money a political action committee (PAC) can contribute to a candidate for public office. Common Cause, the organization which supported the limitations, got no support from any legislator up for reelection.

   "Golly, the legislature sure is mean," said Fred Frosted, a spokesperson for Common Cause.

   "That's tough," said Bubba Stud, a lobbyist for Nasty Chemical Corporation.

5. Noun. All organizations that try to influence decisions by government.

   "The Lobby sure is confusing." said Melvin Generalization, sweepingly. "I can never tell what it wants government to do."

6. Noun (archaic). A waiting area, antechamber, or passageway leading from a meeting room to the rest of a building.

   "You get the tickets, Sue, while I park the car. No sense in this precipitation moisturizing both our apparel," said Maxwell Savecoin dryly. "I'll meet you in the lobby."

   "Golly, Max," said Sue Knot brightly, "you sure know a lot of big words."

7. Noun (fictional). A part of the abdomen between the foyer and the vestibule.

   News Item: The popcorn thief surrendered after a quick-witted usher hit him in the lobby.

   "I figured I might hurt my hand, if I hit him in the teeth," explained the usher.

BOX 6.6

LOBBYIST CAN BE DIVIDED INTO FIVE MAJOR CATEGORIES

Contract Lobbyists: Those hired on contract for a fee specifically to lobby. They may represent more than one client.

In-House Lobbyists: Employees of an organization, association, or business who are part-time or full-time lobbyists. They represent only one client—their employer.

Government Lobbyists or Legislative Liaisons: Employees of state, local, and federal agencies who as part or all of their jobs represent their agencies to the legislative and executive branches of state government.

Citizen or Volunteer Lobbyists: Persons who, usually on an ad hoc and unpaid basis, represent citizens and community organizations or informal groups. They rarely represent more than one interest at a time.

Private Individual "Hobbyists" or Self-Styled Lobbyists: Those acting on their own behalf and not designated by any organization as an official representative.

Source: Ronald J. Hrebenar and Clive S. Thomas, eds., Interest Group Politics in the Midwestern States (*Ames, Iowa: Iowa University Press, 1993*), 11.

---

number of lobbyists has grown rapidly. According to Hrebenar and Thomas, there are five major types of lobbyists as we see in Box 6.6

Attendance at Public Hearings

Public hearings are essential and often overlooked opportunities for participation. A public hearing is an official meeting held by a decision-making body to gather information about a problem, or a proposed course of action.

Legislatures at all levels (county, city, school district, or state) hold public hearings as do many state and local administrative agencies. Decision makers may not do exactly what participants in those hearings want them to, but the decision-making process is usually influenced by the testimony presented. Each source, professional lobbyists, experts, and ordinary citizens, is important in its own way.

Part of the skill of lobbying is being able to find out when and where public hearings on one's topics of interest will take place. While notices of public hearings are often published in the newspaper, people active in politics often contact public officials to find out if any hearings are planned on matters of interest to them, and to get on the mailing list of those who obtain advance notice.

Rationale

Not only does attending a public hearing give one the opportunity to express opinions and influence public officials, it also gives one the opportunity to see what the opposition is up to, and to get informal feedback as to the reactions of public officials to you and to the opposition. At the local level, many decisions can be influenced by what goes on at the public hearing before the School Board, or the City Council, or the County Commissioners Court.

Grassroots Lobbying

Grassroots lobbying involves attempting to get others to act, to lobby. It is sometimes called public relations work. Grassroots lobbying is a strategy directed toward increasing the direction of opinions, the number of people aware of an issue, and the intensity of opinion among those who agree with the position for which one is lobbying. It has two dimensions: long-term and short-term.

Short-term grassroots lobbying is action oriented. It attempts to get other people to act very soon, if not immediately. "Mail your message today!

The long-term dimension seldom involves calls for action. It is basically a public relations exercise. Long-term grassroots lobbying often uses advertisements in the mass media to promote the notion that some individual or group is trustworthy and legitimate. Long-term grassroots lobbying is sometimes referred to as "the bank account approach."

By investing in a bank account of goodwill among the general public, an individual or group may be able to make withdrawals later on. A good reputation (credibility, public image) for an individual or a group is a political resource. Organizations can enhance their public image by advertising meaningless "feel good" slogans or by actually doing something altruistic. Individuals can also enhance their reputations though volunteer and charity work.

It goes without saying that community public service is a good thing in and of itself. However, the practical benefits may not be so obvious. When individuals with a bank account of goodwill eventually become involved in a public issue they start out with a little more credibility than those who were too busy to do public service work. Furthermore, those who do volunteer have a lot more personal contact with those who make decisions in that community because they were probably also volunteers.

Rationale

Grassroots lobbying is important because decision makers are accustomed to being contacted by professional lobbyists. However, they are often quite impressed when an ordinary individual takes the time and trouble to contact them about an issue. Because contacts from ordinary individuals are not as common as contacts by professional lobbyists, decision makers often give these contacts from folks "at the grassroots" a little extra weight.

Well-financed interest groups and their professional lobbyists use direct mail and mass media campaigns to encourage ordinary folk to contact public officials. Not all decision makers have become so sophisticated that they disregard hundreds or thousands of letters or cards that say exactly the same thing. If these items were mailed from different addresses by different individuals, even though the cause was a computerized direct mail campaign, the fact that these individuals took the time to put those items in the mail says something about their opinion on the issue.

Two Messages

Grassroots lobbying usually sends two messages to decision makers. The first message is the content, the overtly expressed message. The second message is indirect. Nevertheless, it is just as significant. The indirect message says, "Hey, look at all the people we can get to contact you. Would you like them for or against you in your next election?"

Regardless of the level at which you operate as an individual, you can multiply the weight of your political opinions by bringing along a few friends or encouraging them to contact public officials themselves. When local legislative bodies, for example, find their sometimes empty chambers filled with people concerned with an issue, they have been known to pay extra close attention. Some members may even change their position on an issue in the presence of a significant number of citizens who cared intensely enough (or were mobilized by you) to show up.

Demonstrating

A demonstration is an activity designed to get attention for a cause. It is a symbolic act. Marches, picket lines, sit-ins, or building a shanty on campus are all demonstrations. A picketline may act as a fence to keep workers or supplies out, but it is a symbolic fence.

Since the Boston Tea Party, demonstrations have been part of the American political scene. Attempting to influence decisions by means of attention-getting behavior has become such a frequently used technique that it can probably be considered a conventional form of participation.

Rationale

A demonstration is a tactic with at least one of the following goals: either to increase the number of people aware of an issue or to provide decision makers with evidence of the intensity of opinion on an issue.

The Fox's demonstration helped bring attention to the environmental issue and thus increased the size of the issue public. A march or sit-in helps to indicate the size of the issue public, and the intensity of feeling on the issue.

Individuals or groups that demonstrate are usually short on political resources such as money or prestige. If they had more money they could buy media time. If they had more

In St. Paul, Minnesota, the actual car involved in a drunk-driving accident is placed on a billboard. Mothers Against Drunk Drivers raised the funds to pay for this effort to increase the size of an issue public.

prestige they could get an extended period of time to spend with a decision maker. Sometimes, however, even prestigious figures use demonstration as a tactic to bring attention to an issue.

Risk

Demonstrations can be illegal or legal. Either way, the individual or organization that chooses this strategy takes a risk. If things get out of hand it can make the demonstrators and the cause look dumb, selfish, or even nasty. The Million Man March on Washington, D. C., involved great risk and careful organization.

Greater risks are taken when a group decides to engage in illegal demonstrations. It works sometimes, but only if conditions are right.

Civil Disobedience or Illegal Demonstration

In most states and communities the law requires that in the interests of public safety a parade permit be applied for before marches, parades, or mass demonstrations take place. They have laws dealing with trespass and damage to private property. They may also have other laws that you may regard as wrong.

To demonstrate against the laws one regards as wrong one must usually get permission to do so from the appropriate authorities. Sometimes the authorities may not cooperate. Organizers of demonstrations thus face the choice of not demonstrating at all or demonstrating illegally. The decision to disobey the rules in order to bring attention to one's cause is not an easy one to make.

Civil Disobedience: Conditions for Success

Civil disobedience is a special kind of demonstration. It can be differentiated from demonstrations involving screaming and shouting or violence by the participants by the fact that it is *civil*. Civil disobedience may produce uncivil behavior by spectators or counterdemonstrators but the group seeking to bring favorable publicity to its cause remains disciplined and peaceful. Civil disobedience may break a law, but it doesn't break anything else. A group is likely to be successful in bringing public attention and sympathy to its cause via civil disobedience if all of the following conditions are met:

1. The cause is one perceived by the general public as just. If the law one is breaking conflicts with the basic principles of the larger society, then it makes sense to make the general public aware of this difference. In other words, create a larger issue public. Civil rights demonstrators who sat in at segregated lunch counters during the 1960s were breaking laws that conflicted with the principle of equality, a value supported by the larger society.

2. The public can be made aware of one's actions. If the media is not present, the message is unlikely to get to many people. The media may be somewhere else, reporting other events. That is why one takes a chance with demonstrations, legal or illegal. In short, civil disobedience (as well as uncivil demonstrations) work best on a slow news day when plenty of reporters and camera crews are available.

3. Civil disobedience is most likely to be successful if there is a simple, acceptable remedy. Passing laws prohibiting discrimination were actions that decision makers could take. On the other hand, a demonstration against sickness or against poverty is much less likely to

have immediate effects than one in favor of a particular antipoverty program or a specific bill to fund medical research.

4. The people engaged in civil disobedience are willing to take the consequences of their action. Individual members who hit back, who resist arrest, or violently refuse to be carried away in a police van, are very likely to damage rather than help their cause. The key to successful civil disobedience is passive resistance, whether the demonstration is legal or illegal.

Demonstrators who refuse to take their lumps either don't understand why civil disobedience was chosen as a tactic, or are really attempting to use a different tactic such as rioting or hand-to-hand combat.

Appointmenteering

Appointmenteering is any activity intended to influence political appointments. Many nonelective positions in government are filled by following civil service regulations and procedures. Many, however, are filled by a process of recruitment and selection that is neither systematic nor well publicized.

The term appointmenteering is used to emphasize the fact that there are many appointed positions in state and local government that have a great deal of influence in the political economy and in the wider society. Thus, it matters who gets appointed to the civil service commission or the Zoning Board.

Many of the appointed positions in state and local government involve making decisions that affect other people's income. The local planning and zoning commissioners sometimes make decisions that affect the opportunities for developers to get very rich, or just moderately rich, and may even encourage them to look elsewhere for land to develop. Textbook selection committee members on state or local school boards make decisions that affect the income of not only local publisher's representatives but of whole publishing companies.

Appointmenteering involves most of the same elements that lobbying does, bringing facts and opinions to the attention of decision makers. In this context facts about the record and the qualifications of people you support or oppose are most relevant. Another way to influence appointments is to volunteer to be appointed.

Local governments use lots of volunteer time and talent on various boards and commissions. In many communities the pool of volunteers is rather small. In order to make yourself available, all you need to do is contact a unit of local government to find out which boards and commissions are of interest to you. Then submit your name to the county clerk, city secretary, or the secretary to the superintendent of the schools. In most communities you will find boards or commissions that deal with: the library (an important board to be on if you wish to help prevent censorship or book burning) planning, (land use, transportation, and social services are a few of the things for which there may be specialized planning commissions) zoning (an important board which attempts to separate family style residences from a wide range of other kinds of land use including industrial and commercial while at the same time promoting the most efficient use of land)—as well as a civil service commission, a commission on human rights, a charter review commission, an airport commission, and a variety of commissions created to meet local needs. See Box 6.7 for a list of commissions found in a typical medium-sized city.

BOX 6.7

BOARDS AND COMMISSIONS IN A MEDIUM-SIZED CITY

Airport Commission

Building Code Board of Adjustments and Appeals

Cemetery Commission

Charter Review Commission

City-County Joint Airport Zoning Board

Citizen's Storm Drainage Advisory Board

Civil Service Commission

Commission for Minorities

Commission for Women

Convention Center City-County Task Force

Electric Utility Board

Emergency Medical Service Committee

Ethics Review Commission

Examining Board of Heating and Air Conditioning Contractors

Fair Housing Commission

Historic Preservation Commission

Housing Authority Board

Human Services Agency Board

Industrial Development Cooperation Board

Library Board

Main Street Advisory Board

Mayor's Conservation Committee

Minority Business Enterprise Committee

Municipal Electrical Utility Board

Parks and Recreation Board

Personnel Appeals Board

Planning & Zoning Commission

Plumbing Boards of Adjustments and Appeals

Public Transportation Committee

Senior Citizen's Advisory Board

Sunset Advisory Commission

Tourist Development Council

Zoning Board of Adjustments and Appeals

Source: City Secretary, San Marcos, Texas, (November, 1989).

Electioneering

Electioneering is any activity directed toward influencing electoral decisions by individuals eligible to vote.

At least three different decisions are subject to influence: (1) the decision on whether or not to register, (2) the decision on whether or not to vote, (3) and the decision of how to vote on each item on the ballot. In addition to influencing the voting decision, many electioneering activities also attempt to persuade people to help in the election campaign by contributing money or time or other resources.

Registration

To prevent voting fraud, most democracies require some form of registration but most do it automatically without requiring action by the individual. In this country, the 1993 National Voting Registration Act made it easier to register in those states that had not yet liberalized their voting requirements.

Regardless of the ease of registration, in nearly every state one must re-register to vote if his or her residence has changed since the last election.

Since in any five-year-period almost 50 percent of the American population has changed residence, this means that in any election year several million Americans who failed to reregister have become ineligible to vote.[9] Therefore, one way to promote voting is to promote registering. Thus, drives are an important part of any election campaign.

Voting

Campaigning is critical to voting turnout. The major effort in an election campaign is to bring the election or referendum to the attention of the eligible voters, to convince them that they ought to act. Most campaigns spend a fair amount of money finding out where their supporters are, and then concentrating on getting them to vote. If all the votes in a geographic area are for the other candidate, then not much campaigning will be done there. Contrary to popular opinion, there is much more effort directed toward finding and motivating one's supporters than there is in attempting to convert the followers of the opposition.

Litigation

Litigation is the act of using the court system to influence decisions. In Chapter 13 we will discuss the state and local court systems, but for now we simply suggest that ordinary people can use the legal system sometimes at relatively low cost.

In most cities certain law firms which will take on a few cases involving the public interest at low fees or no fees. They get good publicity if they win. In most states there is also an organization which specializes in giving legal aid to those who cannot afford regular attorney's fees. *Cannot afford*, is a flexible term which can be better defined by contacting your state or local legal aid society.

Using the courts does not mean that you need to accuse someone of a crime or sue them for damages. You may simply ask the judge to issue an order (a writ) that tells someone to stop doing something (writ of injunction) or that tells a public official to do something they should do anyway (writ of mandamus). If the court issues a writ, then the person who refuses to do what it says is in contempt of court. At that point, the behavior of this individual becomes a government matter and you have just acquired an important ally in your effort—the court itself.

In most states there are also small claims courts and justice of the peace Courts which operate without attorneys. If you have a problem that is not likely to be solved by contacting the legislative or executive branches of government keep in mind the fact that the legal system is there for people who can't afford $150 an hour attorney fees, as well as for people who can.

WHO PARTICIPATES?

Nearly every conceivable type of person can and does participate in politics. However, some categories of people participate more than others. To put it another way, there seems to be a considerable amount of unmobilized resources in the American political system. For example, Table 6.1 indicates the difference in voting rates of over 30 percent between those with a college education and those with less than a junior high school education.

While many types of people vote, not nearly as many people get more involved than that. The portion of the general public that is considered to be active is rather small. Milbraith's classic categories of apathetics, spectators, and gladiators is useful still.[10] He considers about one-third of the American adult population to be politically apathetic or passive; in most cases they are unaware, literally, of the political part of the world around them. Another 60 percent play largely spectator roles; they watch, they cheer, they vote, but they do not do battle. The percentage of gladiators, those who are active in working together to solve problems, organizing or regularly attending meetings and serving on local boards and commissions, does not exceed 5 to 7 percent.

Table 6.1

RATE OF VOTING PARTICIPATION AMONG SELECTED CATEGORIES OF AMERICANS IN PRESIDENTIAL ELECTIONS

United States	1988	1992
Total voting age	178 million	186 million
Percent voted	57	61.3

Percentage Voting by Category

Category	1988	1992
Male	56.4	60.2
Female	58.3	62.3
White	59.3	63.6
Black	51.5	54.0
Hispanic surname	28.8	28.9
Age 18–24	36.2	42.8
Age 45–64	67.9	70.0

Education

	1988	1992
8 years or less	36.7	35.1
9–11 years	41.3	41.2
12 years	54.7	57.5
More than 12 years	70.7	68.7

Source: U. S. Bureau of the Census, Current Population Reports: Voting and Registration in the Election of 1992 (Washington, D.C.: U. S. Government Printing Office, 1993).

In order to understand why some individuals participate more than others, it is necessary to deal with three related concepts: opportunity cost or resource investment, the notion that political participation is hierarchical, and the notion that it is cumulative.

The Resource Investment or Opportunity Cost

An activity can be looked at in terms of the political resources that one invests in a political activity or, secondly, it can be seen as political resources used or given up to engage in a political activity. From the first perspective, time spent on a political activity is time invested in building one's community, in good government, in goals one hopes to achieve through electoral victory, or self satisfaction because one has done one's civic duty. From the second perspective, time spent voting or engaging in any political activity is time given up that might have been used to do other things.

Whether or not one engages in political participation has a great deal to do with whether one sees it as an investment or a cost. Furthermore, just as political resources are unequally distributed in any society, so are opportunity costs, Thus, for a night shift worker attending an evening city council meeting means wages lost, while for a daytime worker, it simply means recreational opportunities forgone.

While the cost of or investment in the same activity may have different meanings for different people most activities can be measured in terms of the amount of time involved, the amount of money involved, or the degree of effort.

A Hierarchy of Activities

Table 6.2 slightly overstates the degree to which Americans engage in political activities. After examining the results from a survey of 15,000 people who were questioned about participation, the researchers constructed a smaller sample of 2,517 people which overrepresented activists. Thus, 70 percent of the people in Table 6.5 voted in the presidential election of 1988, whereas in that year the national rate was 57.9 percent of the voting age population.

It levies no great tax on your mental equipment to figure out from Table 6.2 that some activities presented there require a greater investment of time, energy, and other political resources than others. Whether we think of the resources involved in terms of an investment or a cost, activities at the top of the list require more than those at the bottom. Thus, political participation is hierarchical because political activities can be arranged in a hierarchy according to increasing opportunity costs or resource investment.

This hierarchy of activities also indicates that decreasing percentages of the population engage in high investment activities. It is important to note the difference between a hierarchy of activities in which people from all walks of life participate, and a hierarchy of people according to socio-economic status (SES). The first is a ranking of activities in terms of resource investment. The second is a ranking of individuals in terms of their wealth, the status of their occupations, and the amount of formal education they have.

Accumulating Activities

Political participation is also cumulative in that people who participate in activities involving high opportunity costs usually participate in lower cost activities as well. Political participation is cumulative, or additive. The opposite principle would be that of exchange or substitution. As people moved from low cost to high cost activities, they would stop doing the

Table 6.2

A HIERARCHY OF POLITICAL ACTIVITIES

Activity	Percentage
Serving on a local governing board or regularly attending meetings of that board	3
Attending a protest, march or demonstration in past two years	6
Working in a political campaign in past two years	8
Contributing money to a party or candidate	25
Working informally with others to solve a community problem	25
Contacted a public official	35
Voted in last presidential election	70

Source: Sidney Verba, Kay Lehman Schlozman, Henry Brady, and Norman H. Nie, "Citizen Activity: Who participates? What Do They Say?" American Political Science Review, 87:2 (June, 1993), 316.

former. In politics, however, people add on activities, instead of replacing one type with another. Candidates for governor still remember to vote and have been known to express an opinion about politics now and then.

In short, when we say that political participation is hierarchical and cumulative we mean that:

- We are ranking *activities*, not people.
- Activities can be arranged in a hierarchy of increasing opportunity costs, or declining numbers of participants.
- People participating in high opportunity cost activities such as running for office, are also likely to participate in lower cost activities such as voting in presidential elections.

The notion that participation is hierarchical and cumulative is a useful generalization that is accurate most of the time. However, Verba and Nie provide ample evidence that it is not accurate all of the time.

The Verba-Nie Typology of Participants

Verba and Nie analyzed data gathered from interviews with a sample of over 3,000 adult Americans concerning their involvement in four basic modes of political activity: voting, campaigning, communal participation, and personal contacting of public officials. Using statistical techniques they looked for patterns of individual participation and identified six basic types of political participants.

1. The Inactives (22 percent)

This group corresponds to Milbraith's apathetics. Members of this category seldom vote and rarely engage in any other political activities.

2. The Voting Specialists (21 percent)

This term does not mean that members of this category are somehow expert at voting. Rather, it means that voting is about the only activity in which these people participate.

3. Parochial Participants (4 percent)

This category contains such a small percentage of the population that it hardly seems worth mentioning. However, Verba and Nie regard this category as the most interesting.[11] Parochials engage in few activities other than contacting public officials to solve particular problems that affect them personally.

Since it requires a certain amount of initiative and self-confidence to contact a public official, members of this category seem well equipped to participate in the political system in other ways. They seldom do, however. Very few parochials belong to service clubs or community organizations, and (other than voting) they rarely participate in additional political activities which appear to have lower opportunity costs, such as wearing a campaign button, displaying a bumper sticker on one's car or contributing to political campaigns (Table 6.3). In short, the parochials appear to be a category of persons well equipped to contribute to the political system upon which they are willing to make demands.

The discovery of the parochial category suggests first, that political participation is neither cumulative nor hierarchical for everyone. Second, it encourages one to be a little optimistic. Parochials, after all, are only four percent of the sample. This approach seems to be consistent with the somewhat cynical, "what's-in-it-for-me? . . . I-want-mine-now . . . me-first . . . don't-volunteer-just-take" philosophy that the popular media has attributed to a mythical category of Americans called Yuppies.[12] It is refreshing to find that behavior consistent with this philosophy is not widely spread among those who participate in the politi-

---

Table 6.3

INVOLVEMENT IN POLITICAL PARTICIPATION

Activity	Percentage
1. Regularly vote in Presidential Elections	72
2. Always vote in local elections	47
3. Active in at least one organization involved in community problems	32
4. Have worked with others in trying to solve some community problems	30
5. Have attempted to persuade others to vote their way	28
6. Have ever actively worked for a party or candidates during an election	26
7. Have ever contacted a local government official about some issue or problem	20
8. Have attended at least one political meeting or rally in last three years	19
9. Have ever contacted a state or national official about some issue or problem	18
10. Have ever formed a group or organization to attempt to solve some local community problem	14
11. Contributed money to a party or candidate	13
12. Presently a member of a political club or organization	8

Source: Sidney Verba and Norman H. Nie, Participation in American Political Democracy and Social Equality (New York: Harper and Row, 1972), 31.

cal system. Should subsequent research find parochials to be growing in numbers then we might have cause for some concern.

4. The Communalists (20 percent)

The communalists provide further evidence of the need to qualify the notion that political participation activities are cumulative. Communalists participate in many activities involving attempts to deal with community problems. They belong to and are active in various community service and charitable organizations.

As Table 6.4 indicates, there is a wide range of organizations in which Americans report membership. Organizations involved in campaigning or electoral competition are those to which communalists are least likely to belong. They are much more likely to belong to charitable organizations or those involving volunteer activity to offer services in response to community problems.

Communalists vote, but that is about the extent of their role in electoral politics. The communalist may invest political resources such as time, energy and money in the affairs of his or her community but the communalist seldom participates in even those campaign activities that are regarded as having low opportunity costs.

The discovery that there appear to be about five times as many of the cooperation-oriented communalists as there are parochials reinforces our optimism. We'd rather live in a community where communalists outnumber parochials than one in which it's the other way around.

5. Campaigners (15 percent)

This group is the mirror-image of the communalists. Activities that are without competition do not seem to interest them. Verba and Nie suggest that it is the conflict dimension that differentiates the communalists and the campaigners. They are both active in the affairs of the community. They simply tend to deal with different dimensions.

Campaigners are more likely to:

1. try to persuade others how to vote,
2. actively work for a party or a candidate,
3. attend a political meeting or a rally,
4. contribute money to a party or candidate,
5. belong to a political club

Communalists, on the other hand, are more likely than any of the previously mentioned groups to:

1. work with others on a local problem,
2. form a group to work on local problems,
3. be an active member of a community problem-solving organization. The final category identified by Verba and Nie is the complete activists.

6. The Complete Activists (11 percent)

Individuals in this category engage in all dimensions of activity studied. In terms of campaign and community activities the complete activists perform at a higher rate than the other groups in almost every dimension.

Table 6.4

PERCENTAGES OF ADULT POPULATION REPORTING MEMBERSHIP IN SIXTEEN TYPES OF ORGANIZATIONS

Types of Organizations	Percent Reporting Membership
Labor unions	17
School service groups, such as PTA or school alumni groups	17
Fraternal groups, such as Elks, Eagles, Masons and their women's auxiliaries	15
Sports clubs	12
Political groups, such as Democratic or Republican clubs, or the League of Women Voters	8
Veteran's groups such as the American Legion	7
Youth groups, such as Boy Scouts or Girl Scouts	7
Miscellaneous groups not fitting the categories in this list	7
Professional or academic societies, such as the American Dental Association, Phi Beta Kappa	7
Church-related groups*	6
Service clubs, such as Lions, Rotary, Chamber of Commerce, Zenta, or Optimists	6
Hobby or garden clubs	5
Farm organizations, such as the Farmer's Union, Grange, Farm Bureau	4
Literary, art, discussion, or study clubs	4
School fraternities and sororities	3
Nationality groups, such as the Sons of Herman, League of Latin American Citizens, Hibernian Society	2

*This does not include church membership but rather associations emerging around the church or religion.

Source: Sidney Verba and Norman H. Nie, Participation in America, (New York: Harper and Row, 1972), 42.

Among the various dimensions of political orientation that Verba and Nie analyze in relation to their typology is civic-mindedness—the willingness to give time and effort to the needs and problems of the community.[13] Only two types of participants score high in terms of this orientation: the communalists and the complete activists.

Thus the complete activist can be thought of as being a civic-minded campaigner, or a communalist, willing to enter the world of politics in order to promote the common good. If the complete activist seems somehow familiar, it may have something to do with the fact that this whole book is oriented toward encouraging you to become one.

Six Conditions You Can Influence That Increase Participation

When socioeconomic characteristics are held constant, that is when we compare poor whites and poor African Americans, or middle class whites and middle class African Americans (instead of all African Americans and all Caucasians) an interesting fact emerges. African Americans participate at a higher rate than the rest of the American population. A major causal factor for this difference is the existence of African American organizations and leaders who attempt to influence the six conditions we are about to discuss.[14] These conditions are summarized in Box 6.8.

Value Rewards of Participation

An individual is more likely to participate when he or she believes that the rewards of participation are valuable. Political scientists identify three basic types of rewards associated with political participation: **material benefits, purposive benefits**, and **solidary benefits.**[15] Though many activities may involve more than one type of reward, it is still useful to identify the types separately.

Material rewards come in a variety forms with different meanings for different people. Owners of businesses might participate in politics by making campaign contributions, or by supporting candidates in other ways in order to receive government contracts or freedom from regulations which ultimately cost money. Other individuals may participate by attending a rally because there is free food or door prizes there. People may volunteer to work in a campaign in part because today's indispensable volunteer is tomorrow's employee. People are encouraged to join organizations because of discounts on insurance, or equipment, or the availability of a professional journal that provides useful information. Though you may not have material rewards to offer, you may be able to encourage others to participate because of material rewards you know about. Information, as we observed earlier, is a political resource.

Purposive rewards are those that come to individuals who have worked for a particular goal and achieved it. That goal might have been the election of a candidate, the passage of

BOX 6.8

AN INDIVIDUAL IS MORE LIKELY TO PARTICIPATE IF HE OR SHE . . .

1. Values the rewards to be gained.
2. Thinks the alternatives to be important
3. Is confident that he or she can help change the outcome.
4. Believes the outcome will be unsatisfactory without his or her action.
5. Believes that he or she possesses knowledge or skill that bears on the question at hand.
6. Believes the barriers (opportunity costs) are not too high.

Source: Robert A. Dahl, Modern Political Analysis (Englewood Cliffs, NJ: Prentice Hall, 1970), 85.

a state law that requires people to take a course in gun safety before they can buy one, or an item in the city budget that will pay for paving a street.

Purposive rewards operate at two levels: the immediate psychological lift from having accomplished something one worked hard for, and the long term benefits of various kinds that come from better government, smooth streets, or a safer society.

Solidary benefits are those that come from being part of a group of people one enjoys being with. Simply belonging is a psychological benefit that means a great deal to many people. Solidary benefits may also include the fellowship or camaraderie of people engaged in meaningful activity.

One of the functions of a political leader is to shorten the time it takes for others to make the connection between rewards and participation. You can increase the participation of others if you can help them see the rewards of politics. In some situations people with little or no formal education or political experience can benefit from the education and experience of others.

Perceive Significant Differences

An individual is more likely to participate in politics when he or she believes that there are significant differences among political alternatives. The less informed one is about a subject, the fewer distinctions one will be able to make when confronting it.

People who don't know much about the votes of various city council members on specific issues (such as expenditures for street repairs in poor districts) will tend to see city council members as being pretty much the same.

An individual who explains to several dozen citizens in a poor neighborhood the differences in the voting records of the candidates are likely to improve not only the ability of those citizens to see the differences among council members, but also the likelihood that those individuals will participate in the next city council election.

Efficacy or Confidence

The characteristic of believing that one can affect one's surroundings, that one can change things, is called a sense of efficacy. When it involves politics, we call it **political efficacy**. An individual with a high sense of political efficacy is one who believes that he or she can influence the political environment. People with a high sense of political efficacy are more likely to participate in a wide range of political activities.

Efficacy can often be transferred from one subject matter area to another. When people feel good about themselves they are more likely to venture into new areas, such as politics. During the civil rights era African American leaders indicated their awareness of this fact by promoting the phrase, "Black is beautiful." The reasoning was that, "If you are beautiful, then you'll be more likely to register to vote, or sit-in at the lunch counter, or ride in the front of the bus, or even run for sheriff."

Outcome Uncertainty

Some individuals who are confident that the outcome of an event will be satisfactory without their participation may find other things to do with their time. The more uncertain the outcome appears, the more likely people are to participate.

This is particularly important in the late stages of any campaign, whether it's for election, or whether it's a referendum. If potential voters are convinced that their side will win without their vote, or if potential participants are convinced that their side will win without their participation in various volunteer activities, then it is very likely that significant numbers of them will not participate, and the contest may be lost. Thus, it is important for leaders to make followers aware that the race is still close, and every vote counts, and every hour of volunteer activity is needed.

Relevant Knowledge or Skill

Individuals who believe they have something to contribute to a discussion are likely to take part in it. The hard part is convincing those who do have something to contribute in the political arena but don't believe they do.

One way to deal with this situation is to convince individuals that no special skills are needed to engage in the activity involved. "You don't have to do anything for our candidate, just be there. That way the media won't take pictures of empty seats in the auditorium." Occupying a chair is a skill that most people possess. In short, the notion that those with relevant knowledge or skill are more likely to participate, tends to work against participation. Therefore, you must take away the excuse that they don't have any relevant skill or knowledge.

Is this an ordinary citizen, or a $200,000-a-year lobbyist meeting with a legislator? We're too far away to tell, but whether or not one does it for a living or because one cares about a particular issue at a particular time, one is still engaged in lobbying and is therefore a lobbyist if one personally contacts a public official on a public issue. Like local governments, there is a wide variety of lobbyists.

Reasonable Opportunity Costs

An individual is more likely to participate in politics when he or she believes the opportunity costs are relatively low.

Opportunity costs are to a considerable extent a product of the institutional context in which the individual operates. Thus, in some communities you must stand in long lines to vote because those in charge of the election didn't hire enough people to run it, or just didn't plan very well. The opportunity cost of a five or twenty-five minute wait is subjectively measured by one individual as being unreasonable and by another as being perfectly acceptable.

Thus, one of the jobs of a political leader is both to work to lower opportunity costs themselves and to convince those one wishes to participate to perceive that the existing opportunity costs are reasonable.

Much has been written about alienation and apathy as sources of nonvoting in American elections.[16] However, since a large number of Americans are proud of their system and believe it works pretty well, some observers are inclined to interpret their non participation as a sign of satisfaction.[17] The only European Democracy in which voting turnout is lower than the United States is Switzerland, a nation whose citizens are noted for their support of their system.[18] Thus, a certain amount of non-participation can be seen as a vote of confidence in the status quo.

It is reasonable to assume, however, that individuals attempting to motivate the less fortunate are not going to operate on the assumption that nonparticipation is a sign of contentment. Political activists who confront satisfaction or complacency have a delicate job to perform. To overcome the inertia created by the belief that everything is going along just fine, someone must create some dissatisfaction by pointing out things that are wrong with the way things are now—so that we can act to fix them. In so doing, they must avoid appearing to criticize much beyond the things for which immediate action is required.

This is no easy task. People who point out too many things that need correcting are easily written off as chronic complainers, and sometimes are accused of being disloyal to the "American Way." Too often the response is "If you don't like it here, why don'cha go someplace else?"

Each of the six conditions we have discussed can be influenced by an individual working to change the beliefs, feelings, and perceptions of others. In a sense, these conditions can be seen as levers to pry people out of apathy or handles that you can grasp to move people into the political arena.

Institutional Factors: Powell's Paradox

The second set of conditions that influence individual participation consists of the political institutions with which and through which most individuals participate. In discussing voting turnout in America, G. Bingham Powell has observed: "Seen in comparative perspective, American voter turnout presents an interesting paradox. Americans seem to be more politically aware and involved than citizens in any other democracy, yet the levels of voter turnout in the United States are consistently far below the democratic average."[19]

After seeking answers to this paradox, Powell finds a major part of the explanation in the states. As Table 6.5 suggests, the United States and France are the only two democracies that have neither required nor automatic registration. France requires registration for the equivalent of an identity card and this facilitates voting registration.

In the United States, the registration laws of the fifty states determine whether it is easy or difficult to register. According to Powell, if the states were to employ some form of automatic registration then the turnout in national elections would increase by about 14 percent.[20] The National Voter Registration Act will improve things but probably not by 14 percent.

Since Powell's estimate, a number of researchers have examined reforms in the registration system with mixed results. Royce Crocker, for example, examined state level of registration and turnout before and after motor voter (registration at the same location one applies for or renews one's driver's license) and postcard (or mail-in) registration were introduced. In the 23 states with postcard registration and the 10 states with motor voter registration a decline in voting occurred.[21]

Table 6.5

TURNOUT AND REGISTRATION REQUIREMENTS IN TWENTY DEMOCRACIES IN THE 1970S

Method*	Registration Registered	% Eligible Voting	% Eligible
Australia	Required	86	91
Austria	Automatic	88	96
Belgium	Automatic	88	95
Canada	Automatic	68	93
Denmark	Automatic	85	98
Finland	Automatic	82	100
France	Optional**	78	91
West Germany	Automatic	85	94
Ireland	Automatic	77	100
Israel	Automatic	80	100
Italy	Automatic	94	100
Japan	Automatic	72	100
Netherlands	Automatic	82	98
New Zealand	Required	83	95
Norway	Automatic	82	100
Sweden	Automatic	88	97
Switzerland	Automatic	44	85
United Kingdom	Automatic	75	100
United States	Optional	54	61
Spain	Automatic	78	100
AVERAGE	78.45	94.7	

*In order to prevent vote fraud, all twenty democracies use some kind of registration system. The following three types are found among them. Required registration means that eligible voters are subject to fines or penalties if they do not register. Automatic registration means that governments attempt to register all eligible voters who come into contact with government agencies, e.g., when one applies for a driver's license or a hunting license, one is automatically registered to vote.
**Optional means that eligible voters can choose not to register.

Source: Bingham Powell, "American Voter Turnout in Comparative Perspective," American Political Science Review (March, 1986), 38.

Same-day registration in the United States is not the same thing as automatic registration. Furthermore, it hasn't been in place very long in the few states that have it. Nevertheless, some indication of the potential for increased turnout which may occur as states simplify registration procedures is found in Table 6.6 which compares turnout of the four states with same-day registration with the national average turnout for the 1992 presidential election. A difference of 18.5 percent is somewhat more than the 14 that Powell predicted, and reinforces the notion that reforms in voter registration laws in the United States might have some effect in increasing turnout.

Calvert and Gilchrist examined the impact of this increased turnout in one state, Minnesota. They found that the increase in turnout was not significantly associated with socioeconomic status. Thus, it appears that making voting easier does not result in a higher turnout of the have-nots or more votes for the party associated with them, the Democrats.[22] While same-day registration does increase turnout it is more likely to have an effect on the million or more Americans who are disenfranchised because they moved from one residence to another during the 30-day period when in most states it is too late to register to vote.

Another important institutional factor that influences voting turnout is the party system. A more competitive and dynamic party system, according to Powell, would increase voter turnout in national elections by 13 percent. State regulations, as we shall note in Chapter 9, has a considerable influence both on the nature of the party system itself and on the ability of political parties to operate independently of the interest group system.

Powell's Paradox is resolved somewhat by understanding that although we have a political culture and ideology that promotes participation, we have rules and political institutions which do not promote voting. Voting, is only one of many political activities. It is the one, however, that enables many people to pool their limited resources in the hope of influencing their governments.

Table 6.6

VOTING TURNOUT IN STATES WITH SAME-DAY REGISTRATION: 1992 PRESIDENTIAL ELECTION

Registered State	Percent of Voting Age Voting	Percent of Voting
Maine	68.2	74.1
Minnesota	72.1	74.2
North Dakota	76.2	71.1
Wisconsin	n/a	75.3
Four State Average		73.67
National Average		55.2
Difference		18.5

Source: Bureau of the Census, Statistical Abstract of the United States, 1992 (Washington, D.C.: Department of Commerce, 1993), 281. "Registration Laws," The Book of the States, 1994–95 (Lexington, KY: Council of State Governments, 1994), 223.

CONCLUSION

In this chapter we have discussed individual participation and the ways in which politically active individuals can affect the participation of others, primarily by dealing with the way they feel about themselves about and their relationship to the political system.

In previous chapters we have touched on some of the objective conditions that reduce participation. Two of the most salient are, first, the long ballot of Jacksonian democracy which presents so many choices that nonparticipation becomes a logical way to reduce confusion and frustration. Second, the numerous levels of government that confront the individual with a host of officials to elect and a variety of different elections in which to choose them (state, county, city, school board, water district, flood control district, park district, soil conservation district, and so on). For some observers the number of choices presents a real barrier to participation.

The fact remains, however, that until informed individuals participate in the system, reform is not likely to occur. This presents us with an interesting situation: you cannot make the system easier to participate in until you participate in it.

We encourage you to take part in politics, if only to find out for yourself whether or not we have overstated the need for reform. On the other hand, you may find that the agenda for reform in your state is so long that in your lifetime only one or two items can be dealt with successfully. Either way, the fact that you have become an informed participant is still a step in the right direction. The more you play the game of politics, the better you will understand the way it works and this will better equip you to explain, defend, or correct it.

STUDY OBJECTIVES

1. Identify the six facts about participation that the Fox illustrates.
2. Define political participation.
3. Identify the advantages of conventional participation.
4. Identify the six types of participation strategies.
5. Identify the two time dimensions of grassroots lobbying.
6. Identify the conditions associated with success in the use of demonstrations as a political strategy.
7. Explain why political participation can be described as hierarchical and cumulative.
8. Identify the categories of participants in the Verba-Nie typology.
9. Identify six conditions you can change that increase the likelihood that an individual will participate.
10. Explain Powell's Paradox.
11. Give two reasons why Americans vote at a lower rate than citizens of most democracies.

GLOSSARY

Appointmenteering   Any activity intended to influence political appointments.

Cumulative   Means increasing by successive additions, in the case of political participation it means adding activities rather than substituting activities.

Demonstrating   Any activity in which individuals by their presence or action attempt to gain public attention and support for a cause or issue.

Electioneering   Any activity directed toward influencing electoral decisions by individuals eligible to vote. It is sometimes called campaigning. However, since recruitment of candidates is not always included in the definition of campaigning, electioneering has a separate meaning for some political scientists.

Grassroots lobbying   A strategy that involves attempting to get other people to contact public officials on behalf of one's issue or cause.

Issue public   The portion of the general public which is aware enough of an issue to have an opinion on it.

Litigation   The act of using the court system to influence decisions.

Lobbying   Any activity involving personal communication with a decision maker and is intended to influence a decision on a public issue.

Material benefits   Rewards such as income, goods, or services which one receives for participating in an activity.

Opportunity cost   The political resource or resources that one invests in a political activity, or political resources used or given up to engage in a political activity.

Political efficacy   The belief that one can influence one's political environment. It is a characteristic that is found in varying degrees; those with a high sense of political efficacy are those most willing to participate.

Public hearings   Official meetings held by a decision-making body to gather information about a problem, or a propose a course of action.

Purposive benefits   Benefits that come to individuals who have worked for a particular goal and achieved it.

Socio-economic status   (SES) Places individuals in categories according to the prestige of their occupation, their income, and their level of education. Social scientists prefer this term when talking about rich and poor people. Since social scientists are usually middle class, it reduces ambiguity and the pressure to choose sides.

Solidary benefits   These are derived from being part of a group of people one enjoys being with. Simply belonging is a psychological benefit that means a great deal to many people. Solidary benefits may also include the fellowship or camaraderie of people engaged in meaningful activity.

ENDNOTES

1. *Newsweek,* 1970, reprinted in Golombiewski, J. Malcolm Moore, Jack Rabin, *Dilemmas of Political Participation* (New York: Prentice-Hall, Inc., 1973), 76–78.

2. *Time* (August 8, 1988), 8.

3. Sponsored by the Aurora, Illinois, Chamber of Commerce each June.

4. See, for example, the definitions of Sidney Verba and Norman H. Nie in *Participation in America: Political Democracy and Social Equality* (New York: Harper and Row, 1972), 2; M. Margaret Conway, *Political Participation in the United States* (Washington D.C.: Congressional Quarterly Press, 1986), 2.

5. Telephone interview with Tom Hendon, Director of Environmental and Engineering Services, U. S. Reduction Company, January 30, 1989.

6. Robert J. Golombiewski, Malcom Moore, Jack Rabin, *Dilemmas of Political Participation* (New York: Prentice-Hall, Inc., 1973), 8.

7. Saul Alinski, *Rules for Radicals* (New York: Random House, Vintage Books edition, 1972), xxii. See also, *Reveille For Radicals* (New York: Random House, Vintage Books edition, 1969), 54.

8. The notion that radical individuals and organizations are helpful in paving the way for the success of moderates is well developed in Herbert H. Hines, Black Radicals and *The Civil Rights Mainstream, 1954–1970*, (Knoxville: The University of Tennessee Press, 1988), see especially pp. 3–5.

9. Council of State Governments, *Book of the States, 1986–87*, 208.

10. Lester Milbraith, *Political Participation*, (Chicago: Rand McNally, 1965), 16.

11. Verba and Nie, *Participation*, 85.

12. Douglas Foster, "Post-Yuppie America," *Mother Jones* (February/March, 1989), 16–18.

13. Verba and Nie, *Participation*, 85.

14. Ibid., 171.

15. Peter Clark and James Q. Wilson, "Incentive Systems: A Theory of Organizations," *Administrative Science Quarterly*, 6:3 (September, 1961), 126–166. See also Robert Salisbury, "An Exchange Theory of Interest Groups," *Midwest Journal of Political Science* 13:1 (February, 1969), 1–32.

16. See, for example, William Crotty, *American Parties in Decline*, 2d ed. (Boston: Little Brown & Co., 1984), 276.

17. Furthermore, some regard a high rate of participation as a sign of dissatisfaction and a threat to the stability of the system. See, for example, Seymour Martin Lipset, *Political Man: The Social Bases of Politics* (Garden City, NJ: Doubleday, 1960), 185.

18. Bingham Powell, "American Voter Turnout in Comparative Perspective," *American Political Science Review* (March, 1986), 23.

19. Ibid.

20. Ibid., 36.

21. Royce Crocker, (1990). "Voter Registration and Turnout in States with Mail and Motor-Voter Registration Systems" (Washington, D.C.: Congressional Research Service. See also Ruy Teixeira, *The Disappearing American Voter* (Washington, D.C.: Brookings Institution, 1992).

22. Jerry W. Calvert and Jack Gilchrist, "Suppose They Held an Election and Almost Everybody Came!" *PS: Political Science and Politics*, 26:699.

CHAPTER

7

The Media and Public Opinion

POLITICAL PARTICIPATION USING OLD AND NEW MEDIA TO HELP CITY HALL (INSTEAD OF FIGHTING IT)

The planning department of the city of Colorado Springs decided it was time to revise a law about the kinds of work people could do in their homes in residential neighborhoods. Dave Hughes happened to be the only home employed person at the planning commission meeting when this issue surfaced. He felt that the revised ordinance would discriminate against people working out of their homes, some of whom were the victims of layoffs and corporate downsizing.

Hughes raised objections to the ordinance that convinced the commission to table it for 30 days. He then took the three page ordinance draft home and keyed it into his computer and posted it on an electronic bulletin board. He also wrote a letter to the editor of the local paper stating his opposition to the proposed changes in the ordinance. The letter included Hughes' phone number. He received lots of calls and at the next meeting 175 people showed up.

In the meantime, through the electronic mail and bulletin boards people in Colorado Springs worked on revising the ordinance. New ideas were hashed out, language was crafted to clarify intentions and meet objections. When a consensus had been reached, Hughes presented the citizen version of the ordinance to the planning commission. Virtually unchanged, it went from there to the city council where it was passed.[1]

Participation sometimes involves attempting to influence public opinion through the mass media. David Hughes used both his computer and a more traditional activity—to communicate with a larger public. When 175 people showed up for a planning meeting in Colorado Springs decision makers had a pretty good indication that members of the public were aware of and concerned with an issue.

The Hughes success story helps us point out three characteristics of your relationship to public opinion, the mass media (or the media), and politics.

1. The media are important political resources for reaching a larger audience. Hughes' participation extends the notion that should you choose to participate your effectiveness will increase if you bring along a few friends. Hughes effectiveness in the political system increased when he convinced some strangers to show up.
2. Access to some type of media is available to all of us. Hughes' activities in Colorado Springs demonstrates that buying a full page ad in the newspaper or a 30-second spot on television is not the only way to get to the public via the mass media. Dave Hughes influenced public opinion using three types of media: newspaper, telephone, and an electronic bulletin board.
3. Although public opinion and the mass media are closely related, the exact nature of that relationship is not fully understood. According to Larry Bartles:

> The state of research on media effects is one of the most notable embarrassments of modern social science. The pervasiveness of the mass media and their virtual monopoly over the presentation of many kinds of information must suggest to reasonable observers that what these media say and how they say it has enormous social and political consequences. Nevertheless the scholarly literature has been much better at refuting, qualifying, and circumscribing the thesis of media impact than at supporting it.[2]

Perhaps Bartels is being excessively modest, or pessimistic. The point remains that there is much research yet to be done on how the media influence public opinion and the impact of both on state and local decision making. You may wish to participate in that research effort or you may simply want to know enough about the subject to be an informed participant in community decision making. Either way, it is important for you to know something about what the media are and how they relate to public opinion. We begin with public opinion.

PUBLIC OPINION

Public opinion can be defined as the expression of an attitude on an issue or matter of public concern.[3] As Bernard Hennessy observes:

> Words, spoken or printed, are the most common form of expression of opinion, but at times, gestures—the clenched fist, a stiff-arm salute, even the gasp of the crowd—will suffice to express opinion. . . . For public opinion at any given moment of measurement, expression is necessary.[4]

While we agree with Hennessy that if the attitudes or feelings aren't expressed, then they aren't yet public opinion, we are aware that some scholars make no distinction between attitudes and opinions.[5] However one defines public opinion, the move from having a feeling or attitude to actually expressing it is a move that clarifies one's orientation toward an issue or individual. That is why some people have been known to observe, "I really don't know what I think about that until I hear what I have to say on it."

Where Does Public Opinion Come From?

You may recall the story that starts out, "Daddy, where did I come from?" and ends up—after Daddy's uncomfortable lecture about the birds and bees—with the punch line, "Well, yes, Daddy, there is one thing I'm not sure about. Suzy Bradshaw comes from Philadelphia, where do I come from?"

In discussing sources of public opinion one is almost as likely to be as misunderstood as Daddy was. Scholars have identified at least three interacting sources of public opinion. First is the process of political socialization, second is the influence of individual leaders and the information they interpret through the two-step flow of information, and third is the mass media.

The term *mass media* is used in numerous ways. Depending upon the context it can mean: (1) the various organizational methods by which journalists and discussion forums deliver information (and misinformation); (2) the profession of print and broadcast journalism; (3) the technology itself (television, Internet, phone banks), or all of the above. We will try to make clear by context the way in which we are using the term *media* or *mass media*. We will try not to use it as a collective noun. The media are a diverse they, not a monolithic it. As we will attempt to demonstrate, there are many kinds of mass media, and within each type of media there is considerable variety.

Our main focus is on the delivery of political information. It is important to note at the outset that we get information not only when journalists report and anchors read the news, but also during talk shows or discussion forums, and by means of paid advertising.

Political Culture and Political Socialization

In Chapter 2 we discussed political culture and political socialization. Political culture is important to keep in mind as a major force in promoting political stability. Our political culture has given us a set of standards to use in evaluating new information. As Doris Graber has observed, "People who are exposed to the mass media already possess a fund of knowledge and attitudes which they bring to bear on new information."[6]

This doesn't mean that change is impossible, it just means that it takes some work. The process of political socialization, you may recall, is a learning process that itself sometimes involves change. Some scholars view it as a lifelong experience. Others think of it as a process that brings us into early adulthood—a college education being a part of the process that not all members of society are able to enjoy.

After political socialization, according to this view, each generation confronts specific influences such as the workplace, the media, political institutions, and significant events (local, statewide, or national). In *The American Mosaic* Daniel Elazar touches on the fact that political culture is learned in a context involving generations and locations in space and time.

> The smallest communities and the most comprehensive civil societies are alike in that they are shaped by their geo-historical location. No understanding of American politics in any arena—national, state, or local—is possible without taking this phenomenon into consideration.[7]

The early influences of family, church, school, and peers may be reinforced or contradicted in later life. No two individuals share exactly the same socialization and later life experiences. Sometimes, however, a number of people may share an experience that influences their opinions in a similar way. Veterans of a political campaign, individuals who helped build a home through Habitats for Humanity, or volunteers who helped flood victims or fought a forest fire constitute collections of people who share experiences that cannot be fully shared with others.

The Two-Step Flow of Communication

A second way in which public opinion is influenced is through the people who interpret events and ideas for us. These people may be our employers, trusted friends, or political leaders at the local or the state level. We do not turn to these people to tell us what to think on each and every issue. We do, occasionally, seek or willingly receive information from them because we believe they have more complete information or they've thought a little more deeply about some issues than we have.

Thus, we may be influenced indirectly by thinkers, theories, or media sources we've never dealt with firsthand. When opinion leaders interpret journals of opinion and other media sources we've not read, this is called the two-step flow of communication: media to opinion leader, opinion leader to us.

On some issues, of course, you may be an opinion leader. Many discussions of the media and public opinion use the terms opinion leader or elite, and mass. As we noted in Chapter 6, elite status on a given issue does not depend upon wealth or social position. Depending on the issue, you may be an opinion leader, a member of the interpreting elite, or a part of the mass whose opinions are influenced by others.

Given the tendency for people with some formal education to be better equipped to gather and process information, it is very likely that you will become an opinion leader on several issue areas for a significant number of people. That is, if you apply yourself and actually learn something.

Mass Media

The mass media are, among other things, methods of communicating with large numbers of people, the masses. Mass media developed rather late in human history—after mankind began to live in cities. After town criers and bulletin boards came print media—newspapers, and magazines—and now electronic modes of communication; radio, television, and the linkage of computers all over the world called the Internet.

Influential though it may be, the mass media are not immune from the influences of political culture or us. Each journalist, editor, and commentator grew up in a community and was influenced by a state or local political culture. The media influence us by providing news and advertising. The two are not unrelated as we shall observe.

An important fact about the media and influence is that there is a feedback loop. We can influence the media. Our collective decisions to watch or to buy determine which radio and television shows get renewed, which products get produced. Sometimes our letters and phone calls intervene to alter "market-driven" decisions and thus save quality shows or lead to new products. After being cancelled, the network television show *I'll Fly Away* was picked up by public television and survived for another season because so many individuals took the time to express their interest. The non-violent, value-oriented children's show *The*

Magic School Bus is but one example of a program, that was developed to meet the public's demands for quality television for children.

Political socialization, political culture, opinion leaders, and the mass media affect each of us in different and sometimes unpredictable ways. One product of this interaction is an abstraction called public opinion. As V. O. Key observed, public opinion consists of "those opinions held by private persons which governments find it prudent to heed." In a democracy where the opinions of large numbers of people can affect the political careers of individuals and the decisions they make, the study of public opinion is of value to present and future political leaders at all levels—national, state, and local.

Four Characteristics of Public Opinion That Leaders Watch

Four dimensions of public opinion are of particular concern to those who wish to get things done in the intergovernmental system: the distribution (or direction) of opinion on an issue, the degree of public awareness of particular issues, the intensity of opinions, and the stability of opinions. These are the characteristics of public opinion that political leaders watch most closely.

Issue Salience

This can be measured in terms of the percentage of the public aware of an issue or an individual. While there are those who have an opinion about everything, most of us do not. There are many issues of which we are not yet aware.

The portion of the general public that is aware enough of an issue to have an opinion on it can be defined as the **issue public**. An issue public's size can be changed by making the issue more **salient** or noticeable to a larger portion of the populace. By making more people aware of an issue one may also have an impact on the level of government decision makers affected. A neighborhood issue may thus become a citywide, countywide, or even statewide issue. Several participation strategies are directed at increasing the size of the issue public. Foremost among them are demonstrating and grass-roots lobbying.

For individuals who are thinking about running for office, public opinion analysts use the term **name recognition** to identify public awareness of an individual. Potential candidates often have polls taken to discover the percentage of the public aware of their names. Potential candidates with high name recognition (a large issue public) are more likely to decide to run. However, it's better to run when people are aware of one's good qualities, rather than one's negatives. In dealing with positives and negatives we examine distribution.

Direction or Distribution of Opinion

The distribution of opinion can be measured in terms of the percentage of the public who have a particular position on an issue or candidate. To measure the distribution of opinion we calculate the percentage for or against something.

When public opinion polls are presented in the media the "Don't knows" or "Have no opinions" are sometimes left out. This tends to "harden the data," disguise the size of the issue public, and make the distribution of opinion appear more dramatic than it really is. To overstate things a bit: if 20 percent are for a course of action, 10 percent are against, and 70 percent don't care; it is somewhat less than totally honest to only report that the number in support of an issue is twice that of those against.

In discussions of opinion distribution, the term *direction* is sometimes used to indicate the guidance given policy makers. On an issue that is divided 70 percent to 30 percent considerable guidance is given. Public opinion points in a particular direction.

Intensity

Intensity of opinion on an issue can be measured in terms of percentages of the public who feel strongly about their position on an issue. Individuals whose opinions are strongly felt are most likely to express them by taking action in support of them—participating. The fact that some are willing to act implies that others may be almost ready to. Thus, when you participate as an individual, you force decision makers to at consider at least the possibility that you are the tip of an iceberg.

Stability

This is the degree to which the other three dimensions of public opinion remain unchanged. Decision makers who ignore changes in public opinion are in danger of not being reelected. Thus decision makers are sensitive to changes in the size of an issue public, in the distribution of opinion, and in the intensity of opinions.

There is overwhelming evidence that political participation can change opinions. Two of many historical examples of opinion change are the civil rights movement, which changed national opinions on the legitimacy of segregation, and the Anti-Vietnam War movement, which changed public opinion on the efficacy and legitimacy of the war.

A more recent example of a major public opinion shift occurred when the basketball player Magic Johnson announced that he had the human immunodeficiency virus (HIV). According to Pollock, Magic Johnson's public announcement was a major factor in changing the public perception that acquired immunodeficiency syndrome(AIDS) is specifically a homosexual disease.[8] He notes that in 1981 the Centers for Disease Control had adopted the acronym GRID to refer to the syndrome. GRID meant gay-related immunodeficiency. AIDS became the official term a year later.[9] Thus, for the professional community who dealt with the disease it was not specific to the gay community. The perception that it was, however, persisted among the general public. On November 7, 1991 Magic Johnson changed all that. As we have observed before, one person can make a difference. In the Magic Johnson case that observation has both a poignant and an ironic meaning.

Measuring Public Opinion

Public officials have numerous ways of learning about public opinion, the most direct being when a significant number of citizens actually participate through strategies discussed in Chapter 6. The most well known mechanism of public opinion research is, of course, the poll or survey. As an informed participant in the system, it is important for you to know the value of survey research as well as a little bit about ways to tell a good public opinion poll from a bad one.

Survey research is quite labor intensive and involves a good deal of technical expertise. In the movies Judy Garland and Mickey Rooney used to save the orphanage by raising funds through an amateur variety show. Survey research however, is a lot more complicated than "Hey, kids, let's put on a survey!" This is not to say that dedicated amateurs can't do good surveys. It is simply to point out that first, should you choose to attempt a survey, you have some homework to do before you obtain useful results; and second, there are lots of poor quality survey results reported.

Instead of promoting cynicism in regard to either the media or to survey research, we'd like to provide some information to help you be able to make informed judgments about them.

Sources of Survey Information

Survey research is a big business. There are large organizations that do it for a profit and some that do it as part of an academic research effort. Thousands of political consultant organizations do polling for candidates and for interest groups. It is generally from the latter group of pollsters that questionable data or dubious interpretations of data occasionally emerge.

Steps in the Process

Survey research generally involves at least the following steps. All are important, though some are more likely to lead to serious error than others.

1. Identify the universe.
2. Draw the sample.
3. Choose the survey method and write the questions.
4. Administer the questions.
5. Code and enter the data.
6. Interpret the data and report it.

1. *Identify the universe.* The universe is the population about which the polling organization wants to obtain information. In political research we could be looking for all the potential voters or those voters who are most likely to vote. How we define our universe will help define the questions asked or the places we start in attempting to find a sample.

2. *Draw the sample.* The sample is a portion of the universe. Data is collected on the sample and then a prediction is made based on that data about the whole universe. It is critical that the sample be an accurate reflection of the universe.

At this stage we can doom our survey to the collection of information that does not accurately reflect the universe. The horror story of bad samples is the 1932 presidential election survey by the *Literary Digest* which predicted that Alf Landon would defeat Franklin D. Roosevelt. Instead of sampling from the universe of people eligible to vote, they actually sampled from a part of that universe that was unrepresentative of the whole. In the midst of a Depression with thousands of people out of work and many homeless, *Literary Digest* sampled those well off enough to own a phone or a car. If the *Literary Digest* were only interested in the comfortable, then its survey would have been fairly accurate. After all, Alf Landon did get 38.5 percent of the vote. It may come as no suprise that *Literary Digest* is no longer with us. It never recovered from the embarrassment of reporting bad polling results.[10]

The *Literary Digest* sample is one example of bias based on faulty methodology. A phone sample that took place on Sunday morning might miss a lot of churchgoers. A phone sample on a Friday evening in the autumn might miss a lot of parents of teenagers old enough to play the tuba, kick a football, or wave a pom pom.

The best type of sample is also the most expensive to obtain. It is a random sample. A random sample is one that gives every single member of the universe the same likelihood of being drawn in the sample. That takes a lot of doing. One has to know who every single member is, and then make sure—if that individual is drawn—that he or she is contacted even if the surveyor has to wait for the person's release from the hospital or arrival back in town.

One of the worst types of samples are accidental samples. Also known as haphazard samples, they are drawn in an unsystematic way and yield inaccurate reflections of the universe. Man in the street interviews are biased sometimes in ways that aren't readily apparent. People who happen to be at the mall or in the street outside an event may not represent the larger universe about which we want information. These people may be fine folks, but data based on them will not obtain information from people who were at school, at home, at work or even out of town.[11]

In real life we do a lot of accidental sampling. For better or for worse, some of us make generalizations based on information about a single member of a category: one Korean-American, one political science professor, or one auto mechanic. Survey research attempts to provide more accuracy by more systematic sampling of a universe.

3. *Choose the survey method and write the questions.* Polling by telephone is faster and cheaper than door-to-door surveys. Door to door surveys acquire more in depth data than polling by telephone. The method used will determine the cost of the survey as well as the quality and quantity of data used. Questions for a personal interview can be more detailed than for phone interviews partly because of the fatigue factor, and partly because of the ease of terminating a phone interview. Personal interviews allow for open-ended responses which may have to be coded later. They can also make possible probes into subject matter for which questions have been prepared in advance. "Has any member of your family ever been assaulted?" "No." Then a page or so of questions aren't asked and the well-trained interviewer moves on.

Both phone and door-to-door surveys can look for intensity or can simply provide yes or no options. The questions on handgun control until very recently have only provided those limited responses. Intensity thus had to be measured another way, by participation. At least one scholarly article was published that purported to show that many state governments were undemocratic because public opinion polls in those states showed overwhelming support for gun control yet the state legislature did not pass such legislation. Polls that didn't measure for intensity clearly provided misleading results. That many people will respond to a public opinion poll and then never act on their expressed opinions is a point rather central to our arguments about your role in motivating others to participate.

Telephone and door-to-door surveys do not exhaust the possibilities. There are also mailed questionnaires. Although they are cheaper and less labor intensive than telephone and door-to-door surveys, the return rate of useful information is much lower. This is in part because mailed questionnaires are postponable and more easily interrupted. Once one starts a phone or personal interview one usually completes it.

The low rate of return on mailed questionnaires is also a product of the fact that some interest groups or political consultants use mailed questionnaires not to collect information but to raise money, distribute propaganda, or mobilize the recipients of the questionnaire into action. The envelope containing these so-called surveys usually contains other literature and a request for a donation sometimes right on the survey form itself. These direct mailings that claim to be surveys and aren't are particularly annoying to people who regard survey research as a legitimate way to obtain information and to promote informed decision-making.

4. *Administer the questions.* In the haste to get results quickly, surveys sometimes only gather information from the people in the sample who are available on the first call or visit. A more thorough survey uses at least one, sometimes two or three callbacks. The second calls sometimes produce data that changes the picture of the universe the survey provides.[12]

In constructing the survey, it is sometimes necessary to avoid response-set or the influence of previous questions. Tourangeau and Rasinki (1988) report that before asking a question on support for or opposition to the right of women to opt for an abortion, they asked one set of respondents a four-question series concerned with women's rights. Another set of respondents was asked a series of questions concerned with traditional values. The first set of respondents voiced greater support for the right to an abortion than did the second set.[13]

Thus, in administering the survey different sets of questions have to be supplied to different groups of interviewers or interviewers have to be trained to alternate sets of questions as they move through the sample assigned them.

5. *Code and enter the data.* The responses to questions have to be assigned numbers and then entered into a data base on a computer. Transposed numbers, misdoing, and simple data entry errors require considerable attention to proofreading and checking. The spellcheck feature in many wordprocessing systems doesn't check data. Desktop models can now handle a fairly large amount of information. Polling results for a city council race or a school board election could easily be entered on a recent model desktop computer.

6. *Interpret the data and report it.* In 1984 Union Carbide reported on a lengthy survey it had commissioned on public attitudes about the economy. A majority of the respondents had supported tax cuts for business if the business promised to invest the savings in new equipment and new jobs. A large majority favored the reduction of restrictions in antimonopoly laws which prohibit companies from cooperating in research and development projects.

Union carbide then concluded its report on the study with the following observation, "Government is seen as being wasteful, bloated, inefficient, and costly and as an inherently negative factor in economic growth. Americans believe that government programs should be cut back."

Union Carbide exaggerated public dissatisfaction with government's role in the economy just a little. There were no questions in the survey that directly addressed waste or bloat or the alleged negative effect of government regulation on economic growth. What is more disturbing, however, is that Union Carbide did not report the following data on responses to questions that actually were in their survey:

- A few big companies divide up business between them. Agree—66 percent
- When the economy is booming, most of the increase is kept by business in the

form of higher profits, higher executive salaries, and fat expense accounts. The average person does not benefit much. Agree—66 percent

- When the economy goes down, business keeps its profits high and cuts jobs and wages. Agree—66 percent
- Is the federal government doing more than it should, less than it should, or about the right amount to regulate major corporations in areas like product safety and other things that have to do with protecting the public? Agree with "About right" or "Less than it should"—70 percent
- When asked about 10 specific types of government regulation, a majority of the respondents supported present or even stricter government regulations.[14]

The Union Carbide case is a rather extreme example of misinterpretating public opinion polling results as well as gross errors in reporting them. Hundreds of polling organizations conduct thousands of valid polls every year and provide excruciatingly detailed and responsible interpretations of their data. It doesn't happen very often as blatantly as that, but nevertheless it is a good idea to ask a few questions of your own before accepting survey results at face value. The following are some suggestions for your consideration.[15]

Surveying the Polls

1. Who is conducting the poll? Naturally you cannot be expected to memorize a checklist or to discount every poll that isn't conducted by Gallup, Roper, Harris, or the Survey Research Center at the University of Michigan. Knowing who conducted the poll, however, lets you have a source to check if you are going to be seriously influenced by or use in a speech or paper the information provided by the poll.
2. Is this person a legitimate representative of a polling organization? You have every right to know whether or not someone knocking on your door is a legitimate representative of a reputable polling organization. Don't hesitate to ask for identification; the person should also provide a number to call for verification.
3. Who paid for the poll? Candidates pay for polls, interest groups pay for polls, and some polls are sponsored by newspapers or television networks. There is no reason to totally discount a poll just because the sponsor has a policy or election interest in its results. However, knowing the sponsor might give you some guidance about other questions to ask.
4. Are all the questions and their answers reported? The Union Carbide case should be kept in mind. If an organization does not release an entire poll to the press or public, one may reasonably ask why not?
5. What kind of sample was drawn? Was it random, was it accidental? Polls in which people paid money to phone in their answer are not to be taken very seriously.
6. Are the responses reported in percentages or raw numbers? Percentages of those polled are better, and even better is the statistical significance of any differences that the report seems to indicate are impressive.
7. How many nonresponses were there, or what percentage of "don't knows" were there?
8. Is the sample size reported? Is there a statistic indicating the reliability of the poll?

Direct digit dialing by a small group of people working in a phone bank such as this one can reach a respectable sample of people over a fairly short period of time. Precoded forms enable interviewers to scan responses into the computer with a light pen such as that held by the worker in the foreground.

THE MASS MEDIA

If anything demonstrates how quickly our world is changing, and how recently it has changed in major ways, it is the mass media. Not only are newspapers a fairly recent appearance in the history of the human race, but radio and television are almost too recent to be thought of as history. The Internet is still being invented.

The media discussed in the pages that follow are not isolated structures. They interact with one another. TV reporters read newspapers. There are television sets on in newsrooms of most daily papers. In both television stations and newspapers someone is assigned to listen to the police shortwave band on the radio.

The media are subject to change as well. TV stations change network affiliations, sometimes voluntarily and sometimes otherwise. Book publishing companies are bought and sold in a New York minute. When we signed the contract for the first edition of this book it was with Harper and Row Publishers, a house that had been in existence since 1817. Just before we sent our first draft out for review, Harper and Row merged with Little Brown & Company. After the revisions went off to be set in type but before the cover was designed, Harper and Row was purchased by media magnate Rupert Murdoch and merged with Collins publishers of England. The entity that published the first and second editions of our book is HarperCollins, now part of Murdoch's News Corporation Limited.

The nine mass media we discuss are not meant to be an exhaustive list. For example, we do not devote much time to the telephone even though phone banks and the party line in rural America are both mechanisms for communicating with a large portion of a community (whether we are "listened in on" or listened to). Dave Hughes with whom this chapter opened made his letter to the editor more effective by providing his home phone number as a way to promote feedback.

An important fact to remember about the relationship between the media and you is that you read much faster than anyone can talk. Speech occurs at the rate of 120 words per minute. Since we can read at 360 words a minute and up, some at 800 words per minute, and since we seldom have to wait for the words to appear on paper, we can consume much more information by reading than by listening.

This has important consequences in terms of the quantity of information we can get from different media sources. Hunt and Ruben report that at a recent conference on the "Credibility of the News Media" in St. Petersburg, Florida, a print reporter who attended a session transcribed an entire evening news broadcast, set it in type, and put it in newspaper format. *The entire broadcast filled the equivalent of one newspaper page.*[16]

Big Four

There are many ways of categorizing the media. Book publishers use textbook and trade book as two major categories, each of which is then further subdivided. Other divisions tend to have a focus idea and then everything else is in a residual category such as electronic media and *other*, or print media and *other*.

We have chosen to discuss nine types of media and have somewhat arbitrarily classified them in two categories according to audience size. The big four: Television, Newspapers, Magazines, and Radio reach millions of Americans every day. They deliver news, advertising, entertainment, and instruction. As Figure 7.1 indicates, more money is spent in advertising through television than through all other media combined.

An increasing percentage of Americans depend upon television as their only media source for political information. Over 65 percent of the population gets its news from TV, and 49 percent regard it as its most believable source. Second place is newspapers with 42 percent and 26 percent respectively. There are several possible interpretations of these differences, particularly the differences in believing one's source. What is your interpretation?

Naturally, to be effective in the political system we encourage you to include newspapers and magazines in your information diet.

Television

Whether or not it is actually being watched, in the average household the TV is on for several hours a day. The average viewer spends almost eight hours a week at it, compared to a relatively small amount of time reading newspapers or magazines. Whether you try to reach them through television or not, it is important to know how important television is as a news source for most Americans. Almost as important is the fact that television is not equally distributed throughout the country (Box 7.1).

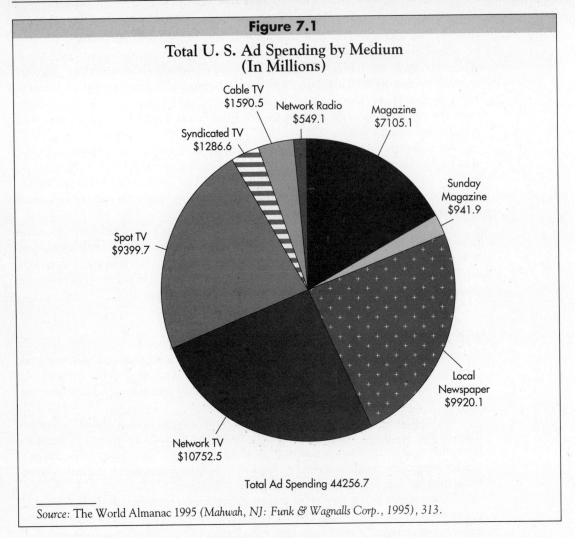

Figure 7.1

Total U. S. Ad Spending by Medium
(In Millions)

Cable TV $1590.5

Network Radio $549.1

Magazine $7105.1

Syndicated TV $1286.6

Sunday Magazine $941.9

Spot TV $9399.7

Local Newspaper $9920.1

Network TV $10752.5

Total Ad Spending 44256.7

Source: The World Almanac 1995 (*Mahwah, NJ: Funk & Wagnalls Corp., 1995*), 313.

Television sets are found in virtually all states and communities, however television stations are not. States like California, Texas, Florida, and New York have several media markets. Other states do not. For example, communities in West Virginia, for several reasons, including the interference caused by mountains, cannot all receive information from a single West Virginia source. Depending upon where one lives in the state, the television programs come from stations in Cincinnati, Pittsburgh, or Washington, D.C. When Jay Rockefeller ran for Governor in 1980 he bought time in all three media markets. On election day people in communities outside of West Virginia were looking for his name on their ballots.[17] However, when the governor of West Virginia calls a press conference, who will show up? There is no guarantee that reporters from television markets outside the state will attend, and hence the importance of the print media for political information not only in West Virginia but elsewhere.

BOX 7.1

DIMENSIONS OF DIVERSITY: PUTTING THINGS IN PERSPECTIVE: THE INFLUENCE OF TELEVISION IN OUR DAILY LIVES

The cable television company that serves Columbia, South Carolina, had a channel in operation a few days before they had programming ready for it. Instead of broadcasting snow and static, they aimed a camera at an aquarium. Once the programming, the Science Fiction Channel, was ready, they put it on. There were so many complaints from people who wanted to have a televised aquarium in their home that the company found another channel and broadcasts this fish tank 14 hours a day.

We assume that none of the fin fans were Neilson or Arbitron families.

Source: The World Almanac 1994 *(Mahwah, NJ: Funk & Wagnalls Corp., 1994), 975*

Newspapers

As of February 1, 1995 there were 1596 daily newspapers in this country, 198 fewer than the previous year. The major trends among daily newspapers are: merger and concentration. Merger means that two or more newspapers in one city are combined into one and readers no longer have a choice. There are fewer cities in America with two newspapers with each passing year. Concentration means that a dozen or so large corporations own most of the daily papers in this country. The larger the newspaper, the more likely it is to be owned by a major chain. Total daily circulation is about 60 million copies for all dailies, but well over half of this is by papers owned by major chains. Along with mergers and concentration of ownership comes a decline in jobs. Today there are fewer newspaper reporters than there are college professors.[18]

Three other trends among newspapers which have state and local political consequences are: a decided turn toward morning rather than afternoon publication, although the latter are still more numerous—996 to 571. Second, more dailies are producing Sunday editions than previously. This is in response to the fact that about two million more Americans take time to read a newspaper on Sunday than during the week. Thus, if you are planning a political event—news conference, demonstration, or rally—you might need to alter the time and day to get the most favorable amount of coverage.

The third trend is an increase in weekly newspaper publication. From 1980 to 1993 the circulation of weeklies went from 12.5 million copies to 55.5 million. About half of these survive on advertising revenue alone and give the paper away free. As Agee, Ault, and Emery observe, "In the files of a small-town weekly are recorded the vital statistics of the town's life—the births and deaths, marriages, social events, and tragedies, and the ludicrous moments that give life zest."[19]

Weekly papers in many rural and suburban communities, even those with metropolitan centers nearby survive and prosper by providing news of the local community that is ignored by the metro dailies. In between the weeklies and the metro dailies are several hundred papers that appear three to five times a week.[20]

Magazines

Magazines are published weekly, monthly, and quarterly and a few every two weeks. *Time* and *Newsweek* appear in about four million homes each week, ranking far behind the top five magazines found in Box 7.2. *Reader's Digest* arrives monthly to some ten million homes and has for decades been the most purchased magazine in the nation.

Political opinion journals such as *Mother Jones*, the *National Review* or *The Nation* are seen by a few thousand readers. These readers, however, are more politically aware and thus make these journals more influential than their circulation figures may suggest. A growing trend in magazine publishing is the metropolitan monthly many of which are patterned after the venerable weekly the *New Yorker* and virtually all of which carry political information.

Magazines present such a wide range of subject matter and in such a wide assortment of packages that no wonder it is difficult for political scientists using survey research techniques to establish a direct link between "Media" and public opinion or political activity. For example, *Esquire* magazine is not generally regarded as must reading for the politically astute. Nevertheless, like many periodicals with a special niche in the media market, it provides insightful commentary. The July 1994 edition featured a copy of Henry Kissinger's *Diplomacy* in an eye-catching cover. More to the point, it included a thought-provoking article on racism, "The Rosewood Massacre" in Florida, and another on angst and drugs, "Kurt Cobain and the Stupid Club."[21] That some of its readers might read these articles and some might not makes specific media influences on attitude virtually untraceable (unless one does extended interviews with a large sample of the American public).

Radio

For a generation raised on television, it is difficult to imagine the importance radio had as an entertainment and information medium from the 1920s until the 1950s. In the 1930s when "Amos 'n Andy" went from a local Chicago show to a national time slot, 7 P.M. EST,

Calvin and Hobbes copyright Watterson. Distributed by Universal Press Syndicate. Reprinted with permission. All rights reserved.

many families adjusted their meal times, and plants altered their closing time so workers could get home to listen to it, even the president adjusted his speaking schedule to accommodate this new phenomenon.[22]

Once television emerged as America's premier communications medium, radio declined as a major source of news and information. That it did not simply become a medium for music and sports broadcasts is due in part to the car radio.

Talk radio, now a political phenomenon with considerable potential, has been around for several decades, almost as long as disc jockeys have been. That's how many talk show hosts started out. Today, talk radio is covered by the two trade magazines—*Radio and Records* and *Talkers Magazine*. It also has a Washington lobby, the National Association of Radio Talk Show Hosts, and a talk show about talk shows.

Starting out as a late night phenomenon it has recently acquired daytime significance and a political importance that many are still trying to figure out. One may reasonably assume cellular phones have helped radio along by making it possible for angry people stuck in traffic to vent their spleen to receptive talk show hosts. According to Randall Bloomquist, the talk radio editor of *Radio and Records*, "The typical talk listener is 50 percent more hostile to the government than the population at large."[23]

According to Morgan Stewart, talk radio's impact is both wildly overrated to the point of hysteria by some observers, while being grossly underrated by others. Current research, he says, indicates that on some issues under the right conditions talk radio is "a formidable grassroots lobbying force."[24]

© *Reprinted by permission: Tribune Media Services.*

The issues tend to be those involving referendums—issues with no partisan cues involved and relatively low levels of information. Radio talk shows tend to be effective in mobilizing people with limited information against something. They are rather weak in promoting in depth examinations of issues, although there are exceptions, "Talk of the Nation" on National Public Radio (NPR) being the first exception that comes to mind.

The right conditions for radio talk shows to be effective are when there are no parties or candidates to provide information, factual or symbolic. In other words, elections in states with strong parties and strong candidates are less likely to be influenced by talk show hosts than elections without either one.

Political consultants are already advising their candidates to set up phone banks, not only for the traditional calling of potential voters, but also to flood talk shows with requests to speak. This seems to run in the face of the well known fact that callers are screened. As Rush Limbaugh the current king of talk show hosts, has observed, "People often confuse the role that callers play in a great talk show. The primary purpose is to make *me* look good, not to allow a forum for the public to make speeches."[25]

Five Minor Media

As future leaders of your states and communities, you will often be the first step in the two step flow of communication (Box 7.3). In addition to magazines and newspapers, we hope you read a few books and learn to use the Internet. Although you may not have reason to

---

BOX 7.2

MASS MEDIA NUMBERS: A COMPARISON OF CIRCULATION AND AUDIENCES OF MAJOR SOURCES OF INFORMATION

Television
(Ninety-eight percent of American households have at least one set)
Total households with TV   94,135,104
U. S. households with cable television   58,834,440
Average per person viewing time 17.5 hours per week

Newspapers
Average daily circulation, all papers   59,811,594
Average Sunday circulation   62,565,574
Biggest single circulation Wall Street Journal   1,818,562

Magazines
Top five general magazines—, Reader's Digest, TV Guide, The Conde Nast Select, National Geographic, Better Homes and Gardens
Total monthly circulation 58.2 million

Rank and Circulation of Top News Magazines
 Time (# 11)   4,103,772   (Weekly)
Newsweek (# 19)   3,156,192   (Weekly)

Source: The World Almanac 1995 (Mahwah, NJ: Funk & Wagnalls Corp., 1995), 305–310.

BOX 7.3

ADVERTISING SPENDING THROUGH MAJOR MEDIA 1991

(Millions of dollars)

Magazines	6,515.2
Sunday magazines	794
Newspapers	6,837.3
Network radio	578.7
Network TV	9,456.2
Local TV	8,751.2
Syndicated TV	1,850.4
Cable TV	1,211.6
Total	$35,994.6
Total for television	$21,269.4

Television = 59 percent of total spending

Source: The World Almanac 1994 *(Mahwah NJ: Funk & Wagnalls Corp., 1994),* 299

use the wire services in your professions, it's worth knowing a little bit about how they fit into the scheme of things.

Books

Approximately 40,000 books are published annually of which about half are textbooks. A portion of the other half, trade books, are about political subjects. These affect our political system in the same way that journals of opinion do, through the two step communication process. There are several useful overviews of the mountain of literature with which we can only aspire to become familiar. Among them are magazines such as the *New York Times Book Review* (which is part of the *New York Times* but is also sold separately in many book-stores), and *The Book Review Digest.*

Internet

The Internet is a system of computers linked by phone lines, hard wire, and sometimes satellite transmission that reaches around the world. On most college campuses the computer center, and many offices, are linked to the Internet. Individuals can tie into the Internet using a modem and phone lines either by subscribing to one of many commercial services such as CompuServe or America On Line, or, if they have an account at a university computer by tying into it via a modem. Many city libraries now offer a freenet service.

The Internet is a mechanism with tremendous potential for political participation. As our Colorado Springs example showed, people can work together to solve a problem in a substance-oriented way without confrontations, high cost media buys, or identifying some person or group as the bad guys. For people impatient with the slow speed of communication by speech, electronic bulletin boards and e-mail offer the opportunity to learn much from many sources quickly.

The Internet also offers opportunities for mischief (Box 7.4). Consequently state and local governments are now revising their law codes in order to define new types of crime as well as devising ways to prevent or detect crimes.

News Services

News services were originally known as wire services because their reports came over the telegraph wires. Although the information supplied by news services often arrives via the Internet, many people still call them wire services. News services are agencies, like the As-

---

BOX 7.4

DIMENSIONS OF DIVERSITY: CRIME AND DETECTION ON THE INTERNET

One day in 1992 John Norstad, a technical services specialist at Northwestern University's Academic Computing and Network Services, received an e-mail message from a colleague in Wales. The Welshman suspected that he had obtained a virus from some computer games he had downloaded from Stanford University's archives.

Norstad, who is a member of MASH, a network of virus analysts, put the word out and soon action was taking place on many fronts. A MASH member at Stanford took the games out of the archives and started looking for their source, which turned out to be the computer at Cornell. As Norstad and other MASH members worked on finding a way to defeat and remove the virus, reports were pouring in about infected computers elsewhere in the United States, Japan, and Europe.

A MASH member at Cornell discovered the group of students who planted the virus. The New York state police visited the sleeping quarters of the students and invited them to discuss things at the station. Eventually the students were convicted of second-degree computer tampering, fined, and sentenced to community service, for which they had plenty of time since Cornell expelled them.

According to Norstad, at least one of the students has been rehabilitated and helps discourage experimentation with viruses. The culture associated with Macintosh users features less mischief-making, says Norstad, than the IBM environment where underground bulletin boards and even booklets describe how to create a virus. Norstad has personally contributed to the relatively virus free Macintosh environment by creating and giving away at no cost a very effective award winning program called Disinfectant©.

For a free copy via Internet contact [j-norstad@ nwu.edu] or send a self-addressed and stamped envelope and a floppy disk (800 or 1440 K) to John Norstad, AC&NS, Northwestern University, 2129 North Campus Drive, Evanston, IL 60208–4311.

Source: Stephanie Russell, "Unsung Hero of the Mac World," Northwestern Perspective (Fall, 1994), 2–8.

sociated Press or Reuters which employ or contract with hundreds of reporters all over the world. The agencies sell stories to radio, television, and newspapers that lack the resources to assign reporters to them. "Rip-n-read" is radio jargon for wire service stories. Wire service stories are written in the traditional inverted pyramid. They start out with who, what, when, where and why. In subsequent paragraphs the writer develops details. Busy editors can cut them almost anywhere without the need to reedit the copy to make sure essentials are not missing.

Wire services are influential for at least two reasons. First they help set the agenda for countless news operations by the prominence they give to particular stories, by a daily listing of things they plan to cover—the "Daybook," and because they are trusted as being non-biased by both the journalistic community and by political leaders and staff.[26]

Recordings

Each year 875 million records, tapes, and compact discs are sold. The money available to pop stars that can be used for political contributions and the opportunity to promote issues via concerts live and televised is an important feature of the political power of the recording industry.

Movies

Documentaries provide political information overtly, while the feature films, approximately 270 per year, which are shown in more than 10,000 local theaters also provide covert messages about a variety of issues.[27] The films of one actor alone, Tom Hanks, have influenced the attitudes and level of information of millions of people about the AIDS epidemic, mental retardation, and homophobia.

FUNCTIONS PERFORMED BY THE NEWS MEDIA

In the following discussion our frame of reference is essentially the big four, with special attention to the news media as opposed to the media as vehicle for advertisements. That the various media are sometimes vehicles for commercials is worth more than passing mention. While it is annoying to have to fold or tear out the stiff stock inserts in magazines (whether or not they have been imprinted with exotic scents), it is also annoying to see political commercials on television that deliver half-truths or play on fear in order to sell a candidate or issue position.

Unfortunately, the stiff stock ads don't turn some people off of the free enterprise system while the political advertisements may further the impression that politics is dirty and thus discourage some people from political participation.[28] The media do attempt from time to time to enforce the canons of good taste in deciding which advertisements they will accept. Recently a number of stations in Texas were forced by court order to accept political advertisements showing the bloody matter and tissue resulting from abortions. The stations preceded the ads with warnings to the viewer and were allowed to determine the time of day when the ads ran.

According to Lazersfeld and Graber, the news media perform at least four important functions for our state and local political systems: surveillance, interpretation, socialization, and civic.[29]

Surveillance (Watchdog)

In serving the function of surveillance the media are operating at two levels: public and private.

Public Surveillance: Information and the Public Agenda

According to Doris Graber, the media serve the public interest when they "throw the spotlight of publicity on selected people, organizations, and events."[30] For some, publicity is a resource, while for others it is most unwelcome. In either case the publicity provides additional information that can be used to make decisions about supporting a policy or a candidate.

The media influence the public agenda because the same quantity and quality of information cannot be supplied on all subject matter to the public and decision makers. Editors and news directors must apportion the limited resources available to the media. For this reason it is sometimes difficult for social scientists to regard the media as simply a messenger. Messengers usually don't decide what the message will be.

Private Surveillance

The media deliver information of use to individual members of the public in the form of weather reports, consumer news, and economic data. Individuals also benefit from the various political stories they are exposed to by having the opportunity not to listen (one may not want to dance, but one likes to be asked) and the opportunity to be reassured that the world seems to be puttering along as usual with no real dangerous surprises in store. In this sense private surveillance could also be termed private reassurance; except, of course, when crimes are reported in our town or our neighborhood.[31]

Interpretation

The news media provide a valuable service when they put information in context. By telling us about causes and consequences, and speculating about why organizations and individuals are doing things, the media give meaning to data. They are also sometimes reassuring when they put events in an historical context. A columnist who writes about the mudslinging that occurred during the campaigns of Thomas Jefferson and Andrew Jackson provides a service in helping the public put in context the extremists currently active on both sides of some issues. If it has been ever thus, then perhaps the American political system consists largely of generally sane and well-meaning people.

Socialization (Teach)

The media are not only sources of information for adults, they also serve as agents of political socialization for children. Through news stories, entertainment, documentaries, and commercials the media overtly and covertly deliver messages about values and about how individuals obtain power and ought to use it.

One of the major unresolved public issues which will be discussed and analyzed for the foreseeable future is what to do about programming to which children are exposed. The linkage between violence on television and tolerance of or use of violence by children and teenagers is fairly firm. A 1994 White House conference of television producers, advertisers, and government officials reviewed dozens of suggestions. Among these are ratings systems for programs so that parents can monitor television watching, electronic governors set in

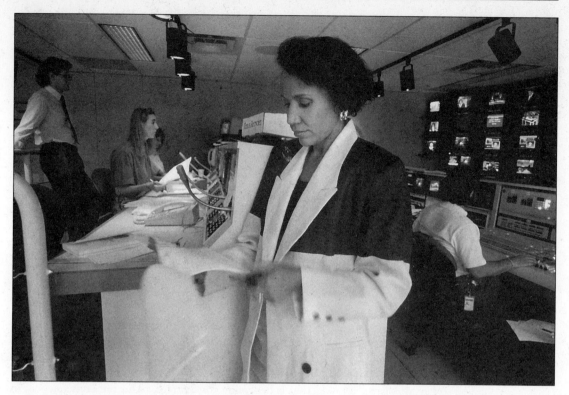

Reneé Poussaint, news anchorwoman, Washington, D.C., reviewing copy before a broadcast. Most TV anchors don't just read what's on the TelePromTer, they often revise what they are to read before the final draft is entered.

the home which lock out certain programs or channels, and efforts to promote more offerings that are constructive as well as entertaining. As noted earlier, the television industry is slowly responding with new educational Saturday morning programming.

Civic

The civic function refers to the efforts of individual members of the media to influence decision makers or the public to solve a problem or right a wrong. Thus when the media inspire, exhort, stimulate, or anger us enough to get us to carry out our duty as citizens and enter the affairs of the polis, the media are performing a civic function.

Howard Kurtz, media critic for the Washington *Post*, believes that there are not enough journalists practicing the civic function in America's newspapers:

> *I am convinced that the finest newspaper stories are infused with the kind of passion that is all too often missing from an increasingly bland profession. Busy readers don't have time for the sort of dull and inconsequential reports that we mass-produce each day, but they invariably respond to journalism that is fueled by commitment.*[32]

Among the examples of the kind of journalism he would like to see more of are: the courageous series on race relations by the New Orleans *Times-Picayune* including a candid examination of the paper's own racist past; the series in the *Albuquerque Tribune*, whose investigative reporters uncovered the identities of five people who had been injected with plutonium by government scientists in the 1940s; and finally, the story by Linda Wheeler of the *Washington Post*, which reported on the death of James Hudson, a part-time maintenance worker at the Lincoln Memorial who died leaving a wife and seven children without a pension or life insurance because the government refused to extend these benefits to part time workers. People responded to Wheeler's story by raising $80,000 for Hudson's family. The government responded by initiating a reexamination of its benefits policy.[33]

PROBLEMS WITH MEDIA

Media bashing is almost a national pastime. It's easy, cheap, and doesn't even require literacy. While we are reluctant to jump on that bandwagon, it does seem reasonable to assume that any human activity can probably be done better and that something as important as the collection and distribution of news about our state and local political systems bears some scrutiny. Furthermore, the appearance of books written by journalists themselves with titles such as *Media Circus*, *Adventures in Medialand*, and The *Media Monopoly* indicates both the willingness to engage in self-criticism and an admission that there is room for improvement.[34]

Concentration, commercialism, anti-labor bias, timidity, sensationalism, and shallow objectivity are some of the items that have been identified by some if not most media critics.

Concentration

The ownership of media production is becoming concentrated. This has consequences in some areas that are readily apparent and in others that have yet to be clearly demonstrated. At the local level the concentration of ownership has led to a reduction in competition.

Newspapers have been dying at an alarming rate. As mentioned earlier, there are very few cities left in which there is competition between two or more daily papers. Newspaper competition is good for the public and good for business. For the public, competition usually means more investigative journalism and more controversial columnists. For business, competition means cheaper advertising rates. As soon as one paper emerges as the only one in a city, its advertising rates are almost sure to go up.

Nationwide, there is an increasing concentration of ownership into a smaller and smaller number of multimedia firms, for example, Times-Mirror (*Los Angeles Times*) owns other newspapers, magazines, book publishers, television stations, and has over a million cable subscribers in 13 states. In 1983 there were 50 national and multinational corporations controlling major portions of the mass media this has been reduced by mergers and acquisitions to 20 in 1992.[35]

When we use the term "mainstream media," we are referring to the major newspapers and magazines that are distributed nationally as well as the networks and the broadcasting stations in the top 100 or so of the nation's 220 media markets. The mainstream media are almost completely owned by conglomerates.

A glance at the large numbers of book publishers and media firms gives the appearance of diversity, yet powerful giants acquire most of the revenue. Of more than 3,000 publishers of books, five produce most of the revenue.[36] The same thing has occurred in the cable industry, which includes some 11,000 cable systems in this country, but seven cable companies, most of which are part of larger conglomerates, have a majority of the 60 million subscribers. According to Bagdikian, "With deregulation of the cable industry in 1984, cities lost a great deal of the power they wielded over cable systems competing for exclusive franchises."[37]

Concentration of power in a few hands is always something to be concerned about, despite the fact that it is possible that such power could be used in a benign fashion. That we are not the puppets of this concentration of power is clear since publishing houses belonging to these empires are a major source of books critical of major media empires.[38]

Commercialism

The term *news hole* refers to the space devoted to news. The rest is advertising, the comics, or specialized information such as the weather and stock prices. Advertising takes up about 60 percent of the space in newspapers.[39] On television there is about 20 minutes of advertising every hour.

Since most media depend upon advertising to exist, there is considerable potential for conflicts of interest. According to the *Wall Street Journal*, journalists "see an increase in the tendency of newspapers to cater to advertisers or pull their punches, when it comes to criticizing advertisers in print."[40]

In conflicts between newsroom and advertising departments sometimes editors and management stand behind their reporters, sometimes they don't. Eugene Roberts, former editor of the *Philadelphia Inquirer*, was told by an advertiser that unless he changed a story, the paper would lose the $70,000 in advertising revenue his company purchased. Roberts didn't kill the story and the advertiser carried out his threat.

On the other hand, Dennis Washburn, a columnist for the *Birmingham News*, was open and honest with the *Washington Journalism Review* which quoted him in an article about how auto dealers pressure newspapers into providing favorable coverage. He admitted that the paper "probably would not jeopardize such a substantial portion of our advertisers unless it was something major."[41] One day after the article appeared Washburn was fired.

Graef Crystal was forced out of two business magazines, *Fortune* and *Financial World*, because of his coverage of the large amounts of money paid to corporate executives, some of whom were "downsizing" their corporations by firing hundreds of lesser paid employees. For example, a major decision-maker in the merger of Time and Warner (which published *Fortune*) was Steve Ross. His compensation was $78 million in salary and stock. According to Crystal, that's enough to have kept on the 600 employees that Ross laid off—including 19 of *Time's* 75 correspondents,—with $48 million to spare. The employees were apparently laid off so that Time Warner could reduce the debt incurred to finance the merger in the first place.[42]

Anti-Labor Bias

In *Through Jaundiced Eyes* William J. Puette, a professor at the University of Hawaii, demonstrates with newspaper headlines, anecdotes, TV news transcripts, movie synopses, and other data the negative portrayal of trade union leaders and organizations by the mainstream media. Three among the many examples are:

1. TV news segments rarely mention unions unless there is a story about wage demands (too high), a possible strike (bad), or internal corruption (typical and bad). When there is a strike, TV usually has a reporter interview people who have been inconvenienced instead of attempting to present the sometimes complicated reasons why the United Parcel Workers or farm laborers used their weapon of last resort.

2. Print media tend to ignore the good news about labor unions—safety regulations, minimum wage laws, health coverage, due process protection, or simply the fact that the isolated worker has a support when there is a disagreement with management. Labor stories, through choice of headlines, sources, and story placement are routinely given a negative slant.

During the baseball strike of 1994 a picture appeared in many papers of a fan wearing a funny looking hat resembling a celery stalk and carrying a sign, "What's all this about a Celery Cap?" Immediately below it a nationally distributed story on the strike began, "Looking like anything but persecuted workers, Cleveland Indians players in BMWs, Porsches and trendy four wheel-drive trucks picked up their belongings from Jacobs Field . . as the strike deadline approached."[43] To their credit a few papers attempted to explain the rather complicated issues involving salary caps, free agency, the length of a career of the average ballplayer, or the profit to investment ratio of baseball owners. Did yours?

This is not to say that the players were right and the owners were wrong. It is simply to point out that to reduce the issues to trivia (greed on both sides) is to miss an opportunity to report the facts and let the individual reader develop a more fully informed opinion.

3. Television dramas, including *Hill Street Blues*, *The Rockford Files*, and *All in the Family*, focus on conflict while making genuine union concerns such as: safety, exposure to dangerous chemicals, fairness (Is requiring single mothers with small children to work the night shift fair?) seem trivial.[44]

Puette argues that since there is no major media source providing a contrasting view, it is no wonder that most Americans accept the biased version presented by the media to be a reflection of the world as it is. As Christopher Cook put it in his review of *Through Jaundiced Eyes*, "If everyone's telling the same lie, then how would we know it's a lie? And how would we know the truth?"[45]

Cook himself tells the story of a phone call he received in his capacity as director of communications for the Texas AFL-CIO. A television reporter was doing a story on unemployment. "I want a real person with a real family" she said. "No problem," Cook responded, "We've got machinists, bus drivers, grocery clerks—all kinds of people."

"Well," said the reporter, "I don't want you to think I have any preconceived ideas, because the story, you know, is about unemployed people. But I want a non-union guy who lives in northwest Austin [a 'nice' part of town] and who once worked for IBM. You know, someone whose *standard of living* has been affected from being out of work."[46]

Cook speculates that, like most TV and print journalists, the "standard of living" oriented reporter who didn't want her story to feature people in poverty from the wrong side of town probably:

1. Learned nothing of labor history or workplace issues during 16 years of school
2. Grew up in a middle-class home where her parents blamed labor unions for many of the nation's problems

3. Assumes any unemployed person dumb enough to belong to a union probably deserved to get laid off.[47]

Lest we give the impression that the foregoing is merely an item about an insensitive reporter, it is important to note that not only are reporters often sent out on stories by a news director whose prejudices may influence the questions asked, but that the story is representative of an industry whose major owners are employers just as the major advertisers are. Whether the news director's or the reporter's prejudices are reflected in the conversation above, the point is that the evidence is strong that antilabor prejudices influence news stories.

Timidity

New York Times vs. *Sullivan* (1964) is a landmark decision on the right of the press to print the truth, even if the story (in this case an advertisement) contains minor errors that are corrected later. It is also a landmark case in the field of civil rights since Mr. Sullivan, a city official, was suing not only the *Times* for libel but also civil rights workers in order to make it too expensive for them to continue seeking social justice in Alabama.

The full-page ad in the *Times* was called an editorial advertisement. The *Times* routinely printed them for organizations advocating causes and attempting to raise funds. The Committee to Defend Martin Luther King Jr. and the Struggle for Freedom in the South sought to raise funds for King's legal defense on a series of attempts by those then in charge of the state and local governments of Alabama to silence the civil rights leader. The ad described the aims of the civil rights movement and the problems it faced. In so doing it made one or two factual errors. The ad included a list of 64 people, including former First Lady Mrs. Eleanor Roosevelt, baseball great Jackie Robinson, and several civil rights leaders of modest means such as the Reverend Ralph Abernathy.[48]

L. B. Sullivan, the Montgomery city commissioner in charge of police, was not named in the ad. However, he sued the *Times* and a number of civil rights leaders for $500,000 each. Other commissioners and eventually the governor joined suit and soon the *Times* faced a legal liability of $3 million, as did each of the codefendants. When Alabama courts ignored the correction and apologies published by the *Times* and decided the case in favor of Sullivan, with a large damages award, they directed the seizure of property of the civil rights leaders including the 1948 Buick belonging to Abernathy.

In 1964 the U. S. Supreme Court reversed the decision and established the fact that officials and corporations that don't like a media report cannot sue that media source into silence simply because the report contains minor errors.[49]

The Sullivan case established the principle that the U. S. Constitution protects news media when they err in attempting to report the truth. This decision provides a little extra backbone for media decision-makers intimidated by the threat of lawsuits from individuals and firms offended by news reports. Nevertheless, some media managers are more timid than they need be in meeting their obligations to inform the public.

Timidity usually involves pulling stories likely to offend advertisers. For example, the *Portland Oregonian* once destroyed thousands of copies of a Sunday edition after one of its salesmen objected to a story advising readers on how to sell a home without a real estate broker.[50] However, in San Antonio, Texas, it went a little further than that.

Apparently the management of KMOL-TV in San Antonio never heard of the Sullivan case. In April 1994, veteran investigative reporter Dan Lauck was ordered to clean out his desk by the end of the day because he refused to read on camera a long apology written by a complaining company's public relations firm. Six weeks earlier, Lauck had quoted on camera a state official who apparently had misunderstood his question. The quote raised the possibility that the company seeking the apology might be culpably linked to an environmental scandal involving the mishandling of contaminated soil. Lauck was quite prepared to set the record straight, but not to admit to intentionally slandering the company or attempting to damage its reputation. KMOL executives, fearing a lawsuit, gave Lauck an ultimatum amounting to "my way or the highway." Lauck left and the news director read the apology on the air during the evening news program to the acute embarrassment of many of the reporters and anchors at the station. Fortunately, Lauck soon found a better job in a much bigger market.

At risk of pointing out the obvious, had Lauck been supported by a collective bargaining agent (a union), the timidity of KMOL's management might have been overcome. Faced with pressure from the union, its backbone might have stiffened and it might have negotiated a little more firmly with the company complaining about a six-week-old story. As it is, the newsroom of KMOL, and thus the San Antonio viewers, lost a reporter for an act that did not damage his ability to rise in his profession.

Sensationalism

"Here's some stuff you might want to know about" is not the usual way the media begin a story. The print media seek conflict, drama, examples of wrongdoing, indecisiveness by public officials, or hypocrisy by the clergy. Decisions involving television news are driven by the preference for the visually dramatic. A talking reporter with a meeting going on in the background—no matter how important its subject matter—is less dramatic than flames shooting out of buildings, smashed autos, wrecked planes, pools of blood, or people on gurneys being loaded into ambulances. Television is not the only purveyor of sensationalism, however. In fact, in the course of examining " Tabloid TV's Blood Lust," sometimes portions of the print media reveal a little "blood lust" of their own while stumbling into unfortunate lapses from journalistic standards.[51]

In a story that provided the opportunity to bash television in general and station WSVN TV in Miami, in particular, both *Time* and *Newsweek* emphasized the dramatic while apparently ignoring facts that might have given their stories balance. The undisputed fact is that a hotel chain in Miami announced in June 1994 that it would henceforth embargo WSVN-TV from the rooms of its guests because of the frequency of violent reports appearing on that station.

A few days later both *Time* and *Newsweek* picked up on this fact and fleshed out their stories by mentioning a study by Joseph Angotti, a Miami University professor, in which the number and types of stories during November 1993 had been tabulated. The percentage of stories that were violent on WSVN during this period was higher than the percentages on the other four English language Miami stations. What *Time* and *Newsweek* did not mention—although the information was available—was that Angotti did a follow-up study in May 1994 that revealed that WSVN had reduced the percentage of stories involving violence from 48 percent in November to 30 percent in May, less than the percentage found on the leading Miami station (WPLG, 32 percent).[52] An ironic twist to *Time's* slanted coverage on WSVN is that the title of its story was "All the News That Fits."

If the media tried a little harder to deliver more news that required an attention span beyond that of a mosquito, would it make any difference?

Evidence that it might, according to some analysts, is the fact that in 1991 when the *Philadelphia Inquirer* (not to be confused with the national tabloid with a similar name) published a lengthy, nine-part series by two investigative journalists on the impact of the federal tax system on the middle class, the paper received 20,000 letters, notes, telephone calls, and requests for reprints. The series was transformed into a best selling book *America: What Went Wrong?*[53]

Shallow Objectivity

The media have also been faulted for giving the appearance of objectivity when they examine an issue from one perspective and then find someone with an obvious bias for an "on the other hand" sound bite. The electronic media are particularly prone to this failure to take responsibility for providing adequate background context in examining major issues of the day. To provide sound bites from two sides is not providing context.

PARTIAL SOLUTIONS

Since the media do not operate unobserved, they therefore do not operate unchecked. There are institutions and processes that counter some of the shortcomings of the media, there is also evidence that the media are doing a better job at serving the public's need for information it can use in making informed decisions, and finally there are some things that you can do to improve the performance of the media.

Checks on Media Misbehavior
Journalistic Standards

Journalists themselves have drawn our attention to many of the problems listed in the previous discussion. The news media have professional organizations that give awards and that identify examples of exemplary work. Two of the major sources of ethical guidance are the Society of Professional Journalists (SPJ) and the American Society of Newspaper Editors (ASNE).

Media Watchdogs

There are three basic types of media watchdogs. The first are the media critics that work for the various major newspapers. They criticize their own papers as well as other papers and other media. The *Washington Post* news critic is the author of *Media Circus*, a book which goes far beyond the previous section in its examination of the shortcomings of the media.

The second type of media watchdog consists of the journalism reviews that specialize in a critical examination of the media. Among the leading journalism reviews are: *The Columbia Journalism Review* (Columbia University), *The American Journalism Review* (University of Maryland), and *The Quill* (Society of Professional Journalists).

The third type of media watchdog consists of organizations and individuals who view the media from a variety of interest and issue perspectives. Some such as the Moral Majority, are concerned with issues of religion and morality. Fairness and Accuracy in Reporting (FAIR), and People for the American Way are concerned about bias in reporting and censorship issues.

FAIR has offices in New York and Los Angeles. It is nonprofit with a small budget and staff. Nevertheless, like the Giraffe Project, it sometimes gets results. In 1990 it did a six month study of the guest list for the highly regarded Public Broadcasting System (PBS) program the *MacNeil/Lehrer News Hour*. FAIR reported that in addition to spending most of its interview time on white males (90 percent of the guests were white, 87 percent male) the *MacNeil/Lehrer News Hour* paid little attention to public interest groups and labor organizations. Together they amounted to a scant six percent of the guest list. Several hundred daily papers picked up this story and *MacNeil/Lehrer* began to reflect a wider cross section of America.[54]

A project in Los Angeles, the Center for Media and Values, has spread the concept of media literacy or critical viewing to communities such as Norman, Oklahoma, Bethesda, Maryland, and Bedford, New York. In Bedford, for example, about 25 parents were trained at the local Episcopal church on how to manage the impact of television advertising on their kids. They were surprised to learn after watching an episode of *Beverly Hills 90210* that about half the commercials were for movies, R-Rated and others—a lesson in media reinforcing its own usage. They also began to notice how commercials for other products used the same production style as the program itself, thus promoting identification of the products with the show and a confusion about what was commercial and what was the drama being sponsored.[55]

Competition Between Types of Media

The media compete for our attention, and sometimes our hard earned cash at the newsstands. FAIR was well aware of this and made sure that press releases for its study of *MacNeil/Lehrer* got to every major newspaper in the country. As we noted in our discussion of *Newsweek*, *Time*, and WSVN-TV in Miami, the print media are critical of the electronic media and can afford more space for it than the electronic media can in reciprocation. Thus, information about the shortcomings of particular stations or particular talk show hosts are quickly made available to the public.

Both print and electronic media have been increasingly active in providing reality checks on state campaign ads by candidates for major statewide offices. The Associated Press provides a regular feature that newspapers and some radio and television stations bring to the attention of the public. A wide open field is the area of reality checks on local campaign ads and literature. Perhaps you could pioneer in this.

An Informed Public

The best check, of course, is an informed public willing to use the tools available to them to hold the media to high standards of conduct. Upset that a favorite show was going to be canceled, Dorothy Swanson in Fairfax, Virginia, wrote letters to the station, to the newspapers, and a few friends to get them to write or call as well. She not only got another year for *Cagney and Lacey* in 1983 but she founded an organization that now has about 2,500 members, Viewers for Quality Television.

Citizens are also using their own video cameras to document concerns that are then given to the press. Since the press is becoming used to buying home videos—reporters at some stations are authorized to pay $50 on the spot for tapes of newsworthy events, getting them for free is an attractive alternative. The press is, however, still resistant to simply paying someone for an interview. That is still a major distinction between straight news reporting and tabloid news reporting, whether print or electronic.[56]

Over the past few years the amount of media coverage given to people and organizations who are making a difference has increased dramatically. The Giraffe Project is but one example of an organization promoting change in media coverage and changes in our society by providing stories of individual successes.

Signs of Improvement

Newsweek reports that in 1994 approximately 10 times as much prime time was allocated to news coverage on television as a decade earlier. Along with celebrity puff pieces numerous examples of solvable state and local problems were identified by shows like *Prime Time Live*—dangerous inbred dogs as a threat to children—and *Eye to Eye*—bad doctors who slip through state regulations as they move from state to state.

While the mainstream media provide a powerful nationalizing (and homogenizing) influence on American culture, reaching rural communities in all 50 states, the new technology has also made it possible for ethnic groups and rural communities to maintain and celebrate their unique additional identities. Jeanie Greene of the Inupiat people in Alaska had the idea of broadcasting amateur video from rural villages via the Rural Alaska Television Network (RATNet). She started producing *Heartbeat Alaska* in 1992 in her apartment. By 1994 the show reached not only 247 rural Alaskan communities but it is also rebroadcast across northern Canada, Greenland, the Russian far east, and Arizona.[57]

One of the keys to solving community problems and to obtaining good press coverage according to DuBois and Lappé is establishing good relationships by providing packaged information, and particularly good visuals. The Southwest Organizing Project (SWOP) in Albuquerque didn't just complain about environmental racism. They researched examples of it and organized a day long tour for the media which had about 12 stops. Reporters and other people on the tours got the opportunity to compare notes, to share stories, and to establish human relationships. After the tours, press sensitivity to and reporting of environmental racism increased, according to Louis Head of SWOP.[58]

You and the Media

Whether you write letters, create organizations, use your video camera, or your computer, you can have an impact on the way that some part of the media operates, on the size of public awareness of an issue, or on the policy options being considered by state and local officials. Naturally, there will be some sweat equity—we never promised you a rose garden.

STUDY OBJECTIVES

1. Identify the media that David Hughes used to influence a decision in his town.
2. Identify the sources of public opinion
3. Identify the two-step flow of communication.
4. Identify the four characteristics of public opinion that political leaders watch most closely.
5. Identify the steps in conducting survey research.
6. Identify the questions you ought to ask in evaluating survey reports in the media.
7. Identify the big four and the little five media.
8. Identify the functions performed by the media.
9. Identify the problems with the media.
10. Identify the checks on media misbehavior.

GLOSSARY

Accidental samples   The least dependable types of samples. They are drawn in an unsystematic way and yield inaccurate reflections of the universe. "Man-in-the-street interviews," are accidental samples biased sometimes in ways that aren't readily apparent.

Internet   A system of computers linked by phone lines, hard wire, and sometimes satellite transmission that reaches around the world. On many campuses the computer center, if not many offices, and sometimes dorm rooms are linked to the Internet via the mainframe computer on campus. Individuals who don't have accounts at a university computer can also tie into the Internet using a modem and phone lines by subscribing to one of many commerical services such as Compuserve or America On Line. Many city libraries now offer a freenet service.

Mass media   Methods of communicating with large numbers of people, the masses. The term is used in numerous ways in different contexts: 1. the various organizational methods by which journalists and discussion forums deliver information (and misinformation), newspapers, radio, television, magazines, and the minor media; 2. the profession of print and broadcast journalism; as a synonym for journalists; 3. the technology itself (television, Internet,) or all of the above.

News services   Agencies, like the Associated Press or Reuters, that employ or contract with hundreds of reporters all over the world. The agencies sell stories to radio, television, and newspapers that lack the resources to assign reporters to them. Originally they were known as **wire services** (many still use that term) because their reports came over the telegraph wires.

Public opinion   The expression of an attitude on an issue or matter of public concern.

Random sample   A sample that gives every single member of the universe the same likelihood of being drawn in the sample.

Salient   Means noticeable. A salient issue is one of which many people are aware.

ENDNOTES

1. Frances Moore Lappé and Paul Martin DuBois, *The Quickening of America: Rebuilding Our Nation, Remaking Our Lives* (San Francisco: Jossey-Bass Inc., 1994), 127–128.

2. Larry M. Bartels, "Messages Received: The Political Impact of Media Exposure," *American Political Science Review* 87:1 (March, 1993), 267.

3. For a similar definition see: Bernard Hennessy, *Public Opinion,* 4th ed. (Monterey, CA: Brooks/Cole Publishers, 1981), 4:

4. Ibid., 6–7.

5. Heckert Asher, *Polling the Public: What Every Citizen Should Know,* (Washington, D.C.: Congressional Quarterly Press, 1988), 37.

6. Doris Graber, *Mass Media and American Politics* 2d ed. (Washington, D.C.: Congressional Quarterly Inc., 1984), 10.

7. Daniel Elazar, *The American Mosaic* (Boulder: Westview Press, 1994), 35

8. Philip H. Pollock III, "Issues, Value, and Critical Moments: Did 'Magic' Johnson Transform Public Opinion on AIDS?" *American Journal of Political Science,* 38:2, 426–444.

9. See Shilts 1987, cited in Pollock, p. 429.

10. Norman M. Bradburn and Seymour Sudman, *Polls and Surveys: Understanding What They Tell Us* (San Francisco: Jossey-Bass Publishers, 1988), 19.

11. Michael Milburn, *Persuasion and Politics: The Social Psychology of Public Opinion* (Belmont, CA: Wadsworth, Inc., 1991), 17.

12. Ibid., 18.

13. R. Tourangeau and K. A. Rasinski, "Cognitive Processes Underlying Context Effects in Attitude Measurement," *Psychological Bulletin,* 1988, 103: 299–314.

14. Norman M. Bradburn and Seymour Sudman. *Polls and Surveys: Understanding What They Tell Us* (San Francisco: Jossey-Bass Publishers, 1988), 158–159.

15. Herbert Asher. *Polling and the Public: What Every Citizen Should Know,* (Washington D.C.: Congressional Quarterly, Inc., 1988), 146–152.

16. Todd Hunt and Brent D. Ruben, *Mass Communications* (New York: HarperCollins, 1993), 278.

17. Thad Beyle, ed., *State Government: CQ's Guide to Current Issues and Activities 1993–94* (Washington D.C.: Congressional Quarterly Press, 1993), 66.

18. John C. Merrill, John Lee, and Edward Jay Friedlander, *Modern Mass Media* 2d ed. (New York: HarperCollins, 1994), 100.

19. Warren K. Agee, Philip H. Ault, and Edwin Emery, *Introduction to Mass Communications,* 11th ed. (New York: HarperCollins, 1994), 127.

20. Ibid., 127–128.

21. Taylor John, "The Rosewood Massacre," and Stephen Wright, "The Big No," *Esquire,* July, 1994, 46–63.

22. Lynne S. Gross, *Telecommunications an Introduction to Electronic Media* (DuBuque, Iowa: Wm. C. Brown. 1988), 46. Cited in Hunt and Rosberg, 237.

23. Morgan Stewart, "Pump Up the Volume," *Campaigns & Elections,* (October/November, 1993), 26.

24. Ibid., 26.

25. Rush Limbaugh, *The Way Things Ought To Be,* Cited in Stewart, p. 26.

26. Thad Beyle, ed., *State Government: CQ's Guide to Current Issues,* 65.

27. Thomas R. Dye, Harmon Zeigler, and S. Robert Lichter, *American Politics in the Media Age* (Pacific Grove, CA: Brooks/Cole, 1992), 85.

28. Divisive election campaigns may reduce voter turnout.

29. The careful reader will note that we have revised Graber's revision of Lazersfeld's original formulation. Lazersfeld assigned three functions to the media: Surveillance, Interpretation, Socialization. Graber added Manipulation. This term, we feel has pejorative connotations which seem absent from Graber's discussion of investigative or muckraking activities associated with this function. That is why, with apologies, we have substituted "Civic" for "Manipulative." See Doris Graber, *Mass Media and American Politics*, 4–11, and Chapter 8, "The Media as Policy-Makers," 259–283.

30. Graber, 5.

31. Ibid., 8–9

32. Howard Kurtz, *The Media Circus: The Trouble With America's Newspapers* (New York: Times Books, 1994), 7.

33. Ibid., 7.

34. Ben H. Bagdikian, *The Media Monopoly*, 4th ed. (Boston: Beacon Press, 1982) .Jeff Cohen and Norman Solomon, *Adventures in Medialand* (Monroe, Maine: Common Courage Press, 1993).

35. Bagdikian, *The Media Monopoly*, ix.

36. Ibid., ix.

37. Ibid., xiii.

38. Benjamin M. Compaine, Christopher H. Sterling, Thomas Guback, J. Kendrick Noble, Jr., *Who Owns the Media? Concentration of Ownership in the Mass Communications Industry*, 2d ed. (White Plains, NY: Knowledge Industry Publications, 1982).

39. Shirley Biagi, *Media/Impact: An Introduction to Mass Media* (Belmont, CA: Wadsworth Publishing, 1994), 17.

40. *Wall Street Journal*, March 6, 1992. Cited in Bagdikian, *The Media Monopoly*, xiii.

41. Kurtz, *The Media Circus*, 140.

42. Bagdikian, *The Media Monopoly*, 4 and 224.

43. Associated Press, "Few Tears Shed as Players Begin Their Summer Vacation," *Austin American Statesman*, August 12, 1994, D4.

44. William J. Puette, *Through Jaundiced Eyes: How the Media View Organized Labor* (Syracuse, NY: Cornell University Press, 1993).

45. Christopher Cook, "Press Gangs," *Texas Observer*, January 15, 1993, p. 19

46. Ibid.

47. Ibid.

48 Anthony Lewis, *Make No Law: The Sullivan Case and the First Amendment* (New York: Vintage Books, 1992), 7 and 11.

49. See Anthony Lewis, *Make No Law: The Sullivan Case and the First Amendment*. (New York: Vintage Books, 1992)

50. Howard Kurtz, *The Media Circus*, 140.

51. " Special Report: Tabloid TV's Blood Lust," *U.S. News & World Report*, July 25, 1994, 46–56.

52. Press release, School of Communication at the University of Miami, June 10, 1994.

53. Donald L. Bartlett and James B. Steele. *America: What Went Wrong?* (Kansas City, MO: Andrews and McMeel, 1992).

54 Lappé and DuBois, *The Quickening of America*, 129–130, 132–133.

55. Ibid., 134–135.

56. Bruce Selcraig, "Buying News," *Columbia Journalism Review*, July/August, 1994, 45.

57. Charles Wohlforth, "Good Morning, Tuntu-Tuyliak: Beyond 'Dance and Dysfunction' in Alaska," *Columbia Journalism Review*, July/August, 1994, 10–11.

58. Lappé and DuBois, *The Quickening of America*, 129–130.

8 *Participation Through Institutions: The Interest-Group Option*

Shellmira Green, a 17-year-old honor student at North Charleston High School in South Carolina was put off by some of the T-shirt slogans being worn by white students. One slogan that particularly annoyed her was, "Made of 100% Cotton, Picked by You."

Ever resourceful, Shellmira found herself a T-shirt that had the Confederate Flag on it. Instead of red, white, and blue for the stars and bars, the flag on her T-shirt featured red, black, and green—the colors of African liberation. When she wore it to school, Shellmira was suspended.

Her mother contacted the North Charleston branch of the National Association for the Advancement of Colored People (NAACP). Now she has a lawyer and has filed a federal civil rights suit.

Many organizations such as the NAACP which provide information, moral support, or social services also attempt to influence the political system by using a variety of strategies, including litigation. Because they try to influence the political system, regardless of what else they do, they can be classified as interest groups.[1]

If you become an active participant in the political system, sooner or later you will join, ally with, or oppose (on some issue or another) a political party, an interest group, or a political action committee (PAC)—probably all three. Dealing with these is not an option. They are everywhere in America. As Alexis de Tocqueville travelling in America in 1830 noted in his report to the people of France:

> In no country in the world has the principle of association been more successfully used, or more unsparingly applied to a multitude of different objects, than in America. Besides the permanent associations which are established by law under the names of townships, cities, and counties, a vast number of others are formed and maintained by the agency of private individuals. . . .
>
> [I]n the United States associations are established to promote public order, commerce industry morality, and religion; for there is no end which the human will, seconded by the collective exertions of individuals, despairs attaining.[2]

To deal skillfully with these organizations, perhaps by even creating one of your own, some background information seems appropriate.

THREE INSTITUTIONS FOR POLITICAL PARTICIPATION

Political parties, interest groups, and PACs are not the only institutions in which you can participate. One can also participate in the three branches of government which will be discussed in Chapters 10 through 14. In this chapter and the next we focus on parties, interest groups, and political action committees. We all examine their similarities, differences, and their roles in the political system.

Interest Groups

We define an **interest group** as an organization which seeks to influence government decisions without taking responsibility for running the government. This definition has three dimensions: organization, seeking to influence government decisions, and not taking responsibility.

The first dimension sets interest groups apart from interests. Not all interests (the unemployed, child abuse victims, college students, residents of a particular neighborhood) are organized to influence government. Interest groups are. Interest groups have structure, leaders, names, addresses, and usually phone numbers. You can mail a letter to an interest group. Interests are harder to correspond with.

The second dimension—seeking to influence government—brings under the definition of interest group many types of organizations that did not start out to influence government. Many religious, charitable, and ethnic organizations, as well as corporations, labor unions, and professional associations were not created to influence government. However, once they attempt to do so, they are treated analytically as interest groups. Thus, when a corporate executive appears before a state legislature to testify against new taxes or regulations protecting workers or the environment, that executive is not likely to be acting as a private citizen. He or she is there to represent an interest group which also happens to be a corporation.

The third dimension of our definition, not taking responsibility for running government, differentiates interest groups from parties. Parties seek to control government through getting their candidates elected. Interest groups seek to influence the decisions made by public officials once they've been elected or appointed.

It seems only fair to point out that this dimension is not included in the definitions of interest groups found in most other textbooks. Furthermore, our attempt to provide a narrowly focused definition for the purposes of informing future leaders about important distinctions between institutions for participation sets our definition apart from the much broader definition used by Hrebenar and Thomas in their excellent five-volume study of interest groups in the states: "any association of individuals or organizations, whether formally organized or not, that attempts to influence public policy."[3] We point this out as a reminder that scholars who study politics often define terms differently because they have different purposes. Hrebenar and Thomas are concerned with being inclusive and comprehensive.[4] In a single textbook covering many institutions and processes we must try to be a little more precise.

Political Action Committees (PACs)

A **political action committee,** or PAC is an organization created to collect money in order to influence elections through campaign contributions. Although PACs have been around for some time, their numbers expanded radically in the past two decades. At the national level they grew from 608 to more than 4,800 by the late 1980s. Since that time the growth overall has slowed somewhat at the national level according to Conybeare and Squire.[5] However, in states and communities where economic development has been taking place and social and economic diversity exists the increase has continued.[6]

PACs and Interest Groups: Similarities Shared

Four similarities are the reason why we will treat PACs as a sub-type of interest groups.

1. They both share the same political goal, influencing government decisions without taking responsibility for the consequences of those decisions. To attempt to do anything to an interest group which has promoted policies that have led to environmental damage, unsafe products, or the proliferation of weapons would be to deny that organization the rights of freedom of speech, freedom of assembly, and right to petition government for the redress of grievances. All three of these rights are guaranteed by the U. S. Constitution and by state constitutions.

   We can under some circumstances hold public officials to account, that is one reason why we need to know who finances their election campaigns, but we cannot hold interest groups to account as voters. We can of course join them in large numbers and try to take them over.

2. PACs and interest groups often share the same roof. With a few exceptions, about 75 percent of the PACs are departments of an interest group. Election campaign laws at the federal level and in many states forbid corporations and labor unions to make contributions from their own treasuries. So they set up political action committees with seperate treasuries or bank accounts and provide them with information useful in fund-raising. Charitable organizations cannot make contributions from their treasuries or they would lose their tax exempt status. Thus they also set up separate organizations.

3. Some PACs behave like interest groups. According to Larry Sabato, "The most important single trend in PAC development is not the swelling of the committees' treasuries but their increased emphasis on political education and grassroots activism."[7] In short, PACs perform many activities traditionally associated with interest groups.

Thus, if it walks like a duck, quacks like a duck, and swims like a duck, let's call it a duck.

4. Interest groups and PACs are similar in that they both help to create and to extend services to PACs. According to a leading scholar on PACs, the U. S. Chamber of Commerce has a PAC called the National Chamber Alliance for Politics (NCAP) which does not make campaign contributions at all.

   Instead of engaging in the one activity with which PACs are commonly identified the NCAP devotes its considerable resources to providing a variety of services to other business-oriented PACs. For example, staff research and analysis of the several thousand candidates competing in primary and general elections for the 435 house seats and the 33 or more senate seats up for election every two years results in the preparation of a list of opportunity races in which business-oriented candidates have a good chance of winning. It has been estimated that getting on the Chamber's opportunity list is worth about $100,000 in contributions from other PACs which follow the Chamber PAC's advice.[8]

Political Parties

A **political party** is an organization that seeks to manage government. In democracies a political party is an organization that seeks to take charge of government through winning elections, rather than through coups and terrorism. When the candidate of a party wins an election then, in a sense, the party "controls" that office. Naturally, the successful candidate has something to say about how he or she is going to operate in that office. However, on issues that matter to the party, in most legislatures members of the party vote together more often than not. Political parties are different from interest groups in four important respects.

1. Parties attempt to control the whole government. Interest groups merely attempt to influence a few particular decisions. If the party in control of government doesn't do a good job, then in theory, we can hold it responsible by electing candidates of the other party in the next election. There is no similar mechanism, even in theory, for holding an interest group responsible. Interest groups that obtain decisions that benefit them at the expense of the public interest can not be punished directly by the general public.

2. Parties offer slates of candidates at the county, state, and national levels. Interest groups do not. They may attempt to influence particular elections. They may even influence the process by which individuals seek party nominations. But an interest group does not nominate a slate of candidates to appear on the ballot under its label.

3. Parties are heavily regulated by state governments. Interest groups are not. The election codes of most states describe in some detail the way parties are supposed to operate, how they are to nominate candidates, and how they are to choose their officers. Except for requiring PACs to report how much money they receive and contribute to candidates, and requiring that lobbyists register and report expenditures, few states regulate the internal operation of interest groups in any significant way. Unlike party leaders, interest group leaders may make decisions on the use of group resources without consulting their members, and leadership selection is not regulated at all.

4. Parties are organized geographically from the precinct level to the national level. While some interest groups such as state medical associations may be organized on

the county level, very few interest groups are organized at all major geographic levels in the electoral system (precinct, ward, county, state, national) as are parties.

Although political parties are significantly different from interest groups they do share at least three features. First, they are organizations. True, some parties appear to be more organized than others. Will Rogers once observed, "I belong to no organized political party. I am a Democrat." Nevertheless, both major parties in each state have some kind of structure, officers, formal rules for conducting business, and state and local party headquarters that are open during election years, if not permanently.

A second similarity shared by both parties and interest groups is that they create PACs. In each house of Congress and in several state legislatures, the members in both parties have organized PACs, which raise funds intended to help the party keep the seats it has and attempt to gain more.

A third similarity was noted at the outset of this chapter; they are both institutions that promote political participation among their members In this similarity, however, there is a major difference. Political action committees attempt to promote participation among their members and, thus, are somewhat selective in their efforts via direct mail to promote political participation. Not everyone received a copy of the letter that caused President Bush to resign from the NRA, just people on their mailing list. Political parties, on the other hand, are virtually the only institutions in the political system that attempt to mobilize the general public to participate in the electoral process. Powell's Paradox, you may recall, addressed the relationship between a viable political party system and popular participation in elections (see Chapter 6). According to Powell, participation in general elections would increase by more than 10 percent if we had a stronger political party system in the United States at the state and local level. We will touch on this issue later on in Chapter 9 when we deal with the responsible party model.

THE VARIETY OF INTEREST GROUPS

There are many types of interest groups. No one classification scheme captures them all, and many groups belong in more than one category. The categories which follow are merely an attempt to explore the variety of interest groups and to provide some understanding of their role in the political system.

Public Interest Groups

Jeffrey M. Berry defines a public interest group as "one that seeks a collective good, the achievement of which will not selectively and materially benefit *only* the membership or activists of the organization."[9] In other words, public interest groups seek benefits that are available to the general public and are not limited to their members. Public interest groups also usually have several topics within the issue area upon which they focus. Common Cause and the League of Women Voters, for example, are primarily good government organizations seeking to promote open records, to reduce the effect of money in politics, and to encourage informed participation.

This definition does not mean that all other groups are against the public interest. It simply suggests that if they have a view of the public interest it is not shared by the public or that the public interest is not the primary focus.[10]

Included in the broad category of public interest groups are consumer, social justice (civil rights, and poverty), and environmental organizations. Women's organizations of general membership including the League of Women Voters and the National Organization for Women are also included in this category for reasons too numerous to mention.

Two of the best known public interest organizations are Common Cause, and the Public Interest Research Group. Common Cause was created in the 1970s by John Gardner, a former member of President Johnson's Cabinet. The Public Interest Research Group was created by Ralph Nader, a lawyer whose book, *Unsafe at Any Speed*, revealed dangerous flaws in the Chevrolet Corvair. The Public Interest Research Group is a staff-run organization that seeks contributions from foundations and the general public. Common Cause is a membership organization. Over 200,000 individuals across the nation belong to Common Cause.

Public Interest groups such as Common Cause, Ralph Nader's Public Interest Research Group, the Sierra Club, or the Environmental Defense Fund do not claim to be infallible judges of the public interest. What they do claim is that on various issues such as air pollu-

Ralph Nader is, depending upon one's point of view about seat belts, air bags, and other protections for consumers and workers, one of the good guys or one of the bad guys. Here he is giving an address at Ulster County Community College in Stone Ridge, New York.

tion, water contamination, unsafe drugs, and unsafe cars, the public has not had an opportunity to consider *all* the facts.

Thus, the public interest groups are seeking as much to get members of the general public to take the time to learn about these issues, and make up their own minds on these issues, as they are attempting to tell the public what is good for them. One of the functions of public interest groups is to create coalitions of individuals and interest groups that can agree on "the public's" side of a specific issue. In the process of seeking to create such coalitions, many voices are heard. Some organizations periodically poll their members to discover the issues that are paramount to them.

In short, public interest groups are concerned with getting certain issues on the public agenda. If, after careful consideration, the general public decides to tolerate air pollution and unsafe cars, as trade-offs for economic growth and cheap transportation, then it is possible that public interest groups will have done their job on those issues and turn to others. There are plenty of important issues on which the public appears to need more information.

Community Organizations

A considerable body of literature supports the notion that de Tocqueville's observations of America in the 1830's are still appropriate. Thousands of Americans are joining or creating community organizations of all sizes to do everything from taking back the streets from drug dealers to building better playgrounds for school children.[11] Some represent the disadvantaged, some represent middle class homeowners, some represent exclusive neighborhoods. Some deal only with city or county government, others operate from the neighborhood to the state level.

In an appendix to their *Quickening of America*, Lappé and DuBois list what they call, only a handful of the thousands of organizations nationwide that are making our democracy come alive to solve real problems."[12] Their "handful" includes the names, addresses, phone and fax numbers of over 100 organizations—many are regional, and state offices that are coordinating centers for dozens of local organizations. If you are interested in creating or getting involved in a community organization, two directories you may wish to consult are:

> David Walls, *Activists Almanac: The Concerned Citizen's Guide to the Leading Advocacy Organizations in America* (New York: Fireside Press, 1993).
>
> Sandi Brockway, ed., *Macrocosm USA: An Environmental, Political, and Social Solutions Handbook with Directions* (Cambria, CA: Macrocosm USA, Inc., 1992).

Neighborhood organizations have a stake in state and national policies in such fields as housing, historic preservation, urban redevelopment, economic development, and social justice.

Thus, far from being small-time or parochial, they are the grass roots organizations through which communities solve problems with and without government help.

Ethnic Organizations

Ethnic organizations are interest groups that help to keep ethnic groups and ethnic identity alive. Often ethnic organizations operate as community organizations, in neighorhoods where the population is fairly homogeneous. Ethnic organizations are interested in a wide range of issues that affect economic opportunities, political representation, and neighborhood issues such as police protection, public services, and education. It is important to note that not all ethnic organizations agree on every issue such as economic development (may provide jobs for some, but in the process, damage a neighborhood). Bilingual education which is appealing to Hispanic groups has less appeal to Asian and black organizations. In 1994 about 50 percent of the black voters in California supported the controversial proposition 187 which was intended to deny services to illegal immigrants—most of whom are Hispanic.

The difference between an ethnic group and an ethnic organization (or ethnic interest group) is essentially the same as the difference between an interest and an interest group. The difference is organization. Ethnic groups are not organizations. However ethnic interest groups are. To identify with an ethnic group involves an emotional commitment. To join an ethnic interest group involves committing additional political resources such as time, and even money.

Among the better known ethnic interest groups are the National Association for the Advancement of Colored People, The League of Latin American Citizens, B'nai B'rith, and the American Indian Movement. In addition to ethnic interest groups which are overtly political, many churches provide an organizational base for ethnic political activity.[13] Thus, some organizations could be classified as both religious and ethnic.

Organizations of Religious and Moral Concerns

Included in this category are local churches, synagogues, and temples of various denominations; the organizations which link them at district, regional, state, and national levels; and various associations to which several denominations may belong such as the National Council of Churches.

Religious organizations attempt to influence government at all levels on many issues such as social justice, hunger, racism, poverty, human rights, and the separation of church and state. In addition to traditional church-based organizations there are a number of groups that link television evangelists and secular conservative organizations.

Intergovernmental Organizations

Many organizations represent either units of government or public officials. They include the National Association of Counties, the U. S. Conference of Mayors, the National League of Cities, the International City/County Management Association, the National Governors Association, and the National Conference of State Legislatures.

Two of the several intergovernmental interest groups that publish reference works of use to professionals, scholars, and private citizens are the Council of State Governments and the International City/County Management Association. The CSG publishes *The Book of the States*. It contains numerous tables comparing the governments and policies of the several states. *The Book of the States* is revised every other year and is found in the reference section of most libraries. Also found there is *The Municipal Yearbook*, published by the ICMA, which contains articles on topics of current interest to local officials as well as tables and charts reporting on surveys of city government structure, policies, and expenditures.

In addition to publications, intergovernmental interest groups promote the sharing of ideas and information through workshops, conferences, and annual conventions. They also coordinate efforts to influence other levels of government. A state association of mayors, for example, keeps its members informed of bills before the legislature that may affect cities.

Labor Unions

Labor unions tend to be found in larger economic enterprises where personal friendships and family-style relationships between employers and employees are hard to maintain. Among the central concerns of labor unions in the political arena is the issue of the legal right to bargain collectively with management. Collective bargaining agreements occur after a majority of the employees, by secret ballot, have created or selected an organization to represent them in negotiating with the employer. These elections are protected by the National Labor Relations Act. A majority vote can end the collective bargaining arrangement as well.

As noted in Chapter 7, one of the major contributers to our view of American society and politics is the mass media and it has a decided bias against labor unions. For this reason it seems appropriate at this time to attempt to explain a common problem for all interest groups which is particularly vexing for labor unions.

The Free-Rider Problem

The fact that workers need to organize in order to bargain effectively with management, which is already organized, leads us to a classic problem facing any interest group that attempts to obtain benefits, or collective goods. Collective goods are those that anyone can enjoy whether or not he or she contributed to the process of acquiring them. Thus, legislation that an interest group obtains and that leads to cleaner air benefits everyone, whether they contributed to the interest groups or not. Many of us are free riders when it comes to some beneficial social reforms, although most of us try to contribute or "pay our dues" in one area or another.

Agency, Union, and Closed Shops

There are three ways to increase the likelihood that employees who benefit from a collective bargaining arrangement will contribute to the organization that does the bargaining.

In an agency shop no one is required to join the union but they are required to help pay the costs. Thus some workers who belong to the union pay full dues, while others who don't join may simply pay an agency fee.

In a union shop after a certain period of time every new worker must join the union. One cannot be a free rider for more than 60 to 90 days.

In a closed shop one cannot get a job unless one already belongs to the union. Closed shops are generally found only in the Northeast, and parts of the Midwest.

The arrangement that unions oppose and the business community prefers is one in which no employee is required to contribute either a fee or dues to the collective bargaining agent. This is generally known as a right to work law. It promotes free-ridership. Free riders are seen as the key to breaking up labor unions: "Hey, why pay dues when I can get all these benefits for nothing?"

Clearly, the term "right to work" indicates who has won in states where those laws exist. In union states more colorful terms are sometimes used to describe "right to work" laws.

In addition to representing employees in particular shops, mines, and factories, many local unions combine to form statewide and nationwide organizations. These organizations promote legislation designed to help both union members and have-nots. Thus, many labor unions lobby for legislation to provide public housing, mass transit, minimum wages, strict regulation of child labor, education assistance, Social Security, and medical assistance for the disadvantaged.

Business

Individual businesses compete with one another in the free enterprise system. Different types of businesses have different policy objectives. For example, General Motors and other large electricity users are currently lobbying the California Public Utilities Commission to allow for competition in the delivery of electricity through the power grid. The utility companies oppose this, and are joined by some consumer groups who believe that down the road the only people who will benefit from competition in the delivery of power are customers who can use a great deal of it.[14]

On other policy issues, power companies, big power users, and a majority of the business community have many interests in common. Most are employers and do not want labor unions protected, or workman's compensation laws too generous. Nearly all have to spend time and money dealing with various government regulations. They all are subject to various kinds of local, state, and national taxes. Many seek government assistance in a variety of ways and at all levels: from getting permission to block city streets for trucks to unload or equipment to work conveniently, to government loans and tax breaks.

There are three basic types of business interest groups: (1) individual firms, (2) trade associations, and (3) peak associations.

Individual Firms

This category includes large enterprises which may operate at local, state, and national levels such as General Motors, Exxon, or Boeing Aircraft, as well as smaller businesses of various sizes, many of which operate only at the local level.

Trade Associations

In any town there are a variety of businesses (automobile dealerships, flower shops, and grocery stores) each of which can be linked to others like it across the state or at the national level through a trade association. In recent years, trade associations have developed to link similar firms in large cities and metropolitan areas.

Peak Associations

These organizations include businesses in different fields that still have many shared interests. The U. S. Chamber of Commerce which is organized at the state and local level is perhaps the best known. It represents a wide range of firms. Others are the National Association of Manufacturers, also organized in many states, and the Business Roundtable which tends to represent very large corporations.

Local chapters of many business organizations are as much social organizations as they are economic or political. Here local business people gather to share experiences as employers, as taxpayers, and as people competing with big out-of-town enterprises.

Professional or Occupational Associations

This category contains numerous groups. Some of them, like the American Medical Association and the American Bar Association are very influential at the local, state, and national levels.

Most professional and occupational associations have essentially the same political goals: control over entry to the profession/occupation, control over standards in the profession, and the development of mechanisms through law or custom that provide economic benefits for those already in the profession/occupation.

A major goal of many professional/occupational interest groups is to get the state legislature to create a board or commission to "regulate" them. The members of the board are usually practitioners of the occupation/profession and have close ties to the interest group to which most practitioners belong.

While it is true that some professional/occupational interest groups represent people who are nearly always employees—teachers, nurses, and college professors, for example—many of the more affluent and powerful professional organizations represent people who are both professionals *and* business owners.

Most have a private practice that is essentially a business. In addition to owning or leasing an office, furniture, sophisticated phone systems, and office equipment, this business also has employees. As business owners, lawyers, accountants, and physicians have interests in profit, labor-management relations, investment tax policies, and government regulation which align them with the business community (Box 8.1).

Agricultural Organizations

This category of interest group includes organizations that represent individuals and enterprises associated with farms, dairies, orchards, ranches, and food processing plants. Among the variety of agricultural groups there are two more or less clear patterns: general and commodity.

The three largest general organizations are the American Farm Bureau Federation, the National Grange, and the National Farmers Union. Each of these organizations is stronger in some regions than others, and has closer ties to some crops than to others.

Among the commodity organizations are the big three marketing cooperatives that link dairy farming: the Associated Milk Producers Incorporated, Mid-American Dairies,

---

BOX 8.1

UNION SHOPS FOR LAWYERS IN RIGHT TO WORK STATES

In many states the professional association for lawyers (the state bar association) is actually in charge of determining who gets to practice law and who doesn't. This is sometimes called an "integrated bar." In this context, the term "integrated" has no relationship whatsoever to how many female, African American, or Hispanic lawyers practice law in that state. It means the professional association for lawyers is integrated with government. In integrated bar states, obtaining a law degree and passing the exam designed and administered by the bar association isn't enough. One must also be admitted to the bar, and one must pay dues to the bar association.

This "union shop for lawyers" is often found in "right to work" states. It is one of the interesting features of state politics that many of the states that give this kind of control to the state bar association do not give it to organizations of blue collar workers.

and Dairymen Inc. Each of these is organized at the state level, and is stronger in some regions than others.

While federal farm programs are of great interest to these organizations, many things that state and county governments do affect them as well. At the county level, government may or may not provide adequate office space for the County Extension Agent or vote funds for acquiring or maintaining a fair grounds and show barns to assist in the marketing of the counties' agricultural produce.

As our partial list indicates, a considerable variety of interest groups are operating in the several states and communities. The Hrebenar-Thomas survey of interest groups in the 50 states indicates 10 major trends in interest group activity over the past decade. They are summarized in Box 8.2

FUNCTIONS PERFORMED BY INTEREST GROUPS

A function is a contribution to the maintenance of a system. Thus we differentiate activities performed by interest groups such as lobbying, electioneering, appointmenteering, and so on, from the effect that these activities have on the political system. Among the functions performed by interest groups which help our political system to operate the way it does, five are particularly important. They are informing, representing, balancing, symbolizing, and mobilizing.

Informing

Interest groups bring information to decision makers who lack the staff resources to get it for them. Giving testimony at public hearings is an important part of the job of a lobbyist. Some of this testimony involves raw data, and some of it involves interpretations of what that data means.

In most state legislatures and local governments staff resources are not available to research all the issues. There are barely enough staff members to handle the flow of paperwork involved in bill drafting, reporting on hearings, and coordinating amendments and revisions. Thus, technical information on complex tax issues, or on the economic consequences of environmental regulation are valuable to decision makers. It doesn't matter whether it comes from an ordinary citizen, from a group representing have-nots, or a group representing haves. Technical information is a valuable resource.

Obviously it is not the only thing that influences decisions. Information about the political consequences of certain decisions is also important. Interest groups can supply this. That is one reason why the political consulting business has grown so much in recent years. Public opinion polling conducted by consultants paid by interest groups provides data about what the public wants, what it will tolerate, and how much discretion seems available to decision makers on certain issues.

Representing: By Interest Groups

A system of representation based on geographic districts is likely to overlook interests that do not form a majority in any particular electoral district. Interest groups provide a means for those who constitute a numerical minority to obtain representation in the decision-making process.

BOX 8.2

STATE-LEVEL INTEREST-GROUP POLITICS IN COMPARATIVE PERSPECTIVE

The ten major trends over the past decade in state-level interest groups in virtually every state:

1. A substantial increase in the number of groups active in state capitals.
2. A simultaneous expansion in the range or types of groups that attempt to affect public policy in the states.
3. The rise of public-service unions (especially teachers and public-employee associations), state and local government agencies as lobbying forces, and public interest and citizens groups.
4. An increased intensity of lobbying, because of the increased number and wider range of groups spending more time and money on lobbying state government than ever before.
5. More sophisticated interest-group tactics, which now include public-relations campaigns, networking (using a member contact system), and grass-roots lobbying, as well as coalition-building, newsletters, and more active participation in campaigns.
6. A phenomenal rise in the use of political action committees (PACs) by certain groups as a means of channeling money to favored candidates. Business, labor, and professional groups account for the bulk of PACs and their contributions.
7. Notable changes in the background and style of contract lobbyists (those hired for a fee specifically to lobby). The wheeler-dealer is being replaced by the technical-expert lobbyist, and more and more contract lobbying is being done by multiservice lobbying firms, law firms, and public relations companies.
8. An increase in the public monitoring of interest-group activity, as evidenced by the passage and strengthening of lobby laws and campaign finance and conflict of interest regulations.
9. Major shifts in interest-group power in the states, whether individual groups or groups as a whole. Business is having to share power with an increasing range of groups. Group influence as a whole appears to have increased, among other things, from the decline of political parties.
10. The role of interest groups within state political systems has expanded overall, in part due to the decline in parties.

In sum, with many states the interest group system is becoming more and more like that operating in the nation's capital.

Source: Ronald J. Hrebenar and Clive S. Thomas, eds., Interest Group Politics in the Midwestern States (Ames, IA: Iowa University Press, 1993), 17–18.

If 10 percent of a state population feels strongly about something, unless that 10 percent forms a majority in some particular constituency, they cannot even elect one representative in most state and local election systems. While it is true that in a close election race 10 percent of the vote is a significant number, many elections are not all that close. Furthermore, unless that interest organizes to try to prove that it was their 10 percent that made the difference between winning and losing, the significance of its vote will be lost. Winning candidates like to think of "all the people" as having spoken, not 41 percent plus some interest's 10 percent.

An interest group that combines (aggregates) the resources of 10 percent of the population in terms of campaign contributions, and volunteer activity, is much more likely to get the attention of the candidates. They may even compete for the endorsement (formal expression of support) by an interest group. Interest groups that have the attention of a candidate during the campaign, usually have access to that candidate when he or she becomes an officeholder. In this way, interest groups can represent numerical minorities.

Balancing

In *Federalist Paper #10,* James Madison stated his fear that powerful interest groups might be inclined toward what he called, "The Mischiefs of Faction," that is the tendency to seek goals that are, "adverse to the rights of other citizens or to the permanent . . . interests of the community." Some scholars of the modern era have suggested that this potential problem can be held in check by two kinds of counter-balancing interest groups: real and potential.

Real interest groups may promote the public interest as a direct goal or it may be a consequence of other less public spirited motivations. They may inform the public or appropriate officeholders of what the other side is attempting. Organized labor may thus counterbalance various business groups, environmentalists act as a check on industries that pollute, consumer groups act as a check on producers, or one business organization may oppose legislation that another is supporting.

Potential interest groups, according to David Truman, also keep interest groups from pushing the political system out of balance. Truman maintains that interest groups are aware that if they go too far in the pursuit of their own goals then members of the general public will organize in protest and may successfully compete with them for influence over government decisions. These nonexistent, potential groups, says Truman, thus act as a check on abuse of power by the interest groups that do exist.[15]

Symbolizing

Symbols can promote self-respect, can encourage individuals to believe in themselves and in the system that really doesn't seem to be working for them. Interest groups serve as symbols for individuals that they are not alone and that their values and their problems are shared by others.

Ethnic, cultural, religious, and other organizations increase the likelihood that their members will participate in the political system in a positive way. These organizations do so by providing these individuals with a positive identity, and the certain knowledge that they are not alone, that there is an organization to channel their talents and resources as well as their grievances into the political system.

The symbolizing function is performed in many ways, by pooling resources to build, buy, or rent a meeting place; by publishing newsletters informing members of events, individual achievements, and group victories; and by organizing meetings and social or ritual occasions to increase group solidarity and commitment.

Mobilizing

Mobilization is the process of getting people to act, to move from passive watching to active participation. In one sense this is simply another way of looking at grassroots lobbying. Interest groups influence decisions important to them by getting their membership and supporters to act, to write letters, to attend rallies, to contact decision makers, and to vote.

In another sense, mobilization is an important function that keeps a political system dynamic, alive, and open. Some interest groups recruit and train new leadership, and bring new people, new energy, new ideas, and fresh insights that make the state and local governments more responsive and thus more effective in serving community and individual needs.

INTEREST GROUPS AS INSTITUTIONS

Particular interest groups and parties may come and go, but the general practice of creating such organizations is well established at the national, state, and local levels. Both James Madison and Alexis de Tocqueville regarded them as necessary parts of our political system, as do we.

Box 8.3 indicates the many factors that vary from state to state and influence the ability of interest groups to affect public policy and the way they attempt to do so.

The last item in Box 8.3 is consistent in every state in one regard; interest groups are regulated far less than are parties. It is worth considering why this is so, as we will in the next chapter. At present we simply note that attempting to regulate the power of interest groups is a legitimate effort, though it may be difficult to regulate all interest groups the same way, given the variety of sizes, resources, and levels of activities. In the next section of this chapter we will discuss problems associated with interest groups to which regulation may be at least a partial solution.

Regulating Institutions

Madison was concerned about the damage that organized interests could do to the political system. He believed that there needs to be a method for "curing the mischiefs of faction," that is, the damage that interest groups can do by promoting policies that benefit a special interest at the cost of the public interest. As we noted in our definition, there is no way for us to use the ballot box to remove an interest group from power as we can remove a political party from power. Nevertheless, Madison felt that finding a way to limit the damage that can be done by special interests is an important job of government. In *Federalist #10* he observed that, "The regulation of these various and interfering interests forms the principal task of modern legislation."[16]

A few years later the insightful de Tocqueville referred to interest groups as associations. He was impressed by the way Americans made use of them, although he made it clear that our rudimentary parties and interest groups could be threats to the general good, as well as promoters of it. Even for an enlightened nineteenth century aristocrat like de Tocqueville, the grant to the common people of the opportunity to form political associations was seen not as a right but as a privilege, to be taken away or modified when abused. De Tocqueville was concerned that associations could too quickly be converted into conspiracies and cabals against the public order. He was very impressed by the way Americans joined together in organizations to raise barns, establish charities, and assist people who had suffered unforeseen loses through fire or flood. Americans he felt had learned how to use this privilege. Recent events might give him cause to reconsider.

He observed with some foresight that, "The unrestrained liberty of association for political purposes is the privilege which a people is longest in learning how to exercise."

BOX 8.3

MAJOR FACTORS INFLUENCING INTEREST-GROUP SYSTEMS IN THE STATES

The following seven factors influence the way interest groups are organized, the strategies and techniques they use, the resources available, and their success in influencing public policy in the several states.

1. *State Policy Domain*. The constitutional/legal authority of a state affects which groups will be politically active. The policies actually exercised by a state affect which groups will be most active.

2. *Political Attitudes*. Especially political culture and political ideology viewed in terms of conservative/liberal attitudes. Affects the type and extent of policies performed; the level of professionalization of the policy making process; acceptable lobbying techniques; and the degree to which interest groups are regulated.

3. *Level of Integration/Fragmentation of the Policy Process*. Factors such as the strength of political parties; power of the governor; number of directly elected cabinet members; or the use of initiative, referendum, and recall, will influence the number of options available to groups. Strong parties, strong governors, and the absence of plebiscatory democracy decreases the opportunities for interests groups to influence policy making, while more fragmentation increases them.

4. *Level of Professionalization of State Government*. Has an impact on the extent to which public officials need group resources and information. Also affects the level of professionalization of the lobbying system. The more professional the legislature and bureaucracy the more independent political leaders are of interst groups and the more professionally interest groups behave.

5. *Level of Socioeconomic Development*. Increased socioeconomic diversity results in a more diverse and competitive group system; a decline in the dominance of one or a few groups; new and more sophisticated techniques of lobbying, such as an increase in contract lobbyists, lawyer-lobbyists, multiclient/multiservice lobbying firms, grass-roots campaigns, and public relations techniques; and a general rise in the professionalization of lobbyists and lobbying.

6. *Level of Campaign Costs and Sources of Support*. As the proportion of group funding increases, especially that from PACs, group access and power increase.

7. *Extensiveness and Enforcement of Public Disclosure Laws*. Including lobby laws, campaign finance laws, PAC regulations, and conflict-of-interest provisions. Increases public information about lobbying activities that has an impact on the methods and techniques of lobbying; this in turn has affected the power of certain groups of lobbyists.

Source: *Ronald J. Hrebenar and Clive S. Thomas, eds.*, Interest Group Politics in the Northeastern States *(University Park, PA: Pennsylvania State University Press, 1993), 13–14.*

Thus, for two of the major contributors to modern American political theory, the notion of regulating both parties and interest groups seemed quite legitimate. An interesting term paper topic might be a comparison of state regulations of parties and of interest groups in your state. If your state is typical, parties are much more heavily regulated than are interest groups.

PROBLEMS ASSOCIATED WITH INTEREST GROUPS

Whether we call them "mischiefs of faction," as did Madison, or think of them as abuses of privilege as did de Tocqueville, there are at least seven problems associated with interest groups about which informed observers of the political system ought to be aware.

Irresponsibility

Interest groups by definition are not responsible, not accountable to the general public. They are not held accountable for the results of the government decisions they influence. When lobbyists for an interest group get a wrinkle written into a tax law that makes it more profitable to close down a mine or a factory and write off the losses than it would be to keep the enterprise going, we cannot hold the interest group responsible for the jobs lost and the human suffering that results. The elected officials might be held responsible, but not the lobbyists.

Many interest groups are not even responsible to their members. As Box 8.4 indicates, dues-paying members and voluntary contributors are but one source of funding for interest groups. Thus, when members unhappy with the actions of group leaders leave the group, substitutes for lost dues can be found from other sources. While many interest groups depend heavily on dues, many do not. The fundraising letter that caused President Bush to resign from the NRA raised over a million dollars.

The realities of mass mailed solicitations are such that many organizations can survive on less than a 10 percent response to each 200,000 item mailing. Thus, rejection by 90 percent of those solicited still leaves interest group leaders with the ability to claim that they have received several thousand contributions and letters supporting their position.

Government by the Few

Robert Michels observed the tendency for small numbers of people within organizations to run them. He called it the **Iron Law of Oligarchy**.[17]

Michels was saying much more than the fact that large numbers of people have to choose representatives to handle the details of day-to-day organization. What Michels was concerned with was the fact that in many organizations small numbers of individuals take over organizations and abolish the linkages that hold them accountable to the membership. Elections are held at inconvenient times, nomination becomes a complex or secret process, election procedures are introduced such as proxy voting which allows one person to cast votes for many other people.

On the face of it there is nothing wrong with the fact that, once in office, many interest group leaders tend to stay there for an entire career. One way to recruit talented people and get a commitment from them to the organization is to offer job security. However, when the procedures for making sure that the leaders are doing what the members want begin to erode, then job security takes on ominous features.

If many organizations run by small elites that are not responsible to their membership exist in a society, that may present no great problem. However, when those organizations marshal considerable political resources to influence the selection of government officials and the decisions those officials make, then that may become a problem. Government unduly influenced by irresponsible organizations can become irresponsible government.

Undemocratic Decision Making

No one expects corporations and financial institutions to be run democratically. Many act as interest groups and organize PACs to raise funds "voluntarily." Box 8.5 represents an exception, not the rule. Thus, it is no surprise that undemocratic institutions operate in our political system.

However, we might have some expectations about interest groups that are voluntary membership organizations. Common Cause provides an example of how an organization can give its membership the opportunity to influence the selection of issues and strategies on which group resources will be expended. Every year a detailed survey of membership positions on issues is taken. The questions have neutral wording, and members can indicate the direction and intensity of their opinions on these issues.

The results of the poll are printed in an issue of *Common Cause Magazine*. Furthermore, many issues of the magazine contain pro and con debates on an important public question that is likely to be of concern to the membership. Thus, the leadership of Common Cause is as concerned with accurately reflecting the opinions of its membership as it is.

Common Cause is, however, as much a departure from the norm as is the behavior of the bank official in Box 8.6. The much more common practice of leaders in interest groups is to use the journal of the interest group to promote a hard-line, uncompromising position on issues; and to send out mailings that are disguised as surveys but that are not really legitimate efforts to survey opinion. Many "surveys" mailed out by interest groups are actually efforts to mobilize members to take action and at the same time to raise funds.

BOX 8.4

FIVE MAJOR SOURCES OF INTEREST GROUP FUNDS

1. Member dues and contributions
2. Selective benefits
3. Television and direct mail solicitations
4. Publications and fees
5. Foundations and wealthy contributors
6. Government grants

Source: Jeffrey M. Berry, The Interest Group Society (Boston: Little, Brown & Co., 1984), 88–90.

BOX 8.5

INTEREST GROUP DEMOCRACY: COMMON CAUSE

Common Cause is not the only democratically run interest group: it does, however, offer a basis for asking questions about other interest groups which claim to be so.[18] Each year Common Cause does two things that few other interest groups do.

First, it distributes a mailed questionnaire to its members giving them the opportunity to identify the issues that concern them. The questions are worded to seek information, not to influence. No inflammatory rhetoric is used as in some interest group polls. The results of this poll are reported in *Common Cause Magazine* and are a major source of guidance for the board of directors and the executive director in terms of allocating resources in the coming year.

This contrasts significantly from the usual method of interest group communication with members. In many, if not most, interest groups the leadership chooses the issues and then presents one side to the membership through literature designed to motivate both contributions and letters to government officials.

A second way in which Common Cause differs from most interest groups is that its members nominate and elect the 60-member board of directors by mail. The terms are staggered. No one has to make decisions on 60 offices all at once. Months before elections are scheduled, the Washington Office of sends out requests for nominations, then prepares and distributes brief biographical sketches of each candidate for the board of directors, and ballots for voting.

Democracy through the mails is not the only, nor the best method, of choosing leadership. Some interest groups choose their leadership through a system of state, regional, and national conventions. Both methods indicate that interest groups can be operated democratically.

Misrepresentation: The Selective Benefits Problem

Selective benefits attract both members and customers. Selective benefits are items or services that are provided to individuals for belonging to an organization. Some people are more likely to pay dues to join an interest group if they get something in return. These selective benefits may include journals (professional and recreational), discounts on various purchases (insurance, travel, medicine, and items used in one's business whether one is a farmer or a physician).

The selective benefits problem is that many interest group members are really customers, not members. They belong primarily because they purchased a package of selective benefits, not because they joined up to promote a cause or enjoy the company of other group members. Table 8.1 provides some basis for making these observations. The Farmers Union is an organization that represents farmers whose landholdings are relatively small (in effect, the traditional family farm). As Table 8.1 indicates, the Farmers Union would lose about half of its membership if it stopped lobbying. The members apparently are aware of what the organization stands for and that is a major reason why they belong to it.

The Farm Bureau Federation is both a major insurance company and a group that looks after the interests of large corporate farms, collectively referred to as agribusiness. If it stopped lobbying, the Federation would still keep over 75 percent of its membership. Why? Because most of them are insurance customers, not serious supporters of policies that benefit

BOX 8.6

RAISING PAC MONEY WITH GENTLE PERSUASION

When the president of Mutual Bank in Boston found out that some of the bank's 64 officers had failed to contribute to the banking industry's state and federal political action committees (PACs), he fired off a memo to all of them, saying in no uncertain terms why they should ante up:

This is unacceptable. . . . All of you are fully aware of the importance to this bank of the issues being voted on this year. I hope none of you is so naive as to think that political contributions—even those from PACs, despite all the pious rhetoric—do not play a vital part in the progress of such matters. . . . Every single officer of this institution should—must—consider it a part of his or her position to contribute . . . Even if you give substantially to individual candidates, you should, as officers of this bank, all support the PACs.

Before the memo, only 19 of 64 officers had been persuaded to contribute to the banking industry PACs; afterwards the number jumped to 48.

Source: Common Cause Magazine (January/February, 1985), 8.

agribusiness. Many, if not most, Farm Bureau "members" are not concerned and perhaps not even in agreement with the policy stands the leadership of that organization takes. Since Farm Bureaus in most states do not poll their "members" on issues, we will never know.[19]

The implications of this for you as a future decision maker are pretty important. When spokespersons for groups financed largely by the sale of selective benefits tell you that their membership wants something, a good question to ask is, "How do you know what your members want?" Perhaps it might be appropriate to ask well funded interest groups to poll their members occasionally, using of course unbiased questions, perhaps even hiring a professional polling organization to design and conduct the poll.

Table 8.1

TWO MINNESOTA FARM ORGANIZATIONS—MEMBERS OR CUSTOMERS?

Item	Percent Farm Bureau Members	Percent Farmers Union Members
1. If organization provided lobbying but no services, would drop out	56	45
2 If organization provided services but no lobbying, would drop out	23	46

Source: Terry M. Moe, The Organization of Interests (Chicago: The University of Chicago Press, 1980), 205–217.

Diversity

Given the consensus reaching back to Madison and de Tocqueville that regulation of interest groups is a legitimate and necessary function, the sheer numbers and variety of types of interest groups makes it extremely difficult to design a method of regulation that is rational, effective, and fair. It doesn't mean we shouldn't try.

All states regulate political parties. This is easier because there aren't very many of them. However, the task of regulating the "mischiefs of faction" is more complex in the case of interest groups.

One exception to the limited regulation of interest groups is the fact that the government does regulate labor unions to assure they are run democratically and that members get a chance to hear both sides of issues on which the power and influence of the organization is brought to bear. If we are to design laws for other interest groups that govern their leadership selection and their decision-making processes, how should churches or religious organizations be treated?

One way might be to exempt religious organizations and use some kind of threshold in terms of economic resources. Thus, a neighborhood organization or a public interest group might not have to spend scarce resources on member surveys as Common Cause does. On the other hand, an organization with a budget of over $60 million such as the National Rifle Association might be required to spend some of it on unbiased member surveys and on increasing the level of information about both sides of issues of concern to NRA members, as well as NRA leaders.[20]

Paralysis of Government: Hyperpluralism

Hyperpluralism is the process by which well-financed interest groups operating as a loose network of mutually supporting seekers of self interest can ultimately lead to a situation in which particular groups gain control of the portion of the government that most closely affects them. The officials in charge, whether appointed or elected, agree with the interest group that put them there and helps keep them there.

This can, as Theodore Lowi suggests, result in the paralysis of government. No action is taken in the public interest because it might interfere with some particular group's private interest. Interest groups can thus be issued licenses to pollute streams, underground water supplies, and the air; produce unsafe products, maintain unsafe working conditions for employees, and engage in competitive practices that destroy small businesses or destroy institutions which benefit the general public such as mass transit systems, parks, beaches, and other recreational areas.

One rather egregious example of ways in which interest groups have helped to close doors on policies and programs at the state and local level which might have been in the public interest involves mass transit.

Early in this century, at a critical stage in the development of urban transportation when a variety of policy choices were available, a consortium of corporations heavily influenced the decision-making process by buying up and then destroying electric trolley systems in about 50 large American cities. When they did this, there weren't all that many large American cities. Thus they set a pattern for how things would be done in other cities as they grew. In 1949, in a Chicago courtroom in a Federal Court a jury found General Motors guilty of conspiracy in restraint of trade. General Motors was fined $5,000 and its treasurer was fined one dollar.[21] The 50 light rail mass transit systems were never rebuilt.

San Francisco is one of the few remaining cities in America which has a trolley system that was not destroyed by the conspiracy devoted to the expanded use of gasoline and diesel-powered vehicles.

The current condition of mass transit in American cities is not wholly due to the effect of this conspiracy. However, by destroying electric trolley car systems, by channeling talent and energy to other methods of moving people and goods, the conspiracy doubtless shaped the options considered and the decisions made. At that time in our history, the governments of the several states and cities affected were unable to deal with this assault on the public interest.

The implications of a strong mass transit system for reducing urban sprawl and the inefficient use of time and fuel are too many to develop here. However, it seems fairly obvious that urban sprawl has been rather expensive for state and local taxpayers which foot the bill for education, police, fire, sewer, and water services as populations spread haphazardly across the landscape.

The Business Bias

One of the most important features of the interest group system is that it is unbalanced. There are more business interest groups than any other kind. Furthermore, as we have already indicated, many people who practice high prestige professions are, in effect, operators of business enterprises—law firms and medical practices. On the whole, in struggles between business and nonbusiness groups, business interest groups are better equipped. They have more money, more prestige, more resources to offer elected and appointed government officials. Business interests can employ experienced, skilled, full-time professionals to communicate their position on various issues and write their salaries and expense accounts off as part of the cost of doing business.

This imbalance should come as no surprise, but one does need to confront it early on and take it as a feature of the interest group system, rather than the result of some evil plot. In a landmark survey of state political systems, Sarah McCally Morehouse examined the dominant types of interest groups in each of the fifty states and the degree to which interest groups as a whole influenced the state political system.[22]

One of the most important findings of this survey was that regardless of the comparative strength of the interest groups in each state political system, in virtually every state, business groups predominate. They are regarded by legislators, journalists, executive officials, and other informed sources as having more influence on the political system than other types of interest groups. Second, in states where interest groups are strongest, business interests are even more predominant. The stronger the interest group system, the stronger are business groups within it. In states where interest groups are relatively weak, business organizations constituted 58 percent of the interest groups, where interest groups are strong the business percentage goes up to 75 percent.[23]

The fact that the interest group system is biased in favor of businesses would not be very important if most Americans were the owners of or executives in businesses. However, most Americans are employees and/or consumers. Thus, there are times when the interests of the business community and the interests of the general public do not coincide. If the strongest institutions in the political system are biased in favor of business, then it is reasonable to question whether the general public interests will be adequately looked after.

CONTROLLING THE MISCHIEFS OF FACTION

There are four basic methods of limiting the damage interest groups can do to the political system while enabling interest groups to continue to make positive contributions to the political system. They are: disclosure, regulation, public financing, and strengthening other institutions.

Disclosure

Disclosure involves letting the public know about sources of money, and uses of money in attempting to influence public decisions. Disclosure requires interest groups (as well as parties and candidates) to make clear where they get their financial resources and what they do with them. By requiring that the use of money in politics takes place in the public eye, instead of behind the scenes, disclosure requirements may help voters and public officials decide whether or not they want to support a given candidate or course of action.

At the very least, disclosure may suggest to some that a careful look be taken at a proposal or candidate receiving heavy financial support from a particular interest group. The two activities interest groups engage in which are most subject to disclosure requirements are electioneering and lobbying.

Disclosure may be more effective when there is an adequately financed independent agency that both enforces the reporting requirements and makes information about contributions easily available to the public before the election. Only twenty-two states have such agencies.[24]

Disclosure can occur, of course, without doing much good. Collecting file cabinets full of reports that enterprising citizens, journalists, and scholars may read only if they come to the office of the secretary of state in the state capital and request them, is better than no disclosure at all. This arrangement is much better in a small state than in a large one.

Disclosure can be even more effective, however, if periodic reports are published which can be more easily digested and transformed into newspaper stories, or questions to ask at candidate forums. In a few pioneering states campaign reports from candidates and from PACs are availiable on the internet. Does your state do this?

Regulation

This approach involves requiring an interest group to do something or forbidding it to do something. Usually regulation involves the amount of money an interest group (or PAC) can contribute to a candidate or party.

Some state regulations make it illegal for corporations and labor unions to contribute directly to a candidate from company funds or from union dues. That is one reason why PACs are created, to provide a fund raising organization separate from the corporation, union, or interest group.

Other limitations may involve the internal operation of the interest group itself. The Landrum-Griffin Act is a federal law that requires labor unions to make detailed reports of union constitutions and rules. Furthermore, certain types of persons are forbidden to hold union office: ex-convicts, Communists, and people with conflicting business interests (a union member who owned a printing company might be tempted to benefit his or her own business via his or her control over union funds). One of the intentions of the Landrum-Griffin Act was to make union leaders accountable to union members.[25]

The same kinds of controls over the internal affairs of various wealthy PACs and large interest groups might further accountability in those organizations as well. Thus far, however, little effort has been made to require by law that elections (in organizations other than unions and political parties) are held democratically, that members who disagree with interest group leaders get the opportunity to be heard by the rest of the membership, or that both sides of important issues be presented in interest group journals and other mailings.

Public Funding

Public funding of elections has become a favorite target of talk show hosts and other defenders of a status quo that favors recipients of PAC largesse and those with personal fortunes to invest in their own campaigns. In *Buckley* vs. *Valeo* the Supreme Court struck a blow to campaign reform that makes it difficult to impose spending limits unless they are tied to public funding. Thus, public funding of at least part of a candidate's campaign is not to provide "welfare for politicians" but rather to make it possible to limit campaign expenditures or make the refusal to accept public funding and limits a campaign issue. In this way the escalating cost of campaigns and the role of money in politics might be held to reasonable limits.

The federal government, 17 states, and a few cities, provide resources for the election campaigns of certain candidates or their parties. Candidates who meet certain qualifications indicating that they have a significant amount of public support can receive funds, if they promise to adhere to limitations on their campaign expenditures.

In 13 states taxpayers indicate whether or not they wish a portion of their state income taxes to be placed in a fund for public funding of election campaigns. In seven states taxpayers can add a contribution called a surcharge to the state campaign financing fund. In California the surcharge sum is matched by the state.

In some states these funds are turned over the political parties, in others they are given directly to candidates for various offices, usually statewide rather than legislative. In Utah the county central committee of the party designated by the voter gets 50 percent of the checkoff funds. Hawaii appropriates funds for all nonfederal elective offices. New Jersey provides funds only for the gubernatorial election, while three other states make funds available to campaigns for more than one state office.[26]

In Seattle, Washington, and Tucson, Arizona, candidates for city council and for mayor receive public funds if they agree to limit the total amount of money they spend in their campaigns.[27]

As we have observed before, money is not the only political resource. Instead of providing funds in exchange for limits on candidate expenditures, at least one city is considering the provision of free time on cable TV; office space, and polling, printing, and secretarial services.[28]

Strengthen Other Institutions

While it is not a perfect relationship because many factors are involved, the stronger the interest groups in a state, the weaker are other institutions such as political parties, the legislature, and the executive branch of government. In the face of interest group domination they are less able to govern, to deliver on campaign promises, and to promote policies for the have-nots.

Thus, if you wish to limit imbalance in a state political system between interest groups and other institutions, you would probably not want to introduce reforms that weaken other institutions. You might even attempt to: (1) dilute the relative influence of interest groups by raising the level of education and awareness of the general public, (2) strengthen other institutions such as political parties, (3) increase the resources available to state and local legislatures, and (4) make it easier for the governor to hold the heads of executive agencies accountable to the chief executive rather than to the interest groups with which they deal most closely.

In the chapters to follow, we will discuss these institutions and ways to strengthen them. The purpose of strengthening other institutions is not to obliterate interest groups, or even render them powerless, but simply to let them continue doing the good things they do well, while preventing them from advancing the mischiefs of faction.

CONCLUSION

In this chapter we have identified two types of institutions through which you can influence government: interest groups and political parties. We have attempted to demystify PACs, treating them essentially as interest groups. We have broadly sketched the wide variety of interest groups involved in state and local politics, but our list of types is by no means exhaustive.

Our discussion of the advantages and disadvantages of interest groups doubtless was not intended to suggest that interest groups (and PACs) are illegitimate institutions or that they should be removed from the political system. We simply bring attention to the possibility that the political system is out of balance. The balance could be corrected slightly if other institutions, such as parties and some part of government, were better able to promote the public interest. At present these other institutions are ill equipped in many states and communities to help interest groups correct their own problems.

Take for example, the problem of misrepresentation. There are many businesspeople who would be appalled by the extreme positions taken by interest group leaders in the name of their sector of the business community, just as there are many responsible gun owners who are embarrassed by, or at least unsympathetic to, some of the positions taken by the National Rifle Association. When interest groups predominate, parties and government have little opportunity to require interest group leaders to act more responsibly to their followers.

These observations will be tested in the pages to come. Naturally, since we choose the evidence, it won't be an unbiased test. Therefore, we urge you to conduct your own tests in the course of deciding how you are going to participate in politics.

STUDY OBJECTIVES

1. Identify the three dimensions of our definition of interest group.
2. Compare and contrast interest groups and parties.
3. Identify four similarities between PACs and interest groups.
4. Identify the difference between an interest and an interest group.
5. Identify the three major types of business interest groups.
6. Identify the major issue that concerns labor unions.
7. Identify two publications associated with intergovernmental interest groups.
8. Identify a public interest group, differentiate it from one or more of the other types.
9. Differentiate between an ethnic group and an interest group.
10. Identify the functions performed by interest groups.
11. Identify the seven problems associated with interest groups.
12. Identify four ways to reduce the effect of problems associated with interest groups (controlling the "mischiefs of faction").

GLOSSARY

Disclosure   involves letting the public know about sources and uses of money, in attempting to influence public decisions. Disclosure requires interest groups (as well as parties and candidates) to make clear where they get their financial resources and what they do with them.

Ethnic organizations   Interest groups that help to keep ethnic groups and ethnic identity alive.

Interest group   is an organization that seeks to influence government decisions without taking responsibility for running the government.

Iron Law of Oligarchy   The tendency for small numbers of people within organizations to run them.

Litigation   The use of the legal system to influence public decisions.

Political action committee (PAC) An organization created to collect money in order to influence elections, largely through campaign contributions.

Political party An organization that seeks to control government. In democracies a political party is an organization that seeks to control government through winning elections, rather than through coups and terrorism.

Potential interest groups Groups which, according to some theorists, will emerge from the general public if existing interest groups misbehave excessively. The effectiveness of this threat is demonstrated in part by the level of air pollution, homelessness, and fairness of state-local taxes. In other words, your assessment of the condition of society is a measure of your assessment of the effectiveness of potential interest groups.

Real interest groups Simply another term for interest group. It is used in the discussion of potential interest groups to differentiate that which could be from that which is.

ENDNOTES

1. Associated Press, August 28, 1994.

2. Alexis de Tocqueville, *Democracy in America*, vol. 1, trans. Henry Reeeve (New Rochelle, NY: Arlington House, 1966), 177.

3. Ronald J. Hrebenar and Clive S. Thomas, eds. *Interest Group Politics in the Northeastern States* (University Park, PA: Pennsylvania State University Press, 1993), 9.

4. Ibid., 10.

5. John A. C. Conybeare and Peverill Squire, "Political Action Committees and the Tragedy of the Commons," *American Politics Quarterly*, 1994, 22:2, 154.

6. David Lowery and Virginia Gray. "The Nationalization of State Interest Group System Density and Diversity," *Social Science Quarterly*, 1994, 75:2, 368–369.

7. Larry J. Sabato , *PAC Power: Inside the World of Political Action Committees* (New York: W. W. Norton and Company, 1984), 165.

8. Ibid., 47.

9. Jeffrey M. Berry, *Lobbying For The People: The Political Behavior of Public Interest Groups* (Princeton, NJ: Princeton University Press, 1977), 7.

10. Some authors use the term *Public Interest Group* to refer to organizations that represent units of government, or government officials. Deil S. Wright, for example, *Understanding Intergovernmental Relations* (North Scituate, MA: Duxbury Press, 1978), 61. While it is true that we are all in big trouble if these organizations do not keep the public interest in mind, we have chosen to use Berry's definition.

11. France Moore Lappé and Paul Martin DuBois, *The Quickening of America: Rebuilding Our Nation Remaking Our Lives* (San Francisco, CA; Jossey-Bass, Inc., 1994), 301–305.

12. For a discussion of QCCO and its successful confrontation with the powerful Port Authority of New York and New Jersey see Michael Dorman, "The Bigger They Are," *Empire State Magazine*, 1983.

13. Edgar Litt, *Ethnic Politics in America* (Glenview, IL: Scott, Foresman and Company, 1970), 49–59.

14. *Austin American Statesman*, Austin, TX, August 28, 1994, D 5.

15. David Truman, *The Governmental Process* (New York: Knopf, 1951), 33.

16. James Madison, *Federalist #10*.

17. Robert Michels, *Political Parties* (New York: Dover Publications, 1959), see especially "Democracy and the Iron Law of Oligarchy," 377–393.

18. For an excellent theoretical treatment of Common Cause in the larger interest group context, see Andrew S. McFarland, *Common Cause: Lobbying in The Public Interest* (Chatham, NJ: Chatham House Publishers, Inc., 1984).

19. Mikkel Jordahl, "The Texas Farm Bureau," *The Texas Observer*, Austin, TX, April 19, 1985, 9–12.

20. National Rifle Association, Annual Financial Report for 1987 to the New York Department of State. The NRA's largest opponent is Handgun Control. In contrast to the $69 million revenues of the NRA, Handgun Control's report to the New York Department of State indicates $3 million in revenues.

21. Testimony of Tom Bradley, Mayor of Los Angeles, before the U. S. Senate Subcommittee on Antitrust and Monopoly, Judiciary Committee, U. S. Senate, 93rd Congress, February 26—March 1, 1974. Quoted in Mark Schneider, *Suburban Growth: Policy and Process*, (Brunswick, OH: King's Court Communications, Inc., 1980), 32–33.

22. Sarah McCalley Morehouse, *State Politics, Parties and Policy* (New York: CBS College Publishing, 1981).

23. L. Harmon Zeigler, "Interest Groups In The States," in Virginia Gray, Herbert Jacob, and Kenneth N. Vines, eds. *Politics in the American States*, 4th ed. (Boston: Little, Brown & Co., 1984), 103.

24. *The Book of the States, 1986–87*, 185–189.

25. Richard B. Morris, ed. *Encyclopedia of American History*, 6th ed. (New York: Harper and Row Publishers, 1982) 526.

26. *The Book of the States, 1986–87*, 206–207.

27. *Austin American-Statesman*, July 23, 1985.

28. Ibid., A-10.

CHAPTER

9

Institutions for Participation: Political Parties

PURGING A DEMON

This is the fourth and final chapter directly addressed to participation in the affairs of your states and local communities. It pulls together the threads of an argument that has been laid out throughout the preceding chapters.

The argument is this. Our political systems are out of balance. The system of special interest organizations which is biased toward the haves has increased in numbers and in influence over the past 20 years. The party system which, under the right circumstances, could be biased toward the middle class and the have-nots has declined over the past 20 years.

To correct the imbalance many actions need to be taken. One which seems paramount is to strengthen political parties. In order to present the case for making parties stronger we must not only examine what they are, and what they could become, we must attempt to purge a demon.

That demon is the term "political machine." In other contexts the word machine has a benevolent image. It connotes a smoothly running entity that operates without much interference from its immediate environment. While in politics the term "machine" implies corruption, in other contexts it does not. The "Big Red Machine" was a term once used in reference to the athletic prowess of the Cincinnati Reds Baseball Team. It was never intended to refer to the propensity of one of its superstars to make the occasional wager on sporting events.

The reason for the need to purge the political machine demon is that our political culture and the media constantly reinforce the notion that a strong political party organization is a political machine. Even scholars with eminent pro-party credentials such as Larry Sabato use the term "machine" to describe

253

strong parties—though they are well aware of the difference between Boss Tweed and strong, coherent state and local party organizations.[1]

Politics, after all, has a bad enough rap as it is. To add the burden of cleaning up the term "political machine" is too much to ask. We have no intention of cleaning up that term. We simply intend to suggest that we purge it, that it not be used to describe strong parties, that journalists and essayists who do so be faulted for the use not only of a cliché but also of using an inaccurate one.

We also intend to indicate that there is a difference between a strong party and a Boss Tweed type of political machine. Fortunately, we will have a lot of help from some outstanding scholars specializing in state, local, and party politics.

There is much at stake in our attempt. If parties really do decline or disappear, who will win? As Larry Sabato points out, the following will benefit: special interest groups and PACs, wealthy and celebrity candidates, incumbents, the news media (particularly tabloid television), and political consultants.

Who will lose? That's a question this chapter attempts to answer.

We proceed as follows:

First, we will examine the political machine and the reforms adopted to kill it off. In the process, we will note political parties were done some serious damage.

Second, we will discuss political parties as they are. The good news is that they are alive and well and doing a pretty good job.

Third, we will examine a model system in which strong parties could make government more accountable to ordinary voters than it currently is.

Finally, we will suggest some changes that might be made to correct the balance.

Along the way we will emphasize that we are not facing catastrophe. Our system is pretty good, just the way it is. Our concern is that you be prepared to look critically at attempts to change it in one direction or another. We hope you don't plan to weaken parties further. Whether you choose to strengthen them is up to you.

POLITICAL MACHINES AND THE WEAKENING OF PARTIES

Although we have a two-party system at the state and national level, the party system is weaker than the interest group system in most states and municipalities. In most states the electoral party plays almost no role in determining who the party's candidates will be in the general election. In most city elections party labels do not even appear on the ballot.

In order to understand why these conditions exist we must review the place of patronage-based nineteenth-century urban political machines and the reform movement in American political history. We begin with a "dirty" word—patronage.

Patronage

Patronage, to put it mildly, is a much-abused word. It is so heavily laden with negative connotations that a paragraph or two is necessary in order to gain some perspective. We begin by pointing out that patronage is a rather ancient practice. The Latin root for patronage is *patronus*, or protector. That word in turn comes from the Latin word for father, *pater*.

A patron is someone who protects, supports, or advances the cause of something or someone else. Its basic idea is similar to the more fashionable term today—mentor.[2] The nature of a patronage relationship varies with the context in which it is found. Patrons are customers in stores and restaurants. They are the financial supporters of art museums and of charitable enterprises. Sometimes specialized words are used to describe patrons. Backers of Broadway shows are called "angels." In some police departments the patron who looks after the career of a subordinate is called a "rabbi." Rabbi means "teacher" and teachers or patrons provide guidance, insight, and information about other people, about how to get things done, and where the opportunities lie.

Although parents care for their children and may, in their old age, be cared for by them, no one seriously advances the parent-child relationship as merely one involving the exchange of child-rearing for old-age benefits. However, it is quite common for people to be cynical about patron-client relationships. A cynic, you may have heard, is one who knows the price of everything and the value of nothing. It is as unproductive to reduce complex human relationships to self-interested barters as it is naive to deny that there is a variety of dimensions involved in many honorable human relationships.

While we extend the benefit of the doubt to patron-client relationships in the realm of charitable, educational, and religious institutions, political relationships are particularly vulnerable to oversimplification and cynical assessment. Thus, to people with little familiarity with the human relationships involved in politics, patronage is very likely to be seen as illegitimate or corrupt rather than as one way of promoting a number of quite legitimate goals. As Box 9.1 suggests, given the choice between two equally qualified candidates for a job, it seems rational for a person with a job to fill to choose the candidate whose political loyalty and enthusiasm have been demonstrated, or does it?

Either way you are dealing with patronage. Patronage may involve not only making decisions in favor of one's supporters— all other things being equal. It may also include encouraging people to become supporters.

In an abstract world where all other things are equal, it is possible to practice patronage in a moralistic way. In the real world, particularly the world of politics, all other things are seldom equal. Thus, the practice of patronage requires and is sometimes given the benefit of the doubt.

Machine Politics

A **political machine** is an organization that practices machine politics. Usually it does so after taking control of a state or local political party. According to Raymond Wolfinger, **machine politics** and political machines are "two quite different phenomena":

> *Machine politics is the manipulation of certain incentives to partisan political participation: [for example] favoritism based on political criteria in personnel decisions, contracting, and in the administration of the laws. A 'political machine' is an organization that practices machine politics, i.e., that attracts and directs its members primarily by means of these incentives.*[3]

BOX 9.1

THE LOGIC OF PATRONAGE

You are a busy elected official. Among the decisions you have to make this morning is which of two equally qualified people to hire as one of your administrative assistants. Both applicants are of the same gender and ethnic identity, both have attached letters of recommendation and impressive resumes indicating that they worked hard to put themselves through school. Both make the same positive impression. However, applicant A has the following in his/her application file, and applicant B does not:

1. A letter from a county judge in your party testifying that applicant A worked hard for the party during the recent election campaign.
2. A letter from one of the major contributors to your campaign asking you to give "every consideration" to applicant A, and indicating that the contributor is an uncle of the applicant.
3. A note, included by your secretary, that the Governor's office called to put in a good word for the applicant.

Which applicant will get the job?

A. Do you choose the candidate who is connected and thus improve your ties to these people and certainly establish the possibility of reciprocity should you ever want to place someone with them?

B. Do you choose the candidate with no links to other political leaders and thus increase the likelihood that you will be the mentor/patron to whom your new employee owes complete political loyalty?

Wolfinger's distinction between machine politics and political machines contains two important points. First, the term "incentives to partisan participation" clearly implies forms of corrupt patronage. Thus, selective enforcement of the law, or hiring practices based *solely* on partisan loyalty, exceed the ethical boundaries of the ancient and honorable practice of patronage.

Second, influencing individuals *primarily* by means of these incentives is associated with machine politics and political machines. For Wolfinger, and for us, a political machine is an organization that has captured a party. It is not a typical party. It is an organization (an interest group, family, or business) that operates *primarily* by unethical and sometimes illegal means in order to get and keep power. Political parties encourage their followers to vote in each election. Political machines encourage their followers to vote *often* in each election.

Although the political machine can be identified as a corrupted form of political party, a major problem arises when the average citizen and the media frequently refer to any strong party organization as a political machine. Whether they are engaged in poetic license, simile, metaphor, or simply sloppy thinking, the effect is the same. The impression is perpetuated that a strong political party is the moral equivalent of the notoriously corrupt Tweed Ring that robbed New York City taxpayers of millions of dollars in the nineteenth century.

When clearly unqualified individuals are given preference over others for jobs, for contracts, for career advancement, or when laws are broken or procedures designed to ensure fair treatment are ignored, then the practice of patronage and the people engaged in it are corrupted and we move into the realm of machine politics. A considerable portion of the money political machines acquired was not from the taxpayers but from businesses eager to get contracts or be the first to build a warehouse or an office building at a preferred location. The money they spent in bribes then they spend today in lobbying, entertainment, advertising, and "public relations." It costs money to do in the competition. Sometimes the public got good value for its dollars in terms of roads and bridges that held up, sometimes not, just like the Pentagon's expensive hammers and toilet seats.

The point here is not that political machines are to be praised but rather to view them in the context of their time, a time before Social Security, a state funded welfare system, Medicare, Medicaid, and personnel agencies. It's important to note that some of what machines did would be considered by our higher, more enlightened standards as wrong. Part of what it took to get rid of the machines was to change the standards of political conduct.

Little that the machines did in the way of patronage or preferences in letting contracts would have shocked Thomas Jefferson or George Washington. They might, however, look askance at what goes on in some corporate mergers and buyouts.

A corporate raider who sells junk bonds to cooperative banks and insurance firms to finance a leveraged buy-out and proceeds to raid the pension funds of the corporations to pay off the junk bonds, reduce the work force of the captured firm to make it look leaner and more competitive, and sell the company off, leaving thousands of workers out of work and without pensions, is not an individual engaged in praiseworthy behavior—even though much of what he gets away with is legal for now. Clearly we still have some work to do on the moral and ethical use of power—political and economic.

The Structure of Political Machines

The "courthouse gang" in rural counties and the classic urban political machine both practiced machine politics and were variations of the same phenomenon. Nevertheless, the term political machine is usually associated with a specific type of organization that existed in a particular period of American history—the late nineteenth and early twentieth century.

The structure of the fully formed political machine consisted of a hierarchy in which there was a fair amount of top-down discipline from the Boss, through ward leaders, to the hundreds of precinct captains. The Boss usually held an official party position, for controlling party nominations was the key to controlling the machine (Box 9.2). Some, but not all, Bosses held the office of mayor, as did the late Richard M. Daley of Chicago.

Wards were relatively small in area but large in population. They were single-member electoral districts for electing aldermen to the city council. In the typical city there were dozens if not several hundred wards sending representatives to a large city council. The ward leaders, who often served as aldermen, were not merely the representatives of a geographic area of the city; they also represented the dominant ethnic groups in these small electoral units.

Machine bosses attempted to create a ticket of citywide offices that was balanced ethnically, while at the same time running at least one or two "blue-ribbon" middle-class candidates near the top to appeal to the reform elements within the party.

BOX 9.2

WHO WAS BOSS TWEED ANYWAY?

Political machines included honest politicians making the best of a bad thing, and charming rascals who enjoyed the game and intended no one any harm. Some, however, were grossly corrupt. One of the most egregious sinners was William Marcy Tweed (1823–1878), a man who gained control of the Tammany Hall political machine in New York and used it to become very rich.

The amount of money Boss Tweed and his colleagues stole is estimated to have been between $75 and $200 million. In the 1870s, this was enough to operate several state governments for a year. It was a shocking sum. The political cartoons of Thomas Nast, the sensational stories reported in the *New York Times*, and an aroused public embarrassed the federal and state governments into action.

Most members of the Tweed Ring were arrested, indicted, found guilty, and imprisoned. The scandal was kept on the front pages when Boss Tweed escaped prison, fled to Spain, was recaptured, and returned to the United States, where he spent the rest of his life behind bars.

Source: Richard B. Morris, ed., The Encyclopedia of American History, *6th ed. (New York: Harper & Row, 1982), 298.*

The foundation upon which the machine rested was the precinct captain, a party worker who was responsible for getting out the vote in his precinct. Just as important, however, was the precinct captain's service as a link between the people in the neighborhoods and the machine. The precinct captain kept his superiors (ward boss or alderman) advised of opportunities to make public appearances (weddings, funerals, family celebrations as well as less structured occasions). George Washington Plunkitt, a machine politician, indicates both the importance of precinct captains as well as the advantages of being able to assist those in need:

> If there's a fire in Ninth, Tenth, or Eleventh Avenue, for example, any hour of the day or night, I'm usually there with some of my precinct captains as soon as the fire engines. If a family is burned out, I don't ask whether they are Republicans or Democrats, and I don't refer them to the Charity Organization Society, which would investigate their case in a month or two and decide they were worthy of help about the time they are dead from starvation. I just get quarters for them, buy clothes for them if their clothes were burned up, and fix them up til they get things runnin' again. It's philanthropy, but it's politics, too—mighty good politics. Who can tell how many votes one of these fires bring me? The poor are the most grateful people in the world, and let me tell you, they have more friends in their neighborhoods than the rich in theirs.[4]

The relationship between the precinct captain and his boss was personal and nonideological. So was the relationship between the precinct captain and the people he recruited for the machine. Loyalty to the machine was more personalized than loyalty to a party. The machine was men and friendships; the party (particularly the party of the reformers) was policy goals, rules and procedures. Machines represented the fatal flaw of depending upon a government of men, instead of the rule of law.

Politics as a Business

In a sense, the classic urban political machine was an entrepreneurial device for processing favors, friendship, and patronage (or incentives to participation) into votes, and votes into political power. Many machine politicians referred to it as a business, a business for professionals who understood the "real world."

As Plunkitt observed at the turn of the century, "Politics is as much a regular business as the grocery or dry-goods . . . business."[5] If, along the way, useful social functions were performed by the machine, so much the better. Most machine politicians believed they were serving the greater good, just as do most members of the business community.

Functions of the Machines

In a classic study of the role political machines played in urban society, Robert K. Merton described several functions they performed which helped bring order and stability to the rapidly growing urban centers of nineteenth- and early twentieth-century America.[6]

Perhaps other institutions could have operated in their places, perhaps order would have been possible without them; but most political scientists agree that Merton's observations, to which we have added one or two of our own, are valid. There is some dispute, however, whether or not having these functions performed by the machine was worth the delivery cost.

Centralize Decision Making

In times when numerous decisions needed to be made in a hurry, it helped to have someone in charge to make them. Without a mechanism for bringing some sort of discipline to the collection of elected officials created by the Jacksonian long ballot, nineteenth-century urban centers might have become even more disorderly than they were. Particularly difficult for managing urban government was the large city council. Each ward representative or alderman expected to get something out of that budget for his people.

Political machines facilitated negotiations and brought other rewards to the table besides chunks of the budget—party nominations, jobs, recognition, and simply promises of future unnamed rewards. If political machines had to provide economic benefits for every vote on every issue at the council level, or every vote in the wards, they would soon have been bankrupt. Thus one function the machines played was to promote cooperation and sometimes deferred gratification in order to get the city built.

Personalize Government

The need still exists for most of us to relate to people as fellow human beings instead of as role-players. In cities of strangers those who were not equipped with literacy or a very strong self-image appreciated the fact that the precinct captains and the political machine provided a human source of information and support. If impersonal public officials intimidate even you and me, then what was it like for a peasant fresh from rural Poland, Italy, Alabama, or West Virginia?

Integrate Newcomers

It can be argued that the fact that American cities remained American was largely due to the ability of political machines to bring newcomers into the political process, and to make it meaningful. By virtue of stimulating participation and arousing interest in the political process, people of very undemocratic societies such as the Hapsburg Empire and Czarist Russia were gradually brought into the American political system. Political machines were an integral part of the process that gave the melting pot its appeal both as an explanation of America and a mechanism that enabled America to adapt to rapid social change.[7]

Provide Welfare

Political machines were not the only source of help to the poor at the time. There were private charities. However, there was virtually no national commitment to social problems until the Great Depression of the 1930s. Until then, welfare assistance was seen as a private and local matter. Thus, with precious little national- and state-level effort, the assistance offered by political machines was all the more important, however inefficiently it may have been provided.

Reduce Ethnic Conflict

According to Milton Rakove, a student of the Daley machine in Chicago:

> Every ethnic, racial, religious, and economic group is entitled to have some representation on the ticket. Thus, in Chicago, the mayor's job has been an Irish job since 1933. The city clerk's job belongs to the Poles. The city treasurer can be a Jew, a Bohemian, or a black. A judicial slate is made up of three or four Irishmen, two or three Jews, two or three Poles, several blacks, a Lithuanian, a German, a Scandinavian, several Bohemians, and several Italians.[8]

One of the problems facing states and communities today is under-representation of various ethnic groups in the political process. In some cities with large ethnic populations and numerous qualified ethnic attorneys there are few if any ethnic state district judges. That would probably not be the case if strong parties—not political machines—simply strong parties had more control over political nominations.

The Decline of Political Machines

At least seven factors led to the decline of the political machine; these were: (1) reduction in the salience of politics, (2) assimilation and the decline of white ethnic block voting, (3) decline in the use of unskilled labor, (4) rise of the union movement, (5) federal involvement in the welfare system, (6) corruption, waste, and scandals, and (7) success of the reform movement.

Reduction in the Salience of Politics

Politics is no longer the only game in town. It interests many of us, but there are other recreational opportunities, other contests, and other teams to root for. Thus, the salience of politics may have experienced the kind of decline one would expect in a society that has grown more complex and more affluent.

Assimilation and the Decline of White Ethnic Block Voting

The white ethnics who made up the base of support for urban machines have demonstrated less rather than more solidarity, losing potential leaders to mainstream American political and social institutions and losing sons and daughters to the suburbs where their votes don't influence city elections, even if ethnic identities persist for some. The melting pot myth worked for them and in so doing weakened urban machines based on urban white ethnic loyalties.

Decline in the Use of Unskilled Labor

Technological change has led to the mechanization of many construction and maintenance functions performed by city government. This has reduced the number of jobs available for a patronage machine. Given their limited education and vulnerability to easy replacement, unskilled workers were the most likely to trade political loyalty for employment.

Rise of the Union Movement

In the building industry as well as in the public employment sector itself, labor unions have been so successful that union leaders have helped to remove the influence of political machines in the job market. The rise of unions to protect workers from employer abuse also protected the hiring and firing process from outside influence, further reducing the patronage in the gift of political leaders.

Federal Involvement in the Welfare System

Prior to 1932 the federal government used few of its considerable resources to provide aid or to encourage state governments to provide aid to the needy. After 1932, the federal government, working through state and local government, encouraged the development of a system of delivering welfare assistance as an entitlement. The criteria for eligibility were impersonal. They involved neither loyalty nor gratitude to any local political leader or organization.

Corruption, Waste, and Scandals

The skepticism with which the country bumpkin views the city slicker is an almost universal phenomenon. In America, in the nineteenth century, those machine leaders who abused their power and authority did more than increase the rural-urban dichotomy. They contributed to the loss of the legitimacy of the machine, but, more important for us, they contributed to the loss of the legitimacy of the political party.

The corruption, waste, and scandals associated with the machine were a sort of pollution of the political environment that weakened the ability of machine leaders in some cities to claim that the disadvantages of machine rule were outweighed by the advantages.

Political machines did not exist in freestanding isolation. They were part of a system of intergovernments, and they were tolerated, if not actively supported, by a significant portion of the community for the benefits they offered. When scandals about machine corruption, waste, and inefficiency became widely known, they lost public support and came under careful scrutiny by the other governments in the intergovernmental system.

The Success of the Reform Movement

Antimachine, urban reform organizations emerged in the late nineteen-century as part of the larger, more broadly based progressive movement.[9] The progressives protested and attempted to do something about the suffering that occurred as American cities industrialized rapidly and civilized slowly. The broadly based reform movement was concerned about the abuse of the concentration of power in large enterprises. As Richard Hofstadter observed in his Pulitzer Prize winning work, *The Age of Reform:*

> *At bottom, the central fear was fear of power, and the greater the strength of an organized interest, the greater the anxiety it aroused. Hence it was the trusts, the investment banking houses, the interlocking directorates, the swollen private fortunes, that were the most criticized, and after them the well-knit, highly disciplined political machines.*[10]

Just as there were captains of industry who were not robber barons, there were also party leaders who promoted reform. Hazen Pingree in Michigan, Ed Crump in Tennessee, Samuel "Golden Rule" Jones in Ohio, Hiram Johnson in California, and Robert LaFollete in Wisconsin are party leaders who promoted reform by means of their own disciplined party organizations.[11] Nevertheless, the bad actors made it necessary to reform both the free enterprise system and the way democracy worked in America.

While we have included the reform movement as one factor in the decline of the political machine, some scholars discount the reform movement, asserting that the machine simply became obsolete as society changed. Tari Renner has observed, "There is little systematic, empirical evidence to indicate that they actually caused the decline."[12]

Whether its contribution to the decline of the urban political machine was great or small, it seems clear that the reform movement has contributed to the weakening of political parties in several important ways.

First, by linking machines and political parties together in the public mind, the reform movement encouraged an antiparty attitude on the part of any group of enlightened citizens attempting to promote honest effective government. According to Denise Baer, the women's suffrage movement

> *was intimately connected to progressivism and its anti-party impulse. One of the ghosts the contemporary scholarship is haunted by is an inability to appreciate party politics . . . The National Organization of Women (NOW) is so convinced that women have achieved nothing in the reformed party system that it has advocated the possibility of forming a third party.*[13]

The second contribution to the current weakness of parties was the successful institutionalization of structures that render parties virtually irrelevant to the decision-making processes and community activities in the thousands of new cities created since the 1940s. This has denied resources of talent and energy to political parties that might have emerged in new communities, and might have better linked the decision makers in these communities to county, state, and national decision making. The isolation of the "reformed" suburban city has not been without a price.

In sum, by weakening parties, the reform movement has helped to shift the balance in the political system in favor of interest groups.

The Reform Movement

In the context of this chapter we use the term the **Reform Movement** to refer specifically to the collection of individuals and groups who were concerned with defeating political machines in nineteenth- and twentieth-century urban America. The six reform proposals that had the greatest effect upon political parties are: nonpartisan municipal elections, spring municipal elections, the short ballot, at-large election of city council members, nomination of party candidates by direct primary, and the civil service.

Some of their reforms were applied to other units of government. Today in Nebraska, where the movement was particularly strong, not only are urban elections nonpartisan but so are elections to the state legislature. With few exceptions, the direct primary is used to nominate state and county candidates, who are later elected on partisan ballots. The focus of the Reform Movement, however, was municipal election. In order to wreck the urban political machines, the reform movement concentrated largely on making it very difficult for any leader or group of leaders to build or maintain a cohesive, disciplined political party in urban America. Municipal elections were moved away from the general election in November and made nonpartisan, further isolating them from the political processes operating in the rest of the intergovernmental system.

The civil service will be discussed in Chapter 12, which deals with the executive branches of state and local government. In the paragraphs that follow we deal with four reforms: the short ballot—which makes a return to urban machines almost impossible no matter what we do to strengthen parties—and three others that have weakened parties.

The Short Ballot

There were at least three reasons for the short ballot, a reform that had its own organization, The National Short-Ballot Association. The first reason was to simplify the voting decision at both state and local levels and thus correct the mistakes of Jacksonian Democracy. With smaller city councils, with fewer state and local executive officials, the electoral process was simplified and the burden of citizenship would be made lighter. Elections would not involve so many decisions to make, and there would be fewer elected public officials to keep track of.

Not only would the greater good be looked after if the citizens could more easily keep track of government, but also citizens would have less need of a party to recruit and sponsor a slate of candidates. Second, by reducing the number of offices for which nomination had to be made, the machine bosses would no longer play the role of brokers and slate makers. A third reason was to promote accountability by increasing the likelihood that the elected chief executive really would be in charge of the executive branch.

Reformers felt that by creating small councils (seven to nine people), there would develop a more collegial body of local citizens concerned more with the city as a whole. In a small council, reformers believed, representatives would have a better chance to get to know one another and would be more likely to work together in the common interest.

Direct Primary

This reform was intended to reduce the ability of party leaders to influence party nominations. This reform has played a major role in helping to tip the balance between parties and interest groups in favor of interest groups. By reducing the role of the electoral party in the nominating process, reformers opened the door for money and for interest groups to play a larger role. By requiring two campaigns, one for the nomination and one for election, the reformers increased the cost of electoral politics and the influence of those with money.

By aiming at machines and hitting parties, the reformers have established the notion that to strengthen the party is to bring back the worst of the old urban political machines. In introducing the direct primary the reform movement denied the electoral party its most valuable resource for influencing the party in office and for rewarding hard work and loyalty to the party. Now in many states potential candidates look to interest groups and to political consultants to help them set up their own candidate-centered organizations to compete in the primary, and—if successful—operate with only loose coordination with the electoral party in the general election campaign.

Once elected, public officials have absolutely no fear that party leaders will deny them renomination. The party label is won in the primary in part because of name recognition, incumbents are way ahead of challengers on that score; furthermore, incumbents are in a better position to attract campaign contributions from interest groups and corporate PACs.

Nonpartisan Elections

A nonpartisan election is one in which party labels do not appear on the ballot. In some cities where this reform was introduced, parties still contest the election and work hard to inform voters about which candidates represent their party. Chicago, for example, throughout the mayoralty of Richard Daley conducted its elections without party labels on the ballot.

The motivation for keeping any party or group labels off the ballot was to prevent the clients of the machine from having party labels as cues to help them make their decisions. In theory this would make it harder for party leaders to manipulate large numbers of uneducated people.

While nonpartisan elections had mixed results in cities where machines already existed and channels of communication already were in place, it had a large impact on the development of new cities in the West, many of which have grown from villages to urban centers in the past 50 years. One indication of reform success in this area is the fact that over 70 percent of American cities with populations of over 25,000 have nonpartisan elections. Virtually all cities created after 1910 use the nonpartisan ballot.[14]

At-Large Election

The use of the **at-large principle** for choosing representatives to legislative bodies such as city councils or school boards was supported in the belief that it would reduce the parochial influence of ward leaders, each taking a narrow view of city governance. Reformers believed that candidates elected at-large to a city council would have to build a citywide coalition of support and would be more inclined to look after the interests of the whole city, not just a small part of it.

It is worth noting that, once the city council has been reduced in size by the short-ballot, single-member districts are larger and thus the need for at-large elections is significantly reduced.

At-large elections increase the need for money to communicate with the electorate. The mass media and interest groups are the beneficiaries of nonpartisan elections in which at-large candidates need to reach a large constituency. In single-member districts one can walk the neighborhood. In large districts, a whole city (at-large) or even one-seventh of a city (small council) can best be reached by advertisements on the radio, television, in the newspaper, or by direct mail. These advertisements cost money. Interest groups, particularly business interest groups, are most likely to be able to make donations and to see that it is worth the cost of donations to have some candidates running for office who are sympathetic to their needs.

THE PARTY ISN'T OVER

Numerous books have suggested that political parties are a dying institution; among them is one with the title, *The Party's Over*.[15] Weak as they are reputed to be, recent research indicates that state and local parties are still essential institutions for participation. In 1994 Wiehouwer and Lockerbie published a study based on American National Elections Studies (NES) data from 1952 to 1990. Their data shows that our voting turnout levels would be even lower than they are if parties weren't active. "Without their effort turnout would have declined even further than it has in the last few decades."[16]

According to Wiehouwer and Lockerbie, parties contact one-fifth to one-quarter of the electorate in each election cycle. When contacted by parties, individuals have a greater propensity to vote and to engage in other political activities such as attending rallies, giving money, or displaying a bumper sticker or yard sign. Anticipating the "politics is an artifact of economics" argument, they note that, "Even when placed alongside a plethora of control variables, these findings hold up." From 1974 onward the average difference between the contacted and non-contacted in terms of voting has been 23.6 percentage points.[17]

Clearly parties are making a difference. They are making a difference because they organize the activities of individuals who then personally influence the activities of others, directly and indirectly. These activities, according to Huckfeldt and Sprague, not only affect individuals and their families but instigate a "cascading mobilization process." People who haven't been personally contacted are influenced when the yard signs and the bumper stickers appear in their neighbors' yards and driveways.[18]

If parties were stronger, perhaps they would be able to contact more than the 20 percent of the population they reach and increase not only voting but other forms of participation as well. If parties were stronger, perhaps they could counter the influence of the powerful interest groups and thus correct some of the "mischiefs of faction" described in Chapter 8. With these possibilities in mind we examine the state and local party system as it is, and examine some suggestions for making it more effective at mobilizing participation and rendering the 86,000 governments more accountable to individuals and communities.

THE MORE OR LESS TWO PARTY SYSTEM

You may recall that in Chapter 8 we defined political party and indicated four important differences between parties and interest groups. In Chapter 6 we discussed various participation strategies. To quickly review, parties are organizations for political participation. They are defined in terms of, and are almost impossible to analyze apart from, electioneering and governing. Parties, like interest groups and PACs, have names, addresses, and members. These institutions for political participation constitute a system through which individuals and communities can attempt to hold government accountable. The major difference between a party and an interest group is that a party attempts to win control of government through electing a slate of candidates. An interest groups seeks to influence government on a narrower range of issues of special concern to the interest group. There are thousands of interest groups and PACs; there are relatively few parties.

To understand how the party system works today it is worth noting that our nominally two party system includes lots of regions in which one party dominates. Furthermore, at the local level numerous elections are held in which party labels are not allowed on the ballot. Furthermore, party labels do not appear on initiatives, referendums, and recalls either.

Minor Parties

In addition to the Republicans and Democrats, numerous and often locally important minor or "third" parties participate in the American political system. Many of them offer candidates for governor and other major offices, but they seldom have a full slate of candidates for the legislature, the judiciary, or the county offices. Third parties perform a valuable function by keeping various issues before the public, pointing out the shortcomings of the two major parties, and providing an outlet for voters looking for a "none of the above" option.

Some minor parties are successful in getting candidates elected and major parties have adopted one or more of their issues. In the 1994 election for the governor of Alaska, four parties offered candidates for governor: the Democratic, the Republican, the Alaskan Independent Party (which had elected a Governor, Walter Hickle, in 1986), and the Green Party. Only the two major parties offered a full slate of candidates for the other offices.

One Party Regions of and Within States

The two major parties do not have an equal probability of winning every election in every state. Though their goal may be to offer a slate of candidates for every office in every constituency, in practice they don't. There are still numerous one party counties or regions within states reflecting political culture and economic or demographic divisions. A party may habitually lose in one portion of a state, but be virtually invincible in other counties or states. For example, upstate New York is traditionally Republican, whereas New York City, despite occasionally electing a Republican mayor, is traditionally Democratic.[19]

THE FORMAL STRUCTURE OF POLITICAL PARTIES

Frank J. Sorauf's classic observation that each of the two major American parties contains three major components—the party in office, the party organization, and the party in the electorate—is as true today as it was when he made it nearly 40 years ago.[20] Few attempts to describe the American party system fail to incorporate it.

The "New" Party Organizations

In recent years additional dimensions of the party have emerged with mixed results for party coherence and integrity. These include: candidate-centered organizations consisting of party activists and new party members, some of whom leave the party after their candidate fails to get a nomination or get elected; the campaign organizations created by state and national legislators; state and national auxiliary organizations such as the Young Democrats of America, The Young Republicans National Federation, the National Federation of Republican Women, the National Federation of Democratic Women, and policy organizations such as the moderate Democratic Leadership Conference, which includes state and national officeholders, and the Republican Ripon Society.

In an article examining the relationship of political parties and the women's movement, Denise L. Baer finds that the creation at the state and national level of the two women's organizations is a healthy thing for the parties and for the progress of women. Noting that the women's movement seems unduly influenced by the antiparty impulse of the turn of the century progressive reformers, Baer observes, "Women need political parties—and we scholars do women and the women's movement a disservice by ignoring parties in our research."[21]

The new party organizations reflect the coalition tradition of American parties. Since both parties have always attempted to hold their own loyalists while attempting to appeal to the middle of the left-right political spectrum, both parties with a few notable exceptions have been true to the American federal tradition of compromise. More often than not, both parties have attempted to bring in under the "big umbrella" a wide range of interest groups and opinion publics. Both parties reflect the fact that there are numerous crosscutting loyalties in the states and communities. Baer's examination of differences among women scholars on the importance for women of the two parties is but one example.

Although it would appear that these new organizations might create competition for resources of money, energy, and talent, it is equally likely that they have brought in new money, new talent, and new resources. The jury is still out. Herrnson, for example, argues convincingly that the parties have adapted to the new era of candidate-centered campaigns.[22] Clearly the new organizations are important, however, and as numerous scholars indicate, these organizations will continue to be studied and compared to the three traditional dimensions of the party: the party in office, electoral party, and the party in the electorate.

The Party in Office

The party in office consists of officials in government who were either elected under the party label or appointed because of party affiliation. These are the individuals who will attempt to organize the government and take responsibility for running it. Under the best of circumstances it is difficult for the party in office to become unified enough to carry out a comprehensive program as promised in party platforms or campaign literature. In addition to the fact that each party is made up of individuals with their own personalities, career objectives, and values, other sources of difficulty face party leaders in promoting unity in the "party in office. Among them are separation of powers and institutional loyalty.

Separation of powers means that one party may control the governorship but not both houses of the state legislature. During the period from 1965 to 1994 this occurred at least once in virtually every state.[23] Institutional loyalty means that some party members in each branch develop a loyalty to the institution in which they serve. They tend to perceive things differently than fellow party members in other agencies in the executive branch or the other house in the legislature.

Later in this chapter we will discuss some of the mechanisms that make it possible for leaders of the party in government to promote party unity in order to carry out the party's program. At this juncture it is important to introduce the distinction between a party leader and an elected official who happens to have been elected under a party label. In systems where parties are weak, the labels Democrat and Republican don't mean as much as they do in systems where parties actually have a meaningful program and the resources to carry it out.

The Electoral Party Organization

The **electoral party** consists of: (1) activists—individual volunteers who campaign, attend party meetings and social functions, and contribute to the party; (2) officials of the party at the state and local levels; and (3) staff members. The vast majority of the individuals in the electoral party are volunteers. Very few are staff or officials on the payroll.

The Permanent Structures

The chairs and the executive committees at the national, state, county, and precinct levels are the organizational structure of a party. The electoral party in many states is not organized to the grass roots in every geographic area. Table 9.1 indicates the way state chairs would like it to be. In a state with 200 counties, there may be a dozen or more precinct chair vacancies and one or two county chairs open at any given time. Although this is bad news for a state chair and for candidates who would like some party help, the good news is that for individuals eager to learn the political process, it is possible to become a party official fairly easily in some areas. In any event it's extremely easy to become a volunteer.

The basic pattern of organization is for the chair of the executive committee at one level to serve as a member of the executive committee at the next highest level. Thus, a county executive committee would consist of precinct chairs and the county chair. In states with townships, or in states where counties include cities large enough in population to have more than one state senate or congressional district, the pattern would be a little different.

Just as there is variation as well as incomplete development of the party structure in some states, there is also considerable variation in the formality of organization at party headquarters. While most state party headquarters have two or three full-time staff and an office in the state capital, many county and precinct organizations operate out of someone's business office or home. County executive committee meetings held at a kitchen table are not unheard of in suburban and rural areas.

Organizational charts imply hierarchy. In political parties, however, there is as much bottom-to-top influence as there is top-down. County chairs are not hired and fired by state chairs. They are locally elected. If the state chair is involved at all, it is more likely to be as one of the people who cajole and persuade an individual to take the job of county chair in a

---

Table 9.1

PARTY ORGANIZATION

National Committee, Chair, National Committee Headquarters

Fifty state Committees, State Committee Chairs, State Headquarters

In each state: from 10 to 254 County Committees, County Chairs, County Headquarters (Total 3,000 counties)

In some states: a Variety of State Senatorial District, or Township, Town, or Ward Committees

In each county: several Precinct Committees, Precinct Chairs or Captains (More than 100,000 nationwide)

county where the party is weak. Chairs are usually individuals who have been active in the party for a considerable period of time, know the personalities and history of the party level at which they operate, and are respected for "paying their dues" by working hard within the organization.

Periodic Events
The Primary

In most states parties are required by state law to nominate candidates for most public offices by means of primary elections rather than at party conventions.[24] In a **primary election** voters (who may or may not be active in the party) can help determine whom the party will nominate. In many states even party officials such as precinct and county chairs are chosen in the primary.

In primary elections the party has no control over who gets on the ballot. Thus the party's most precious resource—the nomination—is placed at the disposal of outsiders. Any interest groups or individual with funds enough to pay the filing fee can become a candidate for a party's nomination. The requirement of nomination by primary election is a major difference between parties and interest groups. The general public has virtually no role in telling interest groups whom to choose as leaders or how to use their major resources.

Some of the reforms intended to destroy political machines have unintended consequences. In 1986, a tragicomedy of major proportions for the Democratic party in Illinois occurred when two candidates from a far right-wing organization led by Lyndon LaRouche ran in the Democratic primary and received enough votes to win nomination to statewide offices. Party leaders could do nothing about it. They had no control over the nominations. So distasteful was the prospect of dragging them into office on his coattails (as well as running on the same ticket with these candidates and of being associated with the policies they supported) that the Democratic party candidate for governor—former U. S. Senator Adlai Stevenson III—withdrew from the Democratic ticket. He attempted to organize an Independent slate but he had to start so late in the process that to no one's surprise Republicans won in the general election.

Conventions

Political party conventions are held at the precinct, county, state, and national levels. In some states, such as Iowa, the precinct convention is called a caucus. Thus the Iowa caucuses, a feature of presidential election years, are really precinct conventions.

The state convention is a major event in state politics. It is covered by the media statewide, not just in the city where it takes place. Delegates come from all over the state. Friendships from previous conventions and campaigns are renewed and in some cases important decisions are made about the party ticket.

State conventions in 35 states play no role in nominating candidates for state offices. The election laws in those states require primary elections to nominate party candidates. However, in about eight states party conventions still play a major role in the nominating process.

In Indiana the primary nominates candidates for governor and U. S. senator; the rest of the candidates are nominated by the state convention of each party. The situation is similar in Michigan except the primaries are used for all national and some state offices, leaving the conventions with a list of decisions to make that is still significant. In Michigan the candidates for lieutenant governor, attorney general, and secretary of state are nominated at the state convention, as are justices of the supreme court, the state board of education, and the separate governing bodies of the University of Michigan, Michigan State, and Wayne State University.

Endorsing Conventions

A promising political experiment at the state level is a compromise between the convention and the primary as vehicles for nominating party candidates. Endorsing conventions held before the primary provide the openness of primary elections with the integrity of party self-government. Endorsing conventions promote party unity and linkage between the electoral party and the party in government.

Pre-primary endorsing conventions for governor are held in at least six states, and state laws in three others provide for the nomination or endorsement of several officials further down the ballot. At endorsing conventions delegates vote on candidates. The candidate who wins endorsement by a majority of the convention is usually declared the party nominee, unless one of the losing candidates with enough votes (usually at least 25 percent) chooses to force a primary. In any event, if no candidate gets a majority, then a primary is held for that office. In Colorado and Connecticut the pre-primary endorsing conventions are held a month or two before the primary is scheduled.[25]

In Connecticut a clear winner at the convention becomes the party's nominee and does not need to run in a primary unless a rival who received at least 20 percent of the convention vote challenges the endorsed candidate. In Colorado the candidate endorsed by the convention is listed first on the primary election ballot. Thus primary voters in that state can safely assume that ballot position means something in the governor's race— the preference of those active in the party.[26]

Although not all candidates endorsed by the party's convention win the nomination in the primary vote, most do. As a result candidates endorsed by the convention are much more likely to pay attention to the electoral party after they are elected to become part of the party in office. Further differences are noticeable between states that have endorsing conventions and those that do not. States with endorsing conventions are about twice as likely to have uncontested primaries because unsuccessful candidates frequently withdraw from the primary. Uncontested primaries promote party unity.

In states with endorsing conventions, according to Jewell and Olson, less than half of the party nominees for governor had a primary contest to win the party nomination between 1960 and 1986. However, in the rest of the states nearly 80 percent of the primary races for governor were contested.[27]

According to Morehouse, the ability of the electoral party to have such a strong influence on the nomination of a state's highest elective office helps to strengthen the party and increases the likelihood of cooperation between the party in office and the electoral party.[28] This pattern holds for the 1988–1992 period. In only seven states were both parties' candidates for governor unopposed in the primary during this period. Five of those seven states were pre-primary endorsing convention states. In the only endorsing convention state where there was a primary it took place in only one of the two parties; the other made its decision at the convention.[29]

Whether they nominate, or endorse, or neither, state party conventions are still regarded as important institutions. In the interest of brevity we will list only eight reasons why state party conventions are important to a large number of people.

- Obtain publicity for the party and for its candidates.
- Afford prestige to local party leaders who attend them as delegates.
- Provide opportunities for building party unity for the forthcoming campaign.
- Select delegates to the national conventions and to the national committee.
- Select, or certify the selection of, the party members who will serve as the presidential electors, should the party's candidate win in that state.
- Select the chair of the state executive committee (usually ratifying the choice of the party's candidate for governor).
- Confirm or change the rules affecting party operations and organization.
- Ratify or approve a state party platform.

The Party in the Electorate

The **party in the electorate** is essentially those voters who support the party with their votes. There are at least three methods of empirically identifying the party in the electorate. Each method touches on a different dimension of the population eligible to vote: (1) those who say they identify with the party, (2) those who vote in the primary election of a party, and (3) those who usually vote for a party's candidates in general elections. The size of the party in the electorate will depend upon which measures of the foregoing dimensions one uses.

Party Identifiers

Party identification is the sense of and willingness to express a feeling of support for and identity with a political party. Party identity performs two important functions in promoting a stable, coherent political system. One function is performed for the individual and one for the electoral process.

For the electoral process, the fact that 60 percent of the population has a party identity and usually acts on it means that each party starts each election with a fairly predictable share of the vote upon which to build. From its portion of the electorate, each party can recruit candidates and volunteer workers, and appeal for campaign contributions. If each party started each election cycle from zero with no foundation upon which to build, the electoral process would probably involve even more blatant appeals to emotion and even greater use of attention-getting activities than it already does.

For the individual, party identity provides a set of cues for use in making decisions, particularly when no other information is available. Although the number of voting age Americans who identify with parties is smaller than it was 30 years ago when the following words were written, they still ring true.

> In view of the fact that very few Americans have a very deep interest in politics, it is a mild paradox that party loyalties should be so widespread. A partial key to this puzzle is that these identifications perform for the citizen an exceedingly useful evaluative function. To the average person the affairs of government are remote and complex, and yet the average citizen is asked periodically to formulate opinion about those affairs. . . . In this dilemma, having the party symbol stamped on certain candidates, certain issue positions, certain interpretation of political reality is of great psychological convenience.[30]

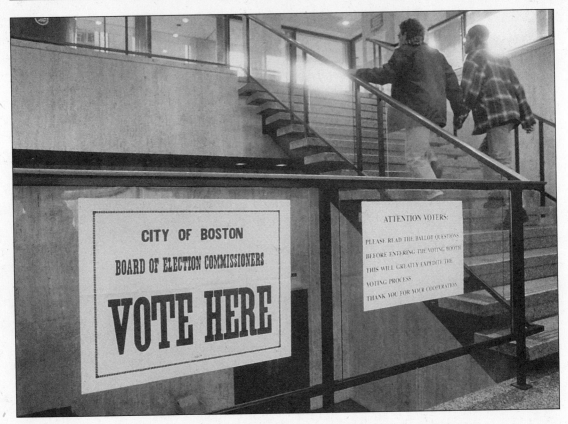

Voting is one of the most basic forms of political participation. Here citizens in Boston exercise their right to vote.

For several decades various polling organizations have used a battery of survey instruments to measure and track changes in the distribution of party identity among the voting age population. In 1993 Green and Schickler reported results from a comparison of data obtained by instruments used by several major polling organizations including Times-Mirror, Gallup, the National Opinion Research Center (NORC), and the Survey Research Center at the University of Michigan. The two most useful were the Michigan seven point scale, data for which is obtained by responses to interviewers' questions, and the NORC seven point self-placement scale derived from respondents' self-placements after viewing options on a card. Green and Schickler recommended a self-placement approach as marginally accurate over the Michigan scale.[31]

Since the various surveys first began, three facts have been established. First, over half of the voting population has consistently indicated an identification with one of the two major parties (Table 9.2). Second, over the years an increasing portion of the electorate is choosing an "independent" identity and, third, fewer party identifiers are indicating a strong attachment to their party. Although the last two trends concern party leaders and political scientists who believe that parties are essential to democracy, neither of these patterns means that parties are dying political institutions (Box 9.3).[32]

BOX 9.3

SEVEN-POINT SELF-PLACEMENT SCALE

Recently researchers compared results from the survey questions used by various polling organizations to measure party identity. Of those tested, the following from the National Opinion Research Center was found to be most reliable.

"On this card is a scale with strong Democrats on one end and strong Republicans on the other, and with independents in the middle. Where would you place yourself on this scale?":

(1) I strongly prefer the Democrats, (2) I prefer the Democrats, (3) I am basically independent but lean toward the Democrats, (4) I am independent, I have no preference for either party, (5) I strongly prefer the Republicans, (6) I prefer the Republicans, (7) I am basically independent but lean toward the Republicans.

Source: Donald Philip Green and Eric Schickler, "Multiple-Measure Assessment of Party Identification," Public Opinion Quarterly, 1993, 57:532.

One interesting finding from the survey work on parties in the electorate is that a few individuals identify with one party in voting at the national level, and the other party in voting at the state and local level. Recent research has indicated the existence of fairly stable dual party identities for about 20 percent of the electorate.[33]

While the significance of this in terms of reported party identity (or independence) has yet to be established, Jewell and Olson suggest that, "Many persons probably call themselves independents because they register with one party (and vote in its primary) while voting

---

Table 9.2

PARTY IDENTIFICATION

Degree of Identity	Percent
Strong Democrats	14
Prefer Democrats	15
Democrat leaner	19
Independent	23
Republican leaner	13
Prefer Republicans	9
Strong Republicans	4
Don't know/refused	4
Total*	101
Number of people surveyed = 507	

*Total exceeds 100% due to rounding

Source: 1973 National Opinion Research Center Data reported in Donald Philip Green and Eric Schickler, "Multiple-Measure Assessment of Party Identification," Public Opinion Quarterly, 1993, 57:508.

more often in the [general election for] the other party."[34] Thus, there may be fewer independents than meets the eye. As Wolfinger and Arseneau observe, many independents are "really closet Democrats and Republicans, not people without attachments to a party."[35]

Voters in Party Primaries

Both parties shrink considerably in size if one measures the party in the electorate in terms of primary election voters. While 65 percent of the voting age population identifies with a party, and about 50 percent vote in presidential elections, on average less than 30 percent of the electorate votes regularly in a party primary.

This smaller category of individuals is a focal point for political consultants and party leaders in all or parts of many states. The primary voter rolls are very useful sources of information about those most likely to vote at all, as well as those most likely to work for a party's candidate. Thus, basic data used for preelection polling and for "get-out-the vote" activities in general elections are the primary voter lists. These lists are usually available for individual voting precincts in each county. They can be purchased in most states at the county clerk's office or the office of the county election administrator.

A recent study of participation in South Bend, Indiana, indicates that approximately 20 percent of the Republicans surveyed indicated that they voted in the Democratic primary. In South Bend and other communities where this phenomenon occurs, primary lists are of limited use for targeting appeals to the party faithful.[36]

Party Identity and General Elections

If we measure the party in the electorate in each state by the number who support its candidates for statewide offices, or elect its candidates to the state legislature, we obtain yet another picture of the party. Whichever of its many dimensions we focus upon, the party in the electorate consists of the people to whom the party in government and the electoral party look for support.

The ability of the electorate to make sure that the parties earn their support depends to a great extent upon the degree to which the rules for conducting elections and organizing government are consistent with a model of political behavior, known as the responsible party model.[37]

Before we examine that model, a disclaimer is necessary. Like all models, it is an abstraction. It exists in perfect form nowhere on earth, much less in the American political system. Nevertheless, the responsible party model provides a goal—government accountable to the electorate—and a number of proposals to realize that goal.

THE RESPONSIBLE PARTY MODEL

The central goal of the **responsible party model** is government held accountable to the public through meaningful elections. Parties can make elections meaningful by performing at least five functions traditionally associated with them:

- identifying and explaining issues to the electorate,
- developing a program on which to campaign for election,
- recruiting and nominating candidates,
- organizing election campaigns,
- organizing government to carry out the program upon which the party campaigned.[38]

The responsible party model is based on the notion of two competing parties, each with a program and a slate of candidates to carry it out. Voters can hold the governing party responsible for its behavior by electing the opposition party in the next election. If voters collectively judge a party's candidates on the party's record rather than on whether a particular representative is a good guy or not, then voters can "throw the rascals out" come election time.

Responsible party theory can be examined several ways. One approach is to attempt to show that it doesn't work.[39] Another approach is to admit that it isn't currently working because it hasn't been tried and then to suggest what could be done to give it a try. We'll take the second approach.

Six Assumptions About Politics in Complex Societies

Responsible party theorists make some assumptions about our local, state, and national political systems that are not intuitively obvious. These assumptions are reasonable but some are debatable. Some we've already provided evidence for others cannot be proved true or false empirically. They are axioms or articles of faith upon which the model is constructed.

The Public Interest Exists

There are some goals which are in the interest of everyone. Large complex societies consist of a variety of people and organizations, each with different needs and wants; each with different views on what the community and government should do. Nevertheless, there are a number of important things upon which we can agree. The struggle to identify the public interest, and obtain agreement on how to achieve it, is a major feature of the political process.

Representative Government Is Necessary for Complex Communities

Direct democracy is appropriate for small communities. It is very difficult to operate in large complex societies.

Direct democracy requires trust and shared assumption about how politics is going to work. Most individuals within large communities are unwilling to take the time to get to know one another and thus establish the rapport and trust necessary for a community to exercise direct democracy. The town meeting setting is not possible with large numbers of people.

A corollary is that plebiscatory democracy (PD) is not direct democracy. As noted earlier, PD lacks a built-in process of face-to-face deliberation involving exploring alternatives, explaining oneself, and reaching compromise.

Thus, representative government is appropriate, if not essential, in complex societies. In this way decisions identifying and promoting the common interest are facilitated.

Mediating Institutions Outside of Government Are Necessary

Even though representative government reduces the burden of decision making for each individual, it is still a heavy burden. As noted in Chapter 3, each individual has three or more units of government to keep track of, and in some units as many as a dozen public officials or more. If initiative, referendum, and recall are available, then the voter has numerous additional decisions to make. In addition, the electoral process itself adds to the variety of decisions facing the individual because there are several types of elections, as Box 9.4 indicates.

Thus, there is a need for organizations that specialize in making elections a manageable, meaningful activity.

Voters Use Cues in Making Decisions

A cue is a guide or even a short-cut to decision making. We don't know anything about each particular restaurant we encounter on our travels, but if it is part of a national or regional chain we have some reasonable expectations about its menu, prices, and the quality of food. The name of or symbol representing the restaurant thus provides a cue. Party labels are similar cues.

Responsible party theory asserts that it is unrealistic to assume that removing party labels improves the quality of decision making. The belief that voters enter the polling place with complete information about each and every candidate and thus have only to register their well-thought-out choices by voting is more elegantly stated as the **rational-comprehensive model** of decision making. It is the unexpressed alternative to the Responsible Party model that we encounter in observations such as: "I don't support a political party. I support an individual."

The notion that the voter should make an independent judgment on each and every candidate for each and every office is both noble and widespread. Unfortunately, in the real world as many voters read down the ballot they soon run out of candidates on whom they have fairly complete information. As they find the exercise of informed judgment more and more difficult with each unfamiliar name and office, they resort to cues, like position on the ballot or names they recognize. In the absence of party labels, these other cues are used as substitutes for political information. Unfortunately, most of these cues have no political significance.

For all its shortcomings, the responsible party model is based on the assumption that party labels are better cues for voters than position on the ballot or name recognition. Party labels are guides to a reference group—a party—which has attempted to apply political criteria in nominating the candidate for the office in the first place.

In elections without party labels it is not unusual for intelligent and reasonably well informed people to use cues such as those found in Box 9.5 in making their voting decision when they lack relevant information.[40] In elections to some offices, these cues become critical factors in determining winners and losers. For many years, when the winner of the Democratic party nomination for any statewide office in Texas was the sure winner in the general election in November, Texas Democrats nominated for the office of state treasurer a man with the same name as a famous bank robber—Jesse James. They also kept in office a man named Tunnel as Railroad Commissioner, and a man named Sadler as Agriculture Commissioner. Eventually Mr. James died, and was replaced by a man named Warren G. Harding.[41]

Given the difficulty of applying the Rational-Comprehensive decision-making model to every candidate for every office, the use of party labels may make sense. "Knee-jerk" party voting seems just as rational and politically relevant as "knee-jerk" voting for whomever is listed first on the ballot, or for people because they have the same names as bank robbers or are called "Bubba" or "Doc." At least, when one votes for a party one is voting for a person with whom one is likely to share a general set of principles. That is the way it is supposed to be—*in theory.*

BOX 9.4

TYPES OF STATE AND LOCAL ELECTIONS*

PARTISAN (Party Labels Serve as Decision Cues)

Jurisdiction or Type	Representative Offices or Subject Matter	Time of Year
General	President, Congress, State, County and Township Legislatures and Executives	November
Municipal	Mayor and Council in a Few Large Cities	Spring

NONPARTISAN (No Party Labels as Decision Cues)

Jurisdiction or Type of Election	Representative Offices or Subject Matter	Time of Year
Municipal	Mayor and City Council in Most Cities	Spring
School District	Board Members in Most School Districts	Spring
Special	Called to replace officials who have resigned, died, been impeached or recalled	Varies
Referendum	Bond Issues, Amendments to City Charters, State Constitutions, Proposed Laws	Varies
Recall	Public Votes to Remove Officials	Varies
Primary **	(Open) The General Public, or (Closed) Party Members, Vote to Choose the Candidates for the General Election in November	Spring-Summer
Run-off	A type of special election held in jurisdictions where a majority rather than a plurality is required to win the nomination in a primary or an election to office. The top two candidates run in this type of election to determine which can get a majority.	

---

* Some elections may combine partisan and nonpartisan elements. In the general election a few judicial offices may be nonpartisan and referendums may also appear on the ballot with no party labels to guide voting decisions. Some special elections use party labels.

**Except for the office of President, the Louisiana primary is essentially the general election for national, state and local offices. All candidates appear on a nonpartisan ballot in a September election. Candidates with a majority win election to office. For offices which did not produce a majority, the top two candidates compete in a November run-off, which, in presidential years, is the same day as the presidential election.

Source: The Book of the States, 1994–95 (Lexington, KY: The Council of State Governments, 1994), 217.

BOX 9.5

CUES USED BY VOTERS IN ELECTIONS WITHOUT PARTY LABELS (THIS INCLUDES PRIMARY ELECTIONS)

After voters have made their decisions on the offices at the top of the ballot, the following cues are often used in the absence of other information—such as the name of the candidate's party:

1. Position on the ballot. Being listed first can be worth about five percent of the vote to a candidate, all other things being equal.
2. Recognition of the name of candidates whom the voter knows in the community.
3. Recognition of the name of candidates because of radio or TV spots, newspaper ads, billboards, or campaign literature.
4. Recognition of the name of a person who isn't the candidate. Some voters know that they aren't voting for that historical person and some aren't sure.
5. Name characteristics such as the name of a person, place, or thing that seems appropriate or even humorous.
6. Name characteristics associated with ethnicity or gender.
7. Nicknames or name characteristics associated with images of folksiness, power, or competence.

Pre-election Coalitions Are Superior

In order to win elections, it is necessary to build coalitions consisting of individuals and organizations with differing agendas but among whom there is some agreement on basic principles. Within each major coalition negotiations and compromises may take place. In a sense, the two national parties are coalitions of individuals, interest groups, 50 state parties which themselves are coalitions of local parties (county, township, and city). The Responsible Party Model assumes that the public is best served when coalitions are created in public before, rather than in secret after, the elections take place. In this way the voter can identify the party whose candidates and issues he or she wants to support.

Parties are Necessary to Mobilize Voters

Fewer voters turn out in elections without parties. One of the major functions of strong political parties is to mobilize the middle class and the have-nots, to use their superior numbers of votes to influence the political system. Thus responsible party theory assumes that the interest group system is biased in favor of the haves, and the party system is biased in favor of the have-nots.

Responsible Party Theory: Competition and Cohesion

The responsible party theory might be called "The Responsible Government" model. Certainly responsible government is its central value. Responsible party theory describes a method for making government accountable to the public through the electoral process. Two or more parties offer candidates who promise to carry out programs. If—once elected—

these officials don't keep their promises, or if what they promised to do doesn't work, then the voters can remove them in the next election and put another party in office. Responsible party theory requires two essential conditions: competition and cohesion.

Competition

Competition between two or more parties is essential for two reasons: to offer an organized alternative and to provide an informed alternative.

Party competition exists when there are at least two parties with a realistic chance of winning control of major government offices in an election. There is a major difference between competition in which two parties compete for the governorship, but not for control of the legislature.

Competition for control of both the executive and legislative branches by two parties means that there will be an organized alternative available if the voters decide to "throw the rascals out" at election time. If there is no alternative then the new set of officeholders is simply a collection of individuals with no plan and no program and no sense of unity to accomplish anything. Neither active individuals, the media, nor interest groups offer the voters an alternative governing party at election time. A competitive party system not only offers alternative policies, it also provides a set of candidates to carry them out.

The second reason why competition is necessary is to provide a set of officials who actually understand how the government works because they've served in it, as the **loyal opposition**. A free press, active individuals, and various interest groups may help in the investigation and publication of government misdeeds and government mistakes. However, they operate outside the major institutions of government. In a competitive party system members of the loyal opposition operate from the inside. Thus, they are in a position to provide an additional degree of insight into the performance of the governing party.

One-party systems are virtually the same thing as no-party systems. In one-party governments there is no mechanism for voters to replace one set of office holders with another. Instead, each voter at each election must make a long series of separate decisions on candidates for each and every office. Under such circumstances, it is very difficult for voters to hold accountable the collection of office holders that constitutes government. Take Arkansas, for example.

According to Diane D. Blair, parties.

> existed in name only in traditional Arkansas Politics. Until very recently the Democratic party, described as one of the most 'moribund and backward in the south,' was a mere holding company under whose name all candidates sought office; and the Republican party 'wavered somewhat between an esoteric cult on the order of a lodge and a conspiracy for plunder.' Arkansas had essentially a no-party system . . . "42

When only one party's nomination is really valuable, that party is not likely to be a cohesive coalition of individuals and interest groups sharing common principles. It is more likely to be a battleground in which all individuals and interests compete for office and influence.

The governing party in a one-party system ends up being the arena instead of a contestant. For the voter, democracy becomes a heavy chore of monitoring the officials one can elect with little or no influence over the rest. Accountable parties broaden the voter's influence.

Cohesion

Party cohesion means that among the three components of the party there is considerable unity. Each of the three components supports the goals of the party. For a party to be collectively responsible to the electorate, the parts must be mutually responsible to one another. This may mean that the party may have to support an occasional unappealing candidate to accomplish greater goals. As one party loyalist put it, "He's an s.o.b. but he's *our* s.o.b." However, party cohesion also means that there are goals and objectives upon which party supporters agree and which they attempt to make apparent to the voters. The responsible party model does not ask the voters for a blank check to be filled in later.

In order to achieve cohesion:

1. Members of the party in office should support the party program despite attempts to influence them by appealing to other loyalties (institution or constituency), values (ideology, religion, or friendship), and interests (personal advancement, campaign resources or the career goals of close associates). The party was put in office to deliver. Members of the party in office who do not support the party should be held responsible to the party in office in the distribution of benefits (committee assignments, pro-

In this rally against police brutality in St. Paul, Minnesota, citizens have organized to take direct action. This form of political participation is protected by the First Amendment's right to "peaceably" assemble.

motions, legislative support). Furthermore, the electoral party should be in a position to deny electoral party endorsement for the next election.

2. The electoral party should use resources effectively to advance the interests of the party. In performing its traditional functions, managing election campaigns and mobilizing voters, the electoral party must support those who support the party. While it may choose to be charitable about withholding endorsement from elected officials who do not support the party, the electoral party must encourage those who do support the party to continue doing so.

3. The party in the electorate should support at least most of the party's candidates in the interests of party unity despite appeals from the other party based on gender, ethnicity, personality, regionalism, friendship, shared values, ideology, issue preferences, or attractiveness of particular candidates.

BRINGING BACK THE BALANCE

Strengthening parties to the point that our system approximates a responsible party system is a goal shared by many individuals and organizations. As the American Assembly observed in its final report, "Many of us are concerned that the balance between parties and interest groups has been upset in recent years . . . and that active steps need to be taken to restore the parties to a more vigorous role in the electoral process.[43]

Although one or two technical points may be new to you, most of our list of suggestions for strengthening parties is based on material already introduced in this and earlier chapters and thus constitutes a review. Our eight reforms by no means exhaust the possibilities raised by much longer lists found in the literature, a literature we urge you to read.[44] These reforms are: (1) partisan municipal elections, (2) indication of party identity at registration, (3) closed primaries, (4) the straight ticket option, (5) promotion of endorsing conventions, (6) requirement that a portion of surplus candidate funds be allocated to state or local parties, (7) provision of free television and radio time to parties during the general election, (8) allocation of resources to parties to organize state legislatures.

Partisan Municipal Elections

Restore party participation in municipal elections. Allowing parties to nominate slates of candidates to appear on the ballot in city elections would enhance both the legitimacy and active base of parties. It would also improve the linkage between individuals and the governments of which they are supposed to be kept informed. This reform would not only help the parties in recruiting and establishing linkages between leaders in the county and city political arenas, it would also be good for the community.

David Price has observed that in addition to helping structure electoral decision making and promoting the accountability of local government, "Local parties [can] play a broader role as 'mediating institutions,' as focal points of community life, and as links between the community and the larger political world."[45] While many precinct and county party members already play a role in the politics of their municipal governments, this 'reform' would increase the likelihood that they would.

There is ample evidence that partisan elections involve higher turnout and would thus promote more participation in municipal elections. In addition, this 'reform' might also promote cooperation between county and municipal officials, as well as place more urban issues on the agendas of state political leaders.

Include Party Identity at Registration

By requiring voters to identify their party, or choose to be independent, at the time of registration the membership base and the awareness of parties are likely to increase, as would general awareness of the party among the general public.[46]

More importantly, however, this reform will make it easier for the party to reach the membership for volunteers and to increase participation on the primary.

Closed Primaries

Adopt **closed primaries.** As a general rule, closed primaries limit participation in the nomination process to individuals who have at least chosen to identify with the party.

Twenty-six states have "closed" primaries.[47] In these states independents who wish to influence party nominations can do so by joining one of them. Otherwise, they can wait until the general election and make their selection from among the slates of candidates nominated by the parties. Nonmembers of interest groups have the same type of choice in influencing the way interest groups operate. They can join or they can remain outside and deal with the results of interest group actions after the fact.

Closed primaries; not only increase party membership and identity, they are also likely to make candidates more aware of the people who make the party work. Consequently, parties are better able to compete with interest groups and PACs for the loyalty and attention of candidates.

The Straight Ticket Option

The straight ticket option makes it easier for a voter to support his or her party. In 20 states the straight ticket option is already available. In 30 states, including those 20, the party-column ballot is used. Both these options make it easier to use the party as a cue to voting. The most awkward ballot, and most likely to discourage voters from even voting on offices further down, is the office block ballot. This type of ballot increases the likelihood that extraneous cues such as location and name recognition will be used in place of party.[48]

Endorsing Conventions

Endorsing conventions give the electoral party a larger role in the nominating process. This in turn increases the ability of party leaders to compete for the attention of successful candidates with interest groups, PACs, and political consultants. In 38 states party conventions play no role at all in the nominating process. In 12 there is some involvement of party leaders in nominations.[49]

This "reform" will improve the ability of the electoral party to promote party cohesion. Potential candidates who have worked hard for the party in the past, or served it well in lesser offices, can be rewarded with endorsements for higher offices. Given the importance of name recognition and the realities of PAC contributions, public officials—elected under the party label—who have not helped the party enact its program will probably not be denied nomination, but by denying endorsements to officeholders party regulars can encourage them to work a little harder on the party's behalf in the next term of office.

Furthermore, even if a primary contest does occur, the use of endorsing conventions could make ballot location more meaningful by reserving first place for the endorsed candidate.

Assign Surplus Campaign Funds to State or Local Parties

Party candidates elected to office under the party label should be required to contribute a portion, say 10 percent, of any surplus campaign funds to the state or local party. In this way the parties will be given resources to recruit and assist candidates to challenge the other party in its safe district, thus increasing competition. Surplus campaign funds are an open invitation to abuse by officeholders who may use them to increase their personal influence within the party or to make it too expensive for anyone else to offer future electoral challenges. Officials who are able to build large war chests become isolated not only from the influence of the party but also from the discipline of the electorate.

A high proportion of the funds contributed by political action committees and wealthy individuals often goes to candidates who don't need it. These candidates are usually incumbents from safe seats, election districts where their party usually wins by comfortable margins—10 percent or more. Many of these candidates often run unopposed. By making funds available to the electoral party to use for the recruitment of candidates to run in districts held by the opposition, and in support of legislators who *do* need party help for reelection, the party system will become more competitive and the candidates elected will pay at least as much attention to advice and counsel from their party as they do to interest groups, wealthy individuals, and political consultants.

By requiring that only a portion of the *surplus* be given, the well-funded incumbents would still be left with a surplus. A fitting irony in this proposal is that PAC funds which have weakened the party system would now be used to strengthen it.

Provide Parties with Free Television and Radio Time

The mass media are an essential part of municipal, county, state, and national elections. Newspapers cannot be required to provide free ads, but radio and television operate via publicly licensed monopolies. The government enforces laws that make it a crime to broadcast on a frequency for which someone has paid a license fee. Thus, as a condition of receiving or keeping a license, the government could require that as a public service each party be given airtime during the month or weeks before the election. With free airtime to allocate, the parties would increase their ability to promote party unity and a more vigorous effort to carry out party platforms once the election is over. This could further reduce the dependence of candidates on PACs for money to buy time.

Give Parties the Authority to Organize State Legislatures

The rules of state legislatures that are not organized along partisan lines could be revised to allow each party caucus to allocate the party's share of committee assignments. In strong party states, the party leaders are the presiding officers. Thus, party loyalty is a factor in making committee assignments. In weak party states, the election of the presiding officers has little to do with party loyalty. Thus, party is not a factor in the committee assignments they make.

Legislators whose committee assignments come from the party are more likely to take getting a party platform voted into law a little more seriously. Furthermore, the election of leaders by secret ballot instead of public roll call vote might promote the rise to legislative leadership of leaders whose power base is within the majority party instead of within a small number of powerful interest groups.

CONCLUSION: CAN PARTIES ADJUST?

Political machines are organizations that gained control of political parties in many American cities during the post–Civil War era and dominated most large cities during the first half of this century. Many of them were so powerful and so corrupt that American political culture has reacted (and sometimes overreacted) to them ever since.

The failure to differentiate political party from political machine creates an image problem for the modern political party. More specifically, it creates problems for those who attempt to promote the notion that strong political parties can serve as counterforces to strong interest groups.

The mass media exacerbate the situation by the indiscriminate use of the term "machine" for virtually any local party, campaign organization, or group that seems to have its act together. As we have already seen, in strong interest group systems one set of interest groups usually predominates. The interests of that set of groups is not always the same as the interests looked after by political parties appealing to the entire electorate for support.

The list of ways to strengthen parties is based largely on features of existing state or local political systems. Thus, in some parts of our federal system, parties are being nurtured by the political system and more often than not the public interest is better served.

The future of political parties as promoters of meaningful electoral choices and as counterforces to the influence of interest groups and PACs is not as grim as it was a few years ago. There is mounting evidence that while political party identity may have declined, the decline is leveling off. Thus, the party in the electorate may be weaker than it was but it isn't going to disappear. Furthermore, the electoral parties in many states are stronger than ever. That is one reason for the increase in the proportion of states that have competitive party systems.

It remains to be seen whether these parties will become cohesive enough to provide voters with meaningful choices and a mechanism for holding government accountable. A great deal will depend upon the willingness of individuals to work within the parties to promote the changes necessary to make government more responsible to the electorate.

STUDY OBJECTIVES

1. Identify the central argument of this chapter.
2. Identify the three components of a political party.
3. Identify the functions of parties.
4. Identify the reasons why we have a two party system.
5. Identify reasons why patronage is a tradition that won't go away.
6. Differentiate machine politics and political machine.
7. Differentiate political party and political machine.

8. Identify the reasons political machines came to power.
9. Identify the functions performed by political machines.
10. Identify the reasons why political machines declined.
11. Identify the cues used by voters in place of party labels.
12. Identify the assumptions upon which Responsible Party Theory is based.
13. Identify the major components of Responsible Party Theory.
14. Identify the major proposals of the reform movement and their effect on political parties.
15. Identify the ways in which state and local political party systems could be strengthened.

GLOSSARY

The at-large principle   This principle apportions all seats in a legislative body to the entire unit of government the legislatures serves. An at-large city council means that all the citizens in the city vote on candidates for that seat. The governor of a state is elected at-large; members of the state legislature, on the other hand, are elected from single member districts.

Closed primaries   These limit participation in the nomination process to individuals who have chosen to identify with the party.

The electoral party   This consists of (1) individuals who campaign, attend party meetings and social functions, and contribute to the party, (2) officials of the party at the state and local levels, and (3) staff members.

Endorsing convention   A convention that takes place before the primary election. In states that use them it promotes party unity and gives the electoral party a larger role in the nominating process. Delegates to the convention vote to endorse one of the people seeking the nomination for governor or any other offices the convention is empowered to endorse. Then voters know which candidate in the primary has the approval of the active party members.

Index of competition   This measures interparty competition within each of the several states. This measure involves three dimensions: proportion of success, duration of success, and frequency of divided control of government.

Loyal opposition   A party loyal to the political system but opposed to the governing party. As the minority party in the legislature, it is aware of the governing process, and is prepared to take over the government if it wins the next election.

Machine politics   The manipulation of certain incentives to partisan political participation: for example, favoritism based on political criteria in personnel decisions, in contracting, and in the administration of the laws.

Mobilize   To arouse, to call to action. A major feature of a competitive two party system is that more voters are mobilized to participate than in a one-party or no-party system.

Nonpartisan elections   These do not have party labels on the ballot as a guide to voters.

One-party systems   These have no mechanism for voters to replace one set of office holders with another. Instead, each voter at each election must make a series of separate decisions on candidates for each and every office.

Open primary   Such a primary enables people to vote in either party's primary regardless of whether one identifies with the party or not.

Party caucus   A meeting of all the members of a party in a legislative body.

Party cohesion   This means that within each of the three components of the party there is considerable unity and that each of the three components supports the goals of the party.

Party identification   The sense of and willingness to express a feeling of support for and identity with a political party.

Party in the electorate   Consists of any or all of the following: (1) those who say they identify with the party, and in some states those who stated their party allegiance when they registered to vote, (2) those who vote in the primary election of a party, (3) those who usually vote for a party's candidates in general elections.

Party in office   This consists of officials in government who were either elected under the party label or appointed because of party affiliation. These are the individuals who will attempt to organize the government and take responsibility for running it.

Patronage   The practice of protecting, supporting, or advancing the cause of something or someone else. In politics patronage means that decisions are made in favor of an individual or a party's supporters. Few critics of patronage make the distinction between situations in which all other things are equal and situations in which favoritism over-rides other important factors such as qualifications for the job or the lowest bid to offer a product or service.

Political consultants   Individuals or firms that offer professional expertise in the new technology of political campaigning.

Political machine   An organization that practices machine politics and usually has taken over an existing local party to do so.

Political party   An organization that attempts to take control of government by means of winning elections.

Primary election   This enables voters (who may or may not be active in the party) to help determine whom the party will nominate for the general election.

Proportional representation   Uses large multimember districts from which are elected numerous legislators according to the percentage of the total vote their party received.

Rational-comprehensive model   A model of decision making that assumes that voters are always informed and rational.

Reform Movement   The collection of individuals and groups who were concerned with defeating political machines in nineteenth- and twentieth-century urban America.

Responsible party model A model of party-governmental relationships that allows the voters to hold government accountable through meaningful elections.

State election code The collection of laws dealing with elections.

ENDNOTES

1. Larry Sabato, *The Party's Just Begun* (Glenview, IL: Scott, Foresman, and Co., 1988).

2. The term *mentor* has less emotional baggage than does *patron*. In Homer's epic the *Odyssey*. Mentor is the name of Odysseus' friend who was entrusted with the education of his son Telemachus.

3. Raymond E. Wolfinger, "Why Political Machines Have Not Withered Away and Other Revisionist Thoughts," *The Journal of Politics* (May, 1972), 365–398.

4. William L. Riordan, *Plunkitt of Tammany Hall* (New York: E. P. Dutton & Co., 1963), 27–28.

5. Riordan, 19.

6. Robert K. Merton, "The Latent Function of the Machine," in *Social Theory and Social Structure*, Robert K. Merton ed. (New York: Free Press of Glencoe, 1957), 71–81. See also Theodore J. Lowi, "Machine Politics: Old and New," *Public Interest* (Fall, 1967), 83–92.

7. William A. Schultze, *Urban and Community Politics* (North Scituate, MA: Duxbury Press, 1974), 176.

8. Milton I. Rakove, *Don't Make No Waves—Don't Back No Losers: An Insider's Analysis of the Daley Machine* (Bloomington, Indiana University Press, 1978), 96.

9. Richard Hofstadter, *The Age of Reform* (New York: Vintage Books, 1955), 5–7.

10. Ibid., 241

11. Hofstadter uses the term "machine" to describe these organizations. Our definition of machine makes the notion of a reform machine something of a conundrum as in "honest crook" or as Plunkitt might prefer, "honest graft." Among the many excellent biographies of these complex and interesting individuals, of special merit are the following: Melvin C. Holli, *Reform in Detroit: Hazen Pingree and Urban Politics* (New York: Oxford University Press, 1969); and William D. Miller, *Mr. Crump of Memphis* (Baton Rouge: Louisiana State University Press, 1964).

12. Tari Renner, "Municipal Election Processes: The Impact on Minority Representation," in *The Municipal Yearbook: 1988* (Washington, D.C.: International City Management Association, 1988), 13.

13. Denise L. Baer, "Political Parties: The Missing Variable in Women and Politics Research," *Political Research Quarterly*, 1993, 570.

14. Charles R. Adrian, "Forms of City Government in American History," in *The Municipal Yearbook: 1988*, 8. See also Eugene C. Lee, "Municipal Elections, A Statistical Profile," in *The Municipal Yearbook: 1963*.

15. Among the works suggesting that parties are in bad shape the best-known include: David Broder, *The Party's Over: The Failure of Politics in America* (New York: Harper and Row, 1971). William Crotty, *American Parties in Decline*, 2d ed. (Boston: Little, Brown & Co., 1984). Everett Carll Ladd, *Where Have all the Voters Gone: The Fracturing of America's Political Parties*, 2d ed. (New York: W. W. Norton & Co., 1982). Thomas R. Dye begins the party chapter of the eighth edition of his widely read textbook, *Politics in State and Communities*, with the heading: "American Political Parties in Disarray" (Englewood Cliffs, NJ: Prentice Hall, 1994), 122.

16. Peter W. Weilhouwer and Brad Lockerbie, "Party Contacting and Political Participation, 1952–90," *American Journal of Political Science*, 1994, 38:226.

17. Ibid., 38: 215.

18. Robert Huckfeldt and John Sprague, "Political Parties and Electoral Mobilization: Political Structure, Social Structure, and the Party Canvass," *American Political Science Review*, 1992, 86:70.

19. Joseph A. Aistrup, "State Legislative Party Competition: A County-Level Measure," *Political Research Quarterly*, 1992, 442.

20. Frank J. Sorauf, *Party Politics in America*, 2d ed. (Boston: Little Brown & Co., 1972), 9–10.

21. Denise L. Baer, "Political Parties: The Missing Variable," 569.

22. Paul Herrnson, *Party Campaigning* (Cambridge, MA: Harvard University Press, 1988).

23. Malcolm E. Jewell and David M. Olson, *Political Parties and Elections in American States* (Chicago: The Dorsey Press, 1988), 226–227.

24. *The Book of the States 1994–95* (The Council of State Governments, Lexington, KY, 1994), 217–218.

25. Ibid.

26. Sarah McCally Morehouse, *State Politics, Parties, and Policy* (New York: Holt, Rinehart, and Winston, 1982), 186.

27. Jewell and Olson, 105.

28. Morehouse, *State Politics*, 186–187.

29. *Book of the States*, 1994–95, 224.

30. Donald Stokes, "Party Loyalty and the Likelihood of Deviating Elections," in Angus Campbell et al., *Elections and the Political Order* (New York: Wiley, 1966), 126–127.

31. Donald Philip Green and Eric Schickler, "Multiple-Measure Assessment of Party Identification," *Public Opinion Quarterly*, 1993, 57:505. Campbell et al., *The American Voter* (New York: Wiley, 1960), 122.

32. See, for example, Sabato, *The Party's Just Begun*.

33. Richard G. Niemi, Stephen Wright, and Lynda W. Powell, "Multiple Party Identifiers and the Measurement of Party Identification," *The Journal of Politics* (November, 1987), 1097.

34. Jewell and Olson, 42.

35. Raymond Wolfinger and Robert B. Arseneau, "Partisan Change in the South, 1952–76," in Louis Maisel and Joseph Cooper, eds. *Political Parties: Development and Decay* (Beverly Hills, CA: Sage Publications, 1978), 197.

36. Robert Huckfeldt and John Sprague, "Political Parties and Electoral Mobilization: Political Structure, Social Structure, and the Party Canvass," *American Political Science Review*, 1992, 86:73.

37. The classic statement is the American Political Science Association, *Toward a More Responsible Two-Party System* (New York: Rinehart and Company, 1950). For a more recent reformulation see David Broder, " The Case for Responsible Party Government," in *Parties and Elections in an Anti-Party Age*, Jeff Fishel, ed. (Bloomington: Indiana University Press, 1978), 22–33. For a devastating critique of the American Political Science Association report, see Evron Kirkpatrick, "Toward a More Responsible Party System: Political Science, Policy Science, or Pseudo-Science?" in Fishel, *Parties and Elections*, 33–55.

38. Jack Plano and Milton Greenberg, *The American Political Dictionary*, 8th ed. (New York: Holt, Rinehart, and Winston, 1989), 85–86.

39. Thomas R. Dye, *Politics in State and Communities*, 8th ed., 123–124.

40. V. O. Key, *Politics, Parties, & Pressure Groups*, 5th ed. (New York: Thomas Y. Crowell Co., 1964), 383, 644.

41. Wendell M. Bedichek and Neal Tannahill, *Public Policy in Texas*, (Glenview, IL: Scott, Foresman and Company, 1982), 136.

42. Diane D. Blair, *Arkansas Politics & Government: Do The People Rule?* (Lincoln: University of Nebraska Press, 1988). This excellent book is one of the first in a series on the states to be published by Nebraska Press. Blair is a Professor at the University of Arkansas and an Arkansas Democratic State Committee member.

43. The Final Report of the Sixty-second American Assembly, 11; this report includes 19 suggested reforms.

44. In addition to the American Assembly's Final Report, many of the papers prepared for it appear in Joel L. Fleishman, ed. *The Future of American Political Parties: The Challenge of Governance* (Englewood Cliffs, NJ: Prentice-Hall, Inc.,1982). Two excellent monographs to which this chapter owes a heavy debt are: David E. Price, *Bringing Back the Parties* (Washington, D.C.: Congressional Quarterly Inc., 1984); Larry Sabato, *The Party's Just Begun* (Glenview, IL: Scott, Foresman, and Co., 1988). The credentials of these two authors are particularly noteworthy. Price is a Political Science professor (Duke University), a former congressman (North Carolina), and former state party chair. Sabato, also a Political Science professor (University of Virginia), has written extensively on Political Action Committees and Campaign Consultants.

45. David Price, *Bringing Back the Parties*, 110–111.

46. Steven E. Finkel and Howard A. Scarrow, "Party Identification and Party Enrollment: The Difference and the Consequence," *The Journal of Politics* (1985), 621.

47. *The Book of the States, 1988–89*, 186–187. Later editions do not update this information.

48. Sabato, *Party*, 224.

49. *The Book of the States, 1988–89*, 184–185.

10

State and Local Parliaments: Legislatures, Boards, and Councils

An Illinois legislator, Representative Larry Wennlund, thought it might be interesting to get some input from ordinary citizens. He announced a contest called, "There Ought to Be a Law," and received over 600 proposals for legislation from all over the state. A high school girl from Joliet proposed that insurance stickers be placed on license plates to make it easier for police to identify vehicles without insurance. Another person suggested a law requiring that mandatory drug and alcohol tests be given to all drivers involved when a death results from an automobile accident. Other proposals were for Sunday elections, for letting pregnant women park in handicapped slots, and for banning people from talking on the phone while driving.

When it comes to passing laws and making policy, legislatures are unique. They are, what one political scientists called, the guts of democracy.[1] John Locke agreed with this assessment, calling the power of the "legislative" the most basic and important. Despite increasingly powerful executives, state legislatures, city councils, school boards, and other legislative bodies are key policymakers. They are also generally accessible to the individual, and, as the above example illustrates, individuals can have a direct bearing on legislation.

Individuals who are familiar with the procedures and organization of legislative bodies can be particularly influential in initiating or blocking government action. We see examples of this every day. Citizens angry about rising utility rates attend the city council meeting to express their displeasure. Students lobby the legislature and testify in public committee hearings to try to prevent tuition increases. A businessman, concerned about the lack of vocational programs offered in local schools, calls a member of the elected school board.

In order to influence legislative bodies, you must understand the functions they perform, how their members are chosen, and how they are organized to do business. Since local legislative bodies differ in many ways from those at the state level, you should be aware of some of the major differences. This chapter examines the functions of legislative bodies and looks specifically at the characteristics of state and local legislatures. It ends with advice and strategies for gaining access to these legislatures.

THE FUNCTIONS OF LEGISLATURES

Legislatures at the national, state, and local level perform unique functions in the American political system. The following discussion examines some of the most important of these functions.

Lawmaking

If you were to ask legislators what the purpose of the legislature is, you would get a variety of answers: "Our job is to represent our constituents." "We resolve important issues through compromise." "We try to find the best way of providing important services to the citizens of this city (or state)." All of these would be correct of course, but the most basic answer is "We pass laws." Lawmaking, or enacting legislation, is the unique task of the legislature.

Legislators themselves perceive lawmaking to be their primary function. One survey asked legislators in Minnesota and Kentucky to rank in importance the functions of lawmaking, oversight, and constituency service. Two-thirds ranked legislating as most important.[2] Almost all the activities of a legislator revolve around the process of making laws. He or she introduces bills, deals with bills in committee, listens to public testimony, consults with lobbyists, constituents and bureaucrats, makes speeches, and even socializes with those interested in a specific law or the lawmaking process.

One should not be misled to believe that legislative bodies do *all* the legislating. Other actors, especially bureaucratic experts, become more highly involved in the lawmaking process as the size and complexity of the city or state increase. The executive often suggests or initiates laws; many bills are actually drafted by executive agencies or interest groups. Bureaucrats use their discretion to implement laws, and their decisions are often formalized as orders or rules. The courts interpret statutory and constitutional laws.

Taxing and Budget-Making

It is important to remember that legislatures, and only legislatures, possess the final authority to tax. This authority, potentially the most abusive held by government, is the key to understanding the dominant role of legislatures in state and local government.

Although budget-making is a form of lawmaking, it is so important it deserves to be mentioned separately. When students think about budgeting, they generally think of a dreary bureaucratic process that is complex, hard to understand and mechanical. While budgeting is a complex process, it is far from mechanical—it is a highly charged political process. Legislatures decide important policy questions when they decide how much citizens will be taxed and what programs government will fund. The budget is a government's ultimate statement of its policy choices. When the state legislature decides to raise teachers' salaries, it is making a statement about the high priority of education. A city council that decides to build a municipal convention center rather than a public housing project is making a statement that economic development and tourism are more important than direct services to the poor. As with lawmaking in general, developing budgets is not the sole function of legislatures. Often state legislatures rely on the governor's plan for taxing and spending while a local legislature will rely on a city manager, school superintendent, or other administrator. Still, the final decisions over the flow of funds are made by legislatures, and their greatest power is the power of the purse.

Oversight

A thoughtful, well-drafted law or budget offers no guarantee that the policy intentions of legislatures will be carried out. To try to insure that this happens, legislatures review and evaluate actions of the executive and oversee the administration of state and local programs. This process of reviewing the implementation of laws and policies is referred to as the **oversight function**.

Until recently, oversight was thought of as the "neglected stepchild" of the policy process. Creating and passing legislation was much more interesting and rewarding than checking to see if that legislation was being implemented properly. In the past few years, however, legislatures are paying increasing attention to oversight. Both state and local governments are going beyond such traditional measures as budget hearings and audits and are applying oversight to the whole legislative process. They are looking more closely at the efficiency and effectiveness of the programs themselves through "performance reviews." Over half the states and many cities have established separate evaluation agencies to conduct oversight of programs and budgets.

Thirty-five states initially established some form of **sunset legislation**. This typically means that unless the legislature acts to renew an executive agency it will cease to exist after a certain date. In general, sunset laws have not resulted in the termination of many agencies, but these laws have been an incentive for agencies to improve their performance.[3] Agencies that know they are going to be reviewed and possibly terminated have an incentive to improve their performance (Box 10.1).

Although legislatures are becoming more aggressive toward oversight, they are still less motivated to perform this function. Oversight often becomes a burden that produces no political rewards. One legislator admits that "most of us are elected to be legislators with the thought that we're there to correct the ills of the world, and we usually start by filing bills on every idea we have."[4] Taking action on these bills means creating public policy, engaging in the excitement of combat, and stimulating the attention of the media.

In contrast, oversight is a boring or tedious process for legislators who must attend lengthy hearings, consider the details of complicated programs, and read voluminous reports. Often they face defensive administrators and entrenched interest groups who distrust their motives and consider them incompetent to judge their programs. In an ideal world the oversight process would be a continuous and integral function of the legislature. In the real world it is often the last to receive attention.

Judicial

Legislatures perform judicial functions directly through impeachment of executive officials and judges and indirectly through the confirmation of judicial appointments. Most state legislatures have the power to remove executive officials and judges through a two-step process. The House of Representatives decides whether to **impeach**, that is, bring formal charges against these officials and the Senate tries them to see if they are guilty. Conviction generally requires a two-thirds vote of the Senate and results in removal from office.

In many states, legislatures influence the judicial process indirectly through the confirmation of judicial appointments. The state senate confirms gubernatorial appointees to the bench usually through a two-thirds vote. Even in states where judges are elected, governors will frequently appoint judges to fill vacancies on state courts. These appointees must also be approved by the senate.

BOX 10.1

SUNSET IN THE STATES: MIXED REVIEWS

Sunset legislation had its birth in Colorado in 1976, and quickly caught the imagination of legislatures throughout the country. By 1980, it had spread to more than 30 states and was highly touted as the promising new instrument of legislative oversight.

It sounded so simple. A number of state agencies—around 30—would be scheduled for termination each year. These agencies would be subjected to a review by the legislature to determine whether or not they should be continued, modified, or terminated, that is, "sunsetted."

The distinguishing feature of sunset, and the reason for its catchy name, was its automatic termination feature. Agencies not specifically reauthorized by statute before the scheduled "sunset" deadline would simply cease to exist. For the first time, the burden of proof for performance and effectiveness was placed squarely on the agency. And for the first time, thorough reviews of the bureaucracy would actually take place. Legislators who were always too busy or too uninterested in oversight, would be forced to review agencies and take positive action to see that these agencies continued to operate.

Like most "reforms," sunset was oversold. It was supposed to reduce the size of state bureaucracies, but the only agencies terminated were small and insignificant. It was supposed to cut down on the increasing costs of state government, but the cost of the sunset review itself was often higher than most anticipated. Additional legislative staff had to be hired to conduct the reviews that required a large amount of time for both the legislature and the agency.

The biggest costs, however, were the political costs. Sunset unleashed a wave of lobbyists who descended on state capitals to protect their favorite agencies and programs. Sunset reviews often opened up enormous controversies. These controversies went beyond questions of how an agency operated; they often revolved around important state policies. Legislators realized the high price of trying to change or eliminate powerful state bureaucracies.

Enthusiasm for sunset waned. By the early 1980s, four states had repealed their sunset statutes or let them fall into disuse. All but five states have made changes to their legislation. No states have adopted sunset laws since 1981.

States that have maintained sunset laws have a lowered level of expectations. Many states modified their statutes to limit the scope of sunset reviews. For example, Kansas and Florida review only regulations and programs, not agencies. Some states extended the length of the review cycle in order to lower the costs of the reviews. A longer review cycle also allows more careful scrutiny of agencies.

As Sunset moves into its second decade, it has become a reasonably effective tool for legislative oversight. Although it does not often result in the termination of agencies, it does result in the modification of existing ones. Agencies anticipating sunset reviews will usually attempt to "get their house in order" to minimize the potential of criticism or changes that an unfavorable review might bring. Sunset does seem to encourage more efficient and effective agency operations. More importantly, the process opens up the possibility of addressing important issues and remedying flagrant bureaucratic abuses. Thus it seems that in a modified form, sunset may be around for a while.

Thus legislatures exercise checks and balances over executive and judicial branches. Impeachment is a final weapon against executive unresponsiveness although it is cumbersome to employ and seldom used. Judicial confirmation means that executives must share control over the appointment of judicial personnel.

Representation

Cities and states share the idea of the nation that they should be governed as republics. You'll recall from Chapter 4 that an important concept of republicanism is the notion of representative government. In Madisonian theory, competent citizens are chosen to represent the community and help it realize its ideals; decision making that is "filtered" through these competent individuals helps preclude tyranny by temporary and irrational majorities. Representatives consider the demands of each issue in light of the whole community. Thus representation is an important function of an elected legislator.

Theories of Representation

Exactly who the legislator represents and how he or she represents them is a controversial matter. Imagine that you have been elected to the state legislature. What would be your philosophy about the way you represent your voters? Would you vote on bills the way you think your constituents want you to vote or the way you think you ought to vote on the basis of your own conscience and judgment? The question is not as simple as it sounds.

There are three classic views of the legislator: the **trustee role**, the **delegate role**, and the **politico role**.[5] In making decisions, trustees claim to follow what they consider right or just, following convictions and principles even if there are times when this means opposing the views of a majority of their constituents. Trustees believes that they are generally in a position to be more knowledgeable about the issues and, therefore, are elected to use their own judgment. Delegates, on the other hand, reflect the views of a majority of their constituents. Their job, as they see it, is to strictly represent the interests of a majority of their voters.

The role of politico combines features of the trustee and the delegate. Depending on the circumstances, a representative may hold the view of trustee on one issue and of delegate on another. If a representative has aspirations of re-election — and most representatives do — he or she cannot afford to consistently ignore constituency views. On the other hand, most voters know very little about most bills. Attempts to mirror the majority view of your constituents makes no sense if there is no majority view.

Those constituents who *do* have a strong and informed view are likely to be an organized minority, that is, a special interest group. The demands of special interest groups may cause conflict in the decisions of a politico. A representative who wants to accommodate special interest group demands may not believe these demands are in the best interest of the entire community. In this situation, a politico must choose between the role of trustee or delegate.

Certainly the concept of representation is complex. As one state legislator observed, ". . . each member casts a vote on a bill, resolution, or procedural question based on how he or she reckons that particular problem at that particular moment. Just as the moments change, so do the rationales. . . ."[6]

Responding to Constituents

Representation goes beyond promoting the policy views of citizens. Constituents want a legislator who gives them attention and assurances and attends to their individual needs.

Most state legislators and all local legislators live and work close to those who elect them. As they go about their business, they are expected to mix with their constituents—at work, parties, the barber shop, or the supermarket. They nurture support by listening and responding to individuals' opinions.

Like their congressional counterparts, state and local legislators are spending more and more time helping individual constituents. This individualized assistance is called **casework**. Casework may involve a variety of activities, but a substantial portion of these require that the legislator intervene with a government agency on the constituent's behalf. A single mother may feel she should qualify for food stamps. A college graduate may want a job working for a city or county agency. A parent feels her son or daughter may have been badly treated by a coach or principal. Some legislators enjoy this function of representation not only because they build electoral support, but also because they feel they are having a direct impact on people's lives.

How Representative Is the Typical Legislator?

There are those who argue that in a democracy such as ours, the representatives we elect to public office should mirror society in general. The idea is that people elected to public office should resemble those who vote for them; this makes them more responsive to the needs of the "common" people. A legislature that reflects the social, economic, and cultural composition of society will be more sensitive to the needs of citizens in that society.

Legislators do tend to possess certain characteristics of a majority of their constituents such as ethnicity, race, or religion. Legislators representing a district in which the majority of voters are Roman Catholic are likely to be Catholic themselves. Beyond these basic characteristics, however, legislators are not likely to reflect the general characteristics of their constituency. Your chances of being elected to a legislature increase substantially if you are white, male, Protestant, upper middle class, well-educated, and work in a business or profession that allows you time away for legislative service. Yet the portrait of the "average" legislator has been changing slowly over the years. Women and minorities have gained more seats in state and local legislatures, although their numbers are still not overwhelming. Women held about 8 percent of the 7,500 state legislative seats in 1975; in 1993 this had more than doubled to about 20.4 percent. Minority membership (African Americans, Hispanics, Asian Americans, and Native Americans) now hold about 10 percent of all state legislative seats.[7]

Table 10.1 shows that "attorney" is still the category most represented in state legislatures, comprising 16 percent. The number of legislatures who define their occupation as "legislator" is increasing. Indeed, the category of full-time legislator would total 24 percent if those who list themselves as "retired," "homemaker," or "student" were included. One reason for this increase is the longer session lengths of many state legislatures; being a legislator in many states now resembles a full-time job.

Amending

One function that all state legislatures and most local legislatures have in common is the ability to change fundamental laws that govern state or local government; these laws are embodied in state constitutions and local charters. State legislatures *propose* amendments to state constitutions that are ultimately approved by the voters. State legislatures also have the authority to approve amendments to the U. S. Constitution.

Table 10.1	
TOP FIVE OCCUPATIONAL CATEGORIES OF STATE LEGISLATORS	
Attorney	16%
Full-time Legislator	15
Business Owner	10
Agricultural	8
Retired	7

Source: Rich Jones, The Book of the States (Lexington, KY: Council of State Governments, 1994–1995), 100.

That legislatures have the potential to alter basic laws embodied in constitutions demonstrates the importance of legislative bodies in American democracy.

STATE LEGISLATURES

Until recently state legislatures have had bad reputations. Charges of corruption, malapportionment, and other abuses come frequently from the press and other political observers. Critics also charge that state legislatures are poorly organized and technically ill-equipped to do what is expected of them. They are the prime examples of "institutional lag"—largely nineteenth-century organizations that must address themselves to twentieth-century problems.[8]

In the past several years, however, state legislatures have instituted wide-sweeping changes or "reforms." They have reapportioned themselves, increased their capacity to make informed decisions, and passed laws to reduce ethical problems. The rapid and dramatic transformation of many state legislatures makes them fascinating targets for study.

Not only are state legislatures more progressive these days, they are also more significant actors in our intergovernmental system. Changes in our federal system since the early 1980s have given the states stronger positions. As states have become more prominent, state legislatures have strengthened their positions within the states. State legislatures have assumed more responsibility for state and local matters, and they are also more heavily involved in implementing federal programs.

Historical Changes in the Role of State Legislatures

American state legislatures have been affected by a number of historical changes. Although these changes have been continuous and complex, four historical stages in the role of legislatures can be identified.

Stage One: Early Domination

Early in American history, legislatures were the symbol of America's democratic struggle against an arbitrary British crown. For 25 years after the Declaration of Independence, state legislatures dominated. Governors represented political tyranny to American citizens who viewed the American Revolution as a revolt against executive authority.

Stage Two: Gradual Decline

For the next 100 years in American history, state legislatures suffered a gradual decline. The decline was primarily the result of two factors: the strengthening of executive power and the incompetence and corruption of legislatures themselves. As memories of autocratic royal governors faded, states gradually realized the need for stronger executives. Slowly, hostility toward governors was replaced with a growing trust in executive power. States took steps to strengthen their governors and created a variety of new executive offices that augmented the role of the executive branch in state affairs.

However, state legislatures themselves brought about their own decline. This reduction in influence and legitimacy is associated with the era of Jacksonian democracy. In response to social and economic changes as America industrialized, when Jackson became president, a new breed of state legislature had appeared on the scene. Jackson himself was elected president because of the support of the new urban masses of the East and the increased population of the Western states. With the rise of Jackson and the common man, the character of people serving in state legislatures changed profoundly. Gradually, as democratization progressed, service in the legislature ceased to be an activity that appealed to those with formal education and high social status. Most competent educated men therefore moved into business or other professional activities.

The incidence of corruption and bribery in state legislatures seemed to increase toward the end of the nineteenth century. The new industrial giants that emerged in the latter half of the nineteenth century—manufacturing, oil, mining, investment, to name a few—were well aware of how greatly they could be hurt or helped by what state legislatures did. Many of these business leaders were as prone to give bribes as state legislators and urban city councilmen were to accept them.

Stage Three: The Progressive Movement

The most predictable response to abuse of power by governmental bodies is to limit that power. So it was with the reformers who addressed the corruption and incompetence of state legislatures. The Progressive movement emerged around the turn of the century led by William Jennings Bryan, Robert M. La Follette, Theodore Roosevelt, and Woodrow Wilson. These reformers helped institute several measures that limited the power of legislatures and put it in the hands of the people.

The Progressives introduced the referendum, the recall, and the initiative. These measures, which were discussed in Chapter 4, gave people more direct control over policy and elected officials. Many state constitutions were revised. Legislative sessions in many states were limited to one every two years (biennial sessions). Reformers assumed that the less often legislators got together the less damage they could do! By 1940 only four states had annual legislative sessions. Less frequent legislative sessions provided one reason for lower salaries, and many states restricted legislators' pay. Debt limitations were introduced to control the financial power of legislatures.

Stage Four: The Age of the Executive

Prompted by Progressive reform, interest in the period from the mid–1930s to the mid–1960s focused on state executive organization and administration. During this period new or revised state constitutions enhanced the powers of governors. The latter were given longer terms, more appointment power, more control over budgets, and greater resources to

Paid lobbyists who represent organized interests and legislators interact frequently. Often, lobbyists give legislation invaluable information, although their influence is a point of political controversy.

manage larger bureaucracies. Meeting biennially, state legislatures were dependent on the executive for information, staff support, and direction. Often legislatures voted yes or no to gubernatorial requests with little revision. They rarely proposed substitute legislation or "marked up," that is, amended legislation in committee.[9]

The Modern State Legislature and the Rise of Professionalism

Facing stronger executives with fewer resources of their own, the word used most often to describe state legislatures was "amateurish." Throughout the first half of the twentieth century part-time "amateur" legislatures continued to be the standard. Legislators were poorly paid, sessions were short and infrequent, staff support was in short supply, and in many states legislators had no office space. About 30 years ago things began to change.

Reapportionment

The most important reason for criticism of state legislatures was their failure to reapportion. **Apportionment** is the allocation of legislative seats to geographic areas; it means that the boundaries of legislative districts (both state legislative districts and U. S. Congressional districts) are drawn about equal in population. **Reapportionment**, therefore, refers to the process of redrawing the boundaries of state and congressional districts to reflect changes or shifts in the population. For years states experienced gradual population shifts from rural to urban areas. Yet legislatures continued to be dominated by rural legislators who had little interest in addressing the problems and concerns of urban areas. Often rural residents felt that city people were not as virtuous, clean, or God-fearing as those living in rural areas and didn't really deserve state aid.

State legislatures are responsible for redrawing the geographical boundaries of voting districts in the two houses of the state legislature as well as for their state seats in the U. S. House of Representatives. Reapportionment is supposed to take place every 10 years after the census is taken. But as time passed almost every state failed to perform this function. Reapportionment may sound like a technical process—entering new census data into the appropriate computer program can easily and quickly yield evenly distributed districts. It is *not* a technical process, however, but a complicated and controversial political process that takes months, even years of planning, bargaining, and scheming to accomplish. It sends waves of anxiety among legislators who almost always have nothing to gain and everything to lose from uncertain results.

Until the 1960s the courts refused to force state legislatures to act, maintaining that reapportionment was a political issue that should be settled by political rather than legal means. Finally, in 1962 the Supreme Court heard the landmark case **Baker v. Carr** and ruled that malapportionment in the lower house of the Tennessee state legislature was a violation of the equal protection clause of the Fourteenth Amendment to the U. S. Constitution. Thus challenges to legislative apportionment in Tennessee and in other states were issues that should be addressed by federal courts.[10] In 1964 the Court handed down six closely related decisions that ultimately led to the redistricting of nearly every state legislature in the United States.[11] These decisions established the **doctrine of "one person, one vote,"** that is, the idea that state legislative districts must be equal in population according to the most recent census.

Even after the reapportionment requirement, legislative boundaries are often subject to gerrymandering to give unfair advantage to the party in control. **Gerrymandering** is the practice of drawing the lines of the legislative districts so as to magnify the power of a particular group. It is usually perpetrated by the dominant political party to give electoral advantage to their representatives. Figure 10.1 shows a hypothetical example of gerrymandering. A geographic area might have an equal number of Republicans and Democrats (in our example there are six of each). In the first box, the district lines are drawn so that Republicans form a majority in three of four districts; in the second box, Democrats control three of the four districts. In the third box, the districts are divided so that Republicans and Democrats each control two districts. Contrary to what you might expect, the straightforward solution in the third box is not always easy to achieve.

When gerrymandering occurs, the injured party will generally sue in federal court. Courts will sometimes strike down legislative reapportionment plans if the plaintiffs can

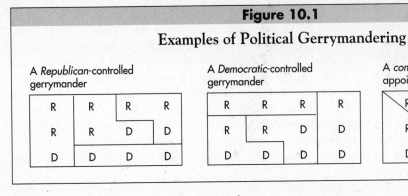

Figure 10.1

Examples of Political Gerrymandering

A *Republican*-controlled gerrymander

A *Democratic*-controlled gerrymander

A *compromise solution* to the appointment districting task

prove that gerrymandering was deliberate. The courts are quickest to invalidate **racial gerrymandering**, or reapportionment plans that obviously discriminate against the election chances of minorities. A reapportionment plan that dilutes minority votes either intentionally or unintentionally is a violation of the Federal Voting Rights Act and the Fourteenth Amendment's equal protection clause, and is, therefore, illegal and unconstitutional.

The courts are not as eager to invalidate **political gerrymandering**, that is, reapportionment plans that discriminate against a political party. In fact, before the early 1980s, federal courts refused to hear cases involving political gerrymandering. Lately the courts have become more receptive to charges of political gerrymandering, although they have yet to invalidate a redistricting plan on that basis. In 1986, the Supreme Court declared in the case *Davis v. Bandemer* that partisan gerrymanders could be unconstitutional. However, the Court upheld the Indiana redistricting plan that was being challenged and failed to spell out clear standards that political parties could use to challenge a plan. In 1989, the Court again failed to invalidate a California redistricting plan that gave obvious advantages to Democrats running for the U.S. House of Representatives (Box 10.2).

Reapportionment has made a difference in the way state funds are allocated. The distribution of state aid has shifted to favor urban areas. As urban constituencies gain representation, there is more emphasis on spending for the kind of services urban dwellers demand: education, welfare, health, and hospitals.[12] Democrats have gained some seats mostly in Northeastern states, and a marked increase in the representation of ethnic minorities has accompanied the increase in urban representation.

Despite these changes, the effects of reapportionment are not as dramatic as many thought. Reapportionment was largely a liberal cause—studies had shown that cities were much more liberal than rural areas. However, shifts in the population in the last two decades have largely been from cities to suburbs. Wealthy suburbs tend to elect Republicans who side with rural representatives against more state involvement in urban problems.

Legislative Professionalism

In the late 1960s and 1970s, a series of important reforms revitalized and modernized state legislatures.[13] Prior to their revitalization, legislatures were unrepresentative, malapportioned, dominated by rural areas of the state, generally uninformed, and easily dominated by governors and special interests. State legislatures met infrequently, many only once every two years. Legislative service was poorly paid so that only wealthy individuals or those with

BOX 10.2

PARTISAN GERRYMANDERING IN CALIFORNIA

After the 1980 census, California Republicans felt that they were the victims of a flagrant case of gerrymandering and many agreed. The state's redistricting plan abolished or merged several GOP districts, shored up weak Democratic seats, and created several open seats that were obviously opportunities for Democrats.

Population growth in California during the 1970s guaranteed two additional seats in the U. S. House of Representatives. Most of this increase occurred in Republican-minded suburban areas. Yet after the 1982 elections, the Democrats' 22–21 margin in the state's U. S. House delegation jumped to 28–17. So effectively were the districts redrawn that in 1984 Republican candidates won a higher share of the aggregate House vote in California, but could pick up only one seat.

After numerous challenges, the Republicans filed suit in federal court. But the case, *Badham v. Edu*, was dismissed by a federal district court in the spring of 1988. The dismissal was upheld by the Supreme Court in January 1989. The Court's decision was a big disappointment for Republicans who felt that the California case was about as good an example of partisan gerrymandering as they would get.

Despite these cases, the Court's willingness to review partisan gerrymandering cases guarantees that there will continue to be litigation in this area.

occupations where they could afford to take time off were encouraged to run for the legislature. Most state legislators had no staff support, and many had no office space.

The "reapportionment revolution" of the 1960s was the first stage of transformation; representation in state legislatures is now equally distributed. Along with reapportionment, however, state legislatures took steps to modernize themselves. For example, we are witnessing longer and more frequent sessions. Most states have switched to annual sessions; only seven states meet biennially. Legislators are receiving higher salaries with more substantial benefits (Box 10.3). Only six states still impose constitutional restrictions on legislative salaries. Staff support is increasing in both quantity and quality. There are now more than 33,000 staffers working in state legislatures, 40 percent of them full-time professionals.[14] Computers and modern information systems are now routinely part of the state legislative process. In addition, many more legislators identify themselves as professionals. Until recently, state legislative service was purely part-time for lawyers, independent businessmen, farmers, independently wealthy individuals, or anyone who had extra time to devote to public service. As discussed earlier in this chapter (see Table 10.1), the number of legislators who define their occupation as "legislator" is increasing. A recent survey of state legislators conducted by the National Conference of State Legislatures found more than half of the legislators in New York and Pennsylvania define their occupation as "legislator."

The biggest changes tend to be in the large and industrialized states. The legislatures of California, Illinois, Massachusetts, Michigan, New Jersey, New York, Ohio, Pennsylvania,

BOX 10.3

DIMENSIONS OF DIVERSITY: LEGISLATIVE SALARIES — LET'S TAKE A CLOSER LOOK

Between 1973 and 1993 legislators in eight states, North Dakota, Idaho, Louisiana, Arkansas, Connecticut, Washington, Pennsylvania, and Kansas voted themselves salary raises of over 500 percent. Is that shocking and shameful or what?

Maybe so, maybe not. The consumer price index went up 234 percent from 1973 to 1993. Thus, raises of twice that could be out of line. How much were those raises anyway?

The biggest percentage raise took North Dakota legislators from $265 a year to $9,000 a year. The biggest dollar raise was in Pennsylvania. Salaries there went from $7,200 a year to $47,000. It appears that Pennsylvania legislators came out all right.

What do other big states pay their legislators? What do most states pay? The three largest states—California, Texas, and New York—pay their legislators $52,000, $7,200, and $57,500, respectively. The median state legislator's salary is about $12,000 a year. That is, 25 states pay less, two pay $12,000 (Idaho and Nebraska), and 23 pay annual salaries of less than $12,000.

Since legislative salaries have always been the subject of controversy, it is important to put them in context. Increasing popular protest in recent years means that it is unlikely that there will be any significant raises in the years to come in any of the states. This is not good news for legislators in Alabama, Rhode Island, and New Hampshire. In those states there have been no raises for 20 years. The state motto of New Hampshire is "Live Free or Die." At $100 a year, its state legislative motto seems to be "Work Free, or Quit."

Source: Charles Mahtesian, "When the Voters Freeze Your Pay," Governing (December 1993), 34–35.

and Wisconsin have lengthy sessions, relatively high legislative salaries and many members whose primary profession is "legislator." But modernization is occurring in some small states as well. Alabama, Connecticut, Mississippi, and North Carolina have improved or expanded legislative office space and staff. Alabama, Kentucky, and North Carolina recently made major improvements in their legislative computer information systems. In Table 10.2 we identify the most and least professional state legislatures. Most professional legislatures were those that paid higher salaries, had longer sessions, and had more staffers to assist members.

Legislative Staff

Perhaps the most significant development in the modern legislature is the increase of personal staff assistance. Legislative staffing was originally very centralized—staff was organized in one or a few central agencies which performed all legislative support functions. Often legislative leaders exercised strong control over staff and used staffing or lack of it to reward or punish members. This is still true in many states. But in recent years staffing has become more decentralized and more specialized. About half the states provide professional or support personnel for individual legislators. Separate committee staffs exist to some extent in

Table 10.2

PROFESSIONALISM LEVELS OF STATE LEGISLATURES

Rank	State	Level	Rank	State	Level
1	New York	.659	26	Louisiana	.185
2	Michigan	.653	27	Oregon	.183
3	California	.625	28	South Carolina	.178
4	Massachusetts	.614	29	Virginia	.170
5	Pennsylvania	.336	30	Maine	.161
6	Ohio	.329	31	Mississippi	.160
7	Alaska	.311	32	Nevada	.160
8	Illinois	.302	33	Alabama	.158
9	Colorado	.300	34	Kansas	.152
10	Missouri	.287	35	Rhode Island	.148
11	Hawaii	.276	36	Vermont	.145
12	Wisconsin	.270	37	Indiana	.139
13	Florida	.255	38	Tennessee	.135
14	New Jersey	.255	39	Georgia	.133
15	Arizona	.250	40	West Virginia	.125
16	Oklahoma	.250	41	Idaho	.119
17	Connecticut	.233	42	Montana	.110
18	Washington	.230	43	Arkansas	.105
19	Iowa	.225	44	Kentucky	.101
20	Texas	.210	45	New Mexico	.098
21	Maryland	.204	46	South Dakota	.083
22	North Carolina	.203	47	Utah	.082
23	Minnesota	.199	48	North Dakota	.075
24	Delaware	.192	49	Wyoming	.056
25	Nebraska	.186	50	New Hampshire	.042

Source: Peverill Squire, "Legislative Professionalization and Membership Stability," Legislative Studies Quarterly 17 (February, 1992): 69-79. Copyright Comparative Legislative Research Center. Reprinted with permission.

many legislatures. Staffers are also noticeably more partisan. Often staff is hired on a partisan basis to work for legislative caucuses, leaders, and individual members. Following the pattern of Congress, legislators in some states now have offices and staff in their home districts to help them attend to the needs of their constituents. Although these district offices are not established for blatantly partisan reasons, they certainly contribute to the legislator's reelection.

The Debate over Professionalism

The goal of reformers who worked to professionalize legislative bodies was to encourage more informed, more deliberative, and more independent legislatures. Legislators would have adequate time to consider measures before them. Salary increases would help retain good people. Specialized and personalized staffers would help legislators handle increasing amounts of legislation more competently and service constituents more conscientiously. Legislators would also become less dependent on special interest groups for information since they themselves would be better informed. With higher salaries, they would more likely isolate themselves from the pressure and support of powerful economic interests. Professionalization also meant increased legislative independence from executives.

Despite the optimism of these arguments, there is increasing speculation about the benefits of professionalism. Some question the efficiency of full-time legislatures. They argue that legislators don't use the extra time to educate themselves and still put off making critical decisions until the last minute. Others feel that part-time citizen legislators are more in touch with their constituents. Michigan state representative Vic Krouse says that "When you spend all your time in Lansing, you're more influenced by the lobbyists than by your constituents."[15] One argument holds that career legislators are more dependent on special interest groups precisely because serving in the legislature is their job. Legislators with only one means of livelihood will place more emphasis on winning reelection and raising money to win.[16]

This debate is not resolved by asking if professionalism has any impact on the kinds of policies state governments produce. Research on this question yields mixed results. One study showed that professional legislatures tend to produce more liberal redistributive policies.[17] This is not surprising since the most professional legislatures tend to be in urban industrialized states. However, other scholars found legislative reforms to have little measurable impact on policy.[18]

The Movement for Term Limits

The complexity of state problems may necessitate legislators who devote full-time to the job of state government, but it is becoming apparent that this trend does not appeal to voters. Americans traditionally have distrusted the notion of a "professional politician," and recently they have taken steps to reverse the trend toward professionalism. In 22 states, voters have approved limits on the terms of their state legislators. Although there is some variety in the types of the limits states have imposed, the most common legislative limitation is eight years, two terms for an office with a four-year term and four for an office with a two-year term.[19] While the U. S. Supreme Court struck down state imposed limits for members of the U. S. Congress, limits for state legislatures are still in effect.

There is little doubt that term limits will increase the rate of legislative turnover. One recent study asked "How many state legislators currently serving would be affected by a term limitation, if such a limitation had been imposed eight years ago?"[20] The researcher looked at both the 15 states that had imposed limits at the time as well as the 35 states that had not. Table 10.3 shows that, on average, well over half the legislators in the 15 states that had imposed term limits would have been affected by an eight-year limit (48.5 percent and 64.3 percent for lower and upper houses, respectively). These figures were very similar for the other 35 states (51.3 percent and 61.3 percent for lower and upper houses, respectively). Thus we can conclude that a significant number of state legislators will find their legislative careers affected, if not ended, by term limitations.

Proponents of term limits argue that limits will end political careerism and attract civic-minded "citizen" legislators to a short but productive "stint" in public office. Opponents, on the other hand, say that term limits will create the unwanted return of amateur legislators whose inexperience leaves them at a disadvantage against bureaucrats and lobbyists. They also claim that term limits are undemocratic since they deny voters the right to choose their representatives. Despite these arguments, opponents find themselves outnumbered by proponents of term limits; recent polls show that about three-quarters of the American public supports term limits.

The Structure and Organization of State Legislatures
Bicameralism

Bicameral or two-house legislatures are characteristic of every state but Nebraska (Box 10.4). Every state calls its upper house the senate, and most states call their lower house the house of representatives. Several states including California, New York, Nevada, and Wisconsin call their lower house the assembly.

Ostensibly the rationale behind the two-house legislature is that it is designed to foster a more deliberative process.[21] Since both houses must pass legislation, rash or careless action is less likely. In reality, most state legislatures have a bicameral legislature because Congress set the example. However, one cannot compare the need for bicameralism in Congress with that in state legislatures. The congressional model resulted from the need for a compromise between the big and little states at the Constitutional Convention of 1787—The Great Compromise. The U.S. Senate was established to satisfy the small states' desire for equality, while the U.S. House was established to satisfy the big states' desire for representation based on population. There were no such compelling political circumstances for the states. Indeed, the United States Supreme Court declared that representation in *both* houses in state legislatures had to be based on population.[23]

BOX 10.4

NEBRASKA AS A MODEL OF REFORM?

Nebraska is the only state with a unicameral or one-house legislature. For years, this meant that Nebraska's legislature was simply a matter of curiosity; these days observers are starting to look at a unicameral legislature as a new and better way to operate.

The one-house legislature is being considered as a real option for reform in some states. California, Iowa, and Maine are considering the move to a unicameral legislature even though no formal recommendations have been presented.[22] In these states, and in others, there is growing frustration with "gridlock" that comes from divided government. Indeed, this frustration threatens to overcome the argument that a two-house legislature provides safeguards through checks and balances.

Supporters argue that the simplified structure of a one-house legislature brings government more directly to the people; it is easier to understand and, therefore, easier for the average citizen to influence. They also claim that a unicameral system results in greater accountability for legislators and greater cooperation between legislators and executive.

Opponents argue that a unicameral legislature can be more easily swayed by lobbyists because the latter need to persuade fewer people. They also point out that a unicameral system does not always allow for careful consideration of a bill before it becomes law.

Faced with budget reductions and increasingly complex demands, many states are looking for new solutions. Thus, for some reformers, the unicameral legislature is an option worth considering.

306 • CHAPTER 10/STATE AND LOCAL PARLIAMENTS: LEGISLATURES, BOARDS, AND COUNCILS

Table 10.3

RETURN RATES FOR THE FRESHMEN STATE LEGISLATORS ELECTED IN 1985–1986 FOR STATES WITH EXISTING TERM LIMITATIONS

State	Lower Chambers			Upper Chambers		
	Class of 1985–1986	Still in Office 1991–1992	% Left Still in Office	Class of 1985–1986	Still in Office 1991–1992	% Left Still in Office
Arizona	9	3	33	2	2	100
Arkansas	20	11	55	5	5	100
California	3	2	67	1	1	100
Colorado	21	10	48	8	4	50
Florida	16	7	44	3	2	66
Michigan	16	8	50	2	0	0
Missouri	27	17	63	5	3	60
Montana	33	13	39	12	7	58
Nebraska				14	10	71
Ohio	15	12	80	7	6	90
Oklahoma	23	9	39	4	1	25
Oregon	18	6	33	6	5	83
South Dakota	19	8	42	8	2	25
Washington	26	13	50	10	7	70
Wyoming	14	5	36	9	6	67
Total	260	124	*48.5%	96	61	*64.3%

RETURN RATES FOR THE FRESHMEN STATE LEGISLATORS ELECTED IN 1985–1986 FOR STATES WITHOUT TERM LIMITATIONS

State	Lower Chambers			Upper Chambers		
	Class of 1985–1986	Still in Office 1991–1992	% Left Still in Office	Class of 1985–1986	Still in Office 1991–1992	% Left Still in Office
Alabama	26	13	50	9	6	67
Alaska	20	3	15	5	2	40
Connecticut	40	17	43	15	3	20
Delaware	7	5	71	1	0	0
Georgia	23	13	57	7	6	90

State	Lower Chambers			Upper Chambers		
	Class of 1985–1986	Still in Office 1991–1992	% Left Still in Office	Class of 1985–1986	Still in Office 1991–1992	% Left Still in Office
Hawaii	12	5	42	3	2	67
Idaho	35	9	26	16	8	50
Illinois	25	16	64	7	6	90
Indiana	12	5	42	6	5	83
Iowa	12	9	75	7	5	71
Kansas	23	15	65	10	7	70
Kentucky	22	14	64	8	5	63
Louisiana	28	19	70	7	5	71
Maine	41	19	46	11	4	36
Maryland	2	1	50	3	3	100
Massachusetts	29	16	55	8	2	25
Minnesota	30	13	43	0	0	0
Mississippi	44	31	70	17	15	88
Nevada	13	5	38	6	5	83
New Hampshire	160	52	33	8	3	38
New Jersey	18	8	44	8	5	63
New Mexico	18	8	44	18	11	61
New York	21	17	81	10	10	100
North Carolina	43	20	47	19	9	47
North Dakota	34	17	50	8	3	38
Pennsylvania	23	18	78	7	7	100
Rhode Island	24	17	71	27	17	63
South Carolina	30	18	60	21	14	67
Tennessee	24	14	58	6	4	67
Texas	37	19	51	2	2	100
Utah	20	5	25	3	2	67
Vermont	40	12	30	7	3	43
Virginia	9	6	67	6	5	83
West Virginia	39	7	18	7	2	29
Wisconsin	30	16	53	10	9	90
Total	1014	482	*51.3%	313	246	61.3%

*Column averages

Source: Cynthia Opheim, "The Effect of State Legislative Term Limits Revisited," Legislative Studies Quarterly 19 (February, 1994): 49–59. Reprinted with permission.

We generally take for granted the superiority of a two-house legislature, but there are some drawbacks to be considered. Although careless or stupid action is less likely, wise or sensible action is more difficult to accomplish. The biggest problem in modern legislative bodies is slowness or inability to act. The passage of bills is a slow, often tortuous procedure made even more complex by two houses. Lest we think that unicameral (one-house) bodies are rare, we should remember that all city councils and other local governing boards are unicameral bodies.[24]

Size

The size of the legislature varies a great deal from state to state. The average upper house has about 40 members; the average lower house has about 113. Not surprisingly, the smallest legislature is the unicameral body in Nebraska. Only 49 members serve in its single house. More surprisingly, tiny New Hampshire has the largest legislature with 400 members. One reason for this may be the tradition in some New England states for every town to be represented.

Large size does not mean that a legislature will be more democratic or more representative. Indeed, larger bodies must often become more oligarchic or dictatorial. In a large group it becomes necessary for a few individuals to assume power in order for the group to accomplish anything. Certainly small groups tend to be more personal and informal, and it is easier for individuals to exercise direct influence on decision making. If you doubt this, consider the differences in the two houses of Congress. While the House of Representatives with its 435 members is heavily regulated by procedural rules (there is even a Rules Committee), the Senate with its 100 members is much more informal.

Larger legislative bodies must organize themselves to get anything done. Size therefore means organizational complexity. A complex organization is less responsive to the public in general and more responsive to special interest groups. Special interest groups have the resources, time, and motivation to learn what it takes to operate in a large and complex system. The general public, however, is often too intimidated or too unconcerned to make the effort it takes to participate in such a system. Thus bigger does not always mean more democratic or more representative.

Leadership Structure

Leadership in a majority of state legislatures, as in Congress, is based primarily on party. The two most important leaders are the speaker of the house and the president or president pro tem of the Senate. The major and minor parties in each house select a majority and minority leader. These officers are assisted by majority and minority whips. These leaders and whips sometimes have assistants.

One interesting difference in state and national government is the role of the lieutenant governor. Although the lieutenant governor is an officer of the executive branch, he or she still presides over the senate in 30 states. Several states recently curtailed the lieutenant governor's power. Eleven states ratified constitutional amendments rescinding the lieutenant governor's authority as presiding officer of the senate.

In most states the lieutenant governor, like the vice president of the United States, presides over the senate, receives assignments from the governor, and waits in the wings for a chance at being governor. However, in some states the lieutenant governor exercises substantial power. In Texas, the lieutenant governor is the major force in the legislature, controlling committee assignments and chairs, assigning bills to committee, and serving as the key figure in budget negotiations. This power is not given to the lieutenant governor by the Texas Constitution, but it has evolved because Texas until recently was not a viable two-party system—there is no competition from minority leaders.

Shyness and modesty are not qualities that will propel one to leadership in a state legislature. Members must campaign aggressively to win support from a majority of their party members or chambers. In states with viable parties, leaders are chosen by party caucuses after the general election and before the start of the legislative session. When the legislature meets, the candidate of the majority party is chosen on a straight-line party vote to be speaker of the house or president of the senate. The candidate of the minority party then becomes minority leader. In states without active parties, the two leaders must win support from majority coalitions.

Leaders' primary responsibility is to move bills through the legislative process. To do this effectively they must manage the committee system by influencing the number and types of committees, determining the number of majority and minority members, and referring bills for deliberation. Most important, leaders control the appointment of the chairs and members of standing committees. Friends and allies are placed on strategic committees while those who have been less than loyal are banished to less powerful domains (see Box 10.5).

It is the responsibility of leaders of the majority party to move major bills and resolve conflicts that might endanger the passage of key legislation. This is not an easy task. The minority party and its leaders may find it useful to oppose the leaders in the hope of creating issues that will help them in the next election. Problems with crucial legislation such as the budget or education bills are not easily resolved, especially if funds are short. Effective leaders attempt to resolve conflicts before they arise; often it is necessary to meet with opposition leaders and members behind the scenes to work out important stumbling blocks.

Legislative Committees

Imagine that you have been elected to the state legislature. Chances are, you will have knowledge and experience in a few areas. If you are from a rural area you may be an expert on agricultural policy; if you are a teacher you are likely to be familiar with educational issues. You will have neither the time nor the knowledge to study thoroughly the vast array of policy questions that state legislatures consider.

State legislative committees allow specialization, making it possible to give every subject some degree of expert treatment. As our society grows more technological and complex, such specialized treatment becomes more necessary.

Committees are critical to legislative decision making because they provide the mechanism for screening legislation. Legislators review bills assigned to their committee and decide whether these bills should be killed, revised, or voted out with a favorable recommendation. Bills that are never placed on the agenda are simply put aside, or pigeonholed. In most states, bills that are given a favorable recommendation by the committee are very likely to be passed on the floor.

To help them make decisions, committee members seek and receive information from a variety of sources, including the staff of the committee (if there is one), interest groups, lobbyists, and administrative agencies. If the bill is important enough, the committee will hold public hearings and listen to testimony from interested parties. Although lobbyists and bureaucrats are likely to be the ones who testify, concerned citizens may ask or be asked to

BOX 10.5

THE SAGA OF WILLIE BROWN

Willie Brown was speaker of the California Assembly from 1980 to 1994, longer than anyone else. Brown, a Democrat and black, was elected speaker by forging a coalition of his supporters and House Republicans. His election came after years of struggle and persistence.

In 1974 Brown, then chairman of the powerful ways and means committee, competed against Leo McCarthy for the leadership position. McCarthy won a majority in the Democratic caucus, and Brown then asked his supporters to back McCarthy in a unanimous vote. Nevertheless, McCarthy stripped Brown of his chairmanship of ways and means. After the 1974 elections, Brown renewed his challenge. Although the majority of Democrats stood behind McCarthy, Republicans cast a solid vote for Brown. McCarthy, however, won reelection.

Two years later in 1976 Brown tried once again to unseat McCarthy with Republican support and again failed. McCarthy vented the full power of the Speaker on Brown, removing him from all important committee assignments and relegating him to a relatively minor role. But in 1980, by virtue of his political skills and his status as a an African American leader, Brown was again playing a major role in California politics. Shortly thereafter, he was elected speaker.

Brown was initially elected speaker with the support of House Republicans, a move they later came to regret. Brown eventually solidified support in the Democratic caucus. Although this support ebbed and waned in recent years, Brown managed to hold his position, largely by being what he termed "a members' speaker"; his goal was to keep members happy and facilitate the passage of their bills. Ironically, voters in California have managed to do what Brown's opponents could never accomplish. In 1991 voters approved a referendum limiting terms for state legislators, and it seems that Brown will become a casualty of term limits. However, since the law does not limit politicians from running for other offices once their terms are up, it is likely that we will continue to observe Brown somewhere in California's political landscape.

give information and opinions. For example, when state legislatures consider increased tuition fees, college students often testify.

Committee systems vary in power and organization. In some states committees are passive about screening legislation, allowing almost all bills to reach the floor for consideration. In others they are very restrictive. In general, committees are more important in state houses than state senates because the house is larger and more impersonal; representatives are more specialized and have less contact with their colleagues.[25] States vary in the number of committees, but the range for houses and senates is 10 to 20.

Following the suggestion of reformers, the overall number of legislative committees has been reduced in the last few years. Some states formally limit the number of committees to which members can be assigned so that legislators can concentrate on fewer issues and become more specialized. Nevertheless, even a few assignments can sometimes be difficult.

Legislators often devote more time to committees that they perceive to be more important to their interests.

Multiple committee assignments serve an important function in addition to allowing specialization; they also allow the legislative leadership to exercise power. In almost all states leaders appoint both members and chairs. Though they will often try to appoint members to committees for which they are best qualified, the number one criterion for committee assignments is political support. Leaders occupy positions on the most powerful committees such as budget or appropriations, and appoint their friends and supporters to these choice assignments as well. The more committees that are available, the more they can be used for reward or punishment.

Although the power that state legislative leaders exercise over members may seem arbitrary and undemocratic, it does help state legislatures to be more efficient. More important, it allows the public to assign responsibility to the legislature. Legislative leaders and the parties or factions they represent are held accountable for the decisions made by the state legislature.

Greater accountability in state legislatures becomes apparent when we compare the committee system in state legislatures with that in Congress. Congressional committee chairs get their jobs by virtue of seniority, not by being in favor with the leadership. Although members are appointed to congressional committees by the leadership, once appointed, they generally continue to serve as long as they wish. The independence of congressional committees from the leadership makes Congress a kind of "headless horse." While the public may be disillusioned about the performance of Congress in general, it is rarely possible to assign blame to congressional leaders or parties, because they have little control over the actions of committees and subcommittees.

The Role of Parties

Although Chapter 9 provided a thorough description of the role of parties in the states, the specific role of parties in state legislatures deserves some attention. We have already seen that most state legislatures are organized and managed along party lines, and most legislative leaders are also party leaders. But the strength of parties and their degree of competitiveness vary from state to state. In a majority of states one party or the other tends to dominate. The most consistent case of one-party dominance has been the Democratic control of Southern legislatures. A dominant party often becomes highly factionalized, however, and may split into ideological, regional, or urban/rural wings. Some states, such as California, Pennsylvania, Iowa, and New York, have strong party competition.

In the last few years parties have become more important in the legislative process. Evidence for this is provided by party caucuses for both majority and minority parties that exist in most state legislatures. In addition to selecting leaders, caucuses may perform other functions in varying degrees. One of these functions is **positioning**, or taking official positions on important issues raised before the legislature. Positioning can vary in frequency and in the firmness of the stands taken. For example, in about one-fourth of the states, binding votes may be taken in party caucuses requiring party members to vote as a bloc on the house or senate floor.[26] Attempts to bind occur only in the most partisan of states, however, and in most cases members of the party caucus will try to build a consensus on an issue. Another function of the party caucus is providing members with information about bills and legislative strategy. Members exchange views with one another; leaders get feedback from rank and file; and rank and file get opinions and cues from leaders. Strategies and tactics for passing or killing legislation are planned so that the caucus position is advanced.[27]

How a Bill Becomes Law

The lawmaking function in state legislatures is a complicated process governed by a series of complex and detailed rules and procedures. Although some of the details vary from state to state, the lawmaking process can be summarized in general. In many states, the process resembles that of Iowa as presented in Figure 10.2. One thing becomes clear as we examine the process of passing a bill into law: It is much easier to kill a bill than to get it passed. The legislative process in the states gives an advantage to determined majorities or minorities who feel strongly that a bill should *not* be passed. Numerous obstacles create a hazardous course for the small percentage of bills that are eventually signed into law by the governor.

Introducing Legislation

There are many different sources of influence on legislators: interest groups, executive agencies, the governor, and, as we have pointed out often in this text, the determined individual. Hence the ideas for initiating legislation, as well as the drafting of the bills themselves, may come from sources other than the legislator. However, legislators have the sole power to introduce and sponsor legislation.

The first step is for the legislator to submit ideas in writing to the bill-drafting agency of the legislature, which drafts and types it in the proper legal form. The legislator files this typed version of the bill with the clerk, who reads aloud the title of the bill in what is called the **first reading**. The bill is then assigned to a standing committee by the presiding officer of the chamber where it is introduced (bills may be introduced in either the house or senate in sequence or at the same time). For example, bills relating to law enforcement will be referred to the criminal justice committee while those that deal with taxes are referred to the committee on ways and means. Assigning bills to standing committees is a source of power for the presiding officers, who may assign a bill to a sympathetic or a hostile committee depending on their view of the bill.

Committee Action

To a large extent, the fate of a bill assigned to committee is determined by the chairperson of the committee because the chair decides on the committee's agenda. If the chairperson chooses, he or she may decide to put the bill at the bottom of the committee's agenda; chances are that the committee will never get to the bill, which will die from inaction. Bills that are considered by the committee are usually given public hearings at which lobbyists and other interested individuals may testify. After deliberating, the committee may take one of several possible actions: (1) report the bill favorably in its original form, (2) report the bill favorably with amendments, (3) report favorably a "substitution" or revised form of the original bill, or (4) report the bill unfavorably. An unfavorable report will in most cases effectively kill the bill. Committees, in the view of most legislators, act as screening mechanisms, and legislators are reluctant to challenge the actions of most committees. Because legislatures are becoming more complex and specialized, committee decisions are often *the*

Figure 10.2

How an Idea Becomes a Law

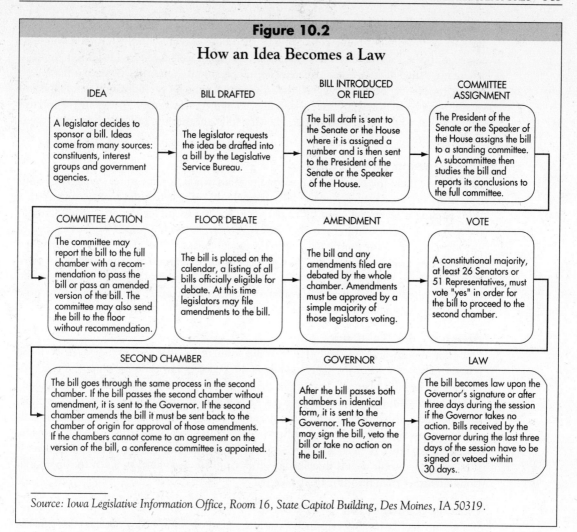

IDEA

A legislator decides to sponsor a bill. Ideas come from many sources: constituents, interest groups and government agencies.

BILL DRAFTED

The legislator requests the idea be drafted into a bill by the Legislative Service Bureau.

BILL INTRODUCED OR FILED

The bill draft is sent to the Senate or the House where it is assigned a number and is then sent to the President of the Senate or the Speaker of the House.

COMMITTEE ASSIGNMENT

The President of the Senate or the Speaker of the House assigns the bill to a standing committee. A subcommittee then studies the bill and reports its conclusions to the full committee.

COMMITTEE ACTION

The committee may report the bill to the full chamber with a recommendation to pass the bill or pass an amended version of the bill. The committee may also send the bill to the floor without recommendation.

FLOOR DEBATE

The bill is placed on the calendar, a listing of all bills officially eligible for debate. At this time legislators may file amendments to the bill.

AMENDMENT

The bill and any amendments filed are debated by the whole chamber. Amendments must be approved by a simple majority of those legislators voting.

VOTE

A constitutional majority, at least 26 Senators or 51 Representatives, must vote "yes" in order for the bill to proceed to the second chamber.

SECOND CHAMBER

The bill goes through the same process in the second chamber. If the bill passes the second chamber without amendment, it is sent to the Governor. If the second chamber amends the bill it must be sent back to the chamber of origin for approval of those amendments. If the chambers cannot come to an agreement on the version of the bill, a conference committee is appointed.

GOVERNOR

After the bill passes both chambers in identical form, it is sent to the Governor. The Governor may sign the bill, veto the bill or take no action on the bill.

LAW

The bill becomes law upon the Governor's signature or after three days during the session if the Governor takes no action. Bills received by the Governor during the last three days of the session have to be signed or vetoed within 30 days.

Source: Iowa Legislative Information Office, Room 16, State Capitol Building, Des Moines, IA 50319.

decision in a legislative body. Still, if there is enough sentiment in favor of a bill, an extraordinary majority vote of the members (usually two-thirds) will force the bill out of committee to the floor for a vote.

In many cases, legislative committees are broken down into subcommittees that represent specific areas within a committee's jurisdiction. Thus bills assigned to a committee may then be assigned to a subcommittee; the subcommittee may take any of the actions that we described as possible for committees. At this point, you may have a clearer appreciation for the obstacles faced by a bill on its tortuous journey through the legislative process.

Rules Committee

Most bills reported favorably by the standing committee go to the floor of the legislative house. Bills that involve an expenditure of money, however, may be referred to another committee such as appropriations, finance, or ways and means, that assesses the cost of the legislation. If the bill is being considered by the house of representatives, then it will most likely go to a **rules committee** (or calendars committee as it is referred to in some states), where it is scheduled for house debate. The rules committee has the power to kill a bill by scheduling it so far down the agenda that there is not time for consideration before the end of the session. In some instances, standing committees fearful of the wrath of interest groups report a bill out of committee, knowing full well that the bill will die in the calendars committee.

Consideration on the Floor

Once on the floor, the bill is given a **second reading** which in some states signals the beginning of debate on the merits of the bill. After the bill is debated and perhaps amended, a **third reading** is taken, followed by a final vote. In a bicameral legislature, the bill must go through a similar process in each chamber. If versions of the bill passed by the two houses are different, one house must concur with the amendments of the other. If this concurrence does not take place, then the bill goes to a **conference committee**, where representatives from each house will try to iron out the differences. At this point it is still possible for the bill to be killed if members of the conference committee cannot work out a compromise that ultimately can be approved by both houses.

Action by the Governor

Once both houses approve the bill in the same form, it is ready to go to the governor. If the governor approves, he or she signs the bill, and it becomes law. In most states the governor may allow the bill to become law by not signing it within a certain number of days (usually seven to ten). If the governor disapproves, he will **veto** the bill (except in North Carolina, the only state which does not give the governor veto power). This action effectively kills the bill unless two-thirds of the members of each house vote to override his veto. In many states, the governor is given special veto power to deal with the money bills. This power is the **line-item veto**; it means that the governor can veto individual items in the appropriations bill rather than rejecting the whole bill.

Passing a Budget Bill

In the state legislative process, the budget is the most important "law" that is passed by the legislature. Whereas many of the details of state budgets are described in Chapter 16, here we will concentrate briefly on a description of budget-making in the legislative process. In putting together the budget, legislators consider estimates of available revenue to decide whether they will have to make the most painful of political decisions: raising taxes to meet spending demands. They consider requests from state agencies as well as requests from various sources for funding of new programs.

At a very early stage in considering the budget proposals, the revenue and spending portions are separated and sent to entirely different standing committees in each house for careful scrutiny. The spending portion becomes one or more appropriations bills. It is sent to the appropriations or budget committee. Some appropriations committees are rather large and include the chairs of all the major subject matter standing committees. This committee and its subcommittees then hold hearings on the proposed appropriations bill or bills. The revenue, or tax, portion is sent to tax committees — usually called ways and means — in each house.

It is not uncommon for individual legislators to submit additional spending bills which also make their way to the appropriations committee. These bills may fulfill campaign promises, or may be at the requests of individual constituents, campaign contributors, local governments within a legislator's district, or executive or judicial agency officials whose programs were left out of the budget submitted to the legislature.

LOCAL LEGISLATURES

Chances are your first and most direct political experience in our intergovernmental system is your attempt to influence a local governing board. Not only are local legislatures much more accessible than their state and national counterparts, they make decisions that have direct and immediate impact on local citizens. County and city board members adopt budgets that specify the services people receive and the amount of taxes they pay. They see or fail to see that streets are maintained, health care is provided, police and fire protection are sufficient, and garbage is collected. They regulate the use of land, the operation of schools, and the disposal of wastes.

There are important differences between state and local legislatures. Local legislatures are usually unicameral rather than bicameral bodies. The concept of separation of power between legislative and executive authority is not as distinct in local legislatures. Some local legislatures have executive responsibilities— the extent of those responsibilities varies from one local government to another. In many local legislatures the chief executive presides: The mayor presides over the city council; the county judge presides over the county commission. With the exception of the lieutenant governor, who serves as presiding officer of some state senates, executive and legislative authority are more well defined at the state level.

As we learned in Chapter 5, the lawmaking authority of local legislatures is limited by state constitutions and state laws. Hence local governments are entirely creatures of the state. State governments delegate powers to local governments for reasons of convenience and because it is politically popular with the citizens of the state to do so. Local governing boards, unlike state legislatures, act within the authority of state constitutions and state legislatures.

In this chapter we focus largely upon the legislatures of the two general purpose governments: the county and the city. However, since special and school districts possess taxing and spending authority, the boards that govern them merit some attention as well.

County Boards
Expanding Role of County Government

Counties are set up by the state to serve as the state's administrative arm. Until the depression of the 1930s, counties concerned themselves primarily with carrying out state programs such as tax assessment and collection, law enforcement, judicial administration, road maintenance, administration of state and county elections, and record-keeping. For the last decade or more, however, counties have been the fastest growing general purpose governments in terms of budgets, employees, and constituents, and have expanded their activities to provide more local services. Counties run parks and recreation centers, libraries, airports, utility systems, economic development programs, hospitals, and a host of services that old-time county commissioners would never have imagined.

Presiding officers of state legislative chambers often have considerable power. Here the Speaker of the House presides over a vote.

Organization of County Boards

Counties vary in size and in how county government is organized. Although an elected county board or board of supervisors is the official governing body of the county, county board members or commissioners are elected **at large** by all the voters in the county or **by district** from voters in different districts within the county. Many large metropolitan counties, such as Palm Beach County, Florida, where the population has tripled since 1960 to 800,000, have gone to electing board members at-large with an appointed county administrator. This system is meant to professionalize the operations of county boards that find themselves tangled in metropolitan growth. Of the nation's 3,106 counties, about one-quarter are run by an appointed manager while about 13 percent now have an elected executive.[28]

The variety of size and organization of counties is highlighted by the variety of titles given to county boards and their members. Some county boards are called **courts** and have names such as **court of county commissioners** or **commissioner's court.** In Texas, county boards are called **county commissioner's courts** and are presided over by the county judge. In California, county boards are referred to as Boards of Supervisors. County board members are jurors in Louisiana, freeholders in New Jersey, and county legislators in New York. One New York county legislator remarked, "If I tell somebody from New York I'm a commissioner, they think I'm the dog catcher."[29] Although county boards are legislative bodies, their power to legislate is severely restricted by the state. Instead of making new laws or ordinances, they are generally concerned with carrying out state laws and setting the county budget. Indeed, many county boards are given no ordinance-making power by their state governments.

The power of county boards is also limited by many separately elected officials who run their own departments without supervision from any authority higher than the voting public. These officials, like the board, are local administrators for the state. For example, the sheriff enforces state law and operates a county jail, and the county clerk registers voters, administers state and local elections, and keeps important records such as births, deaths, marriages, and divorces. With popular support and state authority, these officials may feel free to make their own decisions about personnel and procedures. However, the power of county boards over county departments has expanded as counties have come to have more and more local functions. New departments whose functions are primarily local in nature owe their existence to the county, not the state.

County boards also have some power over elected officials through the budget. The board gives these officials their money and may also have the power to revoke, amend, or shift appropriations once they are made. Though they rarely exercise it, most boards have the authority to approve every expenditure made by county officials.[30] But county boards have to be very careful about punishing officials through the budget since these officials may quickly and convincingly blame the board if services deteriorate. A county sheriff who is denied funds by the board will make sure the voters know who is to blame for an increase in the crime rate.

City Councils

As you learned in Chapter 5, municipal governments are somewhat different from county governments. County governments are created by the state to localize the administration of state policy; municipalities result from actions by local constituents who want to see services provided to the local community. Municipalities come in all sizes in all states. All municipalities are governed by local legislatures called councils or commissions.

City councils are usually small, with five to nine members. In general, the larger the city the larger the council, although some large cities such as Boston and Dallas have councils of only seven to nine members. Council members usually serve part-time, meeting once a week or less. The salaries paid to these local legislators reinforce their amateur status in that most receive either nominal fees or nothing at all. "Professional" city councils do exist in some larger cities. Members meet frequently and are paid enough to make service to the city a job. Council members in Austin, Texas, for example, meet several times a week in televised sessions and receive a salary and allowance of almost $35,000 a year.

Election of City Council Members

City council members are chosen by voters in separate **district elections** or by the voters of the whole city in **at-large elections**. Each system has advantages and disadvantages. Most studies have concluded that district elections give more representation to ethnic minorities and to the poor who often live in well-defined areas of the city. At-large elections diffuse the strength of these groups and make it harder for them to elect a representative. One study examined several factors that might affect black representation on city councils and found that the switch from an at-large to district or "ward" election system is the most important factor in increasing black representation.[31] Because of this, federal courts have tended to look unfavorably on recent attempts by cities to switch from district to at-large systems; in some cases the courts have forced some cities to modify at-large elections to guarantee minority representation on the council.

District elections allow members of the city council to be in closer contact with constituents and to attend to the specific needs of the district. Supporters of district elections also argue that at-large elections make it easier for wealthy people to dominate city government since the wealthy and well-educated have the time to become involved in politics and the money it takes to win a citywide campaign.

Supporters of at-large elections argue that council members in at-large systems are forced to think about the community as a whole, not simply the selfish needs of their own districts. This emphasis on the interests of the whole city is what has led many reformers to urge the adoption of at-large elections. Just as the latter encourage participation by the wealthy and well-educated, they also result in better-qualified council members. At-large systems, say their proponents, result in more informed decision makers who evaluate what is best for the entire community.

You'll recall from Chapter 9 that at-large elections were the result of actions by progressive reformers in the early twentieth century who wanted to dilute the power of party bosses over certain districts or wards within the city. Often the voters in these wards were largely poor immigrants who were organized and mobilized by party machines. Thus many historians and political observers point out that at-large election systems were initiated to give the middle and upper-middle classes more power in city politics.

Although council members are elected by the at-large system in approximately 60 percent of municipalities, this pattern is less common as the size of a city increases. Table 10.4 shows the results of a sample of almost 4,000 cities. As you can see, the proportion of municipalities using at-large systems declines as the population declines.

In addition to at-large systems, reformers have called for nonpartisan elections. Nonpartisan elections—those in which the party affiliation of the candidates does not appear on the ballot—grew dramatically during the 1920s and 1930s. Over 70 percent of the cities use them, and they are found in every state except Hawaii. As noted in Chapter 9, nonpartisan elections were supposed to be a solution to the corruption of the urban party machines. Party bosses who controlled powerful party organizations dominated city government in large cities like Chicago. More and more middle-class voters developed a distaste for these machines and demanded changes. Reformers argued that nonpartisan elections would not only reduce corruption, they would also focus the voter's attention on issues and candidates rather than on party affiliation.

Nonpartisan elections have some effects that reformers might not have anticipated. Incumbency has become more important. With party eliminated as a cue on how to vote, people rely more on the familiarity of the candidate. This gives an advantage to incumbents, who have greater name recognition. Like at-large elections, nonpartisan elections are also class-biased in favor of the middle and upper classes; this is because nonpartisan elections discourage participation by lower-class voters. References to party give poorer, less educated people more understanding and interest in elections. Parties also help to support the campaigns of those without money or connections. The Democratic party in particular gives "organizational encouragement" to poor and uneducated voters. It seems clear that nonpar-

Table 10.4

METHOD OF ELECTION IN MUNICIPALITIES

	Election Method (%)		
	At-large	District	Mixed
Population of city:			
500,000 and over	38	13	50
250,000-499,999	26	10	65
100,000-249,999	46	13	42
50,000-99,999	47	10	43
25,000-49,999	53	13	34
10,000-24,999	56	12	33
5,000- 9,999	59	13	28
2,500- 4,999	63	12	24

Source: International City/County Management Association, The Municipal Yearbook, vol. 60 (Washington, D.C.: International City/County Management Association, 1993), 68.

tisanship works to the advantage of the Republican party, since Republicans typically have higher voter turnouts and rely less on organized efforts to stimulate participation.

Forms of City Government

Legislative bodies in city government are usually found in one of three major forms: the **council-manager form,** the **mayor-council form**, and the **commission form**. The major difference among these forms is the location and responsibility of executive power. Each form places executive power in a different place and gives the legislative body different amounts of executive authority.

The **council-manager** form (Figure 10.3) is the fastest growing form of city government, and like at-large and nonpartisan elections, was a product of the reform movement that began in the 1920s and 1930s. In theory, the council makes decisions and a city manager is hired to see that those general policies are carried out. The city manager is a professional, that is, someone who has technical expertise about budgets and management and may even have a graduate degree in public administration. The manager is hired and may be fired at any time by the council.

Under this system, mayors are generally weak. They preside over the council, but rarely have the power to hire and fire anybody, even the manager. The manager works for the council, not the mayor. To be effective, the manager must be able to detect and serve the council consensus in administering city policies. Thus the council-manager form of government is very vulnerable to conflict. If the council's decision is not clear or changes, the manager may find that he or she has misread the council. This places the manager's job in jeopardy.

The council-manager form is most popular in mid-sized cities with populations ranging from 25,000 to 250,000. Cities with less than 25,000 usually find it too expensive to hire a manager. Cities with more than 250,000 have a number of conflicting groups interested in city administration, making a consensus harder to achieve. City managers work best in cities where there is a broad consensus in the way local government should work. As cities become larger, a broad consensus is harder to achieve because the number of interest groups increases. Larger cities also tend to have more heterogeneous populations which put conflicting demands on city government and administration, especially if the council is elected from districts rather than at large.[32] By contrast, in mid-sized cities, especially those where the ethnic and political composition of the population is relatively homogeneous, such as many suburban cities, the city manager form of government is much more popular.[33]

The advantage of the council-manager form of government is that an "expert," the manager, helps city government run efficiently and professionally. However, there are disadvantages. Although in theory the manager implements council policy, in reality the manager often originates and sets policy behind the scenes. This occurs because council members often do not have the technical expertise of the manager so that the city bureaucrats may feel the need to go along with the manager's recommendations on policy and budget. This is not what proponents of representative democracy have in mind.

The **mayor-council** system maintains the traditional separation of powers between the legislative and executive branches of government, but these governments differ substantially in the amount of formal power given to the mayor. Therefore, these governments can be classified as strong-mayor or weak-mayor systems.

A **strong mayor-council** system usually calls for a full-time mayor and a part-time council (Figure 10.4). The council may be full time in large cities. The mayor is elected at

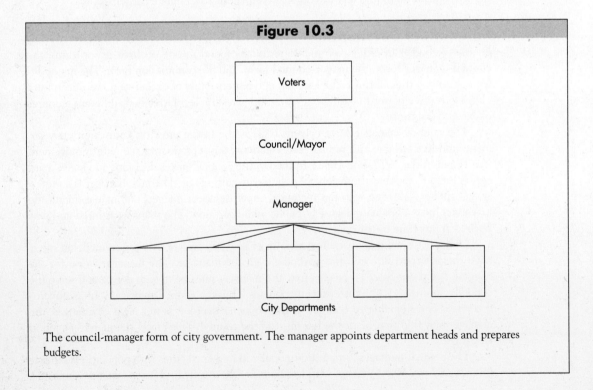

Figure 10.3

The council-manager form of city government. The manager appoints department heads and prepares budgets.

large and has a very strong executive role. He or she assumes the responsibilities of a manager, appointing department heads, administering city programs, hiring and firing city employees, preparing the budget and evaluating city agency performance. A strong mayor may also have extraordinary veto power that can be overridden only by a two-thirds or three-fourths majority of the council. The mayor's power and independence from the council are underscored by a large staff of administrative assistants, auditors, legal counsels, city planners or other professionals. Strong mayors are generally found in large cities. Large cities need a strong mayor who combines administrative and political power to hold a city with many powerful and heterogeneous interests together. A city manager has trouble dealing with powerful interests because he or she is an appointee, not a political figure.

A **weak mayor-council** system places legal restrictions on the mayor (Figure 10.5). Although the mayor may have influence, it is not through his or her formal powers. The council, not the mayor, has control over the budget. The mayor's appointment power is limited; the council appoints key department heads directly. In addition, the mayor may be required to submit all his appointments to the council for approval. Weak mayors are usually found in small towns where the business of government is limited. Small towns may have little need for city managers or strong mayors.

The **commission form** is the least common major form of government; it is found in approximately 100 cities around the nation. The distinguishing characteristic of the commission form is its union of executive and legislative powers. It consists of elected council members or commissioners who are also the heads of key executive departments. The typical city has five commissioners who head five departments. One commissioner, for example, may head the public safety department—fire and police services. Another may direct parks and recreation. Commission members wear two hats. As members of the legislative body, they set policy for the municipality. At the same time they act as department heads, hiring and firing personnel and preparing budgets.

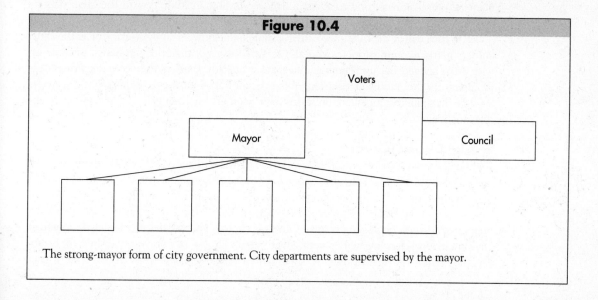

Figure 10.4

Voters

Mayor

Council

The strong-mayor form of city government. City departments are supervised by the mayor.

Figure 10.5

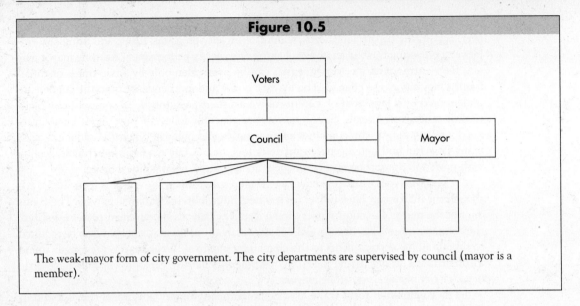

The weak-mayor form of city government. The city departments are supervised by council (mayor is a member).

The advantage of this decentralized system is that the persons in charge of making policy—the commissioners—are also in charge of carrying it out. Commissioners don't have to worry that bureaucrats are violating the intent of the policy or that top-level administrators are getting too much power. However, there are problems. Elected commissioners are full-time politicians and do not always have the competence or the expertise to be department heads. Municipal departments handle complex and technical problems and often require administrators with engineering, accounting, planning, budgeting, and management skills. Since the mayor has no real power, there is no executive to coordinate the various departments. Commissioners tend to adopt a live-and-let-live attitude toward the other departments so that there is little accountability and no system of checks and balances.

Another major disadvantage of the commission form of city government is the difficulty of getting commissioners, who also serve as heads of major departments, to come up with a city budget. Because commissioners are strong advocates of their own departments, it is difficult for them to make decisions about the allocation of scarce resources for the city as a whole. In some instances, commissions have been unable to develop a budget after weeks of wrangling.

Special District Boards

Although special districts are called a variety of names—district, authority, corporation—all are governed by boards. With the exception of school districts, most special district boards are appointed by city or county officials. Since special districts are usually established to provide services that require high levels of expertise, many feel that "professionals" should be appointed to their governing boards. Once appointed, boards vary in the degree to which they are independent of their "parent governments." Some city or county boards, for example, may require special districts to submit their budgets for approval. If a special district board's members are elected, the board is likely to be an autonomous unit of government, raising and spending its own funds without interference from general purpose governments.

The typical board is made up of three to five members serving three- or four-year terms. Most of the board members are part-time, meeting only once or twice a month. Compensation for service may be minimal or nonexistent. Board members usually serve more than one term since they are reappointed or reelected without opposition. Elected members often step down before the election so that a successor can be appointed to fill the vacancy. The successor then has the advantage of running for election as an incumbent.

Recruitment of special district board members illustrates the lack of visibility that is characteristic of special districts (Chapter 4). The public is often unaware of these boards and uninformed about their functions even though special district boards possess significant powers, including the most significant of all: taxing authority.

School District Boards

The most numerous of the special district boards are **school boards**. The vast majority of school districts are "independent," that is, they are administratively and fiscally independent of any general purpose government. Independent school districts are organized much as council-manager municipal governments are. Voters elect the members of the board on an at-large basis, and elections are usually nonpartisan. The school superintendent is hired by the school board as a professional administrator of the schools and, like a city manager, can be fired by the board at any time.

Unlike most special district boards, school boards are highly visible. Some say that "school boards are the essence of grass-roots democracy."[34] They represent the strongly held belief of local control of the schools. Popularly elected boards provide comfort for citizens who fear that "outside experts"—school superintendents and other administrators—may overstep their bounds. Although the at-large system of electing school boards encourages boards dominated by elites or "prominent" citizens, broad support exists for school boards in their present form.

OBTAINING ACCESS

Imagine that you are a student at a state university faced with the possibility of tuition increases that you or your parents cannot afford. The state legislature has not raised tuition for some time, and some legislators feel that an increase is due. What are some of the strategies that you might use to influence the legislature's decision? How can you get the ear of certain key legislators to let them know the hardships this increase will create for you and thousands of other college students in your state? Remember that even though our example focuses on state legislatures, the strategies described here apply to local legislatures as well.

Strategies of Influence
Letters, Phone Calls, and Personal Visits

The first thing you will probably do is find out the name of your state representative and write him or her a letter. You should try to make the letter appear personal, that is, handwritten or typed with your signature. Personal letters usually have more impact on an elected representative than impersonal or form letters. You will want to get as many of your friends to write as you possibly can because the larger the number of letters the more influence they will have. In fact, a letter-writing campaign is what you are really trying to achieve.

If you really hate writing letters or want to do something in addition to writing a letter, you can call your legislator. Chances are you will not speak to your representative, but to a legislative aid who will promise faithfully to relay your feelings to the representative. Again, get as many friends as possible to call. It is also a good idea to call more than once if you have the time and money. If you are persistent, you will probably get to speak directly to your representative (Box 10.6).

The next step is to write and/or call key legislative leaders and committee chairs, such as those that chair the house and senate committees on higher education. These people are probably far more crucial in determining tuition increases than your own legislator (unless you are lucky and she or he is one of them). You should be aware that they are less likely to be influenced by your calls and letters since you do not determine their electoral fate.

If you have the determination, time, and energy, you may want to try to see your representative in person. This may not be that hard to do. In most states, representatives spend a lot of time in their districts and attend all sorts of public events; their presence at these events is usually publicized. Find out where they will be and show up yourself. Since public officials attend these events to try to get and keep votes, most will not mind giving you a minute or two to express your feelings. It is usually more difficult to see a legislator in his or her office at the capitol (if he or she has one), although it is certainly possible. Be sure the secretary or legislative staffer knows that you are a constituent; this important fact will encourage a legislator to work you into a busy schedule.

Campaign Work

If you are really concerned about the possibility of higher tuition fees, you will want to get into the political ball game a little sooner and a little more seriously. Individuals and groups experienced at politics know that the most important influence is established *before* a legislator is elected to office.

There are two ways to gain access to legislators during the election process. The first is through campaign contributions. Legislators, like most of us, are inclined to help those people who help them. With this in mind, you may want to make a contribution to your representative's campaign. To be really effective, however, you will have to organize other students concerned about tuition increases and form a political action committee—a PAC. You will give your PAC a catchy name, one that forms a clever acronym such as STUPAC: Student's Political Action Committee. You and your friends who form this PAC will solicit voluntary contributions from other students. You will have to decide, as a committee, how the funds you have collected will be spent. A wise way to distribute the funds would be to give a percentage to your own representative and then distribute the rest to key legislative figures.

The second way to be effective in the election process is to volunteer to work in a legislative campaign. This may involve stuffing envelopes with campaign literature, making phone calls, registering other students to vote, or just hanging around the campaign headquarters. As you work in the campaign you will get to know those people close to the candidate, as well as the candidate. Obviously, this is going to help you gain access to your representative.

BOX 10.6

TIPS FOR EFFECTIVE LOBBYING

You *can* affect legislation by letting your representative know how you feel on an issue, especially if you do it in the right way.

Here are suggestions for an effective personal letter or visit:

- State that you are a constituent/voter/supporter (if true).
- Cite specific bill numbers, so that staff members can better find and trace them.
- Give personal examples and creative arguments that might lend new light to an old subject, but keep it short and concise.
- Get other constituents to write personal letters. The more constituent mail legislators receive, the more they pay attention.
- Consider sending a telegram. Carefully timed and targeted telegrams are real attention-getters. Few people can help but yield to the pressure of 50 to 75 telegrams from local constituents, especially when they all come the morning of *the vote*.
- A personal visit with your representative is, of course, much better than a letter. It demonstrates dedication, and the sort of commitment that is irresistible to most elected people. If you plan to visit the capitol or city hall, here are some tips to make you visit effective and positive.
- Make an appointment.
- Have a short, written statement available outlining your views.
- Dress as if you were going to court or to a job interview. Your issue is more important to you than your freedom of attire.
- Study the voting record of those whom you will visit. Be informed.
- Be polite and friendly with administrative aides. They read your letters and are informed on the issues and their employer's position. If they like what you have to say, they can insure an audience with the elected official.
- Stick to one issue.
- Do not debate, argue, intimidate, or threaten. Do not get offended by ignorance on your issue.
- Beyond a doubt, the most influential way to visit your representative is to be accompanied by a major contributor, known campaign volunteer, or personal friend of the legislator. These people are going to be persuasive because they have already established points of credibility and agreement.
- Send follow-up letters thanking the legislators for their support, or telling them you hope they will reconsider their positions.

Notice that campaign work involves an element of risk that your candidate may not get elected and the opposing candidate will not feel obligated to support your cause. There are ways to minimize this risk. For example, PACs sometimes contribute to *both* candidates. However, it is important to remember that, like a lot of other things, the greater the risk, the greater the return. A representative who knows that you helped him or her when help was needed the most is going to be more receptive than is one who first hears from you when he or she is deciding an important issue.

Public Testimony

A crucial time for deciding whether to increase tuition fees comes when the house and senate committees on higher education meet. Because members of these committees specialize on matters of higher education, their colleagues in the legislature are inclined to honor their recommendations. To help gather information and formulate recommendations, committees hold public hearings and invite interested individuals to testify. If you are lucky, the chairperson of the committee is opposed to any tuition increases and places the tuition increase bill at the bottom of the committee's agenda (a place reserved for unwanted bills that never come up).

When and if the tuition increase bill does come up, you may be asked by the committee to testify. By this time you will have written, called, or talked in person to your legislator. You may have also made a name for yourself by organizing a PAC or working in an election campaign. You are seen by some as a knowledgeable, certainly an interested individual, one whose views deserve formal consideration. But keep in mind that the committee will also be hearing from those who feel a tuition increase is warranted.

Organizing a Group

You can see that individuals who are committed and energetic can gain access to legislative decision making, but it is also apparent that individuals who form an *organization* are likely to be more influential than those who act alone. Organizations are able to contribute more money and time to a cause. They are usually able to hire "professionals," that is, lobbyists, who are experienced at influencing legislators. Individual members of organizations can rely on each other for the motivation it takes to participate in the political process. Even if your involvement in politics is only temporary—to oppose higher tuition fees—you will be more effective if you persuade others to get involved with you.

CONCLUSION

Legislatures at all levels—federal, state, and local—have common functions. All make laws, approve taxing and spending policies, and oversee the actions of the bureaucracy. All are traditionally the most representative and democratic institutions in government.

Modern state legislatures have done a great deal to overcome their reputations as corrupt and ineffective bodies. Reapportionment means that urban problems are getting more attention, although population growth in conservative white suburbs has reduced the influence of urban interests. The professionalization of state legislatures, particularly those in large urban states, has increased their capacity to make competent decisions. Legislators have higher salaries and more staff and are staying in session longer; many more are identifying themselves as professionals.

There is an ongoing debate, however, over the effectiveness and desirability of legislative professionalism. Some feel that part-time "citizen" legislatures are closer to the people and less susceptible to pressure from organized interest groups. The movement to limit the terms of legislators is a direct result of voter dissatisfaction with professional legislatures.

All state legislatures but one (Nebraska) are bicameral, and their size varies from state to state. Leadership in most state legislatures is based on party, and leaders enjoy a much more powerful role in state legislatures than their counterparts in Congress. State legislative leaders control the assignment of committee chairs and memberships, and often use this power to discipline unsupportive members. Although this power may seem arbitrary, it does give state legislatures more accountability in comparison to Congress.

Unlike state legislative bodies, local governing boards are unicameral and are authorized by a higher authority: the state. County boards exercise some legislative functions, but are primarily administrative arms of the state. Most county boards function without any centralized executive authority, although recently some large urban counties have appointed or elected county administrators. Variations in municipal boards depend on the extent to which they exercise executive powers. Although the emergence of a professional city manager is apparent in many mid-sized cities, strong mayors are more likely to govern large cities in which there are many powerful and competing interests.

The system of electing city council members has a dramatic impact on how the city is governed or, more specifically, on who has power in city government. Reforms of the 1920s and 1930s called for nonpartisan, at-large elections to reduce the influence that powerful party machines had on districts or wards within the city. These reforms gave advantages to incumbent politicians and were class-biased in favor of the middle and upper-middle classes. At-large elections diffuse the power of minorities and the poor, who tend to be concentrated in certain areas of the city. Nonpartisan elections eliminate the ability of parties — the Democratic party in particular — to mobilize poor and uneducated voters.

Individuals who are determined to influence decisions of state and local governments use a variety of participatory strategies to influence in the legislative process. These strategies include letters, phone calls, personal visits, campaign work, or testifying before legislative committees or local governing boards. This is fitting in light of the fact that legislatures were orginally designed to be the most democratic of political institutions in American politics.

STUDY OBJECTIVES

1. Identify functions that are performed by legislatures.
2. Identify three classic views of representation.
3. Identify the four historical stages in the development of state legislatures.
4. Define reapportionment. What have been the consequences of reapportionment of state legislatures?
5. Define legislative professionalism, that is, explain what makes a legislature professional.
6. Describe arguments for and against term limitations for legislators.
7. Explain why one could argue that the leadership and committee systems of most state legislatures make them more accountable than the U. S. Congress.

8. Identify the three major forms of city government.
9. Explain why most school boards resemble the council-manager form of city government.
10. Identify effective strategies for gaining access to state and local legislatures.

GLOSSARY

Baker v. Carr, 1962   The landmark Supreme Court ruling that malapportioned districts may violate the equal protection clause of the Fourteenth Amendment. It also established that federal courts have jurisdiction over lawsuits challenging the apportionment of legislative districts.

Casework   The individual assistance legislators give to their constituents; the most frequent example is intervention with a government agency on the constituent's behalf.

Commission form of city government   The least common form consisting of elected council members who are also the heads of key executive departments.

Conference committee   A joint legislative committee where representatives from the house and senate try to iron out the differences in a bill.

Council-manager form of city government   The fastest growing form of city government. A professional city manager is hired to carry out the decisions of the city council.

Davis v. Bandemer, 1986   The case in which the Supreme Court declared for the first time that partisan gerrymandering could be unconstitutional. However, the court has yet to invalidate a redistricting plan on that basis.

Delegate role of representation   The model of representation in which elected representatives attempt to mirror the views of a majority of their constituents.

District election   The system of electing representatives to the city council or county board who represent districts within the city or county.

Gerrymandering   The practice of drawing the lines of the legislative districts so as to magnify the power of a particular group, usually the dominant political party.

Impeachment   Bringing formal charges against executive officials and judges. In state legislatures and Congress this is done by the house of representatives.

Line-item veto   The power of the governor to veto individual items in the appropriations bill rather than rejecting the whole bill.

One-person, one-vote doctrine   The principle established in a series of Supreme Court decisions that state legislative districts must be equal in population according to the most recent census.

Oversight   The legislature's function of reviewing the way laws and policies are implemented by the bureaucracy.

Politico role of representation   The model of representation that combines features of the trustee and delegate role. Representatives attempt to mirror the views of their constituents when those views are strongly and clearly expressed, but otherwise use their own best judgment.

Reapportionment   The boundaries of legislative districts (both state legislative districts and U.S. Congressional districts) are drawn so that they are about equal in population.

Rules committee   The powerful committee found in most legislative houses of representatives that schedules bills for debate on the house floor.

Strong mayor-council form of city government Found in many large cities. It consists of a strong full-time mayor elected at-large and a part-time city council.

Sunset laws   Enacted in a majority of states, these laws mean that unless the legislature acts to renew an executive agency, it will cease to exist after a certain date.

Trustee role of representation   The model in which representatives use their own best judgment to decide the issues at hand.

Weak mayor-council form of city government   Found in most small towns. It consists of a mayor whose formal powers are limited by a strong city council.

ENDNOTES

1. Alen Rosenthal, "The Legislative Institution—In Transition and at Risk," in *The State of the States*, ed. Carl E. Van Horn (Washington, D.C.: CQ Press, 1993), 115.

2. Richard C. Elling, "The Utility of State Legislative Casework as a Means of Oversight," *Legislative Studies Quarterly* 3 (August, 1979), 353–379.

3. ACIR, *The Question of State Government Capability* (Washington, D.C.: Advisory Commission on Intergovernmental Regulations, 1985), 116. See also Cynthia Slaughter (now Opheim), "Sunset and Occupational Regulation: A Case Study," *Public Administration Review* 46 (May/June, 1986), 241–45; and Landon Curry, Cynthia Opheim, and Patricia Shields, "Sunset as Oversight: Establishing Realistic Objectives," *American Review of Public Administration* 24 (September, 1994): 253–268.

4. Ralph Craft, "Successful Legislative Oversight: Lessons from State Legislatures," *Policy Studies Journal* 10 (Autumn, 1981), 161–71.

5. John C. Wahlke, Heinz Eulau, William Buchanan, and Leroy C. Ferguson, *The Legislative System* (New York: Wiley, 1962), chapters 12 and 13.

6. Chase Untermeyer, "The Lone Star Legislature," in Wendell M. Bedichek and Neal Tannahill, *Public Policy in Texas*, 2d ed. (Glenview, IL: Scott, Foresman and Company, 1986), 204.

7. Victoria Van Son, ED., *CQ's State Fact Finder: Rankings Across America* (Washington, D.C.: Congressional Quarterly Press, 1993), 293–97.

8. Alexander Heard, "Introduction—Old Problems, New Context, The American Assembly," *State Legislatures in American Politics*, Alexander Heard, ed. (Englewood Cliffs, NJ: Prentice-Hall, 1966), 1, 2.

9. John N. Lattimer, "The Changing Role of Legislative Staff in the American State Legislature," *State and Local Government Review* 17 (Fall, 1985), 244–250.

10. *Baker* v. *Carr*, 309 U. S. 186 (1962).

11. *Reynolds* v. *Sims*, 377 U. S. 533 (1964); *WMCA, Inc.* v. *Lomenzo*, 377 U. S. 633 (1964); *Maryland Committee for Fair Representation* v. *Tawes*, 377 U. S. 656 (1964); *Donis* v. *Mann*, 377 U.

S. 678 (1964); *Roman* v. *Sincock*, 377 U. S. 695 (1964); *Lucas* v. *Forty-fourth General Assembly of Colorado*, 377 U. S. 713 (1964).

12. H. George Frederickson and Yong Hyo Cho, "Legislative Apportionment and Fiscal Policy in the American States," *Western Political Quarterly* 27 (March, 1974), 5–37.

13. See Citizen Conference State Legislatures, *State Legislatures: An Evaluation of Their Effectiveness* (New York: Praeger Publisher, 1971) for a comprehensive report on the status of state legislatures and recommendations for modernization. This report was also summarized and published by John Burns, *The Sometime Governments: A Critical Study of American Legislatures* (New York: Holt, Rinehart, and Winston, 1981).

14. Rich Jones, "The State Legislatures," in *The Book of the States*, vol. 29 (Lexington, KY: Council of State Governments, 1992–1993), 125.

15. Quoted in Andrea Paterson, "Is the Citizen Legislator Becoming Extinct?" in Thad L. Beyle, ed. *State Government: CQ's Guide to Current Issues and Activities, 1987–88* (Washington, D.C.: Congressional Quarterly, 1987), 77.

16. Sherry Bebitch Jeffe, "For Legislative Staff, Policy Takes a Back Seat to Politics," *California Journal* (January, 1987), 42–45.

17. Eric M. Uslander and Ronald E. Weber, "The 'Politics' of Redistribution: Towards a Model for the Policy-Making Process in the American States," *American Politics Quarterly* 3 (April, 1975): 130–170.

18. Leonard Ritt, "State Legislative Reform: Does It Matter? *American Politics Quarterly* 1(October, 1973): 499–510; Albert K. Karnig and Lee Sigelman, "State Legislative Reform and Public Policy: Another Look," *Western Political Quarterly* 28 (September, 1975), 548–552.

19. Gerald Benjamin and Michael J. Malbin, "Term Limits for Lawmakers: How to Start Thinking about a Proposal in Process," in *Limiting Legislative Terms*, edited by Gerald Benjamin and Michael J. Malbin (Washington, D.C.: Congressional Quarterly Press, 1992), 12.

20. Cynthia Opheim, "The Effect of State Legislative Term Limits Revisited," *Legislative Studies Quarterly* 19 (February, 1994), 49–59.

21. Malcolm E. Jewell and Samuel C. Patterson, *The Legislative Process in the United States*, 3d ed. (New York: Random House, 1977), 116.

22. See Robb Douglas, "Going Nebraska's Way," *State Government News* 35 (December, 1992), 14–15.

23. *Baker* v. *Carr*, 369 U. S. 186 (1962).

24. Robert S. Lorch, *State and Local Politics: The Great Entanglement*, 2d ed. (Englewood Cliffs, NJ: Prentice-Hall, 1986), 149–50.

25. Rosenthal, *Legislative Life*, 182.

26. Samuel C. Patterson, "Legislators and Legislatures in the American States," in *Politics in the American States*, Virginia Gray, Herbert Jacob, and Kenneth B. Vines, eds. (Boston: Little, Brown, & Co., 1983), 165.

27. Alan Rosenthal, "If the Party's Over, Where's All that Noise Coming From?" *State Government* 57 (1984): 50–54.

28. Rob Gurwitt, "Cultures Clash as Old-Time Politics Confronts Button-Down Management," *Governing: The States and Localities* (April, 1989), 47.

29. John Herbes, "17th-Century Counties Struggle to Cope with 20th-Century Problems," *Governing: The States and Localities* (May, 1989), 42.

30. Lorch, *State and Local Politics: The Great Entanglement*, 229.

31. Richard L. Engstrom and Michael D. McDonald, "The Election of Blacks to City Councils: Clarifying the Impact of Electoral Arrangements on the Seats/Population Relationship," *American Political Science Review* 75 (June, 1981): 344–354. For an excellent source of research on the impact of district versus at-large elections, see Peggy Heilig and Robert J. Mundt, *Your Voice at City Hall* (Albany: State University of New York Press, 1984).

32. See Rob Gurwitt, "The Lure of the Strong Mayor," *Governing* (July, 1993), 36–41.

33. John J. Harrigan, *Political Change in the Metropolis*, 4th ed. (Glenview, IL: Scott, Foresman & Co., 1989), 95–96.

34. Richard D. Bingham, *State and Local Government in an Urban Society* (New York: Random House, 1986), 404.

CHAPTER

11

Chief Executives: Are They Really in Charge?

As the first Republican to govern Massachusetts in 20 years, Governor William Weld inherited a fiscal mess in 1991. The state's projected deficit was $2 billion and its bond rating was in a downward spiral. A mulititude of state programs begun in an era of prosperity were entrenched in government. Weld embraced the notion of "entrepreneural government" and promised to "reinvent the way state government functions." He proceeded to privatize many state services, such as hospitals and prisons, to save money. He also cut spending for social programs substantially and delivered on his promised cut in the state income tax—from 6.25 percent to 5.95 percent. He supported a business-coalition plan to reform the educational system in Massachusetts; the plan included school-based management and a choice program for the public schools.

In many ways, Governor Weld represents the new image of the modern governor. He is an activist governor with a prominent agenda that dominates state politics.

Over the course of American history, executives have gradually strengthened their role in state and local politics at the expense of legislatures. In our modern urban society government has become larger and more pervasive. The need for full-time professional executives to manage government operations has increased. Since legislatures and local boards are composed chiefly of part-time amateurs, we depend heavily on chief executives and bureaucrats to offer the proper solutions to our problems. Like Governor Weld of Massachusetts, most chief executives are not shy about promoting their ideas and solutions, and most legislatures expect this from executives.

This chapter focuses on chief executives at both the state and local levels. Special attention is given to governors, mayors, city managers, and school district superintendents. The chapter examines what these chief executives do, why they have become more powerful, their evolving role in our intergovernmental system, and how individuals can influence their decisions.

THE FUNCTIONS OF CHIEF EXECUTIVES

Symbolic

Chief executives are our most visible politicians. Even those citizens who know or care little about politics can usually identify the governor, mayor, or superintendent of schools. These executives symbolize their respective units of government; they are celebrities who receive a great deal of media attention and scrutiny.

Being a symbol is important for a chief executive because it enhances his or her **informal power**. Unlike **formal powers**, which come from legal and constitutional provisions, informal power refers to influence—the power to persuade.[1] Because chief executives have so much exposure to the mass public, they have more opportunity to influence public opinion. Modern chief executives are cognizant of the potential for influence of their "office," and most seek to build and embellish their symbolic role. They spend a significant portion of their time acting out this role through public appearances. Public officials, especially elected ones, are likely to support an executive who is backed by the force of strong public opinion (see Box 11.1).

BOX 11.1

"THE NEVER-ENDING CAMPAIGN"

Thomas H. Kean's rookie year as governor of New Jersey was a disaster. Kean took office in 1982 by fewer than 2,000 votes out of two million cast in a disputed election. After a year, polls showed that less than half of the voters approved of the job he was doing. His prep school accent (St. Marks and Princeton) and personal shyness did not endear him to the regular working man or woman in New Jersey. However, by the end of his second term, no one doubts that he could have easily won a third term; Kean had become one of the most popular governors in New Jersey history.

Kean turned things around by mounting a campaign, not for office this time, but for public support. He used the tools of electioneering—television, radio, personal appearances—to build support for himself and, by extension, for his policies. He held a series of televised "town meetings," made television commercials that promoted the state's tourism industry and featured celebrities such as Bill Cosby and Brooke Shields, and produced a slogan that became his trademark: "New Jersey and you—P-u-h-f-e-c-t together." His skillful use of electronic media and genuine likability quickly translated into heightened personal popularity. That, in turn, enabled him to assert his will with the legislature more successfully.

Chief executives—presidents, governors, mayors—have learned that you have to stay popular if you want to govern. To their advantage, they have what one politician called "the big mike," that is, the visibility of their office. As the Kean example shows, they have numerous opportunities to mount campaign-style operations for duties that are a regular part of their jobs.

Source: Paul West, "They're Everywhere! For Today's Governors, Life Is a Never-Ending Campaign," Governing (March 1990), 51–55.

Informal power can come from sources other than the chief executive's symbolic function. For example, a governor who commands a strong and dominant party will find his or her influence enhanced. A mayor or school superintendent with a forceful personality will generally have more success in persuading others to see his or her point of view. Serving as the most important symbol of one's government, however, clearly gives chief executives a unique advantage.

Administrative

The first responsibility of the chief executive is to administer laws by managing bureaucracies that constitute the executive branch. Executives direct and coordinate the activities of executive branch agencies so that policy goals can be achieved in an efficient manner. They also formulate new programs and modify old ones. Finally, chief executives interact with legislators, interest groups, and others who are inevitably involved in the implementation of public policy.

Executives are often held responsible for the actions and performance of the bureaucracy, but the amount of control they exercise over state or local bureaucrats is tempered by other factors. The size of the bureaucracy may make it difficult for executives to manage. Whereas the city manager of Salem, Oregon may oversee about 100 people, the governor of California is responsible for 6,000 state employees.

But executives' administrative responsibilities involve more than the technical difficulties of managing large organizations. Their management responsibilities are emeshed in politics—bureaucratic politics. Often agencies have entrenched interests that come from administering programs over a long period of time. Agency alliances with interest groups and other interested constituencies as well as with legislators or board members may dilute the ability of the chief executive to direct these agencies.

To a large degree, executive control of the bureaucracy may depend on the extent of the executive's appointment power. Unlike the president, however, state and local chief executives are often dealing with department heads who are independently elected and thus have independent power bases. The civil service movement—a major reform in state and local government in the twentieth century—has also tempered executives' control over bureaucracy. Even when a chief executive has extensive appointment power, problems may arise. If executives make appointments strictly on a merit basis, they risk alienating loyal party members. If executives employ the concept of patronage as the guiding principle for appointments, weak or incompetent appointees may be the result.

Chief executives must share their administrative power with legislatures. As we learned in Chapter 10, legislatures and boards have final authority over state and local budgets. This fact means that bureaucrats will always, to some degree, be responsive to legislatures. This becomes significant when the chief executive and legislature or board disagree on substantive policy or program questions and goals. Thus executives' ability to manage the bureaucracy may depend on their relationship with the legislature.

Legislative

In your introductory political science classes you learn that legislatures are responsible for passing laws and executives are responsible for executing these laws. Before long you recognize that this neat distinction of responsibilities does not accurately describe modern American government.

State and local chief executives are often described as "chief legislators," because of their prominent role in producing legislation. They are their government's chief agenda-setters. Their visibility allows them to set the direction of public policy, and legislative bodies often respond to the chief executive's "agenda." Most executives assume their office with some type of **program**, that is, a series of policy proposals they and their advisors have developed during the campaign. The most important of these proposals become the executive's real agenda; this agenda reflects the chief executive's broad philosophy and goals. For example, a governor comes to office prepared to slash state spending and exercise "fiscal responsibility." A newly elected mayor is prepared to push for more stringent environmental regulations in the face of what he or she perceives as excessive or reckless commercial development projects.

Executives generally possess several advantages in dealing with legislatures. The prestige and influence that comes from their symbolic function has already been discussed. In addition, they generally have superior staff resources and are much more likely to be full-time professionals.

Chief executives also play a dominant role in legislating when they execute the laws because the manner in which a law is implemented often determines the very nature of the law. Chief executives and the bureaucrats who work for them often have a great deal of discretion in interpreting and applying laws. For example, a state legislature may decide that certain professions need to be regulated, but the regulatory agency determines specific rules for licensing and monitoring of a profession. Or, a local superintendent and principal are charged with interpreting and implementing a local school board's policy of limited corporal punishment. The power of executives and bureaucrats to make rules that have the force of law is discussed in more depth in Chapter 12.

Fiscal

Because chief executives occupy the central positions in state and local administrations and have the general responsibility for their management, they can take a broader view of fiscal resources and spending priorities. Consequently, executives are generally charged with proposing changes in taxation and preparing budgets. These changes and proposals are submitted to legislatures, councils, or boards for review and final approval.

Chief executives may also have a broader view of resource and spending patterns because they generally have broader constituencies. A governor represents the whole state; a mayor speaks for all the citizens of a city. While it is possible that executives will be swayed by narrow interests or parochial concerns, they are more likely to consider the effects of policy on the whole community.

Budgets are an important means of administrative control for executives. Most chief executives review the budget requests of departments and agencies and make final budget recommendations to legislatures or boards. Without such control, executives are handicapped in any test of wills with their bureaucracies. Although chief executives' power and influence over the budget varies, it is important for administrative agencies to have the support of the executive. This support often makes it possible to continue and expand agencies' programs. Even more important, agencies who find themselves out of favor with executives may face the prospect of executive veto power.

GOVERNORS

In recent years the importance of the states and their elected leaders has grown, not only in the states themselves, but also within the context of our federal system of government. As the federal government has reduced its responsibility for domestic programs and services, the gap has been filled in part by the states. As the example of Governor Weld at the beginning of this chapter illustrates, this trend has pushed the governorship into the leading position in the states. Governors are taking the initiative in sorting out the responsibilities the states will continue to perform and in pursuing the traditional functions of the states, such as education and criminal justice.

Historical Development of the Role of Governor

Governors have not always exercised the power and leadership that they do today. Historically there has been a gradual trend toward centralization of gubernatorial power. This trend has evolved through four historical stages.

Early Legislative Dominance

The governors of the original 13 colonies were King George III's appointees. As agents of the crown, these royal governors were symbols of tyranny to American colonists. The early experience with these royal governors left its mark; Americans are still notoriously suspicious of executive authority.

Unpleasant memories of colonial governors prompted early architects of state constitutions to fashion the office of governor as a "powerless ceremonial officer." Most governors were selected by their own state legislatures to serve one-year terms. Most had no veto power and virtually no appointment power.[2] In contrast, state legislatures or "assemblies" acquired courageous reputations by standing up to tyrannical governors during the colonial period. Thus early American history was a time of state legislative dominance.

The 1800s and Jacksonian Democracy

The nineteenth century saw conflicting patterns in executive authority. Widespread corruption and incompetency in state legislatures brought on disillusionment with legislative power, and many people began to realize that stronger governors were needed to check the power of legislatures. Some standard changes were made to increase the governors' powers. The governor became an elective position, with terms of two or four years and governors' powers were broadened to include the veto.

But the enhancement of executive power in the early nineteenth century was followed by restrictions on that power. The movement toward "popular democracy" which characterized the Jacksonian period brought about the **long ballot**. This meant that most state executives were elected independently and removed from control by the governor. These **unintegrated** or **plural executives** became the norm in most state constitutions in the 1800s. Thus even as governors gained independence from legislatures, they were able to exercise little control over their own branches of government.

The Progressive Era

Toward the end of the nineteenth century widespread corruption in state and local government brought demands for reform. Most of the corruption was blamed on the abuse of political parties. As Chapter 9 describes, the dominance of the patronage or "spoils system" meant that elected officials appointed people to government jobs who were of questionable integrity or were plainly incompetent to hold government jobs. Progressive reformers pushed through a series of reforms that were supposed to "depoliticize" government. New policies aimed at limiting the power and abuses of political parties were put into effect in a number of states. Civil service systems were created to replace patronage with **merit systems,** and government commissions and boards were established that operated outside the control of elected officials.

Civil service systems and independent commissions were supposed to isolate executive bodies from partisan political influence. This meant these bodies were isolated from the person who is supposed to be responsible for them: the elected chief executive. Typically governors had no power to appoint members to these boards and commissions nor remove them. Being governor was like being the manager of a large business, but without the power to hire and fire key personnel. Meanwhile, as urbanization and industrialization continued at a rapid pace throughout the first half of the twentieth century, the demand for government services generated larger state bureaucracies.

The Age of the Executive

The first radical shift of power for governors occurred in 1918 when Governor Al Smith of New York commissioned a study on the reorganization of state government. Reforms proposed by Smith and subsequently adopted included a four-year term for the governor; gubernatorial appointment of all statewide officials except the lieutenant governor, attorney general and comptroller; and preparation of an executive budget by the governor for submission to the legislature.[3]

The real increases in executive power came in the 1950s and 1960s. Two factors contributed significantly to the growth of governors' power during this period. The first was the effort by many states to revise their constitutions. Governors often led the movement for state constitutional revision and in the process made sure their own interests received a hearing. These new constitutions included the reforms initially adopted by Governor Smith of New York, as well as others. The second factor to enhance gubernatorial power was the "reapportionment revolution" of the early 1960s. Rural legislators had traditionally viewed strong executive power suspiciously. Redistricting corrected the overrepresentation of rural interests in state legislatures and gave urban constituencies more representation. But most important, the need for strong executive power became more and more apparent as state and local governments assumed greater responsibilities. Strong governors were the logical results of stronger, more active governments.

The Modern Governor

Between the 1940s and the 1960s state governments were the object of a great deal of criticism and scorn. Characterized by corruption, malapportionment, and incompetence, states were referred to by such unflattering terms as the "weak sisters" and the "fallen arches" of the federal system. In 1961 *New York Times* columnist James Reston wrote that "state capitols are over their heads in problems and up to their knees in midgets."[4] Among the "midgets" Reston referred to were no doubt many state governors who possessed reputations as unprofessional "good-time Charlies."[5]

But times have changed. Gradually the states have taken steps to reform their political institutions. Governors have become creative and experienced professionals who use both their formal and informal powers to transform their states. Modern governors have been compared to company CEOs who oversee sizeable budgets, manage large organizations, and persuade their states to adopt new ideas and innovations. Most states have said "goodbye to good-time Charlie" and hello to "a thoroughly trained well-regarded, and capable new breed of state chief executive."[6]

Institutionalization of the Governorship

Governors are extraordinarily busy officials; their schedules are typically frenetic.[7] They generally delegate some of their responsibilities to their staff. The size of the governors' staff and the roles performed by staffers vary from state to state. In general, the governors of small less populous states have smaller staffs than those of large populous states. Thus governorships in smaller states tend to be more **personalized**, while govenorships in larger states tend to be more **institutionalized.**

Gubernatorial staffers perform a number of important functions: speech writer, press secretary, budget officer, policy advisor among others. Recent governors tend to be less likely to appoint campaign staffers to their personal staffs. This reflects a heightened awareness of the importance of staff and their abilities,[8] since a person who knows how to direct a political campaign may not always be an expert in running the government. It also means that governors have a larger pool of knowledgeable staffers from which to select. More recent capable executives and more powerful gubernatorial offices have attracted better individuals who want to serve as staffers in the governor's office.

Intergovernmental Responsibilities

As the federal government struggles with the federal budget deficit, states are assuming more and more responsibility for government programs and services. This has not been an easy process for the states who have, to a certain degree, weaned themselves from federal grant dollars. Federal grants to state and local governments grew from $7.9 billion in 1962 to an estimated $199 billion in 1993.[9] Until recently, federal grants constituted a rising portion of state and local budgets. In 1955 they made up 11.8 percent of the revenues for state and local budgets. By 1982, this percentage had increased to 25.4.[10] However, by the early 1990s, federal assistance to the states declined significantly to make up about 14 percent of state and local reserves.

The states have responded unevenly to cutbacks in federal funding.[11] But a number of states, led by progressive governors, have not only moved to provide programs mandated by the federal government, but have fashioned innovative solutions to problems that Washington has not addressed. While states have long been recognized as policy experimenters or "laboratories of democracy," their assertiveness in policy leadership has grown in recent years. As two political scientists recently stated, "Policy innovation . . . is the beloved stepchild of the states, adopted from neglectful national parents."[12] There is no doubt that younger, more educated, more assertive governors whose formal powers have been strengthened are largely responsible for this surge of new activity.

Governors are adopting new strategies in their attempt to assume more control of intergovernmental affairs. For example, they are equipping themselves to be the chief lobbyists for their state governments. They are establishing Washington liaison offices to assist them in handling relations with the national government. In 1994, 36 states had such offices.

The National Governor's Association, the most important of the governors' organizations, has been significantly strengthened. It has changed from a part-time, largely ineffective annual conference to an association with substantial influence in the national political arena These developments are helping governors to play a much more active role in our intergovernmental system.

Recruitment, Tenure, and Compensation

In general the formal qualifications to be governor are not very restrictive. Most states stipulate age and citizenship requirements. More than four-fifths of the states have a minimum age requirement of 30 years, and 36 states require the governor to be a U. S. citizen. Forty-three states require state residency with requirements of residence before an election ranging from one month to 10 years. Twenty states add that the governor must be a "qualified voter," while a few prohibit persons convicted of bribery, perjury, or "infamous crimes" from serving as governor. Some states have unusual or antiquated requirements. Montana prohibits persons of "unsound mind" from being governor, while Kentucky has a ban on dueling.[13]

It is the unwritten requirements for governor that restrict most average citizens from the job. Governors are characteristically white male Protestants who are married with children. They are generally well educated with a career in law or business, substantial experience in public office, and the support of their state's party officials. Most governors are middle-aged; in 1994, the average age of governors at the time of their first elections was 50.1 years.[14] There is some evidence that younger governors are better governors. One study compared 117 "outstanding " governors from 1950 to 1975 with their colleagues who were judged to have performed less well. These performances were correlated with factors such as prior political and governmental experience, legal training, education, age, formal powers of the office, and various state characteristics. Among these factors, the strongest predictor of performance was the governor's age upon taking office.[15] Although the authors admit that their findings are tentative, this study provides evidence that age is not a barrier to effective leadership.

The ability to lead effectively is also influenced by a governor's **tenure**—the length and frequency of gubernatorial terms. A governor serving only a two-year term or who cannot be reelected is immediately weaker than one who does not suffer these restrictions. The length of gubernatorial terms varies significantly. Governors in only two states—New Hampshire and Vermont—still have two year terms. Only one state, Virginia, restricts the Governor to a single four-year term. The term limits movement, discussed in Chapter 10, has affected gubernatorial as well as legislative terms. Most states limit their governors to two four-year terms either consecutively or absolutely. Only 13 states place no restrictions whatsoever on how many terms any individual may serve as governor.[16]

Although more is not necessarily better with respect to the length of time in office for a governor, short or restricted terms do hamper his or her ability to complete an agenda. A new governor typically spends the first year in office getting adjusted to the demands of being chief executive. Governors elected under two-year terms must immediately begin thinking about reelection, while those elected under restrictions on successive terms may quickly find themselves "lame ducks." Governors regarded as most successful are those who can set long range goals and see them through to completion.

It is possible for most legislatures to remove governors before the end of their term through the process of **impeachment.** The usual method of impeachment is for the lower house to impeach, that is, bring formal charges against the accused, and the senate to hold a formal trial. If the accused is convicted in the senate, he is removed from office. Eighteen governors have been impeached and eight have been convicted.

The good news for governors is that they are much better paid than they used to be. The median salary for governors in 1955 was $15,000 as compared to $80,000 today. Salaries range from $130,000 for the governor of New York to $55,850 for the governor of Montana. While these are not exorbitant figures they are high enough to attract competent and professional candidates.

The Governor as Manager

As chief executives of their states, governors have formal responsibility for a host of bureaucracies that control enormous amounts of money, employ thousands of people, undertake a variety of government programs, and have a direct impact on the lives of large numbers of people. Like private business managers, governors want to see these bureaucracies perform well and efficiently at the lowest possible cost. Unlike private managers, however, governors operate with a host of **constraints** that may limit their ability to manage their own branch.

The most obvious constraint on the governor's ability to manage is the separation and sharing of powers with the legislature and the courts. Unlike a private sector CEO, a governor generally has to get legislative approval to change the primary tasks or structure of executive agencies and departments. Since the legislature has final authority over administrative agency budgets, agencies often respond to the mandates of the legislature which may or may not conflict with those of the governor (Box 11.2).

Often governors try to direct or change agencies that are allied with organized interest groups. These organized interests form the agency's "constituency," and will generally oppose any effort by a chief executive to change the organization or responsibilities of "their agency." Consequently, governors may find that changes they feel are essential to improving the performance or reducing the costs of an agency are resisted by key legislators who are responding to the pleas and complaints of client groups adversely affected by the proposed changes.[17]

Despite these constraints, today's governors are enjoying greater executive control. More staff resources, expanded appointment authority, and greater control of the budget process are narrowing the gap between the governor's responsibilities for management and the actual capacity of the governor to meet those responsibilities. Although executive management of the state bureaucracy encompasses a number of activities, the following four powers are among the most important: appointment, organization, budget, and crisis resolution.

Appointment Power

The power most fundamental to governor as manager is the power of appointment. As Michael Dukasis, former governor of Massachusetts stated, a governor's success "depends heavily on the quality and caliber of people he appoints."

However, gubernatorial appointment is limited by a number of factors. In nearly every state there are other officials who are elected by the voters of the state, who share executive power, and who are quite independent from the governor. These elected executives make up the **plural executive** and generally include the lieutenant governor, the secretary of state, the attorney general, and state treasurer. In addition, some top administrative officials

BOX 11.2

COMPARING GOVERNERS TO CEOs

In this age of "reinventing government," reformers often call for government leaders to emulate business leaders in managing resources more effciently. Indeed, observers have often compared governors to CEOs of large corporations. Both governors and CEOs manage large numbers of employees. But corporate management systems cannot be directly applied to state government. Why? Governors manage a breadth of issues and subjects that would surprise the private-sector chief executive. The typical responsibilities of the business executive—financial management, labor relations, marketing and personnel management—are also the core responsibilities of the governor. However, governors must function under the constant surveillance of a large board of directors—legislators—many of whom inevitably are adversarial. One former governor often asked his business associates, "How would you like to have your board of directors around every single day for 200 days?"

The biggest difference between private and public management can be summed up in one word: politics. Business leaders do face *internal* political problems and obstacles. But the latters' risks and rewards, their incentives, and their bottom lines are all dictated primarily by the market. Political leaders face formidable internal and *external* political obstacles. They must overcome internal obstacles, that is, legislators, agency heads, etc., without many of the formal powers of a CEO. For example, governors are not always allowed to hire and fire personnel. Governors must also overcome external obstacles, that is, they must persuade interest groups and the public at large that their policies are the right ones.

Although similarities do exist, comparisons of the CEOs and governors should be made cautiously.

are appointed by boards or commissions rather than by the governor. Table 11.1 shows that, of the 2,079administrative positions, less than half (42 percent) are appointed by the governors, while 41 percent are appointed by boards, agency heads, or the legislature, and 12 percent are separately elected. There is considerable variation among the states as to the percentage of upper level officials the governor may appoint, ranging from a low of only 20.5 percent in South Carolina to a high of 86.8 percent in New York.

In addition to top administrative positions, governors have the power to appoint members of many regulatory or advisory boards and commissions that make up the state bureaucracy. But here the governor's power may also be limited: most appointees serve fixed terms and cannot be removed, that is, "fired" by the governor except for cause. Removal for cause means that the governor must prove that the appointee was not carrying out his or her duties. In a few states, removal may even require approval by the legislature.

In some states many subcabinet officials in the state's bureaucracy may be selected through a **civil-service** or "merit system." This means that people who show they have the qualifications for a government position are hired, promoted, and fired by an independent civil service commission. Although civil service reform encourages the hiring of qualified people, it hinders the governor's power to manage the bureaucracy. It is difficult for the governor to control the bureaucracy if he has no power to hire and fire bureaucrats.

Table 11.1

HOW STATE ADMINISTRATIVE OFFICIALS ARE SELECTED
(EXCLUDING GOVERNOR)

State	Total Officials	Separately Elected	Appointed, but Not by the Governor	Civil Service	Appointed by the Governor
Alabama	44	6	24	0	14 (31.8)
Alaska	40	1	24	0	15 (37.5)
Arizona	44	4	24	2	14 (31.8)
Arkansas	38	5	17	1	15 (39.4)
California	44	7	6	0	31 (70.4)
Colorado	41	4	5	16	16 (39.0)
Connecticut	45	5	14	9	17 (37.7)
Delaware	41	5	20	0	16 (38.0)
Florida	45	7	25	0	13 (28.8)
Georgia	42	8	18	0	16 (38.0)
Hawaii	39	1	6	11	21 (53.8)
Idaho	43	6	23	0	14 (32.5)
Illinois	37	5	7	0	25 (67.5)
Indiana	45	6	15	0	24 (53.3)
Iowa	44	6	18	0	20 (45.4)
Kansas	43	5	25	0	13 (30.2)
Kentucky	40	6	18	0	16 (40.0)
Louisiana	40	7	5	7	21 (52.5)
Maine	44	0	25	0	19 (43.1)
Maryland	45	5	23	1	16 (35.5)
Massachusetts	43	5	4	0	34 (79.0)
Michigan	42	3	10	17	12 (28.5)
Minnesota	43	4	24	0	15 (34.8)
Mississippi	38	7	24	0	7 (18.4)
Missouri	43	5	25	0	13 (30.2)
Montana	42	4	3	21	14 (33.3)

One study showed that governors have mixed feelings about civil service systems. On the one hand, governors feel civil service regulations provide continuity in state government and free them to think about key appointments and major issues. On the other hand, governors are opposed to extending civil service reform to top administrative officials because it makes these officials less responsive to the governor's policy goals.[18]

Organization Power

The power to create and abolish agencies and to reassign duties and functions among agencies and departments allows the governor to emphasize his own programs and priorities. Governors restructure executive departments through **executive orders**. In the last 20 years governors have issued executive orders aimed at reorganizing the upper levels of the bureaucracy and generally streamlining the executive branch.

In most states, legislatures still have primary authority over reorganization of the bureaucracy. However, 22 states now grant the governor some type of formal reorganization

State	Total Officials	Separately Elected	Appointed, but Not by the Governor	Civil Service	Appointed by the Governor
			Table 11.1 (Continued)		
Nebraska	39	5	15	0	19 (48.7)
Nevada	43	6	16	0	21 (48.8)
New Hampshire	40	0	16	3	21 (52.5)
New Jersey	42	0	21	2	19 (45.2)
New Mexico	43	5	22	0	16 (37.2)
New York	28	4	3	0	21 (75.0)
North Carolina	47	9	23	0	15 (31.9)
North Dakota	41	10	16	0	15 (36.5)
Ohio	42	5	17	0	20 (47.6)
Oklahoma	39	7	17	3	12 (30.7)
Oregon	41	5	24	0	12 (29.2)
Pennsylvania	43	4	1	0	38 (88.4)
Rhode Island	42	4	18	0	20 (47.6)
South Carolina	40	8	29	0	2 (5.0)
South Dakota	41	5	17	0	19 (46.3)
Tennessee	42	1	19	0	22 (52.3)
Texas	40	5	32	0	3 (7.5)
Utah	40	3	23	0	14 (35.0)
Vermont	39	5	17	3	14 (35.8)
Virginia	46	2	6	0	38 (82.6)
Washington	41	8	15	0	18 (43.9)
West Virginia	39	5	8	8	18 (46.1)
Wisconsin	47	5	17	10	15 (31.9)
Wyoming	39	5	18	0	16 (41.0)
Totals	2079	245	842	114	879
50-state percentage		12%	41%	5%	42%

Source: Data taken from Council of State Governments, The Book of the States, 1992–93 (Lexington, KY: Council of State Governments), 76–81.

authority. In most of the 22 states the governor is allowed to propose executive branch reorganization plans that take effect unless disapproved by the legislature.[19]

Reorganization of the bureaucracy may be sorely needed, but governors will quickly realize the disadvantages of comprehensive reorganization efforts. Reorganization is likely to disrupt the routines of the bureaucracies, cause a loss of morale among administrative officials, and cause the departure of key personnel. It also opens up the door for power struggles or "turf battles" among agencies. These and other frustrations cause even the most energetic and progressive governors to hesitate before taking on the bureaucracy.

Budget Power

Almost all governors are given sole responsibility for preparing the first draft of the budget and submitting it to the legislature. This means that the state budget director is responsible to the governor directly or through an intervening agency head appointed by the governor. Only three states (Mississippi, South Carolina, and Texas) require their governors to share this budgetary power with other officials.

There are two reasons that preparation, presentation, and execution of the budget by the governor are important. First, by overseeing the initial draft of the budget, the governor is assured that this draft reflects his or her overall philosophy on taxing and spending. Thus the governor sets the agenda for legislative debate and compromise. This gives the governor an advantage despite the fact that the legislature exercises final statutory authority over the budget. Second, initial control of the budgetary process gives the governor some control over the bureaucracy. Administrators who cooperate with the governor may discover that their slice of the budget pie is somewhat greater than that of uncooperative or hostile administrators.

The governor's budget generally carries a good deal of weight with the legislature because the governor, unlike the legislature, is in a position to weigh the needs of the entire state. Beyond this, governors are generally equipped with more staff resources. Legislators who feel compelled to dispute the governor's recommendations will find themselves at a disadvantage in terms of data and expertise. The governor's budget office is more likely to be equipped with professional staff who are able to research the needs of the state and evaluate the performance of administrative agencies.

Despite these staff resources, the governor's influence over the budget does vary considerably from state to state. In states with strong parties and strong governors, the governor is expected to take the lead in getting his party platform enacted. The budget, in those states, is the source of funds for the platform upon which the governor and his party campaigned for office. Thus the governor plays a much more dominant role than governors do in states where parties are weak and the governor was elected in a campaign with little policy content. In strong party states, the governor's budget message is the first step in showing whether or not promises made in the campaign will be kept.[20]

Crisis Resolution Power

Governors are often called upon to respond to sudden demands that may be placed on them by natural or political crises. The former may include floods, hurricanes, ice storms, earthquakes, while the latter might include responses to strikes or riots. Whenever an emergency response is required, the governor is viewed as the person in charge. Often governors' response to emergencies is made through a concurrent "military" role; the governor is the commander-in-chief of the state militia or the "national guard" as it has come to be known in the states. The governor may call out the National Guard to protect property and preserve order if the situation seems to demand it. Many governors have found that emergencies preoccupy their administration and take up a great deal of time.[21]

The Governor as Chief Legislator

As the key representative for all the people in his state, the governor is expected to lay out a legislative program or agenda early in his or her administration. Often this program emerges during the governor's campaign for office; it is usually formalized in the governor's initial address to the legislature and in subsequent "State of the State" speeches. Education reform, job development, tax reform, drug abuse prevention, expanded health care are all examples of problems that a governor may want to pursue aggressively.

Christine Todd Whitman, the Republican governor of New Jersey, performs what has become a crucial task for governors—selling her ideas to the public through a "constant media campaign."

Strategies of Influence

A successful governor knows that to influence effectively the legislature, she or he must use two different strategies. The first strategy utilizes the formal powers of the governor such as appointment power, budgetary power, and the veto. The second strategy utilizes informal or persuasive techniques. Persuasive power comes naturally from being governor; the office itself suggest respect and leadership.

Using the strategy of informal techniques means the governor will take advantage of the public's opinion that he set the state's governmental agenda. Indeed, a smart governor takes steps to educate the public and involve key public opinion leaders in the policymaking process. A case in point is former Governor Richard Riley of South Carolina, a state where the governor's formal power over the legislature is very weak. Governor Riley, determined to enact sweeping educational reforms in his state, established two blue-ribbon task forces on educational improvement made up of legislators, educators and top business leaders. In preparing for the legislative session, Riley mobilized all his informal powers, especially public relations, media access, and personal popularity. He held public forums across the state to "stir up" the citizens for education reform. His efforts resulted in the Education Improvement Act of 1984, a sweeping reform of the state's educational system.[22]

Governor Riley provides an example of the governor's use of the "bully pulpit," that is, the visibility that comes with the office. Governors are regarded with a certain awe by the general public; when they speak, people listen. Their informal powers have been strengthened by the advent of the electronic media, especially television. Governors repeatedly appear on television and periodically hold press conferences to express their positions. Legislators seldom have the same opportunities to bask in statewide recognition (see Box 11.1).

Governors also try to persuade the legislature by lobbying. Though most are not as obvious about this activity as the governor of Ohio who formally registered himself as a lobbyist before the legislature, a governor will always spend "at least a portion of his time influencing legislation." Governors are assisted in their communications with the legislature by a legislative liaison officer and staff, although these staffers may not be formally titled "legislative liaisons." Examples of lobbying activities that a governor and his staff might engage in are talking to individual members of the legislature, discussing the legislative calendar with the legislative leadership, recruiting witnesses to testify before legislative committees, encouraging agencies or interest groups to lobby, and, on occasion, even preparing floor speeches for supportive legislators.

The Veto

The power to veto bills passed by the legislature was the one resource traditionally held by most eighteenth-century governors. Today the power is stronger and more flexible than ever (Table 11.2). All states but North Carolina give governors the power of veto; 43 states give governors **item veto** power.[23] The latter allows the governor to veto a single item within an appropriations bill rather than vetoing the entire bill. Ten states have adopted a hybrid form of item veto in which the governor may reduce the dollar amount of a specific budget item without eliminating that item altogether. Fifteen states now provide for the **executive amendment**, in which a governor may veto a bill but then send it back to the legislature with recommended changes. If the legislature agrees to the governor's suggestions, he or she will sign the bill into law.

In 15 states the governor can **pocket veto** a bill when the legislature is not in session by withholding his signature for a specified time period. However, in three of the 15 states the legislature may reconvene to override the veto. If it does not, the bill dies.

It is possible for the legislature to override the governor's veto, but in all states this requires more than a simple majority of those elected. Consequently, legislative override of a veto is rare: the percentage of overrides for all states is always less than 10 percent. In some states legislative override of the governor's veto almost never occurs. For example, during John Carlin's two terms as governor of Kansas, he signed 3,085 bills and vetoed 129. Every one of his vetos was sustained.

The governor's power to veto is a formidable weapon, and often the threat of a veto is enough to kill or alter a bill to the governor's liking. Governors do not exercise the veto authority frivolously. When surveyed, a large majority of them agreed with the statement that "bills should be signed unless the governor has very strong objections." Governors will generally exercise the "courtesy of notification," once they decide to veto a bill. This means that they will usually notify affected legislators and agency heads.[24] However, in almost all

Table 11.2

STATES RANKED BY GOVERNOR'S VETO

Very Strong	Strong	Medium	Weak
Alaska	Alabama	Florida	Indiana
Arizona	Arkansas	Idaho	Maine
California	Kentucky	Kansas	Nevada
Colorado	Tennessee	Louisiana	New Hampshire
Connecticut		Massachusetts	North Carolina
Delaware		Montana	Rhode Island
Georgia		New Mexico	Vermont
Hawaii		Oregon	
Illinois		South Carolina	
Iowa		Texas	
Maryland		Utah	
Michigan		Virginia	
Minnesota		Washington	
Mississippi		West Virginia	
Missouri		Wisconsin	
Nebraska			
New Jersey			
New York			
North Dakota			
Ohio			
Oklahoma			
Pennsylvania			
South Dakota			
Wyoming			

Source: Council of State Governments, The Book of the States, 1992–93 (Lexington, KY: Council of State Governments, 1993), 49–50.

the states the power of the veto is the governor's alone, and once a decision is made on a bill, it stands.

Leading Stronger Legislatures

In the past few years there has been a modernization of state legislatures. Chapter 10 describes how legislatures are becoming more professional, that is, sessions are longer, pay is higher, and staff support is increasing. More time and resources are allowing legislators to concentrate more on overseeing the performance of the executive branch. In addition, reapportionment of legislative districts has resulted in representation of urban constituencies. The result of these changes has been to make legislatures more equal partners with the executive in the formulation of state policy.[25]

In one study the National Governors Association (NGA) studied changes in the institutional powers of governors from 1965–1985. The NGA used six indices to measure the formal powers of governors: the governor's tenure potential, appointment powers, budget-making power, the legislature's budget-changing ability, the governor's veto power, and the governor's political strength in the legislature. The first three indices measured the governor's power within the executive branch, while the second three concern the governor's power relative to the legislature. Each state governor was assigned a point value based on the six indices which indicated the strength of his or her formal powers. Table 11.3 shows these rankings. The most notable finding of the study is that while governors' executive powers have been strengthened in the last 20 years, the governors' powers over the legislature have decreased.[26]

This resurgence of state legislatures is not always advantageous for governors. Legislators are demanding a greater voice in state government; they are increasing the time they spend overseeing and evaluating the activities of the executive branch. But while modernization of legislatures is sure to make a governor's relationship with the legislature more difficult, it is not a completely unwelcome change for governors. Most governors find that informed, competent legislators are more in tune with their view of the state's problems. This is reinforced by the fact that legislatures are more representative of urban constituencies than before. Often urban areas provide the margin of victory that governors need in their statewide election. Thus governors and legislators are more likely to agree that the needs of these urban areas should be addressed.

Table 11.3

A COMPARISON OF FORMAL POWERS OF THE GOVERNOR (SCORES IN POINTS)

Very Strong	Strong	Moderate	Weak	Very Weak
Maryland (27)	Connecticut (24)	Alabama (22)	Maine (19)	Texas (16)
Massachusetts (27)	Louisiana (24)	Alaska (22)	Montana (19)	North Carolina (16)
New York (26)	Nebraska (24)	California (22)	New Hampshire (19)	South Carolina (14)
West Virginia (26)	Utah (24)	Georgia (22)	New Mexico (19)	
	Arkansas (23)	Illinois (22)	Virginia (19)	
	Colorado (23)	Iowa (22)	Nevada (18)	
	Florida (23)	Ohio (22)	Washington (18)	
	Hawaii (23)	Pennsylvania (22)	Mississippi (17)	
	Michigan (23)	Arizona (21)	Oregon (17)	
	Minnesota (23)	Delaware (21)	Rhode Island (17)	
	New Jersey (23)	Idaho (21)	Vermont (17)	
	North Dakota (23)	Indiana (21)		
	South Dakota (23)	Kansas (21)		
		Oklahoma (21)		
		Tennessee (21)		
		Wyoming (21)		
		Kentucky (20)		
		Missouri (20)		
		Wisconsin (20)		

Source: Office of State Services, "The Institutionalized Powers of the Governorship: 1965–1985 State Management Notes," (Washington D.C.: National Governors Association, 1987).

The Governor as Party Leader

A governor's success as party leader is vital to his success as governor. As a candidate, the future governor must put together a coalition to win his party's nomination; as governor he must put together a legislative coalition to win approval of his policies. The governor's chances for success are enhanced if he has a majority of his party members in the legislature as long as this majority is not too large. If it is too large, then different groups in the legislative party will form "factions" and will likely disagree with each other. The best of all worlds for a governor is to represent a unified majority party in a state with a competitive two-party system. Because members of the governor's party must compete against members of the other party, it is in their best interests to support the governor and help him be successful. Because he is the leader of their party, this helps to ensure their success as well. It is worth noting that the governor's role as leader of his party can put him at a disadvantage in a state with divided government, that is, a state where members of his party are a legislative minority.

The influence of the governor over his legislative party is also determined by his skills at leading his party. All governors have certain resources with which to influence party members, but their skill at using them marks the difference between a successful and unsuccessful governor. Successful governors will use **patronage**, the power to make appointments and distribute favors, to their advantage. For example, the governor might appoint the friend of a legislator to a government position or to a judgeship. Or he might award a contract to a firm in which the legislator is interested. Governors often campaign for their supporters in the legislature. Gubernatorial appearances at a rally or luncheon may make it easier for a legislator to raise money for his or her campaign. All this is to help the governor establish allies in the attempt to sway the legislature.

COMPARING TWO FORMER GOVERNORS: RONALD REAGAN AND BILL CLINTON

Ronald Reagan and Bill Clinton are the only two American presidents to have been governors of their respective states for more than five years. Comparing the two gives us insight on how a governor's management style and political philosophy interact, and how the two ultimately affect state government. Reagan and Clinton had very different views on how government should be run and the role of government in running it. Their different philosophies of government ultimately resulted in very different management styles, styles that worked well for the two former governors.

Ronald Reagan's philosophy of government is well known. He believed that government programs undermine individual initiative; he felt that a sound and prosperous society depends on the cumulative acts of individuals pursuing self-interests. Reagan felt that the free enterprise system should provide services and jobs in the state whenever possible and that government should be run efficiently and in a businesslike manner.

Reagan developed a formal management system that served his philosophical position well. He was a talented spokesman and persuasive campaigner, but he had almost no management experience. His response was to establish management practices that did not depend on his active management of daily affairs. This system included three important practices: a powerful chief of staff, a strong cabinet, and a routinized decision-making system.

Two of Reagan's chiefs of staff, Bill Clark and Ed Meese, established a formal communication line to the governor and made most key management decisions themselves. Staff members and appointees did have some access to Reagan, but the governor's time was strictly scheduled by the chief of staff. Reagan himself almost never went outside his formal communications channels. He gently turned people toward procedures when they tried to gain access to him outside the routine. One staff person said that if he tried to get a decision directly from the governor, Reagan would say, "Have you talked to Meese?"[27]

Reagan held formal cabinet meetings twice a week. He endorsed the idea of making decisions with a cabinet because it was similar to a corporate board of directors, an arrangement in line with his philosophy. Issues were brought to the attention of the cabinet through "mini-memos," one-page briefs that summarized the issue. All cabinet officers studied these memos and were expected to participate in debate and discussion. The cabinet meeting was the only place where Reagan would hear arguments. He expected his officers to debate the issues in public and then support the group's decision, once made. Reagan himself almost always went along with the group's decision, even if he was not in complete agreement with it.

The highly systematic use of subordinates was, for the most part, advantageous to Reagan. It complemented his lack of management skills and allowed him to do what he did best: exercise his highly effective personal and media skills. The strong chief of staff and formal communication channels allowed an inexperienced manager to function without impairing bureaucratic routines.

Reagan's routinized management style resulted in policy consequences as well. His "closed" style did not encourage ideas or foster innovation. New ideas and new ways of doing things had to be filtered through formal decision-making procedures and the comments and scrutiny of cabinet officials and staffers. The failure to encourage innovation would have been a disadvantage to some chief executives, but Governor Reagan was not interested in making sweeping changes or experimenting with new programs.

Governor Bill Clinton of Arkansas, on the other hand, was so enthusiastic about charging ahead with innovations he thought would help his state, that he was defeated for reelection after two years. Clinton learned a lesson from this defeat, developed a more cooperative spirit, and was reelected two years later. With an ambitious agenda that included comprehensive changes in the state's school system, and business and consumer reform, he served a total of 12 years as governor of Arkansas. Like Reagan, he developed a management system that complemented his style and policy goals.

Clinton's style of management was not nearly as routinized as that of Reagan. The governor of Arkansas sought and got the advice of a myriad of advisors including his wife, Hillary, a Yale law-school graduate. He was fond of talking face to face with a number of different people with different views before reaching decisions. With some of his most important policy initiatives he would establish task forces and solicit advice from the general public. For example, in his efforts to overhaul Arkansas' public school system, Clinton sent Mrs. Clinton to hold hearings in all of the state's 75 counties. He also raised money from the business community for ads in the media.

Clinton's open style reflected his desire for big changes in Arkansas. It encouraged innovation and flexibility, and it gave him a great deal of control over both the details of his proposals and the negotiations and political manuvering it took to get these proposals approved.

LOCAL CHIEF EXECUTIVES

Chances are, your most direct and frequent encounters with political leaders will be with lo-cal executives. Local governments provide citizens with some of their most important and immediate public needs: education, heath care, roads, sanitation services, police and fire protection, and recreational facilities. Local chief executives—mayors, city and county managers, and school district superintendents—have final responsibility to see that these services are effectively delivered. These local leaders, like all chief executives, are often in the limelight. Mayors attend the grand openings of industrial plants that will bring jobs and economic development to their cities; school superintendents speak at sports banquets to honor their school district's athletes. Like chief executives in general, they use this public exposure to enhance their persuasive power. However, like all chief executives, they bear the brunt of voter dissatisfaction if local problems develop.

Counties: Headless Horsemen

The county is a pervasive form of local government: counties exist in all the states but Con-necticut and Rhode Island. A county, unlike a city, is not created by local inhabitants to serve their unique local needs. Counties serve as an administrative arm of state govern-ments. Originally counties stuck to their role as local agents of the state and administered state services such as law enforcement, road maintenance, and welfare services. However, in Chapter 5 we learned that counties are choosing to operate or provide additional services such as libraries, hospitals, airports, and fire protection. This is especially true of counties in densely populated, urbanized states.

Commission Form of County Government

The most obvious generalization about county chief executives is that there are none. Sev-enty-five percent of the nation's counties still have a **commission form** of government. There is an elected county board and a number of independently elected officials. These elected officials often consist of a judge, sheriff, treasurer, clerk, auditor, coroner, and tax as-sessor. In general, none of these elected officials has centralized authority over the others. In a few states, the county judge presides over the county board but has few real executive powers like the power of appointment or the power to veto board actions. In many states the judge is no longer an official of the county but has been designated by the state to be part of the state judiciary.

Centralizing and Professionalizing County Government

As counties have taken over a larger range of activities and services, there has been a move-ment to restructure county government. Changes implemented by some county govern-ments have centralized executive authority and/or made it more professional. The two forms of county government that incorporate these changes are: the **council-administrator form** and the **council-elected executive form**.

The council-administrator form of county government is the fastest growing type of organization in American counties. It is a product of the municipal reform movement that resulted in the council-manager form of city government discussed in Chapter 10. An elected council creates policy and appoints a professional administrator (manager) to carry it out. The county manager is a trained public administrator who takes over the day-to-day management of the county, hires and fires county employees, and prepares budgets. The county manager is completely answerable to the county board and can be fired at the board's discretion.

The council-administrator form results in the professionalization of county government. It allows a highly trained specialist to provide professional leadership and frees county commissioners from the day-to-day management of the county. It is also the most likely change to be adopted at the county level because it requires no substantial changes in the structure of county government—the jobs and power of county commissioners are not threatened, and voters are not asked to approve radical changes. However, it is subject to the same criticisms as the council-manager form of city government. The thrusts of these criticisms, described in detail in Chapter 10, is that a professional administrator is not as closely in tune with the needs of the community.

The council-elected executive form of county government provides for an elected commission and an elected county executive or "county board president." The latter differs from the traditional county judge or county board chairman traditionally chosen by his peers at the first board meeting. The elected county board executive or president is the formal head of the county and frequently has appointment and veto powers that resemble those of a governor or strong mayor. A few counties combine both the council-administrator form and the council-elected executive form so that an elected county board president or the county board will appoint a professional manager.

Mayors

Whatever the political realities of municipal government, both the public and the media assume the mayor is *the* chief executive. Mayors perform the most visible duties of city government: appearing at meetings, dinners, and ribbon-cutting ceremonies, presiding over council meetings, handling emergencies, and meeting with state and federal leaders. Citizens with complaints about potholes in streets or crime in their neighborhood are most likely to go to the mayor.

Chances are, a person who wants to be mayor is not expecting to get rich or have a full-time professional career. Unlike most other state and local chief executives, mayors are generally part-time officials. Most devote about 20 hours a week to the job and earn an average salary of about $10,000. The larger the city, the more likely the mayor's job will be full-time, although this is not always the case. During his four terms, San Antonio mayor Henry Cisneros earned about $10,000 a year and supplemented his income teaching courses at local universities. In recent years, the job of big-city mayor has become more of a stepping stone to higher office than it used to be. For example, former Mayor Richard Lugar of Indianapolis went on to serve in the U. S. Senate while Pete Wilson, former mayor of San Diego, was elected to the U. S. Senate and, subsequently, Governor of California.

Strong and Weak Mayors

In Chapter 10 we learned that mayors can be either strong or weak depending on the form of city government. Under the **commission form** and the **council-manager form** of city government, mayors are usually weak. They remain members of the council or commission, and their formal powers are usually limited to presiding over the council and serving as symbolic leaders of their cities. Most have no authority to veto council actions and do not appoint the heads of city departments. Often a mayor in a council-manager system will work closely with a manager so that the two form a kind of governing team. In larger cities, the mayor is often the dominant member of the team, while the manager dominates in smaller cities.[28]

The **mayor-council form** of city government can be classified as either **weak mayor** or **strong mayor** systems. In weak mayor systems the mayor's appointment power is limited; some or all of his appointments may have to be approved by the council. The council, not the mayor, is likely to have control over the budget. In contrast, strong mayors often have many of the same executive powers as a governor: significant appointment power, budget power, reorganization power, and veto power. The formal strength of a mayor is closely related to the size of a city; the strongest mayors are generally found in the largest cities, which are also the cities most likely to have strong mayor government. Indeed, as large cities grow more racially diverse and resources more scarce, there is growing appeal in an executive who is able to "take charge" (Box 11.3).

It is important to remember, however, that all mayors have some informal influence that comes with the office. A mayor with a forceful personality and a flair for media attention can have a great deal of influence with the council and other city officials. The potential use of **informal** resources is available to all chief executives. Some of the most highly respected mayors to hold office in America—Henry Cisneros of San Antonio, Pete Wilson of San Diego, and Emanuel Cleaver of Kansas City, Missouri—all operated in weak-mayor systems.

The Roles of the Mayor

There are significant differences in the way mayors perform their job. These differences are likely to be based on two factors. The first factor is the extent of the mayor's *legal and political resources*. Does the mayor have sufficient revenue to launch new innovative programs? Is he or she a full-time mayor? Is there sufficient staff resources for the mayor to engage in policy planning, political work, and relations with the state and federal government?[29] The second factor is the mayor's *subjective view of his or her role as mayor*. A newly elected mayor may feel that her mission is to change the basic goals and policies of the city. She may want to develop new programs or reorganize city government. On the other hand, a mayor may feel that her role is to deal individually with existing city problems without initiating new directions or goals. For a better understanding of these differences, we can divide the mayor's role into four types of leadership: the ceremonial mayor, the caretaker mayor, the program entrepreneur, and the crusader-mayor.[30]

The **ceremonial mayor** is not likely to have a great deal of legal or political power, nor does he or she have the desire to establish broad new goals and reshape city policy. This type of mayor has a modest staff and handles most problems individually. He or she generally relies on old friends and colleagues for support rather than trying to aggressively build new coalitions. The prototype of the ceremonial mayor is a personable gregarious person who enjoys personal contacts with his constituents and welcomes the opportunity to perform ceremonial tasks.

The **caretaker mayor** is similar to the ceremonial mayor in many ways. He or she does not a establish an agenda with long-term goals but rather concentrates on simply maintaining traditional services or enhancing services that will produce political payoffs. Much of his or her time is spent attending to people with demands or complaints. But the caretaker

BOX 11.3

BRINGING BACK THE STRONG MAYOR?

The city of Dallas has recently considered the unthinkable: abandoning the city manager form of government. The reason for the change: politics. Dallas has changed dramatically since it first adopted the city manager plan in 1931. For years the city was run by the business community; its political leadership was drawn exclusively from the prosperous white neighborhoods of north Dallas. The manager form of government, with its emphasis on efficiency, was a reflection of the city's homogeneity.

These days things are more complicated. There are many more claimants to power including the city's Hispanic and African American groups, citizen associations, environmental groups and others. There is a growing feeling that it may take strong leadership, i.e., a strong mayor, to forge a consensus. Dallas is not alone in considering a change to a strong mayor system. St. Petersburg, Sacramento, and Dade County, Florida, which includes Miami, are all looking gingerly at a more powerful chief executive.

Many believe the situation in Dallas symbolizes the end of municipal reform as it has been practiced in America for the better part of this century. As originally conceived, the reformed city should have a small council whose members are elected at large, whose mayor performs largely ceremonial duties, and whose manager runs the operations of city government is a businesslike fashion. This notion of reform was supposed to eliminate the corruption and patronage-mongering that had afflicted cities with strong mayors. The problem was that this produced city government whose leaders were relatively insulated from the electorate.

While most city-manager systems have been greatly modified to make them more responsive, there is a feeling in some places that "reforming reformism" is not enough. In the face of poverty, homelessness, gangs, corroding streets, and general civic squabbling, a strong authority figure is an attractive alternative.

Source: Rob Gurwitt, "The Lure of the Strong Mayor," Governing (July 1993). 36–41. See also Terrell Blodgett, "Beware the Lure of the "Strong Mayor," Public Management (January 1994), 6–11, for an excellent rebuttal of Gurwitt's article.

mayor has a bigger staff than that the ceremonial mayor and is likely to delegate more authority to others.

The mayor may decide to act as a **program innovator,** that is, someone who establishes major goals and pushes for new or expanded programs to meet these goals. Only a portion of his time is spent reacting to events or complaints; the rest is used to carry out long-range objectives. The policy innovator makes waves. Changing the priorities of city government is going to upset entrenched interests.[31] Therefore, the program innovator will spend much of his or her time building alliances with major interest groups: the business community, federal agencies, the city council, organized labor, universities, and others. He is likely to have a large professional staff and will delegate authority to the staff as well as to established bureaucracies.

The **crusader-mayor** is similar to the program innovator, but he or she lacks the legal and political resources that the latter possesses. This type of mayor is very active and ambitious and has long-range goals for the city, but relies more on the force of his or her personality and persuasive powers. The crusader mayor lacks the power to control city bureaucracies and motivates the public behind him or her with a dramatic or crusading style of leadership.

These types are ideals, and mayors cannot always be neatly classified as one of the four. However, they are useful to illustrate how the structure of the institution combines with the individual mayor's personality to create a style of leadership.

Mayors and the Intergovernmental System

Mayors determined to set and achieve long-range goals quickly realize that their success, in large part, lies in the hands of other governments. The most important of these governments is the state, which has legal authority over local governments. Many of the decisions that affect a mayor's ability to deal with city problems are made in the state's capital. For example, a mayor who wants to establish or maintain important city programs relies on state aid for a large percentage of the revenues to fund these programs. The new interest in urban problems that has characterized state governments since the redistricting revolution of the 1960s has been both a blessing and a problem for mayors. On the one hand, states are more financially supportive of the efforts of cities to deal with urban problems. On the other hand, the trend lately has been for states to centralize decision making and reduce the autonomy of local officials.

In the 1960s local governments began to rely heavily on federal aid to finance job training, criminal justice, and health care programs. During the Reagan and Bush administrations this aid was steadily reduced. Many mayors were hopeful when Bill Clinton was elected president in 1992. As a former governor for 12 years, Clinton was sympathetic to the difficulties forced on state and local governments by the reductions in federal aid. Unfortunely, the huge growth in the federal deficit that occurred in the 1980s precluded any significant increase in aid to local governments. Mayors, just as before, found that they were forced to do more with less, or in some cases—for example, Mayor Rendell of Philadelphia—less with less.

Despite his dependence on the state and federal government, the biggest constraint on the mayor's power is probably other local governments that are beyond his control. In most cities, huge policy areas are assigned to completely independent special district governments which are not even part of city government. These "functional fiefdoms" are often run by a board of appointed officials who are independent from the mayor and city council and quickly develop their own set of vested interests. As we noted in Chapter 5, the proliferation of these special districts fragments the policy-making process and makes it difficult to assign political accountability to any one official or government body. Thus the need for more unified leadership is probably the single best argument for strengthening the power of the mayor.

Mayors and Economic Development

For the past few years cities have been developing strategies for economic development that make them attractive to private industry. Reductions in federal aid forced the cities "to wean themselves from dependence on federal aid and to prepare themselves for free-market competition."[32] Thus cities are behaving like entrepreneurs, striving for success in the national market competition.

Mayors spend a considerable amount of time engaged in "ceremonial" duties. Here, former mayor Tom Bradley of Los Angeles performs a ribbon-cutting ceremony with Magic Johnson, the basketball star.

Mayors play a critical role in the entrepreneurial strategies of the cities, and many mayors have been elected on "economic development platforms." Mayors push for programs that would attract industry either directly or indirectly. For example, the mayor might persuade the city council to offer a firm tax incentives, below-market loans, or to upgrade the transportation or educational system to attract industry to the city. Big city mayors all over the country have led efforts to revitalize or "redevelop" downtown areas. This revitalization will entice businesses to locate in the city rather than a suburb; it will also lure tourists to the city. All of these economic development strategies are designed to enhance the community's "business climate."

Members of the business community are usually very involved in the politics of economic development. Mayors have created public-private partnerships or **quasi-public organizations** to promote economic growth. These organizations, typically made up of the mayor, city officials, and prominent members of the business community, will often plan and work together to achieve a particular project or simply plan development strategies in general. For example, Denver's former mayor, Federico Pena, worked very closely with the "Denver Partnership," a downtown development corporation to collaborate on a downtown master plan. The purpose of the plan was to direct and promote development in and around the central business district. A 27 member panel consisting of city officials, business inter-ests, and community leaders served as the steering committee for the project. However, the Denver Partnership provided three-quarters of the initial funding and two-thirds of the staff for the project.[33]

A mayor's efforts to attract or revitalize industry usually has wide support. However, these efforts are not conflict-free. Neighborhood groups will sometimes react suspiciously at economic development projects that threaten to disrupt their neighborhood; they also may resent the time and resources devoted to economic development policies at the expense of neighborhood services. One of the most important challenges for mayors in the 1990s is to create a consensus support for development policies that benefit landowners and develop-ers, and in addition, generate a fiscal surplus that will be shared with the rest of the city (Box 11.4).

City Managers

The city manager holds a unique position in local government. Managers provide leader-ship but do not generally possess independent political power. They depend on elected offi-cials for continued employment but are not political appointees. The manager is a trained professional public administrator who both assists and leads the council. Although man-agers establish contacts with leaders in the community, the manager is generally unable to build a power base to stand against the council in battles of will. His or her job is to inform elected officials, recommend what action these officials should take, and implement the policies that they establish.

Although an increasing number of women are entering the field, the typical city man-ager is a white male in his thirties or forties with a college degree. His average tenure is about five years. In earlier years when managers were seen strictly as technicians, they tended to have engineering backgrounds. Today, however, a city manager is likely to have a degree in the social sciences, specifically a bachelor or masters degree in public administration.

The Modern Role of the City Manager

The change in the credentials of city managers reflects the change in the nature of the job. While managers do administer city policies and manage city employees, they are taking a more active role in *making* policy. In council-manager cities, most policy originates with the manager since he or she presents a range of alternatives to the council and recommends a course of action. Managers are usually very powerful because they possess a near-monopoly of technical information; almost all contacts with the municipal bureaucracy take place through the manager. Many managers prepare the city budget with little or no input from council members, and council members often vote yes or no, that is, "up or down" on the manager's budget proposal.

These days many city managers are also expected to play the role of broker, that is, they are expected to lead negotiations among competing interests. This role of broker or negotia-tor suggest that managers must have political as well as managerial skills. Indeed, in a recent survey city managers identified the role of "facilitator for action and policy" as that most characteristic of the managers' job.[34]

Relationship with the Council

In Chapter 10 we discussed advantages and disadvantages of the different forms of munici-pal governments. A mayor-council system with a strong mayor is often the most appropriate

BOX 11.4

NEED NEIGHBORHOOD SERVICES? TRY HIRING THE NEIGHBORS

Tom Fink, the mayor of Anchorage, Alaska, has found one answer to the problem of maintaining municipal services in the face of declining revenues. He has enlisted neighborhoods to provide neighborhood services. This neighborhood-based service delivery goes back to 1974, when the city contracted with a local group of users to maintain and operate the recently built midtown ice-skating arena. A new arena, serving the city's northern area, is now managed by a nonprofit community corporation.

Fink points to numerous success stories. The Anchorage Softball Association provides daily infield maintenance at two neighborhood softball complexes. The city continues to maintain the outfield areas on a less frequent basis. In return for baseball field and stadium maintenance provided by the local summer league baseball teams, the city pays the lights at the stadium—a pretty good deal when the days lengthen to 18 hrs. Community leaders in the predominantly low-income neighborhood of Mountain View have organized volunteers to spot and report zoning volations, remove abandoned vehicles and trash poles, and refurbish and maintain neighborhood recreation centers and parks. Municipal assistance has come in the form of design expertise and donated plants, cooperation and training from municipal zoning officals, and free dump passes for people willing to haul their own trash to the municipal landfill.

In all the cases, both the city and the organization benefit. The neighborhood gets services it wants and needs, and the cost to the city is far less than that of hiring full-time workers to do the job. For example, the city is paying $60,000 over a four-year period for maintenance of the ski trails. If the city had to do the work itself, the cost, including employee benefits, would be more like $280,000.

Fink points out that there are possible pitfalls. Union difficulties may arise from the displacement of municipal employees. Anchorage officials have always been careful not to replace employed workers with the less costly alternative. The idea has worked best when services have expanded into new neighborhoods that could not be staffed by the city itself under existing budget constraints.

Another pitfall is the possible lack of consistent leadership within the neighborhood groups taking on the obligation to provide services. Fear that the group will not perform is the reason government hesitates to enter into such an agreement in the first place. The experience of Anchorage flies in the face of that belief largely because certain individuals have made these partnerships work. As Fink says, "Our successes have depended largely on the tireless effort of serveral dynamic individuals. Long-term continuation of the effort, should those individuals depart, could be problematic." Just as we point out consistently in this text, individuals *do* make a difference in government.

Source: Tom Fink, "Need Neighborhood Services? Try Hiring the Neighbors," Governing: The States and Localities (October 1989), 86.

form of city government for a large city because the mayor is best equipped to hold many powerful interests together. But a strong mayor-council system institutionalizes conflict in a traditional separation-of-powers arrangement. Neither the council nor the mayor can impose solutions on the other so that resolution of conflict is often difficult.

A more harmonious relationship exists between the city manager and council. No formal separation-of-powers exist, and its absence creates an atmosphere where a cooperative relationship between council and executive is possible. Other factors encourage harmony. Because the council appoints the manager, the two share similar goals for their community. Managers, who can be fired at will by the council, will almost always work to advance the latter's goals. A survey of city officials in both council-manager and mayor-council cities showed that council-manager cities had significantly smoother relationships between the executive and the council. Table 11.4 indicates that *all* council members responding in the council-manager cities reported that the council and manager have a good working relationship, but only 56.5 percent of the council members in strong mayor-council cities share this opinion of the relationship between the council and the executive. A very large majority (76.9 percent) of the council members in council-manager cities reported that the manager generally provides the council with sufficient alternatives for making policy decisions, while only 29 percent of the council members in the mayor-council cities reported satisfaction with the range of alternatives. Council members in council-manager cities have more confidence in executive expertise and in the executive's ability to handle citizen complaints.

This data should not give one the idea that conflict between manager and council does not exist. The fact that a city manager holds his job for only an average of about five years tells us that all is not paradise. Managers may resent council involvement in what they feel is their traditional role. Just as managers are becoming more involved in policymaking, so politicians are more involved and assertive in service delivery or the implementation of policy. Political problems may arise for a manager. Managers may create alienation from some members of the council if they become identified with one faction of a badly divided council. Managers are "bureaucrats," and hence they are sometimes criticized for stereotypical bureaucratic behavior—waste and inefficiency or being too rigid. A manager's unwillingness to be flexible may anger council members who are elected and who may be willing to bend policies for the good of their political futures.

School Superintendents

The job of the school superintendent is often a paradox: he or she is among the most respected and yet the most controversial of public administrators. Deference to the superintendent comes from the fact that he possess a large degree of professional expertise on education. Since Americans place a great value on education, they are likely to respect educational "experts." On the other hand, education is a sensitive and value-laden process. Educational policy-making involves teachers who want to be paid sufficiently for their professional efforts and who want to be part of the policymaking process. It involves parents who want their children to learn to read, write, and compute, but also want them to learn specific values. It involves taxpayers who want the whole process to be done at a reasonable cost.

Table 11.4

COUNCIL-EXECUTIVE RELATIONS

Form of Government*

Description	Council-Manager		Strong Mayor-Council	
	Council Members Agree(%)	Department Heads Agree (%)	Council Members Agree (%)	Department Heads Agree (%)
The council and manger (or mayor) have a good working relationship.	100.0	75.7	56.5	52.1
The manager or mayor provides the council with sufficient alternatives for policy decisions.	76.9	90.9	29.1	56.2
The council effectively draws on the expertise of the professional staff.	76.9	76.1	54.2	47.9
Intervention by a council member is necessary to get an adequate response to a citizen's complaint.	34.6	7.5	66.7	14.6

*The forms of government included six council-manager and five strong mayor-council cities.

Source: International City Management Association, The Municipal Yearbook, vol. 55 (Washington, DC: International City Management Association, 1988), 25. Reprinted with permission.

What Superintendents Do

Superintendents are hired by what is usually an elected school board to be a professional manager of the school district. The superintendent's responsibilities fall into four broad categories: personnel, financial management, administration, and curriculum and instruction. Hiring and firing a high school principal, recruiting a basketball coach, promoting a teacher to an administrative position, or hiring and firing the school system's budget director are all part of the superintendent's **personnel** responsibilities. As part of the **financial** responsibilities, superintendents, along with their staff, propose the district's budget and submit it to the board for approval; they also authorize expenditures for allocated funds. Superintendents **administer** the day-to-day operations of the school district which could mean anything from authorizing a school drug search to deciding individual school bus routes. Finally, superintendents are primarily responsible for recommending and implementing changes in the schools' **curriculum**—organizing grade levels, deciding which courses to cut, or choosing which extracurricula activities to offer. Superintendents, depending on the school district, will have varying amounts of responsibility for each of these areas.

A superintendent, like a city manager, is a professional administrator who is not expected to engage in partisan politics. In the minds of most Americans, he is a politically neutral figure, and he makes an effort to project an image of a person whose only interest is setting the best course for public education. But in reality the superintendent probably has a set of goals for the school district, and the success of these goals depends upon political support from the board and from the community. Thus, like all chief executives, superintendents use their informal powers which come from visibility and association with the public. Although they do not rub his elbows in the grimy world of partisan politics, they do make frequent public appearances, give speeches to civic groups, issue press releases, and belong to several community organizations. As the authors of an important study note referring to the rule of a superintendent "He appeals to the public on a subtle level by projecting himself as the foremost authority in the community over a policy area where knowledge rather than political influence should prevail."[35]

Relations Between Superintendents and Boards

The typical local school board is composed of laypersons serving on a part-time basis. This and the fact that school districts have become larger and more complex to operate means that boards are deferring more and more to the expertise and recommendations of the superintendent. This is especially true in large urban, heterogeneous school districts that require large bureaucracies to run.

The tendency of superintendents to dominate boards does not mean that relationships between the two are always harmonious. Indeed, the average tenure for urban superintendents is now less than three years, shorter than that of city managers. The trend in the last few years has been increasing conflict between boards and superintendents. Several factors account for these disagreements. The superintendent may develop the attitude that he is the expert and view the school district as a personal possession resenting any attempt of the board to infringe on his authority. Conflict may arise from how the superintendent and the board view their respective roles. One study showed that in many areas, *both* parties felt they should have more authority.[36] For example, both superintendents and school boards felt they should have more authority over personnel matters. Thus this area of a superintendent's responsibility is ripe for a collision with the board. Newly elected board members may not understand the extent of their authority and feel that their role includes managing the day-to-day responsibilities of the district. Finally, certain issues in education policy that are especially controversial have generated conflict between boards and superintendents. Prominent examples of these issues are school desegregation and sex education.

Certain policies and procedures instituted by a school board or superintendent can help prevent or relieve potential conflict. To clarify the role of the board and the superintendent, it is a good idea for a district to have a district policy manual that defines the specific responsibilities of each. A clear definition of roles and responsibilities will help to resolve some conflict. Another helpful tactic is to discuss a problem as soon as it is identified. Not doing so means the problem may fester and become bigger. One method for identifying problems is regular performance reviews for superintendents. These reviews make it possible for the board to raise their concerns before they become major issues. Boards also need to review their own performance periodically to see if they are fulfilling their own roles properly. The superintendent should be involved in this review process.[37]

CONCLUSION

Chief executives at all levels—federal, state, and local—have common functions. All serve as symbols for their respective governments and in doing so command a certain amount of informal persuasive power. All chief executives administer public policy and direct and coordinate the actions of public bureaucracies. Most are responsible for initiating major policy goals and preparing and presenting budgets to legislative bodies.

Although Americans have harbored a general suspicion of executive authority, the strength of state executive power has been significantly enhanced since the 1950s and 1960s. This enhanced authority is evident in large populous states where there tends to be large gubernatorial staffs, that is, institutionalized governorships.

However, recent evaluations of gubernatorial power reveal that while the formal powers of governors over executive branches have increased, the powers of governors vis-a-vis legislatures have decreased.

Today's governors tend to be younger and more aggressive about pursuing innovative policy goals. The decline in federal aid to the states has forced the latter to assume more initiative and responsibility for public programs. Although the states have responded unevenly, many progressive governors have demonstrated impressive leadership and entrepreneurial skills.

Among local chief executives, there is a great deal of variation in the strength and centralization of authority. While counties have traditionally decentralized executive authority in county commissions and other elected county officials, some large urban counties are adopting a manager or elected executive to manage county government. The authority of the mayor varies from the weak mayor, found primarily in councilmanager and commission forms of city government, to the strong mayor found in mayor-council cities.

There are significant differences in the way mayors perform their job. The differences are usually attributable to the amount of legal and political resources mayors possess and their subjective view of what their role of mayor should be. Some view their role as primarily ceremonial while others actively initiate new programs or new strategies for governing. Mayors, like governors, find themselves constrained by other governments, not the least of which are special district governments or "functional fiefdoms," that exist beyond the control of general purpose governments.

The city manager is a professional manager who both assists and leads the elected city council. In addition to their administrative duties, managers have assumed more policy making and "brokering" special interests. Because managers, unlike strong mayors, do not operate within a system of separation of powers, they generally enjoy more harmonious relationships with councils.

While most special district managers operate in the shadowy confines of invisible special district governments, school superintendents are highly visible and often controversial. The superintendent enjoys a reputation as a respected professional. At the same time, his or her administration of the most sensitive of public policies makes him or her vulnerable to criticism from both school boards and the general public. While tension between superintendents and elected school boards is increasing, certain policies and procedures are useful in preventing or relieving conflict.

STUDY OBJECTIVES

1. Identify four functions performed by chief administrators.
2. Identify two developments in the 1950s and 1960s that were important in enhancing the power of governors.
3. Identify the four stages of the historical development of the role of governor.
4. Identify constraints on the governor's appointment power.
5. Explain two reasons why it is important for governors to have responsibility for preparing and submitting the first draft of the state budget.
6. Distinguish the difference in formal versus informal strategies a governor might use to get what she/he wants and give examples of each.
7. Describe the four roles of mayors.
8. Discuss the duties and responsibilities of city managers. Identify the basis for harmony between city managers and city councils. Identify potential causes of conflict between these managers and councils.
9. Identify the four broad responsibilities of school superintendents.

GLOSSARY

Commission form of county government   An elected board and a number of elected officials such as county judge, county sheriff, or county clerk.

Council-administrative form of county government   An elected council who appoints a professional administrator to carry out council policy.

Council-elected executive form of county government   An elected commission and an elected county executive or "county board president."

Executive amendment   Allows the governor to veto a bill and send it back to the legislature with recommended changes. If the legislature agrees to the governor's suggestions, he or she will sign the bill into law.

Executive order   A rule or regulation issued by the governor that has the effect of law. Executive orders are used to create or modify the organization or procedures of administrative agencies.

Formal powers   The governor's powers that come from legal and constitutional provisions.

Impeachment   The bringing of formal charges against an executive official or judge. An official who is impeached and convicted is removed from office.

Informal powers   A chief executive's power to influence or persuade by virtue of holding his highly visible office.

Institutionalized governorship   The existence of staff and bureaucracies established to assist the governor. It is usually found in larger states.

Item veto   Allows the governor to veto a single item within an appropriations bill rather than vetoing the entire bill.

Merit system   Sometimes referred to as "civil service," means that people are hired for government jobs on the basis of their qualifications.

Patronage   Sometimes referred to as the "spoils system," means that parties have power to dispense government jobs to the supporters of party politicians and policy.

Personalized governorship   The lack of staff or bureaucracies to assist the governor. It is usually found in smaller states.

Program   A series of policy proposals that governors or mayors and their advisors develop during the campaign.

Plural executive   An "unintegrated executive," means that most high-level executive officials are independently elected by the voters of the state.

Pocket veto   A special veto power exercised by the governor at the end of a legislative session whereby bills not signed by the governor die after a specified time.

Tenure   The length and frequency of terms of elected officials.

ENDNOTES

1. The concept of "persuasive power" was most clearly described in Richard E. Neustadt's definitive study of the presidency, *Presidential Power* (New York: John Wiley and Sons, 1960, 1980).

2. Regina K. Brough, "The Powers of the Gubernatorial CEO: Variations Among the States," *Journal of State Government* 59 (July/August 1986): 59.

3. Regina K. Brough, "Strategies for Leaders Who Do Not Have a Lot of Power," *Journal of State Government* 60 (July/August, 1987): 157.

4. Quote taken from David Wessel, "Can-Do Capitals: States Enlarge Roles As Congress Is Unable to Solve Problems," *Wall Street Journal* (June 28, 1988), 1.

5. Larry Sabato, *Goodbye to Good-Time Charlie: The American Governorship Transformed* (Washington, D.C.: Congressional Quarterly Press, 1983), 19.

6. Ibid., 57.

7. See, for example, "A Day in the Life of a Governor," Center for Policy Research, *Governing the American States—A Handbook for New Governors* (Washington, D.C.: National Governors' Association, 1978), 10–20.

8. Thad L. Beyle, "Governors' Views on Being Governor," in Thad L. Beyle and Lynn R. Munchmore, eds., *Being Governor: The View from the Office* (Durham, NC: Duke University Press, 1983), 30. Also published in *State Government* 52 (Summer 1979).

9. ACIR, "The Question of State Government Capability," (Washington D.C.: Advisory Commission on Intergovernmental Relations, 1985), 6; U. S. Department of Commerce, *Statistical Abstract*, 13th ed., 1993, 297.

10. "The Question of State Government Capability," ACIR, 7.

11. Richard P. Nathan and Fred C. Doolittle, *The Consequences of Cuts: The Effects of the Reagan Domestic Program on State and Local Government* (Princeton, NJ: Princeton University: Urban and Regional Research Center, 1983).

12. Ann O'M. Bowman and Richard C. Kearney, *The Resurgence of the States* (Englewood Cliffs, NJ: Prentice-Hall, 1986), 27.

13. Sabato, *Goodbye to Good-Time Charlie*, 19,20.

14. Calculated from *The Book of the States*, Council of State Governments (Lexington, Kentucky, 1994–95), 50–51.

15. Lee Sigelman and Roland Smith, "Personal, Office and State Characteristics as Predictors of

Gubernatorial Performance," *Journal of Politics* 43 (February, 1981): 169–180.

16. Thad L. Beyle and Rich Jones, "Term Limits in the States," *The Book of the States*, (Lexington, KY, Council of State Governments, 1994–95), 30.

17. James K. Conant, "Gubernatorial Strategy and Style: Keys to Improving Executive Branch Management," *Journal of State Government* 59 (July/August, 1986): 82.

18. Thad L. Beyle and Robert Dalton, "Appointment Power: Does It Belong to the Governor?" in *Being Governor: The View from the Office*, edited by Thad L. Beyle and Lynn R. Muchmore (Durham, NC: Duke University Press Policy Studies, 1983), 113.

19. Although the U. S. Supreme Court has ruled the legislative veto violates the separation of powers provision of the federal Constitution, the ruling does not apply to states.

20. Sarah McCally Morehouse, *State Politics, Parties, and Policy* (New York: Holt, Rinehart, and Winston, 1981), 250–1251.

21. See Milton Shapp's comments in Center for Policy Research, *Reflections On Being Governor* (Washington, D.C.: National Governors Association, 1981), 34.

22. Richard C. Kearney, "How a 'Weak' Governor Can be Strong: Dick Riley and Education Reform in South Carolina," *Journal of State Government* 60 (July/August, 1987): 150–56.

23. "State Veto Procedures," *Congressional Digest* (February 1993), 40–42.

24. Beyle, "The Governor as Chief Legislator," 140.

25. See William Pound, "State Legislative Careers: Twenty-Five Years of Reform" in *Changing Patterns in State Legislative Careers*, edited by Gary F. Moncrief and Joel A. Thompson (Ann Arbor: University of Michigan Press, 1992).

26. Office of State Services, "The Institutionalized Powers of the Governorship: 1965–1985," *State Management Notes*, (Washington, D.C.: National Governors Association, 1987).

27. Gary Hamilton, *Governor Reagan, Governor Brown: A Sociology of Executive Power* (New York: Columbia University Press, 1984).

28. David R. Morgan and Sheilah S. Watson, "Policy Leadership in Council-Manager Cities: Comparing Mayor and Manager," *Public Administration Review* 52 (September/October, 1992): 438–446.

29. Jeffrey Pressman, "The Preconditions for Mayoral Leadership," *American Political Science Review* 66 (June, 1972): 512–513, 522.

30. For an extensive discussion of these catagories see Pressman, "The Preconditions for Mayoral Leadership"; John P. Kotter and Paul R. Lawrence, *Mayors in Action: Five Approaches to Urban Government* (New York: Wiley, 1974), chapter 7; and John J. Harrigan, *Political Change in the Metropolis*, 4th ed. (Glenview, IL: Scott, Foresman and Co., 1989), 202–205.

31. Robert L. Lineberry and Edmund P. Fowler, "Reformism and Public Policies in American Cities," *American Political Science Review* 61 (September, 1967), 701–16.

32. Dennis R. Judd and Randy L. Ready, "Entrepreneurial Cities and the New Politics of Economic Development, in *Reagan and the Cities*, edited by George E. Peterson and Carol W. Lewis (Washington, D.C.: Urban Institute Press, 1986), 210.

33. Ibid., 226.

34. Morgan and Watson, "Policy Leadership in Council-Manager Cities, 442.

35. L. Harmon Zeigler and M. Kent Jennings with G. Wayne Peak, *Governing American Schools: Political Interaction in Local School Districts* (North Scituate, MA: Duxbury, 1974), 152.

36. Donald T. Alvey and Kenneth E. Underwood, "School boards and Superintendents: How They Perceive Each Other," *Education Digest* 51 (February, 1986): 46–49.

37. J.G. Hayden, "Superintendent—School Board Conflict: Working It Out," *Education Digest* 52 (April, 1987): 11–13

12

The Many Limbs of the Executive Branch

Every year thousands of college students apply for financial aid at their university financial aid office. If you are one of these students, you may have noticed a few things about that office. For example, you may have talked to a financial aid officer who was an expert in describing financial aid opportunities. You were informed that in order to "qualify" for financial aid, you had to meet certain criteria. You probably got the distinct impression that there was no special treatment for those who did not meet these criteria. You filled out lots of complex forms and gave them back to people who processed many forms exactly like yours. You noticed that the employees in the financial aid office dealt with lots of students in situations similar to yours.

The financial aid office at your college or university is an example of a bureaucracy, and the people who work in it are bureaucrats. There are millions of bureaucracies: the Ford Motor Company, the Catholic Church, and your university are all examples of bureaucracies. Bureaucracies are the most efficient method known for organizing large numbers of people in pursuit of a goal; they are designed for efficiency.

Government bureaucracies are part of the executive branch; employees of the executive branch—bureaucrats—are charged with implementing laws initiated and approved by chief executives and passed by legislatures. These employees work in agencies, bureaus, departments, divisions, and offices collectively referred to as bureaucracies. Hence bureaucrats are the public officials most likely to come into contact with average citizens. A real estate salesman who wants to be licensed, an out of work carpenter who claims unemployment compensation, or a high school senior seeking admission to a state university all deal with public bureaucracies and bureaucrats.

Since the Great Depression and Franklin Roosevelt's New Deal of the 1930s, the size and scope of federal, state, and local governments have increased dramatically. The growth in government programs has been accompanied by an expanding bureaucracy to do the work. Most attention and criticism of this trend has focused on the "bloated" federal bureaucracy, but in recent years growth of state and local bureaucracy has exceeded that at the federal level. In 1953, 63 percent of all public employees worked for state and local governments; in 1993 the figure was 83 percent.

The expanding size of administration is but another source of the irritation and suspicion that Americans have always felt for bureaucracy. Yet the size of bureaucracy is a direct result of the services that citizens demand. We expect state and local governments to provide us free public education, investigate cases of child abuse, maintain recreational parks, solve crimes and put people in jail, and regulate utility companies. It is the employees of our state and local government executive branches who do all these things.

Criticism of bureaucrats derives not so much from what they do but from the conflicting standards of performance that we expect them to meet. The public expects bureaucrats to be both *effective* and *responsive*. These two goals are not the same; they may even contradict each other. Effectiveness is the degree to which an administrator's decisions are more likely than alternative choices to bring about the outcomes that are desired, that is, to make policies work.[1] We expect the employees of public agencies to make their decisions on the basis of technical expertise and not on the basis of pressure from politicians. We demand the managers of public bureaucracies to run their agencies smoothly and effectively, that is, "run them like a business."

Responsiveness is the extent to which decisions by bureaucrats reflect the preferences of the community or the officeholders authorized to speak for the public.[2] When bureaucrats implement public policies, we insist that they be sensitive to the needs and demands of the public and accountable to elected politicians who represent this public. There are times when the most effective decisions are not the most responsive. For example, the parole and probation of criminal offenders may be more effective in the rehabilitation of these offenders than incarceration. Chances are, however, that the public prefers, if not demands, the latter. Yet the failure of state and local government employees to meet either of these two goals inevitably evokes the wrath of the public and their elected representatives.

In this chapter we will examine the functions bureaucracies perform, how state and local executive branches are organized to do business, the role of state and local bureaucracies in our federal system, and how individual citizens may participate in bureaucratic decision making. Finally, we will discuss ideas and reforms that are designed to make state and local bureaucracies more effective and/or responsive (see Box 12.1).

FUNCTIONS OF BUREAUCRACY

In theory, the job of the executive branch is to implement and enforce policies made by legislatures and chief executives. But in practice, the activities of executive agencies go far beyond this technical division of responsibilities. Bureaucrats *do* execute policy. But they are also involved in making policy and in reviewing its impact. For this reason we will examine three major functions of bureaucracy: administration, rule-making, and adjudication.

Administration

Administer is another word for execute, enforce, or apply. The oldest job of executive branches is to administer laws and policies established by policymakers. Once these policymakers decide on a policy or course of action, they must direct an executive agency to put that policy into effect. The agency makes specific decisions that are needed to put the policy in place and assumes the day-to-day tasks of carrying it out. For example, a county commis-

BOX 12.1

THE PROBLEMS OF THE TEXAS STATE BOARD OF INSURANCE

In January, 1989, the Texas State Board of Insurance found itself the target of two of the toughest politicians in Texas: Attorney General Jim Mattox, an all but announced candidate for governor, and State Senator John Montford, a former Marine officer and prosecuter. Charges of waste, cronyism, and patronage were echoed by Mattox's remark that the agency was carrying on an "incestuous relationship with the industry it regulates." Montford, chairman of the powerful Senate State Affairs Committee, initiated hearings to investigate the agency and called for the resignation of its three commissioners.

The two politicians and other critics of the insurance board believe that the board has been "captured" by the interest it was supposed to regulate. In other words, the Insurance Board was controlled by the insurance industry in Texas. Instead of regulating the insurance industry to protect the interest of the public, its critics charged the Insurance Board was taking a pro-industry position. At the very least, the board was overlooking abuses by individual insurance companies or was failing to enforce state regulations that companies violated.

Although **capture** of state regulatory agencies does not always occur, several factors inevitably encourage it. The most important factor is the need for insurance regulators to be "experts." Selling insurance these days is a complicated business. Thus many of those charged with regulating the insurance industry are from the industry itself. Who else is going to be as familiar with the business as insurance executives? Who else is going to be as *effective* at insurance regulation?

Chances are, when these executives finish their stint as appointed insurance commissioners, they will return to their insurance companies. Going from industry to regulatory board and back to the industry is known as the **revolving-door syndrome**. The syndrome helps to account for the allegations of capture of regulatory agencies by the industries they regulate.

The process of capture illustrates the problem of conflicting standards for bureaucracy. On the one hand, we want those who regulate the private sector to be effective, that is, knowledgeable about what they are doing. On the other hand, we want these executives and the bureaucrats who work for them to respond to the interest of the public in general. Sometimes, as the problems of the Texas State Board of Insurance reveal, it is hard to live up to both standards.

sion may decide to allocate county funds for a park and recreation center; the county parks and recreation department is responsible for collecting user fees from persons who use the facility and for overseeing its maintenance. A state that is required to implement federally mandated controls on the use of pesticides may assign regulation to a state agency that spells out for chemical firms, farmers, and aerial spraying firms just what pesticides can be used and the limits on that use. Thus policymaking without administration means no policy at all.

Rule-making

In addition to executing policy, modern bureaucracies are playing an increasingly stronger hand in *making* policy. Industrialization, urbanization, and the technological complexity of our society means that decisions by elected officials require the help of experts. Legislatures, especially the part-time variety that are found in many state and local governments, are simply not able to address many technical problems with specific solutions. To execute these specific solutions, legislatures delegate authority to executive agencies to draft rules or guidelines. These rules lay out specific actions to be taken to achieve the goal of the policy. For example, most state legislators agree on the need to regulate medical services. Without regulation the public may be harmed by unqualified or unscrupulous doctors, some making exaggerated claims for "cures" and treatments, and some by simply playing roles for which they have no training. Yet most state legislators know very little about the highly technical field of medicine. Hence, regulation of physicians is the responsibility of the state medical board.

The delegation of authority to executive agencies is referred to as **bureaucratic discretion.** Some say that the delegation of broad rule-making authority to administrative agencies is one of the most important characteristics of contemporary American government.[3] Bureaucratic discretionary authority *is* a cause for concern. Because agency rules or "regulations" have almost the same impact as laws, the authority to make these rules gives bureaucracy **quasi-legislative power.** Critics worry that the bureaucracy has become a "fourth branch" of government, and that bureaucratic discretion violates the principle of separation of powers. They are worried that powerful executive officials who make these rules are not responsive either to elected representatives or to the public. Still, delegation of authority to the bureaucracy is a necessity of modern government. The large number of problems that face elected officials and the technical nature of solutions to these problems force bureaucratic experts to assume responsibility. Furthermore, legislators depend on experts from bureaucracy for advice in revising old and making new laws.

Revising Rules: Adjudication

Just as legislatures have willingly yielded legislative power to administrative agencies, so have courts given them judicial power. Agencies decide more cases and controversies than are decided by courts of law. A disagreement that results from an agency rule is generally decided by the rule-making agency itself. A court may eventually hear a case involving a disputed agency rule, but only *after* the agency reviews and rules on the case. For example, a welfare client deprived of benefits or a public housing tenant faced with eviction may demand a hearing by the agency. These hearings resemble court trials; an aggrieved party is usually represented by counsel and may bring in sympathetic witnesses to testify in his behalf. If, after the hearing, the protesting party is still not satisfied, he may appeal to the courts.

The power of administrative agencies to judge cases involving agency rules is referred to as **quasi-judicial power.** Agencies are given this power because the number of rules subject to dispute and the technical nature of these rules makes it necessary for bureaucrats to assume a central role in their interpretation.

The significance of administrative agencies becomes obvious when one considers that they combine all three traditional institutional functions—legislative, executive, and judicial. Agencies make rules that have the force of law, they execute these rules, and they judge the validity of their own rules.

THE NATURE OF BUREAUCRATIC ORGANIZATION

To effectively administer laws passed by legislatures and rules established by agencies, state and local executive branches possess many of the characteristics of classic bureaucracies.[4] With varying degrees, these characteristics include division of labor, expertise, hierarchical organization and standardized procedures:

1. Division of labor. The responsibilities of bureaucrats are subdivided in various ways so that agencies are like people on an assembly line, each having a specific function to perform.
2. Expertise. The division of labor in bureaucracies allows employees to become experts in their specific area. Bureaucrats give concentrated attention to specific problems and deal day in and day out with the same tasks. Employees of public bureaucracies are likely to have job security, and most expect to spend their working careers in their agency or department. Thus long years of experience add to their expertise.
3. Arrangement of the various units of the bureaucracy in a hierarchy, that is, a pyramidal form of organization. Authority flows down from a single top administrator—a governor or mayor—and responsibility flows up the pyramid.[5] Almost everyone in any bureaucracy has a boss and, unless one is at the bottom of the hierarchy, some subordinates.
4. Standardized procedures. State and local bureaucracies, like all bureaucracies, operate by fixed rules and regulations, that is, "by the book." Communications are generally formalized through memos, and permanent records are kept of bureaucratic actions. All of these formal rules help bureaucracies to function routinely.

According to people who study organizations, these characteristics help to assure that public services are delivered effectively. However, as we've already noted, an organization that is effective may not be politically responsive to the public in general. Hence, state and local bureaucracies deviate from these classic characteristics. The managers of executive branches are not usually experts and career bureaucrats, but are elected or appointed officials. State and local bureaucratic structures may not follow the perfect pyramidal form of organization placing final authority and responsibility in the hands of a governor or mayor. In short, state and local executive branches deviate from the classic characteristics of bureaucratic structure to enhance accountability to the public and to the elected officials that represent the public.

ORGANIZATION OF STATE EXECUTIVE BRANCHES

Students of American national government know that the federal executive branch is organized in a cabinet style structure that gives the president the authority to appoint and remove the heads or "secretaries" of cabinet level departments. Although 36 states have so-called "cabinet systems," very few give the governor authority to appoint or remove important cabinet level officials.[6] As Table 12.1 shows, the Lieutenant Governor, Secretary of State, Attorney General, and Treasurer are generally constitutionally created positions and are elected by the public. In states with Jacksonian constitutions the voters elect department heads in other policy areas such as agriculture, commerce, or education. As noted earlier, a consequence of the election of these **plural executives** denies the governor control over the executive branch, fragments decision making, and ultimately makes fixing responsibility difficult for the electorate.

The Lieutenant Governor

One of the most confusing roles in state executive branches is that of lieutenant governor, who in many states has both executive and legislative functions. The lieutenant governor usually presides over the state senate, casting a tie-breaking vote when necessary. In some

Table 12.1

METHODS OF SELECTION OF STATE EXECUTIVE OFFICIALS

State	Lieutenant Governor	Secretary of State	Attorney General	Treasurer
Alabama	E	E	E	E
Alaska	E	*	GB	*
Arizona	*	E	E	E
Arkansas	E	E	E	E
California	E	E	E	E
Colorado	E	E	E	E
Connecticut	E	E	E	E
Delaware	E	GS	E	E
Florida	E	E	E	E
Georgia	E	E	E	*
Hawaii	E	*	GS	*
Idaho	E	E	E	E
Illinois	E	E	E	E
Indiana	E	E	E	E
Iowa	E	E	E	E
Kansas	E	E	E	E
Kentucky	E	E	E	E
Louisiana	E	E	E	E
Maine	*	L	L	L
Maryland	E	GS	L	L
Massachusetts	E	E	E	E
Michigan	E	E	E	GS
Minnesota	E	E	E	E
Mississippi	E	E	E	E
Missouri	E	E	E	E
Montana	E	E	E	CS
Nebraska	E	E	E	E
Nevada	*	L	E	E
New Hamshire	*	L	G	L
New Jersey	*	GS	GS	GS
New Mexico	E	E	E	E
New York	E	GS	E	GS
North Carolina	E	E	E	E
North Dakota	E	E	E	E
Ohio	E	E	E	E
Oklahoma	E	GS	E	E
Oregon	*	E	E	E
Pennsylvania	E	GS	E	E
Rhode Island	E	E	E	E
South Carolina	E	E	E	E
South Dakota	E	L	E	E
Tennessee	*	L	SC	L
Texas	E	GS	E	E
Utah	E	*	E	E
Vermont	E	E	E	E
Virginia	E	GB	E	GB

(Continued)

	Table 12.1 (Continued)			
State	**Lieutenant Governor**	**Secretary of State**	**Attorney General**	**Treasurer**
Washington	E	E	E	E
West Virginia	*	E	E	E
Wisconsin	E	E	E	E
Wyoming	*	E	G	E

*No specific chief administrative official or agency in charge of function.

E = elected by public; G= appointed by governor; GS = appointed by governor and approved by senate; GB = appointed by governor and approved by both houses of legislature; CS = Civil Service; L = elected by legislature; SC = elected by state supreme court.

Source: Council of State Governments, The Book of the States, 1992–93 (Lexington, KY: Council of State Governments, 1993), 76.

states this official assumes more important legislative functions, and the power to appoint committee chairs, schedule debate, and assign bills to committees can make a lieutenant governor a powerful force in state politics.

Executive Role

In most states the lieutenant governor's primary executive responsibility is to succeed the governor if the governor dies, retires, is impeached, or becomes incapacitated. This position in the line of succession makes the office of lieutenant governor the main stepping-stone to the governorship, and many view it as a kind of training ground for governors. Indeed, the list of lieutenant governors who "moved up" to higher office reads like a *Who's Who of American Government*: Governor Mario Cuomo of New York; former Senator Thomas Eagleton of Missouri; Governor Charles Robb of Virginia; and Senator Paul Simon of Illinois.[7] Nonetheless, the office bears the brunt of criticism and jokes because its occupant often does little but wait around to assume the job of governor. A recent lieutenant governor of Nevada expressed his frustration at the job when he said that he spent most of his time "checking the obituaries to see if I should be in Carson City."[8]

The office of lieutenant governor is becoming more significant. One of the most important trends is that of electing the governor and lieutenant governor as a team. Rather than have voters select the lieutenant governor as a separate and independent executive, 24 states have the candidates for governor and lieutenant governor of each party run as a team.[9] This encourages compatibility between the two and avoids the embarrassment and friction of having a governor and lieutenant governor from different parties. The lieutenant governor who is a member of a partisan team is much more likely to support the governor and can be an invaluable source of influence over the legislature.

Another noteworthy trend is the increase in the executive or administrative role of lieutenant governors. Thirty states now authorize the governor to delegate executive duties to the lieutenant governor, and governors in other states have done it without explicit authority. Although governors who run as a team are more likely to assign their lieutenant governors executive responsibilities, almost all do so to some extent.[10] Some states even make the lieutenant governor the head of one or more executive departments. In Indiana, for example, the lieutenant governor is director of the Department of Commerce and Commissioner of Agriculture. In Georgia, the lieutenant governor sits on the state's Economic Development Council, the State Finance and Investment Commission and the Georgia Building Authority.[11]

Legislative Role

In the 20 states where the lieutenant governor runs independently of the governor, he or she presides over the state senate in all but one (Louisiana). In the 22 states where the two officials run as a team, the lieutenant governor presides over the senate in 13.[12] The legislative role of the lieutenant governor is a controversial one. Critics believe this role detracts from her or his executive responsibilities, undermines support for the governor's authority, and is inconsistent with the doctrine of separation of powers. Supporters of a powerful legislative role for the lieutenant governor claim that it allows her to serve as a liaison between the executive and legislative branches, keeping lines of communication open.

Department Heads and Top Administrators

The governor and lieutenant governor are assisted in the administration of state government by executives who supervise the state bureaucracy. These officials may be the heads of executive departments such as commerce, health, or agriculture and are often referred to as "commissioners." Top administrators may also supervise state boards, agencies, or regulatory commissions. These department heads and top administrators occupy a crucial position in state government because they serve as middlemen between the governor and the civil servants or career bureaucrats.

Selection of Administrators

Although constitutionally created positions such as attorney general, secretary of state, and state treasurer are selected by voters, most department heads, agency directors, and state board members are appointed by the governor with the consent of the state senate. Some of these officials may be selected by a state board or commission. The governor's appointment of state board or commission members may not give him the control over these organizations that this power implies. This is because appointments are made on a staggered long-term basis—terms are usually six years. The governor fails to have a majority of his own appointees for the first two years of his term, and carry-over appointees from the previous administration continue to exercise control over board policy.

Because a majority of top level administrative officials are patronage positions, that is, appointed by the governor, they encourage bureaucratic responsiveness to the policies and programs of the governor, but what is supposed to work in theory is not always achieved in reality. Executives have difficulty controlling departments or agencies for several reasons. The sheer size of the agency may make it hard for the director to keep up with what is going on. Even more important is the fact that the department head or director is a "temporary" employee while middle managers and lower level bureaucrats are permanent civil service employees. The latter have more knowledge and experience and may be reluctant to follow directions from someone they see as a stranger and an amateur.

Profile of the Modern State Administrator

What kind of person occupies top-level administrative positions in state government? Are these administrators representative of the public in general? How have the characteristics of state administrators changed over the years? Given the fact that much of our experience with state government involves contacts with the agencies and departments these administrators supervise, these are important questions. A continuing study conducted by the American State Administrators Project (ASAP) helps to answer these questions. The study surveyed state agency heads every five years from 1964 through 1988 and reveals important data concerning the representativeness and professionalism of these executives.[13]

The democratic ideal suggests that public organizations should maintain work forces that are representative of the people they serve. We can see from Table 12.2 that state agency heads do not reflect the characteristics of the public at large. The latest survey in 1988 shows that the majority of these administrators are white males with graduate degrees. However, we can also note that over the past 20 years women and minorities have made some progress. For the first time since the surveys began, almost 20 percent of the respondents in 1988 were women, and the percentage of black respondents doubled.

The study also indicates that state administrators are becoming younger and more educated. In 1978, the median age of agency heads dipped below 50 years for the first time, and the trend toward younger administrators continued in 1984 and 1988. The graduate degree seems to be a growing prerequisite for administrators. The self-educated executive who learns by "hard knocks" solely "on the job" is becoming a thing of the past.[14]

The Civil Service

Most employees in state executive branches are not political appointees but are part of **civil service** or **merit systems.** This means that these employees are hired because they take a test to prove that they are qualified to perform a particular job; employment is based on merit rather than political connections or **patronage**.

Federal Influence

Civil service reform was first initiated by the federal government with the passage of the Pendleton Act in 1883. Reformers were disgusted by what they perceived as abuses of patronage or the "spoils system," where incompetent people were given government jobs primarily because of their connections with politicians and political parties. The act itself, however, was stimulated by the assassination of President James A. Garfield in 1881 by a disappointed office seeker. Passage of the Pendleton Act stimulated the growth of state civil service systems. New York promptly established a Civil Service Commission that same year in 1883 and Massachusetts followed in 1884.

In 1939 the federal government provided the most important impetus for states to adopt merit systems. The federal Social Security Act passed in that year requires governments receiving federal-aid money to use a merit system for staffing agencies that implement programs with that money. Today all the states and many cities have some form of civil service system.

The federal government further influenced state and local personnel practices with passage of the Hatch Act in 1939. The act forbids federal employees from participating in partisan political activity, that is, running for political office, managing political campaigns, cir-

Table 12.2

PERSONAL AND BACKGROUND CHARACTERISTICS OF STATE ADMINISTRATORS

	1964%	1968%	1974%	1978%	1984%	1988%
Age						
Under 40	13	14	17	22	25	22
40-49	28	29	31	33	33	41
50-59	35	38	33	31	28	27
60 and over	24	19	19	14	14	10
Mean	52	50	50	48	47	41
Median	53	51	50	49	47	43
Sex						
Male	98	95	96	93	89	82
Female	2	5	4	7	11	18
Ethnic Background						
White	98	97	96	92	90	90
Black	1	1	2	2	5	5
American Indian				1	0.7	0.4
Asian	1	2	2	4	3	2
Hispanic	0	0	0	1	2	2
Education						
High School or less	15	7	4	3	2	2
Some college	19	18	13	11	6	7
Bachelor's degree	25	15	18	15	15	17
Some graduate study	25	16	17	14	14	17
Graduate degree	40	45	47	56	63	57

Source: American State Administrators Project, cited in Deil S. Wright, Jae-Won Woo, and Jennifer Cohen, "The Evolving Profile of State Administrators," Journal of State Government (January/March, 1991), 30–38. Reprinted with permission, copyright by the Council of State Governments.

culating petitions and other similar activities. Following the federal lead, legislatures in all the states adopted "Little Hatch Acts" of their own to limit the political activity of state employees. Although all the states prohibit this activity, some are more restrictive than others.

How Merit Systems Work

Recall that a merit system means people will be hired and paid according to the work they do rather than the political pull they have. Thus the first step to installing a merit system is **job classification**. Jobs are grouped into different categories according to the type of work performed and are arranged hierarchically. Jobs that require the most training, expertise, and responsibility are at the top of the hierarchy, while those that require the least are at the bottom. The classification of jobs is also necessary in order to construct exams that test the competency of those competing for the jobs. Applicants are evaluated on the basis of their exam scores, academic credentials, and job experience. Other criteria such as military service or affirmative action may also be considered. In most states supervisors follow the so-called **rule of three**, meaning that they will hire one of the top three applicants.

After a period of time—usually five years—the individual in a civil service position in given **tenure**. This means that the individual can only be fired for reasons that are specified in state law. Tenure makes it very difficult for a supervisor to fire an employee. To dismiss a civil service employee, cause for dismissal must be presented to a civil service commission. Examples of cause for dismissal include repeated failure to follow an administrator's directive or a misuse of official power. The rationale behind tenure is that it protects nonpolitical employees—civil service employees—from interference by and pressure from politicians (see Box 12.2).

The primary advantages of the Civil Service have always been that it provides constancy and expertise. These reforms and others are efforts to address its major disadvantages: inefficiency and unresponsiveness.

Civil Service Commissions generally run state merit systems. These are nonpartisan independent boards whose members are usually appointed by chief executives and approved by legislative bodies. The Commission's responsibilities include describing and classifying jobs, designing tests, and laying out rules for promotion, retirement, dismissals, and other personnel matters.

BOX 12.2

THE STATES AND CIVIL SERVICE REFORM

As one political writer noted, the term *civil service* conjures up "images of gross overstaffing, government inflexibility, warrens full of dyspeptic shirkers and featherbedding bureaucrats who have become expert a manipulating Byzantine systems to their full career advantage."[15]

Indeed, civil service systems have reputations of inefficiency, inflexibility and unresponsiveness. Although it is only fair to point out the millions of state and local government civil servants who are doing good work under difficult circumstances, it is also true that there is room for improvements.

A number of states are attempting to reform civil service systems. Reforms include the following:

- **Broadbanding** This term refers to the creation of a set of occupational "families" in place of the current system of narrow and complex job classifications. For example, Florida has had 23 categories of administrative assistant in its job classification system, each with a slightly different set of qualifications. Broadbanding would combine these classes and allow more flexibility in hiring for these positions.

- **Decentralization** In the past one centralized office—a personnel agency—has had responsibility for all aspects of hiring and firing civil servants. There is now a move to decentralize the hiring function to give more control to individual agencies and managers. The latter, in some cases, write their own job descriptions and do their own hiring, looking only to the central agency for advising.

- **Expanding or Abolishing the "Rule of Three"** Along with decentralization, some states have dumped the rule of three and have given managers more flexibility in hiring.

The Pros and Cons of Merit Systems

The value of a professional bureaucracy, familiar with the day-to-day operations of government, is obvious. These employees provide the continuity and expertise that are often missing in states where governors and legislatures are transient and part-time. The taxpayer likes to know that public employees are qualified and competent to perform the functions they are hired to perform.

However, the disadvantages of the merit system have also become obvious. Employees in a civil service system may not respond willingly to elected or appointed managers. Protected by tenure, they feel little incentive to promote a manager's goals—they can simply "wait him out." Thus civil service employees are insulated from political pressure, but they are also insulated from political or "democratic" control. The ability of those officials we elect to political office to govern effectively is restricted by a permanent and politically independent bureaucracy.

The permanence and expertise of professional bureaucrats also gives them power over elected and appointed officials. Bureaucrats are experts on procedures and programs within their own areas of specialization. Legislators and top level administrators depend on bureaucratic "experts" for information. All this means that bureaucrats, those government officials least accountable to the public in general, are playing an increasing role in policymaking.

The Pros and Cons of Patronage Systems

A **patronage** or "spoils" system means that elected chief executives confer government positions (as well as contracts or other special favors) to those who have supported their election effort. In most cases, these supporters are members of the chief executive's party. In general, the disadvantages of a merit system comprise the advantages of a patronage system. Government employees are very responsive to elected officials because their jobs and careers depend on the good will and success of the official who appoints them. The chief executive is able to surround herself with loyal subordinates who support her views and help her redeem her campaign pledges.

As we learned in Chapter 9, strong parties, those with the authority to provide inducements or rewards for party workers are likely to be more responsive to the public in general. This is because if the party in power does not deliver on its promises, it is possible for the voters to "throw the rascals out." Thus patronage systems emphasize responsiveness.

The primary disadvantage of patronage systems is the lack of continuity and expertise. Dispensing jobs to loyal supporters does *not* guarantee that these supporters are qualified to perform the increasingly complicated functions of modern government. Nor does it give them the experience to learn these functions; even popular chief executives step down from office after a few years. Thus patronage systems may sacrifice effectiveness for responsiveness.

Reorganization of State Executive Branches

Throughout the twentieth century governors have engaged in executive branch **reorganization**—that is, reshaping how departments, agencies, boards, and commissions are organized. There is no doubt that reorganization was long overdue. States had hundreds of state agencies standing alone, often without any central direction and coordination. This fragmentation of power and responsibility made it hard for governors to achieve their policy goals. Critics charged that agencies possessed overlapping functions and often duplicated services.

In a federal system such as ours local government performs vital functions. The Jackson, Mississippi, City Hall is the seat of municipal government.

Thus reorganization was meant to address both political and administrative concerns. Governors would have more control over state bureaucracy, and the latter would be run more effectively and efficiently.

Most of the major efforts by states to reorganize their executive branches resulted from similar activities at the federal level. At the national level reorganization followed three major studies: the Taft Commission, 1910–1913, the Brownlow Committee initiated by President Franklin D. Roosevelt in 1937, and the Hoover Commission, 1947–1949.[16] The most recent wave of state executive reorganization, prompted by the Hoover Commission and by reapportionment, was the most extensive. Between 1965 and 1977, 21 states launched major reorganization efforts, and virtually all the rest undertook some reorganization.[17]

Goals of Reorganization

Although states did not always adopt them, the following goals were set up as the "standards" of reorganization:

1. Concentrate more authority and responsibility in the hands of the governor. The governor should have more appointment and removal power.

2. Consolidate boards, agencies, and commissions into a few departments with broad functional responsibilities. The heads of these departments should be appointed by the Governor, not elected.

3. Abolish boards and commissions used for administrative work and replace them with single executives.

4. Coordinate staff services—budgeting, accounting, purchasing, personnel—into a single department. In the language of bureaucracy, the personnel, finance, legal, and other such units of a bureaucratic organization constitute its *staff* services.

5. Ensure there is an independent audit of the executive branch, preferably by a legislatively appointed auditor.

6. Provide for a governor's cabinet, whose members he or she appoints, to advise the governor on policy matters and to help eliminate duplication and overlap of functions.[18]

Although the response in the states has been uneven, substantial progress has been achieved in goals number one, two, four, and five. There is no doubt the power of governors' has been strengthened. Between 1964 and 1981, all but eight states reduced the number of top executive officials that are elected. North Carolina reduced its elected executives from 110 to 10; Nevada from 42 to 6. In most of these cases, election was replaced by gubernatorial appointment. As Chapter 11 points out, many governors were also given the power to reorganize their executive branches through executive orders. Consolidation of agencies has taken place particularly in the areas of environmental protection, transportation, and human services. By 1979, two-thirds of the states had an independent auditor designated by the legislature.[19]

Changes have been much less extensive for goals number three and six. Multimember boards and commissions are still widely used in state government, although some have been consolidated. A number of states did provide for a cabinet system—38 by 1992.[20] However, the creation of a cabinet system took second billing to the decision to appoint, rather elect department heads. A governor who does not have the power to appoint cabinet secretaries is not likely to view his cabinet as a useful advisory body. Thus goal number one—the concentration of authority in the hands of the governor—was a much more significant goal than the creation of cabinet systems per se.[21]

Resistance to Change

Implementation of the preceding reorganization goals seems like such a logical and rational thing to do, one may wonder why the goals have not been universally adopted. The reason is because reorganization is a highly *political* process. There is often strong support for maintaining separately elected officials so that people can have more direct influence or because that is the traditional way of doing things. Recall that Americans have always been suspicious of centralized executive power. Certainly agency heads will resist consolidation into a larger department that threatens their authority. Special interest groups often have a close working relationship to a specific agency (perhaps have even captured the agency) and do not want to see it subsumed into a larger, less accessible department. These and other obstacles mean that proponents of reorganization face a difficult task.

An Example of a State Bureaucratic Organization: The Texas Public Education System

One of the most important areas of policy administered by state and local bureaucracies is education policy. All 50 states have local school districts and authorize local school boards to govern them. Although these local boards administer important day-to-day policy, their authority is limited severely by state legislation.

The bureaucratic arrangements in most states reflect the control that the state exercises over local school districts. In almost every state government, the primary policymaking body is the state board or commission of education. The board is assisted by the chief executive official, usually called the commissioner or superintendent of public education. The implementation of state education policy is the responsibility of the state department of education, which usually is a very large bureaucracy.

The Texas Public Education Bureaucracy

Because the organization of the public education bureaucracy in Texas is typical of that in many states, it is useful in illustrating the administration of this complex state and local policy. Figure 12.1 illustrates how Texas organizes the bureaucracy to implement public education. The legislature and the state board of education have broad decision-making power for public education in Texas. The state board of education, whose members are elected for four-year overlapping terms from 15 districts, establishes general rules and guidelines, approves organizational plans, submits budget recommendations to the legislature and governor, and contracts for the purchase of textbooks. The legislature approves the budget for the state's share of the cost of public education.

Much of the decision making concerning education is left to the Texas Education Agency (TEA) and the local school boards. The TEA, whose administrators are appointed

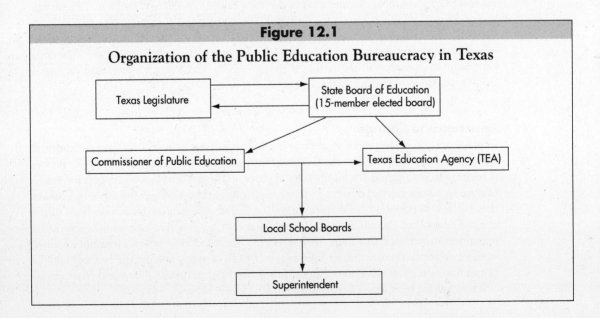

Figure 12.1

Organization of the Public Education Bureaucracy in Texas

Texas Legislature

State Board of Education (15-member elected board)

Commissioner of Public Education

Texas Education Agency (TEA)

Local School Boards

Superintendent

by the state board, handles such general policy maters as curriculum, teacher certification, and school accreditation. The chief administrator of the TEA is the Commissioner of Education, who is appointed to a four-year term by the state board. The commissioner, an experienced educator assisted by a professional staff, acts as a kind of state superintendent, making recommendations to the lay state board.

The day-to-day operation of public schools is the responsibility of locally elected school boards. These boards approve local school budgets, set tax rates, arrange financial audits, make personnel decisions, establish local salary schedules, and approve construction contracts. Because local school boards are composed of part-time laypersons, one of their most important decisions is to hire a professional, that is, a superintendent, whose job is to manage the daily operation of the district.

Where Do You Fit In?

Pondering the organization and functions of this large state and local bureaucracy may intimidate the average citizen, but individuals determined to influence education policy are given a variety of opportunities to do so in our example. The members of the major policy-making bodies—the legislature, the state board of education, and the local school boards—are elected. All make policy in open accessible forums. In addition, many of the day-to-day decisions that affect citizens most directly are made at the local level. Local boards and officials are generally sensitive to the values and concerns of their immediate communities. Although citizens do not elect a superintendent, the fact that the superintendent is a local official makes him or her one of the most accessible bureaucrats.

REFORMING THE BUREAUCRACY: CURRENT ISSUES

As state and local bureaucracies continue to grow, politicians and academics recommend changes that they believe will make these bureaucracies more effective and responsive. Reforming or "reinventing" the bureaucracy has become especially compelling in recent times. A deep recession in the early 1990s, a steady reduction in federal aid, the ongoing transformation of the business sector to make it more competitive in an international market were all factors that put more pressure on government to become more efficient and productive.

The following discussion examines reforms that have been in place for some time as well as those that have emerged in the newer attempts to reinvent government. Among the most prominent are the notion of entrepreneurial government, budget reforms, the development of state and local employee unions, the contracting out of public services to private firms, more openness and participation in state and local governments, and new legislative strategies for controlling the bureaucracy.

Entrepreneurial Government

In 1992 David Osborne, a free-lance journalist from Boston and Ted Gaebler, a former city manager-turned-consultant, collaborated on a book *Reinventing Government: How the Entrepreneurial Spirit is Transforming the Public Sector.*[22] The authors' primary thesis is that top-down, bureaucratic, rule-driven governments be replaced with institutions that are flexible, that treat constituents like customers, that treat employees (or bureaucrats) as if they were the owners of their programs, and, like entrepreneurs in the traditional business sense, are sometimes willing to take risks to find more efficient and effective ways of operating. They write that "slowly, quietly . . . new kinds of public institutions are emerging. They are lean, decentralized and innovative. They are flexible, adaptable, quick to learn new ways when conditions change. They use competition, customer choice and other nonbureaucratic mechanisms to get things done as creatively and effectively as possible."[23] The authors provide example after example to illustrate the notion of entrepreneurial government.

The notion of entrepreneurial government is not without its critics. The latter argue that it rests on premises that are far from proven. These premises assume that government and the private sector are similar and respond similarly to management incentives and a competitive market environment. This assumption is antithetical to classic theories of public administration. These theories posit that public and private institutions exist for fundamentally different reasons and that public and private employees are motivated by different forces. Critics also point out that in allowing bureaucratic managers more power to be flexible, there is less control over these managers by democratically elected officials. Taking risks with the taxpayers' money is not always as desirable as it is with private capital. (see Box 12.3).

Despite its critics, the notion of "entrepreneurial government" has influenced many of the areas of reform described below. As we discuss these reforms we will note its influence.

Budgeting and Budget Reform

Budgeting means planning how to spend money, and, as you might guess, it is the heart of governing. Deciding "who gets what" through a budget is our leaders' way of planning what government does and what are its most important functions.

The Budget Process

In all but three states the governor has responsibility for planning the state budget and submitting it to the legislature. Thus the budget is the governor's potent weapon in controlling state administration. The governor's budget plan reflects proposed expenditures in a **fiscal year.** A fiscal year means a financial year not a normal calendar year. For example, many states have fiscal years that begin July 1 and end June 30. The traditional reason for fiscal years is that legislatures generally met in the spring. By summer the decisions over state agency budgets were finalized so that these agencies could begin spending money.

Once the governor's budget is submitted (if not before), the intensely political process of approving the budget swings into gear. State agencies, organized interest groups, and other interested parties intensely lobby the legislature to make sure their share of the budget pie is retained or increased. Legislators who are supposed to think about the interest of the state or city in general are bombarded with information and arguments from narrow well-organized special interests.

Although some zealous legislators with a cause will work for extreme changes in the budget, most prefer not to deviate from the status quo in any radical fashion. To do so is to invite the wrath of bureaucrats and special interests who find themselves threatened by big changes in the budget. For this reason, the budgeting process has traditionally been incremental. **Incremental budgeting** is a relatively comfortable process for most of the actors involved. The proposed budget is based upon figures in last year's budget plus a little more. Agencies might request money for a few new programs and overestimate the amount

BOX 12.3

THE BENEFITS AND RISKS OF ENTREPRENEURIAL GOVERNMENT

Nowhere are the pros and cons of entrepreneurial government illustrated more dramatically than in Visalia, California. Fans of *Reinventing Government* will recall Visalia as the place where co-author Ted Gaebler promoted his notions of entrepreneurialism in government. During the eight years Gaebler was city manager there, Visalia came to be known as "the most entrepreneurial city in America." Ironically, Visalia has now become one of the first city governments to repudiate the philosophy.

In the 1980s Visalia adopted many innovations in the spirit of reinventing government. These included a radically new budgeting system which allowed the city manager to respond quickly as circumstances changed. The system eliminated all line items within departmental budgets—freeing managers to move resources around as needs shifted. Second, it allowed departments to keep what they didn't spend from one year to the next, so they could shift unused funds to new priorities. These innovations allowed Visalia's Parks and Recreation Department to save $60,000 and to seize an unexpected opportunity to acquire an Olympic size pool for its high school.

However, the same budget and managerial flexibility contributed to a real estate fiasco for the city. In the late 1980s the city made plans to lease the land for a new downtown Radisson Hotel to developers. However, as the developers ran into problems, the city began to lend them money and guarantee further loan payments to other lenders in exchange for a share of the hotel's revenue. But the developers proved incapable of securing funding, and the city negotiated new loan guarantees in return for an even bigger cut of the prospective profits. By the time the hotel was finished in 1990 with some $1 million in cost overruns, it was clear the city would have to buy out the project. The city assumed debts of $12 million in addition to some $8 million it had already spent or committed.

Clearly this is a cautionary tale. It is a reminder that the risks of entrepreneurship can bring gain or loss.

Source: David Osbourne and Ted Gaebler, Reinventing Government: How the Entrepreneurial Spirit is Transforming the Public Sector *(Reading, MA: Addison-Wesley, 1992), 2–5; Rob Gurwitt, "Entrepreneurial Government: The Morning After," Governing (May 1994), 34–40.*

needed for old ones. Governors and legislators review agency requests and make some cuts. Agencies get what they need, governors and legislators get credit for holding down spending, and everybody is satisfied though not thrilled by the whole process.

Once money is **appropriated** by the legislature, the final step in the budget process is to make sure the money is spent in the way the legislature intended. One way to do this is to put an agency's money into several accounts called **line items**. Agencies are then restricted to spending funds only on those things delineated in the line item. Another way of checking on bureaucrats is through **auditing**, that is, the process of looking at agency expenditures to see if they are legal and accurate. Auditing in most states is performed by an official selected by the legislature. In about a dozen states the auditor is popularly elected. Both election and appointment by the legislature are methods that help to ensure the auditor is independent of the executive branch agencies that he or she is charged with checking.

Budget Reforms

Pressure to reduce state spending, dissatisfaction with incrementalism and with the restrictiveness of line item budgeting all provide impetus to reform the budget process.

One attempt to avoid or minimize incrementalism initially implemented in the 1970s was **zero-based budgeting (ZBB)**. Zero-based budgets require agencies to justify every element of their budget every year. Although this was a good idea in theory, ZBB has proven in practice to be too cumbersome and time-consuming, too easy for managers to manipulate, and highly political. In most cases ZBB has been discarded or has been adopted in some hybrid form that invariably reverts back to incrementalism.

The most recent attack on incrementalism has come in both state and federal comprehensive **performance reviews**. The latter involve efforts—usually led by a highly visible elected official—by politicians and management consultants to thoroughly review bureaucratic operations to identify areas of waste, inefficiency, and overlapping services. The most highly publicized of these reviews was the National Performance Review managed out of Vice-President Al Gore's office with additional temporary quarters for nearly 200 consultants and federal employees located nearby. The review yielded a 168 page report with recommendations it claimed would save $108 billion over five years. State governments, such as Texas and Florida, have implemented their own comprehensive reviews that have yielded similar sweeping recommendations.

These performance reviews differ from the normal auditing process; they are much more far reaching and their recommendations are often highly controversial and politically sensitive. For example, the performance reports invariably recommend eliminating supervisory positions and give managers that remain more power and discretion over agency operations. The recommendations in the reports are sometimes criticized for being politically unrealistic. Nevertheless, they have become popular tools for counteracting the abuses of incrementalism.

Osborne and Gaebler, in their book *Reinventing Government*, propose a **mission-driven budget system**.[24] The thrust of this system is that line-items should be discarded or consolidated to allow more flexibility for managers. The authors use the analogy of a family budget to argue that line item budgeting is too restrictive. In a family budget, money is set aside for the mortgage, car payments, groceries, etc. But if the washing machine breaks, you find the money to fix it by using money from other "lines." Public managers do not have this same flexibility; moreover, they have no incentive to save money in their respective lines, because if they do, the legislature may give them less the next year. Mission-driven budgets will allow managers to use money where it is most needed to meet the overall goals and mission of the agency.

State and Local Employee Unions

In recent years public employee unions have increased in size and political influence. Today about 40 percent of state and local employees belong to unions although union membership is most prevalent among local employees particularly clerks, teachers, policemen, fire fighters, and nurses. Two of the largest unions are the AFL-CIO affiliate, the American Federation of State, County, and Municipal Employees (AFSCME), and the Service-Employees International Union (SEIU). Teachers make up nearly one-fifth of all state and local employees and many are represented by NEA, the National Educational Association.

State and local employee unions have grown for a number of reasons. Public employees have followed the lead of other groups such as minorities and women who have organized to protect their rights and promote their interests. The most important reason for the growth of unions is probably economic. For years public employees perceived their pay to be inferior to that of similar workers in the private sector, and for a while this perception was accurate. Between 1975 and 1981 pay gains in the public sector lagged behind those in the private sector by about 8 percent.[25] However, in recent years, whether from the influence of unions or for other reasons, pay has increased by about the same percentage in the two sectors in most states.

Comparing Public and Private Unions

Like their private counterparts, public unions in 36 states organize state and local employees and represent workers in **collective bargaining** with management to try to improve pay and working conditions (see Figure 12.2). Whereas private unions try to get job security for workers, this is not as great a concern for public unions whose workers may be protected through the civil service system.

Public unions face three primary obstacles in their attempts to bargain with management: (1) denial of the right to strike, (2) the problem of "elusive authority," and (3) the ability of governments to resist union pressure. Strikes by federal employees and by almost all state and local employees are illegal. The rationale behind this prohibition is that public workers generally provide essential services; denial of these services causes serious disruptions in the community. Anyone denied the services of police, fire protection, garbage disposal, or school teachers would probably agree with this rationale. Nonetheless, laws against striking are difficult to enforce and illegal strikes often do take place. Workers who strike must ultimately be prosecuted and punished by elected officials. Very few politically sensitive public officials are willing to imprison or fine striking teachers or fire fighters.

Public unions face the problem of "elusive authority." This means it is difficult for public union representatives to work out complex or sensitive agreements with management because "management" often means the legislature or other elected board. In a state or local agency the immediate manager—the agency head—is merely an agent of the legislature or board and has no real authority to bargain with the union.

The third problem for public employee unions is the ability of governments to resist pressure. Unlike private businesses, governments have continuing sources of revenues through taxes and are not pressed to produce profits. Therefore, they can choose to ignore or postpone worker demands or "wait out" strikes. The fact that revenues are raised through taxes adds to government's resistance. Very few elected officials are enthusiastic about granting salary increases to state and local employees if it means calling for tax increases.

However, public unions do possess three important advantages over private unions: more flexibility in management's position, Access to information, and political clout. Just as elected officials may not have the incentive to punish illegal strikers, neither do they always have the incentive of private managers to resist worker demands. Elected mayors who are in office for one or two terms may not have the desire or perseverance to stand up to powerful

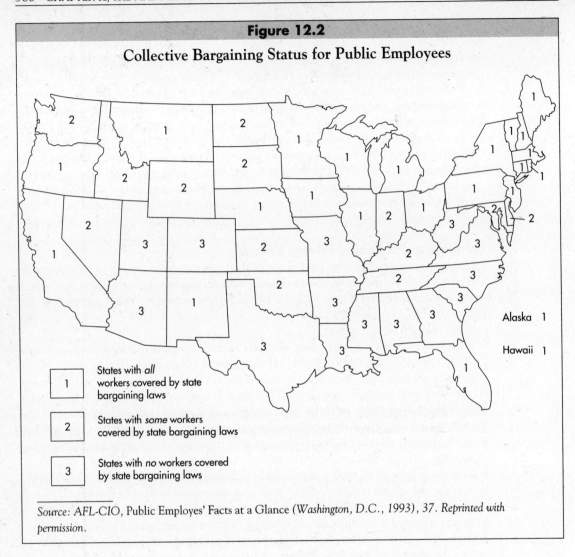

Figure 12.2

Collective Bargaining Status for Public Employees

Alaska 1

Hawaii 1

1	States with *all* workers covered by state bargaining laws
2	States with *some* workers covered by state bargaining laws
3	States with *no* workers covered by state bargaining laws

Source: AFL-CIO, Public Employes' Facts at a Glance (Washington, D.C., 1993), 37. Reprinted with permission.

city unions. They are likely to feel pressure from disgruntled citizens denied police protection or garbage collection because of city strikes, or they may make long-term concessions such as greater pension benefits in lieu of immediate wage increases.

Another advantage for public unions is access to information. Open records laws mean that public employee unions have access to information about budgets that are not always readily available to private unions. This information may give them an advantage in the bargaining process.

Perhaps the most important advantage for public employee unions is their political clout. Although these unions have engaged in lobbying and political action, many have increased this activity in recent years and have become powerful political forces. A good example is New York's Civil Service Employees Association (CSEA). The CSEA represents

250,000 government workers across the state, has its own lobbyist, and is taking an increasing role in the state's elections.

Unions Challenge Merit

State and local employee unions are the object of criticism from several sources. Conservatives argue that public unions are unacceptable because they compromise the sovereignty of democratic government. Why should those who work for democratically elected leaders have an important role in making decisions?

Unions are also the object of criticism from "good government" liberals who claim that they interfere with the concept of merit. First, these critics argue that across-the-board salary increases that unions desire for their members negate the whole idea of giving increases only to those who deserve them. Second, they use the same argument to criticize the union's practice of demanding that seniority (rather than merit) be the basis of promotion and leadership. Finally, they are concerned that unions bring government employees back into the world of partisan politics. Recall that the primary goal of a merit system is to remove those who implement government policy—bureaucrats—from the realm of policymaking.

Union supporters reply that the competition among workers in a merit system lowers worker morale, that seniority is related to merit, and that politics already influences personnel decisions in many so-called merit systems. They also contend that merit is difficult to measure (see Box 12.4). What some might call merit may be simply be favoritism on the part of those who recommend and make promotion decisions. And finally, they argue that without an organization representing them, public employees will not be treated fairly by their employers.

Contracting Out Public Services: Privatization

One of the most significant developments in state and local government in recent years has been the increasing trend toward **privatization**—providing public sector services through private sector contracts.

Contracting with private firms has been practiced by state and local governments for quite some time. States contract with private companies to build highways; the federal government gives contracts to private corporations to build weapons systems. However, in recent years the prevalence and scope of private contracting has increased. Examples of other services carried out under private contract are garbage collection, street repair work, utility billing, vehicle towing and storage, emergency medical service, public hospital management, building and grounds maintenance, and data processing. Some local governments even contract out for police and fire protection and several states are exploring the possibility of privately run prison systems.

Arguments for Privatization

Almost all of the arguments in support of contracting out are couched in terms of classic conservative economic principles. Supporters claim that contracting with private companies shrinks the size of government and reduces the cost of providing public services. Privatization reduces the "natural monopoly" that government enjoys in providing services. Proponents of entrepreneurial government argue that efficiency is enhanced because several private firms, or "suppliers," compete among themselves and with the government to provide the service at the lowest possible cost.

BOX 12.4

PUBLIC UNIONS PUSH FOR COMPARABLE WORTH

Is the job performed by an office secretary as valuable as that performed by a highway repair worker? The job of a nurse as valuable as that of a garbage truck worker? Those who support the concept of comparable worth charge that salaries for many jobs are lower, not because they require less skills, training, or experience, but solely because they are traditionally performed by women.

The concept of comparable worth means that different jobs can be objectively compared to determine their relative value to the employer, and that jobs that are of the same value should be paid equally. Thus comparable worth goes beyond the policy of "equal pay for equal work." It demands equal pay for jobs of "equal value."

In recent years state and local employee unions have taken up the cause of comparable worth. They have pressured state and local governments to conduct evaluations of different jobs to determine if salaries should be boosted in job classes that are traditionally female. Unions have made some progress at the bargaining table. In 1986, American Federation of State County Municipal Employees (AFSCME) and the city of Chicago reached a $1.2 million agreement to raise salaries in about 60 job classes. Several states and municipalities, including Minnesota, Wisconsin, Iowa, New Jersey, and the city of Los Angeles, have comparable pay plans in place as the result of legislation or collective bargaining. Progress has been made in court as well. The best-known comparable worth case, involving state workers in Washington and the AFSCME, ended in 1985 with an out-of-court settlement worth an estimated $482 million. Pay raises for 34,000 employees in female-dominated jobs are being phased in over a period of six years.

Although the implementation of comparable worth has been primarily limited to the public sector, it faces vigorous opposition from business groups. These groups fear the concept, and its accompanying costs, will filter into the private sector. Opposition also comes from those who resent the threat of higher taxes to pay for higher government wages. All of these opponents argue that it is impossible to make objective comparisons among jobs that are not the same.

The issue of comparable worth is a controversial one—a political hot potato that is likely to be debated in state and local government for quite some time.

The results of some studies provide impressive support for privatization. One study of private versus public garbage collection found that private service cost about 30 percent less than public service, and was just as effective.[26] Another study looked at eight different services that were contracted out in the five-county Los Angeles area: street cleaning, janitorial services, residential garbage collection, payroll, traffic-signal maintenance, turf maintenance, and street-tree maintenance. For all of the services except payroll, public sector expenses were higher ranging from 37 percent more for tree trimming to 96 percent more for street maintenance.[27]

Arguments Against Privatization

Critics claim the most serious problem of contracting out is the potential loss of control that may occur as government gives more and more responsibility to the private sector. Will a private garbage collection firm be as responsive to citizens who complain about inadequate service as a municipal agency? Does a state really want to surrender authority over its prison system to a private company? Too much privatization leads to a loss of government responsibility, and consequently, a loss of citizen control.

There are other concerns. Public unions resist privatization because of the threat it poses to public workers, and they have cause to be worried. The loss of jobs by government workers who are displaced by private contractors is sometimes unavoidable. A related question is the effect that privatization has on minorities and affirmative action. Government employment has been an especially valuable means of progress for minorities. There is no guarantee that this progress will continue when jobs are shifted from the public to the private sector.

Some critics even question the efficiency argument of those who support an expanded role for the private sector. Competition is not always present; a few large firms may dominate. The most obvious example of this is the enormous waste and inefficiency that we have witnessed by defense contractors. Moreover, critics maintain that for every story lauding the efficiency of private enterprise, there is an example of inefficiency, waste, and corruption. One example is New York's Human Resources Administration who cancelled several contracts for custodial and printing services because of large cost overruns. What happens, continue critics, when private firms fail to live up to their contracts? Governments may be left with serious disruptions of service because of poor performance by private firms or because these firms face bankruptcy after bidding too low in order to win contracts.

State and local governments should approach privatization with caution. There are situations when contracting out will reduce cost and increase efficiency. It can also bring fresh ideas and approaches into established programs. The possibility of contracting out may even stimulate public employees to perform better. But governments should be aware of its limitations and potential problems.

Openness in Government

Bureaucracies by their very nature are undemocratic. Bureaucrats are supposed to follow rules, that is, "go by the book" without attention to the individual preferences of their clients. Most employees in a government agency are not elected and some are not always concerned about being responsive to prevailing political attitudes. They prefer to make decisions based on their technical expertise and out of the interfering and uninformed view of the general public. When mismanagement or abuse of discretionary authority does occur in a public agency, there is a tendency for bureaucrats to close ranks and protect themselves against the prying eyes of the press and public. Although bureaucrats are supposed to be responsive to elected leaders, we have already seen that many civil service or career bureaucrats are insulated from real control by elected officials.

In the last few years there has been persistent pressure by organized citizen groups such as Common Cause to open up government decision making and make it more accessible to the general public. Reforms began at the federal level and have gradually spread to the states. These changes have made both state and local legislatures and executive agencies

Bureaucrats are almost always "experts" who perform specialized services. Here a doctor working in a city lab tests supplies purchased by New York City.

more accessible to the average citizen, and they have also made it easier to detect misman-agement or abuse in public agencies. The four most important reforms are open meetings or sunshine laws, open records laws, increased protection for whistle-blowers, and citizen par-ticipation requirements.

Sunshine laws require that public bodies—legislative committees, city councils, state or local agencies and other similar bodies—open all meetings to the public except in special circumstances that are specified by law. Examples of these special circumstances might be sensitive personnel questions or a discussion of legal strategies involved in a lawsuit. In such circumstances the board or agency may meet in privately in "executive session." Although all states have adopted open meetings laws, some are more rigorous than others. Most states require advance notice of meetings, and many require that detailed minutes of the meetings be made available to the public.

Sunshine laws allow the public to participate in the decision-making process of legislative committee members and public bureaucrats. Open meetings requirements mean that the often critical decisions made by executive agencies are open for comment and scrutiny. For example, a state public utility commission that decides on a request for a multimillion dollar rate increase must face the rate-paying public in its deliberations.

There is growing concern, however, that having meetings open to the public is not such a good idea. Often those who attend public meeting are special interest groups. It is much harder for a legislator or bureaucrat to resist the pressure from these groups when they are present and breathing down his or her neck. Other factors have lessened the enthusiasm for open meetings. Meeting in private saves time; it also allows public figures the chance to ask "dumb questions" and not be embarrassed. Most important many claim that it is easier to compromise and devise solutions to difficult and politically sensitive problems without the watchful and critical eye of the press or special interest groups. Despite these problems, sunshine laws are alive and well in state and local governments.

Open records laws allow access to most of the records and information held by public agencies. States generally exempt certain records from public scrutiny. For example, access to the grades of an individual attending a state college is generally denied on the basis that it violates individual privacy. Although states do vary in the extent they encourage and enforce freedom of information, in recent years most states have strengthened their open records laws.

Whistle-blowers are individual bureaucrats who open up to public view the abuses or mismanagement of their agencies. They refuse to go along with or perpetuate policies they feel are damaging to the public and lay aside ambitions for promotion and relations with colleagues to challenge the status quo. Indeed, in the past whistle-blowers were almost always denied promotions within their agencies or were even fired (see Box 12.5).

BOX 12.5

A WHISTLE-BLOWER SPEAKS UP

Irwin Levin is an example of a determined individual who bucked the system. Levin, of New York City, New York, was a Senior Supervisor in the Brooklyn field office of Special Services for Children. Levin complained persistently to his superiors about the negligence, incompetence and gross errors of judgment by overloaded or inexperienced welfare workers assigned to cases of suspected child abuse. He discovered 11 children had died who could have been saved had the city made meaningful changes in the system. When no one responded, Levin went to the press with confidential files. For his actions he was fined, suspended without pay for four months, demoted and transferred.

After several years Levin was finally vindicated, but the problem of ineffective social services remains.

Source: The Giraffe Gazette, vol. 3, no. 4 (Summer, 1987)

In 1978 the federal Civil Service Reform Act strengthened protections for whistle-blowers and many states followed suit. However, whistleblowers are far from invulnerable. Even if they receive legal vindication, they almost always continue to be ostracized by their colleagues.

Citizen participation procedures encourage individuals to get involved in public decision making. These procedures have been established through local ordinance, state law, and through requirements or "strings" in federal grant-in-aid programs to state and local governments. State and local agencies are being advised by citizen advisory committees; some state governments and almost all local governments are holding public hearings over proposed budgets and other nonfiscal matters such as zoning changes. Some cities and counties, especially those over 100,000 in population, are using citizen surveys to provide representative samples of citizen views. Forty-eight states have administrative procedures acts which govern rule-making by administrative agencies and allow for citizen input into the rule-making process.

Some observers note the disadvantages that accompany the proliferation of citizen participation procedures. They are time consuming and costly. Even more important, the citizens who are drawn to the citizen participation processes are not truly representative of the general public, they tend to represent special interest groups. Some public officials feel that the procedures are merely "pro forma," that is, they exist to fulfill a desire for more citizen involvement but don't really work. Despite these criticisms, it is still true that democracies are *supposed* to be characterized by a full and free interchange of information between the people and their elected representatives and appointed administrators. Expanding citizen participation procedures allows us to come closer to this ideal.

Legislative Control of the Bureaucracy

State and local legislatures are supposed to oversee their respective bureaucracies to make sure that policy is implemented the way the legislatures intended. This legislative **oversight** has become more important as legislatures delegate more authority to executive agencies. As we discussed earlier in this chapter, state legislatures often appoint auditors to monitor the spending of administrative agencies. In recent years state legislatures have devised other legal tools to help them control expanding bureaucracies. Here we discuss two of the most important tools: sunset laws and the legislative veto.

Sunset Legislation

Pioneered by Colorado in 1976, Sunset laws specify that agencies be "sunsetted," that is, terminated unless the legislature passes a law to recreate them. A typical sunset process might work like this. The legislature would review the state insurance board, the state agency charged with regulating the state's insurance industry. After an extensive review, the legislature would pass a bill recreating the state insurance board perhaps with some changes. If for some reason the legislature failed to enact a law recreating the board it would cease to exist. After an established period, usually 10 or 12 years, the state insurance board would come up for "sunset review" again. The innovative part of this whole process is that, for the first time, it is the responsibility of the agency to prove that there is a need for its existence.

Thirty-six states and some municipalities initially adopted sunset laws. The typical sunset process has the legislature examine a specific number of agencies, usually 20 to 30—during a legislative session. Some states have "comprehensive" sunset laws meaning that all or almost all state agencies are reviewed. Some states restrict sunset review only to regulatory agencies.

When it was first instituted, sunset held out the promise of shrinking government; unnecessary or wasteful agencies would be allowed to die. However, most studies have found that sunset rarely results in the abolition of agencies. Hence some states have suspended or repealed their sunset laws. Sunset's supporters point out that expectations that it would significantly shrink the size of government were unrealistic. In most cases, it tends to result in moderate changes in the operating procedures of agencies and, in some cases, improved performance.[28]

Legislative Veto

As state legislatures delegate more and more authority to the bureaucracy to make rules and interpret statutes, steps have been taken by some legislatures toward greater review of these rules. Twenty-nine states have established the legislative veto which means that the legislature—often a legislative committee—has the authority to veto rules that are not reasonable or do not meet the original intent of the legislature. The legislative veto was also exercised by the U. S. Congress until 1983 when the Supreme Court declared it unconstitutional. The Supreme Court ruling put some doubt on the future of the often controversial use of the legislative veto in the states.

Not surprisingly the legislative veto tends to be used in states with full time legislatures that have the time and staff resources to carefully review actions by state agencies. Proponents of the legislative veto argue that it provides a check on bureaucratic excesses and enables the legislature to ensure that agency regulations are consistent with legislative statutes. Critics charge that it violates the principle of separation of powers and serves as a tool for powerful special interests who wish to block controversial programs.[29]

CONCLUSION

The first and oldest job of the executive branch is to implement and enforce policies made by legislatures and chief executives. The hands-on job of implementing policy is performed by bureaucrats that work in executive agencies, bureaus, commissions, or boards. The size and scope of these state and local bureaucracies are expanding in response to the growing demands on government in recent years.

In addition to implementing laws and policies, executive agencies are given discretionary authority by legislatures to design rules and regulations. These rules act as guidelines laying out the specific details necessary to put policies into effect. Agencies also adjudicate disputes involving their own rules, that is, they decide initially if their own rules are reasonable. Appeals to a court are possible, but generally are permitted only after one has exhausted the administrative review process.

Bureaucracy is often the object of criticism. The criticism comes not so much because bureaucrats are stupid or lazy, but because they are judged by the different and often conflicting standards of effectiveness and responsiveness. Although bureaucrats may function with competence and effectiveness, they may not always be sensitive and responsive to the demands of the public or to the elected officials that represent the public.

To achieve responsiveness and accountability to elected officials, reformers feel that governors should be given the power to appoint top executives. These executives, acting as intermediaries between the governor and career bureaucrats, will work to achieve the policy goals of the governor. Gubernatorial appointment, however, provides no guarantee that governors will control state bureaucracies. Staggered terms for appointees and a permanent civil service may discourage the bureaucracy's responsiveness to the policies and programs of the governor.

The establishment of civil service systems in the states was influenced by the institution of a merit system at the federal level. Today about three-fourths of the states have comprehensive merit systems and the rest have limited coverage. Because merit systems help to ensure that public workers are employed on the basis of their qualifications and expertise, these systems encourage a more professional bureaucracy. On the other hand, government bureaucrats protected by tenure are not likely to be as responsive to democratically elected representatives.

Recent surveys indicate that state administrators are becoming younger, more educated, and a bit more representative of women and minorities although the latter still hold only a small percentage of top state administrative jobs.

In recent years there have been a number of reforms and other developments that are designed to make state and local bureaucracies more effective and responsive. Many of these reforms have been proposed in the name of "entrepreneurial government." This notion infuses the operations of public bureaucracy with practices common to business entrepreneurs: competition to improve bureaucratic efficiency, treating employees (bureaucrats) like owners of their programs, and taking risks to increase productivity. Although critics charge that entrepreneurial practices may not be appropriate for public agencies, attempts to "reinvent" government in the spirit of entrepreneurism have been very popular in recent times.

Public employees have been organizing and joining unions in increasing numbers in response to what they perceive as inferior pay to similar employment in the private sector. While public unions lack the legal right to strike in most states, they do possess advantages. Among the most important advantage is their increasing political clout. However, unions face challenges from those who see them as a threat to the concept of merit. Their clout is also being undermined by the increasing tendency for state and local governments to contract out services to private firms.

Pressure from Common Cause and other "good government" groups has resulted in more openess in government. Public bodies, including state and local agencies, are subject to open meetings and open records laws that allow the press and the average citizen access to information. Some are concerned, however, that too much openness may constrain the decision-making process or allow undue influence by special interests.

Legislatures have strengthened their oversight function and have instituted innovations such as sunset legislation. Sunset laws force legislatures to review administrative agencies on a periodic basis. Legislative review is necessary because agencies will automatically go out of existence unless recreated by legislative statute. State legislatures also employ the legislative veto to review agency rules and guidelines although the future of the legislative veto has been put into question by the U. S. Supreme Court's ruling that it is unconstitutional at the federal level.

STUDY OBJECTIVES

1. Explain why conflicting standards of performance—effectiveness and responsiveness—leads to problems for bureaucrats.
2. Identify the three functions of executive branch agencies and boards.
3. Describe two different roles of lieutenant governors. Describe two trends that make lieutenant governors influential executive actors.
4. Define the term civil service. Identify advantages and disadvantages of a civil service system.
5. Identify four goals of reorganization the states have made substantial progress in meeting.
6. Define entrepreneurial government. Identify one criticism of entrepreneurial government.
7. Identify two major budget reforms.
8. Identify three reasons why "good government" liberals argue that unions challenge the concept of merit. Describe the responses union supporters offer to their critics.
9. Define the term privatization. Identify one argument of those who support privatization and one major concern of those who view it skeptically.
10. Identify the four most important reforms providing for openess in government.
11. Identify the most innovative part of a sunset law.

GLOSSARY

Auditing   The process of examining a state or local government agency's expenditures to see if they are legal and accurate.

Bureaucratic discretion   The delegation of authority given to administrative agencies by legislatures. Agencies use this authority to establish legally binding rules or "regulations."

Capture   A regulatory agency comes to be controlled by the industry or interest that the agency is supposed to regulate.

Collective bargaining   Negotiation on the terms and conditions of employment between an employer and a union representing the employees.

Comparable worth   A demand made by women's groups in recent years, means that different jobs can be objectively compared to determine their relative value to the employer; jobs that are of the same value should be rewarded equally.

Effectiveness   A standard applied to bureaucracy, means the degree to which an administrator's decisions are more likely than alternative choices to bring about the desired outcomes.

Entrepreneurial government   The notion that government bureaucracy should be more flexible and productive; like business, public bureaucracy should pursue its goals in a competitive environment, putting customers (or clients) first.

Fiscal year   Designates the normal yearly cycle of a budget year *not* a calender year.

Incremental budgeting   The process of proposing budgets based upon figures in last year's budget plus a little more.

Legislative veto   The legislature—often a legislative committee—has the authority to strike down agency rules that do not meet the original intent of the legislature.

Merit system   The system of hiring government employees based on their qualifications; employment is based on merit rather than political connections or patronage.

Mission-driven budget system   The abolition of line items in a public budget to allow managers more flexibility to spend the agency's money.

Open records laws   Allow citizen access to most of the records and information held by public agencies.

Oversight   The process conducted to make sure that administrative agencies implement policies the way the legislature intended.

Performance review   A highly visible comprehensive review of bureaucratic operations to identify areas of waste, inefficiency, and overlapping services.

Planning-Programming-Budgeting System (PPBS)   The budget reform that emphasizes the overall goals of agencies rather than year to year spending items.

Plural Executive   The chief executive officials and department heads are elected, making them independent of control by the chief executive.

Privatization   The process of providing public sector services through private sector contracts.

Quasi-judicial powers   The power of administrative agencies to judge cases involving agency rules or "regulations."

Quasi-legislative powers   The authority of the bureaucracy to make rules or "regulations" that have the force of law or legislation.

Reorganization   Reshaping, usually through executive order, how departments, agencies, boards, and commissions are organized.

Responsiveness   A standard applied to bureaucracy, means the extent to which decisions by bureaucrats reflect the preferences of the community or the officeholders authorized to speak for the public.

Revolving door syndrome   The process in which bureaucrats come from industry to regulatory board and back to industry. The syndrome is one of the reasons that agencies are "captured" by the industries they regulate.

Sunset laws   A form of oversight, specify that agencies be "sunsetted," that is, terminated unless the legislature passes a law to recreate them.

Tenure   The right to hold a position or office free from arbitrary dismissal. Public employees in the civil service and teachers achieve tenure after serving a probationary period.

Whistle-blower   An individual who exposes to public view the abuses or mismanagement in his or her own agency.

Zero-based budgeting   A budget reform that has agencies justify every element of their budget, every year. In reality, agencies generally will start with 90 percent of their budgets rather than a zero amount.

ENDNOTES

1. Francis E. Rourke, *Bureaucracy, Politics, and Public Policy*, 3rd ed. (Boston: Little, Brown & Co., 1984), 6.

2. Ibid.

3. Gary C. Bryner, *Bureaucratic Discretion: Law and Policy in Federal Regulatory Agencies* (New York: Pergamon Press, 1987), 1.

4. The "classic" characteristics of bureaucracy are often taken from Max Weber, see H. H. Gerth and C. Wright Mills, trans., *From Max Weber: Essays on Sociology* (New York: Oxford University Press, 1946), pp. 196–239.

5. Richard C. Elling, "State Bureaucracies," in *Politics in the American States: A Comparative Analysis*, 4th ed., edited by Virginia Gray, Herbert Jacob, and Kenneth N. Vines (Boston: Little, Brown & Co., 1983), 250.

6. ACIR, *The Question of State Government Capability* (Washington D.C.: Advisory Commission on Intergovernmental Relations, 1985), 149.

7. Arthur English and John J. Carroll, "The Lieutenant Governor: New Directions for a Neglected Office?" Paper delivered at the 1988 meeting of the Southern Political Science Association, November 3, 1988, p. 2.

8. Lt. Gov. Myron E. Leavitt of Nevada, *U. S. News and World Report* (November 5, 1979), 53–54. Taken from Larry Sabato, *Goodbye to Good-Time Charlie: The American Governorship Transformed*, 2d ed. (Washington, D.C.: Congressinal Quarterly Press, 1983), 74.

9. Laura M. Zaremba, "Governor and Lieutenant Governor on Same Ballot," *Comparative State Politics* 15 (February 1994): 1.

10. Thad L. Beyle and Nelson C. Dometrius, "Governors and Lieutenant Governors," in *Being Governor: The View from the Office*, edited by Thad L. Beyle and Lynn R. Muchmore (Durham N.C.: Duke University Press, 1983), 148.

11. English and Carroll, "The Lieutenant Governor: New Directions," p. 10.

12. Ibid., p. 8.

13. Deil S. Wright, Jae-Won Woo, and Jennifer Cohen, "The Evolving Profile of State Administration," *Journal of State Government* (January/March, 1991), 30–38.

14. Ibid.

15. Jonathan Walters, "How Not to Reform Civil Service," *Governing* (November, 1992), 30.

16. ACIR, *The Question of State Government Capability*, p. 144.

17. Thomas H. Clapper and Thad L. Beyle, "Organizing State Government to Be Managed," in *State Government: Congressional Quarterly's Guide to Current Issues and Activities, 1987–88*, edited by Thad L. Beyle (Washington, D.C.: Congressional Quarterly, Inc., 1987), 125. This article also appeared in the *Comparative State Politics Newsletter*, August 1986, p. 13.

18. A. E. Buck, *The Reorganization of State Governments in the United States* (New York: Columbia University Press, 1938), 14.

19. ACIR, *The Question of State Government Capability*, pp. 147–49.

20. Thad L. Beyle, "The Executive Branch: Organization and Issues, 1992–93," *Book of the States* (Lexington, KY: Council of State Governments, 1994), 66.

21. ACIR, The *Question of State Government Capability*, pp. 148–49.

22. David Osborne and Ted Gaebler, *Reinventing Government: How the Entrepreneurial Spirit is Transforming the Public Sector* (Reading, MA: Addison-Wesley, 1992).

23. Ibid, p. 2.

24. Ibid., pp. 117–119.

25. Bureau of Labor Statistics, Richard E. Schumann, "State and Local Government Pay Increases Outpace Five-year Rise in Private Industry," *Monthly Labor Review* 110 (February, 1987): 18–20.

26. E. S. Savas, *Privatizing the Public Sector: How to Shrink Government* (Chatham, NJ: Chatham House, 1982), 93.

27. Barbara J. Stevens, ed., *Delivering Municipal Services Efficiently: A Comparison of Municipal and Private Service Delivery—Summary* (Washington, D.C.: U.S. Department of Housing and Urban Development, June, 1984).

28. See Cynthia Slaughter (now Opheim), "Sunset and Occupational Regulation: A Case Study," *Public Administration Review* 46 (May-June, 1986): 241–245; Landon Curry, Cynthia Opheim, and Patricia Shields, "Sunset as Oversight: Establishing Realistic Objectives," *American Review of Public Administration* 24 (September 1994): 253–268.

29. David C. Nice, "Sunset Laws and Legislative Vetoes in the States," *State Government* 58 (Spring, 1985): 27–52.

13

The Pursuit of Justice and Order: Law and the Courts

Stephanie Roper was kidnapped, raped, and murdered in 1982. Her attackers were arrested, tried, and convicted of first-degree rape and first-degree murder, but received a sentence which permitted the possibility of parole in eleven years and seven months. Her parents, shocked by potentially short sentences and court procedures that permitted the defendant's family to plead for mercy but denied the Ropers' request to read a victim-impact statement, began a movement to champion victims' rights.

The Ropers' approach has been twofold: on one hand they have organized legislative efforts producing 38 laws and a victims' rights constitutional amendment on the ballot in 1994. At the same time, they have created a foundation providing direct therapeutic support to crime victims and their families. Families and individuals who have been victims, directly or vicariously, can attend meetings, find counseling, and find solace in the testimony and encouragement of others who have survived difficult experiences. The Ropers are people who, with vision and courage, have changed their communities for the better. By channeling their own pain into healing experiences for others, as so often happens, Roberta and Vince Roper report that they healed themselves.

The central goal of government in a liberal democracy is justice. Justice must be the outcome of its legal processes if a government is to retain its legitimacy. Creating legal institutions whose outcomes are seen as legitimate is necessary in any democracy. This chapter will focus on law, the means by which justice is achieved, and examine some of the institutions that undertake to create and dispense justice in the process of administering the law. A second emphasis will be the theme of this book: Can the court system be reinvented and transformed by the entrepreneurial spirit?

Justice is commonly thought to be the goal of the legal process in which law is created, interpreted, and enforced. If everyone agreed on what constitutes a just outcome of that legal process, the enforcement of law would be a much easier task indeed. The good news is that there is a considerable amount of agreement, without which we could not survive as a nation-state. The sobering news is that our citizens will never agree on everything. In part, this simply reflects the human condition. But it also reminds us that we are one of the most diverse societies on the face of the earth, certainly the most heterogeneous liberal-democ-racy to last 200 years on this planet.

The following pages will attempt to demonstrate how we survive as a diverse people by examining (1) the different kinds of law used to promote order and justice; (2) the structure of the state and local court systems; (3) the role of lawyers and bar associations; and (4) the methods for selecting and removing judges.

LAW AND JUSTICE

Law and justice are not synonymous. Justice involves acting in terms of values and ideals. Law involves acting in terms of rules and procedures. Justice may be thought of as fair treat-ment, but justice is not an inevitable consequence of law. One mark of civilized people is their resolve to make justice an outcome of their legal system.

Law involves a process for making rules and pursuing justice. Since justice is best pur-sued calmly and systematically, a major feature of any legal system is the maintenance of or-der. Sometimes law represents a compromise between competing interests, but at other times law supports some interests at the expense of others.[1] Therefore, law originates from both consensus and conflict, depending on the issue and the times. In a liberal democracy, we can use political resources to influence lawmaking, law enforcement, and the interpreta-tion of law.

Our legal system is based upon **the rule of law**. This means that legal questions or de-bates or conflicts refer at some point to a written document and are resolved in a formal process. Citizens may disagree about what is meant by that written document, but their dis-agreements are resolved in a formal process which occurs in a court of law, and all sides agree, more or less, to abide by the decision. The rule of law is a major ingredient in the pur-suit of justice in civilized society.

LAW IN A FEDERAL SYSTEM

The federal Constitution is the supreme law of the land, and although states also have constitutions, the states may not make laws in violation of the federal Constitution. If states do so, and if the laws are challenged, state laws will be struck down as unconstitutional.

Two doctrines mesh state and federal law. Both derive from the federal Constitution. The first, **the full faith and credit clause** of the Constitution, applies to civil matters. It re-quires that each state recognize contracts made in other states. Thus a will made in Oregon will be valid in Florida, and a contract signed in Arizona must be honored in New York. The second, **the doctrine of incorporation** applies the federal Bill of Rights to the states by using the due process clause of the Fourteenth Amendment. As a result of the application of this doctrine, no person may be deprived of the rights guaranteed in the Bill of Rights with-out due process of law.

One example of the doctrine of incorporation is the application of most of the rights contained in the first ten amendments of the federal constitution—the Bill of Rights—to state as well as federal courts. Those rights, called **civil liberties**, are promises that the state will not arbitrarily and capriciously abridge the freedom of individuals. Civil liberties promise that individuals cannot be imprisoned by a unjust government, like that of the

British in the colonies prior to our Revolutionary War. In return, the state demands that citizens obey its laws.

Among the civil liberties are those deemed very important by the citizens of the United States: (1) the right to assemble; (2) the right of free speech; (3) the right to be free from cruel and unusual punishment, (4) the right to be free from unreasonable search and seizure, (5) the right to be free from self incrimination; and (6) the right not to be deprived of life or liberty without due process of law.

At times, judges have decided that a *practice* at the state level is in violation of the federal Constitution, even though it has been common in state courts for some period of time. For instance, the rule that illegally gathered evidence could not be used in a criminal trial, known as the exclusionary rule, was the law only in federal courts. However, in a 1960 ruling, **Mapp v. Ohio,**[2] the Supreme Court decreed that the practice of admitting illegally obtained evidence in state criminal trials was a violation of the due process clause of the Fourteenth Amendment to the Constitution. As a result of this ruling, the exclusionary rule was incorporated into the laws of all states.

THE FORMS OF LAW

The American legal system contains four major categories of law, all of which have evolved in light of the federal Constitution and have developed in response to particular demands of a modern democracy (Table 13.1). The first, **common law** is based on the system of law that originated in medieval England. Common law is created when judges apply a general principle, often found in the precedents in other cases, to situations not fully covered by statute law. *Stare decisis*[3] is the judicial practice of applying a previously used legal principle to a set of facts to settle a legal dispute. **Equity law**, the second of the four categories of law, is also judge-made law and arises from the attempt to prevent a wrong which cannot be remedied by damages.[4] A request for equity is a request for fairness; it is often a request that some action be prevented on the grounds that to permit the action would make it impossible to achieve equity at a later date.

Statutory law is law written and enacted by a legislature. When they conflict, statutory overrides common law, although many statutes are based on common law. All criminal law is statutory law.

Administrative law refers to the statutes, regulations, and orders that govern public agencies. State legislatures and local governing boards often create administrative agencies to enforce their legislative intentions; administrative law, also created by legislatures, to govern these agencies, discourages abuse by employees of public agencies.

Another important distinction that organizes our thinking about law is the dichotomy between civil and criminal law. **Criminal law** is made up of codes that prohibit (and occasionally require) certain behaviors. Criminal laws contain sanctions or punishments to be applied if the law is violated. The sanctions may be fines, confinement, or execution.

Criminal law is statute law; there are no common law crimes. Criminal law is prosecuted by local, state, and federal governments; the government or state is the complainant and the accused person becomes the defendant. The majority of criminal law cases are handled by state courts.

Criminal law can be divided into two categories, felonies and misdemeanors. The exact qualities of a felony vary from state to state, but in general felonies are crimes punishable by death or more than a year in prison. Examples of felonies are murder, rape, robbery, and arson. Misdemeanors are all other crimes and are considered to be less serious than felonies. Penalties usually range from fines to jail terms of less than a year. Examples of misdemeanors are traffic violations, petty theft, and disorderly conduct.[5]

Civil law includes every legal action other than criminal proceedings. Examples of civil law are contract law which applies to the nature of agreements between individuals or corporations; domestic or family law which applies to husband, wife, and child relationships; and tort law which covers the civil wrongs, not based upon contracts, allegedly done by one or more citizens against another. An example of an action brought under domestic law

Table 13.1

THE FORMS OF LAW

Type of Law	Definition	How Made	Application	Advantages/ Disadvantages
COMMON LAW	Body of law resulting from and based upon judicial decisions.	Created by judges using *stare decisis*	Only in civil law situations.	Flexible, practical. Applies old law to new situations. No readily available compendium of rulings.
EQUITY LAW	Evolved from equity courts of England. Involved an appeal to the king to right an injustice in common law.	Created by judges to prevent an intermediate wrong or provide relief from ongoing wrong.	Only in civil law situations.	Flexible. Some states have separate equity courts; others do not.
STATUTORY LAW	It is law written as statute by legislators.	Written and enacted by legislatures interpreted by judges.	In criminal or civil law situations.	Overrides common law when it conflicts with it. Difficulty in writing laws which cover all situations.
ADMINISTRATIVE LAW	It is a form of statutory law that contains specific statutes, orders, and regulations governing public agencies.	Legislative: written and enacted by legislatures, interpreted by Supreme Court Justices.	In criminal or civil law situations.	Gives the public some control over abuse by public officials whose behavior can be supervised and regulated. Considered only by the Supreme Court.

would be divorce, the request for dissolution of a marriage; an example of an action brought under tort law would be libel,[6] the accusation that an individual was maliciously defamed in print by another.

Although the two categories of civil and criminal law are mutually exclusive, a specific behavior can be penalized under both systems. For example, rape is a criminal offense, and a rapist may be convicted in a criminal court. A woman who has been raped can also bring a civil suit against the rapist in order to recover damages. Motor vehicle theft is also a criminal offense, but the person whose car has been stolen could file a civil suit against the thief to recover damages.

THE JUDICIARY: COURTS AND CASES

Despite complaints about judicial activism, the American judiciary is a set of passive institutions. Courts and judges do not initiate legal action, nor do they initiate legislation. Rather, they must wait for citizens or agents of the state to bring business to them.

The method by which justice is sought in the American court system is called the **adversarial system** of justice or adversarial process. In the ideal, it assumes that in the contest between two well-prepared adversaries, the plaintiff and defendant, the truth will emerge. Each case is a dispute to be settled in a court of law following a set of rules, with each side having certain rights and duties. Each side is expected to present its best case; the hope is that as a result of this proceeding, the truth will emerge and justice will be achieved.

The business of judges and courts can be classified in terms of two dichotomies: (1)civil and criminal cases and (2)original and appellate jurisdictions. Some courts deal with all four categories and some specialize. Each category has a vocabulary and procedures that distinguish it from others. However, all four employ the adversarial ideal in the search for justice.

Civil Cases

Civil cases begin when an attorney files a complaint on behalf of the **plaintiff**, against a respondent. The plaintiff is the complaining party and may also be known as the petitioner or the appellant. The **respondent** is also known as the appellee or defendant. To initiate a civil case, the attorney for the plaintiff must accomplish three things: (1)choose the appropriate court, (2)have the complainant sign a **summons** or complaint against the respondent that gives notice requiring the respondent to appear in court to answer charges, and (3) explain the charges to the court and request a remedy.

It is sometimes necessary early in the proceedings to issue a **subpoena** to compel the presence of the respondent. Should the respondent fail to appear, the court may hold that person in contempt of court and levy additional penalties. A **subpoena** *duces tecum* requires the respondent to bring something, usually records or other possessions, to the court. Both forms of subpoena must always be served in person.

When the defendant appears in court, he or she must enter a plea. The defendant may admit the truth of the complaint, or the defendant may deny the complaint and begin the process of defense. Unless the defendant is able to repudiate the jurisdiction of the court or disallow the legality of the complaint, or unless the state or plaintiff withdraws the charge, the case will proceed.

Discovery, the next step in civil cases, takes place outside the courtroom. Discovery is the formal and informal exchange of information between the sides in the law suit. When the discovery occurs in a formal setting, it is called a **deposition**, where the questions and answers are officially and accurately recorded in sworn testimony. Written questions, called **interrogatories**, may also be submitted with a request for written answers during discovery.

The pretrial stage follows discovery. Because going to trial is a time-consuming and financially draining operation for participants, including the court, procedures have developed to reduce its likelihood. Many judges require pretrial hearings or conferences between the two parties in hopes that their differences can be settled prior to trial. Arbitration between the two parties may also be used. Many courts require arbitration in some situations for at least two reasons. First, it helps to reduce the civil caseload and second, there may be other paths to justice than one which results in a winner and a loser.[7] If no decision can be reached through pretrial hearings or arbitration, the case will go to trial.

During the trial, both sides present their case in its best light. In civil cases, a **preponderance of evidence**, the superior weight or quality of evidence, is the principle by which verdicts are decided.[8] Common law required a petty trial jury of twelve persons, and a verdict required a unanimous decision. Today some civil cases are decided by a judge and verdicts do not have to be unanimous, but they must be more than a simple majority. In the interest of efficiency, juries now can number as few as six members.

The verdict or finding in civil cases involves decisions on the points raised by the plaintiff and, if appropriate, an assessment of damages and court costs. A plaintiff may win the case but receive little or no damages and even have to pay all or part of the court costs in addition to attorney's fees.

We have an adversarial system of law and justice in the United States. Each case is a dispute to be settled in a court of law following a set of rules, with each side having certain rights and duties. Each side is expected to present its best case; the hope is that as a result of this proceeding, the truth will emerge and justice will be achieved.

Criminal Cases

Criminal cases are brought to the court's attention when the state attempts to charge an individual with a crime. Charges may be brought in two ways: (1) by **indictment** or **true bill**,[9] a charge drawn up by a prosecutor and brought by a **grand jury**, a group of approximately 12 to 23 individuals chosen by the prosecutor, and (2) by a **bill of information**, an accusation made under oath by a prosecuting attorney before a court.[10] All states use grand juries, and most states permit a bill of information to bring charges in some, if not all, criminal cases.

The next step is the same in both civil and criminal cases: the defendant must indicate a plea in the case. In a criminal case, the plea is entered at the **arraignment** where the defendant hears the charges against him or her and enters a plea of guilty or not guilty. Bail may also be set, and the defendant may be freed by paying a certain amount of money to guarantee his or her appearance at the trial.

If "not guilty" is the plea entered, the process of defense begins. The defendant may try to deny the court's jurisdiction or the legality of the complaint in order to get the state to drop the charge.

The pretrial stage comes next. In criminal cases, a common feature of the pretrial stage is **plea bargaining**. Plea bargaining is a process in which the prosecutor and the defendant, through the defense attorney, negotiate the punishment to be assigned in return for a guilty plea.

Plea bargaining may be thought of as operating under two different models: (1) the consensus model and (2) the concessions model.[11] In the consensus model, the most commonly used process, prosecutors, defense attorneys, and judges can be thought of as the courtroom workgroup sharing agreements about the "worth" of certain kinds of cases.[12] Certain cases and charges have a standard worth, "a going rate." Cases involving serious crimes committed by defendants with prior records are worth more than others and typically result in a plea of guilty with a more severe penalty.

The second model, the concessions model, operates when the worth of a case is unclear because the case is not routine. The defendant may have information with which to bargain in order to gain concessions from the prosecution. The sides "haggle" with one another, each side getting and giving concessions in the process of arriving at the plea. The defendant's attorney communicates the outcome of the bargaining process to the defendant, and they decide whether to plead guilty or to go to trial. If the defendant is unwilling to plead guilty, the case will be taken to trial.

Plea bargaining is advantageous to prosecutors, defense attorneys, and defendants since it eliminates the cost and uncertainty of a trial.[13] It is frequently encouraged by judges as well, though often in covert ways. Former judge Abraham Blumberg reports that some judges help cooperating defense attorneys by arranging a "slow plea of guilty," which is a brief "mock" trial presided over by the judge for the benefit of an attorney whose clients insist upon demonstrating their innocence in a trial.[14] Cooperating attorneys may also earn favorable sentences for their clients from judges in return for guilty pleas and the circumvention of trial.

In criminal cases, the most common disposition of a felony arrest which is not rejected or dismissed is a guilty plea, not a trial. Data gathered from a number of urban courts in 1987 show that approximately 54 percent of all felony arrests ended in guilty pleas, while only three percent ended in trials; 43 percent of felony arrests ended in dismissal or rejection of the indictment. Guilty pleas outnumber trials by a margin of 18 to 1.[15] Many authors argue that too often the criminal courts are, in fact, dispositional, that is tending toward efficient processing of offenders, rather than adversarial.[16]

If a case does go to trial, two assumptions guide the process in the criminal court: (1)the defendant is assumed to be innocent until proved guilty; and (2)guilt must be proved beyond a reasonable doubt. The burden of proof is on the state to demonstrate that the defendant is guilty. In addition, the criteria for guilt are more rigorous than in civil cases.

An adversarial system of justice is a very inefficient system for resolving civil or criminal disputes. It is often more cost effective and less time consuming for each side in the dispute to negotiate a settlement, with each party giving up something to get something else, than to fight to a costly resolution in a court of law. As a result, plea bargaining in criminal cases and pretrial negotiation in civil cases are common. The trials that occur are only a fraction of all cases in which trials could take place. Whether you want to promote this kind of negotiated justice is something to consider. It is one of several issues affecting the search for justice that will confront you as a future decision maker.

THE JUDICIARY: COURTS AND JURISDICTIONS

Because the United States has a dual system of governments, federal and state, it also has a dual court system. Not only does the federal government make and enforce law, but all 50 state governments make and enforce law, as well. State court systems are created by state constitutions, discussed in Chapter 4, and other than in the appellate process where the leap from state to federal courts is made, state courts are separate from the federal system.

The vast majority of cases are filed in state courts. More than 90 million cases were filed in state courts in 1992. By comparison, slightly fewer than 275,000 cases (approximately 226,900 civil cases and 47,500 criminal cases) were filed in federal courts in that same year. Thirty-two states have seen an increase in civil filings since 1990, and domestic relations cases make up more than one-third of all civil cases. Felony criminal filings are also rapidly rising in most states. (See Table 13.2 for the number of court filings in state courts for 1983, 1987, and 1992.)[17]

State court systems vary in the names given the different courts, and they vary in terms of structure. Nevertheless, there is a general pattern of hierarchical structure shared by state courts systems which Figure 13.1 represents. At the top of each system is a court of last appeal, variously known by one of several names, including Supreme Court and Court of Last Appeals. The second level of courts is the appellate courts; beneath them are the trial courts and specialized trial courts.

State court systems can be described as being organized in four ways, which vary in terms of simplicity and uniformity of jurisdiction (see Table 13.3). **Simplicity of jurisdiction** means that subject matter jurisdiction does not overlap between levels. **Uniformity of jurisdiction** means that all trial courts at each level have identical authority to decide cases.[18] A **consolidated court structure** is the name given to a system that has trial courts consolidated into a single court with jurisdiction over all cases and procedures. Six states have a consolidated court system with a two or three-tier court system. The courts at each level have distinct boundaries and separate budgets, with centralized rule-making authority. A **complex court structure** has several general jurisdiction courts or numerous limited jurisdiction courts with overlapping jurisdictions. Fourteen states have complex court systems.[19] While consolidation of court systems will not solve all problems faced by the courts, it can

Figure 13.1

The General Structure of the State Court Systems

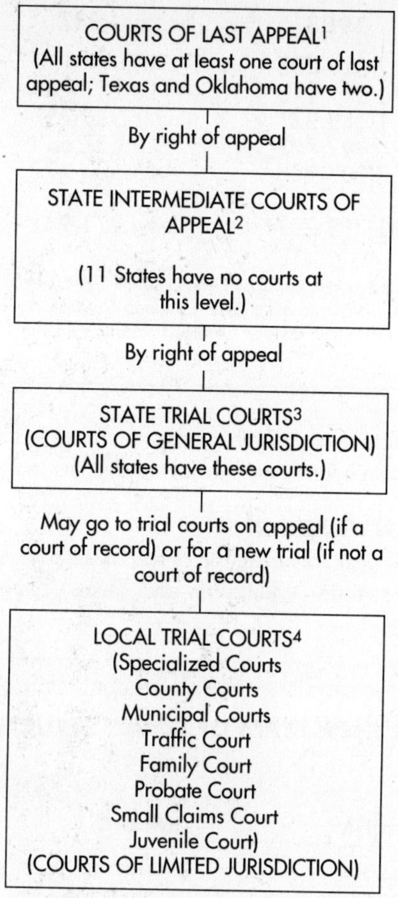

COURTS OF LAST APPEAL[1]
(All states have at least one court of last
appeal; Texas and Oklahoma have two.)

By right of appeal

STATE INTERMEDIATE COURTS OF
APPEAL[2]

(11 States have no courts at
this level.)

By right of appeal

STATE TRIAL COURTS[3]
(COURTS OF GENERAL JURISDICTION)
(All states have these courts.)

May go to trial courts on appeal (if a
court of record) or for a new trial (if not a
court of record)

LOCAL TRIAL COURTS[4]
(Specialized Courts
County Courts
Municipal Courts
Traffic Court
Family Court
Probate Court
Small Claims Court
Juvenile Court)
(COURTS OF LIMITED JURISDICTION)

---

[1]Also known as Supreme Court, Supreme Court of Appeals, Supreme Judicial Courts, Court of Appeals, and Court of Criminal Appeals.

[2]Also known as Court of Appeals, Intermediate Court of Appeals, and Court of Criminal Appeals

[3]Also known as Superior Court, Chancery Court, Circuit Court, District Court, and Court of Common Pleas

[4]These courts have limited jurisdiction, though they may have original jurisdiction and may be courts of record.

Source: Brian J. Ostrom, et al., State Court Caseload Statistics: Annual Report 1992 (National Center for State Courts, 1994).

reduce the confusion that exists in many state court systems.[20] (See Figures 13.2 for a consolidated state court system and 13.3 for a complex state court system.)

Fifteen states have a **mixed court structure,** which means that within their structures, there are two court levels with overlapping jurisdictions. Fifteen states have a **mainly con-**

Table 13.2

STATE COURT CASE FILINGS FOR 1983, 1987, AND 1992

	1983	1987	1992
Civil	12,839,400	16,027,139	19,707,374
Criminal	10,511,116	11,271,768	13,245,543
Juvenile	1,142,271	1,338,737	1,730,721
Total	24,492,787	28,637,644	34,686,638
Traffic	57,287,920	65,634,297	59,102,721
Total, including traffic	81,781,707	94,271,941	93,789,359

Sources: Carla Gaskins, Eugene Flango, and Jeanne Ito, Case Filings in State Courts, 1983, Bureau of Justice Statistics (Washington, D.C.: U.S. Government Printing Office, 1984), 2; State Court Caseload Statistics: Annual Report 1987 , (Williamsburg, VA: National Center for State Courts, 1989), 18, 20; State Court Caseload Statistics: Annual Report 1992 , (Williamsburg, VA: National Center for State Courts, 1994), 5.

solidated court structure which means that each has at least one level with two courts, but the limited jurisdiction courts have uniform jurisdiction.[21]

Courts of Last Appeal

State courts of last appeal are at the top of the hierarchy. All states have at least one court of last appeal, and two states (Oklahoma and Texas) have two courts, one to handle civil

Table 13.3

STATES AND THEIR TYPES OF COURT STRUCTURES, 1994

Consolidated	Complex	Mixed	Mainly Consolidated
Illinois	Arkansas	Alabama	Alaska
Idaho	Arizona	Colorado	California
Iowa	Delaware	Hawaii	Connecticut
Massachusetts	Georgia	Michigan	Florida
Minnesota	Indiana	Montana	Kansas
South Dakota	Louisiana	North Dakota	Maryland
District of	Mississippi	Nebraska	Maine
Columbia	New York	New Hampshire	Missouri
	Ohio	New Mexico	North Carolina
	Oklahoma	Rhode Island	New Jersey
	Oregon	South Carolina	Nevada
	Pennsylvania	Utah	Virginia
	Tennessee	Vermont	Washington
	Texas	West Virginia	Wisconsin
		Wyoming	

Source: Brian J. Ostrom, et al., State Court Caseload Statistics: Annual Report 1992 (Williamsburg, VA: National Center for State Courts, 1994), 166.

cases, the other to handle criminal cases. Called Supreme Courts in 45 states, and by various names (Supreme Judicial Court, Court of Appeals, Court of Criminal Appeals) in the other states, these are the last courts at the state level to which appeals may be made.

Courts of last appeal do not accept all cases appealed to them from the intermediate appellate level.[22] They only accept cases based on questions of law. That is, they decide whether the law was accurately interpreted or fairly applied. They decide whether the defendant received justice. Courts of last appeal may find common law, examine statutory interpretation, or interpret the state constitution. The United States Supreme Court, which hears only a fraction of the cases appealed to it, demands that state remedies be exhausted before it will hear a case. Thus, those few cases selected to be heard by the United States Supreme Court have been heard previously in state courts of last appeal.

Intermediate Courts of Appeal

State intermediate courts of appeal hear cases that are appealed from the lower courts. Appellate courts do not have original jurisdiction; they can only hear cases that have been appealed to them from a lower court. While appeals to the state court of final appeal can be made from the state intermediate appellate courts, most cases are not appealed beyond the intermediate appellate courts because of the cost of such appeals and the acceptance rate by the final court.

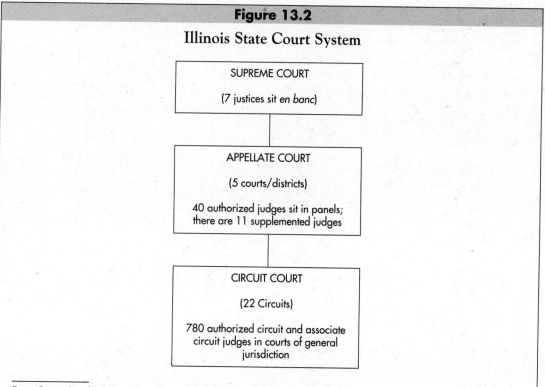

Figure 13.2
Illinois State Court System

SUPREME COURT

(7 justices sit *en banc*)

APPELLATE COURT

(5 courts/districts)

40 authorized judges sit in panels;
there are 11 supplemented judges

CIRCUIT COURT

(22 Circuits)

780 authorized circuit and associate
circuit judges in courts of general
jurisdiction

State Court Caseload Statistics: Annual Report 1992 (Williamsburg, VA: National Center for State Courts, 1994), 185.

Figure 13.3

New York Court Structure, 1992

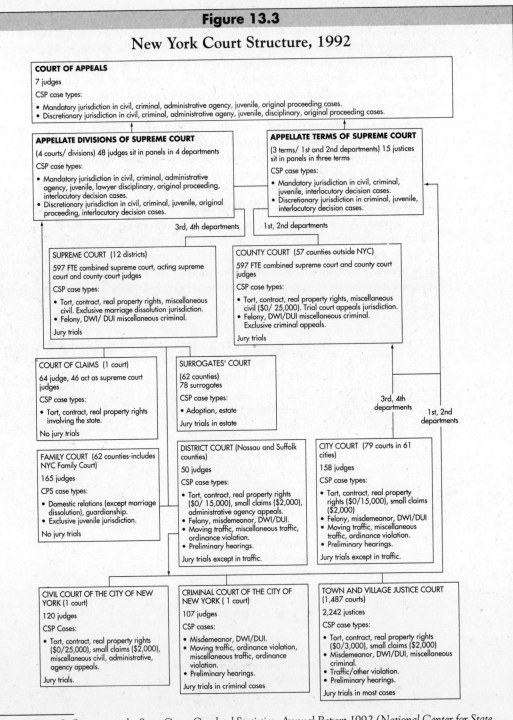

COURT OF APPEALS

7 judges

CSP case types:

- Mandatory jurisdiction in civil, criminal, administrative agency, juvenile, original proceeding cases.
- Discretionary jurisdiction in civil, criminal, administrative ageny, juvenile, disciplinary, original proceeding cases.

APPELLATE DIVISIONS OF SUPREME COURT

(4 courts/ divisions) 48 judges sit in panels in 4 departments

CSP case types:

- Mandatory jurisdiction in civil, criminal, administrative agency, juvenile, lawyer disciplinary, original proceeding, interlocutory decision cases.
- Discretionary jurisdiction in civil, criminal, juvenile, original proceeding, interlocutory decision cases.

APPELLATE TERMS OF SUPREME COURT

(3 terms/ 1st and 2nd departments) 15 justices sit in panels in three terms

CSP case types:

- Mandatory jurisdiction in civil, criminal, juvenile, interlocutory decision cases.
- Discretionary jurisdiction in criminal, juvenile, interlocutory decision cases.

3rd, 4th departments

1st, 2nd departments

SUPREME COURT (12 districts)

597 FTE combined supreme court, acting supreme court and county court judges

CSP case types:

- Tort, contract, real property rights, miscellaneous civil. Exclusive marriage dissolution jurisdiction.
- Felony, DWI/ DUI miscellaneous criminal.

Jury trials

COUNTY COURT (57 counties outside NYC)

597 FTE combined supreme court and county court judges

CSP case types:

- Tort, contract, real property rights, miscellaneous civil ($0/ 25,000). Trial court appeals jurisdiction.
- Felony, DWI/DUI miscellaneous criminal. Exclusive criminal appeals.

Jury trials

COURT OF CLAIMS (1 court)

64 judge, 46 act as supreme court judges

CSP case types:

- Tort, contract, real property rights involving the state.

No jury trials

SURROGATES' COURT

(62 counties)
78 surrogates

CSP case types:

- Adoption, estate

Jury trials in estate

3rd, 4th departments

1st, 2nd departments

FAMILY COURT (62 counties-includes NYC Family Court)

165 judges

CPS case types:

- Domestic relations (except marriage dissolution), guardianship.
- Exclusive juvenile jurisdiction.

No jury trials

DISTRICT COURT (Nassau and Suffolk counties)

50 judges

CSP case types:

- Tort, contract, real property rights ($0/ 15,000), small claims ($2,000), administrative agency appeals.
- Felony, misdemeanor, DWI/DUI.
- Moving traffic, miscellaneous traffic, ordinance violation.
- Preliminary hearings.

Jury trials except in traffic.

CITY COURT (79 courts in 61 cities)

158 judges

CSP case types:

- Tort, contract, real property rights ($0/15,000), small claims ($2,000)
- Felony, misdemeanor, DWI/DUI
- Moving traffic, miscellaneous traffic, ordinance violation.
- Preliminary hearings.

Jury trials except in traffic.

CIVIL COURT OF THE CITY OF NEW YORK (1 court)

120 judges

CSP Cases:

- Tort, contract, real property rights ($0/25,000), small claims ($2,000), miscellaneous civil, administrative, agency appeals.

Jury trials.

CRIMINAL COURT OF THE CITY OF NEW YORK (1 court)

107 judges

CSP cases:

- Misdemeanor, DWI/DUI.
- Moving traffic, ordinance violation, miscellaneous traffic, ordinance violation.
- Preliminary hearings.

Jury trials in criminal cases

TOWN AND VILLAGE JUSTICE COURT (1,487 courts)

2,242 justices

CSP case types:

- Tort, contract, real property rights ($0/3,000), small claims ($2,000)
- Misdemeanor, DWI/DUI, miscellaneous criminal.
- Traffic/other violation.
- Preliminary hearings.

Jury trials in most cases

Source: Brian J. Ostrom, et al., State Court Caseload Statistics: Annual Report 1992 (National Center for State Courts, 1994), 204.

Intermediate appellate courts have different names in different states, including Court of Appeal (in twenty-eight states) and various names in other states. Eleven states have no intermediate appellate courts, and four states have two major courts at this level.[23] Some states have an intricate system of appellate courts with numerous judges; notice the elaborate appeals process pictured in Figure 13.3 for New York state.

State Trial Courts

State trial courts, the next level of courts, have *general jurisdiction*, which means they can hear any type of case that comes up in their area, civil or criminal. They are courts of *original jurisdiction* because cases start or originate there, and they may also hear cases appealed to them from lower courts and administrative tribunals. When appeals come from the local trial courts and most administrative tribunals, the cases are heard **de novo**, as completely new cases. State trial courts carry the responsibility for much of the work in state courts and therefore have broad authority.

Within each state are several territorial jurisdictions called districts or circuits. The state trial court within the district has jurisdiction in the territory. Among the common names for these courts are Circuit Court (16 states), Superior Court (15 states), and District Court (15 states). These courts hear both civil and criminal cases.

Local Trial Courts

Local trial courts are courts of *limited jurisdiction*, which means they can hear only specific kinds of cases (i.e., Juvenile Court, Traffic Court, Probate Court) or cases that occur within a particular area (i.e., County Court, Municipal Court). County courts are established by state governments and deal with violation of state and local ordinances and laws. Municipal courts are established by cities to deal with violations of local ordinances and state laws. These courts deal almost exclusively with criminal violations; most of their time is taken up by misdemeanor traffic violations. Many towns do not want to bear the cost of municipal courts and do not establish them.

Both county and municipal courts may be courts of original jurisdiction. They are also generally the first *courts of record*. Courts of record have three characteristics: (1)transcripts of the proceedings are available; (2)decisions are appealable; and (3)judges preside over the proceedings.

These courts solve local problems. Such courts as Traffic Court, Juvenile Court, and Family Court serve a specific community and may alleviate local social problems. Among the most successful of such courts are the Small Claims Court where citizens can settle minor disputes involving relatively small sums of money. Individuals plead their case to the judge without the services of a lawyer. These courts are streamlined and permit the quick dispensation of justice. (For a discussion of how and when to use a Small Claims Court, see Box 13.1.)

Justice of the Peace Courts

The Justice of the Peace Court is the lowest court at the state level and is presided over by the Justice of the Peace, often called the J. P. Those individuals who become J. P.s are not required to be lawyers or to have any particular training prior to being elected (usually) or being appointed (less often) to the post. Some states do require training when the Justice of the Peace takes office. His or her duties vary, but customarily involve civil cases of less than

BOX 13.1

THE SMALL CLAIMS COURT

If you believe that you have been cheated, but the amount of loss is not enough to justify hiring a lawyer, you do have one other option. You can take your grievance to small claims court where you will be able to represent yourself for only the small cost of filing fees. To find the small claims court, look in the telephone book. If you see no listing under Municipal or County headings, call the Justice of the Peace or a County Court Clerk for the location of the Small Claims Court. In some areas, small claims cases are handled by the Justice of the Peace.

When you find the small claims court, there will be forms to complete and a small filing fee. There is usually someone there to help you complete the forms, and to give advice about the court process. The following guide may help you decide whether to file in small claims court.

To file in small claims court

1. Your claim must be based on a sound legal concept. . . .
2. You must have evidence to support your claim. . . .
3. Your claim must be within the dollar limitation of the jurisdiction of the court. . . .
4. You must file your claim within a specified period of time. . . .
5. You must file your claim with the court that has jurisdiction over your case. . . .
6. Many courts require and common sense dictates that you contact the other party and attempt to resolve the dispute before going to court. . . .
7. In injuries to property or person, you must be able to prove that intentional or negligent behavior was the cause of the injury."

Source: Gayle L. Niles and Douglas H. Snider, Woman's Counsel: A Legal Guide for Women (Denver: Arden Press, 1984), 32–34.

$300, misdemeanors, and other services for a fee. These services may include conducting marriage ceremonies, certifying death, and notarizing documents.

Cost of the State and Local Court Systems

The burden of funding the court system in the United States is carried by state and local governments. State and local governments funded 91 percent of all court payrolls in the United States in 1985, and the same governments funded over 80 percent of all prosecution and legal service payrolls in that year. Salaries for public defender offices are funded almost exclusively by state and local governments.[24]

In comparison to corrections and police protection, judicial systems are among the least costly agencies in the justice system. Table 13.4 reveals the costs of a court system to state and local governments. Notice that courts account for less than 18 percent of all justice system costs at the local level; the court system accounts for one-quarter of the cost for the entire justice system at the state level.

Table 13.4

THE COST OF JUSTICE SYSTEMS AND COURT SYSTEMS AT THE STATE, LOCAL, AND MUNICIPAL LEVEL BY NUMBER EMPLOYED AND PAYROLLS, OCTOBER 1985, 1990

	1985		1990	
	Total Employment	October Payroll (dollars, in thousands)	Total Employment	October Payroll (dollars, in thousands)
Total State Justice System	443,383	878,889	56,3076	1,439,207
Total Local Justice System	885,560	1,698,005	959,335	2,433,120
Total State Court System Only	177,049	323,022	190,142	469,024
Judicial (Courts Only)				
State	61,082	151,678	68,090	214,515
Local (County and Municipal)	115,967	171,344	122,052	254,510
County	88,291	134,529	97,622	205,028
Municipal	27,676	36,815	24,430	49,482
Prosecution and Legal Services				
State	23,926	53,164	29,046	84,805
Local (County and Municipal)	54,025	111,763	58,408	166,613
County	35,657	72,154	40,049	109,516
Municipal	18,386	39,609	18,358	57,097
Public Defense				
State	6,003	12,307	7,255	208,85
Local (County and Municipal)	5,733	13,607	7,363	23,458
County	5,476	12,956	7,038	22,350
Municipal	257	651	325	1,108

Source: Timothy J. Flanagan and Katherine M. Jamieson, Sourcebook of Criminal Justice Statistics, 1987, Bureau of Justice Statistics, (Washington, D.C.: U.S. Government Printing Office, 1988), 15; Timothy J. Flanagan and Katherine Maguire, Sourcebook of Criminal Justice Statistics, 1991, Bureau of Justice Statistics (Washington, D.C.: U.S. Government Printing Office, 1992), 23, 28.

THE JUDICIARY: LAWYERS AND JUDGES

Most judges are lawyers, and if you are interested in becoming a judge, you should plan on going to law school and becoming a lawyer first. The following discussion about lawyers may help you decide if law is a career you'd like to pursue, but be sure to read Box 13.2 to learn about law school before you decide.

Lawyers: Gatekeepers of the Legal System

The classic image of the attorney in the courtroom—tireless, moral, partisan, and above all, concerned with justice—is also the stuff of many books and movies. But real lawyers are average people with typical life problems which, as is true of all persons in the legal system, may encourage them to find solutions that may fall short of the romantic ideal portrayed by Perry Mason. This is not to demean lawyers, nor to impugn their motives. They are, in fact, pivotal to the pursuit of justice in the United States.

The number of persons practicing law increases every year. In May, 1994, the Department of Labor reported more than 869,000 lawyers and judges working in the United States, up from 716,000 in June, 1987. Of those lawyers, 649,000 were males, and 212,000 were females.[25] But as the number of lawyers increases, the distribution of legal services and the public's perception of the legal profession continue to be problems of concern for the nation's legal system. (To see what the public thinks of attorneys, see Table 13.5. Notice that public opinion has changed little over time.)

Lawyers "Man" the Litigious Society

Lawyers are the "principle gatekeepers" for noncriminal cases since would-be litigants must seek their services; their control over civil litigation may be thought of as a monopoly.[26]

Table 13.5

PUBLIC RATINGS OF THE HONESTY AND ETHICAL STANDARDS OF OCCUPATIONS, 1988, 1992 (AS INDICATED BY ANSWERS TO THE QUESTION, "HOW WOULD YOU RATE THE HONESTY AND ETHICAL STANDARDS OF THE PEOPLE IN THESE DIFFERENT FIELDS?")

	Percent Answering "Very High" 1988/1992	Percent Answering "High" 1988/1992	Percent Answering "Average" 1988/1992	Percent Answering "Low" 1988/1992	Percent Answering "Very Low" 1988/1992	Percent Answering "No Opinion" 1988/1992
Druggists	14/14	52/52	29/28	2/3	1/1	2/2
College teachers	10/10	44/40	35/38	5/4	1/1	5/7
Police officers	10/8	37/34	39/42	8/10	3/4	3/2
Lawyers	3/3	15/15	45/43	23/25	10/11	4/3
Realtors	3/2	10/12	47/55	27/22	7/4	6/5

Sources: Sourcebook of Criminal Justice Statistics 1988, Bureau of Justice Statistics *(Washington, D.C.: U.S. Government Printing Office, 1989),* 192; Sourcebook of Criminal Justice Statistics 1992, Bureau of Justice Statistics, *(Washington, D.C.: U.S. Government Printing Office, 1993),* 168.

BOX 13.2

SO YOU WANT TO BE A LAWYER?

If you want to be a lawyer, you must overcome a series of obstacles. The first is earning a bachelor's degree with a very good grade point average. You do not have to major in any particular area, although certain classes, those which emphasize critical thinking skills, logic, and writing, will help you once you get into law school.

Getting into law school is the second obstacle. Law schools use grade point average and scores on the Law School Admission Test (L.S.A.T.) as important criteria for admission. They also may consider other criteria, like improvement in grade point average, college activities, ethnic background, a personal interview or written essay (often requested on admission forms), and letters of recommendation. Very prestigious law schools may consider the college where the bachelor's degree is earned and the difficulty of your undergraduate curriculum.

You should also take the L.S.A.T. seriously because law schools do. Some students take courses to prepare for the exam. You must decide if your pocketbook will permit such a course; you must also decide if your skills require such a course. Write the Law School Admissions Council/ Law School Admissions Services at Box 2000, Newtown, Pennsylvania, 18940–0989 or call (215) 968–1001 for more information about law school admissions.

Deciding which law schools you should apply to is important. You should consider where you want to practice law, and then decide whether you want to attend a law school with a national reputation or a state or local law school which may or may not be prestigious in your state. Consider whether you need to attend school at night or part time, and check to see which law schools permit you to do so. Consider whether you can earn an additional degree while you earn the law degree. Be sure to apply to several law schools in case you are not admitted to the school of your choice.

Once in law school, your life will change dramatically. You will learn the case law approach, a method of examining related cases that focus on an area of law, then applying the information in those cases to the case you are studying. Law school professors expect you to find the material and think about the material on your own. They do not tell you what you should know, but they will call on you in class and expect you to have the answers. Law school is very anxiety provoking until you learn the case method, how to study, and how to be prepared for class.

If you want to be a lawyer in order to make a great deal of money, then law school is where you should make your mark. Starting salaries for lawyers are high for those students in the upper 10 percent of a class (an average of over $30,000 in most large cities), but mediocre students can expect "to devote considerable time and energy to securing a first job they consider acceptable."

Once finished with law school, you will have to pass a state bar exam to become a lawyer. You may work in a law firm as a clerk or research assistant prior to taking the exam, but "passing a bar" admits you to the practice of law. In 1987, more than 40,000 persons became eligible to practice law, adding to the more than 700,000 already practicing law. It should be obvious that the competition between lawyers is significant.

The Official Guide to U.S. Law Schools 1988–1989 (Newtown, PA: Law Access Publications, 1988), 31, 5.

While many of them work for governments (state, local, and federal) and private industry, the significant majority of lawyers are in private practice. Lawyers make their livings by representing clients in actual and potential law suits. As a result, more than *nineteen million* civil suits were filed in state and local courts in 1992.[27] The frequency with which law suits are filed and the number of readily available attorneys to do the filing produces the belief that disputes should be settled in court. As a result, the courts are glutted with law suits, to which time, money, and effort must be allocated. The question which must be asked is whether justice can be the result of this overloaded legal system.

Nevertheless, the dissemination of legal services to those who need them in civil matters is uneven. Surprisingly, it may be that middle income individuals are less adequately represented on a regular basis than any other economic level. The business community is likely to be best served, and the poor in large cities are also likely to be well served by various government agencies.[28] Many middle class individuals must rely on word-of-mouth information from friends and acquaintances when choosing a lawyer; they may have to rely on the same attorneys who wrote their wills, instead of a specialist for their cases. Other middle income individuals may be unable to afford an attorney's fees and so may be unable to obtain legal assistance.

A number of authors have been interested in the degree to which private attorneys represent the interests of their clients or themselves, particularly in the criminal courts. In such analyses, the distinction is made between courthouse regulars and out-of-town attorneys. Defense attorneys who regularly appear before the same judges, and who must negotiate with the same prosecutors, are likely to become more concerned with their relationships with the courtroom workgroup than with their client's welfare.[29] Members of the workgroup share a similar problem: all must manage their burdensome caseloads and attempt to keep the justice system working. This provides the impetus to dispositional justice, the efficient processing of cases through the criminal justice system, by emphasizing plea bargaining. There is some evidence that this situation also occurs in the practice of civil law when the attorney's client or case cannot command a large fee.[30]

Attorneys who come in from other communities as "hired guns" have little to lose in their relationships with local justice officials and are more likely to fight for the interests of their clients; on the other hand, outsiders may be unaware of the rules and expectations in the local court, putting them at a disadvantage in negotiations and rulings.[31] This is true whether the case is in civil or criminal court. In this case, attorneys are obligated to do what they can to secure a positive verdict for their client.

Lawyers are the only individuals permitted to practice law or conduct out-of-court legal business (see Box 13.3).[32] In more than half the states, lawyers are required to be dues-paying members of the state bar in order to practice law in that state.[33] This system is known as the **integrated bar**, a name taken to avoid the negative connotations of a union shop. The integrated bar is, despite the name, a closed shop, which means that people must join the union, in this case the bar, if they want to work. A voluntary bar, which exists in fewer than half the states, does not require membership in order to practice law, but attorneys still must pass a bar exam if they are to practice law in those states.

State legislatures establish bar associations, but typically place them under the control of the state judiciary. The first unified or integrated state bar was established in North Dakota in 1921, and the idea became popular in state legislatures during the Depression when voluntary bar associations were unable to sustain sufficient membership.[34] The integrated bar makes powerful political groups of state bar associations since the dues collected may be used to fund any number of activities, including lobbying for proposed legislation, legal aid programs, and improvements in the justice system. Bar associations are also typically responsible for testing would-be lawyers, accrediting law schools, and disciplining attorneys. Bar associations may also respond to the economic and social problems of particular states in order to ameliorate those problems.[35]

The power of integrated bar associations to propose legislation or to lobby for legislation is one reason that they are under attack by numerous groups, including state legislatures who are beginning to demand that bar associations become voluntary. Indeed many people support the idea of voluntary bar associations in those states with mandatory associations, arguing that the required dues may be used to support programs that many dues-paying attorneys do not support.[36]

As we shall see in the next section, bar associations are especially powerful in the states with the Missouri Plan method of judicial appointment. Critics of the Missouri Plan say that it trades influence of political parties for the influence of bar associations. Integrated bar associations with unified views of appropriate judicial appointments are thus even more powerful. Such power makes the complete demise of the integrated bar unlikely, but does insure a continued attack on it.

Judges: The Individuals in Charge

The classic image of the judge—impartial, unemotional, rational, and, above all, fair—is also the stuff of many books and movies. But judges are individuals, after all, with their own life experiences and world views. Are judges more similar to one another than they are to the average American, and if so, why is that the case? The following sections on judges are intended to help answer this question, as well as provide some insight into the judge's contribution to the search for justice.

Although judges have traditionally enjoyed high status, in recent years they have also been publicly criticized, leading to demands for judicial accountability. In large part these are criticisms of federal judges and their rulings on civil rights and civil liberties, but local courts are not without their critics. (For example, notice from Table 13.6 that many people believe their local courts are too lenient with offenders. Notice also that their opinions changed little in four years.) The demands for judicial accountability tend to focus on how judges are selected.

Who Becomes a Judge?

Judges traditionally have been male attorneys from upper middle class or upper–class families who had been active in politics and demonstrated party loyalty. State courts are still heavily dominated by "men and whites," and although there are signs that this is likely to change with the increase in the number of women and minorities graduating from law school, white males still predominate in the prestigious state appellate courts.[37] In 1985 women accounted for less than eight per cent of all judges at each level of state judiciaries.[38] Judges also tend to be middle class or upper–middle-class individuals since most of them have had the education and finances to successfully complete law school. As Henry Glick points out:

"Most judges also are 'local boys who made good.' Recruitment politics generally requires a close tie to state and local politics, resulting in judges who have always been close to home.

BOX 13.3

THE PARALEGAL: ANOTHER CAREER IN THE JUDICIARY

It is not necessary to become a lawyer or a judge in order to work in law. The Labor Department estimates that the fastest growing occupation for the next 10 years is the paralegal profession. Not only does the employment picture look optimistic for paralegals, but the average national salary is between $22,000 and $25,000, with a Dallas law firm paying some paralegals nearly $100,000 (though this is very unusual).

A paralegal is a legal assistant, someone who is trained to help lawyers research cases and prepare briefs. Paralegals may even prepare preliminary versions of legal documents and interview witnesses. They are often central to activity in a law firm or administrative agency, and the work is important as well as exciting.

There are three routes to becoming a paralegal: (1) two-year Associate of Arts programs, (2) four-year baccalaureate programs; and (3) professional certification. Associate degree programs typically involve a two-year training program and can begin after graduating from high school. They are housed in community colleges, universities, and "proprietary" schools (profit-making businesses offering training and similar in nature to beauty schools or truck driving schools).

Some colleges and universities have established four-year degree programs that offer in-depth training as well as a liberal arts education. Most certificate programs require at least a year of college work, and some require a bachelor's degree for admission. Completion of all work for graduation may take up to two years. Certification programs are also offered at colleges, universities, and proprietary schools.

Recommending one kind of program over another would be a mistake because different practices and views exist in different parts of the country. To decide which program is for you, talk to paralegals working where you want to work. Ask where they went to school and which kind of program they recommend. Ask about job opportunities in the area. If the Department of Labor is correct, there should be many opportunities!

Source: Paul Marcotte, "$100,000 a Year for Paralegals?" The Paralegal, vol. 4, no.2, 1988, 1; Alice Fins, Opportunities in Paralegal Careers (Lincolnwood, IL: VGM Career Horizons, 1985).

There are some exceptions, especially in the fast growing states, but lawyers who leave home probably have a difficult time establishing sufficient ties to a new community to make them acceptable as local judges. Winning elections or an executive appointment usually requires careful nurturing of a political career. This means developing contacts, establishing a record of service to a political party, holding lesser posts in the community, and being well known to fellow lawyers and other prominent groups. Consequently, state judges normally have been born and raised in the same state as the court on which they serve, and have held one or more nonjudicial political jobs such as state legislator and prosecuting attorney or have been a local judge. They are also likely to be a member of the political party that dominates politics in their area. In short, they are typically political insiders and long-standing local residents."[39]

Table 13.6

1987/1991 ATTITUDES TOWARD THE SEVERITY OF LOCAL COURTS (AS INDICATED BY ANSWERS TO THE QUESTION, "IN GENERAL, DO YOU THINK THE COURTS IN THIS AREA DEAL TOO HARSHLY OR NOT HARSHLY ENOUGH WITH CRIMINALS?")

	Percent Who Said "Too Harsh" 1987/1991	Percent Who Said "Not Harsh Enough" 1987/1991	Percent Who Said "About Right" 1987/1991	Percent Who Said "Don't Know" 1987/1991
National Sample	3/4	79/80	12/11	6/5
Females	3/3	80/81	11/11	6/5
Males	4/5	78/78	14/12	6/5
Whites	2/3	81/80	12/12	5/5
Minorities	7/10	70/76	14/8	9/5
College students	3/4	77/78	14/12	6/6
High School students	3/5	84/82	9/9	4/4
Grade school students	5/2	71/78	18/17	7/3
Republicans	2/2	86/82	10/11	2/5
Democrats	4/5	78/79	13/12	6/4
Independents	4/5	76/79	12/10	8/6
18–20 years	0/3	76/70	17/20	7/7
21–29 years	4/8	78/77	9/9	8/5
30–49 years	4/4	78/80	13/11	5/3
50 years+	2/3	82/81	12/12	4/3
Professionals	2/3	80/78	13/11	5/7
Clerical workers	2/3	81/80	12/12	5/5
Manual laborers	5/5	78/82	11/11	5/3
Farmers	2/0	82/89	12/8	2/3

Source: Sourcebook of Criminal Justice Statistics, 1992 (Washington, D.C.: U.S. Government Printing Office, 1993), 196–197.

How Are Judges Selected?

The selection of judges is a major issue confronting those concerned with justice. There are two basic approaches to judicial selection: election and appointment. Federal judges acquire their positions exclusively through appointment, but states use both election and appointment. Those who advocate election of judges argue that this process makes judges accountable to citizens. Those who advocate appointment of judges argue that the judiciary should be independent of popular opinion and loyal only to the law. On the other hand, both appointment and election of judges involve a certain amount of risk. One method permits the person who appoints to choose unfit, political associates to be judges; the other raises the issue of whether judges will remain independent of popular opinion or political contributors, thereby reducing the impartiality of the judiciary.

Six methods for selecting judges are (1)partisan elections; (2)nonpartisan elections; (3)appointment by governor; (4)merit selection at some level of the judicial system; (5)legislative elections; and (6)selection by sitting judges.[40] These methods have been variously combined in attempts to produce merit selection plans with all of the strengths of both appointment and election. Under the **California Plan**,[41] the governor nominates one person for each judgeship. If that person is confirmed by the Commission on Judicial Appointments, he or she becomes a judge who must stand for election at the next general election. This election is a referendum on the record compiled while in office; the judge does not have an opponent. If elected, the judge sits on the bench for a 12-year term, and may be reelected as often as the electorate returns a majority of positive votes.

The **Missouri Plan**, an amendment to that state's constitution in 1940,[42] also combines both election and appointment. It has been more popular than the California Plan. Nonpartisan nominating boards nominate three qualified candidates for each vacant judgeship. The governor appoints the judge from these nominations. After a period of time, not less than a year, the judge stands for election in an unopposed, nonpartisan ratification by the electorate. If ratified, the judge secures the position for a period of years, depending on the level of the judgeship. Fourteen other states have developed variations on the Missouri plan, including permitting judges to run opposed on partisan or nonpartisan ballots at some point after initial ratification, for some of the judgeships in the state.[43]

Judges in courts of last appeal are chosen by a variety of methods, including partisan election (10 states), nonpartisan election (12 states), and some version of the Missouri Plan (14 states). They serve terms of from 6 years to life. In 17 states, the term is 6 years; in 12 states, it is 8 years, and in 12 other states it is 10 years.[44]

The Chief Justice in courts of last appeal is chosen in different ways (see Table 13.7). In 19 states, the Chief Justice is chosen by the other justices; in 11 states the Chief Justice is appointed by the governor and in 6 of those, the consent of the legislature is also necessary. In 8 states the Chief Justice is elected; and in 7 states the Chief Justice is the judge with seniority of service.

Table 13.7

STATES AND THREE METHODS OF SELECTING COURTS OF LAST APPEAL JUDGES

Missouri Plan	Partisan Election	Nonpartisan Election
Alaska	Alabama	Georgia
Arizona	Arkansas	Idaho
Colorado	Illinois	Kentucky
Florida	Mississippi	Louisiana
Indiana	New Mexico	Michigan
Iowa	North Carolina	Minnesota
Kansas	Oregon	Montana
Maryland	Tennessee	Nevada
Missouri	Texas	North Dakota
Nebraska	West Virginia	Ohio
Utah		Washington
Oklahoma		Wisconsin
South Dakota		
Wyoming		

Source: The Book of the States, 1994–95, 190–192.

Table 13.8

STATES AND THEIR METHODS OF SELECTING COURTS OF INTERMEDIATE APPEAL JUDGES

No Court	Missouri Plan	Partisan Election	Nonpartisan Election
Delaware	Alaska	Alabama	Georgia
Maine	Arizona	Arkansas	Idaho
Mississippi	Colorado	Illinois	Kentucky
Montana	Florida	New Mexico	Louisiana
Nebraska	Indiana	New York	Michigan
Nevada	Iowa	North Carolina	Minnesota
New Hampshire	Kansas	Pennsylvania (initial)	North Dakota
Rhode Island	Maryland	Texas	Ohio
South Dakota	Missouri		Oregon
Wyoming	Oklahoma		Pennsylvania (retention)
Utah	Tennessee		Washington
West Virginia			Wisconsin
Wyoming			

Source: The Book of the States, 1994–95, (Lexington, KY: The Council of State Governments, 1994), 190–192.

Intermediate appeal judges are chosen in the same fashion as the justices in the courts of last appeal in all but 2 states, but 11 states do not have intermediate appellate courts (see Table 13.8). Judges in existing courts serve terms of from 6 years to life. In 16 states, the term is 6 years; in 10 states it is 8 years, and in 7 states it is 10 years. Trial court judges are selected in a number of ways, but the Missouri Plan (11 states), partisan election (11 states) and nonpartisan election (18 states) are the most common methods of selection. Terms of office range from 4 years (9 states), 6 years (25 states), 8 years (8 states).[45]

Does It Matter How Judges Are Selected?

Are there any differences between appointed and elected judges? A final answer is not yet available, but evidence suggests that significant differences do not result from the two selection systems. A study of state supreme court justices in four states found that adoption of a particular judicial role—liberal lawmaker versus conservative law-interpreter—was based upon personal values and appeared to be unrelated to methods of judicial selection.[46] It is likely that the type of selection makes little difference in who becomes a judge since, regardless of the method, selection is made from the same general group of people: middle-class lawyers with political contacts.

Does either type of selection produce superior judges? Again, the answer to this question is that the selection process probably makes little measurable difference, if any, in the average quality of judges.[47] Studies show that sitting judges are rarely rejected by voters under the merit plans—the Missouri or California Plans—and that judges voted into office are almost always returned to office.[48] Since the group from which these judges were originally selected contained similar types of persons, there is no reason to believe that, on average, these two processes lead to significantly different outcomes.

The major difference between partisan election (and governor appointment) and merit plan selection has to do with who has the most influence in each selection method. Political parties are most influential in states where judges are elected or appointed by the governor with little meaningful challenge by others, (i.e. the California Plan). But in states which emphasize some variation on the Missouri Plan with a nonpartisan nominating body selecting a pool of qualified candidates, the group most often represented in the nominating process has a great deal of power. That group is usually the state bar, and its influence is institutionalized in such plans. Where the Missouri Plan is used, bar politics have replaced party politics when the selection of judges is at issue.[49] Neither electing judges or appointing them under the Missouri Plan had been shown to produce demonstrably more competent or less biased judges; neither, however, has either system had the deplorable results predicted by their opponents.[50]

How Important Is the Influence of Judges' Party Affiliation?

In general, one would expect judges to be effected by both public opinion and partisan politics. Yet, a study hypothesizing that Democratic judges, being more sympathetic with the "underdog," would sentence convicted rapists more leniently than Republican judges did not produce data to support that hypothesis in Montana.[51] Republican and Democratic judges were not significantly different with regard to sentencing of rapists in Montana from 1987 to 1989. The failed hypothesis was explained in terms of other political variables, primarily the fact that Montana has a non-partisan judicial election system. In this system, judges are elected or, if a vacancy occurs, appointed by the governor from a pool selected by a judicial nominating committee. Thus, governors have less influence and judges may be less influenced by partisan politics.[52]

On the other hand, other analyses of the judicial behavior of all elected appellate judges suggest that there are "basic decision-making differences between Democratic and Republican judges in courts selected under partisan nomination and election procedures."[53] While party affiliation does not explain all appellate judicial behavior, it explains more than any other variable, including age, gender, class, or ethnicity.[54]

To summarize, judges' party affiliation is most likely to influence judicial decisions when judges are elected in partisan elections or governors appoint them, at least initially. The implication of these findings is that voters may be able to influence court systems in those states permitting the election of judges at some point in the process, *if* they know the judges' party affiliation and the meaning of that affiliation in the state in which they live. This is important because appellate judges, whether at the intermediate or final level, make decisions that are policy oriented. Their decisions have implications for policies concerning the rights of the poor and the wealthy, women and men, adults and children, taxpayers and welfare recipients, as well as criminals and victims. If research continues to show the relevance of party affiliation to judicial decision making, then individuals who want judges to be accountable to the electorate rather than independent of it should lobby on behalf of reforms that permit partisan elections.

Nevertheless, except in a few highly publicized cases (e.g., Justice Rose Bird in California) citizen participation in judicial elections is rare. Reasons for this lack of participation vary, but a lack of knowledge about candidates' judicial behavior is the most common explanation. "The overriding conclusion of the national-level judicial elections literature is that the citizen is uninformed."[55] Systematic print media coverage of judges' decisions is unusual. Television news is even less likely to provide such information. While organizations like the League of Women Voters often supply synopses of candidates' characteristics, (i.e., party affiliation, education, and a "job philosophy" statement) along with a picture of the candidate, such abbreviated information may do no more than provide a racial or gender cue with which to make election decisions.[56]

One final point about judicial elections is necessary. While there is little scholarly data about costs of campaigns, one study indicates that the average budget for a 1988 Texas supreme court campaign was more than $750,000.[57] There is also a renewed interest in the V. O. Key notion of "friends and neighbors" politics as a method of explaining judicial election results. Put another way, heavier voting by citizens from a candidate's local area may predict election results, especially in the absence of other partisan cues. Given the viability of this idea, one researcher has taken it one step farther: that friends-and-neighbor politics may predict judicial behavior. If judges are dependent on substantial support from voters from their home base, then it may be that judges are more dependent on those voters for campaign finances, and thus are more likely to be sensitive to the interests of local voters.[58] Further research in this area is, of course, necessary, but as the cost of judicial elections increases, such research becomes even more necessary.

How Are Judges Removed from Office?

Like judicial selection, the removal of judges is an issue of judicial accountability. States have more than one method for removing judges. The most common methods are impeachment, removal by the court of last appeal, and the use of a special court selected on a case-by-case basis. Charges that can lead to removal are the claim that judges can no longer fulfill the obligations of the job because of illness or accident, or that they have been convicted of a felony. Forty-three states permit the impeachment of judges, by far the most common method of judicial removal. Thirty-six states allow the court of last appeals to remove judges as a result of recommendations made by various judicial commissions or for cause.

Just as the trend is away from gubernatorial appointment of judges, it is also away from gubernatorial removal of judges. Two states permit the governor to remove judges, and one state permits the governor to remove judges for criminal convictions. Governors can remove judges with concurrence of two-thirds of the legislature in nine states.

While an emphasis on accountability leads to the election of judges, the right to recall judges through election exists in only five states. Seven states permit the state legislature to remove judges by legislative resolution or a two-thirds vote of both houses of the legislature. Two other states permit the removal of district judges by a local tribunal.[59]

Data from 1987 indicate that judges are rarely removed from the bench.[60] Ninety-two percent of all 5,827 complaints against state judges were dismissed as frivolous or unfounded. Some 126 judges in 27 states were privately or publicly censured. Another 21 judges in 9 states were removed from office. Another 112 judges voluntarily retired. Given the number of judges in state courts, the likelihood that a judge will be removed either for misconduct or health reasons is small.[61]

A citizen swears to "tell the truth, the whole truth, and nothing but the truth." If attorneys on both sides ask the right questions, then juries of fellow citizens are able to decide whose version of the truth they accept.

REINVENTING STATE AND LOCAL COURTS IN THE 1990s

One of the most compelling issues facing state courts is equal access to justice. As such, it is an issue that can be addressed by the entrepreneurial spirit embodied in a reinvention of the court. If that reinvention is not complete, and it is not, it has nevertheless begun.

As part of any reinvention, state and local courts would develop measurable performance standards; such standards have been described by the National Center for State Courts in two publications, *Trial Court Performance Standards* and *Measurement of Trial Court Performance: 1990 Supplement to the Trial Court Performance Standards with Commentary*, both published in 1990. These standards, which focus on performance rather than resource management, a clear reflection of the reinvention orientation, have been adopted in some jurisdictions in several states, including Arizona, California, Florida, Illinois, New Jersey, Ohio, Virginia, and Washington. "These standards require trial courts to be open and accessible and to eliminate unnecessary barriers to justice services, whether economic, physical, or procedural."[62]

A number of states have set out to examine the potential barriers to access which include racial and gender bias, as well as poverty and physical disabilities. Final reports in those states have concluded that racial bias can be reduced by increased minority representation on judicial selection boards and affirmative action programs for court and law enforcement officials. Gender bias task forces often develop innovative approaches, including legislation and the education of judges about family violence, for resolving domestic violence situations.

Disabilities may reduce access to the court in at least two ways. Physical aspects of court buildings which make entrance to and movement through buildings—one need only imagine the steep marble stairs that are at the center of many state and local court buildings—are sources of frustration to the mobility disabled. In addition, other disabilities (blindness, deafness) historically have made jury participation difficult if not impossible. The Americans with Disabilities Act encourages affirmative steps to reduce or eliminate discrimination resulting from disabilities and is likely to have an impact on the courts in the near future.

Poverty and inadequate income may inhibit access to the courts. Despite the fact that attorneys are usually provided in criminal cases, the quality of representation is suspect. In Harlem the public defender's office was reorganized to be more efficient and responsive to community needs. Some states have created task forces to examine indigent defense. A third response to securing access for the poor is alternative dispute resolution (ADR).

Alternative dispute resolution (ADR) may be the clearest reflection of the entrepreneurial reinvention of American courts. It involves informal mechanisms for resolving arguments and thus channels such disputes out of the courts and into mediation. Mediation is an informal process involving one or more mediators and two or more disputing parties. The mediators' obligation is to help the disputants talk to one another and arrive at a voluntary, mutually agreeable solution. This approach can be used for almost any dispute including divorce and custody arguments; conflicts between neighbors or roommates or businesses; and compensation for minor crime injuries. In San Francisco, Community Boards using voluntary mediators now resolve more disputes than the Municipal Court.[63]

Reinvention of the court systems would also involve strategic planning and a market orientation. Planning initiatives are ongoing in a number of states including Arizona, California, Colorado, Delaware, Georgia, Hawaii, New Hampshire, Maine, Massachusetts, Michigan, Utah, and Virginia.[64] Rather than merely reacting to present contingencies, court systems in these states are attempting to strongly influence their futures through planning.

A market orientation can be seen in state courts in a number of ways. Courts are surveying their customers—attorneys, litigants, and citizens—to ask how the courts are perceived. Maine has adopted total quality management throughout its judicial system. Rules that punish litigants who abuse court processes have been adopted in many states.[65] These are the kinds of changes that indicate that courts are ahead of other parts of the justice system in responding to the entrepreneurial mandates of the 1990s.

CONCLUSION

These proposals for court reform result from discussions concerning the kind of court system that Americans want. These are extraordinarily important discussions, in which citizens of a democracy should participate so as to maintain the rule of law and to secure justice. The search for justice is a constant quest to secure the goal that sets civilized individuals apart from those who have little or no regard for human rights or civil liberties. The search involves all governmental institutions, including law enforcement and corrections. It is to these two institutions that we now turn.

STUDY OBJECTIVES

1. Identify the differences between law and justice.
2. Explain the importance of civil liberties and list those you consider important in your own life.
3. Identify the differences between common law, statutory law, equity law, and administrative law.
4. Identify the differences between civil and criminal law.
5. Delineate the steps in the civil court process.
6. Delineate the steps in the criminal court process.
7. Identify the four systems of state court structures.
8. Identify and discuss the levels of state court systems.
9. Identify the six ways in which judges are chosen.
10. Delineate the differences between judges chosen under the Missouri Plan and those who are elected.
11. Describe the importance of political parties for the election of judges.
12. Identify the various kinds of jurisdictions that apply to courts
13. Identify the cases that are handled in state and local courts.
14. Identify the following terms:
    due process
    subpoena
    bill of information
    discovery
    interrogatory
    alternative dispute resolution
    summons
    subpoena *duces tecum*
    grand jury
    deposition
    integrated bar

GLOSSARY

Administrative law The statutes, regulations, and orders that govern public agencies.

Adversarial system System of justice or adversarial process assumes that justice and the truth will emerge as a result of a contest, governed by Constitutional guarantees of due process, between two well-prepared adversaries, the plaintiff and defendant.

Arraignment Occurs when the defendant hears the charges against him or her and enters a plea of guilty or not guilty.

Bill of information An accusation against an individual made under oath by a prosecuting attorney before a court which may begin the criminal process against that person.

California Plan A method of selecting judges in which the governor nominates one person for each judgeship. If that person is confirmed by the Commission on Judicial

Appointments, he or she must stand for election at the next general election and, if elected, sit on the bench for a 12-year term.

Civil law   has two common uses. It may refer to statutory law. It may also refer to all law that is not criminal law.

Civil liberties   The legal rights guaranteed all citizens by the Bill of Rights, including (but not limited to) the right to free speech, the right to trial by a jury of one's peers, and the right to be free from unreasonable search and seizure.

Criminal law   Statute law, made up of codes that prohibit (and occasionally require) certain behaviors, that can result in sanctions or fines, confinement, or execution.

Codes   Collections of laws or a complete set of interrelated laws.

Common law   Judge-made law.

Contempt of court   Applied to an act that lessens the dignity of the court, interferes with the work of the court, or is a willful disobeying of a judge or court order. It may result in punishment by fine, incarceration or both.

De novo   "Completely new." A de novo trial is a new trial, ordered by a judge or an appeals court, which begins again from the first.

Deposition   The taking of sworn testimony outside of court during the discovery portion of a law suit.

Dispositional justice   The tendency, common in criminal justice bureaucracies, to emphasize efficient processing of cases through plea bargaining.

Discovery   A formal and informal exchange on information between two sides in a law suit.

Doctrine of incorporation   Application of the federal Bill of Rights to the states by using the due process clause of the Fourteenth Amendment.

En banc   The practice of having all justices of a court sitting and hearing the same case. Most state courts of last appeal sit en banc. (Sometime the term is also spelled "in banc" or "in bank.")

Equity law   Law made by judges in an attempt to prevent a wrong.

Full faith and credit clause   The Constitution requires that each state recognize contracts made in other states.

Grand jury   A group of approximately 12 to 23 individuals chosen by the prosecutor whose task it is to review criminal charges and bring formal indictments.

Indictment   A formal accusation of a crime made against a person by a grand jury. The grand jury usually acts at the request of a prosecutor.

Injunction   A judicial ruling that prohibits an action.

Integrated bar   A state bar system which requires lawyers to be dues-paying members of the bar in order to practice law in that state.

Interrogatories   Written questions submitted with a request for written answers during discovery.

Justice   Often defined as fair treatment.

Mapp v. Ohio   A landmark decision by the Supreme Court of the United States ruling that the practice by states of admitting illegally obtained evidence in state criminal trials is a violation of the due process clause of the Fourteenth Amendment to the Constitution.

Missouri Plan   A method of selecting judges. Nonpartisan nominating boards nominate three qualified candidates for each vacant judgeship and the governor appoints from these nominations. After a period of time the judge stands for election.

National Center for State Courts   Located at 300 Newport Avenue, Williamsburg, Virginia, 23187–8798, this organization gathers and freely disseminates data and other information about state trial courts.

Law   It is a rule, statute, or ordinance issued by a unit of government. It is also used in a general sense to refer to the entire body of principles, rules, and statutes which has been created by the various legislative bodies and government agencies.

Paralegal   A legal assistant, working in a law firm or administrative agency, who is trained to help lawyers research cases, prepare briefs, and even prepare preliminary versions of legal documents and interview witnesses.

Plaintiff   Also known as the petitioner or the appellant, the plantiff is the complaining party in a civil case.

Plea bargaining   A process in which the prosecutor and the defendant, through the defense attorney, negotiate the punishment to be assigned in return for a guilty plea.

Preponderance of evidence   Defined as the superior weight or quality of evidence, is the principle by which verdicts are decided in civil cases.

Respondent   The appellee or defendant, the party against whom a complaint has been filed in a civil case.

The rule of law   A system of governing in which decisions are made based upon a set rules that are written and known to many.

The rule of men   A system of governing in which decisions are made based upon the whims of individuals, rather than a set of rules.

Stare decisis   Latin for "Let the decision stand," this is the judicial practice of applying a previously used legal principle to a set of facts to settle a legal dispute.

Statutory law   Law that is enacted by a legislature.

Subpoena   A court's order to a person that he or she appear to testify.

Subpoena duces tecum   A court order that a person appear and bring certain documents when he or she testifies.

Summons   A writ delivered by an authorized person to inform the recipient that a lawsuit has been filed against the recipient.

Writ of mandamus   A judicial ruling that commands an action to be done.

ENDNOTES

1. Richard Quinney, *The Social Reality of Crime*, (Boston: Little, Brown &Co., 1970), 35.

2. 81 S. Ct. 1684 (1961).

3. *Stare decisis* is Latin for "let the decision stand."

4. Jack C. Plano and Milton Greenberg, *The American Political Dictionary*, (New York: Holt, Rinehart and Winston, 1989), 232.

5. Ibid., 233, 243.

6. Libel can also be prosecuted as a criminal offense, though this is rare.

7. See Marica J. Lim, "The State of the Judiciary" in *The Book of the States, 1986–87 Edition*, (Lexington, KY: The Council of State Governments, 1987), 149.

8.Danile Oran, *Law Dictionary for Nonlawyers* (St. Paul: West Publishing Co., 1985), 234.

9. The prosecutor carries the charges to the grand juries. If the grand jury believes that the charge is unwarranted, it can issue a no true bill and thus no one is indicted.

10. Plano and Greenberg, *The American Political Dictionary*, 235.

11. James B. Eisenstein, Roy B. Flemming, and Peter F. Nardulli, *The Contours of Justice: Communities and Their Courts* (Boston: Little, Brown & Co., 1989), 120–121.

12. Herbert Jacob, *Urban Justice: Courts, Lawyers, and the Judicial Process* (Boston, Little, Brown & Co., 1978), 174–181.

13. See, for a discussion of plea bargaining as a method of achieving justice, Arthur Rosett and Donald R. Cressey, *Justice by Consent: Plea Bargains in the American Courthouse* (New York: J. B. Lippincott Co., 1976).

14. Abraham S. Blumberg, *Criminal Justice: Issues and Ironies* (New York: New Viewpoints, 1979), 236, 257–262.

15. Barbara Boland, Catherine H. Conly, Paul Mahanna, Lynn Warner, Ronald Sones, *The Prosecution of Felony Arrests, 1987* (Washington, D.C.: Bureau of Justice Statistics, United States Government Printing Office, 1990), 3.

16. For a discussion of this issue, see Blumberg, *Criminal Justice: Issues and Ironies, 1979*; Herbert Jacob, *Urban Justice: Law and Order in American Cities* (Englewood Cliffs, NJ: Prentice Hall, 1973); Jerome Skolnick, *Justice Without Trial* (New York: John Wiley, 1975).

17. *The Statistical Abstract of the United States, 1993* (Washington, D.C.: United States Government Printing Office, 1994), 205.

18. Brian J. Ostrom, et al. *State Court Caseload Statistics: Annual Report 1992* (Williamburg, VA: National Center for State Courts, 1994), 165.

19. *State Court Caseload Statistics: Annual Report 1987* (Williamsburg, VA: National Center for State Courts), 17. Ostrom et al. *State Court Caseload Statistics: Annual Report 1992*, 5, 11, 43, 171.

20. G. Alan Tarr, "Court Unification and Court Performance: A Preliminary Assessment," *Judicature* (vol. 64, no. 8; March 1981), 356–368.

21. Ostrom et al. *State Court Caseload Statistics*, 166.

22. The distinction made here is between appeals based on questions of fact and based on questions of law. Questions of fact refer to the facts of the case. Was the murderer driving a red or green car? Did the burglar steal a piano or a bassoon? These kinds of disputes are not settled in courts of last appeal. Rather, such courts examine the fairness of the trial, the appropriateness of the judge's rulings, or the admissibility of the evidence.

23. Computed from *The Book of the States, 1994–95*, (Lexington, KY: The Council of State Governments, 1994), 186–187.

24. Timothy J. Flanagan and Katherine M. Jamieson, *Sourcebook of Criminal Justice Statistics*, U. S. Department of Justice, Bureau of Justice Statistics, (Washington, D.C.: U.S. Government Printing Office, 1988), 15.

25. *Employment and Earnings*, Bureau of Labor Statistics (Washington, D.C.; GPO, June, 1988), 30; *Employment and Earnings*, Bureau of Labor Statistics (Washington D.C.; U.S. Government Printing Office, May, 1994), 50.

26. Herbert Jacob, *Urban Justice: Law and Order in American Cities*, (Englewood Cliffs, NJ: Prentice-Hall, 1973), 35.

27. *State Court Caseload Statistics, Annual Report, 1992* (Williamsburg, VA: National Center for State Courts, 1994), 5.

28. Jacob, *Urban Justice: Law and Order in American Cities*, 44; James S. Eisenstein and Herbert Jacob, *Felony Justice: An Organizational Analysis of Criminal Courts* (Boston: Little, Brown & Co., 1977), 285.

29. See Blumberg, *Criminal Justice: Issues and Ironies*, 227–246; Eisenstein and Jacob, *Felony Justice: An Organizational Analysis of Criminal Courts*, 50.

30. Douglas Rosenthal, *Lawyer and Client: Who's in Charge?* (New York: Russel Sage, 1976.)

31. See, for instance, Alan Dershowitz, *Reversal of Fortune* (New York: Random House, 1985); F. Lee Bailey, *The Defense Never Rests* (New York: Stein and Day, Publishers, 1971) .

32. William C. Louthan, *The Politics of Justice* (Port Washington, NY: Kennikat Press, 1979), 82.

33. See Dayton D. McKean, *The Integrated Bar* (Boston: Houghton Miffiin Co., 1963) for a discussion of the history and ethics of integrated state bars.

34. Myrna Oliver, "Bar Wars," *California Lawyer* (Jan/Feb 1988), 30–33.

35. For a discussion of one such response by the Minnesota bar, see J. Kenneth Myers, "The Role of the Bar in Troubled Times—A Minnesota Perspective," *Alabama Law Review*, 38:3, 637–657.

36. Mark Thompson, "Is a Voluntary Statewide Bar in the Works?" *California Lawyer* 81 Jan/Feb 1988, 34–35.

37. Henry R. Glick, *Courts, Politics, and Justice* (New York: McGraw-Hill, 1983), 87; Harry P. Stumpf and John H. Culver, *The Politics of State Courts* (New York: Longman, 1992), 56.

38. Karen L. Tokarz, "Women Judges and Merit Selection under the Missouri Plan," *Washington University Law Quarterly*, 64:15.

39. Glick, *Courts, Politics, and Justice*, 87–88.

40. Harry Abraham, *The Judicial Process: An Introductory Analysis of the Courts of the United States, England, and France* (New York: Oxford University Press, 1986), 23. Selection by sitting judges is used only to choose Chief Justices of the Supreme Courts in 18 states.

41. Adopted in 1934 by a voter initiative and referendum.

42. Abraham, *The Judicial Process*, 38.

43. Computed from *The Book of the States, 1994–95* (Lexington, KY: The Council of State Governments, 1994), 184–202.

44. Ibid., 184–202 and Jamieson and Flanagan, *Sourcebook of Criminal Justice Statistics: 1988*, 110.

45. Computed from data in *The Book of the States, 1994–95*, 184–202.

46. John T. Wold, "Political Orientations, Social Backgrounds, and Role Perceptions of State Supreme Court Judges," *Western Political Quarterly* 27:239–248.

47. Stumpf and Culver, *The Politics of State Courts*, 48.

48. Abraham, *The Judicial Process*, 40–41; Adlai E. Stevenson, "'Reform' and Judicial Selection," *The American Bar Association Journal* (November, 1978), 1683–1685; Henry Robert Glick and Kenneth N. Vines, *State Court Systems* (Englewood Cliffs, NJ: Prentice-Hall, 1973), 46–50.

49. Jacob, *Urban Justice: Law and Order in American Cities*, 72.

50. Stumpf and Culver, *The Politics of State Courts*, 48.

51. Barbara M. Yarnold, *Politics and the Courts* (New York: Praeger, 1992), 32–35.

52. Ibid., 36.

53. Philip L. Dubois, *From Ballot to Bench* (Austin: University of Texas Press, 1980), 248.

54. Ibid.

55. Gregory S. Thielemen, "Local Advantage in Campaign Financing: Friends, Neighbors, and Their Money in Texas Supreme Court Elections," *The Journal of Politics* 55:472–478.

56. Nicholas P. Lovrich, Charles H. Sheldon, and Erik Wasmann, "The Racial Factor in Non-partisan Judicial Elections," *The Western Political Journal* 41:807–816.

57. Anthony Champagne, "Judicial Reform in Texas," *Judicature* 72 146–59.

58. Gregory S. Thielemen, "Local Advantage in Campaign Financing, *The Journal of Politics* 55:472.

59. Computed from data in *The Book of the States 1994–95* , 184–202.

60. Stumpf and Culver, *The Politics of State Courts*, 52.

61. Ibid.

62. Erick B. Low, "Assessing the Judicial System: The States Response" in *The Book of the States, 1994–95 Edition*, 168.

63. David Osborne and Ted Gaebler, *Reinventing Government: How the Entrepreneurial Spirit is Transforming the Public Sector* (New York: Penguin Books, 1993), 51.

64. Erick B. Low, "Assessing the Judicial System: The States Response" in *The Book of the States, 1994–95 Edition*, 178.

65. Ibid., 177

14

The Pursuit of Justice and Order: Crime, Victims, Police, and Prisons

At age 27, Catherine Sneed was told that she was dying from kidney disease. Once a high school dropout and a welfare mother of two children, she had earned a college degree and had a counseling job in the San Francisco County Jail. Instead of dwelling on the unfairness of her life circumstances, Catherine asked her boss, the sheriff in charge of the jail, for what seemed like a last request. Might she and jail inmates revive the weed-filled field that had once been the jail farm? He agreed, and today the eight-acre vegetable garden feeds up to 5,000 people a week at homeless shelters in the Bay area. In addition to the jail garden, inmates have also acquired more land to work as a result of a donation by local businessman Elliott Hoffman.

Approximately 150 inmates work daily in the jail's organic garden, and former inmates earn a living in the donated acreage. Attendance in drug or alcohol rehabilitation programs, school, and regular meetings with counselors or probation and parole officers are required of the former inmates. Neighborhood teenagers are hired to work in the garden as well. Although recidivism figures are unavailable, work in the gardens is a reward, not only for the gardeners, but also for the community that benefits from its bounty. Inmates and former inmates report that their sense of self-worth is created and restored while working in the soil, producing food for their community. Catherine Sneed knew that even men and women convicted of crimes are transformed by the capacity to make a contribution. And why not? Indeed, if we could all see into hearts of all humankind, wouldn't we find that desire to make a contribution, to make a difference in our communities, in most of us?

Oh, and by the way, while creating the gardens, Catherine Sneed's kidneys began to work normally.

CRIMINAL JUSTICE

A government that tolerates high levels of criminal activity cannot long maintain its legitimacy. Yet societies must provide some measure of justice for their residents, even those accused of crimes, if legitimacy is to be maintained. One question for this chapter is what is meant by justice in our criminal justice system. A second question is the theme of this book: Can the justice system be reinvented and transformed by the entrepreneurial spirit?

Various definitions of justice exist. For the prosecutor and the victim, justice is achieved by deterrence and retribution. During a criminal trial the prosecutor asks the jury to convict the accused to deter others from committing crimes. At the end of those trials, the victim or the victim's loved ones may argue that the convicted person should be punished as harshly as the victim was abused in retribution for the suffering inflicted.

For the accused, justice means fair treatment. Justice is achieved through a process which ensures that the government has not illegally punished the defendant. After conviction, justice is punishment which is not inhumane or cruel or unusual. A convicted person's family may argue in favor of rehabilitation because the accused is "sick" and should be in a facility that can help him or her return to a normal life. Without a doubt, justice has many definitions for members of this society!

These conflicting definitions about the appropriate consequences of a criminal trial reflect but a small portion of the disagreement about the nature of justice in America. The question of whether we should seek deterrence, retribution, rehabilitation, or some combination is one for which there is no simple answer. Nevertheless, we must ask difficult questions and examine some difficult—and surprising—facts in order to make the choices that face us in the future.

CRIME AND VICTIMIZATION

National polls frequently show crime to be an issue of great concern to Americans. Yet crime, like poverty, is a permanent feature of society. The issue is not whether or when we will eliminate crime, but how much of it we can tolerate, and how much personal wealth and freedom we will sacrifice to "fight" crime. This section will examine the nature and extent of criminal behavior in the United States; subsequent sections will scrutinize efforts by individuals working together to reduce the debilitating effects of crime.

While crime is a national problem, reducing crime is the responsibility of state and local governments. Funding the "war" on crime is also the responsibility of state and local governments, with little help coming from the federal government.[1] Controlling crime and providing justice within limited budgets is a challenge for governments and for the individuals who assist in the undertaking. Reinventing the justice system is indeed a challenge under these constraints.

What Is Crime?

Crime is the violation of statutory, criminal law; all criminal laws provide for some form of punishment. Criminal statutes clearly delineate the nature of each crime, permitting police officers, attorneys, and judges to make distinctions between similar acts. Murder is more than the killing of one human being by another. To be defined as murder, the killing must be willful, and it cannot be justified by the situation: it cannot be self-defense or the defensible killing of a citizen by a police officer in the line of duty. Similarly, burglary is not simply stealing; in fact, a burglary may involve no theft at all! To be defined as burglary, the act must include unlawful entry of a structure with an intention to commit some felony. (See Box 14.1 for the definitions in the Crime Index.)

How Are Crimes Counted?

There are two methods of counting crimes in the United States: (1) police reports as tabulated by the Federal Bureau of Investigation, and (2) victimization reports as compiled by the Bureau of Justice Statistics.

The Federal Bureau of Investigation has gathered crime statistics from police departments in the United States since 1930, and now publishes crime report summaries every three months. Each year, the F.B.I. publishes the *Uniform Crime Reports*, an annual summary of the crime statistics received from police departments in the United States.

The Federal Bureau of Investigation reports two different forms of crime data: crimes reported and arrests made. "Crimes reported" refers to crimes originally reported by citizens or by the police. "Arrests" refers to the number of arrests, not the number of persons arrested. If a man reports that he was both robbed and beaten, that report counts as two crimes, one crime of robbery and one crime of assault; if three individuals are arrested for robbing and beating the man, those arrests count as three arrests for robbery or three arrests for assault (or some combination of three robberies and assault), depending on the local police department's method of counting and reporting crime. It is important to recognize, however, that most crimes are not reported to police; as a result, another method of measuring the amount of crime, victimization studies, has been developed.

Victimization studies consist of research about victims, and are a second method of counting criminal activity. The Bureau of Criminal Justice Statistics began gathering victimization data in 1972, and now publishes an annual report summarizing the data. The data are collected in a national survey of households.[2] Individuals who are interviewed or who complete questionnaires in this random sample of U. S. households are asked if they or a member of their household has been a crime victim. Those who answer yes to this question are asked if a report was been made to the police. The answers from this sample are extrapolated to the entire population. Thus, the Bureau of Justice Statistics (B.J.S) not only provides information about household victimization, but also provides information about crime reporting by citizens to the police.

The B.J.S reports criminal incidents and victimizations. A **criminal incident** is a "specific criminal act involving one or more victims."[3] A **victimization** is a specific criminal incident that affects one person. An incident may involve a number of crimes, but the incident is counted only once and is categorized by the most serious crime. In the example of the man who was both robbed and assaulted, the Bureau of Justice Statistics would report that criminal incident as one robbery and as one victimization. Thus, more crime occurs than is reported in the B.J.S. annual report (and in *The Uniform Crime Report*).

How Much Crime Occurs in the United States?

All of the statistics you will read in this chapter are estimates about the amount of crime based on police reports or victim interviews. No one really knows how much crime occurs in the United States. The number of crimes counted depends on the method for counting crimes. The Federal Bureau of Investigation reports less crime than does the Bureau of Jus-

BOX 14.1

UNIFORM CRIME REPORT DEFINITIONS

The Federal Bureau of Investigation amasses data from more than 95 percent of the police departments in the United States every year and publishes it in a document entitled, *Crime in the U.S.* This publication is usually referred to as the *Uniform Crime Reports*, and contains information about crimes reported to the police, persons arrested, and law enforcement personnel. The definitions are used to define the Crime Index, those crimes considered by the F.B.I. to be the most serious crimes in the United States

Murder and nonnegligent manslaughter . . . is the willful (nonnegligent) killing of one human being by another. The classification of this offense, as for all other Crime Index offenses, is based solely on police investigation, as opposed to the determination of a court, medical examiner, coroner, jury, or other judicial body. Not included in the count for this offense classification are deaths caused by negligence, suicide, or accident; justifiable homicides; and attempts to murder or assaults to murder, which are scored as aggravated assaults . . .

Forcible rape . . . is the carnal knowledge of a female forcibly and against her will. Assaults or attempts to commit rape by force or threat of force are also included; however, statutory rape (without force) and other sex offenses are excluded . . .

Robbery is the taking or attempting to take anything of value from the care, custody, or control of a person or persons by force or threat of force or violence and/or putting the victim in fear . . .

Aggravated assault is an unlawful attack by one person upon another for the purpose of inflicting severe or aggravated bodily injury. This type of assault is usually accompanied by the use of a weapon or by means likely to produce death or great bodily harm. Attempts are included since it is not necessary that an injury result when a gun, knife, or other weapon is used which could and probably would result in serious personal injury if the crime were successfully completed . . .

Burglary [is] the unlawful entry of a structure to commit a felony of theft. The use of force to gain entry is not required to classify an offense as burglary. Burglary . . . is categorized into three subclassifications: forcible entry, unlawful entry where no force is used, and attempted forcible entry . . .

Larceny-theft is the unlawful taking, carrying, leading, or riding away of property from the possession or constructive possession of another. It includes crimes such as shoplifting, pocket-picking, purse snatching, thefts from motor vehicles, thefts of motor vehicle parts and accessories, bicycle thefts, etc., in which no use of force, violence, or fraud occurs. In the Uniform Crime Reporting Program, this crime does not include embezzlement, "con" games, forgery, and worthless checks . . .

(Continued)

BOX 14.1 (Continued)

Motor *vehicle theft* is defined as the theft or attempted theft of a motor vehicle. [T]his offense category includes the stealing of automobiles, trucks, buses, motorcycles, motor scooters, snowmobiles, etc. This definition excludes the taking of a motor vehicle for temporary use by those people having lawful access . . .

Arson is defined . . . as any willful or malicious burning or attempting to burn, with or without intent to defraud, a dwelling, house, public building, motor vehicle or aircraft, personal property of another, etc. Only fires determined through investigation to have been willfully or maliciously set are classified as arsons. Fires of suspicious or unknown origins are excluded.

Source: Uniform Crime Reports for the United States 1992, Federal Bureau of Investigation, U. S. Department of Justice, (Washington, D.C.: U. S. Government Printing Office, 1993), 13, 23, 26, 31, 38, 43, 49, 53.

tice Statistics. For instance, the F.B.I., using data that came to the attention of police departments, reported 1,932,270 violent crimes in 1992, but the Bureau of Justice Statistics, based on victim reports, estimated that 6.6 million violent crimes occurred.[4] Table 14.1 summarizes the statistics for 1992 reported by both agencies.

Table 14.1

CRIMES OF VIOLENCE AND PROPERTY OFFENSES AS REPORTED BY THE F.B.I. FOR 1991-1993 AND THE B.J.S., 1991, 1992*

	F.B.I. 1993	F.B.I. 1992	F.B.I. 1991	B.J.S. 1992	B.J.S. 1991
All Crimes	14,140,952	14,438,191	14,872,883	33,649,340[f]	34,730,000[f]
Rape[a]	104,806	109,062	106,593	140,930	173,000
Robbery[b]	659,757	672,478	687,732	1,225,510	1,145,000
Aggravated Assault[b]	1,135,099	1,126,974	1,092,739	1,848,530	1,609,000
Burglary[b]	2,843,808	2,979,884	3,157,150	4,757,420[d]	5,138,000[d]
Motor Vehicle Theft	7,820,909	1,610,834	1,661,738	1,958,780	2,112,000
Larceny	1,561,047	7,915,199	8,142,228[c]	8,101,150[e]	8,524,000[e]

*This is the last year for which the B.J.S. has reported victimization rates, as of this printing.
[a]Includes attempts and completed acts; does not include statutory rape.
[b]Includes attempted and completed acts.
[c]Includes all larcenies reported to police.
[d]Includes only household burglaries.
[e]Includes only household larcenies.
[f]Refers to the number of victimizations, not the number of crimes.

Sources: Uniform Crime Reports for the United States 1993, Federal Bureau of Investigation (Washington, D.C.: U.S. Government Printing Office, 1994), 58; Criminal Victimization in the United States, 1992, Bureau of Justice Statistics (Washington, D.C.: U.S. Government Printing Office, 1993), 16.

The Federal Bureau of Investigation and the Bureau of Justice Statistics also provide data concerning the rate of crime and victimization. A **rate** is a measure of the incidence of an event for a base population; the homicide rate is the number of homicides for every 100,000 persons. Rates are useful measures because they permit comparison of different geographical areas or comparisons of the same area over time, regardless of the size of the populations (see Box 14.2).

These differences in the amount of crime reported by the F.B.I. and the B.J.S. suggest that a great deal of crime is not reported by citizens to police agencies. You may wonder why someone would fail to report a crime. Violent crimes are often not reported if they are considered personal or private. Most unreported crime is property crime, and property crime is often not reported when the attempt was unsuccessful or the property was recovered. Fear of reprisal is also a reason commonly given for not reporting crimes to the police.[5] Despite these reasons for nonreporting, the Bureau of Justice Statistics indicates that the proportion of crimes reported to police in 1992 was higher than in 1973, and that almost half of all violent crimes and about 31 percent of all theft crimes were reported to the police.[6]

The variation in crime and victimization rates between areas of the country can be seen in Table 14.2. Although many Americans often think that Eastern states are the most violent, the South contributes disproportionately to the reported rates of homicide and

---

BOX 14.2

THE CALCULATION OF CRIME AND VICTIMIZATION RATES

Crime rates calculated by the Federal Bureau of Investigation are usually based upon a population of 100,000 and are calculated by dividing the number of crimes reported by the population and multiplying by 100,000. If a country of 255,082,000 individuals reports 2,979,900 burglaries in one year, the computation of the *burglary rate* would look like this:

2,979,900/ 255,082,000 =
.0116821 X 100,000 =
1168.2 burglaries per 100,000 inhabitants
or a burglary rate of 1,168.2.

That was, in fact, the burglary rate in the United States for 1992, according to the Federal Bureau of Investigation.

Victimization rates are calculated in much the same way, although they are usually calculated on a population base of 1,000 producing a victimization rate per 1,000 inhabitants. According to the Bureau of Justice Statistics, the rate of robbery in 1991 was 5.6 robberies per 1,000 persons and the rate of rape was .8 per 1,000 persons. According to the Federal Bureau of Investigation's *Uniform Crime Reports*, the national robbery rate was 272.7 robberies per 100,000 persons or 2.72 per 1,000 persons and rape was reported at a rate of 42.3 rapes per 100,000 or .423 per 1,000. In both cases the rates reported by the Federal Bureau of Investigation are approximately half of those reported by the Bureau of Justice Statistics.

Sources: *Uniform Crime Reports for the United States, 1992,* 23, 38; Joan M. Johnson, Criminal Victimization in the United States, 1991 *(Washington, D.C.: U. S. Government Printing Office, 1992),* 3.

Table 14.2

INDEX OF CRIME BY REGION, OFFENSE, AND 1993 POPULATION DISTRIBUTION

Region	Northeast	Midwest	South	West
Population as a percent of the total population	19.9	23.7	34.7	21.7
Crime index total	16.8	20.8	37.8	24.7
Violent crime[a]	19.0	19.1	37.3	24.6
Property crime[b]	16.4	21.0	37.9	24.7
Murder and non-negligent manslaughter	17.1	19.0	41.2	22.7
Forcible rape	13.9	24.6	38.5	22.9
Robbery	25.1	18.9	32.0	24.1
Aggravated assault	16.0	18.7	40.2	25.1
Burglary	15.9	19.4	40.6	24.1
Larceny-theft	15.5	22.3	38.2	24.1
Motor vehicle theft	21.8	17.8	31.9	28.5

[a]Includes murder, forcible rape, robbery, and aggravated assault.

[b]Includes burglary, larceny-theft, and motor vehicle theft.

Source: Uniform Crime Reports for the United States, 1993, Federal Bureau of Investigation, U. S. Department of Justice *(Washington, D.C.: U.S. Government Printing Office, 1994), 59.*

rape. Southern states contain less than 35 percent of the country's population, yet they contribute almost forty-two percent of the reported homicides and 36 percent of the reported forcible rapes.[7]

Another way of thinking about the amount of crime is to examine the change in crime rates over time. The *Uniform Crime Reports* indicates that there are over 5,000 index crimes for every 100,000 persons in the United States. But that rate varied during the last 20 years from a high of 5,950 in 1980 to a low of 4,154 in 1973. From 1983 to 1992, the crime rate increased 9.4 percent, from 5,175 to 5,660, but from 1991 to 1992 the crime rate declined 4 percent, and from 1988 to 1992, the crime rate declined .1 percent.[8]

The Bureau of Justice Statistics reports a victimization rate of 91.2 for personal crimes (rape, robbery, assault, larceny) for 1992; this represents a decline from a high of 130.5 in 1978. The Bureau of Justice Statistics reports a household victimization rate of 152.2 for burglary, larceny, and motor vehicle theft; a decline from the high of 223.4 in 1978.[9] The household victimization rate has been below 200 since 1983.[10]

Who Are the Victims?

A number of stereotypes abound in the media. Were we to believe the world is like what we see on television and the movies or what we read in novels, we would think that white females are the most frequent victims, that minority males are most often the perpetrators, and that murder and rape are the most common crimes. None of these stereotypes is supported by crime data collected by state and local law enforcement agencies (see Box 14.3).

Crime is intraracial; the victim and offender are usually persons of the same race (see Table 14.3 for information on intraracial murders). This point is frequently misrepresented

BOX 14.3

VIOLENCE IN AMERICA: IDEOLOGY AND REALITY

Is the United States becoming a more violent country? A cursory glance at the daily newspaper and the nightly local news reveals support for the suggestion that violence is increasing. Certainly there is evidence that Americans believe violence is increasing. As educated people, it is our obligation to see if that belief is supported by the data.

What data should we examine? By now you know that there are two sources for official statistics about violent crime. Is violence increasing according to the data provided by the Federal Bureau of Investigation or the Bureau of Justice Statistics? The answer is both yes and no.

The F.B.I. reports that the violent crime rate (remember, the rate per 100,000 people) was 417.4 in 1973, 757.8 in 1992, and 746.1 in 1993. That represents an increase of approximately 70 percent, certainly an alarming trend! Nevertheless, additional examination reveals that in 1973 the murder rate was 9.4, and in 1993, the murder rate was 9.5! It is clear then that murder (and nonnegligent manslaughter) does not account for the increase in violent crime. What does?

The brief answer is the dramatic increase in reported aggravated assaults, from a rate of 200.5 in 1973 to 440.1 in 1993. Not only is this a dramatic increase in the rate, but the number of aggravated assaults (420,000 in 1972 and 1,135,000 in 1993) is sufficiently large to lift the entire category of violent crime to the 1993 level. The reported forcible rape rate increased from 24.5 to 40.6, and the reported robbery rate increased from 183.1 to 255.8, but there were 104,810 reported rapes, 659,760 reported robberies, and 24,530 reported murders in 1993. Notice that there were more aggravated assaults reported than murders, rapes, and robberies combined.

What is the Bureau of Justice Statistics answer to the question of whether the United States is becoming more violent? In 1972, the personal crime victimization rate (remember, the rate per 1,000 people) for crimes of violence was 32.6; in 1992 it was 32.1. The victimization rate for rape in 1972 was 1; in 1992 it was .7. The victimization rate for robbery in 1972 was 6.7; in 1992 it was 5.9. The victimization rate for assault in 1972 was 25.5; in 1992 it was 24.9. What this means is that the percent of the population being victimized appears not to have changed. Nevertheless, teenagers and blacks are more likely to be victims of violent crime now than in 1972. So is this a more violent country than in 1972? It depends on who is doing the reporting and how the reports are interpreted.

What can be done about the violence in this country? The National Institute of Justice suggests that our goal should be to prevent violent crime, and that the increased use of imprisonment prevented 10 to 15 percent of potential violent crimes by incapacitation. Nevertheless, comprehensive prevention would focus on a number of dimensions, including a reduction in child abuse and provision of preschool enrichment, nonviolent role models, and instruction in alternative ways to express anger. In addition, community policing programs, economic vitalization of low-income areas, and programs to strengthen community organizations must also be addressed. The causes of violence are complex and diverse; the solutions must be diversified, involving "long-term collaboration . . . between local law enforcement, criminal justice, schools, and public health, emergency medicine, and social service agencies. . . . "

Sources: Uniform Crime Reports for the United States 1993, 58; Criminal Victimization in the United States, 1992, 16; *Albert J. Reiss, Jr. and Jeffrey A. Roth*, Understanding and Preventing Violence (*Washington D.C.: National Academy Press*), 1993–1994, 10.

in television dramas and in the media. In crimes of violence with single offenders, whites are victims of white offenders in 80 percent of all cases in which the offender is white; and blacks are victims of blacks in 84 percent of all cases in which the offender is black. Whites are assaulted by whites in eighty-four percent of all assaults, and blacks are assaulted by blacks 83 percent of the time.[11]

Who becomes a victim varies according to the crime. Males are more likely than females to be victims for violent crimes and for thefts, and males are more likely to be offenders. Individuals between the ages of 16 and 19 have the highest violent victimization rates, and blacks are more likely than whites to be violent crime victims, with black males having the highest victimization rates of all groups. Blacks are significantly overrepresented in the category of murder victim. More blacks were murder victims in 1993 than whites, although more white than black females were murdered.[12] White females have the lowest rate of criminal victimization, and never married males have the highest violent crime victimization rate.[13]

For crimes of theft, whites are more likely than blacks to be victims. Males, once again, have higher victimization rates than females, and unmarried males have the highest victimization rates of all. Individuals between the ages of 12 and 20 are most likely to be victims of theft. City dwellers are more likely than suburbanites to be victims of theft, and rural residents are least likely to be theft victims.[14]

Drugs and Crime

The relationship between drug use and crime is complex. Criminal offenders report much higher drug use than persons in the general population, but 60 percent report that use of drugs began *after* their first arrest.[15] Slightly more than half of all property offenders and almost half of all violent offenders reported drug use in the three months prior to criminal acts, and about half of the violent offenders report alcohol use prior to their crimes (see Box 14.4).[16]

Drug use is unlikely to be the cause of criminal careers, but it may be the precipitating event in criminal acts by increasing aggressiveness or decreasing inhibitions.[17] Drug use may also motivate offenders to commit property crimes to buy drugs, as was reported to be the case by about a fourth of all state prison inmates who were incarcerated for property crimes in 1991.[18] The evidence suggests that attempts at reducing crime by simply reducing drug

Table 14.3

MURDER VICTIMS AND OFFENDER RELATIONSHIP BY RACE AND SEX, 1993

	Race of Offender				Sex of Offender		
Race of Victim	White	Black	Other	Unknown	Male	Female	Unknown
White	4,686	849	58	55	5,057	536	55
Black	304	5,393	18	67	4,985	730	67
Other	61	40	137	2	210	28	2
Unknown	11	17	1	22	27	2	22

Source: Uniform Crime Reports, 1993, Federal Bureau of Investigation (Washington, D.C.: U.S. Government Printing Office, 1994), 17.

BOX 14.4

WHO ARE THE OFFENDERS?

Information about persons arrested comes from the Federal Bureau of Investigation's *Uniform Crime Reports*. In general, males are more often arrested than females, and the crimes for which males are arrested are more serious. In addition, while juveniles are frequently depicted as increasingly violent and criminal, the number of juvenile arrests is declining. The following snapshot of arrest data reported for the year 1993 is instructive:

- Eighty-one percent of the persons arrested were males.
- The number of female arrests increased 14 percent from 1988 to 1992 and 2 percent from 1991 to 1993.
- Driving under the influence is the crime for which males are most often arrested, accounting for 11 percent of all male arrests.
- The number of male arrests[19] increased 5 percent from 1988 to 1992, but declined 2 percent from 1992 to 1993.
- The *number* (not rate) of arrests of persons under age 18 increased 22.2 percent from 1984 to 1993.
- The number of arrests of persons who were 18 or older increased 17.6 percent from 1984 to 1993.
- Whites accounted for 67 percent of all arrests in 1993; blacks accounted for 31 percent of all arrests in the same time period.

Source: Uniform Crime Reports for the United States, 1993, *216–218.*

use are likely to be less than successful since crime usually precedes drug use. The problem of crime is seldom subject to simple solutions.

Current State and Local Programs for Crime Reduction

A number of programs to reduce or prevent crime have been implemented at the state and local level. Many of the most innovative have been at the neighborhood level.[20] While no program can eliminate crime, several approaches have reduced the amount of crime in an area, making citizens feel more secure in their homes and more positive about the communities in which they live.

Crime Stoppers

This is a national program, implemented in a community by the citizens and police of that community. The program is intended to encourage citizen participation in crime deterrence by both offering monetary rewards to individuals who provide information about crime and by involving individuals in crime prevention and deterrence and in raising money for the rewards.

Crime Stoppers operates through local newspapers and television stations. "Crimes of the week" are featured and a telephone number promoted; callers who provide information leading to "the arrest and conviction" of those guilty of the crime are promised large sums of money; they are also promised anonymity. Callers who provide information about other crimes also receive money, an amount usually determined by a local citizens advisory board. This board works closely with police detectives to raise money, publicize the program, choose "Crimes of the Week," and deliver the rewards.

Although the impact of Crime Stoppers on crime rates may not be measurable, studies indicate that the program is a cost effective method of solving felony cases that are unlikely to be solved by traditional methods.[21] Police investigators report that Crime Stoppers has been effective in providing evidence to "crack" difficult cases. Nationally, the program is said to have helped to solve more than 92,000 felony crimes, to convict more than 20,000 criminals, and to recover $562 million in stolen property and narcotics.[22] Individuals who want to contribute to crime fighting efforts in their community should consider a Crime Stoppers program.

Neighborhood Watch Programs

These programs are also often called Crime Watch, Block Watch, or Community Alert, as well as Neighborhood Watch, also involve individuals in crime prevention efforts in their neighborhoods and communities. Working with some agency, usually the local police department, residents form block groups and elect a block captain who is responsible for coordinating the efforts and schedules of participants, as well as integrating his or her group with neighboring block groups. Participants organize crime prevention programs, publish awareness newsletters, and designate safe houses for children to run to when danger threatens. The goal of such groups is to increase citizen awareness of the conditions under which crime is most likely to occur and thus reduce the likelihood of crime.

A variety of techniques have been developed in neighborhood watch programs to facilitate citizen awareness about crime, including telephone chains, newsletters, and meetings. Neighborhood watch signs are placed in the neighborhood, and intensified surveillance is encouraged.[23] Local police departments are usually willing to participate in "operation identification" programs that involve engraving of citizens' property with identifying symbols and "operation lock-up" programs which distribute security locks to citizens.[24]

The most common problem faced by block groups is maintaining citizen enthusiasm for the project, but studies of one program in Philadelphia indicate once more the importance of individuals willing to provide proper leadership. Innovative block watch captains, supported by local police officers, can keep programs alive and make significant contributions to their communities.[25]

LAW ENFORCEMENT: THE CHALLENGE OF POLICING A FREE SOCIETY

A discussion of policing will enable us to better understand the principles of limited government and to know what state and local law enforcement officers do while being paid with our tax dollars. Few persons in the United States are more aware of the principles of limited government than police officers, who must deal with the constraints of limited government on a daily basis. Police officers take an oath to maintain the peace and uphold the law, but they must do so in a legal system designed to prevent the abuse of power. The rules that govern police officers (as well as attorneys, judges, correctional officers, and other officers of the court) restrict their ability to intercede in the lives of individuals. Whether these legal constraints also unnecessarily restrict the ability of police officers to protect individuals from crime is an ongoing debate in our society.

An example of the restrictions on police officers is in order. Suppose two police officers, while patrolling an interstate highway, see an old van painted with peace symbols and sporting several bumper stickers which advocate drug use and "free love." A bearded man familiar to the police as a drug dealer is driving the van. In the van with him are three other men with long hair and beards. The police officers suspect, as a result of their experience, that the van contains illegal drugs as well as other illegal items such as burglary tools or stolen goods. But even if the police know that each of the men has a history of drug or burglary convictions, they may not legally stop the van to search it unless they have more than a suspicion. They must have **probable cause**, the right to infringe on the liberty of others because of a belief about their activities resulting from trustworthy information which could be interpreted by a reasonable person to mean that a crime is taking place (or has taken place) and that the person in question is (or was) a participant in that crime.[26]

There are conditions under which the police officers could stop the van. If they knew that a crime had been committed by persons fitting the general description of the men in the van; if one of the men was seen by the police officer throwing a marijuana cigarette out the window; or if the van was clocked going faster than the speed limit, then the police officers could stop the van. Under any of these conditions, as well as others, the police officers would have a right to invade the privacy of the men by detaining them, and in some circumstances the officers could search the men and the van, seize any illegal substances or stolen goods, and arrest the van occupants. These conditions constitute probable cause for believing a crime has been committed.

You may want to know why the police officers cannot simply stop the van if they believe the men have committed or might commit a crime. The reason is that individuals in the United States are protected from arbitrary and capricious interference in their lives by the government and its agents. Most people in the United States believe that it is better to have as much personal freedom or liberty as possible; if police officers were able to intercede easily in the lives of individuals, the personal freedom of individuals would be reduced.

Providing the police with more authority does not necessarily mean that police officers could, by themselves, reduce crime. In fact, police officers are simply part of the larger criminal justice system which has some impact on criminal activity. It is also important to understand that criminal justice systems are themselves simply part of the larger society and that criminal justice systems reflect the political culture of that society.

All other things being equal, according to students of comparative government and criminologists, the more efficient the criminal justice system, the lower the official crime rates in a country. However, it is also the case that efficient, coercive criminal justice systems tend to exist in societies whose people value order more than freedom.[27] We value the individual and individual freedom in this country. It is not likely that Americans would tolerate, without question, the idea of having their homes randomly searched and their property capriciously seized in order to reduce crime, without significant protest and demands for an end to the "police state."

The Number of Law Enforcement Personnel

Fighting crime is a primarily state and local activity. The Bureau of Justice Statistics reported that there are 17,358 state and local law enforcement agencies in the United States;

of those, more than 12,300 are general purpose local police forces, reflecting the emphasis placed by Americans on local control of the police.[28] The duties of these agencies include law enforcement, order maintenance, and service to the community.

The number of law enforcement personnel has remained fairly stable since 1972. In 1987, there were 555,364 sworn officers and 202,144 civilians employed in law enforcement by state and local governments; in 1992, there were 603,954 sworn officers and 204,521 civilians employed in law enforcement by state and local governments.[29] In recent years larger cities have had a higher ratio of law enforcement personnel to the total population than have suburbs and small towns. Cities of 250,000 or more had, on the average, 2.8 law enforcement employees per 1,000 residents, the highest per capita average for all city population groups. The lowest per capita ratio was 1.7 law enforcement employees per 1,000 residents for cities with populations of between 25,000 to 99,999.[30]

Kinds of Law Enforcement Personnel

Law enforcement personnel can be divided into many categories. One basic distinction is between sworn officers and civilians. **Sworn officers** are individuals who have undergone sufficient training to meet state requirements to fulfill all the duties of the police role. These duties include detaining individuals, making arrests, and using deadly force. Civilians are all other employees who work for any law enforcement agency. They include secretaries, many radio dispatchers and lab technicians, as well as crime investigators and other office workers. Civilians make up a quarter of all law enforcement personnel.[31]

It is also possible to classify law enforcement personnel by jurisdiction. Municipal law enforcement personnel usually work in city police departments, but they may be assigned to the city sheriff or prosecuting attorney's office. The duties and activities of municipal law enforcement officers—urban police officers—will be covered in depth later in the chapter.

County law enforcement employees work in sheriff's departments, although a few large cities also have sheriffs who may be independent of or consolidated with the local municipal government.[32] In 1992 there were 3,086 sheriff offices in all states except Alaska and Hawaii.[33] Sheriffs, who are elected in all states except Rhode Island and Hawaii (where they are appointed), typically perform the following duties: (1) maintaining a jail; (2) providing police protection; (3) maintaining court security; and (4) serving process papers.[34]

Nine of 10 sheriffs are responsible for maintaining a jail. Although training is not required to be a sheriff, there are requirements in all states for becoming a sworn officer. Where sheriffs are sworn officers, they are often required to investigate crime, particularly in rural areas that are not patrolled by a police department. Sheriff's departments also provide security in courthouses and courtrooms. In addition, sheriffs may be required to serve papers informing individuals that they have been called as jurors, witnesses, or have legal judgments against them, or to serve a summons.

State police personnel are employees of agencies named either as the State Police, the State Highway Patrol, or the State Department of Public Safety. All states, except Hawaii, have such an agency, and in 1992 there were 52,980 officers employed in those 49 state agencies.[35] Within these agencies, officers are responsible for investigating violations of state statutes, either in association with local police personnel or independent of them. Some state police agencies have specialized departments for investigating the sale and transportation of illegal drugs, white collar crime, or organized crime, depending on the particular problems faced by the state, often as a result of its location. For instance, border states—

Texas, Florida, California—have had specialized state police drug enforcement departments for decades, while northeastern states—New York, New Jersey, Pennsylvania—have maintained state police organized crime departments for decades. In many states, state police agencies have almost complete responsibility for the investigation of white collar crime, including consumer fraud and embezzlement.

Who Becomes a Police Officer?

The women and men who choose law enforcement as a career are average Americans with no unusual personality traits. In recent years, an emphasis on professionalization has led to more sophisticated selection procedures, so that police officers are carefully selected from those persons who aspire to the role. Many states require psychological evaluations of would-be police officers to find individuals who can handle the pressures of police work; professional police departments demand extensive background investigation of applicants for the same reason. In order to select the best officers, police administrators, often with civilians who serve on police commissions or civil service commissions, interview potential police officers, asking about their ideas concerning police work, their anticipated behavior in specific situations, and their views on deadly force and police discretion.

Police officers in state and local municipal departments are typically white males, but civilian employees are primarily females. In 1987, 92 percent of all sworn officers were male,

Police officers fight crime in a variety of ways, often by helping citizens avoid becoming victims. In this case the officer is telling the children how to respond when approached by strangers.

and in 1992, 91 percent were male; however, 64 percent of all civilian law enforcement employees were women in 1987 and in 1992.[36] For state police departments in 1990, the figures were 95 percent male, and 5 percent female. Whites are overrepresented among officers, making up eighty-seven percent of state police officers. Blacks and Hispanics are significantly underrepresented, since 7.5 percent of the officers were black, and 4.4 percent were Hispanic.[37]

What Do Police Officers Do?

More has been written about the activities of the urban police officer than any other individual in law enforcement (except, perhaps, the private detective). Despite their portrayal on television and in the popular press, police officers do not make a felony arrest or fire a weapon on an average tour of duty. On a typical day, in a typical city, the average police officer spends the greatest amount of time on service activities and the least amount of time on law enforcement activities.[38] Patrol officers spend much of their time driving around the city, answering calls from citizens, and initiating calls on their own.

Three basic categories of police officer activity are the **components of the police role** as described by James Q. Wilson in his classic study, *Varieties of Police Behavior*. The three components are

1. law enforcement, which involves all those activities whose obligations end with an arrest or citation and in which law is used as a tool to punish;
2. order maintenance, which involves all those activities designed to restore order or avoid disorder and which may end in arrest, but only if order cannot be secured in any other way ; and
3. service, which involves all those activities designed to please the public by providing aid or service to members of the community.[39]

Serious situations—those involving the law enforcement component—are likely to begin when a citizen "calls the cops." Formal intervention—detaining or arresting a suspect or issuing a citation—is most likely to occur when the police define an individual's activity as serious, either dangerous to the individual or others.

Why Do Police Officers Do What They Do?

Explaining why anyone does anything is tricky business, but police behavior (the ways that police officers act while on duty)—whether they tend to arrest potential lawbreakers, counsel potential lawbreakers, or spend much of their time providing service to the community—has been the subject of a great deal of research. Three aspects of police officers' life have been found to be important in explaining police behavior: (1) training and socialization into the role of police officer; (2) policy established by the police department; and (3) the stress of the daily demands of the occupation.

Training

Training is required of all individuals who become police officers, usually at a county or municipal training center. Most state training requirements stress human relation and crisis intervention skills; weapons training; knowledge of law; and communications. Patrol techniques and criminal investigation skills, however, take up the majority of the training time. Firearm use and self protection are crucial aspects of training, as is mastering the law and its intricacies. The goal of such training is to produce an officer who is courageous and suspicious, who can exercise authority, and who can cope with the constant threat of danger as well as the occasional possibility of corruption.

Socialization

This is the process of learning the norms, values, and roles of a culture. The process of socialization into the police role turns an average individual into a person who can cope with sights and activities few Americans know much about.[40] Police officers see violence and tragedy; they hear curses directed at them; they feel hostility and rejection. At the same time, police officers intercede in troubled situations to help individuals, and they must do so with authority and dispassion.

The ability to handle all aspects of this difficult job must be learned. Much of the learning takes place after formal training in the socialization process where police officers come to learn what is expected of them by those individuals with whom they come into frequent contact: other police officers, good citizens, potential criminals, and momentarily misguided individuals.

Departmental Policy

Having department policy is necessary because police officers must use **discretion**, the right to choose between two or more task-related alternatives regarding their work. Because police officers cannot stop all law violators they see—they simply do not have the time or resources to do so—they must decide when individuals and situations merit official interest.

Remember the example about two police officers who see a van carrying several men suspected of having committed a crime? In the example described, the officers had no legal right to stop the van, but if the van were traveling 10 miles over the speed limit, the situation would require that police officers use discretion. Should they stop the van, or should they direct their attention in other areas that might be more important? Police officers must regularly use discretion under circumstances much more complex and ambiguous than those described in this example.

James Q. Wilson has argued that controlling the discretionary decisions of patrol officers is one of the most important goals of police administrators.[41] To control discretion, administrators create department policy to guide the discretionary decisions of police officers. A particular kind of policy produces a particular style of policing. Since controlling discretion is so important, police behavior can be understood by studying departmental policy and arrest or citation rates. Nevertheless, departmental policy can only provide general guidelines for the exercise of discretion; as a result, discretion has significant implications for civil liberties and the rule of law.[42]

Police officers may exercise discretion by ignoring a situation or intervening in a situation. If intervention is chosen, police officers may do so informally (giving the individual a warning or a lecture), or formally (making an arrest or issuing a citation). If the decision is made to intervene formally, police officers must be aware of the individual's legal rights. If rights are violated, the subsequent arrest or citation may be declared invalid, and the police officer may be subject to disciplinary or legal procedures.

On the other hand, much of what police officers do is done in private, without meaningful public scrutiny; thus, police officers may be able to "get away with" illegal actions against individuals. Civil liberties are secure only to the extent that police departments require officers to ensure them and courts see to it that individuals receive them. The problems involved in policing a democratic society, while maintaining sufficient order for regular commerce, are significant and their solutions are not without cost.

Stress

Stress shapes the role of the police officer in this society. It is the police officer who provides the most visible reminder of the potential for crime and violence, the seamy side of life in the United States.[43] Police work is stressful for several other reasons: (1)the conflict between civil liberties and order; (2)rejection by citizens; and (3)threat of violence and the use of force.

Perhaps the most problematic aspect of police work is the necessity of providing civil liberties while enforcing statutory law. This conflict between fighting crime and protecting civil liberties produces significant role strain among police officers. To cope with this stress, police officers adapt in a number of ways, including becoming overly aggressive, cynical, and unemotional.[44] They also may develop an "us-versus-them" attitude toward individuals and, as a result, withdraw into the police subculture.[45] To the extent that police officers withdraw, they become isolated from the average individual and may lose contact with good citizens.

Isolation increases the stress of police officers. Since police officers remind many people of things they would rather forget, citizens may be less likely to befriend them. This adds to the feelings of isolation and rejection experienced by police officers. This feeling is particularly problematic when police officers think about the risks they take for citizens who seem not to appreciate the work done by them. These feelings of isolation and resentment, coupled with the demand that police officers enforce the law under due process guidelines, make police work very stressful.

Indicators of stress and role strain are higher than average rates of divorce and substance abuse; in 1986, a survey of major departments found that administrators viewed the potential for drug abuse among officers to be so significant that policies and procedures for dealing with the problem had been initiated.[46] Although it is difficult to generate statistics about suicide among police officers, it is generally believed that law enforcement officers are more likely to take their lives than members of many other professions.[47]

The use of force makes the police officer's job very stressful. Police officers have an almost unrestricted right to use force, but Americans devalue the use of force in their own lives (while apparently enjoying its expression in movies and television), preferring education and intellect as methods of solving problems. However, since individuals occasionally use violence, the capacity for a legal response to the illegitimate use of force must exist. But since the use of force cannot be admired lest force become too popular (and therefore frequent), even those who have the legal right to use it suffer a loss of status and prestige for their willingness to take on such an obligation. The phrase, "It's a dirty job, but someone has to do it," surely applies to police work.[48]

Police officers and their families bear many of the costs of police work, but the public also suffers if police officers experience job-related problems. Police work is rarely done in public view, and secrecy sets the stage for abuse of power. The private, stress-related problems of a police officer have the potential to become the public, legal problems of an individual.

Future of Law Enforcement in the United States

A number of proposals have been generated to change police work, some with the hope of making police work more efficient; others with the hope of making it more just. A few intend to reduce the stress experienced by police officers.

More Personnel?

One proposal for reducing the stress experienced by police officers is to increase the number of police officers. More personnel should mean less work and, therefore, less stress. More personnel should also mean more deterrence and, therefore, less crime.

There is some evidence that a dramatic increase in the number of police officers patrolling an area can reduce the amount of reported crime, but the evidence that more officers equates with less crime is far from conclusive. Early flawed studies seemed to demonstrate the relationship between increased patrols and crime reduction (and led to some of the dramatic increases in police department size), but subsequent studies have invalidated this relationship (the Kansas City Preventive Patrol Study) or suggested that the cost of such a crime reduction is more than individuals are willing to pay (the Rand Institute's New York City Subway Study).[49]

Whether more personnel would reduce the stress of overwork is not known. While some police departments are understaffed by national standards, it is not clear that adding police officers reduces the amount of work for each police officer. It may be that adding police officers ultimately produces additional work, since citizens are more likely to "call the cops" if the police are able to come when called.

Take the Handcuffs Off Police Officers?

One of the problems faced by police officers is the role strain caused by the conflict between fighting crime and protecting civil liberties. Some individuals have suggested that this conflict be reduced or eliminated by reducing or eliminating due process. One rather frequent proposal is to reduce the rights of individuals by reducing the scope of the **exclusionary rule**, thus permitting more police intervention and thereby reducing crime. (As noted in a preceding chapter, the exclusionary rule is the legal guideline which says that illegally gathered evidence may not usually be used in a criminal trial.)

During their tenure as attorney generals in the Reagan administration, William French Smith and Edwin Meese asserted that the exclusionary rule, along with the Miranda warning, significantly reduced the ability of police officers to enforce the law, and therefore should be abolished.[50] While the weakening or abolition of the exclusionary rule would, no doubt, make the job of police officers easier in that they would be able to intervene more readily in the lives of individuals, it is not nearly as clear that such intervention would reduce the crime rate. A number of studies indicate that the exclusionary rule has very little impact on crime in either direction.[51] On the other hand, it is obvious that the elimination of the exclusionary rule would make the apprehension of criminals much easier, thereby making the police officers' task of fighting crime more efficient and, presumably, more satisfying.

A recent limiting of the exclusionary rule is the **good faith exception,** that holds that evidence gained when officers unknowingly and in good faith serve an invalid warrant is admissible in court. The good faith exception now applies only to warrants containing errors created by a magistrate. If the exclusionary rule continues to be modified by the good faith exception, it will mean that evidence gathered by police officers who violate the civil liberties of individuals without actually intending to will be admissible in a court of law. It may be that weakening or eliminating the exclusionary rule would reduce the role strain experienced by police officers, thus reducing the stress of the occupation, but it would also, of course, dramatically reduce the freedom and liberty of Americans.

Reinventing Police Work

Changes have been suggested to reduce job stress as well as enhance community safety. These new approaches underscore community involvement as a method of reducing stress and crime at the same time.[52] One suggestion has been that departments implement some version of the **community policing** approach to crime reduction. This phrase is a catch-all term that applies to a variety of methods for deploying police officers, but it is generally an approach for "bringing the police and the community together in a closer working relationship to reduce crime and make communities safer."[53] In some cities, it is similar to the Japanese strategy of giving police officers "semi-permanent" responsibility for a neighborhood or a part of a city.[54] San Diego, California, for instance, is implementing a plan to create 21 "mini-police departments" or police districts, each with neighborhood policing teams. In all cases, officers are expected to become familiar with residents, thereby increasing citizen confidence in the competence of police officers and increasing citizen willingness to provide information and support to the police.[55] Herman Goldstein describes the expectations for police officers in a neighborhood served by community policing:

> Advanced forms of community policing reject many of the characteristics stemming from the emphasis on enforcement. A neighborhood police officer, for example, is expected to have a much broader interest than simply enforcing the criminal law, to exhaust a wide range of alternatives before resorting to arrest for minor offenses, to exercise broad discretion, and to depend more on resourcefulness, persuasion, or cajoling than on coercion, image, or bluff.[56]

Community policing is a crime-fighting strategy. Since the police cannot, by themselves, adequately fight crime, they must secure community involvement if meaningful crime reduction is to occur. Just as important, officers must know members of the community and be familiar with its culture. Advocates of this approach believe that this approach could reduce the isolation and stress experienced by police officers. Police officers support this idea.

> "Some of the regular beat officers are so frustrated and busy they don't care," said Doug Beckham [a Linda Vista, California resident]. "But the neighborhood policing team has time to do follow-up."

> [Neighborhood police officer Mike] Aiken told The Union Tribune that his participation in the neighborhood policing team has given him greater pride in his work. "My pager goes off around the clock. My wife doesn't like it, . . . but I need to know what's going on there. . . . If you're a neighborhood cop, it's more personal to you. You take more pride in it. I know everyone. I love working up there."

> As a result of his involvement in the team, Aiken said he is no longer a "slave to the radio, going from one call to another. It gives us flexibility to understand problems and do something about it."[57]

A similar approach had been called the **community service** approach, designed to mobilize neighborhood support by encouraging citizen participation in neighborhood management. Proponents of this approach believe that police officers should emphasize social work skills while dealing with individuals. Police officers should consider many of their duties as responses to requests for help in dispute settling rather than demands that arrests be made. Police officer integration and feelings of security within the community should result, enabling community members to demand higher standards of behavior from one another. James Q. Wilson, who does not advocate the community service approach, nevertheless argues that properly trained police officers "can help evoke a sense of community and a capacity for regulation where none is now found."[58]

The community service approach is not a crime-fighting approach, but rather a method of helping members of a community police themselves. Self-regulation should lead to crime reduction, proponents argue; perhaps more important for police officers, it could reduce citizen antagonism toward them, thus reducing their feelings of isolation and rejection.

It is important to recognize that changes in police work, while perhaps alleviating some of the stress and frustration found among police officers, are not likely to reduce the overall crime rate significantly. Those communities that experiment with new forms of police work may experience higher levels of order, but it is likely that the truly criminal in those communities will simply move to more accommodating neighborhoods. The crime rate is a national social problem, not a local police problem.

What Can the Individual Do?

Individuals can contribute to local police departments in a number of ways. They can become active in civil service commissions; sit on civilian review boards; join the police reserve units; participate in crime prevention organizations; and support state and local politicians who have similar ideas about law enforcement priorities.

Civil Service Boards Are Staffed by Individuals of the Community

Many municipal police departments are protected by civil service regulations. Cronyism is reduced in these departments because hiring and promotion is done through testing and interview.

Departments governed by civil service regulations often have citizens on their personnel boards who interview aspiring officers. Employment and promotion are important decisions that can influence the course of police work in a city. Individuals interested in becoming involved in their police department should notify local politicians of their local government about their interest.

Individuals Can Also Be on Civilian Review Boards in Some Police Departments

These boards are groups of citizens who review important police actions. Civilian review boards may examine the use of deadly force or undercover operations. Individuals who want to participate on civilian review boards should become involved in local politics and become known in the community as having an interest in these issues.

Police Reserve Programs Are Also Available to Individuals

Some individuals want to do police work, but do not want to make a career of it. They may be candidates for a local police reserve program. In most cases, reserve officers must meet the same employment standards as police officers. Civilian reserve officers are trained in the basics of police work and teamed with police officers. Reserves are expected to donate their time doing routine police work, which occasionally becomes as exciting and dangerous as professional police work. If this sounds appealing to you, contact your local police department to see if a police reserve unit exists. If one does not exist, talk to the chief of police about starting one!

One of the most helpful tasks individuals can do is to participate in crime prevention activities. These activities include but are not limited to those mentioned earlier: joining neighborhood watch programs and Crime Stoppers, or raising money for drug education and prevention efforts. Police officers cannot fight crime without citizen support; significant reductions in crime rate will not occur unless individuals participate in the crime prevention. If crime prevention sounds like something with which you would like to become involved, find out about the programs in your area. If no programs exist, start one!

Finally, individuals who care deeply about police issues, civil liberties, and crime reduction can become involved in the state and local political process. These issues are crucial to the maintenance of democratic societies. Become involved to make your views known. Support candidates who share your views. These activities are the lifeblood of a democratic society.

CORRECTIONS: THE CHALLENGE OF HUMANE AND EFFECTIVE PUNISHMENT

Like other debates in the criminal justice system, the corrections debate centers on whether deterrence, retribution, or rehabilitation should be the goal of corrections. The treatment of incarcerated individuals is as important in a free society as their treatment prior to conviction since almost all persons who enter prison are released back into society, carrying with them the lessons learned in prison. Nevertheless, the first mandate for correctional departments is to control those who have been apprehended and sentenced.

The first goal of all American prisons is **custody**, containing prisoners within the prison. The second goal of all American prisons is **control**, retaining authority over the prisoners' actions within the prison. Correctional officers are trained to respond to threatening situations so as first to maintain custody and then to maintain control. Policy does not permit administrators to accede to prisoners' demands in order to gain the release of correctional officers who have been taken hostage. Custody and control are the most important rules in corrections.

The Types of Correctional Facilities

There are two forms of facilities designed to incarcerate adults for some period of time: jails and prisons. **Jails** are detention facilities designed to hold several kinds of persons for "short" periods of time, including those (1)awaiting arraignment or trial; (2)awaiting sentencing; (3)sentenced and awaiting transport to prison; (4)convicted of probation or parole violations; or (5)given a sentence of less than a year and a day.

Jails held less than 9 percent of all inmates in 1991, but as we will see, both jails and prisons have experienced phenomenal growth in inmate populations during the past decade. In 1983, there were approximately 221,600 adult jail inmates, slightly more than half of whom had not been convicted of the crime for which they were jailed; by 1991, that number had grown to 422,000 and again, slightly more than half had not been convicted of the crime for which they were jailed. Men, since they are most often arrested, are the most common residents of jails; women made up only seven percent of the jail population in 1983 and 9 percent in 1991, reflecting a slight increase in female arrests. Jail populations have a high volume of inmate turnover. In the year ending June 28, 1991, the more than 3,538 local jails reported more than 20 million admissions and releases (see Table 14.4).[59]

Prisons are facilities designed to hold adults sentenced for a year or more. State prisons are typically thought of as having three levels of security: minimum, medium, and maximum. Maximum security prisons, designed to house the most serious felons in the society, pursue the goal of custody with seeming disregard of the consequences for inmates:

> The sixty maximum security prisons in the United States are surrounded by high walls or double fences, accompanied by manned towers. Electronic sensing devices and lights impose unremitting surveillance. The prisons have heavily barred and inside cell blocks with two to six tiers of cells, back-to-back . . . To achieve full custodial control, as well as inmate surveillance, there are frequent searches of cells and inmates for weapons and other contraband . . . Doors which might permit privacy are replaced by grilles of tool-resistant steel. Toilets are open and unscreened . . . Body searches frequently precede and follow visits [by persons outside the prison] . . . Fifty-six maximum security prisons, built between 1830 and 1900 and since remodeled and expanded, are still in use—the backbone of the American prison system.[60]

Medium security institutions commonly have fences rather than walls, and have a variety of types of living quarters. Often inmates live in barracks or dormitories, and their privacy is less frequently invaded by correctional officers. Minimum security prisons also may have barracks or dormitories, but supervision is less than medium security prisons. Inmates may work in fields or farms attached to the minimum security prison.

Prison boot camps have become a popular approach for dealing with young, nonviolent criminals. Thirty states have implemented boot camps for adults, with Georgia and Oklahoma beginning the trend in 1983. There are more than 7,000 available beds, including 1,500 in New York, 800 in Georgia, and 600 in Michigan. Offenders spend an average of 107 days in such camps. Between 8 and 50 percent of the inmates fail to complete the programs.[61]

The belief supporting such camps is that young offenders can be rehabilitated if they receive the kind of treatment experienced by military recruits in basic training. When new inmates arrive at the boot camp, their heads are shaved and rules are distributed. Subsequent rule infractions result in physical punishment, and daily activities include pre-dawn roll calls, marching and exercise drills, physical labor, counseling, and community service. Prison boot camps have the stated goals of reducing recidivism and accomplishing rehabilitation; research as to their effectiveness is inconclusive at this time. Although boot camp inmate attitudes become less antisocial while incarcerated, regular prison inmates also report a decline in antisocial attitudes while in prison.[62]

State jails have also been proposed for Texas. These "jails" are intended to bridge the gap between prisons and community corrections. Prisoners will be sentenced to the state jails under a new class of fourth-degree felonies to serve sentences of up to two years without the possibility of early parole. In addition, they will participate in substance abuse, job training, and educational programs. Legislators sponsoring the approach intend that the jails will avoid the violence and cruelty inherent in standard prisons and will, as a result, permit rehabilitation of inmates.[63]

Private prisons exemplify the entrepreneurial spirit in the criminal justice system. Prisons financed by the state cost more than $250,000 per bed; housing a prisoner averages at least $39,000 per year, including the cost of building the cell amortized over 30 years.[64] Given these costs, states have enlisted the resources found in the private sector which has gotten onto the business of incarcerating inmates in hopes of making a profit. The prison-management business includes 19 companies which have constructed more than 50 facilities housing in excess of 23,000 inmates, almost half of them in Texas.[65]

Proponents of private prisons point out that private enterprise can build facilities more quickly, manage them more efficiently, and save state and local governments approximately 15 percent of the cost. Freer from political whims, private prisons can create innovative rehabilitation programs, while offering modern classrooms and cells. Opponents of private prisons note the possibility that prison-management companies may be in a position to demand higher fees once they become the primary incarcerators of a state's inmates. Whether those in favor of or opposed to private prisons are correct—and they both may be—such facilities have made the dramatic increase in imprisonment possible and continuing (see Box 14.5).

Imprisonment in the United States

The history of imprisonment is somewhat short. Until relatively recently, having a roof over one's head and three meals a day could hardly be considered punishment. Prior to the eighteenth century, mutilation and execution were the most common forms of punishment. In an ironic way, the American Revolutionary War ultimately led to the birth of prisons for two reasons: (1) the developing emphasis on republicanism; and (2) the loss of the colonies as a "dumping ground for convicts."

The loss of the colonies made new forms of punishment necessary. At the same time, the philosophy emphasizing the right of free people to choose their government (and, therefore, to reject an inhumane government) guided political philosophers to a doctrine of utilitarian punishment: that punishment should be only so severe as to dissuade future criminal acts, but no more severe than that lest the persons punished become unfit for living among good individuals.[66] Deterrence became the goal of the correctional system and imprisonment was thought to be a more effective deterrent than execution, since the imprisoned individual would be around as an example of the cost of crime.

The earliest prisons in the United States were the penitentiaries in Pennsylvania requiring solitude and "penitence" (hence the name). The assumption that men (since almost all prisoners *were* men), if given time to reflect on their misdeeds, would reform themselves soon gave way to a harsher view of human potential. Later prisons in the United States were modeled on the Auburn plan, which originally emphasized solitary confinement, but soon gave way to a philosophy of corporal punishment, strict discipline, and arduous labor.[67]

Rehabilitation became the stated goal of many correctional systems after World War II. The rehabilitative ideal, the notion that inmates given the opportunity to change and be rehabilitated could do so, became popular. Various strategies, from individual and group therapy, and behavior modification to job training and educational programs, were implemented.

Robert Martinson officially certified the failure of the rehabilitative ideal in 1974 with his survey of studies concerning rehabilitation.[68] His conclusion, widely reported and very influential, was that rehabilitation attempts in prisons, halfway houses, and reformatories,

BOX 14.5

AIDS IN PRISON

Acquired Immunodeficiency Syndrome (AIDS) and tuberculosis (TB) have become serious problems in the 1990s, in and out of prison. Both pose major problems for prisoners, correctional officers, and administrators. State inmate populations include a higher incidence of persons in the high risk groups—intravenous drug users and males with homosexual contacts. As of October 1987, there were 1,964 reported cases of AIDS in correctional institutions throughout the country. By March, 1993, there were 11,565 inmate AIDS cases in state and federal prisons, with 8,525 of those in state prisons. There were 3,040 cases reported in local jails.

Tuberculosis was thought to be nearly eradicated prior to the appearance of the Human Immunodeficiency Virus (HIV). HIV is the driving force behind the rise of TB, which is now reaching epidemic proportions. James Curran, Deputy Director of the Centers for Disease Control, argues that TB and AIDS are part of a tripartite epidemic, the third disease being drug abuse. TB is a problem within prisons and jails because confinement significantly increases the likelihood that the TB bacterium will be passed on by breathing infected air.

How to house and care for inmates diagnosed with AIDS and tuberculosis is a critical issue. Screening inmates for AIDS without violating their rights is another important issue. Liability issues must be considered as well. If administrators are found liable for failing to protect inmates from AIDS infection while they are incarcerated, taxpayers will have to pay for judgments against those administrators.

Of much concern is what to do with inmates who are released from prison with AIDS. There are no legal justifications for retaining persons in prison past their release dates; moreover, having AIDS is not grounds for incarceration. It may be in the long-term interests of citizens to be concerned about the adequacy of rehabilitation programs if unreformed inmates are released to prey on communities again.

Sources: Theodore M. Hammett, Aids in Correctional Facilities, Bureau of Justice Statistics (Washington, D.C.: U. S. Government Printing Office, May 1988), xvii; Theodore M. Hammett, Lynne Harrold, Michael Gross, and Joel Epstein, 1992 Update: HIV/AIDS in Correctional Facilities, U. S. Department of Justice (National Institute of Justice; U. S. Government Printing Office, 1994), 14; Tuberculosis in Correctional Facilities, U. S. Department of Justice (National Institute of Justice; U. S. Government Printing Office, 1994), 1,2.

were for the most part unsuccessful. Little evidence existed to support the idea that any past or current programs were demonstrably effective in rehabilitating convicted felons. The Martinson report proved to be the death knell of the rehabilitative ideal.

Incarceration in the United States Today

An emphasis on retribution and deterrence marks the current correctional system. Few correctional administrators today espouse rehabilitation as a goal or a possibility. Educational and job training programs do exist, but their primary contribution is to maintain order

Table 14.4

CORRECTIONS IS BIG BUSINESS IN MANY STATES

Nine Largest States	Male Correctional Officers in Adult Systems, 1992	Female Correctional Officers in Adult Systems, 1992	Average Annual Salary of State Correctional Officers, 1992
California	12,809	2,872	$38,604
New York	16,307	1,441	$29,128
Texas	9,920	2,971	$23,385
Florida	8,893	2,658	$18,987
Pennsylvania	4,152	404	$28,479
Illinois	5,921	824	$25,440
Ohio	4,082	860	$23,046
Michigan	6,216	1,498	$28,870
New Jersey	5,114	690	$34,984
State at the top of this category	New York	Texas	Alaska, $41,215
State at the bottom of this category	North Dakota 111	North Dakota 20	South Dakota $15,548
National total	139,751	28,874	$24,239

Source: Kathleen O'Leary Morgan, Scott Morgan, Neal Quinto, eds., Crime State Rankings 1994 (Lawrence, KS: Morgan Quitno Corporation), 128–129, 132.

within the prison. **Warehousing**, confinement which makes no deliberate attempt to change inmates, continues to be the dominant feature of prisons today.

Today's prisons have been shaped by two major societal changes: (1)the rights movements of the 1960s and (2)the expansion of due process by the Supreme Court during the 1960s. The rights movements increased political awareness among all Americans. Blacks and Hispanics became conscious of the value of organized protest. That awareness went into the prison with black and Hispanic prisoners who organized political gangs. White prisoners have done the same, and most prisoners join gangs in state prisons, instead of remaining isolated.

The expansion of due process by the Supreme Court during the 1960s produced an awareness of prisoners' issues. Correctional officers have seen their right to discipline inmates sharply curtailed as federal courts become involved in the day-to-day operations of the prison; one result of this loss of authority is an increase in role strain for correctional officers.

Does Imprisonment Reduce Crime?

The most obvious answer to this question is in the affirmative. Were there no prisons, the criminally motivated would be undeterred. Their frequent criminal behavior would make crime look attractive, even to those who initially were unwilling to commit crimes. Clearly prisons have some crime-reducing consequences.

If, however, the question is framed differently, the relationship between crime and imprisonment is not so obvious. Has the increase in imprisonment produced a similar decrease in crime? The answer to this is probably in the negative. If we examine crime rates and the rates of imprisonment in the 50 states from 1980 to 1992, we find no consistent relationship between crime and imprisonment rates. If increased imprisonment produced decreased crime, there should be a consistent pattern between the two variables, yet there is no such pattern. A safe conclusion is that the causes of crime are so complex that no single solution, no matter how much money is used to implement it, can make a difference in the crime rate.

Who Goes to Prison?

Men who are poor, uneducated, never married, and under 35 make up the greater part of all state prison populations. In 1991 more than half of all persons sentenced to prison had been found guilty of serious crimes (murder, nonnegligent manslaughter, rape, robbery, aggravated assault, or burglary); had never married (55 percent) or were divorced or separated (25 percent); and were 34 years old or younger (67 percent). The percent of all persons incarcerated for drug-related offenses increased to 21.3 percent of the state prison population. Women make up a small part of the inmate population. At the end of 1992, there were 44,010 women in state prisons, less than 6 percent of all state prison inmates.[69]

Blacks are disproportionately overrepresented in prison populations. Black persons make up approximately 12 percent of the population, yet in 1991, blacks accounted for almost half (47.5 percent) of all inmates.[70] California is the only state among the 10 largest in which blacks do not make up more than half of the state inmate population; in a few states, (i.e., Pennsylvania, New Jersey and the southern states of Mississippi, Louisiana, and Georgia) there are twice as many black inmates as white inmates (see Box 14.6).

How Many People Are in Prison?

By the end of 1992 there were more than 800,000 persons in state prisons, for an incarceration rate of 303 sentenced prisoners per 100,000 residents. At the end of 1994 there were more than one million prisoners in United States prisons.[71] This rate reflects a steady increase in the population of state prisons during the last 62 years, but the most dramatic increases in state prison populations have come during the last decade. From 1980 to 1991 the incarceration rate in state prison populations in the Northeast increased from 139 to 248, and in the West the rate increased from 105 to 287. From 1980 to 1992 Alabama's incarceration rate grew from 149 to 404 per 100,000 and Oklahoma's incarceration rate went from 151 to 463.[72] States have now built so many prisons and incarcerated so many prisoners that the United States has the highest incarceration rate in the world (see Figure 14.1).[73]

Why has there been such a dramatic increase in prison populations during the last decade? The answer is complicated, but much of it has to do with new sentencing and correctional philosophies rather than increases in crime rates. Despite a gradually increasing reported crime rate (and a stable victimization rate) from the late 1970s into the 1990s, there has been a demand for more and longer sentences. As a result, less emphasis has been placed on community-based programs, and more emphasis on imprisonment, thus contributing to the increase in prison populations. In addition, the "war on drugs" which began during the Reagan administration, produced an emphasis on punishment as a method of reducing drug use and sales. As a result, one of every three admissions to state prisons since 1990 has been for drug offenses.[74]

BOX 14.6

CALIFORNIA AS THE EXEMPLAR FOR PRISONS AND CRIME RATES

John Irwin and James Austin assert that the dramatic increases in imprisonment of the 1980s and 1990s are unlikely to reduce crime significantly, but are certain to increase dramatically the cost of state governments. In their book, *It's About Time: America's Imprisonment Binge*, they argue that the gains attributed to California's prison system have been, to say the least, misrepresented. Their words follow:

> If we were to pick a state to test the imprisonment theory, California would be the obvious choice, for this state's prison population has increased from 19,623 in 1977 to over 110,000 by 1992. Former Attorney General William Barr believes California should serve as the model for the rest of the country. California, he states, "quadrupled its prison population during the 1980s and various forms of violent crimes fell by as much as 37 percent. But in Texas, which did not increase prison space, crime increased 29 percent in the decade."
>
> A closer examination of the California data presents a very different picture than that cited by Barr. . . . During this period, the size of the prison population increased by 237 percent (from 29,202 to 97,309) and the jail population increased by 118 percent (34,064 to 74,312). Prison operating costs increased by 400 percent, and jail operating costs increased by 265 percent. As of 1990, Californians were paying nearly $3 billion per year to operate the state's prisons and jails.
>
> What has been the impact of this substantial investment in violent crime? Contrary to the claim that the violent crime rate (homicide, rape, robbery, and assault) has dropped, the rate actually increased by 21 percent. Substantial declines did occur, but only for burglary and larceny-theft—a phenomenon that . . . was at least partially attributable to the growth in illegal drug trafficking and shifts in the at-risk population. More interesting is the fact that after 1984 the overall crime rate, and especially violent crimes and auto theft, has grown despite a continued escalation of imprisonment.
>
> California is now so strapped for funds that it must dramatically reduce the number of its parole officers and has been unable to open two brand new prisons, capable of holding 12,000 inmates. The state now has the most overcrowded prison system in the nation (183 percent of rated capacity) and spends millions of dollars each year on court cases challenging the crowded prison conditions. Despite the billions of dollars now being spent each year in locking up offenders, the public is as fearful of crime as it was a decade ago.

Source: John Irwin and James Austin, It's About Time: The Imprisonment Binge (Belmont, CA: Wadsworth Publishing Co. 1994), 156–157.

Because prison populations have increased so dramatically, overcrowding is a significant problem in a number of states. At the end of 1990 state prisons were estimated to be operating at between 18 to 29 percent above capacity. Such overcrowding presents a problem because prisons have nowhere to move inmates while repairing prisons or responding to emergencies.[75] If the population of potential prisoners continues to increase, states have two alternatives: more prisons or alternative sentencing strategies.

Probation

Probation, the practice of deferring prison sentences by permitting the convicted offenders to serve their sentences in the community under the supervision of the court, is an alternative to prison. Probation permits the rehabilitation of offenders who apparently pose no threat to society in the community.

In 1990 the number of adults on probation increased by 5.9 percent, the twelfth year in a row that such an increase occurred.[76] Ironically, the "get-tough-with-felons" policy that has dominated corrections since the mid 1970s, producing larger prison populations has also resulted in larger probation populations. Prisons cannot accommodate all those persons convicted of felonies, and the probation population is increasing at a rate greater than the prison population.

Perhaps more surprising than the size of the probation population is its composition. A new concept has entered the corrections literature: felony probation. Between one-third and one-half of all those persons on probation have been convicted of felonies.[77] But perhaps most surprising to those who believe that harsh punishment is the key to correctional

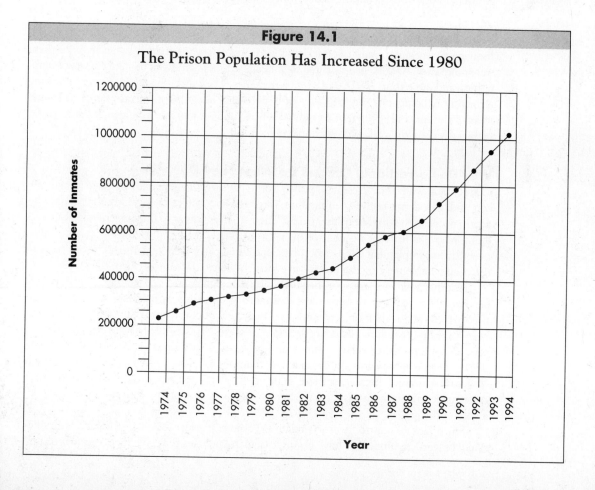

Figure 14.1

The Prison Population Has Increased Since 1980

deterrence is Samuel Walker's conclusion about probation: it is "the one correctional treat-ment program that seems to work" by achieving its stated goals and serving "broader social needs."[78] It does not succeed with every offender, but it succeeds often enough that Walker recommends maintaining the present system with only minor modification.

Probation's success may not be a result of probation itself, but rather the fact that per-sons who receive probation are good risks. It is also probable that avoiding prison and its corrupting effects may actually decrease the likelihood of becoming a career criminal. It is not so much the effectiveness of probation, but the good fortune in avoiding the state prison that produces the rehabilitation. Whatever the reason for its success, probation is one of the more effective correctional practices.[79]

The Correctional Officer

While much has been written about police officers, correctional officers have received much less attention. Yet there is little doubt that the job of the correctional officer is just as stressful as that of the police officer. Perhaps the lack of glamour in prison work contributes to the dearth of popular literature and media attention to the prison guard. While young men and women from all parts of the world may want to become a police officer when they grow up, few grow up dreaming of becoming a prison guard.

Who Becomes a Correctional Officer?

Individuals working in adult correctional facilities are predominantly male. In 1992 there were more than 169,000 people hired by state governments to work in state correctional fa-cilities, and more than 139,000 of those were males. The typical requirements for becoming a correctional officer in a state facility are a high school degree (or its equivalent) and being at least 18 years old. Drug use, a criminal record, and undesirable employment records are reasons for denying work as correctional officer.

Why Do Correctional Officers Do What They Do?

Correctional work is as stressful as police work. The stress experienced by correctional offi-cers and, as a direct result, their families, is related to a failure to include correctional offi-cers in decision making about their work. Their stress is similar to that experienced by a sec-retary who has little or no control over the decisions made by the boss, but who must, nevertheless, implement those decisions. Such situations produce high stress levels because the people implementing the policy have little influence over it (see Table 14.5).

Another source of stress for the guard is role ambiguity and role strain. Correctional of-ficers are expected to maintain order—custody and control—within the prison or jail. Au-thority to carry out their obligations is necessary, yet officers report that their authority has been increasingly reduced by court decisions. As a result, correctional officers must rely on personal aspects of their relationships with inmates to maintain order. At times correctional officers must overlook infractions; at other times they must punish inmates. Making such choices is stressful.[80] Because of these ambiguous task-related demands, correctional officers report uncertainty about what is expected of them and discomfort with the conflicting de-mands of the job.

Since lack of control over job-related decisions produces some of their stress, correc-tional officers' organizations have begun to demand policies that give them greater control.

Table 14.5

BEING A CORRECTIONAL OFFICER IS OFTEN STRESSFUL

Nine Most Populated States	State Prisoners per Correctional Officer, 1992	Turnover Rate of Correctional Officers in Adult Systems
California	6.98	5.5%
New York	3.48	2.5%
Texas	4.75	12%
Florida	4.18	8.6%
Pennsylvania	5.48	5.4%
Illinois	4.69	7.5%
Ohio	7.77	8%
Michigan	5.06	3.5%
New Jersey	3.9	8.5%
State at the top of this category	Oklahoma, 8.67%	Kansas, 32%
State at the bottom of this category	Rhode Island, 2.63	Connecticut, 1.5%
National Rate	4.73	12%

Source: Kathleen O'Leary Morgan, Scott Morgan, Neal Quitno, eds., Crime State Rankings 1994 (Lawrence, KS: Morgan Quitno Corporation), 130–131.

In addition, they have begun to lobby state legislatures for better benefits and job conditions. As the number of correctional officers increases with the growth of prison populations, we can expect officers' political influence to increase as well. This has already become apparent in western states, and with successful leadership, correctional officers may become influential in some state elections.[81]

The Debate Revisited: Deterrence, Rehabilitation, or Retribution?

This section began with a discussion of the debate concerning the ideal goal of prisons. Should prisons be organized to deter, rehabilitate, or provide retribution?

We do not know what, if anything, about the prison experience contributes to rehabilitation; penologists have, for the most part, abandoned the rehabilitative model and its definition of inmates as persons who can be changed for the better. More important, we do know that prisons punish: they deprive prisoners of freedom, dignity, privacy, safety, and heterosexual contacts. That humans can become accustomed to these deprivations (and therefore not be deterred by them) should come as no surprise; one has only to examine the streets of Calcutta or the villages of Ethiopia to know that humans can become accustomed to the direst of circumstances.

Whether prisons provide retribution, or should provide sufficient retribution to satisfy those calling for it, is ultimately a question of values. The instrumental question is whether the individuals who fund state and local governments can afford to fund institutions that require inmates to retain their capacity for violence and to become less civilized in order to survive. While the thought of inflicting suffering on inmates may gratify individuals at some visceral level, the fact remains that almost all of the inmates in prison ultimately leave prison to walk the streets in America again. If we consider the issue in these terms, the question becomes not so much "How much pain can we inflict on them to pay them back for what they have done to us?" but, "What can we do while they are in prison to make them less likely to commit crimes when they leave prison?"

Individuals who care deeply about issues related to imprisonment, civil liberties, and crime reduction must become involved in the state and local political process. These issues are among the most critical in a civilized society, and it is important that citizens be informed about them. It is also important that state legislators be knowledgeable. Individuals must insist that humane treatment of inmates be a part of a legislative program.

The Costs of Justice: Pay Now or Later?

Fighting crime is a major industry in the United States. The fight against crime and for justice is fought primarily by state and local governments. The question is whether we are spending too much or too little, and whether the money could be better spent in other kinds of programs.

State and local governments pay almost all the costs of justice activities in the United States. Expenditures for police protection vary from state to state, but are large nevertheless. Mega-states such as California ($5.4 billion in 1991) and New York ($3.5 billion) spend more for police protection than smaller, less prosperous states like Vermont ($49 million in 1991) and North Dakota ($41 million).[82] Local governments are responsible for the majority of these expenditures; local governments in California paid more than $4.7 billion of the total above. In New York, local governments contributed $3.2 billion, while in Vermont their contribution was $26 million and $33 million in North Dakota (see Table 14.6).

In 1991 the budgets of all sheriff's departments, state agencies, and local police departments totaled more than $32 billion.[83] State and local governments also bear most of the cost of corrections. Over 60 percent of all correctional employees work for state governments; another 35 percent work for local governments.[84] In 1991 state governments paid out more than $17.8 billion for corrections, and local governments, responsible for funding jails and juvenile detention facilities, contributed another $9.5 billion. Michigan, Texas, Florida, New York, and California all paid more than $1 billion for corrections in 1991.[85]

But the cost of justice is more than simply the tax dollars spent on apprehending and imprisoning criminals. There are costs for those persons who work in law enforcement and corrections, and for those who are imprisoned. Finally, there is the cost to the society when inmates, who might have been punished in other ways, are released from prison.

The most significant question is whether it is possible to alleviate the human and monetary costs of reducing crime by a policy of funding programs which increase the likelihood that individuals in our society will have adequate nutrition, education, and health care. Since those in state prisons are less well educated, have often been psychologically deprived, and more frequently have serious health problems than others, it may be possible to reduce the frequency of crime by attacking these problems. Programs that lessen these prob-

Table 14.6

GENERAL EXPENDITURES AND CORRECTIONAL EXPENDITURES FOR THE NINE MOST POPULOUS STATES (IN THOUSANDS OF DOLLARS)

Nine Most Populous States	General Expenditures, 1992	Correctional Expenditures, 1992	Proposed Correctional Budgets, 1993
California	83,360,138	3,226,256	3,178,339
New York	60,869,111	2,008,174	1,426,968
Texas	30,743,796	1,336,280	2,123,889
Florida	24,851,056	1,036,611	1,170,419
Pennsylvania	30,338,335	558,169	604,400
Illinois	23,639,362	625,412	668,834
Ohio	24,106,118	691,342	814,654
Michigan	21,839,665	854,828	1,100,000
New Jersey	24,109,399	659,074	622,342

Sources: The Book of the States 1994–95 (Lexington, KY: The Council of State Governments, 1994), 352; Sourcebook of Criminal Justice Statistics 1993 (Bureau of Justice Statistics (Washington, D.C.: U.S. Government Printing Office, 1994), 14.

lems early in the lives of individuals may reduce those individuals' inclination to commit crimes in later life. While no policy can eliminate crime, policies that reduce human suffering and offer opportunity to pursue the American dream can surely reduce crime. Otherwise we will continue the present strategy of fighting crime, one which is ultimately a strategy of paying too much too late (see Box 14.7).

WHAT WE CAN DO AS CITIZENS IN OUR COMMUNITY

Why did we begin this chapter with a vignette about a woman who teaches jail inmates to create gardens and, in so doing, helps them heal themselves and grow food for the poor? Catherine Sneed provides an excellent example of actions that can be taken by individuals to make the criminal justice system more successful and responsive to neighborhoods. The fact of the matter is that law enforcement and corrections cannot be expected to solve the crime problem by themselves. Citizen involvement in the process is crucial for two reasons: (1) such involvement increases citizen appreciation of the problems associated with law enforcement and (2) such involvement increases citizen commitment to law-abiding behavior.

Why do citizens become more law abiding when involved in the law enforcement process? Suppose all citizens in the United States who consider themselves to be law-abiding citizens were to refuse to purchase any item they *thought* might be stolen, *no matter how good a "deal" they seemed to be offered.* How long do you suppose burglars would continue to steal such items? How long do you suppose "fences" could be willing to buy stolen merchandise from thieves? What do you suppose would be the impact on the crime rate? It should be clear from this example that crime cannot flourish unless "good citizens" permit it to do so. If good citizens are involved daily in a community crime prevention effort, do you imagine that they would be as eager to buy stolen merchandise that has been obtained in violation

BOX 14.7

WHY WOULD ANYONE JOIN A GANG?

It may be difficult for you to imagine that anyone would choose to join a gang or become a criminal, but Martín Sánchez Jankowski says that is exactly the case for most members of gangs. Jankowski, who spent 11 years "hanging out" with 37 African American, Latino, Asian and white gangs in poor (slum) and working class neighborhoods described what he calls gang members as having a **defiant individualist character.** This character has seven self-explanatory components: (1) competitiveness; (2) mistrust or wariness; (3) self reliance; (4) social isolation; (5) survival instinct; (6) a Social Darwinist world view and (7) a defiant air. Jankowski argues that gang members are no more likely to come from single parent families than intact families, and that gang membership is more likely to be a decision made in the mid-to-late teens than earlier. He also suggests that gang members have often rationally calculated the advantages and disadvantages of gang membership and have chosen membership. His words and those of gang members follow.

"Those who had joined a gang most often gave as their reason the belief that it would provide them with an environment that would increase their chances of securing money. Defiant individualists constantly calculate the costs and benefits associated with their efforts to improve their financial well-being (which is not good). Therefore, on the one hand, they believe that if they engage in economic ventures on their own, they will, if successful, earn more per venture than if they acted as part of a gang. However, there is also the belief that if one participates in economic ventures with a gang, it is likely that the amount earned will be more regular, although less per venture.

'Well, I really didn't want to join the gang when I was a little younger because I had this idea that I would make more money if I would do some gigs [various illegal economic ventures] on my own. Now I don't know, I mean, I wasn't wrong. I could make more money on my own, but there are more things happening with the gang, so its a little more even in terms of when the money comes in. . . , Let's just say there is more possibilities for a more steady amount of income if you need it. . . . Others decided to join the gang for financial security. They viewed the gang as an organization that could provide them or their families with money in times of emergency. It represented the combination of a bank and a social security system, the equivalent of what the political machine had been to many new immigrant groups in American cities.

'Hey, the club [the gang] has been there when I needed help. There were times when there just wasn't enough food for me to get filled up with. My family was so hard up and they couldn't manage all their bills and such, so there was some lean meals! Well, I just needed some money to help for awhile, til I got some money or my family was better off. They [the gang] was there to help. I could see that [they would help] before I joined, that's why I joined. They are there when you need them and they'll continue to be.'"

Source: Martin Sánchez Jankowski, Islands in the Street: Gangs and American Urban Society *(Berkeley: University of California Press, 1991), 39–41.*

of their very efforts? Some would, of course; the desire for material possessions is an important part of our culture. But many, if not most, would not. Their commitments to the laws against theft would be strengthened by their efforts, and they would be less willing to encourage theft by purchasing stolen merchandise.

The alternative form of "community crime prevention" is, of course, vigilantism. "Vigilante justice" arises in the United States when citizens lose faith in the criminal justice system. When citizens pursue criminals without regard for the law, they become lawless and similar to those they pursue.

There may be no way to eliminate crime, but if the damaging effects of crime are to be lessened, it will be because individuals organize communities in new and better ways of attacking these problems. As members of a community, we have an obligation to contribute to our community; as property-owning members of that community, we have a monetary motivation for making it the best community possible. Whatever the motivation, communities do not persist nor become better without the involvement of their members.

Citizen involvement in the community offers the best possibility for consistent and sustained crime prevention. In fact, police departments cannot deter crime as efficiently or inexpensively as citizen community watches.

WHAT WOULD A REINVENTED JUSTICE SYSTEM LOOK LIKE?

Can the justice system be reinvented? Can the entrepreneurial spirit be used to change the justice system? In what direction would such a change be aimed? In this section, we will suggest answers to these questions, in light of our previous discussion.

Osborne and Gaebler have a clear view of what a reinvented justice system would look like. Instead of hiring more employees and spending more money, they would put control in the hands of steering organizations, called Public Safety Coordinating Councils, at the state and local level. These councils would include providers (e.g., police chiefs, prosecutors, public defenders) and customers (e.g., neighborhood organizations, school system leaders) who would "steer" their local justice systems.

The councils would be organized in a hierarchical fashion, and the state councils would fund local councils on a competitive basis. Funding would be based on the degree to which the councils empowered community members to prevent crime through strategic planning and managing by data. Incentives would encourage measurement of outcomes (e.g., crime rates, recidivism rates, and court performance), and award extra funding to those communities who performed best.[86]

Can changes like this occur? Of course. Will such changes occur? Certainly, in some cities and states. Will such changes occur in your area? Only if you and other individuals get together and work to secure these changes. The strength and weakness of our system of government is that it rests on the shoulders of individuals. If individuals are committed to creating better justice systems in the places where they live and work, then change—dramatic change—can occur.

CONCLUSION

One of the purposes of order in a society is to provide a suitable context for the pursuit of "the good life," however that may be defined. It is difficult to maintain order in a society as complex and heterogeneous as ours, in part because there are so many views of the good life. Maintaining order in such a society places a significant burden on those persons assigned the task. Police officers and correctional officers are constrained by law and cannot do whatever is most efficient or effective to restore or maintain order; rather, they are required to do what is legal under the state and federal constitutions. Because our society defines justice in terms of individual liberty, police officers may not do whatever is efficient to maintain and restore order on the streets. Because our society defines justice in terms of freedom from cruel and inhumane punishment, correctional officers may not do whatever is efficient to maintain and restore order in the prison.

A criminal justice system like ours has significant costs. There are monetary costs to the taxpayers who must fund the police departments, prisons, and their auxiliary agencies. There are emotional costs to the employees of police departments and prisons. There are emotional and physical costs to the "clients" of police officers and correctional officers, and, at times, physical, emotional, and monetary costs to individuals when the "clients" of police officers and correctional officers are once again returned to the streets.

Alternative forms of police organizations have been suggested as possible ways of making police departments more effective without reducing the liberties of individuals. Some national figures have even suggested the reduction of civil liberties so as to provide more order. Penologists tout alternatives to prison as a way of reducing the debilitating effects of prisons, and others argue for private sector involvement within the prison so as to reduce the costs to taxpayers.

It may be that providing both freedom and order are the goals most difficult to obtain in a democracy. If that is the case, individual understanding of and involvement in the solutions is most critical. For an elaboration of yet another problem, we go to the next chapter.

STUDY OBJECTIVES

1. Identify the alternative definitions of justice.
2. List and explain the two methods of counting crime in the United States.
3. What are victimization studies?
4. Identify the proposals for reducing the costs of police work.
5. What is a rate? How are crime rates calculated?
6. Is crime increasing in the United States? Is violent crime increasing in the United States? Are victimizations increasing in the United States?
7. Explain what is meant by the idea that crime is intraracial.
8. Identify the reasons why police officers act as they do.
9. What is the rehabilitative ideal and what led to its abandonment?
10. What kinds of people become police officers?
11. Identify the causes of police behavior.
12. Identify and describe the different kinds of community policing.
13. Identify the kinds of correctional institutions.
14. List the goals of correctional institutions.
15. Identify the causes of the behavior of correctional officers.
16. List and discuss the characteristics of prisoners in the United States.
17. Discuss probation as a crime-fighting strategy.
18. Identify the proposals for reducing the problems in police and correctional work.
19. Create two answers to the question, "Does imprisonment reduce crime?"
20. List and discuss two reasons why someone would join a gang.
21. Give three reasons for the increase in state prison populations.
22. Identify the following terms:

crime	criminal incident	victimization
discretion	probable cause	recidivism
exclusionary rule	good faith exception	vigilante justice
defiant individualist character		

GLOSSARY

Components of the police role   The concepts created by James Q. Wilson to describe the activities of police officers. The components are law enforcement, order maintenance, and service.

Crime   The violation of statutory, criminal law.

Criminal incident   A concept developed by the Bureau of Justice Statistics to measure victimizations. It is defined as a specific criminal act involving one or more victims.

Community service   This approach to crime reduction is designed to mobilize neighborhood support by encouraging citizen participation in neighborhood management and crime fighting.

Control   Retaining authority over the prisoners' actions within the prison, is the second goal of American prisons.

Custody   Containing prisoners within the prison, is first goal of American prisons.

Discretion   An inevitable aspect of police officers and other law enforcement officials that requires them to choose between two or more task-related alternatives in the course of one's work.

Doctrine of utilitarian punishment   The idea that punishment should be only severe enough to dissuade future criminal acts, but no more severe than that lest the persons punished become unfit for living among good individuals

Exclusionary rule   The legal guideline which says that illegally gathered evidence may not usually by used in a criminal trial.

Good faith exception   The recent exception to the exclusionary rule holds that evidence gained when officers unknowingly and in good faith serve an warrant made invalid by a magistrate is admissible in court.

Lifetime prevalence of imprisonment   The probability of being imprisoned during one's lifetime.

Jails   Detention facilities designed to hold several kinds of persons for "short" periods of time

Prevalence of imprisonment   The probability of being imprisoned on any given day.

Prisons   Detention facilities designed to hold adults sentenced for a year or more.

Prison industries   "Factories within walls," in which prison inmates can work to earn money and keep busy while in prison.

Private prisons   Prisons built, managed, and sometimes owned by private firms or individuals. They represent an alternative to funding prison construction from tax dollars.

Probable cause   The right to infringe on the liberty of others because of a belief about their activities resulting from trustworthy information which could be interpreted by a reasonable person to mean that a crime is taking place (or has taken place) and that the person in question is (or was) a participant in that crime.

Probation   The practice of deferring prison sentences by permitting the convicted offenders to serve their sentences in the community under the supervision of the court. It is an alternative to prison.

Rate   A measure of the incidence of an event for a base population.

Recidivism rate   The rate at which inmates return to prison.

Rehabilitative ideal   The belief that inmates who are given the opportunity to change and be rehabilitated will do so.

Styles of policing   Tendencies on the part of police officers to behave in a certain way. The tendencies, identified by James Q. Wilson, result from department policy. There are three styles of policing: Legalistic, Watchman, and Service.

Sworn officers   Individuals who have undergone sufficient training to meet state requirements to fulfill all the duties of the police role.

Team policing   An approach to crime reduction similar to strategies used in Japan, which gives a group or team of police officers "semi-permanent" responsibility for a neighborhood or a part of a city.

Uniform Crime Reports   An annual summary of the crime statistics received from police departments in the United States published by the Federal Bureau of Investigation.

Victimization   A specific criminal incident that affects one person. An incident may involve a number of crimes, but the incident is counted only once and is categorized by the most serious crime.

Victimization studies   Data about victims gathered in a national survey of a sample of households by the Bureau of Justice Statistics.

Warehousing   The current practice of confining inmates which makes no attempt to rehabilitate or change inmates; instead the goal is simple custody.

ENDNOTES

1. Katherine M. Jamieson and Timothy Flanagan, *Sourcebook of Criminal Justice Statistics, 1988*, Bureau of Justice Statistics, (Washington, D.C.: U. S. Government Printing Office, 1988), 2–23.

2. Kelly H. Shim and Marshall DeBerry, *Criminal Victimization in the United States, 1986*, Bureau of Justice Statistics (Washington, D.C.: U. S. Government Printing Office, 1988), 111–112.

3. Ibid., 1.

4. *Uniform Crime Reports for the United States, 1992*, Federal Bureau of Investigation (Washington, D.C.: U. S. Government Printing Office, 1993), 41; Marianne W. Zawitz, et al., *Highlights from 20 Years of Surveying Crime Victims*, Bureau of Justice Statistics, (Washington, D.C.: U. S. Government Printing Office, 1993), 6.

5. Joan M. Johnson, *Criminal Victimization in the United States, 1991*, Bureau of Justice Statistics (Washington, D.C.: U. S. Government Printing Office, 1992), 100.

6. Zawitz, et al., *Highlights from 20 Years of Surveying Crime Victims*, 32.

7. *Uniform Crime Reports for the United States, 1987*, Federal Bureau of Investigation (Washington, D.C.: U. S. Government Printing Office, 1988), 41.

8. *Uniform Crime Reports for the United States, 1992*, Federal Bureau of Investigation (Washington, D.C.: U. S. Government Printing Office, 1992), 58.

9. Kelly M. Shim and Marshall M. DeBerry, *Criminal Victimization 1987*, Bureau of Justice Statistics (Washington, D.C.: U. S. Government Printing Office, 1988), 3; Zawitz, et al. *Highlights from 20 Years of Surveying Crime Victims*, 6.

10. Shim and DeBerry, *Criminal Victimization 1987*, 3.

11. Ibid., 46.

12.. *Uniform Crime Reports for the United States, 1993*, Federal Bureau of Investigation (Washington, D.C.: U. S. Government Printing Office, 1992), 14.

13. Johnson, *Criminal Victimization in the United States, 1991*, 18.

14. Ibid.

15. *Report to the Nation on Crime and Justice*, 2d ed., Bureau of Justice Statistics (Washington, D.C.: U. S. Government Printing Office, 1988) 50; Christopher Innes, *Drug Use and Crime*, (Washington, D.C.: U. S. Government Printing Office, 1988) 1.

16. *Report to the Nation on Crime and Justice*, 2d ed., *Sourcebook of Criminal Justice Statistics, 1992*, Bureau of Justice Statistics (Washington, D.C.: U. S. Government Printing Office, 1993), 627.

17. Nevertheless, 81 percent of state inmates report that they were not daily users of a major drug during the month prior to arrest and 65 report that they had never been regular users of a major drug. For further information, see Innes, *Drug Use and Crime*, 1.

18. In fact, Charles Silberman reports that methadone maintenance programs may actually increase criminal activity for heroin addicts since "[b]y freeing young addicts of the need to spend most of their time 'chasing the bag,' methadone apparently gave them more time and energy to commit predatory crimes." For more information on this subject, see Charles E. Silberman, *Criminal Violence, Criminal Justice* (New York: Vintage Books, 1980), 244; *Sourcebook of Criminal Justice Statistics, 1992*, 627.

19. Notice that this is not the number of males arrested, since one male can account for a number of arrests, but it is the number of *male arrests*, that is, arrests of males.

20. For a bibliography of community crime prevention programs, see "Topical Bibliography: Community Crime Prevention Programs," (Washington, D.C: National Institute of Justice, no date).

21. Dennis Rosenbaum, Arthur L. Lurigio, and Paul J. Lavrakas, *Crime Stoppers: A National Evaluation of Program Operations and Effects*, (Washington, D.C.: U. S. Government Printing Office, 1987), v.

22. Ibid.

23. James Garofals and Maureen McLeod, Improving the Use and Effectiveness of Neighborhood Watch Programs, *National Institute of Justice* (Washington, D.C.: U. S. Government Printing Office, 1988).

24. If you are interested in learning more about crime prevention, write to the National Crime Prevention Council, Suite 540, 733 15th Street NW; Washington, D.C. 20005.

25. Peter Finn, "Block Watches Help Crime Victims in Philadelphia," in *Research in Action* (Washington, D.C. National Institute of Justice, 1986).

26. *Carroll* v. *United States*, 267 U.S. 132, 45 SCt. 280, 69 L.Ed 543 (125), cert. den. 282 U.S. 873, 51 S.Ct 78, 75 L.Ed 771.

27. Herbert Packer, *The Limits of Criminal Sanction* (Stanford: Stanford University Press, 1968), 150.

28. *Census of State and Local Law Enforcement Agencies*, Bureau of Justice Statistics (Washington, D.C.: U. S. Government Printing Office, 1993) as reported in Kathleen O'Leary Morgan, et al., eds., *Crime State Rankings, 1994*, (Lawrence, KS: Morgan Quitno Corp.), 219.

29. Brian Reaves, *Profile of State and Local Law Enforcement Agencies, 1987*, Bureau of Justice Statistics (Washington, D.C.: U. S. Government Printing Office, 1989),1; *Uniform Crime Reports for the United States, 1992*, 294; *Census of State and Local Law Enforcement Agencies*, Bureau of Justice Statistics, as reported in *Crime State Rankings, 1994*, 222.

30. *Uniform Crime Reports for the United States, 1992*, 289.

31. *Uniform Crime Reports for the United States, 1987*, U. S. Department of Justice, (Washington, D.C.: U. S. Government Printing Office, 1988), 229.

32. *Justice Agencies in the United States: Summary Report 1980*, Bureau of Justice Statistics (Washington, D.C.: U. S. Government Printing Office, 1980),5.

33. *Census of State and Local Law Enforcement Agencies*, as reported in *Crime State Rankings, 1994*, 246.

34. Brian Reaves, *Profile of State and Local Law Enforcement Agencies, 1987*, Bureau of Justice Statistics (Washington, D.C.: U. S. Government Printing Office, 1989), 6.

35. *Census of State and Local Law Enforcement Agencies, 1993*, as reported in *Crime State Rankings, 1994*, 228.

36. *Uniform Crime Reports for the United States, 1987*, 233; *Uniform Crime Reports for the United States, 1992*, 289.

37. *Uniform Crime Reports for the United States, 1987*, 233; "Law Enforcement Management and Administrative Statistics, 1990," Bureau of Justice Statistics (Washington, D.C.: U. S. Government Printing Office, 1992) as reported in *Crime State Rankings, 1994*, 237.

38. James Q. Wilson, *Varieties of Police Behavior* (Cambridge, MA: Harvard University Press, 1968), 5; Jeffrey S. Slovak, *Styles of Urban Policing: Organization, Environment, and Police Styles in Selected American Cities* (New York: New York University Press, 1986), 64–100.

39. Wilson, *Varieties of Police Behavior*.

40. Bernard Locke and Alexander B. Smith, "Police Who Go to College," in Abraham S. Blumberg and Arthur Niederhoffer, eds., *The Ambivalent Force* (Hinsdale, IL: Dryden Press, 1976), 164–168.

41. Wilson, *Varieties of Police Behavior*.

42. Jerome Skolnick, *Justice Without Trial* (New York: John Wiley and Sons, 1975); Paul Chevigny, *Police Power*, (New York: Pantheon Books, 1972).

43. John Clark, "Isolation of the Police: A Comparison of the British and American Situations," *Journal of Criminal Law, Criminology, and Police Science*, 56, (September, 1965), 3.

44. Arthur Niederhoffer, *Behind the Shield: The Police in Urban Society*, (Garden City, NY: Doubleday and Co., Inc., 1969).

45. Skolnick, *Justice Without Trial*.

46. Barbara Manili, Edward F. Connors III, Darrel W. Stephend, John R. Stedman, *Police Drug Testing*, National Institute of Justice, (Washington, D.C. :GPO 1987).

47. See especially, Michael Heiman, "The Police Suicide," *Journal of Police Science and Administration* 3 (September, 1975), 267–273; for a challenge to these assertions, see Arthur and Elaine Niederhoffer, *The Police Family* (Lexington, MA: Lexington Books, 1978) and Gail Goolkasian, Ronald W. Geddes, and William DeJong, *Coping With Police Stress*, National Institute of Justice, (Washington, D.C.: U. S. Government Printing Office, 1985),7–10.

48. Egon Bittner, *The Functions of the Police in Modern Society*, (Cambridge, MA: Oelgeschlager, Gunn & Hain, Publishers, 1980), 37.

49. For an extensive discussion of these issues, see James Q. Wilson, *Thinking About Crime*, (New York: Vintage Books, 1983), 61–68.

50. Edwin Meese, III, "Preparing the Police Agenda for the 1990s," *Law Enforcement News*, vol. XIII, no. 253 (August 18, 1987), 8,11.

51. Samuel Walker, *Sense and Nonsense about Crime*, Monterey, CA: Brooks/Cole Publishing Co.), 91–98.

52. Jerome H. Skolnick and David Bayley, *The New Blue Line: Police Innovation in Six American Cities* (New York: The Free Press, 1986).

53. Jacob R. Clark, "Does Community Policing Add Up?" *Law Enforcement News* (New York: John Jay College/CUNY, 1994) April 15, 1994, 1,8.

54. David H. Bayley, *Forces of Order: Police Behavior in Japan and the United States* (Berkeley: University of California Press, 1992); L. Craig Parker, Jr., *The Japanese Police System Today: An American Perspective* (New York: Kodansha International Ltd., 1984).

55. See especially, Skolnick and Bayley, *The New Blue Line*, and James Q. Wilson, *Thinking About Crime* (New York: Vintage Books, 1983), 71–74.

56. Herman Goldstein, *The New Policing: Confronting Complexity*, National Institute of Justice (Washington, D.C. :U. S. Government Printing Office, 1993), 3.

57. Unknown author, "Going Back to Basics, San Diego Plans Split into 21 Mini-police Departments," *Law Enforcement News*, April 15, 1994, 1.

58. Wilson, *Thinking About Crime*, 13.

59. *Sourcebook of Criminal Justice Statistics, 1992,* April 1993), 598, 605, 594.

60. Leonard Orlando, *Prison: Houses of Darkness* (New York: The Free Press, 1975), 52–53.

61. Doris Layton MacKenzie, "Boot Camps Prisons in 1993," *National Institute of Justice Journal,* National Institute of Justice (Washington, D.C.: U. S. Government Printing Office, November, 1993), 21–28.

62. Ibid.

63. Mike Ward, "State Jails Ordered Back on Track," *Austin American Statesman,* July 16, 1994, 1A,9A.

64. John Irwin and James Austin, *It's About Time: America's Imprisonment Binge* (Belmont, CA: Wadsworth, 1994), 145.

65. R. Michelle Breyer and Mike Ward, "Running Prisons for a Profit" *Austin American Statesman,* September 4, 1994, 1E,8E.

66. Edward L. Ayers, *Vengeance and Justice: Crime and Punishment in the 19th-Century American South* (New York: Oxford University Press, 1984), 37–40.

67. Clemens Bartollas, *Correctional Treatment: Theory and Practice* , (Englewood Cliffs, NJ: Prentice-Hall, 1985), 5–6.

68. Robert Martinson, "What Works? — Questions and Answers About Prison Reform," *The Public Interest,* (Spring, 1974), 22–54.

69. *Sourcebook of Criminal Justice Statistics, 1992,* 623; *Statistical Abstract of the United States, 1993* (Washington, D.C.: U. S. Government Printing Office, 1993), 210.

70. *Statistical Abstract of the United States,* 211.

71. Tom Kuntz, "That's a Long Prison Head Count," *New York Times,* October 24, 1994, E2.

72. *Prisoners in 1992,* Bureau of Justice Statistics (Washington, D.C.: U. S. Government Printing Office, 1993) as reported in *Crime State Rankings, 1994,* 73; *Sourcebook of Criminal Justice Statistics, 1992,* Bureau of Justice Statistics (Washington, D.C.: U. S. Government Printing Office, 1993).

73. "The prison boom bust," *U.S. News and World Report,* May 4, 1992, 28.

74. Robert Famighetti, ed., *The World Almanac and Book of Facts 1994,* (Mahwah, NJ: Funk and Wagnall, 1994), 965.

75. Robyn L. Cohen, *Prisoners in 1990,* Bureau of Justice Statistics (Washington, D.C.: U. S. Government Printing Office, 1993), 3.

76. Timothy J. Flanagan, and Kathleen Maguire, *Sourcebook of Criminal Justice Statistics 1991,* Bureau of Justice Statistics (Washington, D.C.: U. S. Government Printing Office, 1992), 589.

77. Joan Petersilia, *Probation and Felony Offenders,* National Institute of Justice (Washington, D.C.:U. S. Government Printing Office, March, 1985), 1; Samuel Walker, *Sense and Nonsense about Crime,* 175.

78. Walker, *Sense and Nonsense about Crime,* 176.

79. Ibid.

80. James G. Fox, *Organizational and Racial Conflict in Maximum-Security Prisons* (Lexington, MA: Lexington Books, 1982), 29–33.

81. Dan Macallair, "Lock 'Em Up Legislation Means Prisons Gain Clout in California," *Christian Science Monitor,* September 28, 1994, 19; Joyce Purnick, "Prisoners are Piling Up as Guards Dwindle," *New York Times,* September 26, 1994, B3.

82. *Crime State Rankings, 1994,* 180.

83. Ibid.

84. Sue Lindgren, *Justice Expenditure and Employment, 1985,* Bureau of Justice Statistics (Washington, D.C.:U. S. Government Printing Office, March 1987), 3.

85. *Crime State Rankings, 1994,* 189, 192.

86. David Osborne and Ted Gaebler, *Reinventing Government: How the Entrepreneurial Spirit is Transforming the Public Sector* (New York: Penguin Books, 1993), 320.

15

The Pursuit of Justice and Order: Inequality and Relief

At age 17, Charles Ballard became a father and, fleeing his family and responsibility, he joined the Army. Soon he found himself in prison where he confronted the guilt he felt from abandoning his son and examined the wounds created by his father's abandonment of him. Freed from prison, he earned a GED, two college degrees, and custody of his five-year-old son. Working as a social worker, he again saw children without fathers and mothers without husbands. So Charles Ballard took to the streets to find those missing fathers, and after finding them, he started a program to help them become the good fathers they wanted to be.

To be in the program, the young men—fathers—had to live up to only three promises: to legitimize their child, to attend school, and to get a job, no matter how menial. Counselors are successful fathers and husbands who model responsible behavior while on call 24 hours a day to talk over events and feelings when asked to do so. Many believe that gang violence and crime are the expression of anger at missing fathers which is misdirected toward those more accessible. The emphasis is on positive and logical thinking about fatherhood, work, and responsibility. "If you want to change how a man acts, you must change how he thinks about himself, about taking responsibility for his child and respecting the child's mother. When we achieve that, then the rest of the community can be saved."

And Charles Ballard's program is working. In Cleveland, where it began, more than 2,000 young men have been involved in the National Institute for Responsible Fatherhood and Family Development (formerly the Teen Father Program). Seventy percent of them have earned diplomas and 97 percent are providing support for their children! Programs have begun in Washington, D.C., and funding may permit programs in Baltimore, Nashville, Kansas City, and Detroit. And we see once again how one person with vision and courage can make a fundamental difference in a community.

(For more information, you may write The National Institute for Responsible Fatherhood and Family Development, 8555 Hugh Avenue, Dept. P, Cleveland, Ohio 44106.)

POVERTY

Wealth and poverty are relative terms. What is thought of as poor in Mississippi, the poorest state in the United States, might be considered a more than adequate life-style in Bhopal, India. But while most of the poor in the United States have better lives than do the poor in India or Mexico, the poor in this country do suffer in comparison to middle and upper income families. Moreover, the suffering is not merely psychological distress, but very real deprivation of adequate health care, housing, and nutrition, as well as the increased likelihood of being a crime victim. The subject of this chapter is America's poor and attempts by state and local governments to improve the lives of the poor. Also to be considered is the issue of entrepreneurial government and the system of relief.

Social scientists raise a number of questions about the poor. What causes poverty? What can be done about it? Are the poor equally distributed throughout the country? Is aid to the poor equal in different parts of the country? What is impact of poverty programs on the poor? Does the impact of the programs justify their cost? These are among the questions to be answered in this chapter.

While few social scientists believe that poverty can be eliminated, many believe that its more unfortunate effects can be ameliorated. Many people, including some social scientists, believe that poverty can be reduced through government programs. Others think that federal, state, or local governments have no obligation to provide aid to the poor. This chapter begins with an analysis of the nature and causes of poverty, and as well as an examination of some of the programs sponsored by state and local governments to deal with poverty.

What Is Poverty?

The relativity of wealth and impoverishment has given rise to two ways of defining poverty. The first way, an **absolute** definition, defines poverty in terms of an objective standard, usually a governmental measure of subsistence. We will be referring to an absolute measure of poverty, the poverty threshold, throughout this chapter. A second method of discussing poverty is to use a **relative** definition. To use a relative definition means to make a subjective judgment about the meaning of poverty in comparison to the standards of the society. John Kenneth Galbraith, using a relative definition for poverty, has suggested that even if individuals have enough income to survive, they may be considered poverty-stricken if their resulting life style is considered by the community to be unacceptable or degrading.[1]

How poverty is defined is a political issue. The Social Security Administration set the first **poverty line** (now called the poverty threshold) in 1964 by estimating the lowest cost of feeding a family of four. Based upon the Agriculture Department's analysis of the consumption needs of families and a 1955 study showing that families of three or more spent roughly one-third of their income on food, the poverty threshold for families was set at approximately three times the cost of feeding a family. Smaller families and persons living alone have slightly higher costs, a fact that is taken into consideration when calculating the poverty threshold. While modest adjustments have been made to take inflation into account, the poverty threshold remains similar to its original formulation. Thus we may think of the poverty threshold as three times the cost of feeding the members of a household, and thereby create an absolute definition of poverty.

This official definition of poverty is criticized by many. Some argue that the poverty threshold is too low and therefore overlooks many who live in inadequate circumstances, that it fails to take into account the increasing disparity between the poor and the nonpoor, and that it underestimates the amount of poverty in the United States.[2] Others argue that the poverty threshold is too high and therefore includes many who do not need or deserve aid because it ignores government transfer payments (noncash welfare payments like food stamps and Medicaid), encourages underreporting of income, and overestimates the amount of poverty in the United States.[3] Many scholars have concluded that, on balance, the official poverty threshold neither exaggerates nor minimizes the amount of poverty in this country.[4]

The debates about the poverty threshold have produced alternative income and poverty calculations by the federal government. Since poverty status is related to income, what constitutes income is crucial in deciding what constitutes poverty. The official definition for income used in Census Bureau Reports is "money income excluding capital gains before taxes."[5] The Commerce Department, nevertheless, has fifteen alternative definitions for income having to do with such variables as whether capital gains, health insurance supplements, or cash transfers are included in the before-tax definition and whether income taxes, social security taxes, earned income credit, and home equity value are included in the after-tax definition. Of greatest import for the issue of poverty is, of course, whether means-tested government cash transfers and the value of Medicaid are to be included as income for the poor.

An illustration of the political debate concerning the method of calculating the poverty threshold is contained in Figure 15.1. The old calculation measure, used prior to December, 1988, (and used for pre-1989 data in this chapter unless otherwise noted) did not include the value of government transfers like food stamps, Medicaid, and AFDC.[6] When the transfers are included, the number of persons considered to be poor dropped from more than 32 million to less than 25 million in 1988. Advocates for a welfare system argue that the inclusion of such benefits in the measures of poverty masks the suffering of the poor; those opposed to the current welfare system suggest that the benefits are income and should be calculated since they contribute to the standard of living of poor people.

How Many Are Poor?

The United States began to calculate a poverty rate in 1959 when almost 40 million people (22 percent of the population) were poor. In 1992 there were almost 37 million poor people, which means that *one of every seven* persons in the United States is poor![7] Nevertheless, the 1992 **poverty rate**, the percentage of the population below the poverty threshold, was, at 14.5 percent, lower than in 1983 (15.2 percent), the highest rate in the last 20 years.[8]

In 1992 there were eight million poor families; put another way, there were almost 37 million poor persons. Children make up the largest proportion of the poor: one-fifth (21.9 percent) of all children were in families with incomes below the poverty threshold. One quarter of all children under six lived in poor families; perhaps more dramatic, 65 percent of children under six who live in female-headed households are poor. In contrast, the elderly are underrepresented in the poverty population, since they comprise more than 12 percent of the population, but less than 12 percent of the poverty population.

Figure 15.1

Distribution of the Poor in the United States, 1992

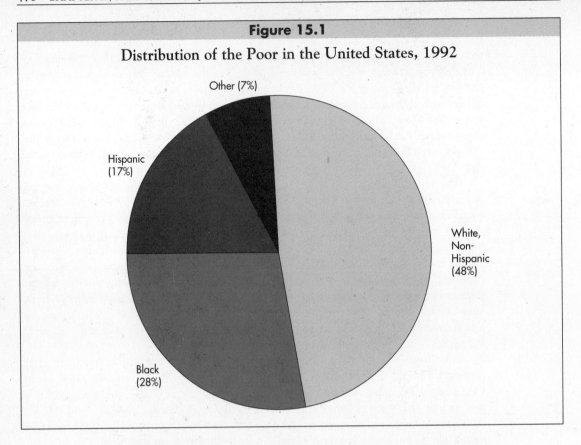

The Causes of Poverty Among the Deserving Poor: Unemployment, Family Disorganization, Low Wages, and the Culture of Poverty

All countries have poverty, but it is important to explain why there are poor in a country as wealthy as the United States. In part, this explanation is necessary in order to decide how best to reduce poverty, but the explanation also determines who among the poor "deserve" help and what the nature of that help will be. Poverty is sometimes characterized as the "just deserts" of a life of sloth, but the causes of poverty, while they may occasionally include laziness, are not exhausted by it. Being poor or becoming poor may be the result of many factors, including and more commonly unemployment, family disorganization, and chronically low wages. In these cases, where poverty is the result of social and economic factors rather than individual failure, we may speak of a class of persons who deserve assistance from the government (see Box 15.1).

Unemployment

Being unemployed is the most common cause of poverty. Half of those who enter poverty do so because someone in their family loses a job or has his or her wages cut.[9] When the government fights inflation by encouraging unemployment, as the Reagan administration

BOX 15.1

WHO ARE THE POOR?

It is possible to think of the poor in dichotomous categories: the deserving and the undeserving poor; the working and the nonworking poor; the occasionally poor and the chronically poor; and the elderly and the young; men and women; blacks and whites. These categories may convey the shape of poverty, but they cannot convey its consequences for the poor.

The majority of poor people in the United States are white, female, and living outside of central cities. In 1992

- more than 14 million children were poor;
- more than 24 million whites were poor;
- one of every eight white persons was poor;
- one third of all female-headed households was poor;
- nine and one-half million black people were poor;
- one of every three black persons was poor;
- six and one-half million Hispanics were poor;
- three of every ten Hispanics was poor; and
- almost eight million families had incomes below the poverty threshold;
- four million poor people were 65 or over
- more than 24 million poor people 16 and over;
- more than nine million poor people worked;
- more than two million poor people worked full-time.

Regionally, the South continued to have the highest percent of poor people;

- the Northeast had the lowest percent of poor people;
- four states (California, Nevada, North Carolina, and Rhode Island) had significant increases in their poverty rates;
- more than a fourth of Mississippi's population was poor;
- 38 percent live in rural areas, and
- 25 percent live in the suburbs.

Eleanor F. Baugher and Martin Shea, Poverty in the United States: 1992, *U. S. Department of Commerce, Bureau of the Census (Washington, D.C. 1993).*

did, poverty follows. From 1980 to 1982 the number of unemployed rose by 3.1 million and the number of persons in poverty increased by 5.1 million.[10] The recession of the early 1980s put almost eleven percent of the population out of work, producing the highest unemployment rate since the Great Depression.

Corporations and businesses do not always consider the welfare of their employees when making business decisions. Nor do they always make provisions for retraining or relocating them. Entire industries, like the auto and steel industries in the 1970s, may reduce their work forces, leading to widespread unemployment in many states. A local industry may relocate to another state, or even a foreign country, where wages are lower. A small business may become insolvent and reduce its work force or even close its doors. An individual may become ill and be unable to work. Unemployment can occur to anyone, and during the 1980s, between 7 and 11 million people were out of work. The 1991–1992 recession put almost 3 million people out of work,[11] and as downsizing continues in a number of industries (e.g., the defense industry), unemployment becomes a threat to the middle-class as well as the lower and working classes.

Family Disorganization

Women and children are the most common victims of family disorganization and victims of poverty. Women are likely to enter poverty when they become the heads of households; 35 percent of female-headed households had incomes beneath the poverty threshold in 1992. Whether the new status is the result of divorce, widowhood, or an out-of-wedlock baby, the status is likely to produce poverty.[12]

The fact that more than half of all poor persons are females is known to those studying poverty. This overrepresentation of females in the poverty figures has been called the **feminization of poverty**, but female headed households have been poor in the United States since poverty figures began being kept in 1959, when almost half of all female-headed households had incomes below the poverty level. In 1992, 11.7 percent of all families were below the poverty level, but 38 percent of all female-headed households and 50 percent of all black female-headed households were below the poverty level.[13]

The feminization of poverty has been exacerbated by so called "man-in-the-house" rules enacted to deny benefits to men able, but unwilling, to work. The enforcement of such

---

Table 15.1

THE POVERTY THRESHOLD FOR A FAMILY OF FOUR AND MEDIAN FAMILY INCOME: SELECTED YEARS[a]

Year	Average Poverty Threshold for a Family of Four	Median Family Income
1960	$3,022	$19,100
1965	$3,223	$21,968
1970	$3,968	$24,662
1975	$5,500	$24,039
1980	$8,414	$23,565
1985	$10,989	$24,072
1990	$13,359	$29,943
1991	$13,394	$30,127
1992	$14,335	$30,786

[a]For years prior to 1981, average threshold for a nonfarm family of four is shown.

Sources: Statistical Abstract, 1988, 422; Mark S. Littman and Eleanor F. Baugher, Poverty in the United States, U.S. Department of Commerce, Bureau of the Census (Washington, D.C.: U. S. Government Printing Office, 1988), 154; Eleanor F. Baugher and Martina Shea, Poverty in the United States: 1992 U. S. Department of Commerce, Bureau of the Census (Washington, D.C.: U. S. Goverment Printing Office, 1993), vii.

rules denied benefits to families with men who were able to work living with their families, and made it costly for fathers to remain with their families during periods of unemployment, thus further weakening familial bonds and increasing the likelihood of female householders.

Being Born into a Poor Family

As noted earlier, almost 22 percent of all children in the United States live in poverty. Some social scientists believe that there is a **culture of poverty**, meaning that the poor are a distinct group with their own rules, ideas, and beliefs. This culture of poverty implies that the poor learn to be poor or fail to learn how to escape poverty, and indeed transmit poverty as a way of life to their children. Culture of poverty theorists believe that poor children are likely to become poor adults who have their own poor children, thus continuing the culture and the cycle of poverty.

The **underclass** is a term that describes a particular group caught in the culture of poverty.[14] Coined by Gunnar Myrdal and popularized by Ken Auletta, the term describes "a third world rural and urban 'underclass' cut off from society, its members lacking 'the education and the skills and other personality traits they need in order to become effectively in demand in the modern economy.'"[15] Members of the underclass have been unable to take advantage of the increases in opportunity resulting from affirmative action, and are thus trapped in poverty. They are trapped in lives that offer them little hope of becoming conventional, middle-class Americans.

Individuals enter poverty for other reasons besides unemployment, family disorganization, or being a member of the culture of poverty. Perhaps most shocking is the fact that some enter poverty, or fail to leave it, even though they work full time.

Low Wages

The **working poor** are rarely mentioned in the media, perhaps because the popular image of the poor is that they do not work, or worse, will not work. That image is, in many cases, false. Of the 23 million poor adults in 1992, 41 percent reported that they had worked during the year, and 10 percent reported having worked full-time for the entire year. For poor family householders (formerly "heads of household"), almost half (49.1 percent) reported that they had worked during the year, and 15 percent reported having worked full-time for the entire year (see Table 15.1). For those who did not work, more than 60 percent said they were retired or disabled, and the others said they were unable to find work or were going to school.[16]

Even poverty-stricken women who have small children work. In 1992 more than half of all women with children under six worked full or part-time, yet remained below the poverty threshold. The majority of those who did not work gave family responsibilities as the reason for not working.[17]

If it seems difficult to believe that someone who worked full time could nevertheless be poor, imagine the situation of a mother of two children who works at a fast-food restaurant for 40 hours a week. Minimum wage is $4.25 an hour. (At this writing, President Clinton has advocated an increase to $5.25.) If she is fortunate enough never to be sick, never to lose working time because of the illnesses of her children, never to suffer the effects of violent crime, and if she can work 40 hours a week, 52 weeks of the year, she would earn $170.00 a week and $8,840 a year. That places her and her children below the poverty threshold for a family of three (one adult and two children) which, in 1992, was $11,186.[18] Regardless of where she stands in relation to the poverty threshold, imagine what a mother faces when she must house, feed, and clothe two children on less than $9,000 a year. Trying to save for college or even for Christmas on that income requires tenacity.

Many individuals in this society live lives on the brink of poverty. As long as they can work, they are able to stay just above the poverty threshold, but they may enter poverty if they become ill, are injured in an accident, acquire a new family member, or are victims of violent crime. Others have no choice concerning their poverty: they are children who have had the misfortune to be born into poverty. For the deserving poor, entering poverty is the result of bad luck.

Failure to Work: The Undeserving Poor?

Do those who fail to work deserve poverty? Are there poor persons who somehow deserve their lot in life because of their lack of effort? And why don't the nonworking poor work? These are the common questions about the poor.

Many of the nonworking poor are not permitted to work. Children make up a significant proportion of the officially poor. Almost 40 percent (39.6 percent) of the poor are under the age of 18. While few suggest that nonworking children should be denied welfare benefits if they do not work, there is much less agreement about what can be expected of women with children. However, with the cost of child care increasing and with health insurance typically unavailable in low paying occupations, it is not clear what women with several small children gain by working at low paying jobs.

But those who are physically able to work must justify their failure to work. Charles Murray has suggested that many of the poor do not work because work and being independent are less attractive than welfare and dependency. In addition, he suggests that the behaviors that help the poor escape poverty have lost the status formerly associated with them.[19] In other words, he suggests that to be dependent and on welfare does not have the social stigma it once had, and that some poor people are not as willing to attempt an escape from welfare as they once were. This is particularly true, Murray argues, for unmarried fathers and fathers-to-be who avoid marriage and contribute to the out-of-wedlock birth rate, thus increasing the number of poor women and children. Welfare makes poverty sufficiently tolerable that the poor do not do all they can to avoid it.

William Julius Wilson suggests, in rebuttal to Murray, that many of the poor do not work primarily because they cannot find jobs for which they have suitable skills.[20] Inadequately educated with few job skills, the poor have traditionally worked as semiskilled or unskilled laborers in central city industrial centers.[21] In the last 20 years, however, advances in transportation and communication have permitted manufacturers, retailers, and construction industries to move from the central city, taking with them the blue-collar jobs commonly filled by the poor. To take the place of blue-collar employers have come information-processing and financial organizations, bringing with them opportunity for professional or white collar employees. Thus the **urban industrial transition** and the resulting decline in employment opportunities have made finding work increasingly difficult for the urban poor. A survey of employers in Atlanta, Boston, Detroit, and Chicago found that only between 5 and 10 percent of the low-skilled job openings were available to applicants with few skills or little work experience.[22] Or in the words of Lynn A. Karoly,

> There are several factors that explain a little piece of the rise in inequality. But the big explanation is that there has been a change in technology that has increased a demand for more skilled

workers. It is not an evil bureaucrat, it is not an evil policy maker or boss who has made this change, but basically people have discovered ways of making things which increase the demand for high-skilled people and decrease the demand for low-skilled people. Since earnings make up the vast majority of family income, inequality of family income also increases. Poverty increases. So it is technology that is driving poverty.[23]

A similar process has been at work in rural areas. The industries common to rural areas—agriculture, timber, mining, oil and gas production—have declined in the last decade and unemployment rates have risen.[24] In addition, incomes have also fallen in rural areas, and fringe benefits, especially pension plans, are less common than in urban areas. Poverty is increasing in rural areas and the gap between urban and rural poverty rates is decreasing (see Figure 15.2).

Thus we are left to ask whether some of the poor fail to work because they don't want to work or because they cannot find work. There is probably some truth to both positions. For some, welfare no longer carries the stigma it once did, and they remain unmotivated to work. Many would work, however, if jobs were available or if they had the skills for the jobs that are available. A local government hoping to deal with the problem of poverty must consider both arguments if it is to develop comprehensive and effective policies for job creation, job training, and new education initiatives to deal with those who, for whatever reason, choose not to work.

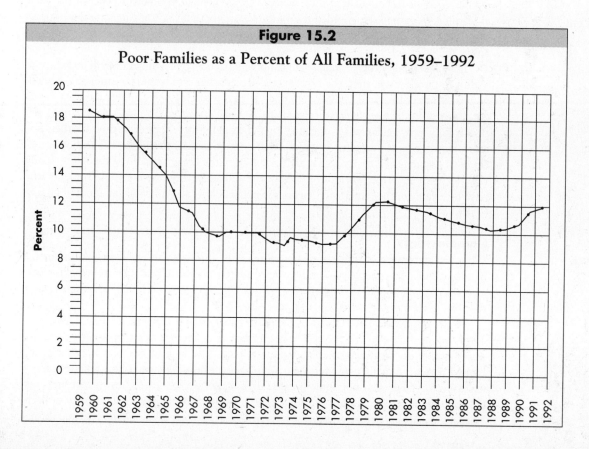

Figure 15.2

Poor Families as a Percent of All Families, 1959–1992

Consequences of Poverty

Being poor has a number of detrimental consequences for the poor and the country in which they live. It means more than simply having a low income and results in more than simply a low standard of living. Being poor means being less likely to become educated, to have a home, to have good health, or to be safe from crime. These are the facts of life for poor people.

Education

One of the first areas in which the poor face a disadvantage is in education. To be successful in school, to learn to read, write, and analyze, children must have sufficient nourishment, rest, health, and parental involvement to be able to demonstrate their native ability. Poverty, hunger, and distracted parents reduce the possibility of success in school.

Poverty reduces the likelihood of being successful in school, and a lack of success in school is directly related to poverty. For householders who have not completed high school, the poverty rate is almost one in four (24.1 percent). For those who have a only a high school diploma, the poverty rate is about 1 in ten (11 percent). Householders with a four-year college degree have a poverty rate of less than 3 in 100 (2.2 percent).[25]

Poverty is related to education in still another way. Important to educational success is the belief that what one does in the classroom will have some payoff; but children who are discouraged by consequences of their own poverty may have insufficient belief in the value of learning, or perhaps heightened fear of the failure that may accompany attempts to master anything, to invest in education. (See the excerpt from *Savage Inequalities* by Jonathan Kozol in Box 15.2.)

If a major goal of the American educational system is to prepare our youth for positions within the work force, then the urban poor face another disadvantage. Inner city schools, with their under-financed classrooms and underpaid teachers, help to "guarantee the future economic subordinacy of minority students."[26] Rural poverty is no less deprivating, and poor rural youth are no better prepared for skilled labor force jobs than their brothers and sisters in the city. If anything, levels of education are lower in rural areas.[27] In both cases, the school systems fail to produce students who have the language skills or the self presentation necessary to secure entry level jobs in the skilled work force. For those students who have little faith in the American Dream, the public school system offers but another chance to fail.

Homelessness

While our stereotype of the homeless is of mentally ill hobos and bag ladies, an increasing number of homeless people are families with children who once owned or were making payments on a home, or rented a decent apartment until eviction. Having lost their homes, they live in their cars, on the street, or in shelters.

Why do individuals and families lose their homes and become unable to find new ones? They become homeless for the same reasons that they become poor: unemployment, low wages, family disorganization, and simple bad luck. The lack of low cost housing in the United States is a major cause for the continuation of homelessness. Many families cannot make a down payment on a home because their wages are too low. They cannot rent suitable housing either because of the size of their family, the cost of rental property or both. The late Michael Harrington suggested that the term "homeless" should be changed to "up-

BOX 15.2

POOR CHILDREN IN AMERICA

The following is an excerpt from *Savage Inequalities* by Jonathan Kozol. The author explores what happens to children when they go to inadequate, racially segregated schools and live in substandard housing in violence ridden neighborhoods. Kozol's point is that children who grow up amid violence and deprived of educational opportunity have little chance of pursuing the American dream, much less achieving it. If at age nine, a child is unfamiliar with the time school begins or the grade he is in, then what importance does he give to school or the subjects it teaches? If school is unimportant, what chance does he have in this society?

This is a conversation with poor children, nine-year-olds Smokey and Serena, seven-year-old Mickey, and Little Sister, a small child whose age is not given, who live in just such a neighborhood in East St. Louis. As this conversation takes place, Mr. Kozol is walking across the children's playground, which is marshy from sewage overflow. Worse, the area is downwind from chemical plants which emit toxic smoke into the environment. Imagine what it would have meant to your life if, at age seven or nine, your family members or friends had been raped or murdered or both. Perhaps hate would have been as casual a topic in your conversations as it is in those of Little Sister, Mickey, and Smokey.

> *None of the children can tell me the approximate time school begins. One says five o'-clock. One says six. Another says that school begins at noon.*
>
> *When I ask what song they sing after the flag pledge, one says, "Jingle Bells." Smokey cannot decide whether he is in the second or third grade.*
>
> *Seven-year-old Mickey sucks his thumb during the walk.*
>
> *The children regale me with a chilling story. . . . .Smokey says his sister was raped and murdered and then dumped behind his school. Other children add more details: Smokey's sister was 11 years old. She was beaten with a brick until she died. The murder was committed by a man who knew her mother.*
>
> *The narrative begins when, without warning, Smokey says, "My sister got killed."*
> *"She was my best friend," Serena says.*
>
> *"They beat her in the head and raped her," Smokey says.*
>
> *"She was hollering out loud," says Little Sister.*
>
> *I asked them when it happened. Smokey says, "Last year." Serena corrects him and she says, "Last week." . . .*
>
> *"The police arrested one man, but they didn't catch the other," Smokey says. Serena says, "He was some kin to her."*
>
> *But Smokey objects, "He weren't no kin to me. He was my momma's friend. . . ."*
> *"Her face was busted," Little Sister says.*
>
> *Serena described the sequence of events: "They told her to go behind the school. They'll give her a quarter if she did. Then they knock her down and told her not to tell what they had did."*
>
> *I ask, "Why did they kill her?"*
> *"They was scared that she would tell." Serena says.*
>
> *"One is in jail," says Smokey. "They caint find the other."*

(Continued)

BOX 15.2 (Continued)

"Instead of raping little bitty children, they should find themselves a wife," says Little Sister.

"I hope," Serena says, "her spirit will come back and get that man."

"And kill that man," says Little Sister.

"Give her another chance to live," Serena says. . . .

"My grandma was murdered," Mickey says out of the blue. "Someone shot two bullets into her head."

I ask, "Is she really dead?"

"She dead all right," says Mickey. "She was layin' there, just dead. . . ."

"I have a cat with three legs," Smokey says.

"Snakes hate rabbits," Mickey says, again for no apparent reason.

"Cats hate fishes," Little Sister says.

"It's a lot of hate," says Smokey.

Source: Jonathan Kozol, *Savage Inequalities* (New York: Crown Publishers, 1992), 12–14.

rooted" because physical shelter is only one aspect of the "homelessness" phenomenon. The most damaging aspect of being "uprooted" is the precarious nature of one's day-to-day living. As he puts it:

A 'home' is not simply a roof over one's head. It is the center of a web of human relationships. When the web is shredded as a result of social and economic trends, a person is homeless even if he or she has an anonymous room somewhere.[28]

It is clear that homelessness is a threat to the well being of a wide variety of people, an increasing number of them single women or women and their children. It is estimated that homeless families, many headed by single mothers, account for between 20 to 30 percent of all homeless people. Children make up about 20 percent of the homeless population.[29] The following testimony from a House Subcommittee on Housing and Urban Development hearing demonstrates the personal nature of the problem:

Ms. Vanover: I have been on the streets for five months now. I started in a very small town in New Hampshire where I held a variety of low paying jobs, barely enough to live on . . . At the time, I was three months pregnant, very hungry for many days. I thank God there was a soup kitchen in the town. After my baby was born, I moved back home for several months. That didn't work out because my mother couldn't afford to feed both me and my baby. I thought maybe going to the big city might give me a better chance to find work. [She and her husband left, leaving the child with her mother in New Hampshire.] My husband is a Vietnam veteran and is having an impossible time trying to get benefits or a job. We have traveled the East coast, through New York, New Jersey, Philadelphia, and Washington, looking for work, but still nothing. It is impossible to find a job without a steady place to sleep. It is a vicious cycle, no mailing address, no telephone, no clean clothes, no showers, no bus fare, no nothing. In a few

Citizens and their governments must respond to the issues signified by signs in the hands of men and women standing on street corners in most U.S. cities. Whether those holding the signs are slackers who could but won't work or people who cannot find work they can do, their signs represent a major shift in the American approach to employment.

other cities there were shelters. Most often there were none. I have stayed in places that would frighten most people. I was frightened.[30]

Poor Health and Shorter Lives

Because poverty reduces access to medical care, the poor often suffer ill health and live shorter lives. A study of more than six hundred women who had cancer surgery at a hospital in Harlem shows a five-year survival rate of only 30 percent. The national average for black women is 60 percent and for white women it is 70 percent. Dr. Harold Freeman, who began offering free breast exams at Harlem Hospital a decade ago, reports that the women patients there see physicians much later than their wealthier female counterparts. "Getting into the medical system for diagnosis and later treatment may to the poor person be more painful that a painless lump."[31] In general, blacks have higher rates of death from cancer, with black males having the highest rates of all Americans.[32]

Readily available health care is especially critical for mothers and children. Perhaps nowhere are disparities between middle income Americans and the poor more apparent than in the infant mortality rates for black and white babies. Black babies are twice as likely to die in their first year, a phenomenon related to a greater percentage of young mothers with poor health habits and poor prenatal care, who then have low birth-weight babies.[33]

Poverty also reduces the likelihood of adequate diet. Good nutrition is necessary for a healthy immune system.[34] A diet high in fat and low in protein is associated with poverty, producing obesity and illness. Black Americans have a life expectancy five and one-half years shorter than that of white Americans, largely because a larger percentage of the black population lives in poverty.[35] Perhaps more ominous, the gap in life expectancy between blacks and whites has once again begun to increase.[36] Poor southern whites have higher than average death rates also, as a result of poverty.[37] An examination of life expectancy tables reveals that the average American Indian, a group that is the "poorest of the poor," dies 20 years earlier than the average non-Indian.[38]

Poverty causes stress, and stress can produce disease. Stress, in itself, is not pathogenic, but chronic stress, which is not channeled into physical exercise or attenuated by social involvement, has a debilitating effect on health.[39] Stress that is handled through the use of alcohol, tobacco, and drugs produces a significantly increased risk of chronic and disabling diseases, such as cancer and heart disease; coupled with a high fat diet, this approach to dealing with stress is deadly.

Criminal Victimization

The poor are most likely to be victims of violent crime, and are commonly victims of property crime as well. The death rate from homicide for white males in 1988 was eight per 100,000, but for black males it was almost 58, having declined from 67 in 1980.[40] One in every 30 black males dies as the result of a homicide, while one in 179 white males will be a homicide victim.[41] Sixty-one of every 1,000 black males are victims of violent crime. For white males, the rate is 38 per thousand; for black females the rate is 31 and for white females, 22 per 1,000.[42]

Household burglary rates and most other household crimes are highest for those with household incomes of less than $7,500.[43] Violent crime rates are highest for the poor as well. Robbery, rape, and assault victims are most common in the income levels below $7,500. Violent victimization rates are higher for the unemployed, the divorced, the never married, and the less educated, all characteristics more common to the poor. [44]

Poverty is so damaging for the poor and the country in which they live that federal, state, and local governments have implemented relief or welfare programs, in one form or another, for the last half century. Delineating the costs and contributions of these programs is the goal of the next section.

Poverty and the Fifty States

The poor are not distributed equally among the states. The South has the greatest proportion of poor persons in the United States. In 1992 Mississippi continues to have the largest percentage of people below the poverty threshold of any state, followed closely by Louisiana; Delaware has the smallest percentage of people below the poverty threshold of any state, followed by New Hampshire. The number of poor (not percent of population) varies between states: California, Texas, New York, and Florida in descending order, have the greatest number of poor persons; Wyoming, Alaska, and Delaware have the fewest number of poor persons (see Figure 15.3).

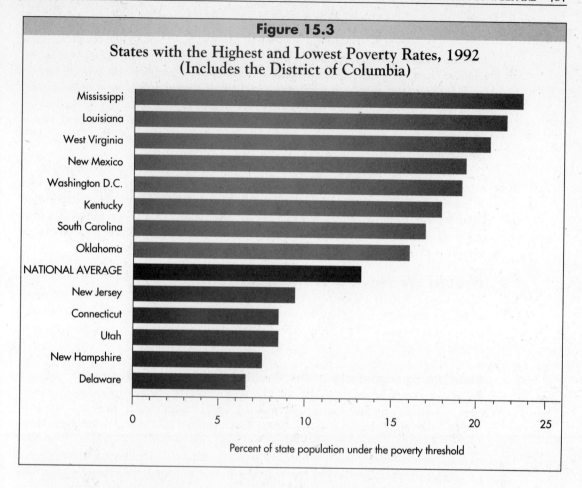

Figure 15.3

States with the Highest and Lowest Poverty Rates, 1992
(Includes the District of Columbia)

Percent of state population under the poverty threshold

THE SYSTEM OF WELFARE

Probably no governmental expense elicits more disagreement than the system of welfare. The disagreement is fueled by misunderstanding and misinformation, but has roots in the fundamental debate over the responsibility of government to the well being of citizens. This section focuses on the dimensions of the welfare system and its cost to state and local governments.

What Is Welfare?

In this chapter, **welfare** refers to means-tested social programs. **Means-tested** government programs are those based on some measure of income. The five major means-tested programs, **Aid to Families with Dependent Children** (AFDC), **Supplemental Security Income** (SSI), **Medicaid,** and **Food Stamps,** use some multiple of the poverty threshold to decide who is eligible for aid. For instance, the Food Stamps program provides food stamps for families if their incomes are less than 130 percent of the poverty threshold. These programs are the typical welfare programs, designed to provide the poor with adequate food and shelter.

Most of the money spent by governments on social programs is not spent in means-tested welfare programs. Instead it is spent in social insurance programs like **Social Security**, **Medicare**, Veterans Benefits, worker's compensation, student loans and unemployment insurance. These social insurance programs, sometimes called **entitlements**, provide support for a wide range of people and are primarily directed toward middle- and upper-income Americans. These social insurance programs are designed to provide a safety net for middle- and upper-income American families should the breadwinner(s) become disabled, unemployed, or die prematurely. These are also the programs intended to help America's elderly secure a dignified retirement. Such programs are not welfare programs.

The yearly government outlay for Social Security is larger than that spent on all means-tested programs put together.[45] Social Security benefits are not means-tested; they are provided regardless of income level. Only 20 percent of the funds distributed in the entitlement programs funded through Social Security go to the poor. Despite the fact that Social Security is not a welfare program, it nevertheless lifts one quarter of the population, the families of the disabled, the elderly, and survivors above the poverty threshold.[46]

Should We Have a Welfare System?

In recent years, this has been a frequently asked question. It has been raised in part because middle-income Americans have begun to question the desirability of paying taxes to support a welfare system. Yet we believe there are some very good reasons for having some form of welfare system.

Maintaining Legitimacy of the Political and Economic Systems

If a government is to maintain the cooperation necessary for achieving national goals, it must be seen as responsive to the needs of its citizens. In every society there are some individuals—the young, the disabled, the elderly — who cannot take care of themselves. Moreover, in our *laissez faire* capitalist economy, low wages and private health insurance produce a tenuous way of life for many. For those citizens who, through no fault of their own, cannot provide for the necessities of life, the government must provide some form of aid to maintain the legitimacy of the polity and the economy.

Human Resource Investment

While there is a persistently poor underclass in the United States, it makes up less than 5 percent of the population at any time.[47] Most poor persons fall into poverty and are able, with temporary relief, job training, or both, to once again become contributing, taxpaying members of their communities.

Humanitarian Reasons

Demonstrating compassion for those less fortunate is a hallmark of civilized societies. While abandoning the disabled and the elderly may be acceptable in a subsistence-level society which cannot support unproductive individuals, a country as wealthy as the United States surely has an obligation to those who become poor despite their best efforts to do otherwise.

The arguments against welfare have primarily to do with its cost. Redistributive policies, those policies which transfer earnings "from higher to lower income segments of the population," have negative consequences for local economies when the low income recipients are not needed by the local economy."[48] While unskilled workers are, at times, needed to work in local industries, this is less often the case when manufacturing enterprises, as noted earlier by William J. Wilson, change their character and location. Nevertheless, the arguments cited in support of aid to the poor have such strong moral claim that governments are willing to honor them.

Federal, State, and Local Governments: Partnership or Rivalry?

Until 1932 state and local governments assumed the responsibility for public assistance. But the Great Depression proved to be too much for most state and local budgets, and the federal government began to help state and local governments provide relief to families and individuals. At the end of the Depression, only the disabled, blind, and orphans remained on the welfare roles.

Assistance to state governments continued without meaningful changes during the 1950s, but the turbulence of the 1960s led to greatly expanded welfare rolls. Lyndon Johnson's Great Society programs declared a war on poverty, and he attempted to fund it and the Vietnam war at the same time. The "war at home" lost support as the war abroad increased in intensity and cost. At the same time, the Johnson administration gave federal aid directly to local welfare programs in the South, bypassing state governments which had blocked the poor from receiving aid. Not surprisingly, state officials became irate at losing the right to administer programs in their states, and the defection of Southerners from the Democratic party, begun as a result of civil rights initiatives in the Kennedy and Johnson administrations, continued in earnest.[49] Subsequent administrations have undertaken to dismantle the Great Society programs, not without some success.

The Reagan administration attempted to reduce federal funding of welfare programs, hoping to require state and local governments to assume more of the cost. The most dramatic revamping of the welfare system since the Great Depression was legislated in 1988. The Family Support Act established the Jobs Opportunity and Basic Skills Program (JOBS) which requires each state to develop programs for poor families with children. The goal of JOBS is to decrease welfare dependency by providing remedial education and job training aimed at groups prone to welfare dependency, primarily members of the underclass. Each state must submit a program to the Department of Health and Human Welfare Services by 1990. It is too soon to know whether this approach will work, although since it provides only a few hundred dollars per recipient per year, there is some doubt that it will accomplish its intent.[50]

In 1987 the federal government provided about 75 percent of the cost of welfare programs,[51] continuing the "war" on poverty as a federally supported struggle. Yet, as will be seen, the federal government cannot ensure that individuals in different states will receive similar levels of assistance; in fact, federalism makes that impossible, and the poor experience deprivation in some states while having a much better standard of living in others.

Nor is the federal government inclined to do more than is necessary in funding state welfare programs. As noted, the Reagan administration attempted to make state and local governments assume more of the costs of welfare. Since this attempt came in the midst of taxpayer revolts in a number of states, it was not completely successful. At the same time, however, the federal government bestowed greater flexibility to states in making major grant allocations. Nevertheless, the appropriate source and amount of funding for welfare programs continues to be a source of friction between governments as well as of concern for those whose lives are constrained by the vagaries of intergovernmental politics.

State governments want the federal government to increase the amount of aid to the states while permitting the states more leeway in administering the programs. There has been some support for this in Congress. Senator Daniel J. Evans, saying that "the current inequalities in AFDC are a national disgrace," argued for establishing minimum benefit and eligibility standards for AFDC and Medicaid, while assuming full responsibility for funding those programs.[52] There is, as one might expect, much opposition to this "nationalization of welfare" suggestion; even many state and local officials argue, as did federal officials during the Reagan administration, that variations in the cost of living between states call for more flexibility at the local level.

The debate between governments concerning who should set welfare levels and who should administer programs is likely to continue. The next section examines those programs and discusses their costs for governments.

Federal, State, and Local Welfare Programs for the Poor

State and local governments receive funds from the federal government through two kinds of grants: categorical grants-in-aid, general revenue sharing grants, and special revenue sharing block grants. **Categorical grants-in-aid** are targeted at special categories of need. Such grants begin when the federal government enacts legislation offering funds to states that meet federal specifications. States then pass legislation bringing them into compliance with the federal legislation. **Special revenue sharing block grants** are federal funds offered to states to replace, at one time, numerous categorical grants-in-aid directed at a particular problem, like job creation or community development. These block grants were used by the Reagan administration to reduce funding for welfare by consolidating previous categorical grants into block grants at a lower funding level.[53]

Currently, there are several government welfare programs, including Aid to Families with Dependent Children (AFDC), Supplemental Security Income (SSI), Medicaid, Public and Subsidized Housing, School Lunches, and Food Stamps. The costs of all programs are shared by federal and state governments, though states pay less than half of the costs of the programs. A brief summary of these programs follows.

Aid to Families with Dependent Children

This is a federal and state categorical grant-in aid program, with state governments paying approximately 45 percent of the cost of the program. AFDC was established by the Social Security Act of 1935, and each state administers its own program. All families with children under 18 with one parent absent are eligible for AFDC cash benefits. In over half of the states, two-parent families are also eligible when the father is out of work. The cost of AFDC to state and local governments is around $7 billion per year. Approximately 11 million persons receive benefits each year; only about one fifth of the 20 million poor adults receive AFDC benefits.[54]

Supplemental Security Income

This program was established in 1972 to provide additional monthly cash payments to impoverished elderly, blind, and disabled persons. The federal government administers this program through Social Security Administration offices. State and local governments pay approximately 20 percent of the cost of this program which, in 1986, was almost 12 billion dollars. More than 11 million individuals, over 4 percent of the population, received benefits.

The nonpoor benefit in numerous ways from SSI. Income received by the poor under this program is used to pay for housing, food, clothing and other items sold by the private sector.

Medicaid

This program was established in 1965 to help cover the medical costs of those persons eligible for AFDC and SSI. In 1992, 47.2 percent of the poor were covered by Medicaid.[55]

In many states Medicaid is extended to the "medically needy," those persons whose incomes exceed eligibility for cash assistance, but are insufficient to pay for necessary medical care. Each state creates and administers its own program within broad federal guidelines. States have a great deal of latitude to determine eligibility and kinds of benefits. Payments that are made directly to those providing the services, generally hospitals and physicians, are also established by the state.

State and local governments paid approximately $20 billion in 1986, providing medical care to more than 21 million persons. By 1992, however, Medicaid expenditures had risen to more than $90 billion, while providing medical care to more than 30 million persons.[56] In the two years between 1990 and 1992, Medicaid costs rose more than 40 percent in the United States, and, as a result a number of states have enacted reforms to control costs. For instance, Oregon's rationed health care system, which limits the number of treatments available to Medicaid recipients, went into effect in 1994. Another strategy, health alliances have been formed in Florida and Washington where the states are acting as "insurance brokers" for small businesses and Medicaid recipients, collecting health premiums from employers and individuals, then negotiating the best prices with health care providers. In this fashion, they will test the utility of health insurance purchasing alliances.[57]

Despite the phenomenal rise in Medicaid costs, the nonpoor benefit in numerous ways from Medicaid. These funds provide income for hospitals, doctors, and related health care agents and agencies, all of whom spend that income in local stores and businesses. Whether the benefits of Medicaid outweigh the disadvantages will continue to be the subject of state and local debate as health reforms are proposed and enacted.

Public and Subsidized Housing

These programs come in a variety of forms. Private sector rent supplements—in which the owner of the rental housing receives the difference between fair market rent and the rent charged to the tenant— are available from the government (federal, state and/or local). Interest reduction programs reduce the amount of interest paid on the mortgage by a home owner so that lower payments can be paid by the poor renter of that home. It takes little imagination to see how these programs benefit the nonpoor. In such situations, property owners have their income supplemented by the federal government.

Public housing projects provide low rent housing for the poor. State and local governments may provide part of the funding for the projects which are under the jurisdiction of the Department of Housing and Urban Development, and they are owned, managed, and run by local housing authorities. Osborne and Gaebler argue that this form of management results in problems for residents of housing projects because it encourages passivity toward events and problems in the projects. Examples of residents who have empowered themselves to run their housing projects suggest that when individuals who live in an area—either public housing projects or privately owned homes—became active in their neighborhoods, order and well being increased.

The National School Lunch

This program is intended to "help safeguard the health and well-being of the Nation's children by assisting the States in providing an adequate supply of foods for all children at a moderate cost."[58] All students, regardless of income, who eat lunches prepared at schools participating in the School Lunch Program receive their meals at reduced prices. Today, school lunches can be free to students whose families have incomes below 130 percent of the poverty threshold, and at reduced prices to students whose families have incomes between 130 and 180 percent of the poverty threshold.

Not only do nonpoor children and their parents benefit from this program with reduced price lunches, but farmers whose products are purchased by the federal government and distributed in the program also benefit.

Food Stamps

This program begun during the 1960s, distributes coupons redeemable for food to families and individuals. Families without elderly or disabled persons must have an income below 130 percent of the poverty threshold to be eligible for food stamps. State welfare agencies administer the program under broad federal guidelines. The federal government provides almost all the funding for food stamps. In 1986 state governments funded 7 percent of the program, costing them about $900 million, and providing benefits to approximately 20 million persons each month.

The nonpoor benefit in numerous ways from the Food Stamp program. Food stamps for the poor are used in local markets to pay for groceries for which they would be unable to pay were it not for the program.

State and local governments also provide assistance by administering various job training and job creation programs. The Job Corps continues to train a small number of disadvantaged young people. A similar program, the Work Incentive Program, assists AFDC mothers to find private sector work. The Comprehensive Employment Fund Training Act (CETA) of 1973 was an attempt to provide job training programs, as well as expand public sector hiring of the poor. It was replaced in 1983 by the Jobs Partnership Training Act, which has the goal of uniting the government and the private sector in local efforts to provide jobs for displaced and disadvantaged workers.

States also receive funds through the Social Services Block Grants which can be used for in-home care of children and the elderly. In addition, states receive funds for the remedial or compensatory education of poor children under the Education and Consolidation Act of 1982.

Who Receives Welfare?

Welfare programs target two categories of people: the disabled, blind, or elderly poor and poor families with children. In 1986 the official poverty threshold for an average family of four was $11,203; in 1992 the poverty threshold was $14,335.[59] Nevertheless, many persons and families whose incomes were below this threshold did not receive welfare payments, and many persons whose incomes were above this threshold did receive government payments. The reason for this paradox is that only 7 of 59 major welfare programs use the poverty threshold as a "means test," a criterion of eligibility; another 20 use some multiple of the poverty threshold as one criterion.[60] Means-tested programs include cash benefits from AFDC, SSI, some veterans benefits, Medicaid benefits, food stamps, free or reduced-price school lunches, and rent subsidies. In a typical month, one in eight Americans participates in one or more means-tested programs (see Figure 15.4).[61]

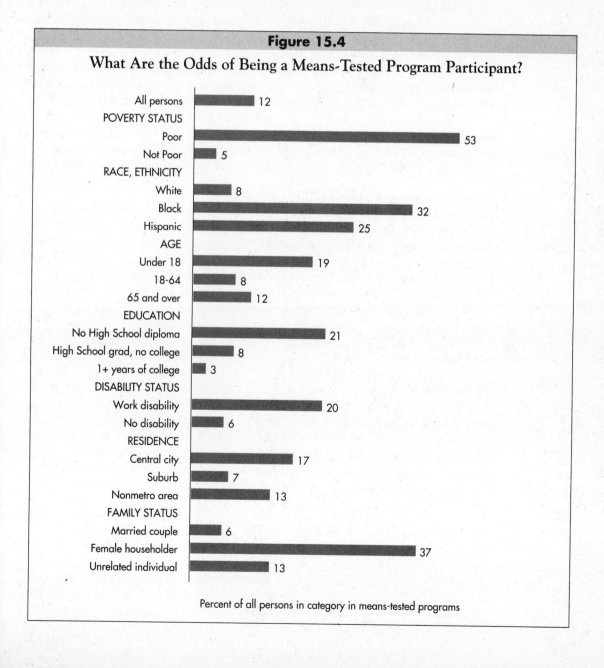

Figure 15.4

What Are the Odds of Being a Means-Tested Program Participant?

Percent of all persons in category in means-tested programs

In 1992, 42.7 percent of persons below the poverty level received means-tested cash assistance, such as Aid to Families with Dependent Children or Supplemental Security Income.[62] Fifty-six percent of those who received cash assistance remained below the poverty threshold when the assistance was added to their income. Two-thirds of the poor received some form of means-tested assistance, other than school lunches, Another 2.4 million received free or reduced-price school lunches, but no other assistance. In all, about 73 percent of the those whose incomes fell below the poverty threshold received some sort of means-tested assistance.[63]

Welfare recipients are typically young and typically female. Women make up 56 percent of the welfare population, since welfare rules favor women with children and the elderly. There are more elderly women than men, so women and children make up the significant majority of welfare recipients. Although blacks and Hispanics have a much greater likelihood of going on welfare than whites, the majority of people on welfare are white.[64] In 1987, 16 percent of all whites, some 31 million persons, received means-tested welfare. Fifty percent of all blacks (more than 14 million individuals) and 43 percent of all Hispanics (more than six million individuals) received means-tested welfare payments of some kind. One in three children received welfare, and one in five elderly persons received welfare. Nationally, approximately one in five persons received some type of means tested welfare.

Does Anyone Ever Get Off Welfare?

Stereotypes of welfare recipients convey a number of myths, including the notion that individuals, once on welfare, remain there for their lifetime, as do their children and their children's children. In fact, the welfare population is much more mercurial. In general, it is estimated that 20 percent of the persons who were poor in 1991 were not poor in 1992. The net increase of poor people during those years is the result of more than six million persons becoming poor, while slightly more than five million moved out of poverty.[65]

Whites are more likely than Hispanics or blacks to exit poverty; whites are also less likely to enter poverty. However, exit rates for whites declined from 30 percent in 1987–1988 to about 23 percent in 1992, while exit rates remained the same for Hispanics and blacks.[66]

Getting married or having a parent who got married increased the likelihood of escaping poverty: individuals who became members of a married-couple family had an exit rate of over 58 percent in 1990–1991, significantly higher than the rate of about 12 percent for those in other kinds of families. As one might expect, working full-time increased the likelihood of exiting poverty: those who worked full-time for two years exited at the highest rate; those who did not work at all had the lowest exit rate. The more persons in the family who worked at least part-time, the greater the likelihood of leaving poverty.[67] Thus it is clear that the reasons for becoming poor and the reasons for exiting poverty are mirror images of one another.

How Much Does the Welfare System Cost?

The distinction between means-tested (welfare) programs for the poor and nonmeans tested (entitlement) programs for all Americans is especially important when calculating the cost of the welfare system. The attack on the welfare system by former President Ronald Reagan, who promised to reduce the federal government's expenditures for social programs, brought this distinction into sharp relief. Those who were eager for the reduction discovered that

Anyone who thinks the work ethic no longer exists in the United States has only to go to an unemployment office and talk to the people standing in line. Though discouraged and worried about their futures, these men and women are nevertheless Americans looking for another chance to participate in the work force.

most of those expenditures went for entitlement programs, not welfare programs. Further, they found that significant cost reductions would have to come from entitlements. This section focuses on the costs of social welfare.

The cost of public welfare programs for state governments was more than $130 billion in 1991. This figure represents more than 12 percent of all spending by state and local governments.[68] The greatest expenditure by state governments is for education, and either highways or public welfare is generally the second most costly category. Thirty-two states spent more for highways than public welfare in 1990.[69]

While all states provide for public welfare, there is significant variation in the amount spent. In 1991 state expenditures for public welfare ranged from $19.6 billion in California to $152 million in Wyoming. As a percentage of the all expenditures, outlay for welfare ranged from more than 18 percent in Massachusetts to less than 6 percent in Wyoming and Nevada.[70]

Not only do general state expenditures vary, but AFDC payments vary by state as well. States are able to set the level of AFDC payments, producing significant variation in the range of payments for a family of four. For 1992 benefits to a family of four were highest in

Alaska ($743) and Hawaii ($633); for the same time period, they were lowest in Alabama ($140) and Mississippi ($122).[71]

Support for the poor is not magnanimous, nor is it universal. AFDC payments to an average household with two children averaged less than $388 per month in federal assistance payments in 1992.[72] Those payments go to families in which approximately one-fifth of all impoverished adults live. Almost 50 percent of the poor were covered by Medicaid in 1992, but 55 percent of all poor adult males and 20 percent of all poor children had no health insurance.[73]

Several answers have already been offered for the grim circumstances of the poor: (1) they do not possess the political power of a PAC or interest group; (2) the political machines that once provided services in large cities have all but disappeared, and with them their services to the poor; and (3) at-large elections reduce the political power of the poor, while (4) nonpartisan elections reduce the participation of the poor, and with the lack of participation comes lack of political power.

These answers do not, however, explain why the poor in some states fare better than the poor in other states. In all likelihood, the answer has to do with the traditional docility of the poor, particularly in Southern states, and the occasional activism of the poor, particularly in Northern and Western states. Piven and Cloward[74] have chronicled the relationship between welfare activism and increases in welfare budgets; thus one can expect that the more pliant the poor, the less likely they are to receive increased benefits. The poor in the South, whose welfare payments traditionally have been lower and less sufficient, are a more passive population; hence politicians at the state and local level do not have to respond as meaningfully to their needs as do politicians in the North and West where the poor have threatened disorder, producing increases in welfare payments.

Welfare myths fuel the debate about welfare. One of the myths, that the poor won't work, has been addressed in this chapter. But there are other myths: that welfare recipients remain on relief forever; that lives of luxury are lived on welfare; that welfare recipients drive Cadillacs to pick up their food stamps, and that women have as many children as possible in order to get more welfare.

These myths are not supported by the data. The majority of AFDC families receive aid for less than three years. As seen earlier, the average AFDC payment is less than $400 a month. On average, the combined value of AFDC payments and food stamps equals 74 percent of the official poverty threshold. Only 7 percent of AFDC families own a car and the average value of the cars owned is less than $2,270. The average AFDC family has total assets of less than $900.[75] The average AFDC family has only two children under the age of 18.[76] Surely these facts to do not support the persistent welfare myths.

Does Welfare Make Any Difference?

Perhaps no debate has been joined more stridently than the debate over the value of welfare. Liberals argue that for many people, welfare is a necessity without which life would be inhumane and survival doubtful. (For a discussion of poverty from a welfare worker's vantage point, read Box 15.3.) Conservatives argue that welfare encourages sloth and perpetuates poverty. Like many such debates, it may be that there is a kernel of truth in both sets of arguments.

Much of the debate about welfare has to do with its usefulness. Does giving welfare to the poor make their lives better or worse? Charles Murray, the leading critic of welfare, argues that welfare policies have actually made life worse. He believes that welfare discourages the effort and aspirations necessary for the poor to escape welfare; in fact, he suggests, the welfare system is a trap, built with good intentions, but having the unintended consequence of encouraging dependency.

A counterargument advanced by John Schwarz is that a number of welfare programs, including the Comprehensive Employment and Training Act and Head Start, have had significant successes.[77] Michael Harrington, whose book *The Other America* revealed the extent of hunger and poverty in the early 1960s, has argued that if the welfare system is a failure, it is because it is underfunded. Had the war in Vietnam not sapped the nation's will to fight the war on poverty, Harrington indicates that poverty could have been significantly reduced in the United States.[78]

There is some evidence that giving money to those who cannot work does reduce poverty. Prior to the mid 1970s, the poverty rate for elderly persons was higher than that for children. Now, however, with Supplemental Security Income, Medicare, and Social Security, the poverty rate among the elderly has declined. The poverty rate of the elderly is now lower than that of children.

The problem of poverty has always been with us, and it will not soon disappear. While providing for any person's every need is probably counterproductive to his own welfare, some kind of aid may be necessary to help the unwilling poor escape poverty and to help their children make better lives for themselves. Many of us want to help those who do not deserve their poverty; but we want to withhold help from those who are poor because of indolence. The question then becomes one of who deserves welfare. Separating the worthy poor from the unworthy poor is important if the welfare system is to have legitimacy in the community.

Work and Education: Dual Approaches to Reducing Welfare Dependency

This question raises the larger issue: how shall we help the worthy poor to help themselves? An emphasis on work characterized the states' approach to reducing welfare dependency during the eighties. **Workfare** programs were hailed as a partial solution to the twin problems of poverty and welfare by both liberals and conservatives during the Reagan years.[79] These programs, which have been successful where work is available despite funding cuts by the federal government, were designed to help the poor find work, then to require that they continue to work. Specially trained personnel helped participants find suitable work, plan transportation, and arrange child care, if necessary. Participation in a workfare program was mandatory; welfare benefits could be reduced or eliminated for those unwilling to participate in the program or to put forth the effort necessary to find and keep a job.

Critics of workfare argue that it is authoritarian and coercive. Its proponents say that current welfare programs are more repressive and that they create dependency and passivity. Workfare, advocates suggest, can actually help the poor develop the skills and values vital to earning a better way of life. This debate has not been resolved, and workfare continues to be proposed as an answer to some of the problems created by welfare systems in the United States.

The Family Support Act of 1988 encouraged states to combine workfare—the early 1980s approach—with an emphasis on education and job skills, the approach of the 1970s. While retaining the emphasis on work as a way out of poverty (and as a way of earning a

BOX 15.3

A DAY IN THE LIFE OF A WELFARE WORKER

In large metropolitan areas welfare workers, school teachers, and police officers see the consequences of poverty daily. What follows is a firsthand account of hunger and poverty, as described by an investigative reporter as she toured a Philadelphia slum with a welfare worker. Although it does not happen every day, this is the kind of experience with which a welfare worker frequently must deal.

"Anna (Jones) and her nine children lived in a boarded-up section of North Philadelphia near Fifteenth Street and Susquehanna Avenue. Paint fell from the walls of tenement buildings, broken windows went unreplaced, and even the shattered glass seemed never to be picked up. . . . These were the streets the Jones kids played in and walked through when they went to school. But when I found them, the children had been going to school less and less. Inside the school's administration office there was a steadily growing fear that these children were in danger of starving to death. The school officials were still a little afraid to say anything definitive, afraid of making a mistake. But one nurse involved with the case admitted that the kids were getting worse. After that, the school counselor wrote a letter to the Department of Welfare explaining that a caseworker found the house unfit for human habitation and that on a recent visit to the house the children were found eating a box of laundry starch.

As we stood shivering in front of Mrs. Jones's house, the counselor explained that there were plenty of other cases like this in Philadelphia—some were worse. In the dark living room, Mrs. Jones sat huddled in a bathrobe, on the only piece of furniture in the house, a torn green couch, partially covered by a dirty sheet. A plastic trash bag covered one of the broken windows but the wind tore through the others, past the living room into the empty kitchen, and down the rubbish strewn, mouse-infested stairway to the cellar.

"Mrs. Jones, do you have any food in the house?" the counselor had asked.

"Yes, I have food."

We looked in the refrigerator. The only thing there was some kind of orange liquid that had spilled and hardened along the bottom shelf and a single can of solidified fat. The kitchen

welfare check), the Act also discouraged forcing the poor into low wage jobs. Instead, states were encouraged to create working relationships between education, job training, and welfare systems, so as to provide the setting for innovative, life changing opportunities.

Under the Family Support Act, some states began to "rethink" their welfare systems. Instead of merely determining eligibility for state and local programs, welfare workers began to think in terms of how to assist the poor to "determine . . . [their] needs and goals, identify barriers to meeting those goals, broker services and act as cheerleaders for clients."[80]

Two cases are illustrative of what combining education and job training with workfare can do. California's Greater Avenues for Independence (GAIN) places an emphasis on training and education, in tandem with child care and other welfare services. A study of welfare parents in six counties found that those parents, typically single mothers with school age children, earned 16 percent more than a control group in their first year in the

BOX 15.3 (Continued)

hadn't one item of food. A pot sat on the hot plate with an old tea bag floating in its cold water.

The children came downstairs dressed in the school outfits given to them by the Department of Welfare at the beginning of the year. These were still quite new, perhaps because the children had attended school so little. They came in silently and lined up, trembling without coats, behind the couch. Their hands were numb with cold, but they stood there, like little Spartans in their mother's army, determined to be loyal to her.

"Are you cold?" I asked.

"No," said a nine-year-old girl, speaking for the group.

"Are you hungry?"

"No."

"When did you eat last?"

"We're not hungry," she said deliberately.

"Does your mother have food?"

"Yes," she said, "She does."

It was as if those kids had memorized a liturgy before their mother brought them down from the bedroom, where they slept on torn, filthy mattresses without sheets or blankets or pillows. Or perhaps hunger and cold had numbed them beyond feeling. The four-year-old didn't move. He simply stared off into space and the seventeen-month-old infant just sat there drinking water from a bottle. I was told she had never uttered a word.

Before I left I saw something in the eyes of one of the children. A desire to communicate something. He was Paul, a boy of eight, but his physical growth had already been retarded by about three years. I bent down, "Would you like to come back to school with us?" I asked, "It's warm at school and there are lunches."

He didn't say anything. He didn't have to. He just looked at me hard, for a long serious moment, then slowly he lifted his hand and gently, tentatively, touched my cold fingers with his. I smiled. His large brown eyes filled with tears. Then he nodded.

Source: Loretta Schwartz-Nobel, Starving in the Shadow of Plenty *(New York: McGraw Hill Book Co., 1981), 41–43.*

program and 24 percent more in their second year of participation. Welfare payments dropped by 7 percent for teen parents by the second year. Ohio's LEAP program provides a $62 per month bonus to teen mothers who stay in school, and it penalizes those who drop out by the same amount. Studies show that 61 percent of the participants maintained attendance or graduated, compared to only 51 percent of a control group.[81]

TO BE CONSIDERED: REINVENTING THE RELIEF SYSTEM

Many of the state and local programs discussed in this chapter are attempts to apply entrepreneurial principles to the system of relief called welfare. It is, nevertheless, worth noting the principles that would be the focus of a reinvented welfare system.

A proposal for changing welfare would empower those it serves to be active and responsible. Public housing would be managed by those who live there, not an absent government landlord. The responsibility for enforcing standards of behaviors in neighborhoods would belong to neighbors, with the help of the police (who help all neighborhoods), not government attorneys and bureaucrats. Kimi Gray remains a classic example of the empowered public housing organizer.[82]

Welfare budgets would be mission driven, rather than service driven. Mission-driven budgets focus on measurable outcomes related to the mission. Data related to mission success (known as performance measures) are routinely gathered. Successes receive continued funding; failures are altered or eliminated. (Robert Stumberg in *Reinventing Government* cautions that it is important to think long-term when measuring success and failure. Rarely do state or local governments analyze results over a several year period. Were they to do so, Stumberg argues, they would better fund programs like Head Start, which returns $5 for every $1 of original investment in lower welfare, crime, education costs, and higher tax revenues.[83])

A reinvented welfare system would emphasize earning rather than spending. For example, job placement programs should be privatized or at least required to compete with private placement programs or be abandoned. That is what happened in Massachusetts where the Transitional Employment Enterprises (TEE) demonstrated its superiority to Kelly Services in training and placing office workers who also happened to be welfare recipients.[84]

On the other hand, there are several reasons to doubt that the relief system can be readily changed. Those reasons have a great deal to do with the people who are on relief. Of those recipients who have been on AFDC rolls for two or more years, two-thirds do not have a high school diploma. Recent research indicates that between 30 and 40 percent of all AFDC recipients fall into the "least proficient" literacy category. Being less proficient in reading and writing increases the likelihood that AFDC recipients will be anxious, depressed, and under motivated to attempt work or education at which they may fail. [85]

As costs to state and local governments increase, there will be continued emphasis on changing systems of relief. Whether that change reflects draconian approaches of eliminating the welfare system or innovative approaches for reinventing the system will be decided by citizens like yourself. Individuals can make a difference in this debate. Read on to see what some have accomplished in their own communities.

CONCLUSION: WHAT WE CAN DO IN OUR COMMUNITIES

Community efforts begin with the ideas of individuals, like Charles Ballard (mentioned earlier in this chapter), who are able to organize others in pursuit of a goal. The individuals who accomplish such goals are no different from you or your friends; they simply have taken a step beyond thinking to doing. Several examples of individuals making a difference in their communities follow. Perhaps they will provide answers to the problems in your community.

The problems associated with teenage pregnancy and motherhood have prompted a number of communities, including Norfolk, Virginia, and Rochester, New York, as well as several in Appalachia and Louisiana, to establish "resource mother" projects.[86] Neighborhood women who have successfully reared their own children are enlisted as counselors for local pregnant teenagers. Their task is to reduce the likelihood of future pregnancies and provide positive maternal role models, and there is some evidence that the program is successful. Lawton Chiles, retired Florida senator says, "Our studies indicate that if a girl has a baby by age 13, she'll have three by age 18. Well, where resource mothers have been used, the repeat rate has been cut in half."[87]

The problems of hunger and homelessness prompted Nancy Bissell and Gordon Packard to organize the Saint Martin's Soup Kitchen in Tucson, Arizona, which fed 240 people a day until the city closed the facility because of neighbors' complaints. Undaunted, Ms. Bissell and Mr. Packard established the Primavera Foundation which renovated a dilapidated motel, hiring 15 homeless men to do so. The motel, which became a home for mentally and physically handicapped people, was followed by a 70-bed temporary shelter. Volunteers provide counseling, meals, and job leads.[88]

Millard Fuller was a millionaire by the time he was 30, so he chose another goal: he decided to eliminate substandard housing in the United States. He founded Habitat for Humanity, an organization having the goal of providing affordable housing to the poor. Joining with Clarence Jordan, he organized Fund for Humanity, a pool of capital to buy housing materials and offer mortgages to those too poor to qualify for bank loans. Volunteers offered their labor, and Fuller recruited national figures, including former President Jimmy Carter, to participate in the project. Today Habitat for Humanity is a national organization that has built more than 4,000 homes since 1976.

An average Habitat home of 1,000 square feet sells for less than $30,000. The average home owner has a mortgage payment of around $150, usually less than the rent for substandard housing in the area. Home owners participate in a sweat equity program: not only they help build their own homes, but they also agree to help build other homes. Fuller insists that Habitat volunteers are not case workers; they are coworkers with home owners in the Habitat for Humanity program.[89]

The children in South Providence, Rhode Island, had no park to play in so Mark Toney organized the children of the area to lobby for a new park. Toney's political organization, Direct Action for Rights and Equality (DARE), helped convince city leaders that a park was necessary. DARE has also registered voters, improved school facilities, and instituted a fuel assistance program for poor families. The strength of DARE comes from an involved, dues-paying membership made up of blacks, Asians, Hispanics, and whites. Toney, who graduated from Brown University, uses classic community organization strategies to encourage local officials to be concerned about DARE's issues.[90]

The farming crisis of the 1980s has led to foreclosure on over 300,000 farms. Helen Waller of Circle, Montana, was appalled by the crisis and decided to do something about the hardships facing farmers. She organized 47 farm groups in 35 states to create Save the Family Farm Coalition, an organization which was responsible for legislation changing the credit provisions of 1987 farm legislation. Now lobbying for the Family Farm Act to be passed in 1990, Waller says you can fight city hall and you can change things in Washington, D.C. She knows because she has done it.[91]

You can make the kind of contributions to your community that Nancy Bissell, Gordon Packard, Millard Fuller, Mark Toney, and Helen Waller have made. Or you may have another idea. What is important is taking the first step, by putting your ideas into action and organizing your community to solve its own problems of poverty.

STUDY OBJECTIVES

1. What two kinds of definitions of poverty do social scientists use?
2. Explain how the poverty threshold was created.
3. List and discuss the major reasons for becoming poor.
4. Describe the culture of poverty.
5. How many people are poor in the United States?
6. Explain how Charles Murray and William Julius Wilson disagree about the causes of poverty.
7. Delineate the characteristics of the underclass.
8. What kinds of people are poor in the United States?
9. What are the consequences of poverty?
10. Why do people become homeless and remain homeless?
11. How are the poor distributed across the states?
12. How do welfare payments vary between the states?
13. What is the difference between welfare and entitlements?
14. How much does the system of welfare cost the federal government?
15. How much does the system of welfare cost state and local governments?
16. What are the consequences of the welfare system?
17. Describe workfare as a solution to welfare dependency.

GLOSSARY

Absolute   Defines poverty in terms of an objective standard, usually a governmental measure of subsistence like the poverty threshold.

Aid to Families with Dependent Children   A federal and state welfare program, established by the Social Security Act of 1935, administered by each state for all poor families with children under 18 with one parent absent. In over half of the states, two-parent families are also eligible when the father is out of work.

Categorical grants-in-aid   Federal strategies of funding state and local governments, with the funds targeted at special categories of needy persons.

Culture of poverty   The belief that the poor are a distinct group with their own rules, ideas, and beliefs. This implies that the poor learn to be poor or fail to learn how to escape poverty, and indeed transmit poverty as a way of life to their children.

Entitlements   Social insurance programs like Social Security, Medicare, Veterans Benefits, worker's compensation, student loans and unemployment insurance that provide a safety net for middle income people.

Feminization of poverty   The fact that females are over represented in poverty figures, a fact that has been known since poverty figures began to be kept in 1959, when almost half of all female-headed households had incomes below the poverty level.

Food Stamps This program, begun during the 1960's, distributes coupons redeemable for food to families and individuals with incomes under 130 percent of the poverty threshold. Administered by state welfare agencies, the federal government provides almost all the funding for food stamps.

Means-tested Government welfare programs based on some measure of income. The four major means-tested programs are, Aid to Families with Dependent Children (AFDC), Supplemental Security Income (SSI), Medicaid, and Food Stamps.

Medicaid This means-tested welfare program, was established in 1965 to help cover the medical costs of those persons eligible for AFDC and SSI.

Poverty threshold (or line) A measure of poverty established by the Social Security Administration in 1964 by estimating the lowest cost of feeding a family of four and multiplying that by three, believed to be the proportion of income spent on food by the average middle income family.

Poverty rate The proportion or percent of the population below the poverty threshold.

Relative A subjective judgment about the meaning of poverty in comparison to the standards of the society. John Kenneth Galbraith has suggested that even if individuals have enough income to survive, they may be considered poverty-stricken if their resulting life style is considered by the community to be unacceptable or degrading.

Special revenue sharing block grants Federal funds offered to states to replace, at one time, numerous categorical grants-in-aid directed at a particular problem, like job creation or community development.

The Supplemental Security Income A means-tested welfare program, was established in 1972 to provide additional monthly cash payments to impoverished elderly, blind, and disabled persons.

Underclass A term coined by Gunnar Myrdal that refers to a third world rural and urban underclass cut off from society, lacking the education, skills and other personality traits needed to take advantage of the increases in opportunity that resulted from affirmative action, and who are thus trapped in poverty.

Urban industrial transition The move from the central city by manufacturers, retailers, and construction industries, taking with them the blue-collar jobs commonly filled by the poor. In their place have come information-processing and financial organizations, bringing with them opportunity for professional or white collar employees, but a loss of opportunity for the urban poor.

Welfare Means-tested social programs.

Working poor The one-third to one-half of all adults whose incomes place them below the poverty threshold, but who do, in fact, work, often fifty weeks or more during the year.

Workfare Programs that require welfare recipients to work to get benefits while acquiring job skills or a high school diploma.

ENDNOTES

1. John Kenneth Galbraith, *The Affluent Society* (New York: New American Library, 1958), 251.

2. One strong argument against the poverty line is that middle class people tend to spend about one-fourth of their income on food. Therefore, many reason, the basic cost of food should be multiplied by four to get the official poverty line. As it is, the poor are doomed to substandard incomes.

3. For an interesting discussion of both perspectives, see Bonnie Szumski, ed., *Social Justice: Opposing Viewpoints*, (St. Paul, MN: Greenhaven Press, 1984), 57–97.

4. William Julius Wilson, *The Truly Disadvantaged: The Inner City, the Underclass, and Public Policy* (Chicago: University of Chicago Press, 1987),171.

5. Robert W. Cleveland, *Measuring the Effect of Benefits and Taxes on Income and Poverty: 1992*, U. S. Department of Commerce, Bureau of the Census (Washington, DC: U. S. Government Printing Office, 1993), vii.

6. Ibid.

7. Robert Famighetti, ed., *World Almanac and Book of Facts, 1994* (St. Martin's Press: New York, 1994), 371.

8. Eleanor F. Baugher and Martin Shea, *Poverty in the United States: 1992*, U. S. Department of Commerce, Bureau of the Census (Washington, DC: U. S. Government Printing Office, 1993), xvii–xviii. William O'Hare, *Poverty in America: Trends and New Patterns* (Washington, DC: Population Reference Bureau, 1989), 43.

9. O'Hare, *Poverty in America's Trends and New Patterns*, 15.

10. Robert B. Hill speaking before the Committee on Ways and Means, House of Representatives, October 26, 1993.

11. Ibid.

12. "When Families Break Up," U. S. Department of Commerce, Bureau of the Census (Washington, DC: U. S. Government Printing Office, 1992).

13. Baugher and Shea, *Poverty in the United States: 1992*, xv.

14. A variety of definitions, few of them concise, have been given for the term *underclass*. Some authors, like Auletta, include the mentally ill and some criminals. For a more scholarly definition, see Sara McLanahan and Irwin Garfinkle, "Single Mothers, the Underclass, and Social Policy," *The Annals of the American Academy of Political and Social Science*, January, 1989, vol. 501, 92–104.

15. Ken Auletta, *The Underclass* (New York: Random House, 1982), 27.

16. Baugher and Shea, *Poverty in the United States: 1992*, xv.

17. Ibid.

18. Ibid., vii. Even at $5.00 an hour she and her children remain below the poverty threshold. In fact, this poor mother would have to work year-round, with no time off for illness or vacation, making more than $5.37 an hour to reach the poverty threshold.

19. Charles Murray, *Losing Ground: American Social Policy 1950–1980* (New York: Basic Books, 1984), 178–179.

20. William Julius Wilson, *The Truly Disadvantaged: The Inner City, the Underclass, and Public Policy* (Chicago: University of Chicago Press, 1987).

21. John D. Kasarda, "Urban Industrial Transition and the Underclass," *The Annals of the American Academy of Political and Social Science*, January, 1989, vol. 501, 26–47.

22. David Whitman, "The Myth of Reform," *U.S. News and World Report*, January 16, 1995, 31.

23. Lynn A. Karoly, speaking before the Committee on Ways and Means, House of Representatives, October 26, 1993.

24. William O'Hare, *The Rise of Poverty in Rural America* (Washington, DC: Population Reference Bureau, 1988), 5.

25. Baugher and Shea, *Poverty in the United States: 1992*, xvi.

26. Wilson, *The Truly Disadvantaged*, 103.

27. O'Hare, *The Rise of Poverty in Rural America*, 9.

28. Michael Harrington, *The New American Poverty* (New York: Penguin Books, 1985), 101.

29. Richard Sweeney, *Out of Place: Homelessness in America* (New York: HarperCollins College Publishers, 1993), 26.

30. As quoted in Rene I. Jahiel, "The Situation of Homelessness" in *The Homeless in Contemporary Society*, Richard D. Bingham, Roy E. Green, and Sammis B. White, eds. (Beverly Hills, CA: Sage Publications, 1987), 97–118.

31. "He explores link to poverty," *USA TODAY*, March 29, 1989, 2A.

32. Rita Rubin, "Black Health," *Dallas Morning News*, February 6, 1989, 6D–7D.

33. Famighetti, ed., *World Almanac and Book of Facts 1994*, 956.

34. Jane E. Brody, "Intriguing Studies Link Nutrition to Immunity," *New York Times*, March 2, 1989, 21, 24, 25.

35. Rita Rubin, "Black Health," *Dallas Morning News*, February 6, 1989, 6D–7D.

36. Philip J. Hilts, "Racial Life Expectancy Gap Widens," *New York Times* News Service, *Austin-American Statesman*, October 9, 1989, A4.

37. Paul Clancy, "Doctor's cancer crusade,"*USA TODAY*, March 29, 1989, 2A.

38. Harrington, *The New American Poverty*, 221.

39. Richard Totman, *Social Causes of Illness* (New York: Pantheon Books, 1979).

40. *The Statistical Abstract of the United States, 1991*, 85.

41. Marianne W. Zawitz, ed., *Report to the Nation on Crime and Justice*, (Bureau of Justice Statistics: Washington, D.C., 1988), 28.

42. Joan M. Johnson, *Criminal Victimization in the United States, 1991*, (Bureau of Justice Statistics: Washington, D.C., 1992), 18.

43. Zawitz, *Report to the Nation on Crime and Justice*, 27; Joan M. Johnson, *Criminal Victimization in the United States, 1991* (Bureau of Justice Statistics: Washington, D.C., 1992), 46.

44. Zawitz, *Report to the Nation on Crime and Justice*, 27; Joan M. Johnson, *Criminal Victimization in the United States, 1991* (Bureau of Justice Statistics: Washington, D.C., 1992), 33.

45. William O'Hare, *America's Welfare Population: Who Gets What?* (Washington DC: Population Reference Bureau, 1987), 3.

46. Congressional Budget Office, "Poverty Status of Families," June, 1987.

47. O'Hare, *America's Welfare Population*, 21.

48. Paul E. Peterson, *City Limits* (Chicago: University of Chicago Press, 1981), 43.

49. Frances Fox Piven and Richard A. Cloward, *Regulating the Poor* (New York: Pantheon Books, 1971).

50. O'Hare, *Poverty in America: Trends and New Patterns*,44.

51. Ibid., 10.

52. ACIR, *Summary of Welfare Reform Hearings–1986*, (Washington, DC: Advisory Commission on Intergovernmental Relations, 1987), 11.

53. Steve Burghardt and Michael Fabricant, *Working Under the Safety Net: Policy and Practice for the New American Poor* (Beverly Hills: CA: Sage Publications, 1987), 158.

54. William O'Hare, *Poverty in America: Trends and New Patterns*, 44.

55. Baugher and Shea, *Poverty in the United States: 1992*, xx.

56. Census Bureau data contained in *State Rankings, 1994* (Lawrence, KS: Morgan Quinto Corporation, 1994), 477–479.

57. Penelope Lemov, "States and Medicaid: Ahead of the Feds," *Governing* (July, 1993), 27–28.

58. Robert W. Cleveland, *Measuring the Effect of Benefits and Taxes on Income and Poverty: 1992*, U. S. Department of Commerce, Bureau of the Census (Washington, DC: U. S. Government Printing Office, 1993), E-1.

59. Mark S. Littman and Eleanor F. Baugher, *Poverty in the United States*, U. S. Department of Commerce, Bureau of the Census (Washington, DC: U. S. Government Printing Office, 1988), 154; Baugher and Shea, *Poverty in the United States: 1992*, vii. The 1992 threshold uses a definition of income based on pre-tax income only, that is, it does not include noncash benefits such as employer provided health insurance, food stamps, or Medicaid.

60. O'Hare, *America's Welfare Population*, 3.

61. "Participants in Assistance Programs," U.S. Department of Commerce, Bureau of the Census Stastical Brief (Washington, DC: U. S. Government Printing Office, November, 1994),

62. Baugher and Shea, *Poverty in the United States: 1992*, xvii.

63. Ibid., xvii–xviii.

64. O'Hare, *America's Welfare Population*, 6.

65. Baugher and Shea, *Poverty in the United States: 1992*, xx.

66. Ibid.

67. Ibid., xxi–xxii.

68. Census Bureau data contained in *State Rankings, 1994* (Lawrence, KS: Morgan Quinto Corp., 1994), 464, 466.

69. *Book of the States, 1992–93*, 641.

70. Census Bureau data contained in *State Rankings, 1994* (Lawrence, KS: Morgan Quinto Corp., 1994), 464, 466.

71. Ibid., 490.

72. Ibid., 464, 466.

73. Baugher and Shea, *Poverty in the United States: 1992*, xx.

74. Frances Fox Piven and Richard A. Cloward, *Regulating the Poor* (New York: Vintage Books, 1993).

75. O'Hare, *America's Welfare Population*, 7.

76. Ibid., 5.

77. John E. Schwarz, *America's Hidden Success: A Reassessment of Twenty Years of Public Policy* (New York: W. W. Norton, 1983).

78. Harrington, *The New American Poverty*.

79. Lawrene M. Mead, "The Logic of Workfare: The Underclass and Work Policy," *The Annals of the American Academy of Political and Social Science*, January, 1989, vol. 501, 156–169.

80. Kathleen Sylvester, "Welfare: The Hope & the Frustration," *Governing* (November, 1991), 52.

81. Kathleen Sylvester, "Two State Routes Out of Welfare," *Governing* (June, 1993), 14.

82. David Osborne and Ted Gaebler, *Reinventing Government: How the Entrepreneurial Spirit is Transforming the Public Sector* (New York: Penguin Books, 1993), 60.

83. Ibid., 206.

84. Ibid., 151–152.

85. David Whitman, "The Myth of Reform," *U.S. News and World Report*, January 16, 1995, 30–34.

86. William Raspberry, "A Good Start in Life," *Austin American-Statesman*, October 17, 1989, A8.

87. Ibid.

88. *The Giraffe Gazette* (Whidbey Island, WA: The Giraffe Project, 1989), vol V., no. 1, 15.

89. Don Winbush, "A Bootstrap Approach to Low-Cost Housing," *Time Magazine*, January 16, 1989, 12–13.

90. William O. Beeman, "Door Knocker Extraordinaire," *Mother Jones* (January, 1989), 29.

91. Pat Dawson, "High Noon in the Heartland," *Mother Jones* (January, 1989), 32–33.

16

Paying for It: The Revenue-Expenditure System

BUDGETS INVOLVE LIFE AND DEATH DECISIONS

Donna Arneson, a 36-year-old single mother with no health insurance, and no savings, was one of several victims of the 1988 decision by the State of Oregon not to provide funds for organ transplants. Although the chances of a successful operation were only about 50 percent, a liver transplant was Mrs. Arneson's only hope to live more than a few weeks beyond the end of the legislative session.

As new surgical techniques, drugs, sophisticated organ donor systems, and aftercare methods have raised the hopes of many doomed to die, the demand for transplant operations has increased dramatically in this decade. The number of heart transplants increased more than 20 fold from 1981 to 1987. Transplant operations cost between $150,000 and $250,000, and thus are beyond the means of most Americans.

The expense of the operations together with the high mortality rate (about 50 percent) make for tough decisions for state officials charged with stretching scarce medical and social service funds as far as possible. Of the 19 medical transplants—bone marrow, heart, liver, and pancreas—that Oregon covered between 1985 and 1988, only nine have survived. During the past two years the Oregon legislature has adopted a series of changes that will provide increased access to basic medical care for about 24,000 low-income people each year. The total cost of these reforms will be over $18 million.

It is possible that these medical expenditures will provide early diagnosis and preventive care to avoid the risk, expense, and high mortality rates of transplant operations. In the meantime those who need those operations and cannot afford them wait to die.[1]

In this chapter we discuss the cost of using government to solve problems that confront our communities and how we pay for it. The price to be paid comes in at least two parts.

One part of the price is called the government **budget**. A budget, as you recall from Chapter 10, is a plan for getting and spending money. State and local governments cannot print extra money the way the federal government can, so they must either revise the budget to reduce expenditures, find more revenue, borrow the money, or find a way to get some other unit of government to pay.

A second part of the price to be paid is the human and social consequences of *not* acting to solve problems, or of not acting fast enough to solve problems—in other words, doing a half fast job of alleviating human suffering. Two familiar observations summarize this second part of the price of failing to deal with serious social, environmental, and human problems. "There is no such thing as a free lunch," and, "You can pay me now, or you can pay me later."

The first, reaffirms the fact that not only does virtually everything have a cost to someone, and the second, reminds us that there is a time frame involved in postponing problem solving. The cost often goes up during the time we delay paying it.

THE BUDGET: A PLAN FOR PAYING FOR IT

The budget is one of the most important sets of decisions that political actors ever try to influence. Decisions about budgets often involve life and death matters. Usually the life and death issues are abstract and distant. When the likelihood of highway death is increased by decisions to cut funds for enforcing the speed limits, or for inspecting trucks and keeping the unsafe ones off the highway, the consequences can be treated as statistics, not as living, dying, or maimed individuals. Sometimes, however, these life and death decisions involve real people whom the decision makers have come to know.

Coby Howard had leukemia which might have been cured or at least sent into remission if he could have obtained a $100,000 bone marrow transplant operation that his family could not afford. He was seven years old in 1987 when he died. To blame the government of Oregon, or even the director of the Oregon Adult and Family Services Department for the deaths of particular individuals is both unfair and unrealistic. These tragedies are happening in every state. Political leaders have to make tough decisions, and they do not make them lightly. Freddye Webb-Petett is the administrator who had to decide on the funding recommendation affecting a whole category of human lives including Coby Howard's. For many years she kept a picture of Coby on her desk to remind her, on a daily basis, of something she was already well aware. Government decisions about money have consequences for real people.[2]

Nine Influences on Government Budgets

Among the many influences on the budget of a unit of government are at least nine that you have encountered in earlier chapters of this book.

1. At each level of government the legislature is the body that passes the budget. At minimum, the legislature passes at least one appropriations bill which, at the state level, is sent to the executive branch for approval. If the existing revenue laws will yield enough to pay for the appropriations, then new tax bills may not be needed. Contrary to the popular notion that legislatures never lower taxes, nearly every year several states refine their

tax systems, raising some taxes and lowering others, even abandoning some as Michigan did with the property tax for schools in 1993.

2. The executive branch plays four roles in the budgetary process at the state level, and at least three at the local level. First, the chief executive at the state level, and in many local governments, prepares the budget submitted to the legislature. He or she is expected to lobby for its approval. Second, once the legislature passes tax bills and appropriations (spending) bills, the chief executive has the power to veto them. In some states the governor has the **line item veto**. This pertains only to appropriations and means that the governor can strike out specific items without having to veto the whole bill. Except for the strong mayor system, most local government constitutions do not give the executive branch a veto.

The third role of the executive branch is that of spending the money appropriated to it. This involves the several agencies in the executive branch which perform a variety of services and enforce regulations. A special set of activities make up a fourth role: collecting the taxes, and accounting for the expenditure of funds through the preaudit and postaudit procedures.

Preaudits occur when an official, called an auditor or comptroller certifies that there is enough money in an agency's budget for a particular kind of expenditure. For example, among the separate categories in a typical agency's budget one finds: supplies, personnel, contracts, and equipment. The money in these categories is not always interchangeable (fungible) and thus it is necessary for someone to certify that the money is going to be spent appropriately.

Periodically, after money has been spent, another auditor, sometimes from a different agency, examines the agency's records to make sure that the money was actually spent appropriately—that the bills have been paid, and that the correct individuals or organizations received the money.

3. The judicial branch is involved in the budget when a court hears challenges to the legality of the way various agencies spend money or collect taxes or fees, when it hears challenges to the constitutionality of tax laws or appropriations laws, and when it tries the cases of individuals accused of breaking tax laws or spending government money inappropriately. Both the judicial and the legislative branches also spend money. They need staff and equipment to perform their functions just as the executive branch does.

4. The political culture affects the budget through the myths and beliefs generally accepted in a region or state about what is appropriate for government to spend money on, and what the most appropriate sources of revenue are. Political culture is one reason why there are so many different patterns of taxing and spending among states that are rich, as well as among states that are poor.[3]

The amount of money spent on a given program is not determined simply by the wealth of the economy in which a unit of government is located. Table 16.1 provides a comparison of the states in terms of welfare expenditure differences and wealth (i.e., ability to afford high welfare payments).[4] The top 10 states in per capita welfare expenditure are printed in bold. The ten states with the wealthiest state-local economies are underlined. Only five states lead in *both* wealth and in welfare expenditure. Nearly all the high welfare effort states—many of which are not wealthy—are states with a moralistic political culture. While it is true that the average AFDC payment in wealthy states is higher than the average among poor states, the variation within each category (poor states and rich states) suggests that politics and political culture have more than a little to do with it.[5]

5. The relative strength of institutions greatly affects the size and shape of a budget. Interest groups and parties attempt to influence how money is appropriated and how revenues are acquired. We have observed earlier that the business community was overrepresented in both weak and strong interest group systems. While companies can play a positive role as in Battle Creek, they can also use influence in the political economy to prevent positive action on issues such as workplace safety, economic regulation, and even on the way funds are raised. Borrowing from, rather than taxing, the haves, is greatly favored as a revenue method by banks and investment law firms. The haves support this approach, but not unanimously.

6. When interest groups predominate in a state with no countervailing political institutions such as strong parties or strong institutions of government, then the budgetary result is often less money spent on programs to benefit the have-nots and less effort made to protect the environment.[6]

7. The personality of and perceptions of each and every decision maker who is involved in the process of designing, passing, and executing the budget affects the role they play in shaping the content of the budget and the way it is administered. To those seeking to influence a particular unit of a government's budget, these factors are very important. Individuals matter.

8. Past budget decisions have an impact on the ones a society has to make in the present. "You can pay me now, or pay me later," says the auto mechanic who is trying to get you to buy an oil change and a new oil filter now, instead of an engine overhaul later. He has a point, since an engine overhaul costs about 50 times as much as the clean oil filter that prevents it. In the context of governmental budgets, we sometimes pay for *not* doing things—by not paying now, we pay much more, later.

9. Decisions made by one government may affect the budgets of other governments. When a school district builds a new school, the city or county will have to deal with the budgetary consequences of increased traffic on nearby roads. In an intergovernmental system each government affects one or more others. When the state legislature assigns functions to local governments without providing them with the resources to pay for them, they are, in essence, passing on tax increases or service cut-backs.

When the federal government borrows huge amounts of money, it affects the ability of other governments to borrow. When the federal government cuts back on social programs it requires state and local government budget makers to confront decisions about taking up the slack, or dealing with the human and political consequences of reductions in programs such as education, health, housing, transportation, and environmental protection.

10. The political activities of individuals and groups influence budgetary decisions. Money is seldom appropriated by legislatures at any level unless it is clear that some individuals want it to happen so much that they will invest political resources (time, energy, talent) to advocate that appropriation.

Redistribution: What Gets Paid for and Who Pays

Decisions on both taxing and spending have a redistributive effect. **Redistribution** refers to government actions that alter the existing pattern of opportunities to live a better life. Although Box 16.1 provides examples of ways in which wealth is transferred from the have-

Table 16.1

PER CAPITA WELFARE EXPENDITURES AND STATE-LOCAL WEALTH

State	Per Capita Welfare Expenditures Dollar Amount	Rank	Rank Percent of Population in Poverty	Rank in State-Local Wealth
Alabama	332	41	19	48
Alaska*	**763**	**3**	**12**	**1**
Arizona	276	48	15	27
Arkansas	402	27	17	49
California	**625**	**7**	**16**	**9**
Colorado	335	39	10	12
Connecticut	**629**	**6**	**9**	**4**
Delaware	378	32	8	6
Florida	343	38	15	18
Georgia	404	25	17	33
Hawaii	421	20	8	2
Idaho	274	49	14	47
Illinois	421	21	14	19
Indiana	405	24	16	37
Iowa	419	22	10	28
Kansas	331	42	12	30
Kentucky	522	13	19	43
Louisiana	431	19	19	39
Maine	**711**	**4**	**14**	**24**
Maryland	434	17	9	14
Massachusetts	**965**	**1**	**11**	**8**
Michigan	**547**	**9**	**14**	**26**
Minnesota	536	11	13	20
Mississippi	335	40	14	50
Missouri	343	37	15	35
Montana	410	23	15	34
Nebraska	371	33	10	25
Nevada	204	50	11	5
New Hampshire	360	34	7	10
New Jersey	**539**	**10**	**10**	**7**
New Mexico	347	36	22	41
New York	942	2	15	17
North Carolina	351	35	14	31
North Dakota	403	26	14	32

(Continued)

Table 16.1 (Continued)

State	Per Capita Welfare Expenditures Dollar Amount	Rank	Rank Percent of Population in Poverty	Rank in State-Local Wealth
Ohio	522	12	13	29
Oklahoma	398	29	17	40
Oregon	392	31	13	21
Pennsylvania	511	14	11	23
Rhode Island	**649**	**5**	**10**	**38**
South Carolina	432	18	16	44
S. Dakota	302	45	14	42
Tennessee	399	28	16	45
Texas	311	44	18	22
Utah	302	46	13	46
Vermont	**610**	**8**	**13**	**15**
Virginia	289	47	10	16
Washington	489	16	9	13
West Virginia	393	30	18	50
Wisconsin	501	15	10	36
<u>Wyoming</u>	<u>331</u>	<u>43</u>	<u>10</u>	<u>3</u>

* The top 10 states in per capita welfare expenditure are printed in bold. The 10 wealthiest states are underlined.

Sources: ACIR, RTS 1991: State Tax Capacity and Effort (Washington, D.C.: Advisory Commission on Intergovernmental Relations, 1993); and U. S. Department of Commerce, Bureau of the Census, State Government Finances: 1991 (Washington, D.C.: United States Government Printing Office, 1992); and Poverty in the United States, 1991 (Washington, D.C.: U. S. Government Printing Office, 1992).

nots to the haves by government action, redistribution is most often used to identify those actions that assist the have-nots.

Redistribution occurs because almost any set of rules is likely to distribute costs and benefits unevenly. For example, the rules of basketball tend to benefit tall people with exceptional leaping ability; the rules for ice hockey do not. A decision by the federal government to fight inflation by maintaining a 5 percent unemployment rate does not affect stockbrokers and carpenters equally, nor does it affect all states and communities in the same way either.

Budget Choices: The Art of the Possible
In making decisions about taxing and spending, chief executives and legislators at the local and state levels face a number of difficult choices even if they decide to spend no more than

BOX 16.1

REINFORCING INEQUALITY: SELECTED EXAMPLES

1. Providing funds for an elaborate highway system linking suburban shopping centers, upper class residential neighborhoods, and downtown offices benefits the haves. The alternative could be to pay for public transportation for the many poor people who don't have cars or vans; or to build people movers in the central cities (like those in airports) to make it easier to get around in the city.

2. A state that spends a lot of money on a low tuition, higher education system on one hand and on a bare minimum elementary and secondary system on the other hand, is engaged in reinforcing inequality. Since upper and middle class children are better prepared at home for even the worst primary and secondary school system (by parents who read to them, buy them coloring books, make them watch *Sesame Street* and correct their grammar), they are much more likely to survive underfunded primary and secondary schools. Thus they will be able to take advantage of the state's opportunities for higher education, while the children of parents with limited education and teaching skills will be less likely to do so.

   Redistribution could be advanced by a well financed state supported system of primary, secondary, and remedial education. This might increase the opportunities for more of the children of the have-nots to overcome the disadvantages of poverty and nonsupportive home environments while they learn sophisticated job skills or make it to college.

3. Spending money on research information and technical assistance to business and investors, instead of on retraining, unemployment benefits, or worker's compensation to those injured or made ill on the job, can reinforce inequality.

4. Borrowing, instead of raising taxes to pay for government buildings and facilities, often reinforces inequality. Millions of dollars in public money are paid to lawyers and brokers who design bond packages so that the public credit can be used to pay more public money in interest to the wealthy individuals who will buy the bonds. In buying bonds the wealthy loan money, at interest, to the public instead of paying taxes to finance whatever it was the bond issue was designed to pay for in the first place. Not only does paying for facilities with bonds triple the cost of the facility, the interest earned by the bondholders is usually exempt from taxation.

last year. These choices can be summarized under four courses of action. First, they can spend the same amount this year as last on every program. In effect, this means cutting each program the same amount, because each year inflation reduces the number of things a fixed amount of money will buy. Thus to buy the same services as the year before, the budget for each program would need to be increased.

The second choice is to take inflation into account, and attempt to keep some programs at the same service level rather than the same dollar level. This means that budget makers will have to decide where to cut, if they do not wish to find new sources of revenue. This choice involves concentrating the cuts in a few programs in order to offer the same level of services in others. Third, budget makers can even improve some services, by cutting others. Fourth, if new problems arise and they often do, whole new programs must be funded out of cuts in other programs.

The choices are not often as simple as spend or don't spend. Avoiding waste, promoting efficiency, and attempting to walk the fine line between responsibility to the next generation while attending to the realities of the present one, is a difficult set of tasks. That is why politics is sometimes referred to as *the art of the possible*. Creating and enacting budgets for state and local governments is the essence of the art of the possible.

The Budget and You

The decisions budget makers have to make about resources are not unlike those made by you in deciding whether or not to become involved in the political system. Not only does participation have a price, so does nonparticipation. Thus, when you choose not to use some of your political resources to influence decisions, you make a decision for which you may pay later.

The observation, "There is no such thing as a free lunch," certainly applies to the politics of state and local governments. We cannot enjoy a life free of politics without paying for it by having others make decisions for us. Part of that price is that some of those decisions may be bad ones. The observation about paying later applies both to political participation and to spending money.

EXPENDITURES: WHERE DOES THE MONEY GO?

State and local governments spend over a trillion dollars a year. This amounts to approximately 17 percent of the gross domestic product (GDP).[7] The GDP is a figure that attempts to represent the total annual output of all the final goods and services in the national economy expressed in terms of market value.[8]

Government Contributions to the GDP

State and local government expenditures are not simply amounts of money taken from the economy. They are contributions to it, and understated contributions at that. State and local government contributions to the GDP are measured by the budgets which include the salaries paid as well as the goods that they produce.

The GDP, does not measure all the value added (or preserved) by government action. The salaries of school teachers, for example, can be measured as part of the GDP. However, the value added to the sum total of knowledge and skill possessed by each student is not measured and thus cannot be adequately included in the GDP. The years of productive labor (and taxpaying) added to lives of individuals talked out of suicide or guided out of drug addiction by social workers or school counselors do not get included either, any more than does the value of the property and lives saved by police, fire, and emergency medical services.

The Growth of Government Spending

When this century began, national, state, and local governments combined spent about 8 percent of the GDP. By 1975 it was about 30 percent and has stayed about that level ever since. While the federal government accounts for much of that increase, the state-local portion more than doubled, from 5 percent to more than 12.

The major reasons for the growth of state and local spending both in percentage terms and in total sums are largely the result of social, economic, and technological changes, including the industrial and automotive revolutions discussed in Chapter 2. It is much more expensive to operate a heterogeneous metropolitan society than it is a homogeneous rural society. Not only are there more people to serve, but the metropolitan setting demands more types of services. Whether or not we need more units of government to offer them is a point we have already discussed in Chapter 5.

Major State And Local Functions: What We Pay For

The Council of State Governments has identified some 82 functions that are performed by many, if not most, state governments.[9] A recent study of city government identified a list of some 67 functions performed by some but not all city governments.[10] Despite the variety of functions performed by state and local government, there are a few that take up most of the money (see Figure 16.1).

The three biggest state expenditures account for nearly 60 percent of the total. They are aid to local governments, welfare, and education. Welfare and education are also the services for which most of the state aid is intended. The three biggest local government expenditure items are education, public utilities, and public safety. Together they account for over half of total local government expenditures.

Table 16.2 indicates something of the wide range of differences in service offerings by large cities. Clark and Ferguson developed a measure of municipal service offerings called the **functional performance index**.[11] It takes into account differences in the cost of services as well as the number offered. Collecting solid waste, for example, is much more labor intensive and involves more equipment and land than does sweeping the streets. A low functional performance score may mean that a city offers a few expensive services, or several inexpensive ones, whereas a high score indicates a fairly comprehensive offering of all or nearly all 67 types of major services.

Table 16.2 indicates both the wide range of service effort put forth by various cities, in general, and a good example of the variation within a single state. In California, three cities—San Francisco, Los Angeles, and San Jose—manifest considerably different levels of service.

Clark and Ferguson also examined demographic, financial, and political data on over 50 cities across the country to determine the causes of and solutions to **fiscal strain**—the inability to meet debt and expenditure obligations with existing revenues.[12] Their major finding was that the process of urban decay is neither irreversible nor automatic. As Table 16. 2 indicates, Baltimore and Boston are northeastern cities with high functional performance scores similar to that of New York. However, neither Baltimore nor Boston experienced the financial crises that New York did in the 1970s, even though they experienced some of the same problems in terms of job losses and demographic changes in the urban population. According to Clark and Ferguson the major reason for the financial stability of Baltimore and Boston was political leadership. Political leadership, even in cities with high service offerings, can deal successfully with fiscal strain.

Fiscal strain determinants are twofold, including both city fiscal policies and private sector resources. Informed analysts should consider each. Our twofold approach shows that population and job loss can bring fiscal strain, but only if local leaders do not adapt. To write off most

Figure 16.1

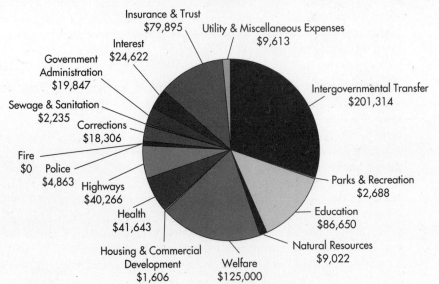

STATE

Insurance & Trust
$79,895

Utility & Miscellaneous Expenses
$9,613

Interest $24,622

Government Administration $19,847

Sewage & Sanitation $2,235

Corrections $18,306

Fire $0

Police $4,863

Highways $40,266

Health $41,643

Housing & Commercial Development $1,606

Welfare $125,000

Natural Resources $9,022

Education $86,650

Parks & Recreation $2,688

Intergovernmental Transfer $201,314

**TOTAL 1992 STATE EXPENDITURE
$668,070**

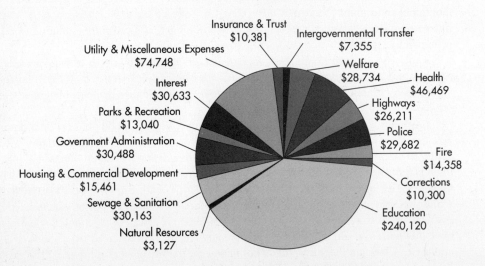

Insurance & Trust $10,381

Intergovernmental Transfer $7,355

Utility & Miscellaneous Expenses $74,748

Welfare $28,734

Health $46,469

Interest $30,633

Highways $26,211

Parks & Recreation $13,040

Police $29,682

Government Administration $30,488

Fire $14,358

Housing & Commercial Development $15,461

Corrections $10,300

Sewage & Sanitation $30,163

Education $240,120

Natural Resources $3,127

**TOTAL 1992 LOCAL EXPENDITURE
$611,270**

Note: Amounts shown are in millions of dollars.

Source: U. S. Statistical Abstract: 1994 (*Washington, D.C.: ACIR, 1994*), 298.

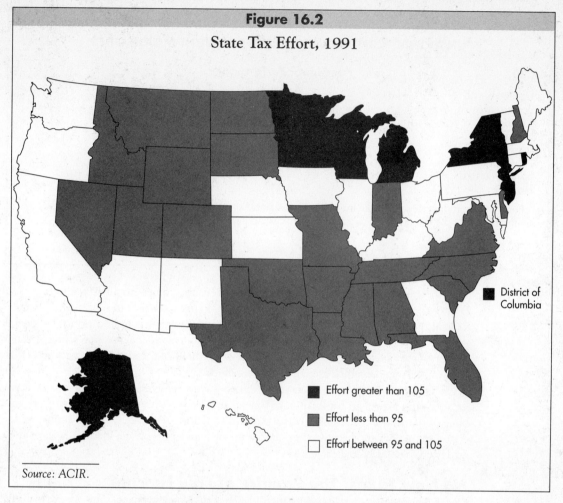

Figure 16.2

State Tax Effort, 1991

District of Columbia

■ Effort greater than 105

▓ Effort less than 95

□ Effort between 95 and 105

Source: ACIR.

older northeastern cities as 'poor risks' is an enormous simplification, denigrating local leaders by assuming that they cannot adapt to private sector changes.[13]

The ability of leaders to lead depends in part upon their personal abilities. Individuals matter, as we've noted a time or two. Leadership is also influenced by the nature of the political system in which they operate. Thus, political culture, and political institutions are major factors in determining whether a particular state or local government will make a major or a minimal effort within the confines of available resources to offer social services and promote redistribution (see Figure 16.2).

THE REVENUE SYSTEM

Our treatment of revenue will be somewhat more extensive than that of spending for at least three reasons. (1) The anti-tax bias of the American political culture; (2) the unfairness of the tax system in nearly every state; and (3) the need to deal with unfamiliar terms and concepts that are critical for an informed analysis of budget issues.

Table 16.2

FUNCTIONAL PERFORMANCE SCORES FOR EIGHT MAJOR CITIES*

City	Functional Performance
Baltimore, MD	567
Boston, MA	409
Chicago, IL	98
Houston, TX	38
Los Angeles, CA	78
New York, NY	583
San Francisco, CA	250
San Jose, CA	44

* Functional performance scores take into account the fact that some services are more expensive to offer than others, thus the *type of* as well as *number of* services is reflected in each city's score.

Source: Terry Nichols Clark and Lorna Crowley Ferguson, City Money (New York: Columbia University Press, 1983), 531.

About half of state and local government revenue comes from taxes, the first item listed in Box 16.2. The percentage of revenue based on taxes rises to 63 percent when we include the 14 percent contributed by federal grants-in-aid which are paid for by federal taxes. Thus taxes are far and away the largest single state and local revenue source. Even a portion of the category, "charges and miscellaneous" includes a variety of user fees and other transactions some of which are virtually the same as taxes.[14]

Thus we will focus most of our attention on the major revenue source, taxes, and leave for your term papers an exploration of sources such as speed traps (fines and fees) or gambling (lotteries and para-mutual betting) as ways of raising revenue. As noted earlier, we focus on taxes not only because they are the major source of revenue, but also because they are levied so unfairly in most states.

No New Taxes: The Promise of Free Lunches

One of the most potent political slogans in America is, "No New Taxes." This appeals to different categories of individuals for entirely different reasons. The net effect of the slogan is usually to preserve the biases built into the existing system of taxes and expenditures, the status quo.

For example, if our tax system relies largely on a percentage of what we spend, then those who can live comfortably without spending all they earn have an advantage. They have money left over each year to devote to untaxed activities such as speculating, saving, or investing. If we allow individuals and businesses to deduct from their taxable income (as business expenses) the money spent giving gifts (honorariums, fees, campaign contributions) directly or indirectly to public officials in order to gain access to them, then we further bias the taxation system (and the political system) in the direction of imbalance.

To individuals who are disadvantaged by the biases of the status quo, the have-nots, the slogan "No new taxes" promises that their current tax burden will not be made even worse. Thus they are encouraged by the slogan to believe that the tax rates affecting them won't increase if a "no new taxes" candidate is elected. With few exceptions, the poor (and the middle class) bear a heavier state-local tax burden than the haves.[15] Since there are so many poor, and since this unfairness is so widespread, the "No new taxes" message has a ready mass audience.

To those who are given advantages by the status quo, "No new taxes," means that there will be no changes in the current mix of taxes. No new *types* of taxes (there are about eight basic types) will be introduced, nor will the emphasis on particular types be changed. The message to them is that the distribution of burdens will not be reformed in the direction of fairness. Clearly the haves are highly motivated to help pay for the television commericials and talk show hosts whose messages promote the notion that "No new taxes" is a good thing for the have-nots.

Lest we be accused of fomenting class warfare here, we hasten to point out that in many states and communities the effort to make the taxation system more equitable has been led by wealthy individuals who knew their taxes would go up if the biases in the taxation system were changed.

From the mid 1970s onward the slogan "No new taxes" has been elevated to the level of a credibility test for political candidates from the White House to the county court house. One of the ironies of this slogan is that compared to the citizens of other industrialized nations, Americans are not heavily taxed. Table 16.3 presents the percentage of the Gross Do-

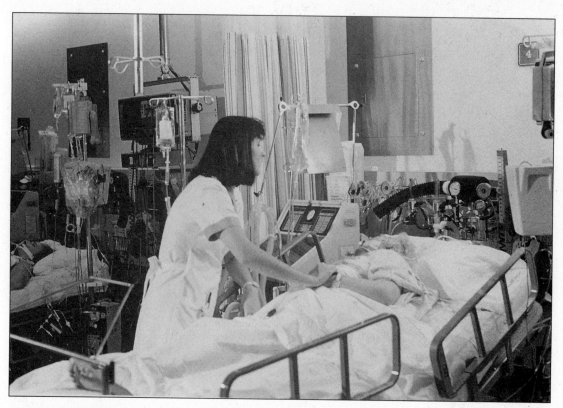

The dramatic increase in Medicaid expenditures has produced cost-controlling reforms in several states. Oregon's rationed health care system limits the number of treatments available to Medicaid recipients, and Florida and Washington act as insurance brokers collecting health premiums and negotiating the best prices with providers.

BOX 16.2

REVENUE SOURCES FOR STATE AND LOCAL GOVERNMENT

1. Eight types of taxes: general sales, selected sales, licenses and fees, property, corporate income, personal income, severance, and estate and gift.
2. Intergovernmental transfers (such as grants-in-aid and shared taxes),
3. A wide variety of government enterprises (such as utilities and transit systems, toll roads and bridges, and state owned liquor stores);
4. The sale of monopoly rights or franchises to enterprises such as cable, taxi, or utility companies.
5. The rent or sale of assets (such as land, buildings, or trees, coal and other natural resources).
6. Interest on money invested.
7. Fines or penalties.
8. Borrowing (usually, but not always, from wealthy individuals, insurance companies, and mutual investment funds).
9. Fees or assessments for services such as park admission, survey work, or snow removal or

mestic Product paid in taxes to all levels of government during 1991 in the seven wealthiest industrial nations. The table clearly indicates that while the range is not all that large—from 29 percent of Gross Domestic Product to 44 percent—the United States is at the lowest end. The problem is not that all taxpayers are overburdened. The problem is the imbalance. The burden is not equally distributed between the have and the have-nots.

The modern anti-tax movement began quietly about 1974 in several medium sized cities across the country. It was particularly strong in cities with a high proportion of middle class voters who, though liberal in the sense of supporting individualism, tolerance, and freedom of opportunity, were conservative in terms of the use of government funds to solve

Table 16.3

TAXES AS A PERCENTAGE OF 1991 GROSS DOMESTIC PRODUCT IN THE SEVEN RICHEST INDUSTRIAL COUNTRIES

Country	Percent of GDP
United States	29.8
Italy	40
Canada	37
France	44
Japan	31
United Kingdom	36
Germany	39

Source: U. S. Bureau of the Census, Statistical Abstract of the United States: 1994 (Washington, D.C.: U. S. Government Printing Office, 1994), 867.

social problems. In 1978 the media focused on Proposition 13 in California, which was directed at property taxes, and the anti-tax movement gained national attention.[16] The fact that property taxes in general have ceased to be an accurate indicator of an individual's wealth, was not the focus of the anti-tax movement; supporters of the movement were not interested in reforming the system of taxes. In effect it was both an anti-government and an anti-tax movement. Instead of making the system of paying for government more just, it sought to reduce both taxes and government.

According to Clark and Ferguson, "No new taxes," is part of the political culture learned by many Americans.

> Americans revolt against taxes when the tax bite is still lower than in many other countries. National factors reinforce fiscal conservatism for Americans: the absence of a feudal past, the correspondingly egalitarian ideology, individualistic Protestantism, the frontier with vast areas of individual farming (reinforcing isolation), abundance of natural resources, isolation from other countries, and few wars.[17]

The price of policies based on the free-lunch myth is indicated in part by the fact that each year we now make $100 billion more in interest payments on the national debt than we did in 1979.[18] In the absence of new revenue, the only way to pay for the tripling of the national debt has been to cut other programs. The effect of tax cuts for the rich and the program cuts for the poor has been a massive eight-year shift toward reinforcement of inequality.[19] Furthermore, since 87 percent of the national debt is owed to wealthy American citizens and financial institutions who buy the government bonds, the debt has further reinforced inequality. According to two respected economists, Heilbroner and Bernstein,

> It seems fair to say, therefore, that the government debt is a net expense for the lower three-quarters of the nation, and a net benefit for the upper one-quarter. Thus one very real but largely overlooked aspect of the interest burden lies in its impact on the distribution of income.[20]

The rest of the nation now provides interest income for the wealthiest one-quarter. At the same time social programs to aid the poorest quarter have been significantly reduced. State and local governments are now in the process of attempting to cope with the consequences of this shift toward inequality. Some governments are trying harder than others.

Types of State and Local Taxes

According to the Advisory Commission on Intergovernmental Relations virtually all tax sources used by state and local governments fall into one of eight categories. They are: General Sales, Selective Sales, Licenses and Fees, Property, Personal Income, Corporate Income, Severance, and Estate and Gift. Table 16.4 indicates the percentage of total tax revenue collected by state and local governments that each of these sources represents.

General Sales Tax

This is a tax on the gross receipts on all retail sales. The tax is collected at the point of sale. The business then pays the state on a monthly or quarterly basis. The state then allocates the local government share, if any.

Selected Sales Tax

This tax is imposed on particular kinds of commodities. Among the items most frequently subjected to a selected sales tax are: motor fuels, alcoholic beverages, tobacco products, insurance premiums, public utility bills, amusements, and pari-mutuel gambling.

Table 16.4

COMPONENTS OF THE REPRESENTATIVE REVENUE SYSTEM IN 1991

Tax Source	Percent of Total
General Sales	19.6
Selective Sales Taxes	7.9
License Taxes	1.9
Personal Income Taxes	16.5
Corporation Income Taxes	3.7
Property Taxes	25.3
Estate and Gift Taxes	0.6
Severance Taxes	.8
Other Taxes	3.0
Rents and Royalties	.4
Lotteries	1.3
User Charges	19.2
Total	100.0

Source: ACIR, State Tax Capacity and Effort: 1991 *(Washington D.C.: Advisory Commission on Intergovernmental Relations, 1993), 7.*

Licenses and Fees Tax

Taxes levied at a flat rate. The purpose is to raise revenue and/or to regulate. Among the most frequently taxed subjects are motor vehicles, motor vehicle operators, corporations, various occupations, firms engaged in the manufacture or distribution of alcoholic beverages, and individuals who hunt and fish.

Property Tax

There are three types of property: (1) real estate (land and improvements on it); (2) movable property (such as cars, paintings, home furnishings, equipment, or unsold commercial inventory); and (3) intangible property (stocks, bonds, securities, and other paper claims on wealth).

Many taxing authorities classify property according to its economic use. A frequently used scheme includes four categories of taxable property: residential, commercial, agricultural, and public utility. Each category may be taxed at different rates. Some categories such as commercial, include real property and movable property, such as heavy equipment.[21]

Personal Income Tax

This is a tax on the net annual income of an individual, after certain deductions are allowed. This tax is only levied on one's income. The principle of taxing according to income or ability to pay is sometimes employed in administering other taxes. Agricultural land, in some states, is not taxed on its market value (which might be quite high) but on the income derived from the crops or livestock raised on it (which might not be very much at all).

In 31 states property tax relief for people with low incomes is provided by means of **circuit breaker laws**. These limit the amount of property taxes that can be collected on an individual's home or apartment. The circuit breaker law is a percentage of the resident's income that can be collected in property taxes regardless of the market value of the residence. After the specified percentage of income is reached the property tax is turned off, just as circuit breakers cut off electricity when the load the wires must carry becomes too heavy.

In 25 of the states that use it, the circuit-breaker applies to renters as well. It is assumed that a specified percentage of a tenant's annual rental payment represents the landlord's effort to pass on all or part of the property tax. In those states the elderly or disabled cannot be asked to pay more than a fixed percent (from 15 to 25 percent) of their net income in property taxes whether they own or rent.[22]

Corporate Income Tax

This is a tax on the net income or profits of a corporation or business firm. A corporation or firm with no profits pays no income tax. Most states levy, and most firms prefer, this tax rather than a corporate franchise or license tax which must be paid regardless of the profitability of the business in a given year.

Estate and Gift Tax

These are taxes imposed on the transfer of property by gift or via a will. These taxes are usually levied on large estates.

Severance Tax

This is a tax that is levied on the act of removing minerals or other natural products from the ground. The most common items taxed are coal, oil, and gas.

Determining the Mix

Numerous patterns emerge from the variety of ways several thousand state and local governments make use of the eight types of taxes. There are differences in the rates charged for each particular tax and in the exemptions or relief allowed. Some units of government do not use certain taxes at all. Six states do not tax corporate income; seven do not tax net personal incomes.[23] Most states have vacated the property tax, leaving it for local governments as a revenue source. In many states certain taxes, such as sales or personal income tax, are optional for particular local governments.

Two of the most important taxation patterns are, first, the tendency for each type of government to use certain types of taxes. States rely largely on income and sales taxes, general purpose local governments (municipalities, counties, and townships) rely largely on property and sales taxes, and school districts in all but a few states rely almost exclusively on property taxes.[24]

The second important feature of any state-local tax system is the dominance of state government. While the economy, and the federal government, have a significant influence on state and local revenues, the major source of decisions about the state-local tax mix in any state is state government, especially the state legislature. State governments have the power to levy taxes, to limit, grant, or deny tax sources to local governments, and to require local governments to perform functions that require revenue. Any discussion of reforming or evaluating the state-local revenue system in the 50 states will tend to focus on the institutions empowered to change the entire system—the state legislatures and the governors.

TEN CHARACTERISTICS OF A GOOD STATE-LOCAL REVENUE SYSTEM

According to the National Council of State Legislatures a good state-local revenue system has 10 characteristics: coherence, reliability, diversity, equity, efficiency, accountability, effectiveness, jurisdictional parity, intergovernmental responsibility, and pragmatism. While some of these criteria require more elaboration than others, all are worth some attention.[25]

In evaluating revenue systems, we naturally focus on taxes, the major source of state and local government revenue. Most of the following concepts can be applied to particular types of taxes as well as to entire revenue systems.

Coherence

A high-quality state-local revenue system should be composed of elements that function well together as a logical system. The state legislature, the major revenue policy maker, should design a reporting system to monitor the effects of state tax decisions on both the economy and on local governments. Particular attention should be paid first to the *exemptions* that the state requires local governments to grant on property taxes. In many states the legislature declares that certain kinds of property or a portion of the value (the first $5,000, for example) of property is exempt or excused from taxation. If a state prevents local governments from using other tax sources, then a property tax exemption can mean a serious reduction in the tax base of a local government. When the legislature also requires (mandates) local governments to offer new or expanded services at the same time that it cuts their revenue base, the legislature is putting these local governments in a double bind.

Reliability

A high-quality revenue system should produce revenue in a reliable manner. Reliability involves stability, certainty, and sufficiency.

Stability means that a tax system should not reinforce downturns in the economy, and at the same time it should help siphon off excess income in inflationary times. Taxes on income and sales do this; taxes on property and various per unit taxes such as licenses do not.

Certainty means that there is a high probability that the tax yield will remain the same from year to year. Taxes on selected items that are not likely to be purchased in poor economic times fail to meet the certainty criterion. A sales tax system that is narrowly based also may fail to meet this criterion. In poor economic times discretionary income for luxury items, clothing, and home furnishing is reduced, but various services and necessities are still purchased. A broadly based sales tax would thus promote certainty.

Sufficiency means that a revenue system includes enough taxes to pay for the services and programs that the community feels are appropriate. A sufficient or adequate tax system should make use of taxes that grow at least as fast as the economy.

Diversity

A high-quality revenue system should have substantial diversification of revenue sources over reasonably broad bases. A diverse revenue system should use a variety of taxes that require every sector of the economy to contribute. The Advisory Commission on Intergovernmental Relations recommends that a state-local tax system should have the following mix of taxes: sales and property should constitute 20 to 30 percent of total revenue, personal income should be 20 to 35 percent of total revenue, and the remainder should come from a combination of corporate taxes, user fees, and selective sales taxes.[26]

Equity

A high-quality revenue system should be fair. Minimum aspects of an equitable system are: a) that it shields genuine subsistence income from taxation, b) that it is proportionate or progressive, and c) that horizontal equity should be observed, that is, all households with the same income should pay approximately the same tax.[27] **Subsistence** means barely ade-

Table 16.5

DISTRIBUTION OF ABILITY TO PAY: PERCENT OF TOTAL PERSONAL INCOME IN THE UNITED STATES RECEIVED BY EACH 20 PERCENT OF HOUSEHOLDS

Category	Top Income of Individuals in Category	Percent of Total Personal Income in Category
Top 20%	Over $100,000,000	44.6
Second 20%	$64,300	24.0
Third 20%	$44,200	16.5
Fourth 20%	$30,000	10.5
Fifth 20%	$16,960	4.4

Note: The top 5 percent received 17.6 percent of the total. The lower limit of the top 5 percent = $106,509.

Source: U. S. Bureau of the Census, Statistical Abstract of the United States: 1994 *(Washington, D.C.: U. S. Government Printing Office, 1994), 471.*

quate to meet the most basic of needs: shelter, food, and clothing. Not included are: medical care, recreation, education, and transportation. It is impossible to shield a subsistence income from a sales tax, but there are methods for shielding the poor from the effects of other types of taxes. Circuit breaker laws can reduce the effects of property taxes on the poor. Using some kind of income tax and then exempting those below a certain income level would increase dependence of a tax system on the ability to pay rather than the necessity to spend.

Vertical equity means that individuals in all income categories bear the same burden (not the same size tax bill). The **tax burden** is the percentage of one's income paid in taxes. This is also known as the *effective rate* (ER).[28]

Table 16.5 presents the distribution of ability to pay taxes in the U. S. economy. The total population is divided into five categories of families according to income received in 1992. Each *quintile* or 20 percent of the population contains the same number of people. However, each quintile does not receive the same amount of income.

The poorest 20 percent of the population receive 4.4 percent of the total personal income earned in 1992, down slightly from 1985. Thus, their ability to pay taxes to pay is rather limited. This quintile includes an estimated 37 million persons below the poverty level in 1992. As you may recall from Chapter 14, the poverty level in 1992 was $7,143 for an individual and $14,335 for a family of four.

On the other hand, the top 20 percent of the population received 45 percent of the total personal income to individuals in the United States The ability of this category to pay taxes is greater than that of the bottom three categories combined.

Thus, as Table 16.5 suggests, the percent of the total income acquired by each of the income categories (or classes) leaves some with a much greater ability to pay than others.

Beyond the notion of "soak the rich, " which is always appealing to those of us who aren't, there are three common sense reasons for vertical equity to be a principle upon which to base a tax system:

1. First, those with high incomes have more to lose if a mutually agreed upon system of law and order, of enforcement of contracts, and of protection of property breaks down. Therefore, they should pay a larger amount—perhaps even a higher percentage of their income—to maintain this system. Taxes are insurance against mob rule or anarchy. When you have more to insure, you pay a higher premium.
2. Second, those with high incomes have more to spend after basic necessities are paid for, therefore their *surplus* is being taxed, not their food, shelter, and clothing budgets as in the case of a subsistence income.
3. Third, many of those with high incomes would willingly contribute a proportionate share of their income to pay for society, but are reluctant to do so unless the rest of those with high incomes do likewise. Therefore, a taxation system requires all to do what some would do anyway.

Since efforts by human beings to hit a target such as tax equity do not always hit dead center, we have three additional terms to use in discussing vertical equity. They are: proportionate, regressive, and progressive. A **proportionate tax** (or tax system) is one that hits the target of vertical equity. A proportionate tax system requires each individual to contribute to the cost of government in proportion to income received. In a proportionate tax system each individual bears the same tax burden (see Table 16.6).

The other two systems depart from proportionality in different directions. A **regressive tax** system misses the target of proportionality in favor of the top income categories. The burden gets lighter as income increases. A **progressive system** misses the target in the direction of redistribution. The burden increases as income increases. The tax burden is lighter for the poor and heavier for the rich.

According to Donald Phares, who has done extensive research on tax equity within the several states, all local tax systems are regressive, and only three state systems are progressive (California, Delaware, and Iowa). In only one state (Delaware) is the total state-local system even mildly progressive. Table 16.6 compares state-local tax systems using an index developed by Daniel B. Suits.[29] Using the most recent data available, Phares calculated the index scores for local, state, and state-local tax systems. According to this index a score of −1.00 means that a tax system is totally regressive, the have-nots pay the entire tax bill. An index score of +1.00 is completely progressive. Although recent tax law revisions in some states may result in slightly different scores, the basic pattern is unlikely to change unless some significant tax reforms are instituted to move state-local tax systems in the direction of equity, perhaps even progressivity.[30]

The regressive nature of most state-local tax systems is associated with the types of taxes upon which the tax system relies for most of its revenue. Regressive systems tend to depend upon property and sales taxes. Progressive taxation systems may use these taxes but they depend to a much greater extent upon corporate and personal income taxes.

While it may be obvious that a tax on incomes will be proportionate or slightly progressive, the regressive impact of sales and property taxes is not intuitively obvious. Property tax regressivity occurs because the value of one's residential property is often unrelated to one's income. For example, many elderly people on modest retirement incomes who live in the house they bought 30 years ago are faced with an unpleasant consequence of urban growth. When they bought that home it was in a residential neighborhood on the edge of the city. Now it may occupy prime commercial land. Since land and property are taxed at their market value, these elderly citizens have property tax bills that do not reflect their in-

Table 16.6

EQUITY OF STATE TAX SYSTEMS

A tax system in which everyone bears the same burden would be represented by no departure from level or zero. Note that all local systems are regressive and the combined state-local tax system is regressive in almost every case. Index scores range from completely progressive +1.00, to completely regressive −1.00. Proportionality is 0.00.

State	Total State	Total Local	State and Local Taxes
Alabama	−0.09	−0.15	−0.10
Alaska	−0.04	−0.08	−0.05
Arizona	−0.09	−0.12	−0.10
Arkansas	−0.08	−0.12	−0.09
California	+0.04	−0.12	−0.04
Colorado	−0.04	−0.11	−0.07
Connecticut	−0.02	−0.13	−0.06
Delaware	+0.06	−0.11	+0.02
Florida	−0.13	−0.12	−0.11
Georgia	−0.05	−0.11	−0.07
Hawaii	+0.00	−0.11	−0.03
Idaho	−0.03	−0.07	−0.04
Illinois	−0.04	−0.08	−0.06
Indiana	−0.04	−0.09	−0.06
Iowa	+0.02	−0.08	−0.02
Kansas	−0.03	−0.07	−0.04
Kentucky	−0.03	−0.13	−0.05
Louisiana	−0.07	−0.07	−0.07
Maine	−0.04	−0.17	−0.07
Maryland	−0.04	−0.11	−0.06
Massachusetts	+0.01	−0.16	−0.06
Michigan	+0.01	−0.12	−0.06
Minnesota	+0.04	−0.15	−0.02
Mississippi	−0.09	−0.14	−0.10
Missouri	−0.04	−0.14	−0.08
Montana	0.00	−0.07	−0.04
Nebraska	0.00	−0.07	−0.04
Nevada	−0.09	−0.11	−0.09
New. Hampshire	−0.06	−0.18	−0.12
New Jersey	−0.03	−0.17	−0.10
New Mexico	−0.09	−0.15	−0.10
New York	+0.07	−0.10	−0.02
North Carolina	−0.04	−0.11	−0.05
North Dakota	−0.02	−0.07	−0.04
Ohio	−0.01	−0.11	−0.05
Oklahoma	−0.03	−0.11	−0.06
Oregon	+0.05	−0.10	−0.03
Pennsylvania	−0.01	−0.16	−0.06
Rhode Island	−0.01	−0.13	−0.06
South Carolina	−0.05	−0.12	−0.06
South Dakota	−0.08	−0.08	−0.08
Tennessee	−0.08	−0.10	−0.09
Texas	−0.13	−0.06	−0.09

(continued)

Table 16.6 (Continued)

State	Total State	Total Local	State and Local Taxes
Utah	−0.03	−0.14	−0.07
Vermont	0.00	−0.20	−0.07
Virginia	−0.06	−0.12	−0.08
Washington	−0.06	−0.10	−0.07
West Virginia	−0.07	−0.10	−0.07
Wisconsin	+0.02	−0.14	−0.03
Wyoming	−0.11	−0.04	−0.07
U. S. Average	−0.04	−0.12	−0.07

Source: Donald Phares, "State and Local Tax Burdens Across the Fifty States," Growth and Change (April, 1985), 39.

comes. For a significant portion of our population, the value of the property they own increases faster than their income.

Many homeowners regard property taxes as almost as obnoxious as the federal income tax. Roger J. Vaughn observes that the problem is at least partially because only real estate is taxed. The value of stocks, bonds, paintings, jewelry, and expensive home furnishings are not taxed.

> Taxpayers, angry about spiralling property taxes, have a hard time knowing who to blame— the assessor, the school board, the city council, or the county board. But much of the blame must be borne by the inequity of the tax itself. Real estate, the only real asset for low and moderate-income households, is but a small share of the assets of the relatively affluent. Yet property taxes are usually limited to real estate, making the tax relatively regressive.[31]

In the business community the may lead to inequities as well. A business which owns a large amount of expensive heavy equipment may have a higher tax burden than one which makes the same profit without using equipment.

Sales tax regressivity occurs not only because it is administratively impossible to shield the poor from its effects, but also because virtually the entire income of a poor family is subject to the sales tax. Poor families must spend all their income each year simply to feed, shelter, and cloth themselves. A wealthy family, even though it enjoys a higher standard of consumption (steaks instead of hot dogs, exclusive restaurants instead of fast food), will still have a goodly portion of its income available for investment, speculation, and savings that are usually not subject to a sales tax.

Even in the 21 states where sales of food or prescription drugs are tax exempt, the relief provided by this exemption reduces but does not remove regressivity. Next time you check your grocery bill, note the relatively modest portion of it actually devoted to food. In states with sales taxes, the rest of your grocery bill—the aspirin, shampoo, soap, dog food, paper towels, scouring powder, and so on—would be subject to the tax. Furthermore, while grocery store food is not taxed, restaurant food is. In the interest of sanity, working parents are likely to treat their families to occasional fast food meals. Thus, not even a poor family's entire food budget is exempt from taxation.

Horizontal equity means that people in the same income category will be taxed at the same rate, regardless of where they live. Not only is there economic inequality among states, there are also inequalities within states. Local governments differ considerably in terms of their ability to pay for services because local governments do not have equal tax bases. A school district which is able to raise revenue because it is located over a large pool of oil will not have to tax homes and businesses at a very high rate. A school district or city with little or no valuable commercial or industrial land will have to levy a higher tax rate upon residential property for its tax base.

The difference in the tax bases of local governments is sometimes called **fiscal disparity**. Within the federal system, the national government and many state governments have made some attempt to take fiscal disparities into account in the design of grant-in-aid programs. A major issue in many state legislatures is whether or not enough effort has been made by the state to deal with fiscal disparities that lead to inequalities in educational opportunity, health care, and other social services.

The consequences of fiscal disparities within any particular state can be reduced if the state government is willing to provide grants, share revenue, or pay for the cost of certain services. A study by the ACIR on the extent to which state expenditure patterns reduced interjurisdictional fiscal disparities indicated considerable variation among the states. State payments were classified as reducing fiscal differences if they directly or indirectly dealt with welfare, medicaid, or were based on local needs such as large school populations.

The states use a variety of methods for promoting horizontal equity. Some states have attempted to reduce disparities with revenue-sharing programs such as that used in North Dakota. In North Dakota five percent of the state's income tax revenue is reserved for a program that distributes funds to local governments according to their level of poverty and the size of the population in the jurisdiction.[32] Massachusetts has assumed full fiscal responsibility for local court costs. The Minnesota Fiscal Disparities Act provides that all additions to the commercial real estate tax base will be shared among the local governments in that metropolitan area. In Hawaii there are no local school districts; education is funded completely by the state.

Efficiency

Within this criterion the National Association of Legislatures has included four related concepts. The first two are closely related. First, the tax system should be understandable to the taxpayer. Second it should be easy to comply with. There should not be many complicated forms and a variety of different tax payment deadlines. One reason for the popularity of the sales tax is that it is relatively easy for a member of the general public to pay and no complicated calculations or forms are required. Income taxes, on the other hand, often require a fair amount of emotional distress and intellectual effort. This complexity and necessary effort are at least partially responsible for the fact that the federal income tax is consistently viewed as the least fair of five of the major taxes collected in the intergovernmental system even though, according to the ability-to-pay standard, it is one of the most fair. As Table 16.7 shows, the state income tax is viewed most favorably. Thus, in many states the public is not resistant to being taxed according to the ability-to-pay. It's the difficulty of understanding and other dimensions of inefficiency that seem to bother people.

The third dimension of administrative efficiency includes the notion of low administrative costs. A tax system that is administratively efficient means that the tax can be collected without using most of the returns to pay for collecting it. This is another reason why

All but five states require retail stores to collect a general sales tax—one of the most regressive taxes of those available to state and local governments. Three of the five states have tax systems that are proportional or regressive.

property taxes are not popular. The property tax involves a series of labor intensive steps every year for each piece of property in a taxing jurisdiction, as Box 16.3 indicates. Few tax systems would be as expensive to set up from scratch today as the property tax system.

Lotteries and pari-mutunel betting are often recommended as nontax revenue sources. While all the issues are more complex than we can deal with here, it is instructive to consider the amount of the "take" in a lottery system which is used up in prizes and in administration (as well as advertising to promote the sale of lottery tickets—the appropriateness of which is worth some thought). After paying for prizes and administrative costs, about 40 percent of lottery ticket sales was left for the state treasuries.[33] Few other taxes would be used very long if 60 percent of the take was devoted to collection costs.

The fourth characteristic of an efficient tax system is that it does not unnecessarily interfere with private economic decisions such as home improvements, industry location, individual savings, or business investment. An economically efficient system should be competitive with tax systems in other states or communities without relying heavily on tax

Table 16.7

RESPONDENTS' ANSWER TO "WHICH DO YOU THINK IS THE WORST TAX—THAT IS, THE LEAST FAIR ?"

Type of Tax	1981	1991
Federal income tax	36	26
Local property tax	33	30
State sales tax	14	19
State income tax	9	12
Don't know	9	14

Source: ACIR, Changing Attitudes on Government Taxes 1991 (Washington, D. C.: Advisory Commission on Intergovernmental Relations, 1991), 4.

incentives that favor certain businesses or industries over others, or upon industry specific taxes that treat one type of business—telecommunications, utilities, banks—differently from others.

BOX 16.3

COLLECTING THE PROPERTY TAX

1. Inspect to see if improvements have increased its market value
2. Calculate market value
3. Notify owner of appraised value
4. Convene an appeals board to hear appeals for changes in appraisal
5. Render decisions on appeals and deal with consequences, sometimes lawsuits
6. Convene public hearing by taxing authority to discuss tax rate; if authority intends to raise tax rate, then notification needs to be published in newspapers and hearings scheduled
7. Deliberate and set a tax rate by taxing authority. After the tax rate is set there may be a referendum to reverse it (sometimes called, a roll-back election)
8. Hold the referendum (election) and await results after the waiting period for roll-back petitions has elapsed, or
9. Calculate tax bill
10. Distribute tax bills
11. Administer appeals, and/or
12. Verify documentation of applications for exemptions such as circuitbreakers, homestead exemptions, farm and ranch property exemptions.
13. Record and deposit payments
14. Collect delinquent payments

Accountability

A high-quality revenue system should be explicit. There should be no hidden tax increases. There should be a notification and appeals process such as that described above. Many states now have "truth in taxation" laws that local taxing authorities must follow. However, few state legislatures deal adequately with the impact of their own decisions on local governments. Thus, state mandates requiring expensive administrative procedures, or requiring that new services be offered at the local level, are not always funded adequately by the legislature.

One way of improving accountability is for **fiscal notes** to be published as part of all proposed state laws. A fiscal note is an estimate of the cost of the proposed law to government, state or local. The fiscal note alerts local governments and their state associations to attend hearings and propose alternatives, or work for appropriations to reimburse expenditures. Otherwise, they must raise local taxes to pay for the state mandated actions, or cut existing services.

Tax expenditure reports are another way to promote accountability.[34] A tax expenditure is the amount of revenue lost by granting an exemption to a tax. Every year interest groups for particular firms or industries seek specific exemptions to various taxes. Some of the loopholes created involve considerable costs to the government. In many cases the problem that the exemption is supposed to solve would be more efficiently and simply dealt with by a spending or loan program.[35]

Effectiveness

A high-quality revenue system should be administered professionally and uniformly, both throughout the state and within individual jurisdictions. Saving money by poorly paying auditors, appraisers, and tax analysts, or by failing to provide adequate resources such as computers, software, and staff is a false economy. If the public becomes aware of the possibility that some are able to escape their fair share of the agreed upon tax burden, then revenues may drop off and the system will become even more expensive to repair later.

One of the criticisms of the use of sales taxes with numerous exemptions is that the average convenience store clerk becomes the person who decides whether some goods are taxable or not. The use of amateur tax collectors results in a variety of tax bills with little relationship to the law or to fairness or efficiency. A local NBC reporter was charged seven different amounts of sales tax on the same basket of goods in seven different pharmacies in New York, where the state exempts from the sales tax "drugs and medicines." Confusion arose from anomalies such as the fact that sterilized cotton is exempt while nonsterilized cotton is not; Prell shampoo is regarded as merely taxable shampoo by some pharmacies while Head and Shoulders is regarded as tax exempt because it is intended to treat dandruff, and so on.[36]

Jurisdictional Parity

A high-quality revenue system should result in enough equalization of the resources available to local governments that they are able to provide an adequate level of services. This is one of several areas where taxing and spending are related. State money is spent, or given in local government grants, so that local jurisdictions with inadequate tax bases do not have to overtax individuals and businesses and thus drive them away.

Despite fiscal disparities, horizontal equity should be maintained not only to make the tax system fair, but also to provide a basic minimum level of services for all the citizens in the state. This is particularly important in the field of human resources and education. A region or community that cannot afford to prepare the next generation for leadership and citizenship is doomed to a cycle of dependency on the rest of the state.

Intergovernmental Responsibility

A high-quality state-local revenue system should minimize intergovernmental tax competition and business tax incentives. The evidence is overwhelming that taxes are not a particularly important factor in business locations. The factors taken most seriously by businesses looking at an area are the quality of life, the availability of markets, raw materials, and labor costs.[37]

Table 16.8 compares the ranking of state-local tax systems in terms of their attractiveness to business with the rankings of states in terms of actual locations of Japanese manufacturing plants. As Table 16.8 indicates, the total number of plants in the 10 states with the most attractive business tax climate is 138, whereas the total for the 10 states with the worst business tax climate was 240. Clearly other considerations than taxes are at work here.

The persistence of the myth that the availability of a tax-subsidy equals plant location, seems due in a large part to the existence of organizations that have a stake in it. As we observed in the interest group chapter, many organizations depend on dues paid by businesses for their income. One of the best ways to demonstrate the value of an organization to its business clients is to promote low taxes. Thus a good deal of the pressure for special treatment for businesses in the tax system—to promote a "good business climate" for new business locations—comes from the numerous business interest groups already in the state or community. According to the National Conference on State Legislatures:

> Tax concessions are not cost-effective. State and local government revenues forgone through tax expenditures are greater than benefits derived by recipient firms. It is unlikely that any form of tax concession can be cost-effective.[38]

Many state and local government tax breaks end up as subsidies for the federal government. The more profitable the business, from not paying local or state taxes, the more corporate income tax the federal government collects. Furthermore, the fact that federal tax law allows firms to claim state and local tax payments as deductible business expenses means that differences in taxes between states or between local governments become even more irrelevant in business locations. The leveling effect of this deduction is sometimes called the **federal offset**.[39]

According to Rasmussen and colleagues, one of the most cost effective ways to attract new business is to provide **loan guarantees,** not tax breaks. A loan guarantee means that the government doesn't loan any money—a bank does—but the government agrees to pay back the loan—if the business fails. Even if 22 percent of the total loaned to various, firms is not repaid, the ratio between the cost of the state guarantee payments to the lending institutions and the benefits received by the businesses is more favorable than any tax incentive.[40]

Table 16.8

SELECTED TAX CLIMATE FACTORS

State	ACIR Business Tax Rating	Japanese Manufacturer Locations
Alabama	5	12
Alaska	20	23
Arizona	11	4
Arkansas	13	6
California	50	167
Colorado	20	1
Connecticut	19	3
Delaware	16	0
Florida	12	5
Georgia	23	39
Hawaii	25	4
Idaho	29	0
Illinois	6	34
Indiana	13	17
Iowa	48	4
Kansas	25	2
Kentucky	9	10
Louisiana	40	0
Maine	39	1
Maryland	35	8
Massachusetts	32	9
Michigan	45	30
Minnesota	49	3
Mississippi	6	0
Missouri	1	5
Montana	43	1
Nebraska	20	6

Pragmatism

A high-quality revenue system should not be used as an instrument of social policy to encourage particular activities such as business investment or personal saving. Taxes are inefficient at rewarding or encouraging behavior. They are almost by definition negative in effect.[41] Thus, a pragmatic tax system is based on the realization that taxes may be used to discourage behavior—smoking, drinking, polluting, gambling but not to encourage it—saving or investment.

Taxes may also be used to reimburse governments for the indirect costs that arise from certain kinds of behavior. For example, the evidence is mounting that working in an office where smoking takes place is a serious threat to one's health. Thus, it seems appropriate for smokers, or companies which profit from their addiction, to contribute more than others to cancer research and to treatment centers for victims of cancer. In sum, using taxes to encourage behavior results in tax expenditures. Using taxes to discourage behavior results in revenue.

While all 10 characteristics of a good revenue system are important to know about, it

Table 16.8 (Continued)

State	ACIR Business Tax Rating	Japanese Manufacturer Locations
Nevada	30	5
New. Hampshire	10	3
New Jersey	4	40
New Mexico	32	0
New York	44	23
North Carolina	13	15
North Dakota	30	0
Ohio	17	18
Oklahoma	42	7
Oregon	37	8
Pennsylvania	34	20
Rhode Island	46	0
South Carolina	7	7
South Dakota *	3	0
Tennessee	2	19
Texas	23	23
Utah	25	1
Vermont	37	1
Virginia	7	9
Washington	36	34
West Virginia	47	2
Wisconsin	41	3
Wyoming	28	0

* South Dakota levies a 6 percent tax on the profits of banks and financial corporations.

Sources: ACIR, Interjurisidictional Competition in the Federal System: A Roundtable Discussion, 1988–89 *(Washington, D.C., U. S. Government Printing Office), 1989.*

may also be worth considering them as goals in terms of participation. Fairness or vertical equity seems particularly appropriate for a political system that values equality of opportunity. Whether or not you decide to work for tax reform, it seems fairly certain that you will pay a price for not doing so in your state, unless you are, or become one of, those who benefit from a regressive system and wish to continue that benefit.

We move from evaluating the components of tax systems at the state and local level to developing criteria for examining whole tax systems at the state and local level.

TAX CAPACITY AND TAX EFFORT: COMPARING THE FIFTY STATES

These two concepts were developed about 20 years ago by the Advisory Commission on Intergovernmental Relations in order to help Congress design grant-in-aid formulas. Many states have adopted them in designing some of their own grant-in aid programs for local governments.

Tax capacity is defined as the amount of revenue that would be collected in a unit of government if each and every one of the eight tax sources were taxed at the average rate.

Tax capacity is a way of measuring the tax base of a unit of government. It is also a measure of fiscal disparity. The concept is so useful that many states are beginning to use tax capacity data in grant-in-aid formulas for local governments.

Tax capacity is reported in billions of dollars. To make comparison easier, the ACIR has created a tax capacity index for each state that takes population into account. It is scaled so that 100 is the per capita tax capacity of the average state. Thus the index score for each state is a percentage of the average state-local tax capacity. As Table 16.9 indicates, Arkansas has a tax capacity that is 73.3 percent of the average, while Wyoming has a tax capacity that is 150.7 percent of the average. In designing a grant program which takes into account, Arkansas might expect a little more help than Wyoming.

Tax effort is an attempt to measure the willingness of state leaders and citizens to pay for government out of available resources. Some state-local systems, of course, don't have a big tax base. Others are comparatively wealthy, but the decision makers in those systems have chosen not to use government to solve problems or have chosen to pay for programs by borrowing. Either way, the next generation is faced with the bills. Tax effort is an attempt to take the tax base (tax capacity) of each state-local system into account in measuring willingness to pay.

A state that realizes its capacity (taxes all eight of its resource bases at the average state rate) will have a tax index score of 100 (or 100 percent of its capacity). A state with an index score of more than 100, is taxing at an above average rate for at least some of the eight tax sources. Both Kentucky and South Carolina are states with comparatively poor tax capacities (83). However the tax effort index scores indicate that Kentucky(100) tries harder to pay its own way than does South Carolina (90). The tax effort index is calculated by dividing the tax revenue (money actually collected in taxes) by the tax capacity.

If one is designing a grant program that takes effort into account, states such as Nevada and New Hampshire with very low tax efforts (73 and 84) might not do very well. Taking both tax effort and tax capacity into account, they would not expect to receive as much help as any of the three states mentioned above. While both Nevada and New Hampshire have tax capacities over 100, Kentucky and South Carolina have much lower tax capacities and much higher efforts.

CONCLUSION: REGRESSIVITY AND REDISTRIBUTION

Fifteen chapters ago we began this book by presenting three simple notions: (1) That individuals matter—that they can change society, help preserve the essential values and institutions in a society in the midst of change; or both; (2) That state and local governments are among the major social institutions in society for helping human beings achieve a higher quality of life; and, if 1 and 2 are even partially true, then it follows; (3) That individuals ought to pay careful attention to their governments and participate in shaping the decisions communities make in deciding what those governments do.

The foregoing chapter has advanced the notion that we can do better in terms of making our revenue systems more efficient and more equitable. If seeking social justice, making the institutions of government more efficient and responsive, and preserving our environment are among your goals, sooner or later someone will ask you how to pay for these goals. Will it mean new taxes? One possible answer is, yes—for the undertaxed. By revising the state-local tax systems in a slightly progressive direction, simply by making sure that the

Table 16.9

TAX CAPACITY AND TAX EFFORT PER CAPITA

	Tax Capacity Index/Rank		Tax Effort Index/Rank	
Alabama	81	48	81	47
Alaska	178	1	119	3
Arizona	94	27	103	10
Arkansas	78	49	82	46
California	115	10	95	25
Colorado	109	12	86	40
Connecticut	130	4	99	20
Delaware	125	6	80	49
Florida	103	18	86	41
Georgia	91	33	95	26
Hawaii	146	2	95	28
Idaho	82	47	94	29
Illinois	102	19	100	14
Indiana	90	37	93	31
Iowa	93	28	100	15
Kansas	93	30	100	16
Kentucky	83	43	100	17
Louisiana	89	39	89	37
Maine	95	24	102	11
Maryland	106	14	103	9
Massachusetts	117	9	101	13
Michigan	94	26	107	8
Minnesota	101	20	112	7
Mississippi	68	51	92	33
Missouri	91	35	85	42
Montana	91	34	78	50
Nebraska	95	25	99	18
Nevada	128	5	73	51
New Hampshire	110	11	84	43
New Jersey	119	8	112	6
New Mexico	87	41	96	24
New York	103	17	156	2
North Carolina	93	31	87	38
North Dakota	91	32	92	34
Ohio	93	29	96	23
Oklahoma	87	40	93	32
Oregon	100	21	97	22
Pennsylvania	96	23	95	27
Rhode Island	89	38	115	5
South Carolina	83	44	90	36
South Dakota	86	42	83	44
Tennessee	82	45	82	45
Texas	97	22	87	39
Utah	82	46	94	30
Vermont	105	15	97	21
Virginia	103	16	91	35
Washington	108	13	99	19

(Continued)

Table 16.9 (Continued)

	Tax Capacity Index/Rank		Tax Effort Index/Rank	
West Virginia	77	50	102	12
Wisconsin	90	36	118	4
Wyoming	134	3	81	48

Source: Advisory Commission on Intergovernmental Relations, RTS 1991: State Tax Capacity and Effort (Washington, D.C.: ACIR, 1993), 76.

rich bear the same burden as the poor, billions of state-local dollars could be raised without increasing the burden of the poor (or the middle class) by one penny.

With that frightening thought we wish you well in your efforts to make your communities even better places in which to pursue your dreams, and better places for the next generation than they were when you found them.

STUDY OBJECTIVES

1. Identify the two parts of the price to be considered in deciding on whether or not to use government to solve problems.
2. Identify the factors that influence the budget.
3. Identify the major steps in the budget-making process.
4. Identify the 10 characteristics of a high quality state-local revenue system, according to The National Conference on State Legislatures.
5. Identify the principles involved in defining and promoting equity in a system of taxation.
6. Approximately what percentage of total personal income do the first and fifth quintiles of the population obtain?
7. Identify the reasons for basing a tax system on the principle of vertical equity.
8. Identify the negative nature of taxation.
9. Compare and contrast expenditures in the spending side of the budget with tax expenditures on the revenue side.
10. Compare and contrast tax capacity and tax effort.

GLOSSARY

Budget   A plan for getting and spending money.

Certainty   There is a high probability that the tax yield will remain the same from year to year.

Circuit breaker laws   These laws limit the amount of property taxes that can be collected on an individual's home or apartment. The circuit breaker is a percentage of the resident's income that can be collected in property taxes regardless of the market value of the residence.

Federal offset A term which refering to the fact that the federal corporate income tax tends to reduce differences in state-local tax systems. Thus, offering tax breaks to businesses may simply produce profits on which the business pays federal taxes.

Fiscal disparity The difference in the tax bases of local governments, and thus their ability to offer services to their residents.

Fiscal notes An estimate of the cost of the proposed law to government, state or local.

Fiscal strain The inability to meet debt and expenditure obligations with existing revenues.

Fiscal year A 12-month period used for bookkeeping purposes. A fiscal year is also known as a budget year.

Functional performance index An attempt to compare the service offerings of major American cities by examining not the amount of money spent, but the mix of services. The index score takes into consideration the fact that some services are more expensive than others to offer.

Horizontal equity People in the same income category will be taxed at the same rate, regardless of where they live, or regardless of whether their income is capital gains or wages.

Line item veto This pertains only to appropriations and means that the governor can strike out specific items without having to veto the whole bill.

Loan guarantee A promise by a unit of government to repay a loan if the borrower defaults on payment. This means that banks will loan money to a business with the assurance that they are not taking any risk. It is a method of subsidizing, and thus attracting, a new business to a community. Given the possibility that the business may fail and leave government holding the bag, loan guarantee programs must be carefully managed.

Pre-audits These occur when an official called an auditor or comptroller certifies that there is enough money in an agency's budget for a particular kind of expenditure.

Progressive system A system in which the tax burden increases as income increases. The tax burden is lighter for the poor and heavier for the rich.

Proportionate tax This requires each individual to contribute to the cost of government in proportion to income received. In a proportionate tax system each individual bears the same tax burden, or has the same effective tax rate.

Redistribution This refers to government actions that alter the existing pattern of opportunities to live a better life. Redistribution is most often used to identify those actions that assist the have-nots.

Stability A tax system should not reinforce downturns in the economy, and at the same time it should help siphon off excess income in inflationary times.

Subsistence Barely adequate to meet the most basic needs: shelter, food, and clothing.

Sufficiency A revenue system includes enough taxes to pay for the services and programs that the community feels are appropriate.

Tax burden The percentage of one's income paid in taxes. This is also known as the effective rate (ER).

Tax capacity The amount of revenue that would be collected in a unit of government if each and every one of the eight tax sources were taxed at the average rate.

Tax effort An attempt to measure the willingness of state leaders and citizens to pay for government out of available resources.

Tax expenditure The amount of revenue lost by granting an exemption to a tax.

Vertical equity Individuals in all income categories bear the same burden (not the same size tax bill).

ENDNOTES

1. Michael Specter, "Oregon Legislators Face Up to the Hard Job of 'Playing God,'" *The Washington Post National Weekly Edition*, February 15, 1988, 33.

2. Ibid.

3. For an alternative interpretation, see Thomas R. Dye, *Politics in States and Communities*. (Englewood Cliffs, NJ: Prentice-Hall, 1988), 476.

4. Ibid.

5. Brizius and Foster, *Almanac of the Fifty States*, 1988, 441.

6. Sarah McCalley Morehouse, *State Politics, Parties and Policy* (New York: Holt, Rinehart, and Winston, 1981), 303.

7. ACIR, *Significant Features of Fiscal Federalism: 1989*, vol. I , (Washington, D.C.: Advisory Commission on Intergovernmental Relations, 2, 12.

8. Plano and Greenberg, 356.

9. Council of State Governments, *Book of the States: 1988–89,*

10. Terry Nichols Clark and Lorna Crowley Ferguson, *City Money: Political Processes, Fiscal Strains, and Retrenchment* (New York: Columbia University Press, 1983), 317–318.

11. Ibid., 53.

12. For a more detailed definition see ibid., 43–50.

13. Ibid., 13.

14. Bureau of the Census, *Statistical Abstract of the United States, 1988* (Washington, D.C.: 1989), 262.

15. Phares, Donald, "The Role of Tax Burden Studies in State Tax Policy," in *Reforming State Tax Systems* (Lexington, KY: National Conference of State Legislatures, 1986), 81.

16. Clark and Ferguson, *City Money*.

17. Ibid., 182.

18. Robert Heilbroner and Peter Berstein, *The Debt and The Deficit* (New York: W. W. Norton, 1989), 26.

19. Congressional Budget Office, *The Combined Effects of Major Changes in Federal Taxes and Spending Programs since 1981*, (Washington, D.C., U. S. Government Printing Office, 1984).

20. Heilbroner and Berstein, *Debt and the Deficit*, 50.

21. ACIR, 103.

22. Steven D. Gold, ed., *The Unfinished Agenda for State Tax Reform*, (Denver: National Conference of State Legislatures, 1988), 171.

23. U. S. Bureau of the Census, *Statistical Abstract of the United States: 1994* (Washington, D.C.: U. S. Government Printing Office, 1994), 305.

24. Gold, *The Unfinished Agenda*, 48.

25. The discussion which follows is based largely on Gold's "Principles of a High Quality State Revenue System," and Steven D. Gold and Corina L. Eckl, "Appendix Checklist of Characteristics of a Good State Revenue System, " in Gold, *Unfinished Business Agenda*, 47–63

26. Robert Kleine and John Shannon, Characteristics of a High Quality State-Local Tax System, (Washington, D.C.: Advisory Commission on Intergovernmental Relations, 1985), 15.

27. Gold, "Principles of a High Quality State Revenue System," 52.

28. Donald Phares, "State and Local Tax Burdens Across the Fifty States," in *Growth and Change* (April, 1985), 34–35.

29. Daniel B. Suits, "Measurement of Tax Progressivity," *American Economic Review*, vol 67:4 (September, 1977), 747–752. Cited in Donald Phares, "State and Local Tax Burdens Across the Fifty States," *Growth and Change* (April, 1985) 42.

30. See, for example, Michael Barker, ed. *State Taxation Policy* (Durham, NC: Duke Press Policy Studies, 1983), Donald Phares, *State-Local Tax Equity: An Empirical Analysis of the Fifty States* (Lexington, MA: Lexington Books, 1973); and *Who Pays State and Local Taxes?* (Cambridge, MA: Oelgeschlager, Gunn, and Hain Publishers, 1980); Joseph Pechman and Benjamin Okner, *Who Bears the Tax Burden?* (Washington, D.C.: Brookings Institution, 1974).

31. Roger, J. Vaughn, "State Taxation and Economic Development," in Michael Barker, ed., *State Taxation Policy*, 48.

32. Barker, *State Taxation Policy*, 46.

33. *Statistical Abstract of the United States: 1994*, 311.

34. Cline, Robert. "Personal Income Tax," *Reforming State Tax Systems*, 207.

35. David Rasmussen, Marc Bendick, and Larry Ledebur, "A Methodology for Selecting Economic Development Incentives," *Growth and Change* (January, 1984), 18–25.

36. Gold, *Reforming State Tax Systems*, 135.

37. Barker, *State Taxation Policy*, 80.

38. Larry C. Ledebur and William W. Hamilton, "The Failure of Tax Concessions as Economic Development Incentives," in Gold, *Reforming State Tax Systems* (Denver: The National Conference of State Legislatures, 1986), 112.

39. Richard D. Pomp, "Simplicity and Complexity in the Complexity of a State Tax System," in *Reforming State Tax Systems* (Denver: The National Conference of State Legislatures, 1986), 112.

40. Ledebur and Hamilton, "The Failure of Tax Concessions as Economic Development Incentives," 113.

41. Gold, *The Unfinished Agenda*, 55.

CREDITS

INDEX